HAWAII 2019

13th Edition

By Martha Cheng, Jeanne Cooper
& Shannon Wianecki

FrommerMedia LLC

Published by
FROMMER MEDIA LLC

Copyright © 2019 FrommerMedia LLC, New York, NY. All rights reserved. No part of this
publication may be reproduced, stored in a retrieval system or transmitted in any form or by any
means, electronic, mechanical, photocopying, recording, scanning or otherwise, except as
permitted under Sections 107 or 108 of the 1976 United States Copyright Act, without the prior
written permission of the Publisher. Requests to the Publisher for permission should be addressed
to Support@FrommerMedia.com.

Frommer's Complete Guide to Hawaii 2019, 13th Edition

ISBN 978-1-62887-390-0 (paper), 978-1-62887-391-7 (e-book)

Editorial Director: Pauline Frommer
Editor: Elizabeth Heath
Production Editor: Lindsay Conner
Cartographer: Roberta Stockwell
Photo Editor: Meghan Lamb
Indexer: Cheryl Lenser

For information on our other products or services, see www.frommers.com.

Frommer Media LLC also publishes its books in a variety of electronic formats. Some content that
appears in print may not be available in electronic formats.

Manufactured in China

5 4 3 2 1

HOW TO CONTACT US

In researching this book, we discovered many wonderful places—hotels, restaurants, shops, and
more. We're sure you'll find others. Please tell us about them, so we can share the information with
your fellow travelers in upcoming editions. If you were disappointed with a recommendation, we'd
love to know that, too. Please write to: Support@FrommerMedia.com.

FROMMER'S STAR RATINGS SYSTEM

Every hotel, restaurant and attraction listed in this guide has been ranked for quality and value.
Here's what the stars mean:

★ Recommended
★★ Highly Recommended
★★★ A must! Don't miss!

AN IMPORTANT NOTE

The world is a dynamic place. Hotels change ownership, restaurants hike their prices,
museums alter their opening hours, and buses and trains change their routings. And all of
this can occur in the several months after our authors have visited, inspected, and written
about, these hotels, restaurants, museums and transportation services. Though we have
made valiant efforts to keep all our information fresh and up-to-date, some few changes
can inevitably occur in the periods before a revised edition of this guidebook is published.
So please bear with us if a tiny number of the details in this book have changed. Please
also note that we have no responsibility or liability for any inaccuracy or errors or
omissions, or for inconvenience, loss, damage, or expenses suffered by anyone as a result
of assertions in this guide.

CONTENTS

LIST OF MAPS

ABOUT THE AUTHORS

Martha Cheng came to Hawaii for a boy and stayed for its food, ocean, and people. She is the former food editor for *Honolulu Magazine* and now writes feature stories for local and national publications on everything from squash farms in Waimea to fly fishing in Maui. Originally from San Francisco, she's a former pastry chef, line cook, food-truck owner, Peace Corps volunteer, and Google techie. These days, she surfs, eats, and writes.

Jeanne Cooper is the former travel editor of the *San Francisco Chronicle*, for whom she writes frequently about Hawaii. Her stories about the islands have also appeared in other Hearst-owned newspapers, magazines, and websites; *Sunset* magazine; and *Elsewhere*, a Sydney media portal. Before helping to relaunch *Frommer's Hawaii*, she contributed to guidebooks on San Francisco, Boston, and Washington, D.C., for *Fodor's*, *Travel & Leisure*, and *Time Out*. A resident of California and the Big Island, she was inspired to study hula by her mother, who lived in Hawai'i before statehood.

Shannon Wianecki has been exploring Hawaii's hidden treasures since her "small kid" days. She contributes to numerous publications worldwide including *Smithsonian*, *BBC Travel*, and *Hana Hou!*, the Hawaiian Airlines magazine. In 2016, the Hawai'i Ecotourism Association named her Travel Writer of the Year and she has twice been a finalist for Best Independent Journalist in Hawaii. When she isn't busy writing about rare plants or fascinating local characters, she's out looking for them with her four-legged sidekick, Spike. She resides on Maui's north shore.

THE BEST
OF HAWAII

There's no place on earth quite like this handful of sun-drenched Pacific islands. Here you'll find palm-fringed blue lagoons, lush rainforests, cascading waterfalls, soaring summits (some capped with snow), a live volcano, and beaches of every hue: gold, red, black, and even green. Roadside stands offer fruits and flowers for pocket change, and award-winning chefs deliver unforgettable feasts. Each of the six main islands possesses its own unique mix of natural and cultural treasures—and the possibilities for adventure, indulgence, and relaxation are endless.

THE best BEACHES

o **Lanikai Beach** (Oahu): Too gorgeous to be real, this stretch along the Windward Coast is one of Hawaii's postcard-perfect beaches—a mile of golden sand as soft as powdered sugar bordering translucent turquoise waters. The waters are calm year-round and excellent for swimming, snorkeling, and kayaking. Two tiny offshore islands complete the picture, functioning both as scenic backdrops and bird sanctuaries. See p. 108.

o **Hapuna Beach** (Big Island): A half-mile of tawny sand, as wide as a football field, gently slopes down to crystalline waters that in summer are usually excellent for swimming, snorkeling, and bodysurfing; in winter, the thundering waves should be admired from the shore, where the picnicking and state camping facilities are first rate. See p. 226.

o **Waianapanapa State Park** (Maui): Maui has many terrific beaches to choose from, but this one is extra special: On the dramatic Hana coast, jet-black sand is pummeled by the azure surf, sea arches and caves dot the shoreline, and a cliffside trail leads through an ancient *hala* forest. Plan to picnic or camp here. See p. 322.

o **Papohaku Beach Park** (Molokai): The currents are too strong for swimming here, but the light-blond strand of sand, nearly 300 feet wide and stretching for some 3 miles—one of Hawaii's longest beaches—is great for picnicking, walking, and watching sunsets, with Oahu shimmering in the distance. See p. 446.

o **Hulopoe Beach** (Lanai): This large sprawl of soft golden sand is one of the prettiest in the state. Bordered by the regal Four Seasons resort on one side and lava-rock tide pools on the other, this protected marine preserve

Waikiki Beach and Diamond Head in Honolulu on Oahu Island

offers prime swimming, snorkeling, tide-pool exploring, picnicking, camping, and the chance to spy on resident spinner dolphins. See p. 471.

o **Poipu Beach** (Kauai): This popular beach on the sunny South Shore has something for everyone: protected swimming, snorkeling, body-boarding, surfing, and plenty of sand for basking—with a rare Hawaiian monk seal joining sunbathers every so often. See p. 531.

THE best AUTHENTIC EXPERIENCES

o **Eat Local:** People in Hawaii love food. Want to get a local talking? Ask for her favorite place to get poke or saimin or shave ice. The islands offer excellent fine-dining opportunities (see the examples below), but they also have plenty of respectable hole-in-the-wall joints and beloved institutions that have hung around for half a century. On Oahu, eat poke at **Ono Seafood** (p. 147), enjoy true Hawaiian food at **Helena's Hawaiian Food** (p. 154), and join the regulars at **Liliha Bakery** (p. 155) for a loco moco. On Kauai, slurp saimin and shave ice at **Hamura's Saimin Stand** (p. 579).

o **Feel History Come Alive at Pearl Harbor** (Oahu): On December 7, 1941, Japanese warplanes bombed Pearl Harbor, forcing the United States to enter World War II. Standing on the deck of the **USS *Arizona* Memorial**—the eternal tomb for the 1,177 sailors trapped below when the battleship sank—is a profound experience. You can also visit the

Juggling fire at a luau on Maui

USS *Missouri* Memorial, where the Japanese signed their surrender on September 2, 1945. See p. 81.

o **Experience Hula:** Each year the city of Hilo on the Big Island hosts a prestigious competition celebrating ancient Hawaiian dance: the **Merrie Monarch Festival** (p. 47), held the week after Easter. On Molokai, reverent dancers celebrate the birth of hula during the 3-day **Ka Hula Piko** festival (p. 459) held in mid-summer. Year-round, local *halau* (hula troupes) perform **free shows** at several shopping centers. On Oahu, check out the **Bishop Museum** (p. 73), which stages excellent performances on weekdays, or head to the Halekulani's **House Without a Key** (p. 171), where the sunset functions as a beautiful backdrop to equally beautiful hula. On Maui, the **Old Lahaina Luau** (p. 426) is the real deal, showcasing Hawaiian dance and storytelling nightly on a gracious, beachfront stage.

o **Ponder Petroglyphs:** More than 23,000 ancient rock carvings decorate the lava fields at **Hawaii Volcanoes National Park** (p. 213) on the Big Island. You can see hundreds more on a short hike through the **Puako Petroglyph Archaeological Preserve** (p. 194), near the Fairmont Orchid on the Kohala Coast. Go early in the morning or late afternoon when the angle of the sun lets you see the forms clearly. On

Lanai, fantastic birdmen and canoes are etched into rocks at **Luahiwa** (p. 468), **Shipwreck Beach** (p. 472), and **Kaunolu Village** (p. 470).

o **Trek to Kalaupapa** (Molokai): The only access to this hauntingly beautiful and remote place is by foot or nine-seater plane. Hikers can descend the 26 switchbacks on the sea cliff's narrow 3-mile trail; a once-in-a-lifetime adventure. Once you've reached the peninsula, you'll board the **Damien Tours** bus (p. 440)—your transport back to a time when islanders with Hansen's Disease (leprosy) were exiled to Molokai and Father Damien devoted his life to care for them.

THE best OUTDOOR ADVENTURES

o **Surfing on Oahu:** Whether you're learning to surf or a pro, Oahu has waves for everyone. Few experiences are more exhilarating than standing on your first wave, and Waikiki offers lessons, board rentals, and gentle surf. During the winter, the North Shore gets big and rough, so stay out of the water if you're not an experienced surfer. But even the view from the beach, watching the daredevils take off on waves twice their height, is thrilling. See p. 117.

o **Witness the Whales:** From December to April, humpback whales cruise Hawaiian waters. You can see these gentle giants from almost any shore; simply scan the horizon for a spout. Hear them, too, by ducking your head below the surface and listening for their otherworldly music. Boats on every island offer whale-watching cruises, but Maui is your best bet for seeing the massive marine mammals up close. Try **Trilogy** (p. 335) for a first-class catamaran ride or, if you're adventurous, climb into an outrigger canoe with **Hawaiian Paddle Sports** (p. 337).

o **Visit Volcanoes:** The entire island chain is made of volcanoes; don't miss the opportunity to explore them. On Oahu, the whole family can hike to the top of ancient, world-famous **Diamond Head Crater** (p. 117). At **Hawaii Volcanoes National Park** (p. 213) on the Big Island, where Kilauea has been erupting since 1983, acres

Waimea Canyon, Kauai

THE welcoming LEI

A lei is aloha turned tangible, communicating "hello," "goodbye," "congratulations," and "I love you" in a single strand of fragrant flowers. Leis are the perfect symbol for the islands: Their fragrance and beauty are enjoyed in the moment, but the aloha they embody lasts long after they've faded.

Traditionally, Hawaiians made leis out of flowers, shells, ferns, leaves, nuts, and even seaweed. Some were twisted, some braided, and some strung. Then, as now, they were worn to commemorate special occasions, honor a loved one, or complement a hula dancer's costume. Leis are available at most of the islands' airports, from florists, and even at supermarkets. You can find wonderful, inexpensive leis at the half-dozen lei shops on **Maunakea Street** in Honolulu's Chinatown and at **Castillo Orchids** (℡ **808/329-6070**),

73-4310 Laui St., off Kaiminani Drive in the Kona Palisades subdivision, across from the Kona Airport on the Big Island. You can also arrange in advance to have a lei-greeter meet you as you deplane. **Greeters of Hawaii** (www.greetersof hawaii.com; ℡ **800/366-8559**) serves the major airports on Oahu, Maui, Kauai, and the Big Island. On Molokai, you can sew your own at **Molokai Plumerias** (p. 437).

of new black rock and billowing sulfurous steam give hints of Pele's presence even when red-hot lava isn't visible. On Maui, **Haleakala National Park** (p. 312) provides a bird's-eye view into a long-dormant volcanic crater.

o **Get Misted by Waterfalls:** Waterfalls thundering down into sparkling pools are some of Hawaii's most beautiful natural wonders. If you're on the Big Island, head to the spectacular 442-foot **Akaka Falls** (p. 200), north of Hilo. On Maui, the Road to Hana offers numerous viewing opportunities. At the end of the drive you'll find **Oheo Gulch** (p. 323), with some of the most dramatic and accessible waterfalls on the islands. Kauai is laced with waterfalls, especially along the North Shore and in the Wailua area, where you can drive right up to the 151-foot **Opaekaa Falls** (p. 507) and the 80-foot **Wailua Falls** (p. 507). On Molokai, the 250-foot **Mooula Falls** (p. 435) can be visited only via a guided hike through breathtaking Halawa Valley, but that, too, is a very special experience.

o **Peer into Waimea Canyon** (Kauai): It may not share the vast dimensions of Arizona's Grand Canyon, but Kauai's colorful gorge—a mile wide, 3,600 feet deep, and 14 miles long—has a grandeur all its own, easily viewed from several overlooks just off Kokee Road. Hike to Waipoo Falls to experience its red parapets up close, or take one of the helicopter rides that swoop between its walls like the white-tailed trop-icbird. See p. 520.

o **Explore the Napali Coast** (Kauai): With the exception of the Kalalau Valley Overlook, the fluted ridges and deep, primeval valleys of the island's northwest portion can't be viewed by car. You must hike the 11-mile Kalalau Trail (p. 511), kayak (p. 535), take a snorkel cruise (p. 533), or book a helicopter ride (p. 521) to experience its wild, stunning beauty.

o **Four-Wheel It on Lanai** (Lanai): Off-roading is a way of life on barely paved Lanai. Rugged trails lead to deserted beaches, abandoned villages, sacred sites, and valleys filled with wild game.

THE best HOTELS

o **Halekulani** (Oahu; www.halekulani.com; *C* **800/367-2343**): When price is no object, this is really the only place to stay. A place of Zen amid the buzz, this beach hotel is the finest Waikiki has to offer. Even if you don't stay here, pop by for a sunset mai tai at House Without a Key to hear live Hawaiian music while a lovely hula dancer sways to the music. See p. 130.

o **Royal Hawaiian** (Oahu): This pink oasis, hidden away among blooming gardens within the concrete jungle of Waikiki, is a stunner. It's vibrant and exotic, from the Spanish-Moorish arches in the common

Disney Aulani Resort, an upscale hotel and entertainment resort by Walt Disney on the island of Oahu in Hawaii

Four Seasons Resort Hualalai

areas to the pink-and-gold pineapple wallpaper in the Historic Wing's guest rooms. See p. 133.

- **Kahala Hotel & Resort** (Oahu): Situated in one of Oahu's most prestigious residential areas, the Kahala provides the peace and serenity of a neighbor-island vacation, but with the conveniences of Waikiki just a 10-minute drive away. The lush, tropical grounds include an 800-foot, crescent-shaped beach and a 26,000-square-foot lagoon (home to two bottlenose dolphins, sea turtles, and tropical fish). See p. 137.

- **Four Seasons Resort Hualalai** (Big Island): The seven pools alone will put you in seventh heaven at this exclusive yet environmentally conscious oasis of understated luxury, which also offers a private, 18-hole golf course, an award-winning spa, exquisite dining, and impeccable service—with no resort fee. See p. 260.

- **Grand Naniloa Hotel Hilo—A DoubleTree by Hilton** (Big Island): Thanks to a $20-million renovation that blended chic, modern furnishings with a focus on hula, this long-neglected icon along scenic Banyan Drive now stands heads and shoulders above any other hotel in Hilo—and is a great value anywhere in the state. The gleaming lobby and bay-view lounge host hula videos, displays, and free shows, while images of dancers by acclaimed photographer Kim Taylor Reece grace all 388 rooms (many with dazzling views) and public spaces. See p. 268.

- **Westin Hapuna Beach Resort** (Big Island): Dramatically resculpted and rebranded as a Westin in 2018, this hidden gem on the Kohala Coast already boasted huge rooms, an enormous beach, and one exceptional restaurant; now it offers a large family pool with separate adult infinity-edge pool, revitalized lobby and new dining outlets, and Westin's luxurious beds and showers. Also consider its gorgeous but pricier sister hotel, the Mauna Kea Beach Hotel (p. 264), part of Marriott's Autograph Collection but independently owned. See p. 263.

o **Andaz Maui** (Maui): This Wailea resort offers a prime beachfront locale, chic decor, an apothecary-style spa, and two phenomenal restaurants, including one by superstar chef Masaharu Morimoto. Accommodations here ramp up the style quotient with crisp white linens, warm wood furniture, and mid-century accents. Wrap yourself in a plush robe and nosh on the complimentary minibar snacks from the sanctuary of your private lanai. At the 'Awili Spa you can mix your own massage oil and body scrubs; yoga and fitness classes are free. See p. 375.

o **Travaasa Hana** (Maui): Nestled in the center of quaint Hana town, this 66-acre resort wraps around Kauiki Head, the dramatic point where Queen Kaahumanu was born. You'll feel like royalty in one of the Sea Ranch Cottages here. Floor-to-ceiling sliding doors open to spacious lanais, some with private hot tubs. You'll be far from shopping malls and sports bars, but exotic red-, black-, and white-sand beaches are a short walk or shuttle ride away. This is luxury in its purest form. See p. 383.

o **Four Seasons Resort Lanai at Manele Bay** (Lanai): This gracious resort on Lanai's south coast overlooks Hulopoe Beach—one of the finest stretches of sand in the state. Guest rooms are palatial, outfitted with museum-quality art and automated everything—from temperature, lighting, and sound system to fancy toilets! The suites have deep soaking Japanese cedar tubs, and views that stretch for an eternity. The restaurants and service throughout the resort are impeccable. See p. 471.

o **Grand Hyatt Kauai Resort & Spa** (Kauai): At this sprawling, family-embracing resort in Poipu, the elaborate, multi-tiered fantasy pool and

Grand Hyatt Kauai Resort & Spa

saltwater lagoon more than compensate for the rough waters of Keoneloa (Shipwrecks) Beach. Don't fret: Calmer Poipu Beach is just a short drive away. Anara Spa and Poipu Bay Golf Course offer excellent adult diversions, too. See p. 467.

o **The Lodge at Kukuiula** (Kauai): Thanks to an array of luxuriously furnished cottages, bungalows, and villas, overnight guests can enjoy all the perks of home ownership at the island's most exclusive resort—including access to its private golf course, unrivaled spa, and fine dining—without the overhead of a multimillion-dollar second (or third) home. See p. 568.

THE best RESTAURANTS

o **Alan Wong's Restaurant** (Oahu): Master strokes at this shrine of Hawaii Regional Cuisine include ginger-crusted fresh *onaga* (red snapper), a whole-tomato salad dressed with *li hing mui* (plum powder) vinaigrette, and *opihi* (limpet) shooters. Alan Wong reinvents local flavors for the fine-dining table in ways that continue to surprise and delight. See p. 155.

o **Sushi Izakaya Gaku** (Oahu): The city is dotted with *izakayas,* Japanese pubs serving small plates made for sharing, and this gem is the best of them all. You'll discover life beyond maguro and hamachi nigiri with seasonal, uncommon seafood, such as sea bass sashimi and grilled ray. Thanks to the large population of Japanese nationals living in Honolulu, the Japanese food here is some of the best outside of Japan. But it's not just straight-from-Tokyo fare at Gaku; the chefs here scour fish markets around town daily for the best local fish. See p. 156.

o **The Pig and the Lady** (Oahu): This casual restaurant, with its traditional Vietnamese noodle soups and playful interpretations of Southeast Asian food, is both soulful and surprising. The soulful: the pho of the day, drawing on recipes from chef Andrew Le's mother. The surprising: hand-cut pasta with pork and *lilikoi* (passion fruit). The best of both worlds: a pho French dip banh mi, with slices of tender brisket and a cup of pho broth for dipping. See p. 152.

o **Ka'ana Kitchen** (Maui): Treat chef Isaac Bancaco's grid menu like a gourmet bingo card; every combination is a winner. Start off with a hand-mixed cocktail and the ahi tataki: ruby-red tuna, heirloom tomato, and fresh burrata sprinkled with black salt and nasturtium petals. The $45 breakfast buffet grants you access to the kitchen's novel chilled countertops, stocked with every delicacy and fresh juice you can imagine. See p. 407.

o **Mama's Fish House** (Maui): Overlooking Kuau Cove on Maui's North Shore, this restaurant is a South Pacific fantasy. Every nook is decorated with some fanciful artifact of salt-kissed adventure. The

Mama's Fish House, Maui

menu lists the anglers who reeled in the day's catch; you can order ono "caught by Keith Nakamura along the 40-fathom ledge near Hana" or deep-water ahi seared with coconut and lime. The Tahitian Pearl dessert is almost too stunning to eat. See p. 416.

- **Tin Roof** (Maui): Celebrity chef Sheldon Simeon won the hearts of *Top Chef* fans not once, but twice. He and his wife, Janice, opened their own humble to-go spot in an industrial Kahului strip mall. Simeon's Filipino-inspired menu is so much fun: buy a 50-cent "dime bag" of house-made furikake to sprinkle on your mochiko chicken. Add a 6-minute egg to your pork belly bowl. You'll want to Instagram yourself eating the chocolate birthday cake bibingka, covered in sprinkles. See p. 392.

- **Merriman's** (Waimea, Big Island): Chef Peter Merriman, one of the founders of Hawaii Regional Cuisine, oversees a locally inspired culinary empire that also includes Monkeypod Kitchen and Moku Kitchen outlets on Maui and Oahu (p. 162 and 150), as well as the Beach House on Kauai (p. 584), famed for sunset photo ops. His original Waimea restaurant, opened in 1988, still merits the drive upcountry from the coast. See p. 281.

- **Umekes** (Kailua-Kona and Waimea, Big Island): The island specialty of diced raw, marinated seafood poke—pronounced *po-kay*—comes in many varieties at this hole-in-the-wall takeout counter, with just as delicious, farm-fresh sides. Chef Nakoa Pabre also runs a handsome sit-down version with full bar, Umekes Fishmarket Bar and Grill (*©* **808/238-0571**), and opened Umekes Waimea in late 2017 (*©* **808/315-8739**) See p. 274.

- **Pueo's Osteria** (Waikoloa, Big Island): Former Four Seasons Hualalai chef James Babian takes his inspiration from Tuscany and, as much

IN HAWAII, mother nature IS STILL IN CHARGE

Recent events in Hawaii remind us that these islands remain very much subject to the whims of Mother Nature. In April 2018, torrential rains on the island of Kauai washed out roads and hiking trails and destroyed or damaged homes and businesses, primarily on the North Shore. While most of the damage has been repaired, several popular North Shore beaches and the Kalalau Trail remain closed at press time.

Then, on April 30, a series of earthquakes and volcanic eruptions began on the Big Island in a remote area well-known for volcanic activity, although not at this scale for nearly 40 years. Dozens of home been destroyed by molten lava, asphalt roads have cracked open and forests set ablaze. As we go to press, the lava flow continues and shows no signs of slowing down. Sections of Hawaii Volcanoes National Park are closed until the crisis is averted. It's important to stress that the lava is only affecting the Puna region of the Big Island; the majority of the Big Island remains open for business, perfectly safe and just as paradisiacal as ever. (Or at least that was the case at press time). See chapters 5 and 9 for more specific information about closures and changes due to these natural events.

For the latest update on the Big Island's volcanic activity, visit https://volcanoes. usgs.gov/volcanoes/kilauea/status.html. For civil defense alerts, including road closures, on the Big Island, visit www.hawaiicounty.gov/active-alerts.

as he can, uses ingredients from local farmers and fishermen, creating exceptionally fresh, well-priced cuisine paired with an intriguing wine list. Another reason to drive 15 minutes up the mountain: The thoughtfully crafted bar menu is served nightly. See p. 280.

○ **Bar Acuda** (Hanalei, Kauai): When the sun goes down, the surfing set freshens up for a night on the town at this stylish tapas bar. Created by Jim Moffat, a former star of San Francisco's culinary scene, Bar Acuda's fare is centered around fresh seafood and seasonal pairings inspired by Mediterranean cuisine. See p. 580.

○ **Red Salt** (Poipu, Kauai): Hidden inside the jewel box of boutique hotel Koa Kea is this equally brilliant dining room, where local seafood and produce shine under executive chef Noelani Planas. The evening sushi bar and tropical breakfasts are also not to be missed. See p. 586.

○ **Eating House 1849 (**Poipu, Kauai): Hawaii Regional Cuisine cofounder Roy Yamaguchi closed the long-lived Garden Island outpost of his signature Roy's brand to open this more casual, plantation-themed restaurant in the open-air Shops at Kukuiula. Returning to his island roots with hearty small plates and family-style dishes made it an instant success, now replicated at two Oahu locations. See p. 586.

○ **Nobu Lanai** (Lanai): Lanai now ranks among New York, Milan, Budapest, and Mexico City as somewhere one can dine at a Nobu restaurant—a measure of how fun a place is, in the immortal words of pop star Madonna. The best way to experience this epicurean phenomenon is to order the *omakase*—the chef's tasting menu—for $120. Each dish is as delicious as it is artful. See p. 481.

THE best OF HAWAII FOR KIDS

o **Aulani, a Disney Resort & Spa, Ko Olina, Hawaii** (Oahu): Disney built this high-rise hotel and spa (with timeshare condos) on 21 acres on the beach, about an hour's drive from Waikiki. It's a great destination for families, with a full children's program, plus areas and activities for teens and tweens. Mickey, Minnie, and other Disney characters walk the resort and stop to take photos with kids. See p. 139.

o **Polynesian Cultural Center** (Oahu): Experience the songs, dance, and costumes of six Pacific islands and archipelagos at the Disneyland version of Polynesia. There are plenty of activities to engage kids, such as spear-throwing competitions and Maori games that test hand-eye coordination. See p. 99.

o **Build Sandcastles on Kailua Beach** (Oahu): This gorgeous beach is kid-friendly, with sand that slopes gently into the water. The waves vary in spots—perfect for the young ones to splash around and older kids to boogie board. The broad stretch of sand is also great for building castles. See p. 108.

Students from University of Hawaii perform traditional Tahiti dance on a canoe at the Polynesian Cultural Center

- **Slumber Party at the Aquarium** (Maui): Kids can book a sleepover in the Maui Ocean Center, staying up into the wee hours to watch glowing jellyfish and other nocturnal animals. See p. 309.

- **Snorkel in Kealakekua Bay** (Big Island): Everyone can enjoy the dazzling display of marine life here on a **Fair Wind** cruise (www.fairwind.com; *©* **800/677-9461** or 808/322-2788), which offers inner tubes and underwater viewing boxes for little ones (or older ones) who don't want to get their faces wet. Two water slides and a spacious boat with a friendly crew add to the fun. See p. 232.

- **Play at Lydgate Park** (Kauai): If kids tire of snorkeling in the protected swimming area of Lydgate Beach, a giant wooden fantasy play structure and bridge to the dunes await, along with grassy fields and several miles of biking trails. See p. 506.

- **Ride a Sugarcane Train** (Kauai): At **Kilohana Plantation,** families can enjoy an inexpensive, narrated train ride through fields, forest, and orchards, with a stop to feed goats and wild pigs. See p. 505.

- **Frolic in a Playful Garden** (Kauai): The "Under the Rainbow" children's garden at Na Aina Kai Botanical Gardens & Sculpture Park offers a hedge maze, treehouse, mini railroad, and wading pool, among other delights. See p. 510.

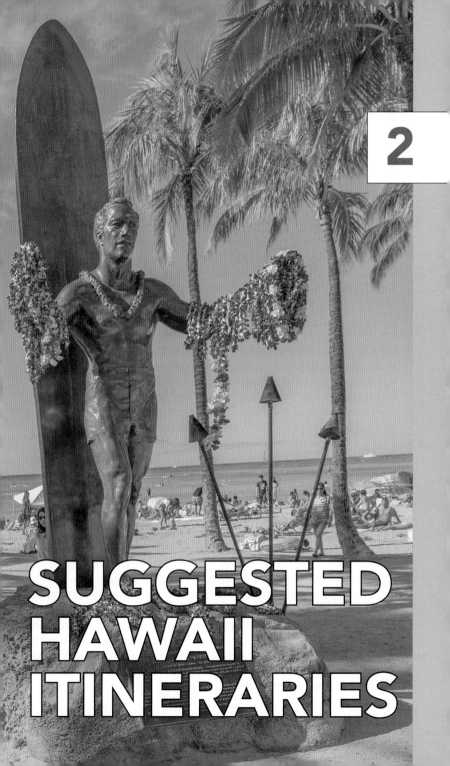

2

SUGGESTED HAWAII ITINERARIES

F or most people, the fetching dollops of land in the middle of the Pacific Ocean are a dream destination— but getting to this remote region can seem daunting. So once you finally arrive, you'll want to make the most of your time. In this chapter we've built six 1-week itineraries for Oahu, Hawaii Island, Maui, Molokai, Lanai, and Kauai, each designed to hit the highlights and provide a revealing window into the real Hawaii.

You can follow these itineraries to the letter or use them to build your own personalized trip. Whatever you do, *don't max out your days.* This is Hawaii, after all—save time to smell the perfume of plumeria, listen to wind rustling through a bamboo forest, and feel the caress of the Pacific.

A WEEK ON OAHU

Oahu is so stunning that the *ali'i,* the kings of Hawaii, made it the capital of the island nation. Below, we presume that you'll be staying in Honolulu, which makes a good base for the rest of the island. Plus, it has the best dining options and a cosmopolitan liveliness unavailable anywhere else in the islands. If you prefer quieter nights, though, opt for a vacation rental in Kailua or on the North Shore and factor into the following itinerary extra time for traveling.

DAY 1: Arrive & Hit Waikiki Beach ★★★

Unwind from your plane ride with a little sun and sand. Take a dip in the ocean at the most famous beach in the world: **Waikiki Beach** (p. 104). Catch the sunset with a mai tai, Hawaiian music, and some of the loveliest hula you'll ever see at **House Without a Key** (p. 171).

DAY 2: Surf in Waikiki & Visit Pearl Harbor ★★★

Thanks to jet lag, you'll be up early; take advantage with an early-morning surf session, aka dawn patrol, when the waves are smooth and glassy. Waikiki has great waves for learning, and a surf lesson (p. 117) will have you riding the waves in no time. The poke at **Ono Seafood** (p. 147) makes a great post-surf meal, and then you'll want to refresh yourself with a lychee-mango-pineapple shave ice drizzled with lilikoi cream at **Waiola Shave Ice** (p. 146). In the afternoon, head to **Pearl Harbor** (p. 81), site of the infamous 1941 attack. For

PREVIOUS PAGE: **Duke Kahanamoku statue at Queen's Beach in Waikiki**

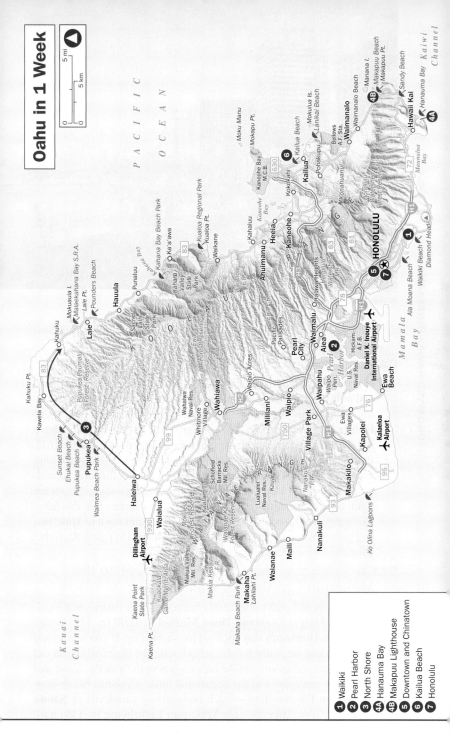

Oahu in 1 Week

1 Waikiki
2 Pearl Harbor
3 North Shore
4A Hanauma Bay
4B Makapuu Lighthouse
5 Downtown and Chinatown
6 Kailua Beach
7 Honolulu

Waikiki Beach

dinner, go local and dine at **Highway Inn** (p. 150) for *kalua* pig, *lau-lau*, *pipikaula*, and *poi*.

DAY 3: Explore the North Shore ★★★

Grab a fried *malasada* (holeless doughnut) dipped in sugar at **Leonard's Bakery** (p. 146) before heading to the **North Shore** (see "Central Oahu & the North Shore," on p. 101). Stop in the quaint town of **Haleiwa** for a pineapple-*lilikoi*-mango treat at **Matsumoto Shave Ice** (p. 101), and grab a picnic lunch from **Beet Box Café** (p. 161). Pick one of the gorgeous North Shore beaches for a day of swimming and sunbathing. **Waimea Beach Park** (p. 111) is a favorite, no matter the season. In winter, if the waves are pumping and conditions are right, head to **Pipeline** (p. 117) and watch pro surfers ride this tube-like wave over razor-sharp reef. Stop in the quaint town of **Hale'iwa** and grab a picnic lunch from **Beet Box Café** (p. 161). Still daylight? Take the longer coastal road back into Honolulu.

DAY 4: Snorkel in Hanauma Bay ★★ & Hike the Makapuu Lighthouse Trail ★★

Get up early and grab some freshly baked morning pastries or a local-style breakfast at **Diamond Head Market & Grill** (p. 158) before heading to **Hanauma Bay** (p. 104) for snorkeling. If you're a strong swimmer and the water is calm (check with the lifeguard), head out past the reef and away from the crowds, where the water's clearer and you'll see more fish and the occasional turtle. Continue beach-hopping down the coastline—watch bodysurfing daredevils at **Sandy Beach** (p. 106). Hike the easy **Makapuu Lighthouse** (p. 119) trail, with views to Molokai and Lanai on a clear day. In winter, you may even see migrating humpback whales. Take the Pali Highway home to Honolulu—and be sure to stop at the **Nuuanu Pali Lookout** (p. 87). For a night out, head to Chinatown, where a slew of new restaurants have opened: Start with a cocktail in the rooftop courtyard at **Tchin Tchin** (p. 152) and move on to dinner at **Senia** (p. 153).

DAY 5: Glimpse Historic Honolulu & Experience Hawaiian Culture

Fuel up at **Koko Head Café** (p. 157), an island-style brunch spot before heading to downtown Honolulu to see the city's historic sites, including the **Iolani Palace** (p. 79). Lunch at **The Pig and the Lady** (p. 152) for modern Vietnamese food, pick up some tropical fruit at one of the many Chinatown vendors, and browse the new boutiques started by Hawaii's young creatives (p. 163). Spend the afternoon at the **Bishop Museum** (p. 73) to immerse yourself in Hawaiian culture, then head up to **Puu Ualakaa State Park** (p. 87) to watch the sunset over Honolulu. For dinner, get a taste of Honolulu's spectacular Japanese cuisine at **Sushi Izakaya Gaku** (p. 156).

DAY 6: Relax at Kailua Beach ★★★

On your last full day on Oahu, travel over the Pali Highway to the windward side of the island. Dig into a stack of *lilikoi* (passion fruit)

Iolani Palace

pancakes at **Moke's Bread and Breakfast** (p. 161) and then spend the rest of the day at **Kailua Beach** (p. 108). It's the perfect beach to kayak or stand-up paddle to the Mokulua Islands (or, as the locals call it, "the Mokes") or simply relax. For your last dinner, dig into the Family Feast at **Mahina and Sun's** (p. 145), which features a whole fried fish with only-in-Hawaii sides.

DAY 7: Marvel at Shangri La ★★★

Head to the **Honolulu Museum of Art** for your tour of **Shangri La** (p. 78), the private palace of tobacco heiress Doris Duke. Filled with Islamic art, the interior is stunning, but so is the location, on a cliff facing Diamond Head. Then, take one last look at Diamond Head and Waikiki . . . from the ocean, aboard the **Holokai Catamaran** (p. 112).

A WEEK ON THE BIG ISLAND OF HAWAII

Because of the distances involved, a week is barely enough time to see the entire Big Island; it's best to plan for 2 weeks—or even better, a return visit. Here's how to see the highlights, changing hotels as you go.

DAY 1: Arrive & Amble Through Kailua-Kona ★★★

Since most flights arrive at lunchtime or later, check into your Kona Coast lodgings and go for a stroll through historic **Kailua-Kona** by **Hulihee Palace** (p. 187) and **Mokuaikaua Church** (p. 188). Wear sandals so you can dip your feet in one of the pocket coves, such as Kamakahonu Bay, within sight of **Kamehameha's historic compound,** and enjoy a sunset dinner at an oceanview restaurant. Don't unpack—you'll be on the road early the next day.

DAY 2: A Morning Sail & Afternoon Drive ★★★

The day starts with a morning snorkel tour (plus breakfast and lunch) aboard the *Fair Wind II* (p. 232), sailing to the historic preserve of **Kealakekua Bay.** After returning to Keauhou Bay, head south to **Hawaii Volcanoes National Park** (p. 213), by way of **Puuhonua O Honaunau National Historical Park** (p. 193) and the **Kau Coffee Mill** (p. 217), for a pick-me-up, and swing by **Punaluu Beach Park** (p. 230) for a black-sand photo op, possibly with basking turtles. Check into lodgings in **Volcano Village** (p. 269) or **Volcano House** (p. 270), where you may dine by the glow of fiery Kilauea.

DAY 3: Explore an Active Volcano ★★★

Stop at the national park's **Kilauea Visitor Center** to learn about current lava flows (if any) and the day's free ranger-led walks. Take **Crater Rim Road** past **Halemaumau Crater** (p. 214) to see **Nahuku,** aka the Thurston Lava Tube (p. 215), and **Devastation**

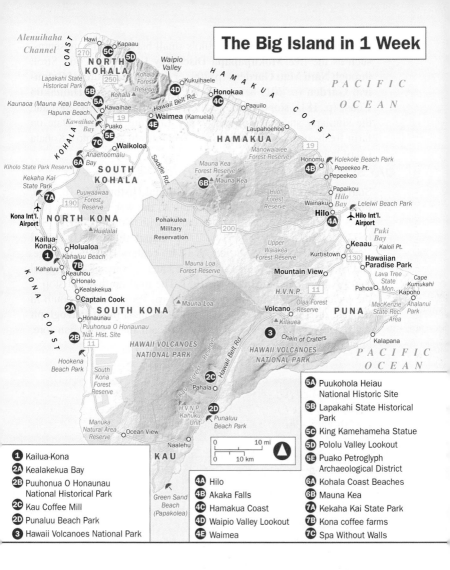

The Big Island in 1 Week

- **1** Kailua-Kona
- **2A** Kealakekua Bay
- **2B** Puuhonua O Honaunau National Historical Park
- **2C** Kau Coffee Mill
- **2D** Punaluu Beach Park
- **3** Hawaii Volcanoes National Park

- **4A** Hilo
- **4B** Akaka Falls
- **4C** Hamakua Coast
- **4D** Waipio Valley Lookout
- **4E** Waimea

- **5A** Puukohola Heiau National Historic Site
- **5B** Lapakahi State Historical Park
- **5C** King Kamehameha Statue
- **5D** Pololu Valley Lookout
- **5E** Puako Petroglyph Archaeological District
- **6A** Kohala Coast Beaches
- **6B** Mauna Kea
- **7A** Kekaha Kai State Park
- **7B** Kona coffee farms
- **7C** Spa Without Walls

Trail (p. 251), before driving down **Chain of Craters Road,** leading to a vast petroglyph field and the 2003 lava flow that smothered the roadway; more lava began flowing in 2016. After sunset, visit the **Thomas A. Jaggar Museum** (open till 7:30pm; p. 215) and its observation deck (open 24 hours) for another look at Pele's power.

DAY 4: Tour Old Hawaii ★★★

It's just a 45-minute drive from Volcano to **Hilo** (p. 181), so after breakfast go to **Imiloa: Astronomy Center of Hawaii** (p. 208), opening at 9am. Then explore **Banyan Drive** (p. 205), **Liliuokalani**

Gardens (p. 205), and one of Hilo's small but intriguing museums, such as the free **Mokupapapa Discovery Center** (p. 206). Stroll through **Nani Mau Gardens** (p. 209) or the **Hawaii Tropical Botanical Garden** (p. 201) before driving along the pastoral **Hamakua Coast** (p. 181), stopping at breathtaking **Akaka Falls** (p. 200) and the similarly stunning **Waipio Valley Lookout** (p. 204). Dine on farm-fresh cuisine in **Waimea** (p. 179) before checking into a Kohala Coast hotel (p. 262).

DAY 5: Explore the Historic Kohala Coast ★★★

Start by visiting **Puukohola Heiau National Historic Site** (p. 194), the massive temple Kamehameha built to the war god, Ku; it also looks impressive on an intimate cruise with **Kohala Sail & Sea** (p. 234). Continue north on Hwy. 270 to **Lapakahi State Historical Park** (p. 195) to see the outlines of a 14th-century Hawaiian village, and have lunch in Hawi or Kapaau; the latter is home of the original **King Kamehameha Statue** (p. 195). The final northbound stop is the picturesque **Pololu Valley Lookout** (p. 196). Heading south in the late afternoon, make the short hike to the **Puako Petroglyph Archaeological Preserve** (p. 194). To learn more Hawaiian lore, book one of Kohala's evening **luaus** (p. 292).

Waipio Valley Lookout

Pololu Valley Beach

DAY 6: Sand, Sea & Stars ★★★

You've earned a morning at the beach, and the Big Island's prettiest beaches are on the Kohala Coast: **Anaehoomalu Bay (A-Bay), Hapuna,** and **Kaunaoa** (see "Beaches," p. 221). Skip the scuba, though, because in the afternoon you're heading up 13,796-foot **Mauna Kea** (p. 196), revered by astronomers. Let an expert with four-wheel-drive, cold-weather gear, and telescopes for stargazing take you there; **Mauna Kea Summit Adventures** (p. 198) or **Hawaii Forest & Trail** (p. 219) are recommended tour guides.

DAY 7: Spa, Beach, or Coffee Time ★★★

On your last full day, visit one of North Kona's gorgeous beaches hidden behind lava fields, such as **Kekaha Kai State Park** (p. 222) or the tranquil cove at **Kaloko-Honokohau National Historical Park** (p. 188) in the morning. In the afternoon, relax with a spa treatment at the Fairmont Orchid's **Spa Without Walls** (p. 263), or tour a **Kona coffee farm** (p. 191) and bring home gourmet beans as souvenirs.

A WEEK ON MAUI

You'll need at least a week to savor Maui's best experiences. We recommend splitting your vacation between East and West Maui, starting with hot and sunny beaches and ending in the rejuvenating rainforest. We've designed this itinerary assuming you'll stay in West Maui for the first 3 days, but it works just as well if you stay in Wailea or Kihei. To minimize driving, move your headquarters to lush East Maui on day 4.

Old Lahaina Luau

DAY 1: Arrive & Explore West Maui ★★★

Upon arrival, fuel up at **Tin Roof** (p. 392) before heading to your hotel. Check in, and then go for a reviving dip at one of West Maui's prime beaches (p. 328). Meander around the historic old town of **Lahaina** (p. 298). Since you were savvy enough to book reservations for the **Old Lahaina Luau** (p. 426) a month in advance, you can immerse yourself in Hawaiian culture as the sun drops into the sea.

DAY 2: Sail to Lanai ★★★

You'll likely wake up early on your first morning here, so book an early-morning trip with **Trilogy** (p. 335), the best sailing/snorkeling operation in Hawaii. You'll spend the day (breakfast and lunch included) sailing to Lanai, snorkeling, touring the island, and sailing back to Lahaina. You'll have the afternoon free to shop or nap.

DAY 3: Sunbathe in South Maui ★★★

Take a drive out to **Makena State Beach Park** (p. 332) and soak in the raw beauty of this wild shore. On the way, pay a visit to the sharks and sea turtles at the **Maui Ocean Center** in Maalaea (p. 309). Linger in South Maui to enjoy the sunset and feast at one of the area's terrific restaurants (recommendations start on p. 404).

DAY 4: Ascend a 10,000-Foot Volcano ★★★

Venture up to the 10,023-foot summit of **Haleakala,** the island's dormant volcano. Witnessing the sunrise here can be phenomenal (as well as mind-numbingly cold and crowded). Aim for a little later and hike in the **National Park** (p. 312), an awe-inspiring experience any time of day. On your way back down the mountain, stop and tour **Upcountry Maui** (p. 311), particularly the communities of **Kula, Makawao,** and

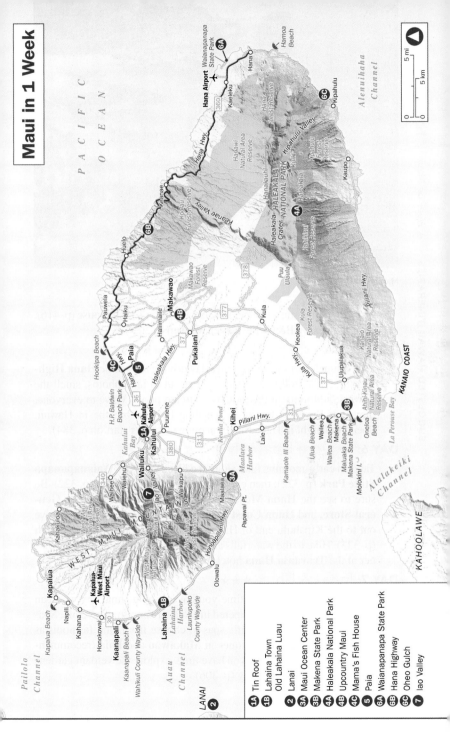

Maui in 1 Week

Legend:
- 1A Tin Roof
- 1B Lahaina Town
- Old Lahaina Luau
- 2 Lanai
- 3A Maui Ocean Center
- 3B Makena State Park
- 4A Haleakala National Park
- 4B Upcountry Maui
- 4C Mama's Fish House
- 5 Paia
- 6A Waianapanapa State Park
- 6B Hana Highway
- 6C Oheo Gulch
- 7 Iao Valley

Makena Cove

Paia. Plan for a sunset dinner in Kuau at **Mama's Fish House** (p. 416). Stay at a nearby B&B or the chic **Paia Inn** (p. 382).

DAY 5: Drive the Hana Highway ★★★

Pack a lunch and spend the entire day driving the scenic **Hana Highway** (p. 317). Pull over often and get out to take photos, smell the flowers, and jump in the mountain-stream pools. Wave to everyone, move off the road for those speeding by, and breathe in Hawaii. Spend the night in Hana (hotel recommendations start on p. 384).

DAY 6: Explore Heavenly Hana ★★★

Take an early-morning hike along the black sands of **Waianapanapa State Park** (p. 322); then explore the tiny town of **Hana** (p. 322). Be sure to see the **Hana Museum Cultural Center, Hasegawa General Store,** and **Hana Coast Gallery.** Stock up on snacks and drive out to the Kipahulu end of Haleakala National Park at **Oheo Gulch** (p. 323). Hike to the waterfalls and swim in the pools. Splurge on dinner at the **Travaasa Hana** hotel (p. 383).

DAY 7: Relax & Shop ★★★

Depending on how much time you have on your final day, you can relax on the beach, get pampered in a spa, or shop for souvenirs. Spagoers have a range of terrific spas to choose from, and fashionistas should check out the boutiques in **Makawao** and **Paia** (recommendations start on p. 423). If you have time, explore the verdant gardens and waterfalls at **Iao Valley** (p. 306).

Molokai in 1 Week

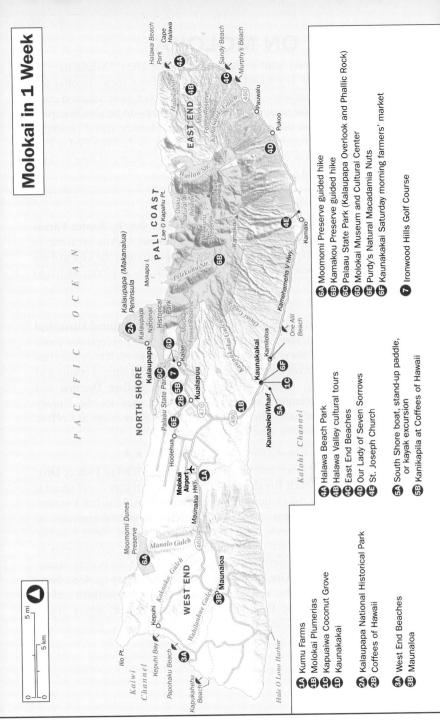

1A Kumu Farms
1B Molokai Plumerias
1C Kapuaiwa Coconut Grove
1D Kaunakakai

2A Kalaupapa National Historical Park
2B Coffees of Hawaii

3A West End Beaches
3B Maunaloa

4A Halawa Beach Park
4B Halawa Valley cultural tours
4C East End Beaches
4D Our Lady of Seven Sorrows
4E St. Joseph Church

5A South Shore boat, stand-up paddle, or kayak excursion
5B Kanikapila at Coffees of Hawaii

6A Moomomi Preserve guided hike
6B Kamakou Preserve guided hike
6C Palaau State Park (Kalaupapa Overlook and Phallic Rock)
6D Molokai Museum and Cultural Center
6E Purdy's Natural Macadamia Nuts
6F Kaunakakai Saturday morning farmers' market

7 Ironwood Hills Golf Course

A WEEK ON MOLOKAI

Some visitors would quail at the thought of spending 7 whole days on Hawaii's most low-key island, which at first glance seems to offer few activities and attractions. But you'll need to plan your vacation carefully—including the season and days of the week—to be able to experience everything on this itinerary, based on a Monday arrival (weekday arrival strongly recommended). If you're staying on the West End or East End, where the most desirable lodgings are, leave plenty of time to drive to Central Molokai attractions.

DAY 1: Arrive & Stock Up

After you pick up your rental car (a must), stop by **Kumu Farms** near the airport (p. 456) for organic produce. While en route to **Kaunakakai** (p. 434) to finish your shopping, enjoy the views of the **Molokai Plumerias** orchard (p. 437), typically in bloom March to October.

DAY 2: Tour Kalaupapa ★★★

Whether you're hiking or flying to **Kalaupapa National Historical Park** (p. 440), you will not be disappointed by the exceptional views and unique history. The effort and expense are worth it to explore this otherwise inaccessible, always impressive site of natural beauty and tragic history, where two Catholic saints, **Father Damien** and **Mother Marianne Cope** (p. 443), helped care for the leprosy patients exiled here. After your return "topside," recharge at **Coffees of Hawaii** (p. 438), which grows its own.

DAY 3: Savor the West End Beaches ★★

Pack a picnic lunch and beach gear—stop at **Molokai Fish & Dive** (p. 447) or **Beach Break** (p. 449) to buy or rent gear—and spend a day exploring the glorious **West End beaches** (p. 446). If it's winter, don't plan on going in the water; instead, enjoy the sightings of whales (at their peak Jan–Mar) or intrepid surfers. Drive into the quiet plantation town of **Maunaloa** to restock your refreshments at the **Maunaloa General Store** (p. 456) or browse the eclectic wares at the **Big Wind Kite Factory & Plantation Gallery** (p. 458). Note that the only public restroom facilities are at the northern end of nearly 3-mile-long **Papohaku Beach Park** ★★★, where you'll want to stay for sunset.

DAY 4: Hike to a Waterfall & into the Past ★★★

Anyone can take the incredibly scenic, sinuous, shore-hugging drive to pretty **Halawa Beach Park** (p. 445), but you'll need reservations (book several weeks in advance) and a picnic lunch for the **Halawa Valley cultural tours** (p. 438) offered by the Solatorio family. After the traditional Hawaiian protocol to welcome visitors and an introduction to the ancient enclave's history, you'll hike to the gorgeous, 250-foot Mooula Falls, where a dip is possible in calm conditions. Since you have your swim gear, stop at the East End's **Sandy** and **Kumimi** beaches (p. 445) on the drive home. You'll also want to make a photo stop at Father Damien's picturesque churches on the eastern half of King Kamehameha V Hwy., **St. Joseph** and **Our Lady of Seven Sorrows** (p. 443).

DAY 5: Paddle, Snorkel, or Watch Whales on the South Shore ★★★

If you haven't explored the teeming marine life and tranquil waters sheltered by the South Shore's enormous fringing reef, then you haven't really seen Molokai at its finest. Depending on your ability, book **a stand-up paddle** or **kayak excursion** with **Molokai Outdoors** (p. 448), or a **snorkel/dive trip** with **Molokai Fish & Dive** (p. 447). The reef typically keeps the water calm even in winter (Dec–Mar), when several outfitters also offer **whale-watching excursions** (p. 444). Unlike on Maui, your boat may be the only one visible for miles around. Head to **Coffees of Hawaii** (p. 438) for the twice-weekly **kanikapila** (jam session) with takes place on the wide lanai Friday (3–6pm) and Tuesdays (10am–1pm). Island kupuna (elders) play old-school Hawaiian music and pop classics—it's not to be missed.

DAY 6: Explore Nature Reserves ★★★ or a Scenic Park & Unique Shops ★★

The best (and only recommended) way to explore the windswept dunes of **Moomomi Preserve** and the miniature trees in the cloud forest atop the **Kamakou Preserve** is via one of the **Nature Conservancy's guided hikes** (p. 450), offered once a month March through October—book as far in advance as possible. If neither hike is available or practical, drive to **Palaau State Park** (p. 442) to check out the Kalaupapa Overlook and Phallic Rock, and stop by the **Molokai Museum and Cultural Center** (p. 438) and **Purdy's Macadamia Nut Farm** (p. 439). Or simply browse the **Saturday morning farmer's market** (p. 456) and quaint stores in Kaunakakai (p. 457).

If this is Sunday, then there's little to do on Molokai—besides going to one of the many churches—and that's the way local folks like it. Now's a good day to revisit a favorite beach or drive up to rustic **Ironwood Hills Golf Course** (p. 449).

A WEEK ON LANAI

The smallest of all the Hawaiian Islands, this former pineapple plantation is now home to a posh resort, a rich and colorful history, and a postage-stamp-size town with some of the friendliest people you'll ever meet. There are enough activities here to keep you busy, but you'll probably be happiest skipping a few and slowing down to Lanai speed.

DAY 1: Arrive & Investigate Hulopoe Bay's Tide Pools ★★★

After settling into your hotel, head for the best stretch of sand on the island (and maybe the state): **Hulopoe Beach** (p. 471). It's generally safe for swimming, and snorkeling within this marine preserve is terrific. The fish are so friendly you practically have to shoo them away; dolphins are frequent visitors. Climb up to the **Puu Pehe** or Sweetheart Rock lookout (p. 478). Dine like a celebrity at **Nobu** (p. 481).

DAY 2: Explore Lanai City & Garden of the Gods ★★★

Head into quaint Lanai City to browse the boutiques (p. 483) and get a colorful history lesson at the **Lanai Culture & Heritage Center** (p. 467). Buckle up for a 3½-hour tour with **Rabaca's Limousine Service.** Let your driver navigate the rough road down to **Polihua Beach** (p. 472), Lanai's largest white-sand beach. On the way back, linger at the **Garden of the Gods** (p. 467) to snap photos of the otherworldly landscape at sunset. Finish your day at the **Lanai City Bar & Grille,** listening to live music and dining by the fire pits out back (p. 480).

DAY 3: Enjoy a Day on the Water ★★★

Spend the day with **Lanai Ocean Sports** (p. 473) on a snorkel sail or scuba adventure along the island's west coast or at **Cathedrals,** one of Hawaii's most ethereal dive sites. At night, savor hand-mixed cocktails and shoot some pool at the **Four Seasons Lanai Sports Bar & Grill** (p. 479).

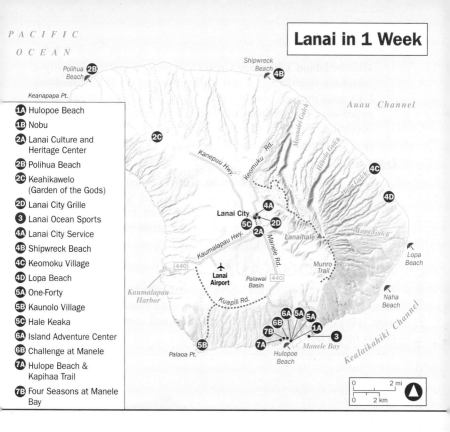

Lanai in 1 Week

Polihua Beach **2B**

Keanapapa Pt.

Shipwreck Beach **4B**

Auau Channel

1A Hulopoe Beach
1B Nobu
2A Lanai Culture and Heritage Center
2B Polihua Beach
2C Keahikawelo (Garden of the Gods)
2D Lanai City Grille
3 Lanai Ocean Sports
4A Lanai City Service
4B Shipwreck Beach
4C Keomoku Village
4D Lopa Beach
5A One-Forty
5B Kaunolo Village
5C Hale Keaka
6A Island Adventure Center
6B Challenge at Manele
7A Hulope Beach & Kapihaa Trail
7B Four Seasons at Manele Bay

2C

Kanepuu Hwy.
Keomuku Rd.

Maunalei Gulch
Hauola Gulch
Hi'i Gulch

4C
4D

Lanai City **4A**
5C **2D**
2A

Kaumalapau Hwy.

Manele Rd.

Lanaihale

Lopa Gulch

Lopa Beach

440

Lanai Airport

Palawai Basin

Munro Trail

440

Kaumalapau Harbor

Kuapli Rd.

Naha Beach

6A **5A** **5A**
6B
7B **1A**
5B
7A
Palaoa Pt.
Hulopoe Beach

Manele Bay

3

Kealaikahiki Channel

0 — 2 mi
0 — 2 km

DAY 4: Four-Wheel It to the East Side ★★★

Lanai is a fantastic place to go four-wheeling. If it hasn't been raining, splurge on an ATV or four-wheel-drive vehicle and head out to the East Side. Get a picnic lunch from **Lanai City Service** (p. 483) and download the Lanai Guide app for GPS-enabled directions, historic photos, and haunting Hawaiian chants. Find the petroglyphs at **Shipwreck Beach** (p. 472) and forge onward to **Keomoku Village** and **Lopa Beach** (p. 469).

DAY 5: Brunch Like Royalty & Visit an Ancient King's Temple ★★★

Fill your belly at **One Forty** (p. 481), where the lavish breakfast buffet's omelet station, juice bar, and *malasada* (Portuguese doughnut) fryer should fuel you for hours. Tackle the rugged 4WD road down to **Kaunolu Village** (p. 470), where King Kahekili and his warriors famously leapt from the cliffs into the sea. Return your ATV or car in town and catch a movie at **Hale Keaka** (p. 486).

DAY 6: Choose Your Adventure & Hit the Spa ★★★

Visit the **Island Adventure Center** to book your preferred activity: a horseback ride through Lanai's upland forests (p. 477), a rambling UTV tour through several cultural sites, or a round of golf at the award-winning **Challenge at Manele** golf course (p. 477). Cap your adventure with a soothing treatment at the **Hawanawana Spa** (p. 480) at the Four Seasons Resort Lanai.

DAY 7: Spend a Day at the Beach ★★

Soak up the sun at **Hulopoe Beach** (p. 471). Grab a book and watch the kids play in the surf. If you feel inclined, follow the **Kapihaa Trail** (p. 477) along the rocky coast. For lunch, wander up to **Malibu Farms** (p. 482) and scan the horizon for dolphins or whales.

A WEEK ON KAUAI

Because much of the Garden Island, including the Napali Coast, is inaccessible to cars, a week will *just* suffice to view its beauty. To save driving time, split your stay between the North and South shores (detailed below) or stay on the East Side.

Hanalei Bay

Kauai in 1 Week

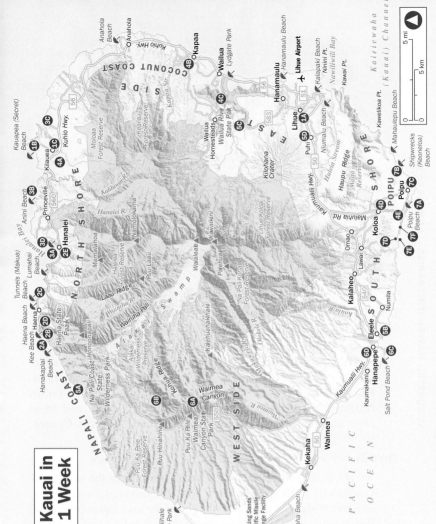

1A Hamura's Saimin Stand
1B Kilauea Point National Wildlife Refuge & Lighthouse
1C Kong Long Historic Market Center
2A Kee Beach
2B Kalalau Trail
2C Makua (Tunnels) Beach
2D Limahuli Garden & Preserve
2E Tahiti Nui
3A Hanalei Bay
3B Anini Beach
3C Na Aina Ka Botanical Gardens
4A St. Regis Princeville
4B Ainana Hou Community Park
4B Kapaa
4C Opaekaa Falls/Wailua River State Park
4D Old Koloa Town
4E Shops at Kukuiula
5A Napali Coast helicopter or boat tour
5B Kauai Island Brewery & Grill
5C Wailua Falls
5D Kilohana Plantation
6A Waimea Canyon
6B Kokee State Park
6C Salt Pond Beach Park
6D Hanapepe
7A Poipu Beach
7B Mahaulepu Heritage Trail
7C Anara Spa at Grand Hyatt Kauai
7D National Tropical Botanical Garden
7E Spouting Horn
7F RumFire
7G The Beach House

33

Helicopter view of Napali

DAY 1: Arrival, Lunch & a Scenic Drive ★★★

From the airport, stop by **Hamura's Saimin Stand** (p. 579) or another **Lihue** lunch counter (see "Plate Lunch, Bento & Poke," p. 576) for a classic taste of Kauai before driving through the bustling Coconut Coast on your way to the serenity of the rural **North Shore** (p. 494). Soak in the views at the **Kilauea Point National Wildlife Refuge & Lighthouse** (p. 509), and then poke around Kilauea's **Kong Lung Historic Market Center** (p. 592).

DAY 2: Hike & Snorkel the North Shore ★★★

Thanks to the time difference between Hawaii and the mainland, you'll likely wake up early. Get a head start driving across the nine one-lane bridges on the way to the end of the road and popular **Kee Beach** (p. 528). If conditions permit, hike at least a half-hour out on the challenging **Kalalau Trail** (p. 511) for glimpses of the stunning **Napali Coast,** or tackle the first 2 miles to **Hanakapiai Beach,** 3 to 4 hours round-trip. After (or instead of) hiking, snorkel at **Kee** and equally gorgeous **Makua (Tunnels) Beach** (p. 529), accessed from **Haena Beach Park** (p. 529). Eat lunch in Haena and then spend time in the jewel-box setting of **Limahuli Garden and Preserve** (p. 510). Return to Hanalei to explore shops and galleries; after dinner, enjoy live Hawaiian music at the venerable **Tahiti Nui** (p. 597).

DAY 3: Adventures in Hanalei ★★★

The day begins on **Hanalei Bay, kayaking, surfing,** or **snorkeling** (see "Watersports," p. 553) or just frolicking at one of the three different beach parks (p. 527). If the waves are too rough, head instead to lagoonlike **Anini Beach** (p. 526). Later, try **ziplining** (p. 554) or **horseback riding** (p. 552) amid waterfalls and green mountains; those who book in advance can tour delightful **Na Aina Kai Botanical Gardens** (p. 510). Savor views of Hanalei Bay and "Bali Hai" over cocktails at the **St. Regis Princeville** (p. 565) before dinner at the hotel or **Bar Acuda** (p. 580).

DAY 4: Nature & Culture en Route to Poipu ★★

After breakfast, head south. Visit Kilauea's **Anaina Hou Community Park** (p. 507) for Kauai-themed mini-golf in a botanical garden or a hike or bike along the scenic Wai Koa loop trail. Stop for a bite at a funky cafe in **Kapaa;** then drive to **Opaekaa Falls** and see the cultural sites of **Wailua River State Park** (p. 506). After crossing through busy Lihue, admire the scenery on the way to **Old Koloa Town** (p. 593), where you can browse the quaint shops

Double rainbow over Kalalau valley, seen from Pihea trail, Kauai

Poipu Beach is one of the most popular tourist areas on the island of Kauai

before checking into your Poipu lodgings. Pick a dinner spot from the many excellent choices in the **Shops at Kukuiula** (p. 594).

DAY 5: Napali by Boat or Helicopter ★★★

Splurge on a **snorkel boat** or **Zodiac raft tour** (p. 533) to the **Napali Coast,** or take a **helicopter tour** (p. 521) for amazing views of Napali, Waimea Canyon, waterfalls, and more. After your boat returns, hoist a draft beer at **Kauai Island Brewery & Grill** (p. 589). For helicopter tours, most of which depart from Lihue, book a late-morning tour (after rush hour). Then have lunch in Lihue and drive to **Wailua Falls** (p. 507) before perusing the shops, tasting rum, or riding the train at **Kilohana Plantation** (p. 505).

DAY 6: Waimea Canyon & Kokee State Park ★★★

Start your drive early to "the Grand Canyon of the Pacific," **Waimea Canyon** (p. 520). Stay on the road through forested **Kokee State Park** (p. 517) to the **Kalalau Valley Lookout** (p. 518), and wait for mists to part for a magnificent view. Stop by the **Kokee Museum** (p. 551) to obtain trail information for a hike after lunch at **Kokee Lodge** (p. 589). Or head back down to hit the waves at **Salt Pond Beach** or stroll through rustic **Hanapepe** (p. 498), home to a **Friday night festival and art walk** (p. 597).

DAY 7: Beach & Spa Time in Poipu ★★★

Spend the morning at glorious **Poipu Beach** (p. 531) before the crowds arrive, and then head over to **Keoneloa (Shipwrecks) Beach** (p. 531) to hike along the coastal **Mahaulepu Heritage Trail**

(p. 551). Later, indulge in a spa treatment at Anara Spa at the **Grand Hyatt Kauai** (p. 567) or take a tour (booked in advance) at the **National Tropical Botanical Garden** (p. 515). Check out the flume of **Spouting Horn** (p. 517) before sunset cocktails at **RumFire Poipu Beach** in the **Sheraton Kauai** (p. 569) and dinner at the **Beach House** (p. 584).

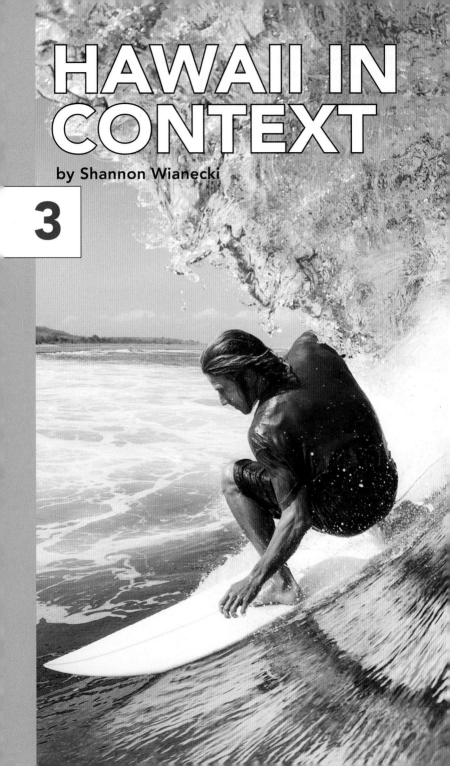

HAWAII IN CONTEXT

by Shannon Wianecki

3

S ince the Polynesians ventured across the Pacific to the Hawaiian Islands more than 1,000 years ago, these floating jewels have summoned travelers from around the globe.

The Hawaiian Islands bask in the warm waters of the Pacific, where they are blessed by a tropical sun and cooled by gentle trade winds—creating what might be the most ideal climate imaginable. Mother Nature has carved out verdant valleys, hung brilliant rainbows in the sky, and trimmed the islands with sandy beaches in a spectrum of colors. The indigenous Hawaiian culture embodies "aloha spirit," an easy-going generosity that takes the shape of flower leis freely given, monumental feasts shared with friends and family, and hypnotic melodies played late into the tropical night.

Visitors are drawn to Hawaii not only for its incredible beauty, but also for its opportunities for adventure. Go on, gaze into that fiery volcano, swim in a sea of rainbow-colored fish, tee off on a championship golf course, hike through a rainforest to hidden waterfalls, and kayak into the deep end of the ocean, where whales leap out of the water for reasons still mysterious. Looking for rest and relaxation? You'll discover that life moves at an unhurried pace here. Extra doses of sun and sea allow both body and mind to recharge.

Hawaii is a sensory experience that will remain with you long after your tan fades. Years later, a sweet fragrance, the sun's warmth on your face, or the sound of the ocean breeze will deliver you back to the time you spent in the Hawaiian Islands.

THE FIRST HAWAIIANS

Throughout the Middle Ages, while Western sailors clung to the edges of continents for fear of falling off the earth's edge, Polynesian voyagers crisscrossed the planet's largest ocean. The first people to colonize Hawaii were unsurpassed navigators. Using the stars, birds, and currents as guides, they sailed double-hulled canoes across thousands of miles, zeroing in on tiny islands in the center of the Pacific. They packed their vessels with food, plants, medicine, tools, and animals: everything necessary for building a new life on a distant shore. Over a span of 800 years, the great Polynesian migration connected a vast triangle of islands stretching from New Zealand to Hawaii to Easter Island and encompassing the many diverse archipelagos in between. Archaeologists surmise that Hawaii's first wave of settlers came via the Marquesas Islands sometime after a.d. 1000, though oral histories suggest a much earlier date.

FACING PAGE: **Surfing in Hawaii**

Over the ensuing centuries, a distinctly Hawaiian culture arose. Sailors became farmers and fishermen. These early Hawaiians were as skilled on land as they had been at sea; they built highly productive fish ponds, aqueducts to irrigate terraced *kalo loi* (taro patches), and 3-acre *heiau* (temples) with 50-foot-high rock walls. Farmers cultivated more than 400 varieties of *kalo,* their staple food; 300 types of sweet potato; and 40 different bananas. Each variety served a different need—some were drought resistant, others medicinal, and others good for babies. Hawaiian women fashioned intricately patterned *kapa* (barkcloth)—some of the finest in all of Polynesia. Each of the Hawaiian Islands was its own kingdom, governed by *ali'i* (high-ranking chiefs) who drew their authority from an established caste system and *kapu* (taboos). Those who broke the *kapu* could be sacrificed.

The ancient Hawaiian creation chant, the *Kumulipō,* depicts a universe that began when heat and light emerged out of darkness, followed by the first life form: a coral polyp. The 2,000-line epic poem is a grand genealogy, describing how all species are interrelated, from gently waving seaweeds to mighty human warriors. It is the basis for the Hawaiian concept of *kuleana,* a word that simultaneously refers to privilege and responsibility. To this day, Native Hawaiians view the care of their natural resources as a filial duty and honor.

WESTERN CONTACT
Cook's Ill-Fated Voyage

In the dawn hours of January 18, 1778, Captain James Cook of the HMS *Resolution* spotted an unfamiliar set of islands, which he later named for his benefactor, the Earl of Sandwich. The 50-year-old sea captain was already famous in Britain for "discovering" much of the South Pacific. Now on his third great voyage of exploration, Cook had set sail from Tahiti northward across uncharted waters. He was searching for the mythical Northwest Passage that was said to link the Pacific and Atlantic oceans. On his way, he stumbled upon Hawaii (aka the Sandwich Isles) quite by chance.

With the arrival of the *Resolution,* Stone Age Hawaii entered the age of iron. Sailors swapped nails and munitions for fresh water, pigs, and the affections of Hawaiian women. Tragically, the foreigners brought with them a terrible cargo: syphilis, measles, and other diseases that decimated the Hawaiian people. Captain Cook estimated the native population at 400,000 in 1778. (Later historians claim it could have been as high as 900,000.) By the time Christian missionaries arrived 40 years later, the number of Native Hawaiians had plummeted to just 150,000.

In a skirmish over a stolen boat, Cook was killed by a blow to the head. His British countrymen sailed home, leaving Hawaii forever altered. The islands were now on the sea charts, and traders on the fur route between Canada and China stopped here to get fresh water. More trade—and more disastrous liaisons—ensued.

King Kamehameha statue

Two more sea captains left indelible marks on the islands. The first was American John Kendrick, who in 1791 filled his ship with fragrant Hawaiian sandalwood and sailed to China. By 1825, Hawaii's sandalwood groves were gone. The second was Englishman George Vancouver, who in 1793 left behind cows and sheep, which ventured out to graze in the islands' native forest and hastened the spread of invasive species. King Kamehameha I sent for cowboys from Mexico and Spain to round up the wild livestock, thus beginning the islands' *paniolo* (cowboy) tradition.

King Kamehameha I was an ambitious *ali'i* who used western guns to unite the islands under single rule. After his death in 1819, the tightly woven Hawaiian society began to unravel. One of his successors, Queen Kaahumanu, abolished the *kapu* system, opening the door for religion of another form.

Staying to Do Well

In April 1820, missionaries bent on converting Hawaiians arrived from New England. The newcomers clothed the natives, banned them from dancing the hula, and nearly dismantled the ancient culture. The churchgoers tried to keep sailors and whalers out of the bawdy houses, where whiskey flowed and the virtue of native women was never safe. To their credit, the missionaries created a 12-letter alphabet for the Hawaiian language, taught reading and writing, started a printing press, and began recording the islands' history, which until that time had been preserved solely in memorized chants.

Children of the missionaries became business leaders and politicians. They married Hawaiians and stayed on in the islands, causing one wag to remark that the missionaries "came to do good and stayed to do well." In 1848, King Kamehameha III enacted the Great Mahele (division).

WHO IS hawaiian IN HAWAII?

Only *kanaka maoli* (Native Hawaiians) are truly Hawaiian. The sugar and pineapple plantations brought so many different people to Hawaii that the state is now a remarkable potpourri of ethnic groups: Native Hawaiians were joined by **Caucasians, Japanese, Chinese, Filipinos, Koreans, Portuguese, Puerto Ricans, Samoans, Tongans, Tahitians,** and other **Asian and Pacific Islanders.** Add to that a sprinkling of **Vietnamese, Canadians, African Americans, American Indians, South Americans,** and **Europeans** of every stripe. Many people retained the traditions of their homeland and many more blended their cultures into something new. That is the genesis of Hawaiian Pidgin, local cuisine, and holidays and celebrations unique to these Islands.

Intended to guarantee Native Hawaiians rights to their land, it ultimately enabled foreigners to take ownership of vast tracts of land. Within two generations, more than 80% of all private land was in *haole* (foreign) hands. Businessmen planted acre after acre of sugarcane and imported waves of immigrants to work the fields: Chinese starting in 1852, Japanese in 1885, and Portuguese in 1878.

King David Kalakaua was elected to the throne in 1874. This popular "Merrie Monarch" built Iolani Palace in 1882, threw extravagant parties, and lifted the prohibitions on hula and other native arts. For this, he was much loved. He proclaimed, "hula is the language of the heart and, therefore, the heartbeat of the Hawaiian people." He also gave Pearl Harbor to the United States; it became the westernmost bastion of the U.S. Navy. While visiting chilly San Francisco in 1891, King Kalakaua caught a cold and died in the royal suite of the Sheraton Palace. His sister, Queen Liliuokalani, assumed the throne.

The Overthrow

For years, a group of American sugar plantation owners and missionary descendants had been machinating against the monarchy. On January 17, 1893, with the support of the U.S. minister to Hawaii and the Marines, the conspirators imprisoned Queen Liliuokalani in her own palace. To avoid bloodshed, she abdicated the throne, trusting that the United States government would right the wrong. As the Queen waited in vain, she penned the sorrowful lyric "Aloha Oe," Hawaii's song of farewell.

U.S. President Grover Cleveland's attempt to restore the monarchy was thwarted by Congress. Sanford Dole, a powerful sugar plantation owner, appointed himself president of the newly declared Republic of Hawaii. His fellow sugarcane planters, known as the Big Five, controlled banking, shipping, hardware, and every other facet of economic life in the Islands. In 1898, through annexation, Hawaii became an American territory ruled by Dole.

Oahu's central Ewa Plain soon filled with row crops. The Dole family planted pineapple on its sprawling acreage. Planters imported more contract laborers from Puerto Rico (1900), Korea (1903), and the Philippines (1907–31). Many of the new immigrants stayed on to establish families and become a part of the islands. Meanwhile, Native Hawaiians became a landless minority. Their language was banned in schools and their cultural practices devalued.

For nearly a century in Hawaii, sugar was king, generously subsidized by the U.S. government. Sugar is a thirsty crop, and plantation owners oversaw the construction of flumes and aqueducts that channeled mountain streams down to parched plains, where waving fields of cane soon grew. The waters that once fed taro patches dried up. The sugar planters dominated the territory's economy, shaped its social fabric, and kept the islands in a colonial plantation era with bosses and field hands. But the workers eventually went on strike for higher wages and improved working conditions, and the planters found themselves unable to compete with cheap third-world labor costs.

Tourism Takes Hold

Tourism in Hawaii began in the 1860s. Kilauea volcano was one of the world's prime attractions for adventure travelers. In 1865 a grass structure known as Volcano House was built on the rim of Halemaumau Crater to shelter visitors; it was Hawaii's first hotel. The visitor industry blossomed as the plantation era peaked and waned.

Queen Liliuokalani statue

SPEAKING hawaiian

Nearly everyone in Hawaii speaks English, though many people now also speak *ōlelo Hawaii,* the native language of these islands. Most roads, towns, and beaches possess vowel-heavy Hawaiian names, so it will serve you well to practice pronunciation before venturing out to 'Aiea or Nu'uanu.

The Hawaiian alphabet has only 12 letters: 7 consonants (*h, k, l, m, n, p,* and *w*) and 5 vowels (*a, e, i, o,* and *u*)—but those vowels are liberally used! Usually they are "short," pronounced: *ah, ay, ee, oh,* and *oo.* For example, *wahine* (woman) is *wah-hee-nay.* Most vowels are pronounced separately, but on occasion they are sounded together with the "long" pronunciation: *ay, ee, eye, oh,* and *you.* For example, Wai'anae on Oahu's leeward coast is *Why-ah-ny.*

Two pronunciation marks can help you sound your way through Hawaiian names. The okina, a backwards apostrophe, indicates a glottal stop or a slight pause. The kahakō is a line over a vowel indicating stress. Observing these rules, you can tell that Pā'ia, a popular surf town on Maui's North Shore, is pronounced *PAH-ee-ah.* The Likelike Highway is *lee-KAY-lee-KAY.*

Incorporate *aloha* (hello, goodbye, love) and *mahalo* (thank you) into your vocabulary. If you've just arrived, you're a *malihini* (newcomer). Someone who's been here a long time is a *kama'āina* (child of the land). When you finish a job or your meal, you are *pau* (finished). On Friday, it's *pau hana,* work finished. You eat *pūpū* (appetizers) when you go *pau hana.* **Note:** Hawaiian punctuation marks are not included in this edition, but you will see them on road signs, menus, and publications throughout Hawaii.

In 1901 W. C. Peacock built the elegant Beaux Arts Moana Hotel on Waikiki Beach, and W. C. Weedon convinced Honolulu businessmen to bankroll his plan to advertise Hawaii in San Francisco. Armed with a stereopticon and tinted photos of Waikiki, Weedon sailed off in 1902 for 6 months of lecture tours to introduce "those remarkable people and the beautiful lands of Hawaii." He drew packed houses. A tourism promotion bureau was formed in 1903, and about 2,000 visitors came to Hawaii that year.

The steamship was Hawaii's tourism lifeline. It took 4½ days to sail from San Francisco to Honolulu. Streamers, leis, and pomp welcomed each Matson liner at downtown's Aloha Tower. Well-heeled visitors brought trunks, servants, and Rolls-Royces and stayed for months. Hawaiians amused visitors with personal tours, floral parades, and hula shows.

Beginning in 1935 and running for the next 40 years, Webley Edwards's weekly live radio show, "Hawaii Calls," planted the sounds of Waikiki—surf, sliding steel guitar, sweet Hawaiian harmonies, drumbeats—in the hearts of millions of listeners in the United States, Australia, and Canada.

By 1936, visitors could fly to Honolulu from San Francisco on the *Hawaii Clipper,* a seven-passenger Pan American Martin M-130 flying boat, for $360 one-way. The flight took 21 hours, 33 minutes. Modern tourism was born, with five flying boats providing daily service. The 1941 visitor count was a brisk 31,846 through December 6.

World War II & Statehood

On December 7, 1941, Japanese Zeros came out of the rising sun to bomb American warships based at Pearl Harbor. This was the "day of infamy" that plunged the United States into World War II.

The attack brought immediate changes to the islands. Martial law was declared, stripping the Big Five cartel of its absolute power in a single day. German and Japanese Americans were interned. Hawaii was "blacked out" at night, Waikiki Beach was strung with barbed wire, and Aloha Tower was painted in camouflage. Only young men bound for the Pacific came to Hawaii during the war years. Many came back to graves in a cemetery called Punchbowl.

The postwar years saw the beginnings of Hawaii's faux culture. The authentic traditions had long been suppressed, and into the void flowed a consumable brand of aloha. Harry Yee invented the Blue Hawaii cocktail and dropped in a tiny Japanese parasol. Vic Bergeron created the mai tai, a drink made of rum and fresh lime juice, and opened Trader Vic's, America's first themed restaurant that featured the art, decor, and food of Polynesia. Arthur Godfrey picked up a ukulele and began singing *hapa-haole* tunes on early TV shows. In 1955, Henry J. Kaiser built the Hilton Hawaiian Village, and the 11-story high-rise Princess Kaiulani Hotel opened on a site where the real princess once played. Hawaii greeted 109,000 visitors that year.

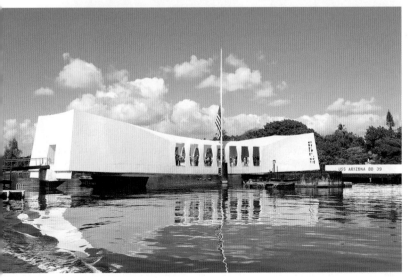

U.S.S. Arizona Memorial at Pearl Harbor

In 1959, Hawaii became the 50th state of the United States. That year also saw the arrival of the first jet airliners, which brought 250,000 tourists to the state. By the 1980s, Hawaii's visitor count surpassed 6 million. Fantasy megaresorts bloomed on the neighbor islands like giant artificial flowers, swelling the luxury market with ever-swankier accommodations. Hawaii's tourist industry—the bastion of the state's economy—has survived worldwide recessions, airline-industry hiccups, and increased competition from overseas. Year after year, the Hawaiian Islands continue to be ranked among the top visitor destinations in the world.

HAWAII TODAY
A Cultural Renaissance

Despite the ever-increasing influx of foreign people and customs, Native Hawaiian culture is experiencing a rebirth. It began in earnest in 1976, when members of the Polynesian Voyaging Society launched *Hōkūlea,* a double-hulled canoe of the sort that hadn't been seen on these shores in centuries. The *Hōkūlea*'s daring crew sailed her 2,500 miles to Tahiti without using modern instruments, relying instead on ancient navigational techniques. Most historians at that time discounted Polynesian wayfinding methods as rudimentary; the prevailing theory was that Pacific Islanders had discovered Hawaii by accident, not intention. The *Hōkūlea*'s successful voyage sparked a fire in the hearts of indigenous islanders across the Pacific, who reclaimed their identity as a sophisticated, powerful people with unique wisdom to offer the world.

Hula

The Hawaiian language found new life, too. In 1984, a group of educators and parents recognized that, with fewer than 50 children fluent in Hawaiian, the language was dangerously close to extinction. They started a preschool where *keiki* (children) learned lessons purely in Hawaiian. They overcame numerous bureaucratic obstacles (including a law still on the books forbidding instruction in Hawaiian) to establish Hawaiian-language-immersion programs across the state that run from preschool through post-graduate education.

Hula—which never fully disappeared despite the missionaries' best efforts—is thriving. At the annual Merrie Monarch Festival commemorating King Kalakaua, hula *halau* (troupes) from Hawaii and beyond gather to demonstrate their skill and artistry. Fans of the ancient dance form are glued to the live broadcast of what is known as the Olympics of hula. *Kumu hula* (hula teachers) have safeguarded many Hawaiian cultural practices as part of their art: the making of *kapa,* the collection and cultivation of native herbs, and the observation of *kuleana,* an individual's responsibility to the community.

In that same spirit, in May 2014, the traditional voyaging canoe *Hōkūlea* embarked on her most ambitious adventure yet: an international peace delegation. During the canoe's 3-year circumnavigation of the globe, the crew sought "to weave a lei around the world" and chart a new course toward a healthier and more sustainable horizon for all of humankind. The sailors met with political leaders, scientists, educators, and schoolchildren in each of the ports they visited. *Hōkūlea* returned home to a hero's welcome in June 2017.

DINING IN HAWAII
The Gang of 12

In the early days of Hawaii's tourism industry, the food wasn't anything to write home about. Continental cuisine ruled fine-dining kitchens. Meats and produce arrived much the same way visitors did: jet-lagged after a long journey from a far-off land. Island chefs struggled to revive limp iceberg lettuce and frozen cocktail shrimp—often letting outstanding ocean views make up for uninspired dishes. In 1991, 12 chefs staged a revolt. They partnered with local farmers, ditched the dictatorship of imported foods, and brought sun-ripened mango, crisp organic greens, and freshly caught *uku* (snapper) to the table. Coining the name Hawaii Regional Cuisine (HRC), they gave the world a taste of what happens when passionate, classically trained cooks have their way with ripe Pacific flavors.

Nearly 3 decades later, the movement to unite local farms and kitchens has only grown more vibrant. The HRC heavyweights continue to keep things hot in island kitchens, but they aren't, by any means, the sole source of good eats in Hawaii.

Shops selling fresh steaming noodles abound in Oahu's **Chinatown.** Francophiles will delight in the classic French cooking at **La Mer** on Oahu and **Gerard's** on Maui. You'll be hard-pressed to discover more authentic Japanese fare than can be had in the restaurants dotting Honolulu's side streets.

Plate Lunches, Shave Ice & Food Trucks

Haute cuisine is alive and well in Hawaii, but equally important in the culinary pageant are good-value plate lunches, shave ice, and food trucks.

The **plate lunch,** like Hawaiian Pidgin, is a gift of the plantation era. You find plate lunches of various kinds served in to-go eateries across the state. They usually consist of some protein—fried mahi-mahi, say, or teriyaki beef, shoyu chicken, or chicken or pork cutlets served katsu-style: breaded, fried, and slathered in tangy sauce—accompanied by "two scoops rice," macaroni salad, and a few leaves of green, typically julienned cabbage. Chili water and soy sauce are the condiments of choice. Like **saimin**—the local version of noodles in broth topped with scrambled eggs, green onions, and sometimes pork—the plate lunch is Hawaii's version of comfort food.

Because this is Hawaii, at least a few fingerfuls of **poi**—steamed, pounded taro (the traditional Hawaiian staple crop)—are a must. Mix it with salty *kalua* pork (pork cooked in a Polynesian underground oven known as an *imu*) or *lomi* salmon (salted salmon with tomatoes and green onions). Other tasty Hawaiian foods include **poke** (pronounced *po-kay*), a popular appetizer made of cubed raw fish seasoned with onions, seaweed,

Ahi poke

Traditional plate lunch

and roasted *kukui* nuts); ***laulau,*** pork, chicken, or fish steamed in tī leaves; **squid** *lūau,* cooked in coconut milk and taro tops; ***haupia,*** creamy coconut pudding; and ***kūlolo,*** a steamed pudding of coconut, brown sugar, and taro.

For a sweet snack, the prevailing choice is **shave ice.** Particularly on hot, humid days, long lines of shave-ice lovers gather for heaps of finely shaved ice topped with sweet tropical syrups. Sweet-sour *li hing mui* is a favorite, and gourmet flavors include calamansi lime and red velvet cupcake. Aficionados order shave ice with ice cream and sweetened adzuki beans on the bottom or sweetened condensed milk on top.

WHEN TO GO

Most visitors come to Hawaii when the weather is lousy elsewhere. Thus, the **high season**—when prices are up and resorts are often booked to capacity—is generally from mid-December to March or mid-April. In particular, the last 2 weeks of December and first week of January, are prime time for travel to Hawaii. Spring break is also jam-packed with families taking advantage of the school holiday.

If you're planning a trip during peak season, make hotel and rental car reservations as early as possible, expect crowds, and prepare to pay top dollar. The winter months tend to be a little rainier and cooler. But there's a perk to travelling during this time: Hawaiian humpback whales are here, too.

The **off season,** when the best rates are available and the islands are less crowded, is late spring (mid-Apr to early June) and fall (Sept to mid-Dec).

If you plan to travel in **summer** (June–Aug), don't expect to see the fantastic bargains of spring and fall—this is prime time for family travel. But you'll still find much better deals on packages, airfare, and accommodations than in the winter months.

on location **IN HAWAII**

Hawaii's iconic landscapes serve as a backdrop for numerous TV shows and films. *Jumanji* is the most recent blockbuster shot in the Aloha State, at Waimea Falls on Oahu and Rainbow Falls on Hawaii Island. Fans of **Lost** might recognize Mokuleia Beach on Oahu's North Shore as the site of the fictional plane crash. Episode three was shot in Oahu's Kaaawa Valley, a lush and remote spot that appears in several movies, including *50 First Dates, Godzilla,* and *Pearl Harbor.* Johnny Depp leaps into Kilauea Falls on Kauai in *Pirates of the Caribbean: On Stranger Tides.* Adam Sandler and Jennifer Aniston luxuriate at the Grand Wailea's pool and pass through the lobby of the Mana Kai on Maui in *Just Go With It.*

The Descendants, Alexander Payne's film about a dysfunctional Hawaii *kama-aina* (long-time resident) family, features a wealth of island scenery and music. George Clooney (as Matt King) and the cast spent 11 weeks shooting in Hawaii; it's easy to trace their trail. Matt King's house is on Old Pali Road in Nuuanu. When King runs down the hill to visit a friend, he's greeted by Poppy, a pygmy goat standing beneath a 50-foot-tall lychee tree. Payne rented the plantation-style house—goat and all—from a local family and shot scenes there without changing a thing. Whether or not you're a film buff, you should definitely pick up a copy of *The Descendants* **soundtrack.** This goldmine of modern and classic Hawaiian music features the very best island voices, from Gabby Pahinui to Keola Beamer, and includes several versions of the hauntingly beautiful anthem "Hiilawe." You won't find a better soundtrack for your Hawaiian vacation.

Shailene Woodley, George Clooney, Amara Miller, and Nick Krause in *The Descendants*

Hey, No Smoking in Hawaii

Well, not *totally* no smoking, but Hawaii has one of the toughest laws against smoking in the U.S. The Hawaii Smoke-Free Law prohibits smoking in public buildings, including airports, shopping malls, grocery stores, retail shops, buses, movie theaters, banks, convention facilities, and all government buildings and facilities. There is no smoking in restaurants, bars, or nightclubs. Most

B&Bs prohibit smoking indoors, and more and more hotels and resorts are becoming smoke-free even in public areas. Also, there is no smoking within 20 feet of a doorway, window, or ventilation intake (so no hanging around outside a bar to smoke—you must go 20 ft. away). Even some beaches have no-smoking policies.

Climate

Because Hawaii lies at the edge of the tropical zone, it technically has only two seasons, both of them warm. There's a dry season that corresponds to **summer** (Apr–Oct) and a rainy season in **winter** (Nov–Mar). It rains every day somewhere in the islands at any time of the year, but the rainy season can bring enough gray weather to spoil your tanning opportunities. Fortunately, it seldom rains in one spot for more than 3 days straight.

The **year-round temperature** doesn't vary much. At the beach, the average daytime high in summer is 85°F (29°C), while the average daytime high in winter is 78°F (26°C); nighttime lows are usually about 10° cooler. But how warm it is on any given day really depends on *where* you are on the island.

Each island has a **leeward** side (the side sheltered from the wind) and a **windward** side (the side that gets the wind's full force). The leeward sides (the west and south) are usually hot and dry, while the windward sides (east and north) are generally cooler and moist. When you want arid, sunbaked, desert-like weather, go leeward. When you want lush, wet, rainforest weather, go windward.

Hawaii also has a wide range of **microclimates,** thanks to interior valleys, coastal plains, and mountain peaks. Kauai's Mount Waialeale is one of the wettest spots on earth, yet Waimea Canyon, just a few miles away, is almost a desert. On the Big Island, Hilo ranks among the wettest cities in the nation, with 180 inches of rainfall a year. At Puako, only 60 miles away, it rains less than 6 inches a year. The summits of Mauna Kea on the Big Island and Haleakala on Maui often see snow in winter—even when the sun is blazing down at the beach. The locals say if you don't like the weather, just drive a few miles down the road—it's sure to be different!

Average Temperature & Number of Rainy Days

WAIKIKI

	JAN	FEB	MAR	APR	MAY	JUNE	JULY	AUG	SEPT	OCT	NOV	DEC
High (°F/°C)	80/27	80/27	81/27	82/28	84/29	86/30	87/31	88/31	88/31	86/30	84/29	81/27
Low (°F/°C)	70/21	66/19	66/19	69/21	70/21	72/22	73/23	74/23	74/23	72/22	70/21	67/19
Rainy Days	10	9	9	9	7	6	7	6	7	9	9	10

HANALEI, KAUAI

	JAN	FEB	MAR	APR	MAY	JUNE	JULY	AUG	SEPT	OCT	NOV	DEC
High (°F/°C)	79/26	80/27	80/27	82/28	84/29	86/30	88/31	88/31	87/31	86/30	83/28	80/27
Low (°F/°C)	61/16	61/16	62/17	63/17	65/18	66/19	66/19	67/19	68/20	67/19	65/18	62/17
Rainy Days	8	5	6	3	3	2	8	2	3	3	4	7

Holidays

When Hawaii observes holidays (especially those over a long weekend), travel between the islands increases, inter-island airline seats are fully booked, rental cars are at a premium, and hotels and restaurants are busier.

Federal, state, and county government offices are closed on all federal holidays. Federal holidays in 2019 include New Year's Day (Jan 1); Martin Luther King, Jr., Day (Jan 21); Presidents' Day (Feb 18); Memorial Day (May 27); Independence Day (July 4); Labor Day (Sept 2); Columbus Day (Oct 14); Veterans Day (Nov 11); Thanksgiving (Nov 28); and Christmas (Dec 25).

State and county offices are also closed on local holidays, including Prince Kuhio Day (Mar 26), honoring the birthday of Hawaii's first delegate to the U.S. Congress; King Kamehameha Day (June 11), a statewide holiday commemorating Kamehameha the Great, who united the islands and ruled from 1795 to 1819; and Admission Day (Aug 16), which honors the admittance of Hawaii as the 50th state on August 21, 1959.

Hawaii Calendar of Events

Please note that, as with any schedule of upcoming events, the following information is subject to change; always confirm the details before you plan your trip around an event.

JANUARY

Waimea Ocean Film Festival, Waimea and the Kohala Coast, Big Island. Several days of films featuring the ocean, ranging from surfing and Hawaiian canoe paddling to ecological issues. Go to www.waimea oceanfilm.org or call ☎ **808/854-6095.** First weekend after New Year's Day.

PGA Tournament of Champions, Kapalua Resort, Maui. Top PGA golfers compete for $8.75 million purse. Go to www.pga tour.com/toc or call ☎ **808/665-9160.** January 3–7.

Pacific Islands Arts Festival, Kapiolani Park, Honolulu, Oahu. This weekend fest features more than 75 artists and crafters, entertainment, food, and demonstrations. Free admission. Go to www.icb-web.net/haa or call ☎ **808/637-5337.** Mid-January.

Ka Molokai Makahiki, Kaunakakai Town Baseball Park, Mitchell Pauole Center, Kaunakakai, Molokai. Makahiki, a traditional time of peace in ancient Hawaii, is re-created with performances by Hawaiian music groups and *halau* (hula schools),

Daylight Saving Time

Most of the United States observes daylight saving time, which lasts from 2am on the second Sunday in March to 2am on the first Sunday in November. **Hawaii does not observe daylight saving time.** So when daylight saving time is in effect in most of the U.S., Hawaii is 3 hours behind the West Coast and 6 hours behind the East Coast. When the U.S. reverts to standard time in November, Hawaii is 2 hours behind the West Coast and 5 hours behind the East Coast.

sporting competitions, crafts, and food. It's a wonderful chance to experience ancient Hawaii. Ceremonial games start at 7:30am. Go to www.visitmolokai.com/wp/events-molokai-events-calendar or call ☏ **800/800-6367** or 808/553-3876. Late January.

FEBRUARY

Kauai Quilt Show, Lihue, Kauai. Quilting became an important creative outlet in the islands after the arrival of Western missionaries. Learn about Hawaii's unique style of applique quilting and view modern takes on this lovely art. Go to www.kauaifestivals.com or call ☏ **808/652-2261.** Throughout February.

Maui Whale Festival, Kalama Park, Kihei, Maui. A month-long celebration of Hawaii's massive marine visitors, with a film festival, benefit gala, harbor party, whale-watches with experts, and the "great whale count." Go to www.mauiwhalefestival.org or call ☏ **808/249-8811.** Throughout February.

Waimea Town Celebration, Waimea, Kauai. This annual weeklong party on Kauai's west side celebrates the Hawaiian and multiethnic history of the town where Captain Cook first landed. This is the island's biggest event, drawing some 10,000 people. Top Hawaiian entertainers, sporting events, rodeo, and ice cream eating and hat lei contests are just a few of the draws. Get details at www.waimeatowncelebration.com or call ☏ **808/651-5744.** Weekend after Presidents' Day weekend.

Sand Castle Esquisse, Kailua Beach Park, Oahu. Pull up a beach chair and watch University of Hawaii School of Architecture students compete against professional architects to see who can build the best, most unusual, and most outrageous sand sculpture. The building takes place 9am to noon; judging is noon to 1pm. Visit http://aias-hawaii.squarespace.com or call ☏ **808/956-7225.** Mid-February.

Chinese New Year, most islands. In 2018, lion dancers will be snaking their way around the state on February 16, the start of the Chinese Year of the Dog. On Oahu, Honolulu's Chinatown rolls out the red carpet for this fiery celebration with parades, pageants, and street festivals. Visit www.chinesechamber.com or call ☏ **808/533-3181.** On Maui, lion dancers perform at the historic Wo Hing Temple on Front Street (http://visitlahaina.com). Call ☏ **888/310-1117** or 808/667-9175.

Narcissus Festival, Honolulu, Oahu. Taking place around the Chinese New Year, this cultural festival includes a queen pageant, cooking demonstrations, and a cultural fair. Visit www.chinesechamber.com or call ☏ **808/533-3181.**

Punahou School Carnival, Punahou School, Honolulu, Oahu. This 2-day event has everything you can imagine in a school carnival, from high-speed rides to homemade jellies. All proceeds go to scholarship funds for Hawaii's most prestigious private high school. Go to www.punahou.edu or call ☏ **808/944-5711.** Early to mid-February.

Buffalo's Big Board Surfing Classic, Makaha Beach, Oahu. Now in its fourth decade, this thrilling contest features classic Hawaiian-style surfing, with longboard, tandem, and canoe surfing heats over several days. Go to www.buffalosurfingclassic.com or call ☎ **808/668-9712.** Mid-February or early March.

MARCH

Whale & Ocean Arts Festival, Lahaina, Maui. The entire town of Lahaina celebrates the annual migration of Pacific humpback whales with this weekend festival in Banyan Tree Park. Artists offer their best ocean-themed art for sale, while Hawaiian musicians and hula troupes entertain. Enjoy marine-related activities, games, and a touch-pool exhibit for kids. Get details at http://visitlahaina.com or call ☎ **888/310-1117** or 808/667-9175. Early March.

Kona Brewers Festival, King Kamehameha's Kona Beach Hotel Lūʻau Grounds, Kailua-Kona, Big Island. This annual event features microbreweries from around the world, with beer tastings, food, and entertainment. Visit http://konabrewersfestival.com or call ☎ **808/987-9196.** Mid-March.

St. Patrick's Day Parade, Waikiki (Fort DeRussy to Kapiolani Park), Oahu. Bagpipers, bands, clowns, and marching groups parade through the heart of Waikiki, with lots of Irish-style celebrating all day. Visit www.fosphawaii.ning.com/page/parade or call ☎ **808/926-1777** (Kelley O'Neil's Pub). March 17.

Prince Kuhio Day Celebrations, all islands. On this state holiday, various festivals throughout Hawaii celebrate the birth of Jonah Kuhio Kalanianaole, who was born on March 26, 1871, and elected to Congress in 1902. Kauai, his birthplace, stages weeklong festivities at various locations around the island; visit www.kauaifestivals.com for details. Week of March 26.

Celebration of the Arts, Ritz-Carlton Kapalua, Kapalua Resort, Maui. Contemporary and traditional Hawaiian artists give free hands-on lessons during this 3-day festival, which also features song contests and rousing debates on what it means to be Hawaiian. Go to www.celebrationofthearts.org or call ☎ **808/669-6200.** Easter weekend.

APRIL

Maui County Ag Fest, Waikapū, Maui. Maui celebrates its farmers and their fresh bounty at this well-attended event. Kids enjoy barnyard games while parents duck into the Grand Taste tent to sample top chefs' collaborations with local farmers. Go to www.mauicountyfarmbureau.org/maui-county-agricultural-festival-2 or call ☎ **808/243-2290.** First Saturday in April.

Buddha Day, Lahaina Jodo Mission, Lahaina, Maui. Each spring this historic mission holds a flower festival pageant honoring the birth of Buddha. Call ☎ **808/661-4304.** First Sunday in April.

Easter Sunrise Service, National Memorial Cemetery of the Pacific, Punchbowl Crater, Honolulu, Oahu. For a century, people have gathered at this famous cemetery for Easter sunrise services. Call ☎ **808/532-3720.** April 1, 2018.

Merrie Monarch Hula Festival, Hilo, Big Island. Hawaii's biggest, most prestigious hula festival features a week of modern (*auana*) and ancient (*kahiko*) dance competition in honor of King David Kalakaua, the "Merrie Monarch" who revived the dance. Tickets sell out by January, so book early. Go to www.merriemonarch.com or call ☎ **808/935-9168.** Late March through early April.

East Maui Taro Festival, Hana, Maui. Taro, a Hawaiian staple food, is celebrated through music, hula, arts, crafts, and, of course, taro-inspired feasts. Go to www.tarofestival.org or call ☎ **808/264-1553.** Last weekend in April.

Big Island Chocolate Festival, Kona, Big Island. This celebration of chocolate (cacao) grown and produced in Hawaii features symposiums, candy-making workshops, and gala tasting events. It's held in the Fairmont Orchid hotel. Go to www.bigislandchocolatefestival.com or call ☎ **808/329-0833.** Late April–early May.

"I Love Kailua" Town Party This 27-year-old neighborhood party fills Kailua Road with local crafts and specialty food booths, live music, jumping castles, and free health screenings. It's a fundraiser for the local Outdoor Circle chapter, which uses the proceeds to preserve trees and natural spaces in Kailua and Lanikai. Visit www.facebook.com/ilovekailua or call ☎ 808/987-9196. Last Sunday in April.

MAY

Outrigger Canoe Season, all islands. From May to September, canoe paddlers across the state participate in outrigger canoe races nearly every weekend. Go to www.ocpaddler.com for this year's schedule of events.

Lei Day Celebrations, Waikiki, Oahu. May Day (May 1) is Lei Day in Hawaii, celebrated with lei-making contests, pageantry, arts, and crafts. On Oahu, the real highlight is the live concert from 9am to 5:30pm at the Queen Kapiolani Regional Park Bandstand. Go to www.facebook.com/leidaycelebration or call ☎ 808/768-3041. May 1.

World Fire-Knife Dance Championships & Samoa Festival, Polynesian Cultural Center, Laie, Oahu. Junior and adult fire-knife dancers from around the world converge on the center for one of the most amazing performances you'll ever see. Authentic Samoan food and cultural festivities round out the fun. Go to www.worldfireknife.com or call ☎ 800/367-7060. Mid-May.

Lantern Floating Hawaii, Magic Island at Ala Moana Beach Park, Honolulu, Oahu. Some 40,000 people gather at Shinnyo-en Temple's annual Memorial Day lantern ceremony, a beautiful appeal for peace and harmony. At sunset, hundreds of glowing lanterns are set adrift. Hula and music follow. Go to www.lanternfloatinghawaii.com or call ☎ 808/947-2814. Last Monday in May.

Memorial Day, National Memorial Cemetery of the Pacific, Punchbowl Crater, Honolulu, Oahu. The armed forces hold a ceremony recognizing those who died for their country, beginning at 10am. Call ☎ 808/532-3720. Last Monday in May.

Maui Windsurfing Race Series, Kanaha Beach Park, Kahului. This annual windsurfing slalom race takes place at Kanaha Beach Park, west of Kahului Airport in central Maui. Go to http://uswindsurfing.org/maui-slalom-series or call Hi-Tech Surf Sports at ☎ 808/877-2111. Late May through June.

JUNE

Obon Season, all islands. This colorful Buddhist ceremony honoring the souls of the dead kicks off in June. Synchronized dancers circle a tower where Taiko drummers play, and food booths sell Japanese treats late into the night. Each weekend a different Buddhist temple hosts the Bon Dance. Go to www.gohawaii.com for a statewide schedule.

Molokai Ka Hula Piko Festival, Mitchell Pauole Center, Kaunakakai, Molokai. This 3-day hula celebration occurs on the island where the Hawaiian dance was born and features performances by hula schools, musicians, and singers from across Hawaii, as well as local food and Hawaiian crafts: quilting, woodworking, and featherwork. Go to www.kahulapiko.com or call ☎ 800/800-6367 or 808/553-3876. Early June.

Honolulu Pride Parade & Celebration, Waikiki, Oahu. Since 1990, Hawaii's capital has celebrated diversity. This annual rainbow-splashed parade features a gay military color guard, roller derby, and high-energy floats. Kapiolani Park hosts daylong festivities. Go to http://hawaiilgbtlegacyfoundation.com or follow @honolulupride on Twitter. Early June.

King Kamehameha Celebration, all islands. This state holiday (officially June 11, but celebrated on different dates on each island) features a massive floral parade, *ho'olaulea* (party), and much more. Oahu: ☎ 808/586-0333. Kauai: ☎ 808/651-6419. Big Island: www.konaparade.org ☎ 808/322-9944. Maui: http://visitlahaina.com or ☎ 808/667-9194. Molokai: ☎ 808/553-3876.

Maui Film Festival, Wailea Resort, Maui. Sundance, Cannes, Tribeca and . . . Maui! Hawaii is home to a major film festival, where movies are screened under the stars at a posh Wailea golf course. Five days of premiere screenings, celebrity awards, and lavish parties. Go to www.mauifilmfestival.com or call ☎ **808/579-9244.** Early or mid-June.

King Kamehameha Hula Competition, Neal S. Blaisdell Center, Honolulu, Oahu. This daylong hula competition features dancers from as far away as Japan, Canada, and Mexico. Go to www.blaisdellcenter.com or call ☎ **808/768-5252.** Third weekend in June.

Kapalua Wine & Food Festival, Kapalua Resort, Maui. Big-time oenophiles and food experts gather at the Ritz-Carlton Kapalua for 4 days of formal tastings, panel discussions, and samplings of new releases. The seafood finale ranks among the state's best feasts. Go to http://kapaluawineandfoodfestival.com or call ☎ **800/KAPALUA** (527-2582). Mid-June.

Lanai Pineapple Festival, Lanai City, Lanai. The local pineapple is long gone, but this 2-day festival celebrates the island's plantation legacy, including a pineapple-eating contest, a pineapple-cooking contest, arts and crafts, food, music, and fireworks. Go to www.lanaipineapplefestival.com or call ☎ **808/565-7600.** Late June/early July.

Ala Moana Fourth of July Spectacular, Ala Moana Center, Waikiki, Oahu. The 15-minute fireworks display is among the largest in the country. People gather on the Ewa parking deck at 4pm for the best view. A concert at 5pm is followed by fireworks at 8:30pm. Shoppers enjoy a 20% discount all week. Go to www.alamoanacenter.com/Events or call ☎ **808/955-9517.** July 3–6.

Makawao Parade & Rodeo, Makawao, Maui. The annual parade and rodeo has been taking place in this upcountry cowboy town for 60 years. Good fun! Go to www.gohawaii.com/maui or call ☎ **808/572-9565.** July 4.

Parker Ranch Rodeo, Waimea, Big Island. Head to the heart of cowboy country for a hot competition between local *paniolo* (cowboys). The arena accommodates 2,000 people and professional caterers supply food. Go to http://parkerranch.com or call ☎ **808/885-7311.** July 4.

Ukulele Festival, Kapiolani Park Bandstand, Waikiki, Oahu. Now in its 47th year, this free concert features a ukulele orchestra of some 800 students, ages 4 to 92. Hawaii's top musicians pitch in. Get the details at www.ukulelefestivalhawaii.org. Mid-July.

Molokai 2 Oahu Paddleboard World Championships, starts on Molokai and finishes on Oahu. Some 200 international participants journey to Molokai to compete in this 32-mile race, considered to be the world championship of long-distance paddleboarding. The race begins at Kaluakoi Beach on Molokai at 7:30am and finishes at Maunaloa Bay on Oahu around 12:30pm. Go to www.molokai2oahu.com or call ☎ **760/944-3854.** Late July.

Queen Liliuokalani Keiki Hula Competition, Neal S. Blaisdell Center, Honolulu, Oahu. More than 500 *keiki* (children) representing 22 *halau* (hula schools) from the islands compete in this dance fest. The event is broadcast a week later on KITV-TV. Go to www.keikihula.org or call ☎ **808/521-6905.** Mid- to late July.

50th State Fair, Aloha Stadium, Honolulu, Oahu. The annual state fair is a great one, with displays of Hawaiian agricultural products (including dazzling orchids), educational and cultural exhibits, entertainment, and local food. Go to www.ekfernandez.com/events/50th.asp or call ☎ **808/682-5767.** Late May through June.

Neil Pryde Hawaii State Championship, Kanaha Beach Park, Kahului, Maui. Top windsurfers compete in the final race of the series. Go to www.facebook.com/Maui-Race-Series-600081173346035 or call Hi-Tech Maui at ☎ **808/877-2111.** Late July or early August.

Mango Festival, Sheraton Kona Resort & Spa, Kailua-Kona, Big Island. Few fruits rival a ripe mango for flavor. Sample multiple varieties, taste mango-laden recipes, and learn how to grow your own at this annual celebration of the golden fruit. Go to www.facebook.com/Mango Festivals or call ✆ **808/936-5233.** Early August.

Puukohola Heiau National Historic Site Anniversary Celebration, Kawaihae, Big Island. This homage to authentic Hawaiian culture begins at 6am at Puukohola Heiau. It's a rugged, beautiful site where attendees make leis, weave *lauhala* mats, pound *poi*, and dance ancient hula. Bring refreshments and sunscreen. Go to www.nps.gov/puhe or call ✆ **808/882-7218.** Mid-August.

Duke's OceanFest Hoolaulea, Waikiki, Oahu. Nine days of water-oriented competitions and festivities celebrate the life of Duke Kahanamoku. Events include longboard surfing, paddleboard racing, swimming, tandem surfing, surf polo, beach volleyball, stand-up paddling, and a luau. Visit www.dukesoceanfest.com. Mid- to late August.

Hawaii Volcanoes National Park Cultural Festival, Hawaii Volcanoes National Park, Hawaii. During this all-day, hands-on celebration, you can practice making lei or traditional Hawaiian musical instruments, watch hula dancers, and learn about rare native plants in the rainforests surrounding Kilauea volcano. See www.nps.gov/havo or call ✆ **808/985-6000.** Late August.

SEPTEMBER

Aloha Festivals, various locations on all islands. Parades and other events celebrate Hawaiian culture and friendliness throughout the state. The parades with flower-decked horses are particularly eye-catching. Go to www.alohafestivals.com or call ✆ **808/923-2030.** Throughout September.

Na Wahine O Ke Kai, Hale o Lono Harbor, Molokai to Waikiki, Oahu. The finale to the outrigger canoe season, this

exciting race starts at sunrise on the remote shore of Molokai and travels 40 miles across the channel to end in triumphant festivities at the Hilton Hawaiian Village. For details, visit www.nawahineokekai.com. Late September.

Waikiki Roughwater Swim, Waikiki, Oahu. This popular 2.5-mile, open-ocean swim traces Sans Souci (Kaimana) Beach between the Natatorium and the New Otani Kaimana Beach Hotel in Waikiki. Early registration is encouraged, but last-minute entries on race day are allowed. Go to www.wrswim.com. Saturday, Labor Day weekend.

Queen Liliuokalani Canoe Race, Kailua-Kona to Honaunau, Big Island. Thousands of paddlers compete in the world's largest long-distance canoe race. Go to www.kaiopua.org or call ✆ **808/938-8577.** Labor Day weekend.

Kapalua Open, Kapalua, Maui. This USTA–sanctioned event features the largest tennis purse for a tournament in the state. Registration includes a tennis tourney, dinner, raffle, and T-shirt (and trophy if you're lucky!). Go to www.golfatkapalua.com/KapaluaTennisEvents.html or call ✆ **808/662-7730.** Labor Day weekend.

OCTOBER

Emalani Festival, Kokee State Park, Kaua'i. This culturally rich festival honors Queen Emma, an inveterate gardener and Hawaii's first environmental queen, who made a forest trek to Kokee with 100 friends in 1871. Go to www.kokee.org or call ✆ **808/335-9975.** Second Saturday in October.

Maui County Fair, War Memorial Complex, Wailuku, Maui. Now in its 96th year, the oldest county fair in Hawaii features a parade, amusement rides, live entertainment, and exhibits. Go to www.mauifair.com or call ✆ **808/280-6889.** Early October.

Hawaii Chocolate Festival, Honolulu, Oahu. Indulge your sweet tooth at this celebration of Hawaiian-grown cacao. Dozens of local vendors share their gourmet creations—everything from truffles and crepes to chocolate-scented soap. Go to http://hawaiichocolatefestival.com. Mid-October.

Ironman Triathlon World Championship, Kailua-Kona, Big Island. Some 1,500-plus world-class athletes run a full marathon, swim 2.5 miles, and bike 112 miles on the Kona-Kohala Coast of the Big Island. Spectators watch the action along the route for free. The best place to see the 7am start is along the Alii Drive seawall, facing Kailua Bay; arrive before 5:30am to get a seat. (Alii Dr. closes to traffic; park on a side street and walk down.) To watch finishers come in, line up along Alii Drive from Holualoa Street to Palani Road. The first finisher can arrive as early as 2:30pm. Go to www.ironmanworld championship.com or call ✆ **808/329-0063.** Saturday closest to the full moon in October.

Hana Hoohiwahiwa O Kaiulani, Sheraton Princess Kaiulani, Waikiki, Oahu. This hotel commemorates the birthday of its namesake, Princess Victoria Kaiulani, with a week of complimentary hula lessons, lei making, ukulele lessons, and more. The crowning touch is the Princess Kaiulani Keiki Hula Festival, which showcases performances by more than 200 *keiki* (children) from *halau* (schools) on the island of Oahu. Go to www.princess-kaiulani.com or call ✆ **808/922-5811.** Mid-October.

Xterra World Championship, Kapalua, Maui. Hundreds of gonzo athletes plunge into the Pacific, jump on mountain bikes, and race through the rainforest to be crowned Xterra world champion (and win $105,000). After the race, athletes and friends celebrate at an awards dinner and adrenaline-fueled Halloween party. Go to www.xterraplanet.com/maui or call ✆ **877/751-8880.** Late October.

Hawaii Food & Wine Festival, multiple locations on Oahu, Hawaii, and Maui. Cofounded by Alan Wong and Roy Yamaguchi (two of the state's most celebrated chefs), this 2-week gourmet bonanza includes wine and spirit tastings, cooking demos, field trips, and glitzy galas. See www.hawaiifoodandwine festival.com or call ✆ **808/738-6245.** Mid-October to early November.

Hawaiian Slack Key Guitar Festival, Kauai Beach Resort, Lihue, Kauai. The best of Hawaii's folk music (slack key guitar) performed by the best musicians in Hawaii. It's 6 hours long and just $10. Go to www.kauaifestivals.com or call ✆ **808/226-2697.** Mid-November.

Kona Coffee Cultural Festival, Kailua-Kona, Big Island. Celebrate the coffee harvest with a bean-picking contest, lei contests, song and dance, and the Miss Kona Coffee Pageant. Go to http://kona coffeefest.com or call ✆ **808/326-7820.** Events throughout November.

Hawaii International Film Festival, various locations throughout the state. This cinema festival with a cross-cultural spin features filmmakers from Asia, the Pacific Islands, and the United States. Go to www.hiff.org or call ✆ **808/792-1577.** Mid-November.

Na Mele O Maui, Maui. A traditional Hawaiian song competition for children in kindergarten through 12th grade, sponsored by the Kaanapali Resort and held at the Maui Arts & Cultural Center. Free admission. Go to www.mauiarts.org or call ✆ **808/242-7469.** Late November or early December.

Maui Jim Maui Invitational Basketball Tournament, Lahaina Civic Center, Lahaina. Elite college teams battle for the ball in this intimate annual preseason tournament. Go to www.mauiinvitational. com. Thanksgiving weekend.

Invitational Wreath Exhibit, Volcano Art Center, Hawaii Volcanoes National Park, Big Island. Thirty-plus artists, including painters, sculptors, glass artists, fiber artists, and potters, produce both whimsical and traditional "wreaths" for this exhibit. Park entrance fees apply. Go to www.volcanoartcenter.org or call ✆ **808/967-7565.** Mid-November to early January.

Vans Triple Crown of Surfing, North Shore, Oahu. The world's top professional surfers compete in thrilling surf events for more than $1 million in prize money. Go to www.vanstriplecrownof surfing.com. Held between mid-November and mid-December, depending on the surf.

Kona Surf Film Festival, Courtyard Marriott King Kamehameha's Kona Beach Hotel, Big Island. An outdoor screening of independent films focusing on waves and wave riders. Go to www.konasurffilm festival.org or call ☏ **808/936-0089.** Early December.

Festival of Lights, all islands. On Oahu, the mayor throws the switch to light up the 40-foot-tall Norfolk pine and other trees in front of Honolulu Hale, while on Maui, kids can play in a "snow zone" and make holiday crafts beneath the Lahaina Banyan tree, glowing with thousands of twinkle lights. Molokai celebrates with a host of activities in Kaunakakai; on Kauai, the lighting ceremony takes place in front of the former county building on Rice Street in Lihue. Call ☏ **808/768-6622** on Oahu; ☏ **808/667-9175** on Maui; ☏ **808/553-4482** on Molokai; or ☏ **808/639-6571** on Kauai. Early December.

Honolulu Marathon, Honolulu, Oahu. More than 30,000 racers compete in this oceanfront marathon, one of the largest in the world, and receive medals and fresh *malasadas* (hole-less doughnuts) as a reward. Check it out at www.honolulu marathon.org or call ☏ **808/734-7200.** Second Sunday of December.

Hawaii Bowl, Aloha Stadium, Honolulu, Oahu. A Pac 10 team plays a Big 12 team in this nationally televised collegiate football classic. Go to www.thehawaii bowl.com or call ☏ **808/523-3688.** Usually December 24.

First Light, Maui Arts & Cultural Center, Kahului, Maui. The Maui Film Festival screens Academy Award–contending films over the holidays. Go to www.maui filmfestival.com or call ☏ **808/579-9244.** Mid- to late December.

OAHU

by Martha Cheng

ahu has it all: wide, sandy beaches; year-round surf; breathtaking ridge hikes; and a vibrant urban city in Honolulu. Home to Pearl Harbor and the only royal palace in the United States, Honolulu is imbued with history. Always deeply mindful of its past, it is also racing into the future. The revitalization of old neighborhoods has sprouted trendy boutiques and attention-grabbing cuisine, and Waikiki, the world-famous vacation playground, continues to refine itself with stylish and luxurious new hotels, and the shops to match. Sure, Oahu may be Hawaii's most crowded island, but its rich human tapestry—locals of myriad ethnic mixes, wealthy Japanese expats, Mainland sun-seekers, surfers from around the globe—makes it unlike any other place in the world.

ESSENTIALS
Arriving

Even though more and more transpacific flights are going directly to the neighbor islands these days, chances are still good that you'll touch down on Oahu first and Honolulu will be your gateway to the Hawaiian Islands. **Honolulu International Airport** sits on the South Shore of Oahu, west of downtown Honolulu and Waikiki near Pearl Harbor. Many major American and international carriers fly to Honolulu from the Mainland; for a list of airlines, see chapter 10, "Planning Your Trip to Hawaii."

LANDING AT HONOLULU INTERNATIONAL AIRPORT

You can walk or take the free airport shuttle from your arrival gate to the main terminal and baggage claim on the ground level. Unless you're connecting to an inter-island flight immediately, you'll exit to the palm-lined street where uniformed attendants can either flag down a taxi or direct you to **TheBus** (www.thebus.org; see "By Bus," below). For Waikiki shuttles and rental-car vans, cross the street to the median and wait at the designated stop.

Passengers connecting to neighbor-island flights take the free shuttle or walk to the large inter-island terminal serving Hawaiian Airlines or to the more distant commuter terminal, which serves smaller carriers such as Island Air and Mokulele Airlines. (For details on inter-island flights, see "Getting Around Hawaii" on p. 601.)

FACING PAGE: **Snorkeling paradise Hanauma bay, Oahu**

GETTING TO & FROM THE AIRPORT

BY RENTAL CAR   All major car-rental companies have vehicles available at the airport. Rental-agency vans will pick you up curbside at the center island outside baggage claim and take you to their off-site lots. It's about a 20-minute drive from the airport to downtown Honolulu.

BY TAXI   Taxis are abundant at the airport, and an attendant will be happy to flag one down for you. The fare is about $25 from Honolulu International to downtown Honolulu and around $35 to $40 to Waikiki. If you need to call a taxi, see "Getting Around," later in this chapter, for a list of cab companies.

BY AIRPORT SHUTTLE SpeediShuttle (www.speedishuttle.com; © **877/242-5777**) offers transportation in air-conditioned vans from the airport to Waikiki hotels; a trip from the airport to Waikiki is $15 per person. You'll find the shuttle at street level outside baggage claim on the median. You can board with two pieces of luggage and a carry-on at no extra charge. Tips are welcome. For advance purchase of group tickets, call the number above or book online.

BY BUS   **TheBus** (www.thebus.org; © **808/848-5555**) is a good option if you aren't carrying a lot of luggage. TheBus nos. 19 and 20 (Waikiki Beach and hotels) run from the airport to downtown Honolulu and Waikiki. The first bus from Waikiki to the airport leaves at 4:46am Monday through Friday and 5:27am Saturday and Sunday; the last bus departs the airport for Waikiki at 1:22am Monday through Friday, 1:24am Saturday and Sunday; buses arrive approximately every 15 minutes. There are two bus stops on the main terminal's upper level; a third is on the second level of the inter-island terminal. *Note:* You can board TheBus with a carry-on or small suitcase, as long as it fits under the seat and doesn't disrupt other passengers; otherwise, you'll have to take a shuttle or taxi. The travel time to Waikiki is approximately 1 hour. The one-way fare is $2.50 and $1.25 for children 6 to 17; exact change only. For more on TheBus, see "Getting Around," later in this chapter.

Visitor Information

The **Hawaii Visitors & Convention Bureau (HVCB),** 2270 Kalakaua Ave., Suite 801, Honolulu, HI 96815 (www.gohawaii.com or www.hvcb. org; © **800/GO-HAWAII**), supplies free brochures, maps, and accommodations guides.

A number of free publications, such as *This Week Oahu,* are packed with money-saving coupons and good regional maps; look for them on racks at the airport and around town. *Another tip:* Snag one of the Japanese magazines scattered around Waikiki. Even if you can't read Japanese, you'll find out about the latest, trendiest, or best restaurants and shops around the island.

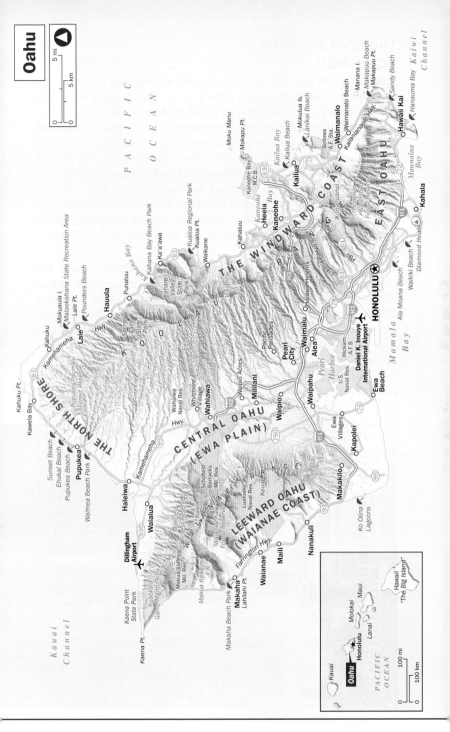

Oahu

5 mi

5 km

PACIFIC OCEAN

Kaiwi Channel

Makapuu Beach
Manana I.
Makapuu Pt.
Waimanalo Beach
Sandy Beach
Waimanalo
Kalanianaole Hwy.
Hanauma Bay
Hawaii Kai
Moku Manu
Mokapu Pt.
Mokulua Is.
Lanikai Beach
Kahala
Kaneohe Bay
M.C.B.
Kailua Bay
Kailua Beach
Kailua
(630)
Kaneohe
Mamala Bay
Heeia
Kahaluu
Koolau Range
H3
Honolulu
Watershed
Forest Reserve
Diamond Head
Waikiki Beach
Ala Moana Beach
HONOLULU ★
Daniel K. Inouye
International Airport
Hickam A.F.B.
Pearl Harbor
U.S. Naval Res.
Alea
Pearl City
Waimalu
Pacific
Palisades
Waipahu
Ewa Beach
(76)
Ewa
Villages
Kapolei
H1
(750)
Makakilo
KOOLAU RANGE

Kualoa Regional Park
Kualoa Pt.
Waikane
Ka'a'awa
Kahana Bay Beach Park
Kahana Bay
Kahana
Valley
State
Park
Punaluu
Punaluu Bay
(83)
THE WINDWARD COAST
Waihole
F.R.
Ewa For. R.
Ewa For. R.

Mokuauia I.
Laie Pt.
Pounders Beach
Laie
Hwy.
Hauula
Sacred
Falls
State
Park
Pupukea-Paumalu
Forest Reserve
Kamehameha
Kahuku Pt.
Kahuku
Kawela Bay
Sunset Beach
Ehukai Beach
Pupukea
Pupukea Beach Park
THE NORTH SHORE
Waimea Beach Park
Kamehameha
(83)
(99)
Haleiwa
Waialua
(930)
Dillingham Airport ✈
Mokuleia
Forest Reserve
Makua Valley
Mil. Res.
Makua Keaau
Kuaokala
Game Mgmt. Area
Kaena Point State Park
Kaena Pt.
Kauai Channel
Makaha Beach Park
Makaha
Lahilahi Pt.
Waianae-Kaala
Forest Reserve
Waianae
Maili
Farrington Hwy.
Nanakuli
LEEWARD OAHU (WAIANAE COAST)
WAIANAE RANGE
Lualualei
Naval Res.
Kaupuni
Schofield
Barracks
Mil. Res.
Ko Olina
Lagoons

Whitmore
Village
Wahiawa
Naval Res.
Wahiawa
Waialua
(80)
Kaukonahua Rd.
Waipio Acres
Mililani
(99)
(750)
CENTRAL OAHU (EWA PLAIN)
Waipio
H2
Kamehameha

PACIFIC OCEAN

Mamala Bay

63

Inset map

Oahu
Kauai
Honolulu ★
PACIFIC OCEAN
Molokai
Maui
Lanai
"Hawaii The Big Island"

100 mi

100 km

The Island in Brief

HONOLULU

Hawaii's largest city looks like any other big metropolitan center with tall buildings. In fact, some cynics refer to it as "Los Angeles West." But within Honolulu's boundaries, you'll find rainforests, deep canyons, valleys, waterfalls, a nearly mile-high mountain range, coral reefs, and gold-sand beaches. The city proper—where most of Honolulu's residents live—is approximately 12 miles wide and 26 miles long, running east-west roughly between **Diamond Head** and **Pearl Harbor.** Within the city are seven hills laced by seven streams that run to Mamala Bay.

A plethora of neighborhoods surrounds the central area. These areas are generally quieter and more residential than Waikiki, but they're still within minutes of beaches, shopping, and all the activities Oahu has to offer.

WAIKIKI ★★   Waikiki is changing almost daily. There's now a Ritz Carlton, and the nearly-new International Marketplace anchored by Saks Fifth Avenue. It's a sign of Waikiki's transformation: faded Polynesian kitsch giving way to luxury retailers and residences. Still, Waikiki tenaciously hangs on to its character: Explore just 1 block *mauka* of Kalakaua Ave., and you'll find hip boutique hotels, hidden hole-in-the-wall eateries, and walk-up apartments and nondescript condos where locals still live.

When King Kalakaua played in Waikiki, it was "a hamlet of plain cottages . . . its excitements caused by the activity of insect tribes and the

Diamond Head and Waikiki Beach

Mainlanders sometimes find the directions given by locals a bit confusing. Seldom will you hear the terms *east, west, north,* and *south;* instead, islanders refer to directions as either **makai** (ma-*kae*), meaning toward the sea, or **mauka** (*mow*-kah), toward the mountains. In Honolulu, people use **Diamond Head** as a direction meaning to the east (in the direction of the world-famous crater called Diamond Head), and **Ewa** as a direction meaning to the west (toward the town called Ewa, on the other side of Pearl Harbor).

So if you ask a local for directions, this is what you're likely to hear: "Drive 2 blocks *makai* (toward the sea), and then turn Diamond Head (east) at the stoplight. Go 1 block, and turn *mauka* (toward the mountains). It's on the 'Ewa (western) side of the street."

occasional fall of a coconut." The Merrie Monarch, who gave his name to Waikiki's main street, would love the scene today. Some 5 million tourists visit Oahu every year, and 9 out of 10 of them stay in Waikiki. This urban beach is where all the action is; it's backed by 175 high-rise hotels with more than 33,000 guest rooms and hundreds of bars and restaurants, all in a 1½-square-mile beach zone. Waikiki means honeymooners and sun seekers, bikinis and bare buns, an around-the-clock beach party every day of the year. Staying in Waikiki puts you in the heart of it all, but be aware that this on-the-go place has traffic noise 24 hours a day—and it's almost always crowded.

ALA MOANA ★★   A great beach as well as Hawaii's largest shopping mall, Ala Moana is the retail and transportation heart of Honolulu, a place where you can both shop and suntan in one afternoon. All bus routes lead to the open-air **Ala Moana Center,** across the street from **Ala Moana Beach Park** ★★. The shopping center is one of Hawaii's most visited destinations for its collection of luxury brands (such as Louis Vuitton and Chanel) and Hawaii-based stores (from Tori Richard to Town & Country Surf).

KAKAAKO ★   This is Honolulu's most rapidly developing neighborhood—a primarily industrial area giving way to new condo buildings, from workforce housing to the island's most expensive penthouses. Sprouting up among the new construction are lively hubs of boutiques and restaurants, including **Ward Village** and **Salt.**

DOWNTOWN AND CHINATOWN ★★   Here you'll find historic Honolulu, including Iolani Palace, the official residence of Hawaii's kings and queens; its business center housed in high rises; and the Capitol District, all jammed in about 1 square mile. On the waterfront stands the iconic 1926 **Aloha Tower.**

On the edge of downtown is the **Chinatown Historic District,** one of the oldest Chinatowns in America and still one of Honolulu's liveliest neighborhoods, a nonstop pageant of people, sights, sounds, smells, and

4

OAHU   Essentials

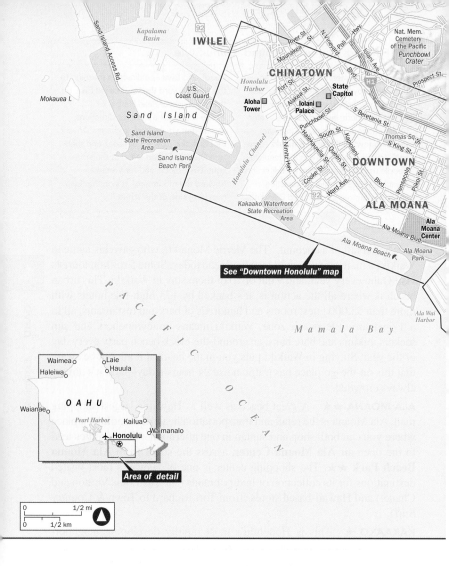

tastes, though not all Chinese. Southeast Asians, including many Vietnamese, share the old storefronts, as do Honolulu's oldest bar (the divey **Smith's Union Bar**) and some of the city's hippest clubs and chicest boutiques. Go in the morning, when everyone shops for fresh goods such as mangoes (when in season), live fish (sometimes of the same varieties you saw while snorkeling), fresh tofu, and hogs' heads.

MANOA VALLEY ★   This verdant valley above Waikiki, blessed by frequent rain showers, was the site of the first sugar and coffee plantations in Hawaii. It still has vintage *kamaaina* (native-born) homes, one of Hawaii's

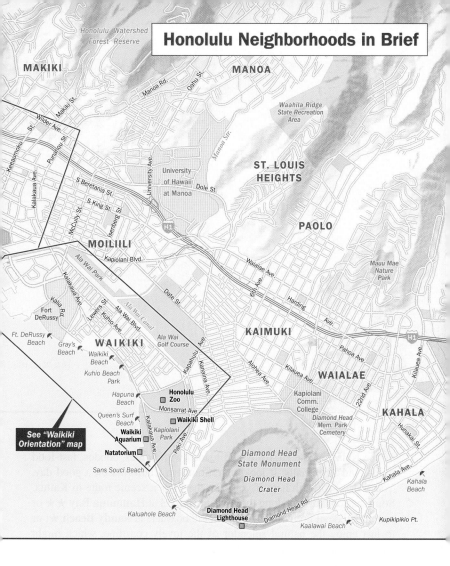

Honolulu Neighborhoods in Brief

premier botanical gardens (**Lyon Arboretum ★**), the ever-gushing **Mā noa Falls,** and the 320-acre **University of Hawaii** campus, where 50,000 students hit the books when they're not on the beach.

TO THE EAST: KAHALA   Except for the estates of millionaires and the luxurious **Kahala Hotel & Resort ★★★**, there's little out this way that's of interest to visitors.

EAST OAHU

Beyond Kahala lies East Honolulu and suburban bedroom communities such as Aina Haina, Niu Valley, and Hawaii Kai, among others, all linked

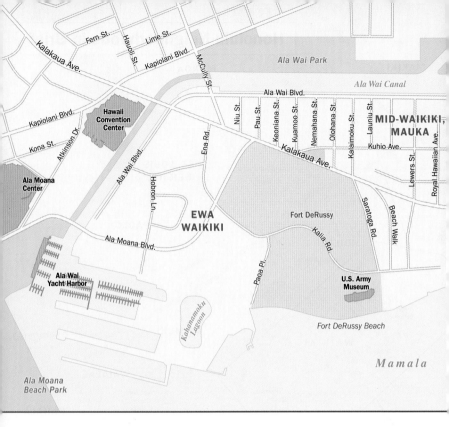

by the Kalanianaole Highway and loaded with homes, condos, fast-food joints, and strip malls. It looks like Southern California on a good day. You'll drive through here if you take the longer, scenic route to Kailua. Some reasons to stop along the way: to snorkel at **Hanauma Bay ★★** or watch daredevil body surfers and boogie boarders at **Sandy Beach ★**; or to just enjoy the natural splendor of the lovely coastline, which might include a hike to **Makapuu Lighthouse ★★**.

THE WINDWARD COAST

The windward side is on the opposite side of the island from Waikiki. On this coast, trade winds blow cooling breezes over gorgeous beaches; rain squalls spawn lush, tropical vegetation; and the fluted Koolau mountain range preens in the background. B&Bs, ranging from oceanfront estates to tiny cottages on quiet residential streets, are everywhere. Vacations here are spent enjoying ocean activities and exploring the surrounding areas. Waikiki is a 20-minute drive away.

KAILUA ★★★   The biggest little beach town in Hawaii, Kailua sits on a beautiful bay with two of Hawaii's best beaches. In the past few years, the

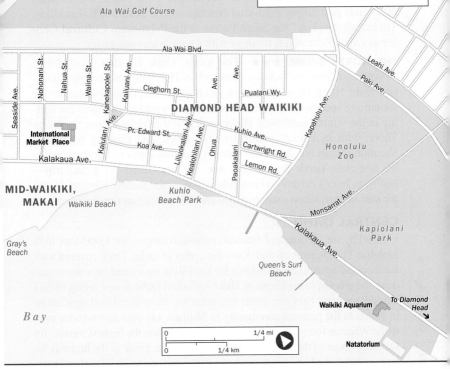

Ala Wai Golf Course

Ala Wai Blvd.

Seaside Ave.

Nohonani St.

Nahua St.

Walina St.

Kanekapolei St.

Kailuani Ave.

Cleghorn St.

Ave.

Ave.

Pualani Wy.

Leahi Ave.

Paki Ave.

DIAMOND HEAD WAIKIKI

Kailani Ave.

Pr. Edward St.

Liliuokalani Ave.

Kealohilani Ave.

Ohua

Kuhio Ave.

Kabahulu Ave.

International Market Place

Koa Ave.

Paoakalani

Cartwright Rd.

Lemon Rd.

Honolulu Zoo

Kalakaua Ave.

MID-WAIKIKI, MAKAI

Waikiki Beach

Kuhio Beach Park

Monsarrat Ave.

Kalakaua Ave.

Kapiolani Park

Gray's Beach

Queen's Surf Beach

Bay

Waikiki Aquarium

To Diamond Head

Natatorium

0   1/4 mi
0   1/4 km

town has seen some redevelopment, with a new Target, Whole Foods, condos, and newer, bigger digs for old favorite shops and restaurants. But in between, there are still funky low-rise clusters of timeworn shops and homes. Kailua has become the B&B capital of Hawaii; it's an affordable alternative to Waikiki, with rooms and vacation rentals starting at $100 a day. With the prevailing trade winds whipping up a cooling breeze, Kailua attracts windsurfers from around the world. On calmer days, kayaking or stand-up paddling to the Mokulua Islands off the coast is a favorite adventure.

KANEOHE BAY ★   Helter-skelter suburbia sprawls around the edges of Kaneohe, one of the most scenic bays in the Pacific. After you clear the trafficky maze of town, Oahu returns to its more natural state. This great bay beckons you to get out on the water; you can depart from He'eia Boat Harbor on snorkel or fishing charters. From here, you'll have a panoramic view of the Koolau Range.

KUALOA/LAIE ★   The upper-northeast shore is one of Oahu's most sacred places, an early Hawaiian landing spot where kings dipped their sails and ghosts still march in the night. Sheer cliffs stab the reef-fringed seacoast, while old fish ponds are tucked along the two-lane coast road that winds past empty gold-sand beaches around beautiful Kahana Bay. Thousands "explore" the South Pacific at the **Polynesian Cultural Center** in Laie, a Mormon settlement with a temple and university.

THE NORTH SHORE ★★★ For locals, Oahu is often divided into "town" and "country"—town being urban Honolulu, and country referring to the North Shore. This coast yields expansive, beautiful beaches for swimming and snorkeling in the summer and world-class waves for surfing in the winter. Laid-back **Haleiwa ★★** is the social hub of the North Shore, with its casual restaurants, surf shops, and clothing boutiques. Vacation rentals are the most common accommodations, but there's also the first-class **Turtle Bay Resort ★★**. Be forewarned: It's a long trip—nearly an hour's drive—to Honolulu and Waikiki, and even longer during the surf season, when tourists and wave-seekers can jam up the roads.

CENTRAL OAHU

Flanked by the Koolau and Waianae mountain ranges, the 1,000-foot-high Leilehua Plateau runs up and down the center of Oahu. Once covered with sandalwood forests (hacked down for the China trade) and later the sugarcane and pineapple backbone of Hawaii, Central Oahu is now trying to find a middle ground between farms and suburbia, from diversified agriculture in Kunia to the planned community in Mililani. Let your eye wander west to the Waianae Range and Mount Kaala, at 4,020 feet the highest summit on Oahu; up there in the misty rainforest, native birds thrive in the hummocky bog. In 1914, the U.S. Army pitched a tent camp on the plain; author James Jones would later call **Schofield Barracks** "the most beautiful army post in the world." Hollywood filmed Jones's *From Here to Eternity* here.

LEEWARD OAHU: THE WAIANAE COAST

The west coast of Oahu is a hot and dry place of dramatic beauty: white-sand beaches bordering the deep-blue ocean, steep verdant green cliffs, and miles of Mother Nature's wildness. Tourist services are concentrated in Ko Olina Resort, which has a Disney hotel and a Four Seasons (new in 2016), pricey resort restaurants, golf course, marina, and a wedding chapel, should you want to get hitched. This side of Oahu is less visited—though that could change as Ko Olina lures visitors from Waikiki—except by surfers bound for **Makaha Beach ★★** and those coming to see needle-nose **Kaena Point ★** (the island's westernmost outpost), which has a coastal wilderness park.

GETTING AROUND

BY CAR Oahu residents own more than 686,000 registered vehicles, but they have only 1,500 miles of mostly two-lane roads to use. That's 450 cars for every mile—a fact that becomes abundantly clear during morning

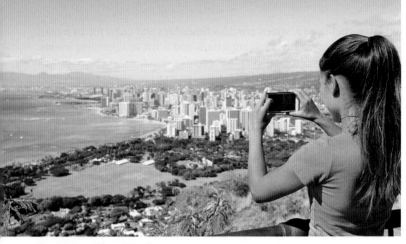

The view from Diamond Head

and evening rush hours. You can (mostly) avoid the gridlock by driving between 9am and 2pm or after 7pm.

All of the major car-rental firms have agencies on Oahu at the airport and in Waikiki. For listings, see chapter 10. For tips on insurance and driving rules in Hawaii, see "Getting Around Hawaii" (p. 601).

BY BUS One of the best deals anywhere, **TheBus** will take you around the whole island for $2.50 ($1.25 for children age 6–17)—if you have the time. To get to the North Shore and back takes 4 hours, twice as long as if you travel by car. But for shorter distances, TheBus is great, and it goes almost everywhere almost all the time. If you're planning on sticking to the Waikiki–Ala Moana–Downtown region, TheBus will save you a lot of car hassle and expense. The most popular route is **no. 8,** which arrives every 10 minutes or so to shuttle people between Waikiki and Ala Moana Center (the ride takes 15–20 min.). The **no. 19** (Airport/Hickam), **no. 20** (Airport/Halawa Gate), and **no. 40** (Waipahu/Ala Moana) cover the same stretch. Waikiki service begins daily at 5am and runs until midnight; most buses run about every 15 minutes during the day and every 30 minutes in the evening.

The Circle Island–North Shore route is **no. 52** (Wahiawa/Circle Island); the Circle Island–South Shore route is **no. 55** (Kaneohe/Circle Island). Both routes leave Ala Moana Center every 30 minutes and take about 4½ hours to circle the island. Be aware that at Turtle Bay Resort, just outside Kahuku, the 52 becomes the 55 and returns to Honolulu via the coast, and the 55 becomes the 52 and returns to Honolulu on the inland route. (Translation: You'll have to get off and switch buses to complete your island tour.) There are express buses available to some areas (for example, **no. 54** to Pearl City, **no. 85** to Kailua and to Kaneohe).

For more information on routes and schedules, call **TheBus** (© **808/848-5555,** or 808/296-1818 for recorded information) or check out **www.thebus.org,** which provides timetables and maps for all routes, plus directions to many local attractions and a list of upcoming events. Taking TheBus is often easier than parking your car.

BY TAXI   Oahu's major **cab companies** offer 24-hour, islandwide, radio-dispatched service, with multilingual drivers and air-conditioned cars, limos, and vans, including vehicles equipped with wheelchair lifts (there's a $9 charge for wheelchairs). Fares are standard for all taxi firms. From the airport, expect to pay about $35 to $40 to Waikiki, about $25 to $35 to downtown, $60 and up to Kailua, about $60-plus to Hawaii Kai, and about $90 to $125 to the North Shore (plus tip). Plus there may be a $4.75 fee per piece of luggage.

   Uber, the taxi-hailing app, has arrived in Honolulu. Use it on your phone to summon and pay for a ride in a private vehicle (standard taxi meter rates, plus a $1 surcharge; gratuity automatically added). If you prefer to go the old-fashioned route, try **The Cab** (www.thecabhawaii.com; ✆ **808/422-2222**) or **EcoCab** (www.ecocabhawaii.com; ✆ **808/979-1010**), an all-hybrid taxi fleet.

[Fast FACTS] OAHU

Dentists   If you need dental attention while on Oahu, find a dentist near you through the website of the **Hawaii Dental Association** (www.hawaiidental association.net).

Doctors   Straub Clinic & Hospital's **Doctors on Call** (www.straubhealth.org; ✆ **808/971-6000**) can dispatch a van if you need help getting to the main clinic or its clinics at the Hilton Hawaiian Village and the Sheraton Waikiki.

Emergencies   Call ✆ **911** for police, fire, or ambulance. If you need to call the **Poison Control Center** (✆ **800/222-1222**), you will automatically be directed to the Poison Control Center for the area code of the phone you are calling from; all are available 24/7 and very helpful.

Hospitals   Hospitals offering 24-hour emergency care include **Queen's Medical Center,** 1301 Punchbowl St. (✆ 808/538-9011); **Kuakini Medical Center,** 347 Kuakini St. (✆ 808/536-2236); **Straub Clinic & Hospital,** 888 S. King St. (✆ 808/522-4000); **Kaiser Permanente Medical Center,** 3288 Moanalua Rd. (✆ 808/432-0000; note that the emergency room is open to Kaiser members only); **Kapiolani Medical Center for Women & Children,** 1319 Punahou St. (✆ 808/983-8633); and **Kapiolani Medical Center at Pali Momi,** 98-1079 Moanalua Rd. (✆ 808/486-6000). Central Oahu has **Wahiawa General Hospital,** 128 Lehua St. (✆ 808/621-8411). On the windward side is **Castle Medical**

Center, 640 Ulukahiki St., Kailua (✆ 808/263-5500).

Internet Access   Outside of your hotel, Starbucks is your best bet for Internet access. The Royal Hawaiian Center shopping mall and International Marketplace also have free Wi-Fi.

Newspapers   Oahu's only daily paper is the *Honolulu Star Advertiser.*

Post Office   To find the location nearest you, call ✆ **800/275-8777.** The downtown location is in the old U.S. Post Office, Customs, and Court House Building (referred to as the Old Federal Building) at 335 Merchant St., across from Iolani Palace and next to the Kamehameha Statue (bus: 20, E, or 19). Other branch offices can be found in Waikiki at 330 Saratoga

Ave. (Diamond Head side of Fort DeRussy; bus: 19 or 20) and in the Ala Moana Center (bus: 8, 19, or 20).

Safety   Be aware of car break-ins in touristed areas and beach parks; make sure to keep valuables out of sight.

Weather   For National Weather Service recorded forecasts for Oahu, call
© **808/973-4380.**

ATTRACTIONS IN & AROUND HONOLULU & WAIKIKI
Historic Honolulu

The Waikiki you see today bears no resemblance to the Waikiki of yesteryear, a place of vast taro fields extending from the ocean to deep into Mā noa Valley, dotted with numerous fish ponds and gardens tended by thousands of people. This picture of old Waikiki can be recaptured by following the emerging **Waikiki Historic Trail** ★ (www.waikikihistorictrail. org), a meandering 2-mile walk with 20 bronze surfboard markers (standing 6 ft., 5 in. tall—you can't miss 'em), complete with descriptions and archival photos of the historic sites. The markers note everything from Waikiki's ancient fishponds to the history of the Ala Wai Canal. The trail begins at Kuhio Beach and ends at the King Kalakaua statue at the intersection of Kuhio and Kalakaua avenues.

Bishop Museum ★★★ MUSEUM   This is a museum for adults and kids alike. For the adults: the original **Hawaiian Hall,** built in 1889 to house the collection of Hawaiian artifacts and royal family heirlooms of Princess Bernice Pauahi Bishop, the last descendant of King Kamehameha I. Today, the exhibits, spread out over three floors, give the most complete sense of how ancient native Hawaiians lived. On display are carvings representing Hawaiian gods and the personal effects of Hawaiian royalty, including a feathered cape worn by Kamehameha himself. In the Hawaiian Hall Atrium, traditions come to life with the daily **hula show** (2pm).

For the kids, there's the 50-foot sperm whale skeleton and the **Richard T. Mamiya Science Adventure Center,** featuring interactive exhibits on how volcanoes, wind, and waves work. There's even a

Bishop Museum

4

OAHU

Attractions In & Around Honolulu & Waikiki

73

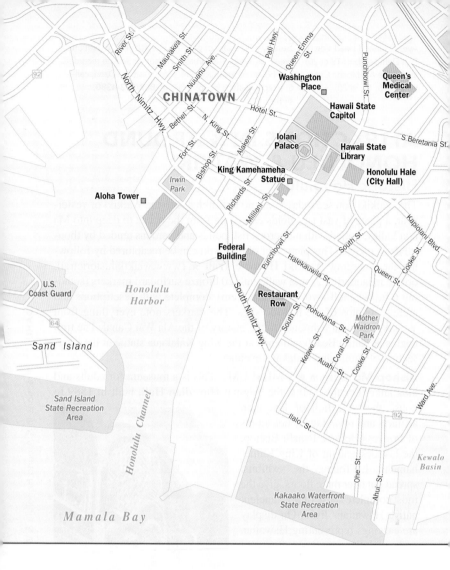

twice-daily "lava pour," demonstrating lava in its molten liquid state and then, as it cools, as brittle volcanic glass. Don't miss the shows at the **J. Watamull Planetarium,** in which you'll explore the current evening sky and take home a star map so you can find the constellations and planets.

Hungry? Check out the museum cafe by Highway Inn, a favorite local restaurant that serves ono (delicious) Hawaiian plate lunches.

1525 Bernice St., just off Kalihi St./Likelike Hwy. www.bishopmuseum.org. ⓒ **808/847-3511.** $23 adults, $20 seniors, $15 children 4–12. Daily 9am–5pm. Parking is $5. Bus: 2.

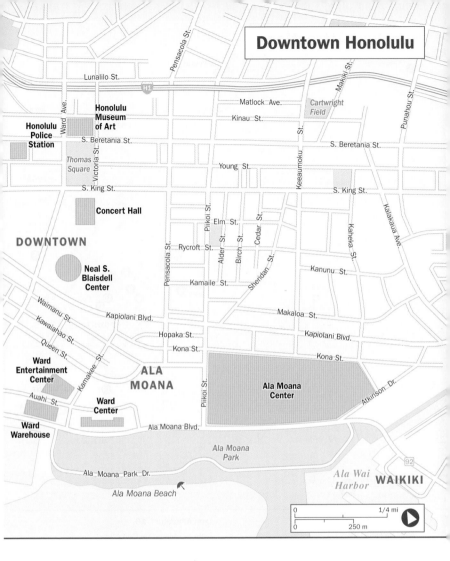

Hawaiian Mission Houses Historic Site and Archives ★ HIS-
TORIC SITE   Centered on the first mission houses built in the 1800s,
what was formerly known as the Mission Houses Museum has undergone
a rebranding. Possibly it's because missionaries have been cast as the bad
white guys who eradicated native Hawaiian culture. Now, instead of
depicting early American missionary life exclusively, the expanded focus
includes collaborations between Hawaiians and missionaries, which
resulted in successes like the printed Hawaiian language and widespread
literacy (by the 1860s, Hawaii had the highest literacy rate of any nation).

Honolulu Attractions

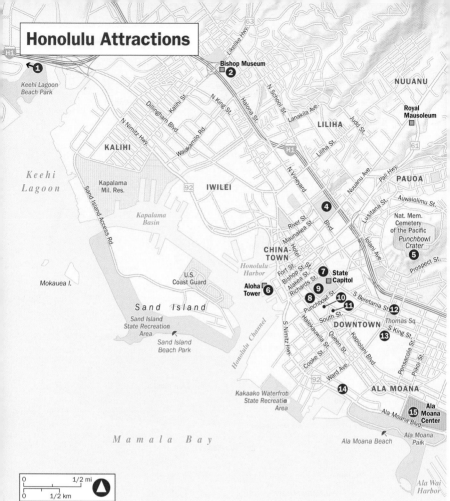

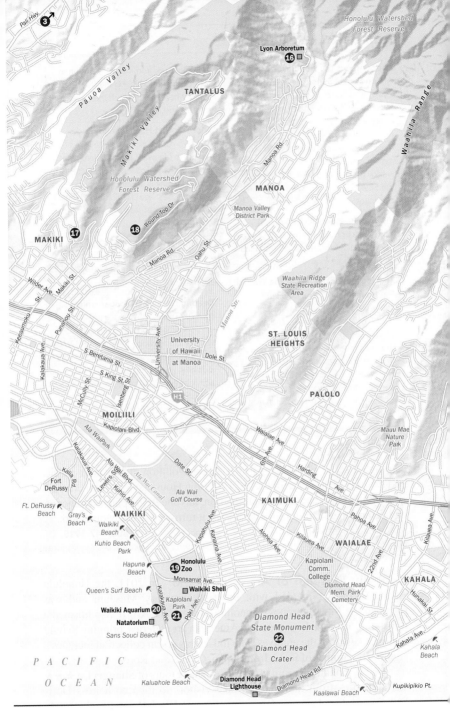

Checking out the Honolulu Museum of Art on Family Sunday (see below) Every third Sunday of the month, the Museum of Art is free, offering a variety of art activities and movies for the kids. Past programs have included sessions making pirate sock puppets and screenings of animated shorts from around the world. You can also take the shuttle to the Spalding House, where the fun continues.

Visiting the Honolulu Zoo (p. 85) Visit Africa in Hawaii at the zoo, where the lions, giraffes, zebras, and elephants delight youngsters and parents alike.

Peeking Under the Sea at the Waikiki Aquarium (p. 86) The aquarium is pretty small, but it has a fascinating collection of alien-like jellyfish and allows for up-close encounters of the endangered Hawaiian monk seal and an octopus that changes color before your eyes. Check the aquarium website for family-friendly activities, including a Behind the Scenes tour, where you'll learn what makes the aquarium run, from habitat creation to fish food, and Exploring the Reef at night tours, where you'll search the ocean reef for eels and octopi.

Snorkeling at Hanauma Bay (p. 104) Checked out the sea life at the aquarium? Now it's time to swim with some of them! The inside of sheltered Hanauma Bay is usually very calm, making it the best spot for first-time snorkelers to swim alongside Hawaii's brightly colored fish.

Eating Shave Ice (p. 146) No visit to Hawaii is complete without shave ice—powdery soft ice drenched in tropically flavored fruit syrups.

Beating Drums in a Tongan Village (p. 99) The Polynesian Cultural Center introduces kids to Polynesian activities, which include canoe paddling and Tahitian spear throwing. They'll even let the kids help cook Samoan staples. The activities go on every day from 12:30 to 5:30pm.

Through a series of programs, such as the evolution of Hawaiian music, and exhibits in the cellar of the 1821 Mission House (saloon pilot crackers and 19th-century bone-saw reproduction, anyone?), the plan is to encourage "emotional learning." Missionaries, it turns out, were people, too. 553 S. King St. (at Kawaiahao St.). http://missionhouses.org. ☎ **808/447-3910.** $10 adults, $8 military personnel and seniors, $6 students and children 6 and over, free for children 5 and under. Tues–Sat 10am–4pm. Bus: 2 and 42.

Honolulu Museum of Art ★ MUSEUM   In 2011, the Honolulu Academy of Art merged with the Contemporary Museum and was renamed the (more apropos) Honolulu Museum of Art. It also finished a reinstallation of the European and American art galleries, bringing to light many pieces from the archives. The museum's Asian collection includes a significant number of items from Japan, China, and Korea.

The Honolulu Museum of Art is also where tours of **Shangri La** ★★★ start. Shuttles from the museum take visitors to tobacco heiress Doris Duke's private palace on a 5-acre sanctuary in Black Point. It's absolutely stunning, packed with Islamic art and intricate tilework from Iran, Turkey, and Syria; textiles from Egypt and India; and custom-painted ceilings by Moroccan artisans. Outside's not so bad either, with ocean views all the way to Diamond Head. Make sure to book in advance—the tours fill up quickly, a testament to this unique wonder. Tours are offered Wednesday through Saturday and take 2½ hours.

Admittedly, I love the **Spalding House** (formerly the Contemporary Museum) more for its views and surrounding gardens than for its art collection. It's in Tantalus, high above the city, and yet only a 10-minute drive from downtown. One of my favorite activities is the Lauhala and Lunch, where you picnic on the expansive lawn overlooking Honolulu. Call ahead to reserve a picnic basket from the Spalding House Café, which comes complete with tatami mats ($40 lunch for two).

900 S. Beretania St. www.honolulumuseum.org. (✆) **808/532-8700;** 808/532-3853 for Shangri La reservations; 808/237-5225 for the Spalding House Café. $10 adults; $5 students, seniors, and military personnel; free for children 12 and under. Shangri La tours $25 ($20 Hawaii residents), children under 8 not admitted, advance reservations a must. Tues–Sat 10am–4:30pm; Sun 1–5pm.

Iolani Palace ★★ HISTORIC BUILDING If you want to really "understand" Hawaii, this 45-minute tour is worth your time. The Iolani Palace was built by King David Kalākaua, who spared no expense. The 4-year project, completed in 1882, cost $360,000—and nearly bankrupted

Iolani Palace

the Hawaiian kingdom. This four-story Italian Renaissance palace was the first electrified building in Honolulu (it had electricity before the White House and Buckingham Palace). Royals lived here for 11 years, until Queen Lili'uokalani was deposed and the Hawaiian monarchy fell forever in a palace coup led by U.S. Marines on January 17, 1893, at the demand of sugar planters and missionary descendants.

Cherished by latter-day royalists, the 10-room palace stands as an architectural statement of the monarchy period. Iolani attracts 60,000 visitors a year in groups of 15; everyone must don booties to scoot across the royal floors. Visitors take either a comprehensive **guided tour ★**, which offers a docent-guided tour of the interior, or a self-led **audio tour.** Finish by exploring the Basement Gallery on your own, where you'll find crown jewels, ancient feathered cloaks, the royal china, and more.

364 S. King St. (at Richards St.). www.iolanipalace.org. © **808/538-1471.** Guided tour Tues–Sat $22 adults, $6 children 5–12; reservations required. Book online or visit the ticket office in the Iolani Barracks on the Palace Grounds. Audio tour $15 adults, $6 children 5–12. Gallery tour $7 adults, $3 children 5–12. Mon–Sat 9:30am–4pm. Children 4 and under allowed only in the Basement Gallery (with an adult). Extremely limited parking on palace grounds; try metered parking on the street. Bus: 2.

Kawaiahao Church ★ CHURCH   In 1842, Kawaiahao Church stood complete at last. Designed by Rev. Hiram Bingham (grandfather of explorer and politician Hiram Bingham III) and supervised by Kamehameha III, who ordered his people to help build it, the project took 5 years to complete. Workers quarried 14,000 coral blocks weighing 1,000 pounds each from the offshore reefs and cut timber in the forests for the beams. This proud stone church, complete with bell tower and colonial colonnade, was the first permanent Western house of worship in the islands. It became the church of the Hawaiian royalty and remains in use today. Some fine portraits of Hawaiian royalty hang inside, on the upper level. English- and Hawaiian-language services are held Sundays at 9am.

957 Punchbowl St. (at King St.). © **808/469-3000.** Free (donations appreciated). Mon–Sat 8am–4:30pm; Sun services 9am. Bus: 2.

Queen Emma Summer Palace ★ PALACE   Hanaiakamalama, the name of the country estate of Kamehameha IV and Queen Emma, was once in the secluded uplands of Nuuanu Valley. These days it's adjacent to a six-lane highway full of speeding cars. This simple, seven-room New England–style house, built in 1848 and restored by the Daughters of Hawaii, is worth an hour of your time to see the interesting blend of Victorian furniture and hallmarks of Hawaiian royalty, including feather cloaks and *kahili*, the feathered standards that mark the presence of *alii* (royalty). Other royal treasures include a canoe-shaped cradle for Queen Emma's baby, Prince Albert, who died at the age of 4. (Kauai's ritzy Princeville Resort is named for the little prince.)

2913 Pali Hwy. (at Old Pali Rd.). http://daughtersofhawaii.org. © **808/595-3167.** $10 adults, $1 children 11 and under. Daily 9am–4pm. Bus: E or 57.

Wartime Honolulu

USS *Arizona* Memorial at Pearl Harbor ★★★ HISTORIC
SITE   On December 7, 1941, the USS *Arizona,* while moored here in
Pearl Harbor, was bombed in a Japanese air raid. The 608-foot battleship
sank in 9 minutes without firing a shot, taking 1,177 sailors and Marines
to their deaths—and catapulting the United States into World War II.

Note: **At press time, the USS *Arizona* was closed to visitors for
structural repairs. Park officials assured us the work would be done
by late fall of 2018, but do check the website to make sure that the site
is open once again.**

Nobody who visits the memorial will ever forget it. The deck of the
ship lies 6 feet below the surface of the sea. Oil still oozes slowly up from
the Arizona's engine room and
stains the harbor's calm, blue
water; some say the ship still
weeps for its lost crew. The
memorial, designed by Alfred
Preis, a German architect
interned on Sand Island during
the war, is a stark-white, 184-
foot rectangular bridge that
spans the sunken hull of the
ship. It contains the ship's bell,
recovered from the wreckage,
and a shrine room with the
names of the dead carved in
stone.

> ## Pearl Harbor Visitor Center: Getting Tickets
>
> The **USS *Arizona* Memorial, USS *Bowfin*
> and Submarine Museum, USS *Missouri*
> Memorial,** and **Pacific Aviation Museum** are
> all accessed via the Pearl Harbor Visitor
> Center. Park here and purchase tickets for all
> the exhibits. (Entry to the USS *Arizona*
> Memorial is free, but you still must get a
> ticket. Better yet, for the USS *Arizona,*
> reserve your spot at **www.recreation.gov** to
> avoid a long wait.) Shuttle buses will deliver
> you to the sites within Pearl Harbor.

Today, free U.S. Navy launches take visitors to the *Arizona.* You can
make an **advance reservation** to visit the memorial at the website **www.
recreation.gov** for an additional $1.50 per-ticket convenience fee. This is
highly recommended; if you try to get walk-up tickets directly at the visitor center, you may have to wait a few hours before the tour. While
you're waiting for the free shuttle to take you out to the ship, get the
audio tour ★★★, which will make the trip even more meaningful. The
tour (on an MP3 player) is about 2½ hours long, costs $7.50, and is worth
every nickel. It's like having your own personal park ranger as your guide.
The tape is narrated by the late Ernest Borgnine and features stories told
by actual Pearl Harbor survivors—both American and Japanese. Plus,
while you're waiting for the launch, the tour will take you step by step
through the museum's personal mementos, photographs, and historic doc-
uments. You can pause the tour for the moving 20-minute film that pre-
cedes your trip to the ship. The tour continues on the launch, describing
the shoreline and letting you know what's in store at the memorial itself.
At the memorial, the tour gives you a mental picture of that fateful day,

USS *Arizona* Memorial

and the narration continues on your boat ride back. Allow a total of at least 4 hours for your visit.

Note that boat rides to the *Arizona* are sometimes suspended because of high winds. Check the World War II **Valor in the Pacific** Facebook page (www.facebook.com/valorNPS) for updated information on boat ride suspensions. Due to increased security measures, visitors cannot carry purses, handbags, fanny packs, backpacks, camera bags (though you can carry your camera, cellphone, or video camera with you), diaper bags, or other items that offer concealment on the boat. However, there is a storage facility where you can stash carry-on-size items (no bigger than 30×30×18 in.) for a fee. *A reminder to parents:* Baby strollers, baby carriages, and baby backpacks are not allowed inside the theater, on the boat, or on the USS *Arizona* Memorial. All babies must be carried. *One last note:* Most unfortunately, the USS *Arizona* Memorial is a high-theft area—so leave your valuables at the hotel.

Pearl Harbor. www.nps.gov/usar. (C) **808/422-3300.** Free. $7.50 for the audio guide. **Highly recommended:** Make an advance reservation to visit the memorial at www. recreation.gov. Children 11 and under should be accompanied by an adult. Wheelchairs gladly accommodated. Daily 7am–5pm (programs run 8am–3pm). Drive west on H-1 past the airport; take the USS *Arizona* Memorial exit and follow the green-and-white signs; there's ample free parking. Bus: 40 or 42; or *Arizona* Memorial Shuttle Bus VIP (C) **866/836-0317**), which picks up at Waikiki hotels 7am–noon ($10 per person round-trip).

USS *Bowfin* Submarine Museum & Park ★ HISTORIC SITE   Ever wonder what life on a submarine is like? Then go inside the USS *Bowfin*, aka the Pearl Harbor Avenger, to experience the claustrophobic quarters where soldiers lived and launched torpedoes. The *Bowfin* Museum details wartime submarine history and gives a sense of the impressive technical challenges that must be overcome for submarines to even exist. The Waterfront Memorial honors submariners lost during World War II.

11 Arizona Memorial Dr. (next to the USS *Arizona* Memorial Visitor Center). www. bowfin.org. ℂ **808/423-1341.** $12 adults, $8 active-duty military personnel and seniors, $5 children 4–12 (children 3 and under not permitted for safety reasons). Daily 7am–5pm (last admission 4:30pm). See USS *Arizona* Memorial, above, for driving, bus, and shuttle directions.

USS *Missouri* Memorial ★ HISTORIC SITE   In the deck of this 58,000-ton battleship (the last one the navy launched), World War II came to an end with the signing of the Japanese surrender on September 2, 1945. The *Missouri* was part of the force that carried out bombing raids over Tokyo and provided firepower in the battles of Iwo Jima and Okinawa. In 1955, the navy decommissioned the ship and mothballed it at the Puget Sound Naval Shipyard in Washington State. But the *Missouri* was modernized and called back into action in 1986, eventually being deployed in the Persian Gulf War, before retiring once again in 1992. Here it sat until another battle ensued, this time over who would get the right to keep this living legend. Hawaii won that battle and brought the ship to Pearl Harbor in 1998. The 887-foot ship is now open to visitors as a museum memorial.

You're free to explore on your own or take a guided tour. Highlights of this massive (more than 200-ft. tall) battleship include the forecastle (or "fo'c's'le," in navy talk), where the 30,000-pound anchors are dropped on 1,080 feet of anchor chain; the 16-inch guns (each 65 ft. long and weighing 116 tons), which can accurately fire a 2,700-pound shell some 23 miles in 50 seconds; and the spot where the Instrument of Surrender was signed as Douglas MacArthur, Chester Nimitz, and "Bull" Halsey looked on.

Battleship Row, Pearl Harbor. www.ussmissouri.com. ℂ **877/MIGHTY-MO.** $27 adults, $13 children 4–12. Mighty Mo Tour (35 min.); Heart of the Missouri Tour (90 min.) $27 extra. Daily 8am–5pm; guided tours 8:15am–4:15pm. Check in at the USS *Bowfin* Submarine Museum, next to the USS *Arizona* Memorial Visitor Center. See USS *Arizona* Memorial, above, for driving, bus, and shuttle directions.

National Memorial Cemetery of the Pacific ★★ CEMETERY
The National Memorial Cemetery of the Pacific (aka Punchbowl) is an ash-and-lava tuff cone that exploded about 150,000 years ago—like Diamond Head, only smaller. Early Hawaiians called it Puowaina, or "hill of sacrifice." The old crater is a burial ground for veterans as well as the 35,000 victims of three American wars in Asia and the Pacific: World War II, Korea, and Vietnam. Among the graves, you'll find many unmarked ones with the date December 7, 1941, carved in stone. Some names will be unknown forever; others are famous, like that of war correspondent Ernie Pyle, killed by a Japanese sniper in April 1945 on Okinawa; still others buried here are remembered only by family and surviving buddies.

The white stone tablets known as the Courts of the Missing bear the names of 28,788 Americans missing in action in World War II.

Punchbowl Crater, 2177 Puowaina Dr. (at the end of the road). Free. Daily 8am–5:30pm (Mar–Sept to 6:30pm). Bus: 2 or 42, with a long walk.

Pacific Aviation Museum ★ MUSEUM The Pacific Aviation Museum is the flashiest (and newest) of the Pearl Harbor exhibits, with its propaganda-esque written histories and signs. There are two hangars: Hangar 37 includes planes involved in the 1942 attack, but the best is Hangar 79, the doors still riddled with bullet holes from the Pearl Harbor strafing. It houses military aircraft, old and new; you can even climb into the cockpit of some of them. On the far end is the Restoration Shop, where you can watch vintage aircraft actively being restored. For an additional $10, sit in a Combat Flight Simulator, like an immersive video game in which you fly a plane and shoot down the enemy.

Hanger 39, 319 Lexington Blvd., Ford Island (next to the red-and-white control tower). www.pacificaviationmuseum.org. © **808/441-1000.** $25 adults, $15 children 4–12; guided behind-the-scenes tour $35 adults, $25 children 4–12. Daily 9am–5pm. See USS *Arizona* Memorial, above, for driving, bus, and shuttle directions.

Just Beyond Pearl Harbor

Hawaiian Railway ★ TRAIN It's like a Disneyland ride . . . through Honolulu's suburbia. It's also a quirky way to see the less-traveled leeward side of Oahu. Between 1890 and 1947, the chief mode of transportation for Oahu's sugar mills was the Oahu Railway and Land Co.'s narrow-gauge trains. The line carried not only equipment, raw sugar, and supplies, but also passengers from one side of the island to the other. About 6 miles of the train tracks have been restored, starting in 'Ewa and ending along the coast at Kahe Point. Don't expect ocean views all the way—you're passing through the heart of suburban Honolulu (yup, that's a Costco and a power plant) before you reach the ocean. Still, the 1½-hour narrated ride is pretty amusing. Even better, book the 3pm rides, and the train stops at Ko Olina resort for ice cream.

91-1001 Renton Rd., Ewa. www.hawaiianrailway.com. © **808/681-5461.** $12 adults, $8 seniors and children 2–12. Parlor Car 64 $25. Departures Sat at 3pm and Sun at 1 and 3pm and weekdays by appointment. Take H-1 west to Exit 5A; take Hwy. 76 south for 2½ miles to Tesoro Gas; turn right on Renton Rd. and drive 1½ miles to end of paved section. The station is on the left. Bus: E or 42, with a 1½-mile walk.

Hawaii's Plantation Village ★ HISTORIC SITE The hour-long tour of this restored 50-acre village offers a glimpse back in time to when sugar planters shaped the land, economy, and culture of Hawaii. From 1852, when the first contract laborers arrived here from China, to 1947, when the plantation era ended, more than 400,000 men, women, and children from China, Japan, Portugal, Puerto Rico, Korea, and the Philippines came to work the sugarcane fields. The "talk story" tour brings the old village alive with 30 faithfully restored camp houses, Chinese and Japanese temples, the Plantation Store, and even a sumo-wrestling ring.

94-695 Waipahu St. (at Waipahu Depot Rd.), Waipahu. www.hawaiiplantationvillage. org. ℂ **808/677-0110.** Admission with guided tour $15 adults, $12 seniors, $8 military personnel, $6 children 4–11. Mon–Sat 10am–2pm. Take H-1 west to Waikele-Waipahu exit (Exit 7); get in the left lane of the exit and turn left on Paiwa St.; at the 5th light, turn right onto Waipahu St.; after the 2nd light, turn left. Bus: 40 or 42.

Gardens, Aquariums & Zoos

Foster Botanical Garden ★ GARDEN   You could spend days in this unique historic garden, a leafy oasis amid the high-rises of downtown Honolulu. Combine a tour of the garden with a trip to Chinatown (just across the street) to maximize your time and double your pleasure. The

giant trees that tower over the garden's main terrace were planted in the 1850s by William Hillebrand, a German physician and botanist, on royal land leased from Queen Emma. Today this 14-acre public garden, on the north side of Chinatown, is a living museum of plants, some rare and endangered, collected from the tropical regions of the world. Of special interest are 26 "Exceptional Trees" protected by state law, a large palm collection, a primitive cycad garden, and a hybrid orchid collection.

Foster Botanical Garden

50 N. Vineyard Blvd. (at Nuuanu Ave.). ℂ **808/522-7066.** $5 adults, $1 children 6–12. Daily 9am–4pm; guided tours Mon–Sat at 1pm (reservations recommended). Bus: 19 or E.

Honolulu Zoo ★ ZOO   Nobody comes to Hawaii to see an Indian elephant or African lions and zebras, right? Wrong. This 43-acre municipal zoo in Waikiki attracts visitors in droves. If you've got kids, allot at least half a day. The highlight is the African Savanna, a 10-acre exhibit with more than 40 African critters, including antelope and giraffes. The zoo also has a rare Hawaiian nene goose, one of the few indigenous animals left in Hawaii.

151 Kapahulu Ave. (between Paki and Kalākaua aves.), at entrance to Kapi'olani Park. www.honoluluzoo.org. ℂ **808/971-7171.** $14 adults, $6 children 3–12. Daily 9am–4:30pm. Zoo parking (entrance on Kapahulu Ave.) $1 per hr. Bus: 8 or 42.

Lyon Arboretum ★ GARDEN   The Lyon Arboretum dates from 1918, when the Hawaiian Sugar Planters Association wanted to demonstrate the value of watershed for reforestation. In 1953, it became part of the University of Hawaii, where they continued to expand the extensive collection of tropical plants. Six-story-tall breadfruit trees, yellow orchids no bigger than a nickel, ferns with fuzzy buds as big as a human head—these are just a few of the botanical wonders you'll find at the 194-acre arboretum. A whole different world opens up to you along the self-guided, 20-minute hike through the arboretum to Inspiration Point. You'll pass more than 5,000 exotic tropical plants full of singing birds in this cultivated rainforest at the head of Manoa Valley.

3860 Manoa Rd. (near the top of the road). www.hawaii.edu/lyonarboretum. © **808/988-0456.** Suggested donation $5. Mon–Fri 8am–4pm; Sat 9am–3pm. Bus: 5.

Waikiki Aquarium ★ AQUARIUM   Half of Hawaii's beauty is its underwater world. Behold the chambered nautilus, nature's submarine and inspiration for Jules Verne's *20,000 Leagues Under the Sea*. You can see this tropical, spiral-shelled cephalopod mollusk—the only living one born in captivity—any day of the week here. Its natural habitat is the deep waters of Micronesia, but former aquarium director Bruce Carlson not only succeeded in trapping the pearly shelled creature in 1,500 feet of water (by dangling chunks of raw tuna), but also managed to breed this ancient relative of the octopus. There are plenty of other fish to see in this small but first-class aquarium, located on a live coral reef. The reef habitat features sharks, eels, a touch tank, and habitats for the endangered Hawaiian monk seal and green sea turtle. The rotating jellyfish exhibit is

Waikiki Aquarium

otherworldly—it's like watching alien life. The aquarium is small; you'll probably need only an hour or less to see everything.

2777 Kalakaua Ave. (across from Kapiolani Park). www.waikikiaquarium.org. © **808/923-9741.** $12 adults, $8 active military, $5 seniors and children 4–12. Daily 9am–4:30pm. Bus: 2 and Waikiki Trolley's Green Line.

Other Natural Wonders & Spectacular Views

In addition to the attractions listed below, check out the hike to **Diamond Head Crater ★★★** (p. 117); almost everybody can handle it, and the 360-degree views from the top are fabulous.

Nuuanu Pali Lookout ★ NATURAL ATTRACTION   Gale-force winds sometimes howl through the mountain pass at this 1,186-foot-high perch guarded by 3,000-foot peaks, so hold on to your hat—and small children. But if you walk up from the parking lot to the precipice, you'll be rewarded with a view that'll blow you away. At the edge, the dizzying panorama of Oahu's windward side is breathtaking: Clouds low enough to pinch scoot by on trade winds; pinnacles of the pali (cliffs), green with ferns, often disappear in the mist. From on high, the tropical palette of green and blue runs down to the sea. Combine this 10-minute stop with a trip over the pali to the windward side.

Near the summit of Pali Hwy. (Hwy. 61); take the Nuuanu Pali Lookout turnoff. Parking lot $3 per vehicle.

Puu Ualakaa State Park ★★★ STATE PARK/NATURAL ATTRAC-TION   The best **sunset view** of Honolulu is from a 1,048-foot-high hill named for sweet potatoes. Actually, the poetic Hawaiian name means "rolling sweet potato hill," for the way early planters used gravity to harvest their crop. The panorama is sweeping and majestic. On a clear day—which is often—you can see from Diamond Head to the Wai'anae Range, almost the length of Oahu. At night, several scenic overlooks provide romantic spots high above the city lights.

At the end of Round Hill Dr. Daily 7am–6:45pm (to 7:45pm in summer). From Waikiki, take Ala Wai Blvd. to McCully St., turn right, and drive *mauka* (inland) beyond the H-1 on-ramps to Wilder St.; turn left and go to Makiki St.; turn right, and continue onward and upward about 3 miles.

WALKING TOUR: HISTORIC HONOLULU

GETTING THERE:	**From Waikiki, take Ala Moana Boulevard in the Ewa direction. Ala Moana Boulevard ends at Nimitz Highway. Turn right on the next street on your right (Alakea St.). Park in the garage across from St. Andrew's Church after you cross Beretania Street. Bus: 2, 13, 19, or 20.**
START & FINISH:	**St. Andrew's Church, Beretania and Alakea streets.**

TIME:	**2 to 3 hours, depending on how long you linger in museums.**
BEST TIMES:	**Monday through Saturday, daytime, when ʻIolani Palace is open.**

The 1800s were a turbulent time in Hawaii. By the end of the 1790s, Kamehameha the Great had united all the islands. Foreigners then began arriving by ship—first explorers, then merchants, and then, in 1820, missionaries. The rulers of Hawaii were hard-pressed to keep up. By 1840, it was clear that the capital had shifted from Lahaina, where the Kingdom of Hawaii was actually centered, to Honolulu, where the majority of commerce and trade was taking place. In 1848, the Great Mahele (division) enabled commoners and, eventually, foreigners to own crown land, and in two generations, more than 80% of all private lands had shifted to foreign ownership. With the introduction of sugar as a crop, the foreigners prospered, and in time they put more and more pressures on the government.

By 1872, the monarchy had run through the Kamehameha line and, in 1873, David Kalakaua was elected to the throne. Known as the "Merrie Monarch," Kalakaua redefined the monarchy by going on a world tour, building Iolani Palace, having a European-style coronation, and throwing extravagant parties. By the end of the 1800s, however, the foreign sugar growers and merchants had become extremely powerful in Hawaii. With the assistance of the U.S. Marines, they orchestrated the overthrow of Queen Liliuokalani, Hawaii's last reigning monarch, in 1893. The United States declared Hawaii a territory in 1898.

You can witness the remnants of these turbulent years in just a few short blocks.

Cross the street from the garage and venture back to 1858 when you enter:

1 St. Andrew's Church

The Hawaiian monarchs were greatly influenced by the royals in Europe. When King Kamehameha IV saw the grandeur of the Church of England, he decided to build his own cathedral. He and Queen Emma founded the Anglican Church of Hawaii in 1858. The king didn't live to see the church completed, however; he died on St. Andrew's Day, 4 years before King Kamehameha V oversaw the laying of the cornerstone in 1867. The church was named St. Andrew's in honor of King Kamehameha IV's death. This French-Gothic structure was shipped in pieces from England. Even if you aren't fond of visiting churches, you have to see the floor-to-eaves, hand-blown stained-glass window that faces the setting sun. In the glass is a mural of Rev. Thomas Staley (the first bishop in Hawaii), King Kamehameha IV, and Queen Emma. Services are conducted in English and Hawaiian. On Sundays at 8am the Hawaiian Choir sings Hawaiian hymns, and at 10:30am the Cathedral Choir, in existence for 150 years, performs.

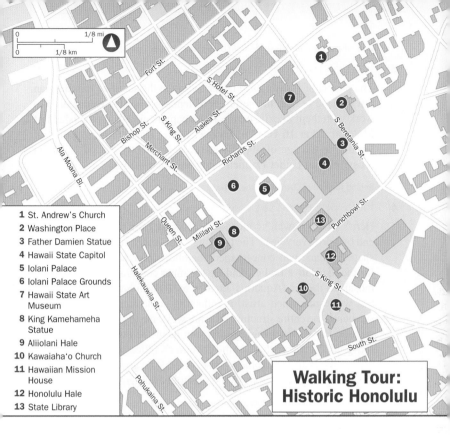

Walking Tour: Historic Honolulu

Next, walk down Beretania Street in the Diamond Head direction to the gates of:

2   Washington Place

This was the former home of Queen Liliuokalani, Hawaii's last queen. For 80 years after her death, it served as the governor's house, until a new home was built on the property in 2002 and the historic residence was opened to the public. Tours are held Thursdays at 10am by reservation only. They're free; fill out the request form at (washingtonplacefoundation.org) at least 2 days in advance to reserve. The Greek Revival–style home, built in 1842 by a U.S. sea captain named John Dominis, got its name from the U.S. ambassador who once stayed here and told so many stories about George Washington that people starting calling the home Washington Place. The sea captain's son married a Hawaiian princess, Lydia Kapaakea, who later became Queen Liliuokalani. When the queen was overthrown by U.S. businessmen in 1893, she moved out of Iolani Palace and into Washington Place, where she lived until her death in 1917. On the left side of the building, near the sidewalk, is a plaque inscribed with the words to one of the most popular songs written by Queen Liliuokalani, "Aloha Oe" ("Farewell to Thee").

Cross the street and walk to the front of the Hawaii State Capitol, where you'll find the:

3 Father Damien Statue

The people of Hawaii have never forgotten the sacrifice this Belgian priest made to help the sufferers of leprosy when he volunteered to work with them in exile on the Kalaupapa Peninsula on the island of Molokai. After 16 years of service, Father Damien himself died of leprosy, at the age of 49. The statue is frequently draped in leis in recognition of Father Damien's humanitarian work.

Behind the Father Damien Statue is the:

4 Hawaii State Capitol

Here's where Hawaii's state legislators work from mid-January to the end of April every year. The building's unusual design has palm tree–shaped pillars, two cone-shaped chambers (representing volcanoes) for the legislative bodies, and, in the inner courtyard, a 600,000-tile mosaic of the sea (Aquarius) created by Tadashi Sato, a Hawaii-born and world-renowned artist. A reflecting pool (representing the sea) surrounds the entire structure. You are welcome to go into the rotunda and see the woven hangings and murals at the entrance; pick up a self-guided-tour brochure at the governor's office on the fourth floor. The public is also welcome to observe the state government in action during legislative sessions (www.capitol.hawaii.gov).

Walk down Richards Street toward the ocean and stop at:

5 Iolani Palace

Hawaii is the only state in the U.S. to have not one but two royal palaces: one in Kona, where the royals went during the summer, and Iolani Palace (*Iolani* means "royal hawk"). Don't miss the opportunity to see this grande dame of historic buildings. Guided tours are $22 adults, $6 children 5 to 12; self-guided audio tours are $15 adults, $6 children 5 to 12; and basement gallery tours are $7 adults, $3 children 5 to 12. It's open Monday to Saturday 9:30am to 4pm; call ℂ **808/522-0832** or book online (www.iolanipalace.org) to reserve in advance, as spots are limited.

In ancient times, a *heiau* (temple) stood in this area. When it became clear to King Kamehameha III that the capital should be transferred from Lahaina to Honolulu, he moved to a modest building here in 1845. The construction of the palace began in 1879 by King David Kalakaua and was finished 3 years later at a cost of $350,000. The king spared no expense: You can still see the glass and iron work imported from San Francisco, and the palace had all the modern conveniences for its time. Electric lights were installed 4 years before the White House had them, and every bedroom had its

Father Damien statue, in front of the Hawaii State Capitol

own full bathroom with hot and cold running water, copper-lined tub, flush toilet, and bidet. The king had a telephone line from the palace to his boathouse on the water a year after Alexander Graham Bell introduced it to the world.

It was also in this palace that Queen Liliuokalani was overthrown and placed under house arrest for 9 months. Later, the territorial and then the state government used the palace until it outgrew it. When the legislature left in 1968, the palace was in shambles. It has since undergone a $7-million overhaul to restore it to its former glory.

After you visit the palace, spend some time on the:

6 Iolani Palace Grounds

You can wander around the grounds at no charge. The ticket window to the palace and the gift shop are in the former barracks of the Royal Household Guards. The domed pavilion on the grounds was originally built as a Coronation Stand by King Kalākaua (9 years after he took the throne, the king decided to have a formal European-style coronation ceremony where he crowned himself and his queen, Kapiolani). Later he used it as a **Royal Bandstand** for concerts (King Kalakaua, along with Henri Berger, the first Royal Hawaiian Bandmaster, wrote "Hawaii Ponoi," the state anthem). Today, the Royal Hawaiian Band, founded in 1836 by King Kamehameha III, plays at the Royal Bandstand every Friday from noon to 1pm.

From the palace grounds, turn in the Ewa direction, cross Richards Street, and walk to the corner of Richards and Hotel streets to the:

7 Hawaii State Art Museum

Opened in 2002, the Hawaii State Art Museum is housed in the original Royal Hawaiian hotel, built in 1872 during the reign of King Kamehameha V. Most of the art displayed in the 300-piece collection was created by local artists. The pieces were purchased by the state, thanks to a 1967 law that says that 1% of the cost of state buildings will be used to acquire works of art. Nearly 5 decades later, the state has amassed almost 6,000 pieces.

Walk *makai* down Richards Street and turn left (toward Diamond Head) on South King Street to the:

8 King Kamehameha Statue

At the juncture of King, Merchant, and Mililani streets stands a replica of the man who united the Hawaiian Islands. The striking black-and-gold bronze statue is magnificent. Try to see the statue on June 11 (King Kamehameha Day), when it is covered with leis in honor of Hawaii's favorite son.

King Kamehameha statue

The statue of Kamehameha I was cast by Thomas Gould in 1880 in Paris. However, it was lost at sea somewhere near the Falkland Islands. Subsequently, the insurance money was used to pay for a second statue, but in the meantime, the original statue was recovered. The original was eventually sent to the town of Kapa'au on the Big Island, the birthplace of Kamehameha, and the second statue was placed in Honolulu in 1883, as part of King David Kalākaua's coronation ceremony.

Right behind the King Kamehameha Statue is:

9 Aliiolani Hale

The name translates to "House of Heavenly Kings." This distinctive building, with a clock tower, now houses the Supreme Court of Hawaii and the Judiciary History Center. King Kamehameha V originally wanted to build a palace here and commissioned the Australian architect Thomas Rowe in 1872. However, it ended up as the first major government building for the Hawaiian monarchy. Kamehameha V didn't live to see it completed, and King David Kalākaua dedicated the building in 1874. Ironically, less than 20 years later, on January 17, 1893, Stanford Dole, backed by other prominent sugar planters, stood on the steps to this building and proclaimed the overthrow of the Hawaiian monarchy and the establishment of a provisional government. Self-guided tours are available Monday through Friday from 7:45am to 4:30pm; admission is free.

Walk toward Diamond Head on King Street; at the corner of King and Punchbowl, stop in at the:

10 Kawaiahao Church

When the missionaries came to Hawaii, the first thing they did was build churches. Four thatched-grass churches (one measured 54×22 ft. and could seat 300 people on lauhala mats; the last thatched church held 4,500 people) had been built on this site through 1837, before Rev. Hiram Bingham began building what he considered a "real" church: a New England–style congregational structure with Gothic influences. Between 1837 and 1842, the construction of the church required some 14,000 giant coral slabs (some weighing more than 1,000 pounds). Hawaiian divers ravaged the reefs, digging out huge chunks of coral and causing irreparable environmental damage.

Kawaiahao is Hawaii's oldest church and has been the site of numerous historic events, such as a speech made by King Kamehameha III in 1843, an excerpt from which became Hawaii's state motto (*"Ua mau ke ea o ka aina i ka pono,"* which translates as "The life of the land is preserved in righteousness").

The church is open Monday through Saturday 8am to 4:30pm; you'll find it to be very cool in temperature. Don't sit in the back pews marked with kahili feathers and velvet cushions; they are still reserved for the descendants of royalty. Sunday service (in English and Hawaiian) is at 9am.

Cross the street, and you'll see the:

11 Hawaiian Mission Houses

On the corner of King and Kawaiahao streets stand the original buildings of the Sandwich Islands Mission Headquarters: the **Frame House** (built in 1821), the **Chamberlain House** (1831), and the **Printing Office** (1841). The complex is open Tuesday through Saturday from 10am to 4pm; admission is $10 adults, $8 seniors and military personnel, and $6 students and children 6 and older. The tours are often led by descendants of the original missionaries to Hawaii. For information, go to www.missionhouses.org.

Believe it or not, the missionaries brought their own prefab house along with them when they came around Cape Horn from Boston in 1819. The Frame House was designed for New England winters and had small windows (it must have been stiflingly hot inside). Finished in 1821 (the interior frame was left behind and didn't arrive until Christmas 1820), it is Hawaii's oldest wooden structure. The Chamberlain House, built in 1831, was used by the missionaries as a storehouse.

The missionaries believed that the best way to spread the Lord's message to the Hawaiians was to learn their language, and then to print literature for them to read. So it was the missionaries who gave the Hawaiians a written language. The Printing House on the grounds was where the lead-type Ramage press (brought from New England, of course) was used to print the Hawaiian Bible.

Cross King Street and walk in the Ewa direction to the corner of Punchbowl and King to:

12 Honolulu Hale

The **Honolulu City Hall,** built in 1927, was designed by Honolulu's most famous architect, C. W. Dickey. His Spanish Mission–style building has an open-air courtyard, which is used for art exhibits and concerts. It's open Monday through Friday.

Cross Punchbowl Street and walk *mauka* to the:

13 State Library

Anything you want to know about Hawaii and the Pacific can be found here, at the main branch of the state's library system. Located in a restored historic building, it has an open garden courtyard in the middle, great for stopping for a rest on your walk.

Head down Beretania in the Ewa direction to Alakea back to the parking garage.

BEYOND HONOLULU: EXPLORING THE ISLAND BY CAR

Urban Honolulu, with its history, cuisine, and shopping, can captivate travelers for days. But the rest of the island draws them out in its promise of wild coastlines and unique adventures.

Oahu's Southeast Coast

From the high-rises of Waikiki, venture down Kalakaua Avenue through tree-lined **Kapiolani Park** to take a look at a different side of Oahu, the arid southeast shore. The landscape here is more moonscape, with prickly cacti onshore and, in winter, spouting whales cavorting in the water.

To get to this coast, follow Kalakaua Avenue past the multitiered Dillingham Fountain and around the bend in the road, which now becomes Poni Moi Road. Make a right on Diamond Head Road and begin the climb up the side of the old crater. At the top are several lookout points, so if the official Diamond Head Lookout is jammed with cars, try one of the other lookouts just down the road. The view of the rolling waves and surfers is spectacular; take the time to pull over. This is also a wonderful place to begin your day early and watch the sun rise.

Diamond Head Road rolls downhill into the ritzy community of **Kahala.** At the fork in the road at the triangular Fort Ruger Park, veer to your right and continue on the palm tree–lined Kahala Avenue. Make a left on Hunakai Street, and then take a right on Kīlauea Avenue and look for the sign, "H-1 west." Turn right at the sign, although you won't get on the H-1 freeway; instead, get on Kalanianaole Highway, a four-lane highway interrupted every few blocks by a stoplight. This is the suburban bedroom community to Honolulu, marked by malls on the left and beach parks on the right.

One of these parks is **Hanauma Bay** ★★ (p. 104); you'll see the turnoff on the right when you're about half an hour from Waikiki. This marine preserve is one of the island's best places to snorkel; you'll find the friendliest fish on the island here. *A reminder:* The beach park is closed on Tuesday.

Around mile marker 11, the jagged lava coast itself spouts sea foam at the **Halona Blowhole.** Look out to sea from Halona over Sandy Beach and across the 26-mile gulf to neighboring Molokai and the faint triangular shadow of Lanai on the far horizon. **Sandy Beach** ★ (p. 106) is one of Oahu's most dangerous beaches, with thundering shorebreak. Bodyboarders just love it.

The coast looks raw and empty along this stretch as the road weaves past old Hawaiian fish ponds and the famous formation known as **Pele's Chair,** just off Kalanianaole Highway (Hwy. 72) above Queen's Beach. From a distance, the lava-rock outcropping looks like a mighty throne; it's believed to be the fire goddess's last resting place on Oahu before she flew off to continue her work on other islands.

Ahead lies 647-foot-high **Makapuu Point,** with a lighthouse that once signaled safe passage for steamship passengers arriving from San Francisco. The automated light now brightens Oahu's south coast for passing tankers, fishing boats, and sailors. You can take a short hike up the **Makapuu Lighthouse Trail** ★★ (p. 119) for a spectacular vista.

Turn the corner at Makapuu and you're on Oahu's windward side, where cooling trade winds propel windsurfers across turquoise bays; the waves at **Makapuu Beach Park** ★ (p. 106) are perfect for bodysurfing.

Ahead, the coastal vista is a profusion of fluted green mountains and strange peaks, edged by golden beaches and the blue, blue Pacific. The 3,000-foot-high, sheer, green Koolau mountains plunge almost straight down, presenting an irresistible jumping-off spot for paragliders. Most likely, you'll spot their colorful chutes in the sky, looking like balloons released into the wind.

Winding up the coast, Kalaniana'ole Highway (Hwy. 72) leads through rural **Waimanalo,** a country beach town of nurseries and stables. Nearly 4 miles long, **Waimanalo Beach ★★** (p. 110) is Oahu's longest beach and popular with local families on weekends. Take a swim here or head on to **Kailua Beach ★★★** (p. 108), one of Hawaii's best.

The Windward Coast

From the **Nuunau Pali Lookout ★**, near the summit of the Pali Highway (Hwy. 61), you get the first hint of the other side of Oahu, a region so green and lovely that it could be an island sibling of Tahiti. With its many beaches and bays, the scenic 30-mile Windward Coast parallels the corduroy-ridged, nearly perpendicular cliffs of the Koolau Range, which separates the windward side of the island from Honolulu and the rest of Oahu. As you descend on the serpentine Pali Highway beneath often-gushing waterfalls, you'll see the nearly 1,000-foot spike of **Olomana,** a bold pinnacle that beckons intrepid hikers, and, beyond, the town of **Waimanalo,** where many of Native Hawaiian descent live. Stop by **Ai Love Nalo ★** (p. 159), for a fruit smoothie or fresh and flavorful renditions of local classics, such as a veggie laulau or poi parfait, layered with seasonal fruit, granola, and coconut flakes.

From the Pali Highway, to the right is Kailua, Hawaii's biggest beach town, with more than 50,000 residents and 2 special beaches, **Kailua Beach ★★★** (p. 108) and **Lanikai Beach ★★★** (p. 108). You can easily spend an entire day in Kailua, which I absolutely recommend, whether to laze on the sand or stand-up paddle to the Mokuloa Islands. But Kailua isn't all beach: Chic boutiques line the streets, such as **Oliver Men's Shop** and the **Aloha Beach Club,** and you can grab a shave ice at **The Local Hawaii** (p. 168).

After whiling away a day in Kailua, allocate another day for exploring the rest of the Windward coast. Take Highway 830N, which goes through Kaneohe and then follows the coast to Heeia State Park. Here, you'll find **Heeia Fish Pond,** which ancient Hawaiians built by enclosing natural bays with rocks to trap fish on the incoming tide. The 88-acre fish pond, which is made of lava rock and had four watchtowers to observe fish movement and several sluice gates along the 5,000-foot-long wall, is now in the process of being restored.

Drive onto **Heeia Pier,** which juts onto Kaneohe Bay. You can take a snorkel cruise here or sail out to a sandbar in the middle of the bay for an incredible view of Oahu that most people, even those who live here, never see. Incredibly scenic Kaneohe Bay is spiked with islets and lined with gold-sand beach parks like **Kualoa Regional Park ★** (p. 111), a favorite picnic spot. The bay has a barrier reef and four tiny islets, one of which is known as Moku o loe, or Coconut Island. Don't be surprised if it looks familiar—it appeared in *Gilligan's Island*.

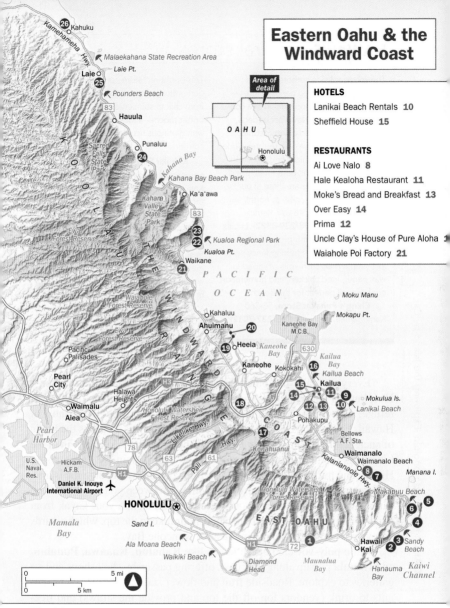

Eastern Oahu & the Windward Coast

Moku Manu

Mokapu Pt.

Kaneohe Bay M.C.B.

PACIFIC

OCEAN

OAHU

Honolulu ✦

Area of detail

Kahuku **26**

Kamehameha Hwy

Malaekahana State Recreation Area

Laie Pt.

Laie ○ **25**

Pounders Beach

83

Hauula

Punaluu
24

Sacred Falls State Park

K O O L A U

Kahana Bay

Kahana Bay Beach Park

Kahana Valley State Park

83

Ka'a'awa

23
22 Kualoa Regional Park

Kualoa Pt.

Waikane
21

THE WINDWARD RANGE

Waiahole Forest Reserve

Ewa Forest Reserve

Kahaluu ○
Ahuimanu **20**

19 ○ Heeia *Kaneohe Bay*

Kaneohe Kokokahi

Kailua Bay

630

Kailua Beach

16

15
14 **Kailua** **11**
12 **13** **9** Mokulua Is.
10 Lanikai Beach

Pacific Palisades ○

Pearl City ○

Halawa Heights ○

Honolulu Watershed Forest Reserve

H3

18

Pohakupu

17

Konahuanui

Bellows A.F. Sta.

Pali Hwy.

Likelike Hwy.

63 **61**

78

Waimalu ○
Aiea ○

Hickam A.F.B.

U.S. Naval Res.

Pearl Harbor

H1

Daniel K. Inouye International Airport ✈

HONOLULU ⊛

Sand I.

Ala Moana Beach

Waikiki Beach

Mamala Bay

Waimanalo
Waimanalo Beach
8 **7**

Manana I.

Kalanianaole Hwy.

E A S T   O A H U

Honolulu Watershed Forest Reserve

Makapuu Beach
5
6
4

1

Hawaii Kai **2** **3** Sandy Beach

Diamond Head

Maunalua Bay

Hanauma Bay

Kaiwi Channel

| 0 | | 5 mi |
| 0 | | 5 km |

The windward side harbors some of Oahu's best remaining general stores—Hawaii's mom-and-pop version of a convenience store or a New York bodega. Here, nostalgia is sold alongside the boiled peanuts by the cash register. Under the same roof, you might find smoked meat and toilet paper, butter mochi and fishing supplies. Here are three of our favorites (listed from south to north):

Waikane Store, 48-377 Kamehameha Hwy. (© **808/239-8522**): Locals pop into this little lime-green store that dates back to 1898. Nothing fancy here, just simple maki sushi rolls wrapped in wax paper, fried chicken, and homemade cookies—all perfect for the beach.

Ching's Punaluu Store, 53-360 Kamehameha Hwy. (© **808/237-7017**):

This bright-red store, run by the third generation, offers all the local favorites—from chili to soft serve. Don't miss the butter mochi—a local sweet treat made with glutinous rice flour. It's pure, chewy comfort.

Kahuku Superette ★★★, 56-505 Kamehameha Hwy. (© **808/293-9878**): Kahuku's shrimp trucks may entice with their potent, garlicky smells, but absolutely don't miss the poke (seasoned raw fish) from Kahuku Superette. If you're not afraid of kimchi, get the special poke: fresh ahi tuna with a housemade, fermented, gingery paste that's sure to waken your taste buds. Want something milder? Try the shoyu poke. This nondescript store is a must-stop for many of Honolulu's notable chefs.

Everyone calls the other distinctively shaped island **Chinaman's Hat,** but it's really named **Mokolii.** It's a sacred *puu honua,* or place of refuge, like the restored Puu Honua Honaunau on the Big Island of Hawaii. Excavations have unearthed evidence that this area was the home of ancient *alii* (royalty). Early Hawaiians believed that Mokolii (Fin of the Lizard) is all that remains of a *mo'o,* or lizard, slain by Pele's sister, Hiiaka, and hurled into the sea. At low tide you can swim out to the island, but keep watch on the changing tide, which can sweep you out to sea. You can also kayak to the island; park your car and launch your kayak from Kualoa Regional Park. It's about a half-hour hike to the top, which awards you views of the Koolau mountains and Kaneohe Bay.

Little poly-voweled beach towns like **Kahaluu, Kaaawa, Punaluu,** and **Hauula** pop up along the coast, offering passersby shell shops and art galleries to explore. Roadside fruit and flower stands vend ice-cold coconuts to drink (vendors lop off the top and provide the straws) and tree-ripened mangoes, papayas, and apple bananas (short bananas with a tart apple aftertaste).

Sugar, once the sole industry of this region, is gone. But **Kahuku,** the former sugar-plantation town, has found new life as a small aquaculture community with shrimp farms. Not of all the shrimp trucks use local shrimp, however—**Romy's** is one of the few, while the perpetually popular Giovanni's cooks up imported, frozen shrimp. Definitely stop for a poke bowl at **Kahuku Superette** (p. 98).

From here, continue along Kamehameha Highway (Hwy. 83) to the North Shore.

Attractions Along the Windward Coast

The attractions below are arranged geographically as you drive up the coast from south to north.

Hoomaluhia Botanical Garden ★ GARDEN   This 400-acre botanical garden at the foot of the steepled Koolau Range is the perfect place for a picnic. Its name means "a peaceful refuge," and that's exactly what the Army Corps of Engineers created when they installed a flood-control project here, which resulted in a 32-acre freshwater lake and garden. Just unfold a beach mat, lie back, and watch the clouds race across the rippled cliffs of the majestic Koolau Mountains. This is one of the few public places on Oahu that provides a close-up view of the steepled cliffs. The park has hiking trails and a lovely, quiet campground (p. 140). If you like hiking and nature, plan to spend at least a half-day here. *Note:* Be prepared for rain, mud, and mosquitoes.

45-680 Luluku Rd., Kaneohe. ✆ **808/233-7323.** Free. Daily 9am–4pm. Guided nature hikes Sat 10am and Sun 1pm. Take H-1 to the Pali Hwy. (Hwy. 61); turn left on Kamehameha Hwy. (Hwy. 83); at the 4th light, turn left onto Luluku Rd. Bus: 55 or 56 will stop on Kamehameha Hwy.; it's a 2-mile walk to the visitor center.

Kualoa Ranch and Activity Club ★★ ACTIVITY PARK   Kualoa Ranch does raise cattle, but people don't come here to see the cows. They come for adventure packages covering numerous activities on its 4,000 acres. Options include horseback riding and ATV rides that take you through the locations where movies like *Jurassic Park* and *Godzilla* were filmed. Get your adrenaline going on the zipline course, which allows you to fly through the treetops at the ranch.

49-560 Kamehameha Hwy., Kaaawa. www.kualoa.com. ✆ **800/231-7321** or 808/237-7321. Reservations required. Various packages available; single activities $23–$95. Daily 8am–3:30pm. Take H-1 to the Likelike Hwy. (Hwy. 63), turn left at Kahekili Hwy. (Hwy. 83), and continue to Kaaawa. Bus: 55.

Polynesian Cultural Center ★ THEME PARK   This is the Disneyland version of Polynesia, operated by the Mormon Church. It's a great show for families, informative and fun (the droll Samoan presentation amuses both adults and children). Here you can see the lifestyles, songs, dance, costumes, and architecture of six Pacific islands or archipelagos—Fiji, New Zealand, Samoa, Tahiti, Tonga, and Hawaii—in the re-created villages scattered throughout the 42-acre lagoon park. You won't be able to see it all in a day, but a day is enough.

Native students from Polynesia who attend Hawaii's Brigham Young University are the "inhabitants" of each village. They engage the audience

Polynesian Cultural Center

with spear-throwing competitions, coconut tree–climbing presentations, and invitations to pound Tongan drums. One of my favorite shows is the canoe pageant, daily at 2:30pm; each island puts on a representation of their dance, music, and costume atop canoes in the lagoon.

Don't miss *Ha: Breath of Life,* a coming-of-age story told through the different Polynesian dances, some full of grace, some fierce, and all thrilling. It's one of Oahu's better shows.

Just beyond the center is the **Hawaii Temple of the Church of Jesus Christ of Latter-day Saints,** built of volcanic rock and concrete in the form of a Greek cross; it includes reflecting pools, formal gardens, and royal palms. Completed in 1919, it was the first Mormon temple built outside the continental United States. An optional tour of the Temple Visitors Center, as well as neighboring Brigham Young University Hawaii, is included in the package admission price.

55-370 Kamehameha Hwy., Laie. www.polynesia.com. ℂ **800/367-7060** or 808/293-3333. Various packages available for $60–$220 adults, $48–$176 children 3–11. Mon–Sat noon–9pm. Take H-1 to Pali Hwy. (Hwy. 61) and turn left on Kamehameha Hwy. (Hwy. 83). Bus: 55. Polynesian Cultural Center coach $22 round-trip; call numbers above to book.

Valley of the Temples ★ HISTORIC SITE   This famous cemetery in a cleft of the pali is stalked by wild peacocks and about 700 curious people a day, who pay to see the 9-foot meditation Buddha, acres of ponds full of more than 10,000 Japanese koi carp, and a replica of Japan's 900-year-old Byodo-In Temple of Equality. The original, made of wood, stands in Uji, on the outskirts of Kyoto; the Hawaii version, made of concrete, was erected in 1968 to commemorate the 100th anniversary of the arrival of the first Japanese immigrants to Hawaii. It's not the same as seeing the original, but it's worth a detour.

47-200 Kahekili Hwy. (across the street from Temple Valley Shopping Center), Kāne'ohe. www.byodo-in.com. ℂ **808/239-8811.** $3 adults, $2 seniors, $1 children 11 and under. Daily 9am–5pm. Take the H-1 to the Likelike Hwy. (Hwy. 63); after the Wilson Tunnel, get in the right lane and take the Kahekili Hwy. (Hwy. 63); at the 6th traffic light is the entrance to the cemetery (on the left). Bus: 65.

Central Oahu & the North Shore

If you can afford the splurge, rent a convertible—the perfect car for Oahu to enjoy the sun and soaring views—and head for the North Shore and Hawaii's surf city: **Haleiwa ★★★**, a former sugar-plantation town and a designated historic site. Although in recent years, Haleiwa has been spruced up—even the half-century old, formerly dusty **Matsumoto's Shave Ice** has new digs now—it still maintains a surfer/hippie vibe around the edges. For more, see "Surf City: Haleiwa," p. 109.

Getting there is half the fun. You have two choices: The first is to meander north along the lush Windward Coast, following the coastline lined with roadside stands selling mangoes, bright tropical pareu, fresh corn, and pond-raised prawns. Attractions along that route are discussed in the previous section.

The second choice is to cruise up the H-2 through Oahu's broad and fertile central valley, past Pearl Harbor and the Schofield Barracks of *From Here to Eternity* fame, and on through the red-earthed heart of the island, where pineapple and sugarcane fields stretch from the Koolau to the Waianae mountains, until the sea reappears on the horizon.

Once you're on H-1, stay to the right side; the freeway tends to divide abruptly. Keep following the signs for the H-1 (it separates off to Hwy. 78 at the airport and reunites later on; either way will get you there), and then the H-1/H-2. Leave the H-1 where the two highways divide; take the H-2 up the middle of the island, heading north toward the town of Wahiawa. That's what the sign will say—not North Shore or Haleiwa, but Wahiawa.

The H-2 runs out and becomes a two-lane country road about 18 miles outside downtown Honolulu, near Schofield Barracks. The highway becomes Kamehameha Highway (Hwy. 99 and later Hwy. 83) at Wahiawa. Just past Wahiawa, about a half-hour out of Honolulu, the **Dole Pineapple Plantation,** 64-1550 Kamehameha Hwy. (www.doleplantation.com; ⓒ **808/621-8408;** daily 9:30am–5pm; bus: 52), offers a rest stop, with pineapples, pineapple history, pineapple trinkets, pineapple juice, and pineapple soft serve. This agricultural exhibit/retail area features a train ride and maze that kids will love to wander through; it's open daily from 9:30am to 5pm (activities start at $6 adults, $5.25 children 4–12).

"Kam" Highway, as everyone calls it, will be your road for most of the rest of the trip to Haleiwa, on the North Shore.

CENTRAL OAHU ATTRACTIONS

On the central plains of Oahu, tract homes and malls with factory-outlet stores are now spreading across abandoned sugarcane fields. Hawaiian chiefs once sent commoners into thick sandalwood forests to cut down trees, which were then sold to China traders for small fortunes.

Kukaniloko Birthing Stones ★ HISTORIC SITE   This is the most sacred site in central Oahu. Two rows of 18 lava rocks once flanked a central birthing stone, where women of ancient Hawaii gave birth to potential *alii* (royalty). The rocks, according to Hawaiian belief, held the power to ease the labor pains of childbirth. Birth rituals involved 48 chiefs who pounded drums to announce the arrival of newborns likely to become chiefs. Used by Oahu's *alii* for generations of births, the *pohaku* (rocks), many in bowl-like shapes, now lie strewn in a grove of trees that stands in a pineapple field here. Some think the site may also have served ancient astronomers—like a Hawaiian Stonehenge. Petroglyphs of human forms and circles appear on some stones.

Off Kamehameha Hwy., btw. Wahiawa and Haleiwa, on Plantation Rd., opposite the road to Whitmore Village.

NORTH SHORE ATTRACTIONS

Puu o Mahuka Heiau ★ HISTORIC SITE   Go around sundown to feel the *mana* (sacred spirit) of this Hawaiian place. The largest sacrificial temple on Oahu, it's associated with the great Kaopulupulu, who sought peace between Oahu and Kauai. This prescient *kahuna* predicted that the island would be overrun by strangers from a distant land. In 1794, three of Capt. George Vancouver's men of the *Daedalus* were sacrificed here. In 1819, the year before New England missionaries landed in Hawaii, King Kamehameha II ordered all idols here to be destroyed.

A national historic landmark, this 18th-century *heiau,* known as the "hill of escape," sits on a 300-foot bluff overlooking Waimea Bay and 25 miles of Oahu's wave-lashed north coast—all the way to Kaena Point, where the Waianae Range ends in a spirit leap to the other world. The *heiau* appears as a huge rectangle of rocks twice as big as a football field, with an altar often covered by the flower and fruit offerings left by native Hawaiians.

1 mile past Waimea Bay. Take Pupukea Rd. *mauka* (inland) off Kamehameha Hwy. at Foodland, and drive 1 mile up a switchback road. Bus: 52, then walk up Pupukea Rd.

Waimea Valley ★ NATURAL ATTRACTION   For nearly 3 decades, this 1,875-acre park has lured visitors with activities from cliff diving and hula performances to kayaking and ATV tours. In 2008, the Office of Hawaiian Affairs took over and formed a nonprofit corporation, Hiipaka, to run the park, with an emphasis on perpetuating and sharing the "living Hawaiian culture." A visit here offers a lush walk into the past. The valley is packed with archaeological sites, including the 600-year-old Hale O Lono, a heiau dedicated to the Hawaiian god Lono, the god of peace, fertility, and agriculture. The botanical collection has 35 different gardens, including super-rare Hawaiian species such as the endangered *Kokia cookei* hibiscus. The valley is also home to fauna such as the endangered *alae ula,* or Hawaiian moorhen; look for a black bird with a red face cruising in the ponds. The 150-acre Arboretum and Botanical Garden contains

Central & Leeward Oahu

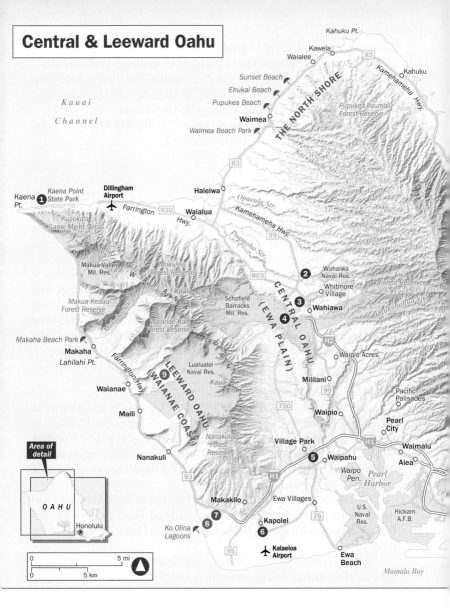

more than 5,000 species of tropical plants. Walk through the gardens (take the paved paths or dirt trails) and wind up at 45-foot-high Waimea Falls—bring your bathing suit and you can dive into the cold, murky water. The public is invited to hike the trails and spend a day in this quiet oasis. Check the website for potential closings due to weather.

59-864 Kamehameha Hwy. www.waimeavalley.net. © **808/638-7766.** $16 adults, $12 seniors, $8 children 4–12. Daily 9am–5pm. Bus: 52.

BEACHES

The Waikiki Coast

ALA MOANA BEACH PARK ★★

Gold-sand Ala Moana (meaning "path to the sea" in Hawaiian) stretches for more than a mile along Honolulu's coast between downtown and Waikiki. This 76-acre midtown beach park, with spreading lawns shaded by banyans and palms, is one of the island's most popular playgrounds. It has a man-made beach, created in the 1930s by filling a coral reef with Wai'anae Coast sand, as well as its own lagoon, yacht harbor, tennis courts, music pavilion, bathhouses, picnic tables, and enough wide-open green spaces to accommodate 4 million visitors a year. The water is calm almost year-round, protected by black-lava rocks set offshore. There's a large parking lot as well as metered street parking.

WAIKIKI BEACH ★★

No beach anywhere is so widely known or so universally sought after as this narrow, 1½-mile-long crescent of imported sand (from Molokai) at the foot of a string of high-rise hotels. Waikiki attracts nearly 5 million visitors a year from every corner of the planet. First-timers are amazed to discover how small Waikiki Beach really is, but there's always a place for them under the tropical sun here.

Waikiki is actually a string of beaches that extends between **Sans Souci State Recreational Area,** near Diamond Head to the east, and **Duke Kahanamoku Beach,** in front of the Hilton Hawaiian Village to the west.

Waikiki is fabulous for swimming, board surfing, bodysurfing, outrigger canoeing, diving, sailing, snorkeling, and pole fishing. Every imaginable type of watersports equipment is available for rent here. Facilities include showers, lifeguards, restrooms, grills, picnic tables, and pavilions at the **Queen's Surf** end of the beach (at Kapiolani Park, btw. the zoo and the aquarium). The best place to park is at Kapiolani Park, near Sans Souci.

East Oahu

HANAUMA BAY ★★

Oahu's most popular snorkeling spot is this volcanic crater with a broken sea wall; its small, curved, 2,000-foot gold-sand beach is packed

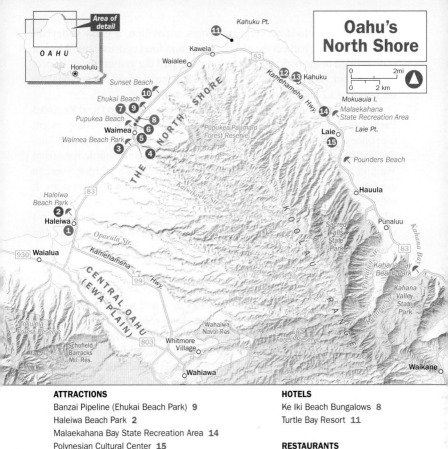

Area of detail

OAHU

Honolulu ⊛

Oahu's North Shore

Kahuku Pt.

Kawela

Waialee

Sunset Beach

Ehukai Beach **10**

Pupukea Beach **7 9**

Waimea **8**

Waimea Beach Park **6**

5

3

4

THE NORTH SHORE

Kahuku **11**

Kamehameha Hwy **12 13**

Mokuauia I. **14**

Malaekahana State Recreation Area

Pupukea Paumalu Forest Reserve

Laie **15**

Laie Pt.

Pounders Beach

Haleiwa Beach Park **2**

Haleiwa **1**

Waialua **930**

Opaeula Str.

Kamehameha Hwy **99**

CENTRAL OAHU (EWA PLAIN)

Kaiwikoele Str.

KOOLAU RANGE

Sacred Falls State Park

Punaluu

Kahana Bay Beach Park

Kahana Valley State Park

Kahana Bay

83

Hauula

Waikane

Mokuleia Forest Reserve

Schofield Barracks Mil. Res.

803

Whitmore Village

Wahiawa Naval Res.

Wahiawa

Ewa Forest Reserve

0 ___ 2mi
0 ___ 2 km

ATTRACTIONS

Banzai Pipeline (Ehukai Beach Park) **9**
Haleiwa Beach Park **2**
Malaekahana Bay State Recreation Area **14**
Polynesian Cultural Center **15**
Puu o Mahuka Heiau **5**
Shark's Cove, Pūpūkea Beach Park **6**
Sunset Beach **10**
Waimea Beach Park **3**
Waimea Valley **4**

HOTELS

Ke Iki Beach Bungalows **8**
Turtle Bay Resort **11**

RESTAURANTS

The Elephant Truck **7**
Kahuku Farms **12**
Matsumoto Shave Ice **1**
Shrimp trucks **13**

elbow-to-elbow with people year-round. The bay's shallow shoreline water and abundant marine life are the main attractions, but this good-looking beach is also popular for sunbathing and people-watching. Serious divers shoot "the slot" (a passage through the reef) to get to Witch's Brew, a turbulent cove, and then brave strong currents in 70-foot depths at the bay mouth to see coral gardens, turtles, and even sharks. (***Divers:*** Beware of the Molokai Express, a strong current.) You can snorkel in the safe, shallow (10-ft.) inner bay, which, along with the beach, is almost always crowded. Because Hanauma Bay is a conservation district, you cannot touch or remove any marine life here. Feeding the fish is also prohibited.

Facilities include parking, restrooms, a pavilion, a grass volleyball court, lifeguards, barbecues, picnic tables, and food concessions. Alcohol is prohibited in the park; there is no smoking past the visitor center. Expect to pay $1 per vehicle to park plus an entrance fee of $7.50 per person (free for children 12 and under and Hawaii residents).

If you're driving, take Kalanianaole Highway to Koko Head Regional Park. Avoid the crowds by going early, about 7am, on a weekday morning; once the parking lot's full, you're out of luck. Alternatively, take TheBus to escape the parking problem: The Hanauma Bay Shuttle runs from Waikiki to Hanauma Bay every half-hour from 8:45am to 1pm; you can catch it at the Ala Moana Hotel, the Ilikai Hotel, or other city bus stops. It returns every hour from noon to 4pm. For information, call ℂ **808/396-4229.** Hanauma Bay is closed every Tuesday so that the fish can have a day off, but it's open all other days from 6am to 7pm in the summer and 6am to 6pm in the winter.

SANDY BEACH ★

Sandy Beach is one of the best bodysurfing beaches on Oahu; it's also one of the most dangerous. It's better to just stand and watch the daredevils literally risk their necks at this 1,200-foot-long gold-sand beach, which is pounded by wild waves and haunted by a dangerous shore break and strong backwash. Weak swimmers and children should definitely stay out of the water here. Lifeguards post flags to alert beachgoers to the day's surf: Green means safe, yellow means caution, and red indicates very dangerous water conditions.

Facilities include restrooms and parking. Go weekdays to avoid the crowds or weekends to catch the bodysurfers in action. From Waikiki, drive east on the H-1, which becomes Kalanianaole Highway; proceed past Hawaii Kai, up the hill to Hanauma Bay, past the Halona Blowhole, and along the coast. The next big gold beach on the right is Sandy Beach. TheBus no. 22 will also bring you here.

MAKAPUU BEACH PARK ★

Makapuu Beach is a beautiful 1,000-foot-long gold-sand beach cupped in the stark black Koolau cliffs on Oahu's easternmost point. Even if you never venture into the water, it's worth a visit just to enjoy the great natural beauty of this classic Hawaiian beach. (You've probably already seen it in countless TV shows, from *Hawaii Five-O* to *Magnum, P.I.*) In summer, the ocean here is as gentle as a Jacuzzi, and swimming and diving are perfect; come winter, however, and Makapu'u is a hit with expert bodysurfers, who come for the big, pounding waves that are too dangerous for most regular swimmers.

Facilities include restrooms, lifeguards, barbecue grills, picnic tables, and parking. To get here, follow Kalaniana'ole Highway toward Waimānalo, or take TheBus no. 22 or 23.

Beaches & Outdoor Activities on Oahu

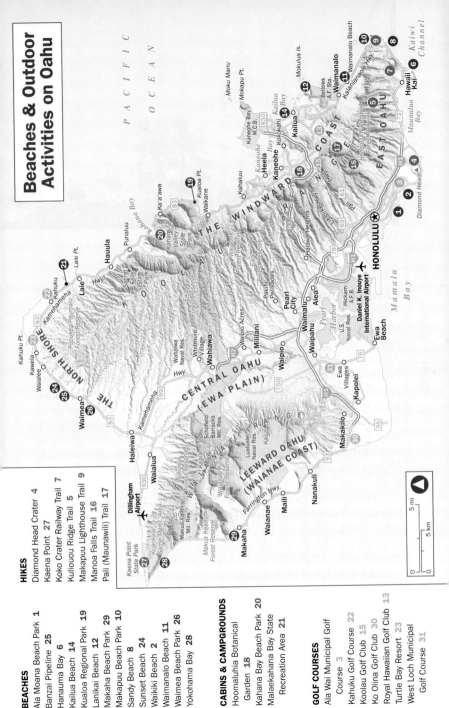

BEACHES

Ala Moana Beach Park **1**
Banzai Pipeline **25**
Hanauma Bay **6**
Kailua Beach **14**
Kualoa Regional Park **19**
Lanikai Beach **12**
Makaha Beach Park **29**
Makapuu Beach Park **10**
Sandy Beach **8**
Sunset Beach **24**
Waikiki Beach **2**
Waimanalo Beach **11**
Waimea Beach Park **26**
Yokohama Bay **28**

CABINS & CAMPGROUNDS

Hoomaluhia Botanical
Garden **18**
Kahana Bay Beach Park **20**
Malaekahana Bay State
Recreation Area **21**

GOLF COURSES

Ala Wai Municipal Golf
Course **3**
Kahuku Golf Course **22**
Koolau Golf Club **15**
Ko Olina Golf Club **30**
Royal Hawaiian Golf Club **13**
Turtle Bay Resort **23**
West Loch Municipal
Golf Course **31**

HIKES

Diamond Head Crater **4**
Kaena Point **27**
Koko Crater Railway Trail **7**
Kuliouou Ridge Trail **5**
Makapuu Lighthouse Trail **9**
Manoa Falls Trail **16**
Pali (Maunawili) Trail **17**

Waikiki Beach

The Windward Coast

LANIKAI BEACH ★★★

One of Hawaii's best spots for swimming, gold-sand Lanikai's crystal-clear lagoon is like a giant saltwater swimming pool that you're lucky enough to be able to share with the resident tropical fish and sea turtles. Almost too gorgeous to be real, this is one of Hawaii's postcard-perfect beaches: It's a mile long and thin in places, but the sand's as soft as talcum powder. Kayakers often paddle out to the two tiny offshore Mokulua islands, which are seabird sanctuaries. Unfortunately, the secret's out about Lanikai, and the small beach is starting to feel more crowded every year; get here early to try to grab a space on the sand. Another reason to come in the morning: The Koolau Range tends to block the afternoon sun. Or for a rare, magical moment, come to watch the full moon rise over the water.

There are no facilities here, just off-street parking. From Waikiki, take the H-1 to the Pali Highway (Hwy. 61) through the Nuunau Pali Tunnel to Kailua, where the Pali Highway becomes Kailua Road as it proceeds through town. At Kalaheo Avenue, turn right and follow the coast about 2 miles to Kailua Beach Park; just past it, turn left at the T intersection and drive uphill on Aalapapa Drive, a one-way street that loops back as Mokulua Drive. Park on Mokulua Drive and walk down any of the eight public-access lanes to the shore. Or take TheBus no. 57A or 57 (Kailua), and then transfer to the no. 70 bus.

KAILUA BEACH ★★★

Windward Oahu's premier beach is a wide, 2-mile-long golden strand with dunes, palm trees, panoramic views, and offshore islets that are home to seabirds. The swimming is excellent, and the azure waters are usually decorated with bright sails; this is Oahu's premier windsurfing beach

SURF CITY: haleiwa

Only 28 miles from Waikiki is **Haleiwa** ★★★, the funky former sugar-plantation town that's now the world capital of big-wave surfing. Haleiwa comes alive in winter, when the waves rise; then, it seems, every surfer in the world is here to see and be seen.

Officially designated a historic cultural and scenic district, this beach town was founded by sugar baron Benjamin Dillingham, who built a 30-mile railroad to link his Honolulu and North Shore plantations in 1899. He opened a Victorian hotel overlooking Kaiaka Bay and named it Haleiwa, or "house of the 'iwa," the tropical seabird often seen here. The hotel and railroad are gone, but the town of Haleiwa, which was rediscovered in the late 1960s by hippies, manages to hold onto some of its rustic charm. Of course, like other places on Oahu, that is changing; some of the older wooden storefronts are being redeveloped and local chains such as T&C Surf are moving in. Arts and crafts, boutiques, and burger joints line both sides of the town. There's also a busy fishing harbor full of charter boats and captains who hunt the Kauai Channel daily for tuna, mahimahi, and marlin.

Just down the road are the fabled shrines of surfing—**Waimea Beach, Banzai Pipeline, Sunset Beach**—where some of the world's largest waves, reaching 20 feet and higher, rise up between November and January. November to December is the holding period for **Vans Triple Crown of Surfing** (http://vans triplecrownofsurfing.com), one of the world's premier surf competition series, when professional surfers from around the world descend on the 7-mile miracle of waves. Hang around Haleiwa and the North Shore and you're bound to run into a few of the pros. Battle the traffic to come up on competition days (it seems like everyone ditches work and heads north on these days): It's one of Oahu's best shows. For details on North Shore beaches, see p. 111.

Kailua Beach

as well. It's a favorite spot to sail catamarans, bodysurf the gentle waves, or paddle a kayak. Water conditions are quite safe, especially at the mouth of Ka'elepulu Stream, where toddlers play in the freshwater shallows at the middle of the beach park. The water is usually about 78°F (26°C), the views are spectacular, and the setting, at the foot of the sheer green Ko'olau Range, is idyllic. It's gotten so crowded over the years that the city council banned all commercial activity on the beach, which has led to a decrease in kayak traffic jams both on the beach and in the water. These days you can usually find a less-occupied stretch of sand the farther you are from the beach park.

Facilities at the beach park include picnic tables, barbecues, restrooms, a volleyball court, a public boat ramp, and free parking. To get here, take Pali Highway (Hwy. 61) to Kailua, drive through town, turn right on Kalaheo Avenue, and go a mile until you see the beach on your left. Or take TheBus no. 57A or 57 into Kailua.

WAIMANALO BEACH ★★★

At almost 6 miles long, this is O'ahu's longest beach and a favorite among locals. Depending on the swell, the water can be a little rougher than at Kailua, making it fun for bodysurfing and boogie boarding. The wide, sandy beach is backed by ironwood trees, which provide shade if you tire of the sun. On weekdays, it will feel like you have the whole place to yourself; on weekends, locals bring out the grills, tents, and fishing poles. *Note:* Make sure your valuables are hidden in your car; break-ins have occurred in the parking lot.

Facilities include restrooms, picnic tables, outdoor showers, and parking. Waimanalo Beach has a different few points of entry—my pick would be the Waimanalo Bay Recreation Area. To get there, follow

Kalanianaole Highway toward Waimanalo and turn right at the Waimanalo Bay sign, or take TheBus no. 57.

KUALOA REGIONAL PARK ★

This 150-acre coco-palm-fringed peninsula is located on Kaneohe Bay's north shore at the foot of the spiky Koolau Ridge. The park has a broad, grassy lawn and a long, narrow, white-sand beach ideal for swimming, walking, beachcombing, kite-flying, or just enjoying the natural beauty of this once-sacred Hawaiian shore, listed on the National Register of Historic Places. The waters are shallow and safe for swimming year-round. Offshore is Mokolii, the picturesque islet otherwise known as Chinaman's Hat. You can swim or wade out to the island (during low tide only) or kayak. A small sandy beach can be found on the backside, and it takes less than half an hour to reach the top of this tiny island.

Facilities at both sites include restrooms, outdoor showers, picnic tables, and drinking fountains. To get to the park, take the Likelike Highway (Hwy. 63); after the Wilson Tunnel, get in the right lane and turn off on Kahakili Highway (Hwy. 83). Or take TheBus no. 55.

The North Shore

WAIMEA BEACH PARK ★★★

This deep, sandy bowl has gentle summer waves that are excellent for swimming, snorkeling, and bodysurfing. To one side of the bay is a huge rock that local kids like to climb and dive from. In this placid scene, the only clues of what's to come in winter are those evacuation whistles on poles beside the road. But what a difference a season makes: Winter waves pound the narrow bay, sometimes rising to 50 feet high. When the surf's really up, very strong currents and shore breaks sweep the bay—and it seems like everyone on Oahu drives out to Waimea to get a look at the monster waves and those who ride them. Weekends are great for watching the surfers; to avoid the crowds, go on weekdays.

Facilities include lifeguards, restrooms, showers, parking, and nearby restaurants and shops in Haleiwa town. The beach is located on Kamehameha Highway (Hwy. 83); from Waikiki, take TheBus no. 52.

Leeward Oahu: The Waianae Coast

MAKAHA BEACH PARK ★★★

When the surf's up here, it's spectacular: Monstrous waves pound the beach. Nearly a mile long, this half-moon, gold-sand beach is tucked between 231-foot Lahilahi Point, which locals call Black Rock, and Kepuhi Point, a toe of the Waianae mountain range. Summer is the best time to hit this beach—the waves are small, the sand abundant, and the water safe for swimming. Children hug the shore on the north side of the beach, near the lifeguard stand, while divers seek an offshore channel full of big fish.

Facilities include restrooms, lifeguards, and parking. To get here, take the H-1 freeway to the end of the line, where it becomes Farrington Highway (Hwy. 93), and follow it to the beach; or take TheBus no. C.

YOKOHAMA BAY ★★★

Where Farrington Highway (Hwy. 93) ends, the wilderness of **Kaena Point State Park** begins. It's a remote 853-acre coastline park of empty beaches, sand dunes, cliffs, and deep-blue water. This is the last sandy stretch of shore on the northwest coast of Oahu. Sometimes it's known as Keawaula Beach, but everybody here calls it Yokohama, after the Japanese immigrants who came from that port city to work the cane fields and fished along this shoreline. When the surf's calm—mainly in summer—this is a good area for snorkeling, diving, swimming, shore fishing, and picnicking. There are no lifeguards or facilities, except at the park entrance, where there's a restroom and lifeguard stand. There's no bus service either.

WATERSPORTS
Boating

One of the best things about Hawaii? The ocean. There are a million ways to enjoy it, but to get far from the shore and see the incredible beauty of the sea, hop on a boat.

Holokai Catamaran ★★   One of the most fun and effortless ways to get in the water is a sail off of Waikiki. Many catamarans launch from Waikiki, but this is our favorite of the "booze cruises." It's the least crowded and rowdy, and the drink selection is the best, with multiple Maui Brewing Co. brews and a decent island cocktail. The **Sunset Sail** is the most popular and festive, with an open bar, while the **Tradewind Sail,** which pushes off in the afternoon, is more mellow. The most romantic? The **Fireworks Sail,** which seemingly takes you right under the weekly Friday-night fireworks show.

Gray's Beach in front of the Halekulani. www.sailholokai.com. ℂ **808/922-2210.** All cruises 1½ hr. Tradewind Sail $35 adults, $25 children. Fireworks Sail $50 adults and children. Sunset Sail $55 adults; $45 children. Bus: 19 or 20.

Wild Side Tours ★★   Picture this: You're floating in the calm waters off the Waianae coast, where your 42-foot sailing catamaran has just dropped you off. Below, in the reef, are turtles, and suddenly in the distance, you see spinner dolphins. This happens almost every day on the 4-hour tours (departing at 8am; check-in 7:30am) operated by the Cullins family, who have swum in these waters for decades. In winter, you may spot humpback whales on the morning cruise, which includes lunch, snorkel gear, instruction, and a flotation device. The other thing that sets this company apart is its small group sizes, limited to 6 on the **Best of the West** tour, and 10 on the **Deluxe Wildlife Charter.**

Waianae Boat Harbor, 85-471 Farrington Hwy., Waianae. www.sailhawaii.com. ☏ **808/306-7273.** Best of the West $195 for age 12 and up (not recommended for younger children). Deluxe Wildlife Charter $175 adults; $145 children. Bus: C.

Bodyboarding (Boogie Boarding) & Bodysurfing

Good places to learn to bodyboard are in the small waves of **Waikiki Beach ★★★, Kailua Beach ★★★, Waimanalo Beach ★★** (reviewed under "Beaches," earlier in this chapter), and **Bellows Field Beach Park,** off Kalanianaole Highway (Hwy. 72) in Waimanalo, which is open to the public on weekends (from noon Fri to midnight Sun and holidays). To get here, turn toward the ocean on Hughes Road, and then right on Tinker Road, which takes you to the park.

See the introduction to this section for a list of rental shops where you can get a boogie board.

Ocean Kayaking/Stand-Up Paddling

Revel in amazing views both above and below the water on the Windward Coast with **Holokai Kayak and Snorkel Adventures ★**, 46-465 Kamehameha Hwy., Kaneohe, at Heeia State Park (www.holokaiadventures.com; ☏ **808/781-4773**). Sign up for a 4-hour guided tour and you'll see the majestic Koolau Range from your kayak. Then, as you head to Coconut Island (aka Gilligan's Island), you'll stop to snorkel and admire the

Bodyboarding at Waikiki Beach

fish and turtles in the almost-always calm Kaneohe Bay. Or, you can go at your own pace with the self-guided kayak or stand-up paddleboard option—they'll point you in the direction of the disappearing sandbar Ahu o Laka, as well as the good snorkel spots. What's even better? Proceeds go to Kamaaina Kids (which runs environmental education programs for children) and improving He'eia State Park.

For a wonderful adventure, rent a kayak or a stand-up paddleboard (SUP), arrive at Lanikai Beach just as the sun is appearing, and paddle across the channel to the pyramid-shaped islands called Mokulua, or the Mokes, as locals call them—it's an unforgettable experience. On the windward side, check out **Kailua Sailboards & Kayaks,** 130 Kailua Rd., a block from Kailua Beach Park (www.kailuasailboards.com; ✆ **808/262-2555**), where single kayaks and SUP boards rent for $59 for a half-day and double kayaks are $69 for a half-day. Note that paddling to the Mokulua Islands is not allowed on Sundays.

If you're staying on the North Shore, go to **Surf-N-Sea,** 62-595 Kamehameha Hwy., Haleiwa (www.surfnsea.com; ✆ **800/899-7873**), where kayak rentals start at $10 per hour and go to $60 for a full day. During the summer months, you can start in Haleiwa and kayak to Waimea Bay. SUP rentals start at $20 per hour and go to $60 for a full day. You can paddle in the bay behind the shop or in Anahula Stream, passing under the iconic Rainbow Bridge.

Scuba Diving

Oahu is a wonderful place to scuba dive, especially for those interested in wreck diving. One of the more famous wrecks in Hawaii is the *Mahi,* a 185-foot former minesweeper easily accessible just south of Waianae. Abundant marine life makes this a great place to shoot photos—schools of lemon butterfly fish and taape (blue-lined snapper) are so comfortable with divers and photographers that they practically pose. Eagle rays, green sea turtles, manta rays, and white-tipped sharks occasionally cruise by as well, and eels peer out from the wreck.

For non-wreck diving, one of the best dive spots in summer is **Kahuna Canyon.** In Hawaiian, *kahuna* means priest, wise man, or sorcerer; this massive amphitheater, located near Mokuleia, is a perfect example of something a sorcerer might conjure up. Walls rising from the ocean floor create the illusion of an underwater Grand Canyon. Inside the amphitheater, crabs, octopuses, slippers, and spiny lobsters abound (be aware that taking them in summer is illegal), and giant trevally, parrotfish, and unicorn fish congregate as well. Outside the amphitheater, you're likely to see an occasional shark in the distance.

Because Oahu's greatest dives are offshore, your best bet is to book a two-tank dive from a dive boat. **Living Ocean Scuba ★**, 1125 Ala Moana Blvd. (www. livingoceanscuba.com; ✆ **808/436-3438**), offers dives for both first-time and certified divers. Living Ocean takes divers to south

EXPERIENCING jaws: SWIM WITH THE SHARKS

Ocean Ramsey and her crew at **One Ocean Diving ★★★** (www.oneocean diving.com; text: ☎ **808/649-0018**) are on a first-name basis with some of the sharks they swim with. That's right, *swim with*, cage free. And you can, too, with little more than a snorkel, mask, and fins on your feet (this is a snorkeling trip, not scuba diving). As you ride the boat out, about 3 miles offshore from Hale'iwa, where sharks are known to congregate, the crew educates you about shark behavior. For one, they're really not that interested in humans. Two, most of the sharks you'll see are sandbar and Galapagos sharks, which are not considered dangerous. And three, if you should see a potentially more threatening shark, such as a tiger shark, they teach you how to conjure your alpha shark: Stay at the top of ocean, and don't turn your back on them. Your guides are always alert and nearby; only three people are allowed in the water at a time. Once I got used to the sight of the sharks around me, I began to admire their beauty and grace. One Ocean Diving hopes to change misconceptions about sharks and bring awareness to their plight as their numbers dwindle. A dive with them is as educational as it is exciting. Rates are $150 a person, and a snorkel mask and fins are provided; must be 4 feet or taller to enter the water.

shore sites such as the **Sea Tiger,** a former Chinese trading vessel that was confiscated for carrying illegal immigrants to Hawaii, and later sunk in 1999 to create a dive site. Divers can penetrate the wreck, which also teems with marine life: whitetip reef sharks, turtles, eagle rays, and plenty of fish. The two-tank boat dives start at $100 per person. While Living Ocean dives primarily from the south shore, they can also help set up dive trips on other sides of the island.

Snorkeling

Some of the best snorkeling in Oahu is at **Hanauma Bay** ★★. It's crowded—sometimes it seems there are more people than fish—but Hanauma has clear, warm, protected waters and an abundance of friendly reef fish, including Moorish idols, scores of butterfly fish, damselfish, and wrasses. Hanauma Bay has two reefs, an inner and an outer—the first for novices, the other for experts. The inner reef is calm and shallow (less than 10 ft.); in some places, you can just wade and put your face in the water. Go early: It's packed by 10am. And it's closed on Tuesdays. For details, see "Beaches," earlier in this chapter.

On the North Shore, head to **Shark's Cove** ★★, just off Kame-hameha Highway, between Haleiwa and Pupukea. In the summer, this big, lava-edged pool is one of Oahu's best snorkel spots. Waves splash over the natural lava grotto and cascade like waterfalls into the pool full of tropical fish. To the right of the cove are deep-sea caves and underwater tunnels to explore.

If you want to rent snorkel equipment, check out **Snorkel Bob's** on the way to Hanauma Bay at 700 Kapahulu Ave. (at Date St.), Honolulu (www.snorkelbob.com; ② **808/735-7944**).

Sport Fishing

Kewalo Basin, located between the Honolulu International Airport and Waikiki, is the main location for charter fishing boats on Oahu. From Waikiki, take Kalakaua Avenue Ewa (west) beyond Ala Moana Center; Kewalo Basin is on the left, across from Ward Centers. Look for charter boats all in a row in their slips; when the fish are biting, the captains display the catch of the day in the afternoon. You can also take TheBus no. 19 or 20 (Airport).

The best sport-fishing booking desk in the state is **Sportfish Hawaii** ★ (www.sportfishhawaii.com; ② **877/388-1376** or 808/396-2607), which books boats on all the islands. These fishing vessels have been inspected and must meet rigorous criteria to guarantee that you will have a great time. Prices range from $875 to $1,399 for a full-day exclusive charter (you, plus five friends, get the entire boat to yourself), from $650 for a half-day exclusive, or from $220 for a full-day shared charter (you share the boat with five other people).

Surfing

In summer, when the water's warm and there's a soft breeze in the air, the south swell comes up. It's surf season in Waikiki, the best place on Oahu to learn how to surf. For lessons, find **Hans Hedemann Surf School** (www.hhsurf.com; ℭ **808/924-7778**) at the Park Shore Waikiki (and, if you're on the North Shore, there's also an outpost at Turtle Bay Resort). Hedemann, a champion surfer for some 34 years, gives private lessons—at $400 for a 3-hour session. (He has taught celebrities such as Cameron Diaz and Adam Sandler.) If the expenditure is beyond your budget, go for a $75 2-hour group lesson (4-person max) taught by other friendly instructors.

Surfboards are also available for rent on the North Shore at **Surf-N-Sea,** 62-595 Kamehameha Hwy., Haleiwa (www.surfnsea.com; ℭ **800/899-7873**), for $5 to $7 an hour. Lessons go for $85 for 2 to 3 hours.

More experienced surfers should drop into any surf shop around Oahu, or call the **Surf News Network Surfline** (ℭ **808/596-SURF**) to get the latest surf conditions. The breaks at the base of Diamond Head are popular among intermediate to expert surfers.

If you're in Hawaii in winter and want to see the serious surfers catch the really big waves, bring your binoculars and grab a front-row seat on the beach at **Waimea Bay, Sunset Beach,** or **Pipeline.**

HIKING

People are often surprised to discover that the great outdoors is often minutes from downtown Honolulu. The island's major hiking trails traverse razor-thin ridgebacks, deep waterfall valleys, and more. The best source of hiking information on Oahu is the state's **Na Ala Hele (Trails to Go On) Program** (www.hawaiitrails.org; ℭ **808/973-9782**). The website has everything you need: detailed maps and descriptions of 40 trails in the Na Ala Hele program, a hiking safety brochure, updates on the trails, hyperlinks to weather information, health warnings, info on native plants or how to volunteer for trail upkeep, and more.

Honolulu-Area Hikes

DIAMOND HEAD CRATER ★★★

This is a moderate but steep walk to the summit of Hawaii's most famous landmark. Kids love to look out from the top of the 760-foot volcanic cone, where they have 360-degree views of Oahu up the leeward coast from Waikiki. The 1.5-mile round-trip takes about 1½ hours, and the entry fee is $5 per car load; if you walk in, it's $1 per person.

Diamond Head was created by a volcanic explosion about half a million years ago. The Hawaiians called the crater Leahi (meaning "the brow of the 'ahi," or tuna, referring to the shape of the crater). Diamond Head was considered a sacred spot; King Kamehameha offered human sacrifices at a *heiau* (temple) on the western slope. It wasn't until the 19th

Hiking Oahu

century that Mount Leahi got its current name: A group of sailors found what they thought were diamonds in the crater; it turned out they were just worthless calcite crystals, but the name stuck.

Before you begin your journey to the top of the crater, put on some decent shoes (rubber-soled tennies are fine) and don't forget water (very important), a hat to protect you from the sun, and a camera. You might want to put all your gear in a pack to leave your hands free for the climb.

Go early, preferably just after the 6am opening, before the midday sun starts beating down. The hike to the summit starts at Monsarrat and 18th avenues on the crater's inland (or *mauka*) side. To get here, take The-Bus no. 58 from the Ala Moana Center or drive to the intersection of Diamond Head Road and 18th Avenue. Follow the road through the tunnel (which is closed 6pm–6am) and park in the lot. From the trailhead in the parking lot, you'll proceed along a paved walkway (with handrails) as you climb up the slope. You'll pass old World War I and World War II pillboxes, gun emplacements, and tunnels built as part of the Pacific defense network. Several steps take you up to the top observation post on Point Leahi. The views are incredible.

MANOA FALLS TRAIL ★★

This easy .75-mile (one-way) hike is terrific for families; it takes less than an hour to reach idyllic Manoa Falls. The trailhead, marked by a footbridge, is at the end of Manoa Road, past Lyon Arboretum. The staff at the arboretum prefers that hikers not park in their lot, so the best place to park is in the residential area below Paradise Park; you can also get to the arboretum via TheBus no. 5. The often-muddy trail follows Waihi Stream and meanders through the forest reserve past guavas, mountain apples, and wild ginger. The forest is moist and humid and inhabited by giant bloodthirsty mosquitoes, so bring repellent. If it has rained recently, stay on the trail and step carefully because it can be very slippery (and it's a long way down if you slide off the side).

East Oahu Hikes

KOKO CRATER RAILWAY TRAIL ★★

If you're looking for quiet, you'll want to find another trail. This is less a hike than a strenuous workout, and it's popular among fitness buffs who climb it daily, people trying to stick to New Year's resolutions to be more active, and triathletes in training. But first-timers and tourists also tackle the 1,048 stairs along the railway track—once part of a World War II–era tram system—for the panoramic views from the Windward Coast to Waikiki. It's a tough hike, but you'll have lots of friendly company along the way, and the view from the top is worth it. As they say, no pain, no gain. It's unshaded the whole way, so try to go early in the morning or in the late afternoon to catch the sunset, and bring plenty of water.

To get to the trailhead from Waikiki take Kalanianaole Highway (Hwy. 72) to Hawaii Kai, turn left at Lunalilo Home Road, and then follow Anapalau Street to the trailhead parking lot; you can also take TheBus no. 22 or 23.

KULIOUOU RIDGE TRAIL ★★

One of Honolulu's best ridge trails, this moderate 2.5-mile hike (each way) starts in the middle of a residential neighborhood, then ascends through ironwood and pine trees, and drops you in the middle of a native Hawaiian forest. Here, ohia lehua, with its distinctive red pom-pom–like flowers grow. Hawaiian legend has it that Ohia and Lehua were lovers. Pele fell in love with Ohia, but when he rejected her advances, she turned him into a tree. The gods took pity on the heartbroken Lehua and turned her into a flower on the tree. According to the story, if you pick a flower from the ohia lehua, it will rain, representing the separated lovers' tears. So avoid picking the flowers, if only to assure clear views at the top of the summit—on a good day, you can see all the way to Waimanalo.

To get there from Waikiki, take Kalanianaole Highway (Hwy. 72) and turn left on Kuliouou Road. Turn right on Kalaau Place and look for street parking. You'll find the trailhead at the end of the road. No bus service is available.

MAKAPUU LIGHTHOUSE TRAIL ★★

You've seen this famous old lighthouse on episodes of *Magnum, P.I.* and *Hawaii Five-O*. No longer staffed by the Coast Guard (it's fully automated now), the lighthouse sits at the end of a precipitous cliff trail on an airy perch over the Windward Coast, Manana (Rabbit) Island, and the azure Pacific. It's about a 45-minute, 1-mile hike from Kalanianaole Highway (Hwy. 72), along a paved road that begins across from Hawaii Kai Executive Golf Course and winds around the 646-foot-high sea bluff to the lighthouse lookout.

The view of the ocean all the way to Molokai and Lanai is often so clear that, from November to March, if you're lucky, you'll see migrating humpback whales.

To get to the trailhead from Waikiki, take Kalanianaole Highway (Hwy. 72) past Hanauma Bay and Sandy Beach to Makapu'u Head, the southeastern tip of the island; you can also take TheBus no. 22 or 23.

Blowhole alert: When the south swell is running, usually in summer, a couple of blowholes on the south side of Makapuu Head put the famous Hālona Blowhole to shame.

Windward Coast Hikes

PALI (MAUNAWILI) TRAIL ★

For a million-dollar view of the Windward Coast, take this 11-mile (one-way) foothill trail. The trailhead is about 6 miles from downtown Hono-lulu, on the windward side of the Nu'unau Pali Tunnel, at the scenic lookout just beyond the hairpin turn of the Pali Highway (Hwy. 61). Just as you begin the turn, look for the scenic overlook sign, slow down, and pull off the highway into the parking lot (sorry, no bus service available).

The mostly flat, well-marked, easy-to-moderate trail goes through the forest on the lower slopes of the 3,000-foot Koolau mountain range and ends up in the backyard of the coastal Hawaiian village of Waimanalo. Go halfway to get the view and then return to your car, or have someone meet you in 'Nalo.

To Land's End: A Leeward Oahu Hike

KAENA POINT ★

At the very western tip of Oahu lie the dry, barren lands of **Kaena Point State Park,** 853 acres of jagged sea cliffs, deep gulches, sand dunes, endangered plant life, and a remote, wild, wind- and surf-battered coast-line. *Kaena* means "red hot" or "glowing" in Hawaiian; the name refers to the brilliant sunsets visible from the point.

Kaena is steeped in numerous legends. A popular one concerns the demigod Maui: Maui had a famous hook that he used to raise islands from the sea. He decided that he wanted to bring the islands of Oahu and Kauai closer together, so one day he threw his hook across the Kauai Channel and snagged Kauai (which is actually visible from Kaena Point on clear days). Using all his might, Maui was able to pull loose a huge boulder, which fell into the waters very close to the present lighthouse at Kaena. The rock is still called Pohaku o Kauai (the Rock from Kaua'i). Like

Black Rock in Kaanapali on Maui, Kaena is thought of as the point on Oahu from which souls depart.

To hike out to this departing place, take the clearly marked trail from the parking lot of Kaena Point State Park. The moderate 5-mile round-trip hike to the point will take a couple of hours. The trail along the cliff passes tide pools abundant in marine life and rugged protrusions of lava reaching out to the turbulent sea; seabirds circle overhead. Do *not* go off the trail; you might step on buried birds' eggs. There are no sandy beaches, and the water is nearly always turbulent here. In winter, when a big north swell is running, the waves at Ka'ena are the biggest in the state, averaging heights of 30 to 40 feet. Even when the water appears calm, offshore currents are powerful, so don't plan on taking a swim. Go early in the morning to see the schools of porpoises that frequent the area just offshore.

To get to the trailhead from Honolulu or Waikiki, take the H-1 west to its end; continue on Hwy. 93 past Mākaha and follow Hwy. 930 to the end of the road. There is no bus service.

OTHER OUTDOOR ACTIVITIES
Biking

Oahu is not particularly bike-friendly, as drivers still need to learn to share the road. But that may be changing with the installation of new bike lanes and the 2017 introduction of **Biki** (www.gobiki.org), Honolulu's bike-share program. At press time, 1,000 bikes had been placed at 100 docking stations throughout metro Honolulu. Modeled after other systems in cities such as Paris and New York, you can purchase single ride passes ($3.50 for 30 minutes) or monthly passes ($15 for unlimited 30-minute rides or $25 for unlimited 60-minute rides). Biki makes short trips, such as from your hotel to the beach, or Waikiki to Chinatown, a breeze.

For a bike-and-hike adventure, contact **Bike Hawaii ★** (www.bike-hawaii.com; ✆ **877/682-7433** or 808/734-4214), which has a variety of group tours, such as mountain biking in Kualoa. This guided mountain-bike tour follows dirt roads and a single track meandering through the 1,000-acre Kaaawa Valley on Oahu's northeast shore, with stops at a reconstructed Hawaiian *hale* (house) and *kalo loi* (taro terrace) for some cultural narrative, plus an old military bunker that has been converted into a movie museum for films shot here (*Jurassic Park, Godzilla, Mighty Joe Young, Windtalkers,* and more). The 6-mile trip, which takes 2 to 3 hours of riding, includes van transportation from your hotel, a bike, helmet, snacks, picnic lunch, water bottle, and guide; it's $130 for adults and $77 for children 14 and under. Want to see views from *mauka* (mountain) to *makai* (sea)? Then sign up for the Rainforest to Reef tour (8½ hours; $170 adults, $110 kids 14 and under) in which you hike in a tropical rainforest to a waterfall, drive up Mount Tantalus and cruise down on bikes, and, finally, set sail on a catamaran in Waikiki to snorkel and soak up the sun.

Golf

Oahu has nearly 3 dozen golf courses, ranging from bare-bones municipal courses to exclusive country-club courses with membership fees running to six figures a year. Below are the best of a great bunch.

As you get to know Oahu's courses, you'll see that the windward courses play much differently than the leeward courses. On the windward side, the prevailing winds blow from the ocean to shore, and the grain direction of the greens tends to run the same way—from the ocean to the mountains. Leeward golf courses have the opposite tendency: The winds usually blow from the mountains to the ocean, with the grain direction of the greens corresponding.

Tips on beating the crowds and saving money: Oahu's golf courses tend to be crowded, so I suggest that you go midweek, if you can. Also, most island courses have twilight rates that offer substantial discounts if you're willing to tee off in the afternoon; these are included in the listings below, where applicable.

Transportation note: TheBus does not allow golf-club bags onboard, so if you want to use TheBus to get to a course, you're going to have to rent clubs there.

WAIKIKI

Ala Wai Municipal Golf Course ★ This is Oahu's most popular municipal course. Translation: it gets really crowded; some 500 rounds a day are played on this 18-hole course. But it's the closest course, and within walking distance, to Waikiki's hotels. It's something of a challenge to get a tee time at this busy par-70, 6,020-yard course, and the computerized tee reservations system for all of Oahu's municipal courses will allow you to book only 3 days in advance, but keep trying. Ala Wai has a flat layout bordered by the Ala Wai Canal on one side and the Mānoa-Pālolo Stream on the other. It's less windy than most Oahu courses, but pay attention to the 372-yard, par-4 1st hole, which demands a straight and long shot to the very tiny green. If you miss, you can make it up on the 478-yard, par-5 10th hole— the green is reachable in two, so with a two-putt, a birdie is within reach.

404 Kapahulu Ave., Waikiki. www.co.honolulu.hi.us/des/golf/alawai.htm. © **808/733-7387** for golf course, or 808/296-2000 for tee-time reservations. Greens fees $55; twilight rates $28; cart $20. From Waikiki, turn left on Kapahulu Ave.; the course is on the *mauka* side of Ala Wai Canal. Bus: 19, 20, or 13.

THE WINDWARD COAST

Koolau Golf Club ★★ This is a spectacularly beautiful golf course, carved out of the tropical rainforest nestled against the Ko'olau mountain range. It's also spectacularly difficult—narrow and winding, with extreme changes in elevation. Legend has it that when Koolau Golf Club first opened, it was so difficult that it was given a slope rating of 162 . . . where the maximum slope rating is 155. The official rating has dropped to a still formidable 152 from the back tees. The windward side's wet conditions don't make it any easier (and now you know why this side is so green and lush). But when things get frustrating, just take a breath, look up at the mountains, and marvel at the beauty that surrounds you. Facilities include a pro shop, driving range, putting and chipping greens, and restaurant.

45-550 Kionaole Rd., Kaneohe. www.koolaugolfclub.com. © **808/236-4653.** Greens fees $145; twilight fees $110. Take H-1 to the Pali Hwy. (Hwy. 61); turn left on Hwy. 83, turn left for Kahiko St., take another left onto Kahiko St., and then turn right on Kiona'ole Rd.; the golf club will be on the right. No bus service.

Royal Hawaiian Golf Club ★★ Here's another gorgeous course, often referred to as the Jurassic Park of golf courses, so named for both the breathtaking scenery and because it's not for the faint-hearted. Designed by Perry and Pete Dye, the club has since been redeveloped by hall-of-fame golfer Greg Norman. Switchback trails lead you up to wide vistas that help take the sting out of losing so many balls. Facilities include a pro shop, driving range, putting and chipping greens, and a snack bar.

770 Auloa Rd., Kailua. www.royalhawaiiangc.com. © **808/262-2139.** Greens fees $160; twilight fees $115. Take H-1 to the Pali Hwy. (Hwy. 61); turn right onto Auloa Rd. Bus: 89.

THE NORTH SHORE

Kahuku Golf Course ★ This 9-hole budget golf course is a bit funky. Don't expect a clubhouse: there's only a dilapidated shack where you check in and minimal facilities consisting of golf club rentals, a few pull carts, and two Porta-Potties. But a round at this scenic oceanside course amid the tranquility of the North Shore is quite an experience nonetheless. Duffers will love the ease of this recreational course, and weight watchers will be happy to walk the gently sloping greens. Don't forget to bring your camera for the views. No reservations are taken and tee times are offered first-come, first-served. With plenty of retirees happy to sit and wait, the competition is fierce for early tee times.

56-501 Kamehameha Hwy., Kahuku. © **808/293-5842.** Greens fees $33. Take H-1 west to H-2; follow H-2 through Wahiawa to Kamehameha Hwy. (Hwy. 99, then Hwy. 83); follow it to Kahuku.

Turtle Bay Resort ★★★ This North Shore resort is home to two of Hawaii's top golf courses. The 18-hole **Arnold Palmer Course** (formerly the Links at Kuilima) was designed by Arnold Palmer and Ed Seay. Now that the casuarina (ironwood) trees have matured, it's not as windy as it used to be, but this is still a challenging course. The front 9, with rolling terrain, only a few trees, and lots of wind, play like a British Isles course. The back 9 have narrower tree-lined fairways and water. The course circles Punaho'olapa Marsh, a protected wetland for endangered Hawaiian waterfowl.

Another option is the par-71, 6,200-yard **George Fazio Course**—the only Fazio course in Hawaii. Larry Keil, pro at Turtle Bay, says that people like it because it's a more forgiving course, without all the water hazards and bunkers of the Palmer course. The 6th hole has two greens, so you can play the hole as a par-3 or par-4. The toughest hole has to be the par-3, 176-yard 2nd hole, where you tee off across a lake with a mean crosswind. The most scenic hole is the 7th, where the ocean is on your left; in winter, you might get lucky and see some whales.

Facilities include a pro shop, a driving range, putting and chipping greens, and a snack bar. Weekdays are best for tee times.

57-049 Kamehameha Hwy., Kahuku. www.turtlebayresort.com. © **808/293-8574.** Greens fees: Palmer Course $195 ($165 for resort guests); twilight rates (after 1pm) $120. Fazio Course $125 ($115 for resort guests); twilight rates $85. Take H-1 west past Pearl City; when the freeway splits, take H-2 and follow the signs to Haleiwa; at Haleiwa, take Hwy. 83 to Turtle Bay Resort. Bus: 52 or 55.

LEEWARD OAHU

Ko Olina Golf Club ★★★   This Ted Robinson–designed course has rolling fairways and elevated tee and water features. *Golf Digest* once named it one of "America's Top 75 Resort Courses." The signature hole— the 12th, a par-3—has an elevated tee that sits on a rock garden with a cascading waterfall. At the 18th hole, you'll see and hear water all around you—seven pools begin on the right side of the fairway and slope down to a lake. A waterfall is on your left off the elevated green. You'll have no choice but to play the left and approach the green over the water. Book in advance; this course is crowded all the time. Facilities include a driving range, locker rooms, a Jacuzzi, steam rooms, a restaurant and bar. Lessons are available.

92-1220 Aliinui Dr., Kapolei. www.koolinagolf.com. © **808/676-5300.** Greens fees $225 ($195 for guests staying at any of the Ko Olina resorts); twilight rates (after 1pm) $160. Ask about transportation from Waikiki hotels. Collared shirts requested for men and women. Take H-1 west until it becomes Hwy. 93 (Farrington Hwy.); turn off at the Ko Olina exit; take the exit road (Aliinui Dr.) into Ko Olina Resort; turn left into the clubhouse. No bus service.

West Loch Municipal Golf Course ★   This par-72, 6,615-yard course located just 30 minutes from Waikiki, in Ewa Beach, offers golfers a challenge at bargain rates. The difficulties on this unusual municipal course, designed by Robin Nelson and Rodney Wright, are water (lots of hazards), constant trade winds, and narrow fairways. To help you out, the course features a "water" driving range (with a lake) to practice your drives. In addition to the driving range, West Loch has practice greens, a pro shop, and a restaurant.

91-1126 Okupe St., Ewa Beach. © **808/675-6076.** Greens fees $55; 9 holes after 1pm $28; cart $20. Book 3 days in advance. Take H-1 west to the Hwy. 76 exit; stay in the left lane and turn left at West Loch Estates, just opposite St. Francis Medical Center. To park, take 2 immediate right turns. Bus: E.

Horseback Riding

You can gallop on the beach at the **Turtle Bay Resort ★★**, 57-091 Kamehameha Hwy., Kahuku (www.turtlebayresort.com; ✆ **808/293-6024;** bus: 52 or 55), where 45-minute rides along sandy beaches with spectacular ocean views and through a forest of ironwood trees cost $85 for age 7 and up (riders must be at least 4 ft., 4 in. tall). Romantic sunset rides are $110 per person. Private rides for up to four people are $130 per person. **Kualoa Ranch ★★**, 49-560 Kamehameha Hwy., Ka'a'awa (www.kualoa.com; ✆ **800/231-7321** or 808/237-7321) also offers 1- and 2-hour horseback tours ($85 and $130, respectively) into the lush Kaaawa Valley, against the backdrop of the Kualoa mountains.

ORGANIZED TOURS

Guided Sightseeing Tours

If your time is limited, you might want to consider a guided tour. These tours are informative, can give you a good overview of Honolulu or Oahu in a limited amount of time, and are surprisingly entertaining.

E Noa Tours, 1141 Waimanu St., Suite 105, Honolulu (www.enoa.com; ✆ **800/824-8804** or 808/591-2561), offers a range of narrated tours, from island loops to explorations of Pearl Harbor, on air-conditioned, 27-passenger minibuses. The Majestic Circle Island Tour ($99 for adults, $80 for children 3–11) stops at Diamond Head Crater, Hanauma Bay, Byodo-In Temple, Sunset Beach, Waimea Valley (admission included), and various beach sites along the way. Other tours focus on Pearl Harbor/USS *Arizona* Memorial and the North Shore.

Waikiki Trolley Tours ★, 1141 Waimanu St., Suite 105, Honolulu (www.waikikitrolley.com; ✆ **800/824-8804** or 808/593-2822), offers four tours of sightseeing, entertainment, dining, and shopping that give you the lay of the land. You can get on and off the trolley as needed (trolleys come along every 2–20 min.). An all-day pass (8:30am–11:35pm) is $45 for adults; a 4-day pass is $65. For the same price, you can experience the 2-hour narrated Panoramic Coast Line tour (Blue Line) of the southeast side of Oahu, an easy way to see the stunning views.

Specialty Tours

Below is a sampling of specialty tours found on Oahu.

CHOCOLATE FACTORY TOUR

Hawaii is the only state in the U.S. to grow cacao commercially, and at bean-to-bar maker **Manoa Chocolate ★★**, 315 Uluniu St., Suite 203 (www.manoachocolate.com; ✆ **808/262-6789**), you can find out more about Hawaii's burgeoning chocolate scene and see what it takes to turn

bird's-eye VIEW: AIR TOURS

To understand why Oahu was the island of kings, you need to see it from the air. **Island Seaplane Service ★★★** (www.islandseaplane.com; ✆ **808/836-6273**) operates flights departing from a floating dock in the protected waters of Ke'ehi Lagoon in either a six-passenger de Havilland Beaver or a four-passenger Cessna 206. There's nothing quite like feeling the slap of the waves as the plane skims across the water and then effortlessly lifts into the air.

The half-hour tour ($179) gives you aerial views of Waikiki Beach, Diamond Head Crater, Kāhala's luxury estates, and the sparkling waters of Hanauma and Kā ne'ohe bays; the 1-hour tour ($299) continues on to Chinaman's Hat, the Polynesian Cultural Center, and the rolling surf of the North Shore. The flight returns across the island over Hawaii's historic wartime sites: **Schofield Barracks** and the Pearl Harbor memorials.

Exploring by seaplane

cacao beans into smooth chocolate bars. You'll taste the beans through every step of the process and be able to compare Hawaii-grown chocolate with chocolate from around the world. A rare treat.

KO HANA RUM TOUR

Discover how rum is made, from grass to glass at **Ko Hana ★★★**, 92-1770 Kunia Rd. #227 (www.kohanarum.com; ✆ 808/517-4067). But this is not just any rum. This is Hawaiian agricole rum, distilled from pure cane juice, fresh-pressed from heirloom varieties of Hawaiian sugarcane. Most rum you see on shelves starts from molasses, whereas at Ko Hana, it begins with sugarcane, and each bottle is labeled with the varietal it was distilled from. The tour in Kunia, in the heart of Oahu's farmland, will not only give you sweeping views all the way to Diamond Head, it will take you through the cane fields, the distillery, and the tasting room to sample white rums alongside barrel-aged ones. Tours are $25 for adults.

FARM TOUR

Take a tractor-pulled wagon ride through the tropical fruit groves of **Kahuku Farms ★★**, 56-800 Kamehameha Hwy. (www.kahukufarms. com; © **808/628-0639**). For the smoothie tour ($16 for adults, $14 for children 5–12), you'll learn about the apple banana (short and tart), *lilikoi* (passion fruit), and pineapple, and then taste them all in a smoothie made on the spot at the cafe. Oh, and don't miss the grilled banana bread topped with made-on-the-farm ice cream and *haupia* (coconut) and caramel sauce.

WHERE TO STAY ON OAHU

Before you go online to book a place to stay, consider when you'll be visiting. The high season, when hotels are full and rates are at their peak, is mid-December to March. The secondary high season, when rates are high but rooms are somewhat easier to come by, is June to September. The low seasons—when you can expect fewer tourists and better deals— are April to June and September to mid-December. (For more on Hawaii's travel seasons, see "When to Go" on p. 49.) No matter when you travel, you can often get a good rate at many of Waikiki's hotels by booking a package.

For a description of each neighborhood, see "The Island in Brief" (p. 64). It can help you decide where you'd like to base yourself.

Remember that hotel and room taxes of 14.962% will be added to your bill (Oahu has a .546% additional tax that the other islands do not have). And don't forget about parking charges—at up to $30 a day in Waikiki, they can add up quickly.

Note that more and more hotels charge a mandatory daily "resort fee" or "amenity fee," usually somewhere between $25 and $30, which can increase the room rates by 20%. Hotels say these charges cover amenities, some of which you may not need (such as movie rentals, a welcome drink, a color photograph of you on the property—drinking that welcome drink, perhaps?) and some which are awfully handy (such as Internet access and parking). We have listed resort charges next to the room rates in the reviews below.

VACATION RENTALS Oahu has few true bed-and-breakfast inns. Instead, if you're looking for a non-hotel experience, your best bet is a vacation rental. You can rent direct from owners via **VRBO.com** (Vacation Rentals by Owner) and **Airbnb.com**. On these sites, you'll find a range of offerings, from $80-a-night studios to unique, off-the-beaten-path lodgings, like a Portlock cottage near Hanauma Bay on the water (listed on vrbo.com) or a North Shore treehouse (listed on Airbnb.com). Make sure to read the reviews before booking so you have a general idea of what you're getting into. Note that for VRBO, unless you purchase

VRBO's Vacation Protection Services, most places won't provide a refund if a rental is not what you expected. Airbnb.com gives renters more peace of mind; it withholds payment until check-in so renters can make sure the listing is as advertised. But I've booked places on both sites, basing my picks on reviews, and I've found the hosts friendly and listings accurate.

Waikiki

EWA WAIKIKI

All the hotels listed below are located between the ocean and Kalakaua Avenue, and between Ala Wai Terrace in the Ewa (western) direction and Olohana Street and Fort DeRussy Park in the Diamond Head (eastern) direction.

Expensive

Hilton Hawaiian Village Beach Resort & Spa ★★   This sprawling resort is like a microcosm of Waikiki—on good days it feels like a lively little beach town with hidden nooks and crannies to discover and great bars in which to make new friends, and on bad days it's just an endless traffic jam, with lines into the parking garage, at the front desk, and in the restaurants. Need an oasis in the middle of it all? Choose the Alii Tower; it has its own lobby lounge, reception, and concierge, and even its own pool and bar; it's like a hotel within a hotel.

But there's something for everyone at the Hilton Hawaiian—I've seen families settling in for a screening of *The Lorax* on the lawn, winter breakers leaving the Tapa Tower (the largest tower) to hit the bars, and well-heeled (literally) tourists returning to the Alii Tower with their shopping bags. Room views can range from a straight-on view of the tower in front to oceanfront, so close to the water you can hear waves lapping. Cheaper rooms are in the Kalia, Tapa, and Diamond Head towers (which are farther from the beach), and the more expensive ones in the Rainbow and Alii, which are closest to the water. I found rooms in all the towers to be spacious, clean, and comfy, so ultimately it may come down to how close you want to be to the beach.

2005 Kalia Rd. (at Ala Moana Blvd.), Honolulu. www.hiltonhawaiianvillage.com. 𝒞 **800/HILTONS** or 808/949-4321. 2,860 units. $220–$550 double; from $499 suite. $35 resort charge per day includes Internet access and movie rentals. Extra person (over 2 adults) $50. Children 17 and under stay free in parent's room. Valet parking $39, self-parking $32. Bus: 19 or 20. **Amenities:** 9 restaurants; 4 bars; year-round children's program; concierge; fitness center; 6 outdoor pools; room service; Wi-Fi (included in resort fee).

Prince Waikiki ★★   These two towers look like they're from *The Jetsons*, especially with the glass-walled elevators zipping up and down the exterior. The hotel completed an extensive remodel in 2017; installing more inviting restaurants and an infinity pool; most arresting of the updates are the 800 pieces of shimmering copper, reminiscent of fish scales, suspended from the ceiling of the hotel lobby. The rooms were also

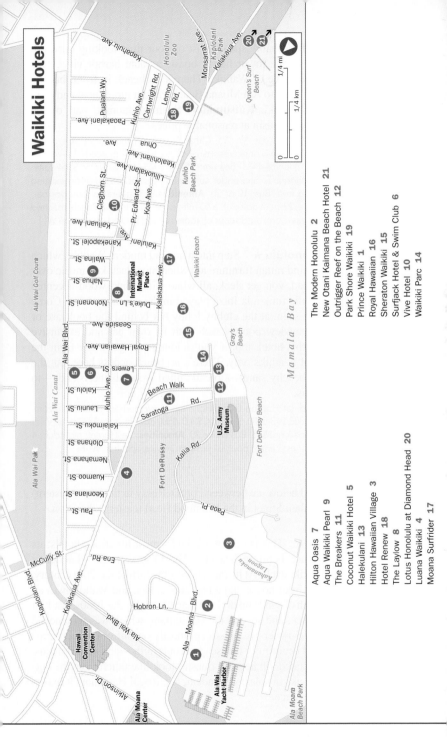

Waikiki Hotels

Aqua Oasis **7**
Aqua Waikiki Pearl **9**
The Breakers **11**
Coconut Waikiki Hotel **5**
Halekulani **13**
Hilton Hawaiian Village **3**
Hotel Renew **18**
The Laylow **8**
Lotus Honolulu at Diamond Head **20**
Luana Waikiki **4**
Moana Surfrider **17**

The Modern Honolulu **2**
New Otani Kaimana Beach Hotel **21**
Outrigger Reef on the Beach **12**
Park Shore Waikiki **19**
Prince Waikiki **1**
Royal Hawaiian **16**
Sheraton Waikiki **15**
Surfjack Hotel & Swim Club **6**
Vive Hotel **10**
Waikiki Parc **14**

updated, but you'll probably spend most of your time looking outward; every room, even on the lower floors, boasts a yacht harbor view. This hotel is on the quiet side of Waikiki. There's no beach in front, but it's about a 10-minute walk to Ala Moana Beach Park, a more local and less-busy beach than Waikiki. **Katsumidori Sushi** restaurant, part of the remodel, offers quality sushi at reasonable prices.

100 Holomoana St. (just across Ala Wai Canal Bridge, on the ocean side of Ala Moana Blvd.), Honolulu. www.princeresortshawaii.com/hawaii-prince-hotel-waikiki. © **888/977-4623** or 808/956-1111. 563 units. $294–$444 double; from $544 suite. Extra person $60. Children 17 and under stay free in parent's room using existing bedding. Self-parking free. Bus: 19 or 20. **Amenities:** 2 restaurants; outdoor bar; babysitting; concierge; 27-hole golf club a 40-min. drive away in Ewa Beach (reached by hotel shuttle); fitness room; outdoor pool; room service; small day spa; free Wi-Fi.

Moderate

The Modern Honolulu ★ Step into a hip and modern Waikiki, which means you won't find rattan furniture anywhere nor slack key music over the speakers. Instead, you get sleek, all white with blond-wood-accented rooms and electronic funk a la Ibiza played in the common areas. Come here to see and be seen, at the clubby lobby bar behind the bookcase or alongside two oceanview pools—each with its own bar and expansive daybeds. Choose this hotel, too, if you're looking to get away from the kids—the top pool is adults only. There's no beach access here, but the pool has its own beachy sand—a blend culled from all the islands—to pretend like there is.

1775 Ala Moana Blvd. (at Hobron Lane), Honolulu. www.themodernhonolulu.com. © **855/970-4161** or 808/943-5800. 353 units. $200–$500 double; from $530 suite. Valet parking only (no self-parking) $35. Bus: 19 or 20. **Amenities:** Restaurant; nightclub; 4 lounges; concierge; fitness center; pool; 24-hr. room service; spa; free Wi-Fi.

MID-WAIKIKI

All the hotels listed below are between Fort DeRussy in the Ewa (western) direction and Kaiulani Street in the Diamond Head (eastern) direction.

Expensive

Halekulani ★★★ This is one of Waikiki's most luxurious hotels; its name means "house befitting heaven." The history of the Halekulani tracks that of Waikiki itself: At its inception at the turn of the 20th century, it was just a beachfront house and a few bungalows, and Waikiki was an undeveloped stretch of sand and drained marshland. By the 1980s, Waikiki was a different place, and so was the Halekulani, which was relaunched by its new Japanese owners as an oasis of mostly oceanfront hotel rooms, marble foyers, and beautifully landscaped courtyards—and so it remains. It's all very understated—it actually doesn't look like much from the outside. But what it lacks in splashy grandeur, a la Royal Hawaiian, it makes up with a quiet elegance.

4

OAHU

Where to Stay on Oahu

The large rooms are done in what the Halekulani calls its signature "seven shades of white." Generously sized tile-and-marble bathrooms and louver shutter doors separating the lanais contribute to the spare yet luxe feel. Of all the hotels in Waikiki, this one feels the most peaceful, abetted by lovely, personable service. It's a true escape.

2199 Kalia Rd. (at the ocean end of Lewers St.), Honolulu. www.halekulani.com. 🄲 **800/367-2343** or 808/923-2311. 453 units. $495–$960 double; from $980 suite. Extra person $125. 1 child 17 and under stays free in parent's room using existing bedding; additional rollaway bed $40. Maximum 3 people per room. Parking $35. Bus: 19 or 20. **Amenities:** 3 restaurants; 3 bars; 24-hr. concierge; fitness center; gorgeous outdoor pool; room service; spa; free tickets to the Honolulu Museum of Art, Bishop Museum, and Doris Duke's Shangri La estate; free Wi-Fi.

Moana Surfrider, a Westin Resort ★★ This is Waikiki's oldest hotel, built in 1901. Even after more than 100 years, multiple renovations, and the construction of two towers in the '50s and '60s, the hotel has managed to retain its original and still grand Beaux-Arts main building. It's so picturesque you're likely to encounter many a Japanese wedding couple posing for a shot along the staircase and in the lobby. I prefer the rooms in the Banyan Wing for their nostalgic character, but these tend to be small in size. Larger rooms with lanais are in the Tower Wing, and although they are as well appointed as any you'll find at other Westin properties, with

AFFORDABLE waikiki: AQUA HOTELS

Inexpensive accommodations are few and far between on Oahu, and especially in Waikiki . . . at least places you'd actually *want* to stay in. But a good bet is the Aqua chain (www.aquaresorts.com), whose inexpensive to moderately priced properties (from $119 a night) are managed by a Hawaii-based company. Hotels vary in quality (with furnishings ranging from dated tropical to bright and modern), but they are generally clean, well maintained, and regularly updated.

Some of the Oahu standouts in the Aqua portfolio include the **Aqua Waikiki Pearl,** 415 Nahua St. (✆ 808/954-7425), right in the middle of Waikiki and about a 10-minute walk to the beach. It has

spacious room options, and I was able to find a 450-square-foot room for $125 online. The **Aqua Oasis,** 320 Lewers St. (✆ 808/441-7781) is just that—a cheery property with a lush courtyard and lounge area as well as clean rooms with city views and plumeria accents. Rates here start at $150. Rooms in the **Luana Waikiki,** 2045 Kalakaua Ave. (✆ 808/955-6000), which Aqua acquired from Outrigger in 2014, start at $159. It offers a pool and suites with a kitchen. Best of the midrange Aqua hotels is the **Park Shore Waikiki,** 2586 Kalākaua Ave. (✆ 808/954-7426), which offers views of Diamond Head and the ocean, starting at just $160 a night.

granite bathrooms and signature Heavenly beds, they don't feel very Hawaii. Of course, to change that, get a room with a view of Diamond Head, or just step out under the giant banyan tree in the courtyard and enjoy the nightly live Hawaiian music and a mai tai.

2365 Kalakaua Ave. (ocean side of the street, across from Kaiulani St.), Honolulu. www.moana-surfrider.com. ✆ **800/325-3535** or 808/922-3111. 793 units. $300–$610 double; from $970 suite. $30 resort charge per day (covers self-parking, Internet, and local calls). Extra person $120. Children 17 and under stay free in parent's room using existing bedding. Valet parking $15 additional. Bus: 19 or 20. **Amenities:** 3 restaurants; bar; babysitting; children's program; concierge; nearby fitness room (about a 2-min. walk down the beach at the Sheraton Waikiki); outdoor pool; room service; Wi-Fi (included in resort fee).

Outrigger Reef on the Beach ★★   You may arrive by car, but the Outrigger reminds you—with the 100-year-old koa wood canoe suspended in the longhouse entryway—that long ago, the Polynesians came to Hawaii by boat, navigating their way only by the stars. The Hawaii-based Outrigger chain has a handful of hotels on Oahu, and this one is its most striking, with lovely Hawaiian cultural touches. You'll find the outrigger theme throughout the hotel, such as in the collection of Polynesian canoe art by Herb Kane, who some call the "father of the Hawaiian Renaissance." (Most notably, he built the double-hulled voyaging canoe the *Hokulea* in 1975, which revived ancient celestial navigation methods. From 2014-2017, the *Hokulea* sailed around the world—without a compass, GPS, or any other modern-day navigational equipment.) But don't worry, at Outrigger Reef, you can have your historical culture and modern amenities too, such as free Wi-Fi, a large pool, and three restaurants, including the new, beachside **Reef Bar and Market Grill** with grill-your-own steaks. Decked out in tasteful Hawaiian decor, rooms are spacious.

Note that **Outrigger Waikiki on the Beach** (www.outriggerwaikiki-hotel.com) has a similar feel and price point to Outrigger Reef on the Beach, but its location in the center of Waikiki and its resident bar—Duke's Waikiki, the area's most happening bar—means it's a little more bustling and noisy.

2169 Kalia Rd. (at Saratoga Rd.), Honolulu. www.outriggerreef.com. © **866/733-6420** or 808/923-3111. 639 units. $200–$450 double. Resort fee $30 includes Wi-Fi and rides on the Waikiki Trolley. Extra person (over 2 adults) $75 per person per night. Children 17 and under stay free in parent's room. Valet parking only (no self-parking) $35. Bus: 19 or 20. **Amenities:** 3 restaurants; 2 bars; babysitting; fitness center; spa; outdoor pools.

Royal Hawaiian ★★★ The "Pink Palace of the Pacific" is as pink as the Halekulani is white. Everytime I step into the Royal Hawaiian, it still takes my breath away. I love its vibrant exoticism—the Spanish-Moorish architecture manifested in graceful stucco arches, the patterned floor tiles, the ornate lamps. Who knew that pink could look so good against Hawaii's blue skies and seas? The historic rooms are my favorite, with the pink and gold-embossed wallpaper and dark-wood furniture. Rooms in the Mailani Tower wing are larger, the colors more muted (although, don't worry, there are still pink accents) and the bathrooms there have fancy Toto toilets. Here, even your '*okole* (rear end) is pampered.

2259 Kalakaua Ave. (at Royal Hawaiian Ave., on the ocean side of the Royal Hawaiian Shopping Center), Honolulu. www.royal-hawaiian.com. © **800/325-3535** or 808/923-7311. 528 units. $350–$535 double; from $490 suite. Extra person $155. Bus: 19 or 20. **Amenities:** 2 restaurants; landmark bar; babysitting; bike rentals; concierge; prefered tee times at area golf courses; outdoor pool; room service; spa; free Wi-Fi. A fitness room and a year-round children's program (are offered next door at the Sheraton Waikiki).

Sheraton Waikiki ★ At 30 stories tall, the Sheraton towers over its neighbors. With almost 2,000 rooms and a location right in the middle of the busiest section of Waikiki, this is not the place to book if you're looking for a peaceful getaway. What you do get: views of the ocean (available in most rooms), the Helumoa Playground pool for kids, and a gorgeous infinity pool for adults. Expect crowds, though. Drinks at **Rumfire** are fun, with great views to match; the **Kai Market** dinner buffet offers a smorgasbord of local flavors. Dining is expensive (as is expected at most Waikiki hotels); for cheap, grab-and-go meals, I like to go to **Lawson Station,** something of a Japanese version of 7-Eleven but with much better food, such as bento boxes, oden, and yummy desserts made by local companies.

2255 Kalākaua Ave. (at Royal Hawaiian Ave., on the ocean side of the Royal Hawaiian Shopping Center and west of the Royal Hawaiian), Honolulu. www.sheraton-waikiki. com. © **800/325-3535** or 808/922-4422. 1,852 units. $295–$495 double; from $705 suite. $35 resort charge per day (includes Internet, and local and long-distance calls). Extra person $120. Children 17 and under stay free in parent's room. Valet parking $45, self-parking $35. Bus: 19 or 20. **Amenities:** 5 restaurants; 2 bars; nightclub; babysitting; bike rentals; children's program; concierge; fitness center; 2 large outdoor pools; room service; Wi-Fi (included in resort fee).

Moderate

The Laylow ★★   Following the Surfjack, the Laylow opened in 2017 for the Instagram jet-set crowd. It's part of the Marriott Autograph Collection, but with under 200 rooms and a lovely midcentury Hawaii aesthetic, it feels like a boutique hotel. Despite its location right next to the International Marketplace and in the middle of Waikiki, the second floor **Hideout** restaurant and lounge creates an oasis edged with tropical foliage, low-slung banquettes, modern wicker chairs, and fire pits. There are even sandy areas to dig your toes into. The rooms capture the same vibe, with minimalist 1960s wood furniture, warmed up with teal-and-pink palm wallpaper.

2299 Kuhio Ave., Honolulu. www.laylowwaikiki.com. © **808/922-6600.** 186 units. $209–$269 double; suites from $279. $25 resort fee. Extra person $35. Valet parking $35. Bus: 19 or 20. **Amenities:** Restaurant; pool; room service; free Wi-Fi.

Surfjack Hotel & Swim Club ★★★   Step back into the golden ages of Waikiki, when Don Ho crooned in Waikiki lounges and the beachfront was dotted with low-slung buildings and bungalows. The Surfjack, new in 2016, was remade from a 1960s budget hotel. Its owners enlisted a considerable amount of local talent, from young designers to established artists, to create a space that screams midcentury-beach house cool, from the "Wish You Were Here" mosaic on the swimming pool floor to the pretty blue and white tiling in the bathrooms to the vintage headboard upholstery by Tori Richard. It's not close to the beach, and the views are mostly of buildings, and yet, it's hard to leave this soulful enclave, where you can get excellent cocktails by the pool or a perfect cup of coffee while you browse the on-site boutique, **Olive and Oliver.**

412 Lewers St., Honolulu. www.surfjack.com. © **855/945-4082** or 808/564-7608. 112 units. $217–$287 double; suites from $287. $25 resort fee (includes Internet and local calls). Extra person $30. Bus: 19 or 20. **Amenities:** Restaurant; pool; room service; Wi-Fi (included in resort fee).

Waikiki Parc ★   This is the Halekulani's younger, hipper sister, located across the street and run by the same management company. The lobby entrance glows blue to the beat of electronica, and the breakfast buffet is served in what used to be a Nobu dining room. The rooms aren't as posh as the rest of the hotel, though—the floors are tile and rooms feel more utilitarian than stylish. But the location—across the street from the beach—is great. Spring for an ocean view; otherwise, you might be overlooking the parking lot.

2233 Helumoa Rd. (at Lewers St.), Honolulu. www.waikikiparc.com. © **800/422-0450** or 808/921-7272. 297 units. $221–$345 double. Extra person $75. Children 17 and under stay free in parent's room. Bus: 19 or 20. **Amenities:** 2 restaurants; babysitting; concierge; fitness center; 8th-floor pool deck; room service; free admission to the Bishop Museum and Honolulu Museum of Art; free Wi-Fi.

Inexpensive

The Breakers ★   In the 1950s and '60s, thanks to statehood and the jet age, Waikiki's low-rise skyline gave way to larger and taller hotels. A lot of the more modest hotels are long gone . . . except for the Breakers. The two-story building, built in 1954, has managed to hold on to its family feel and prime real estate (just a few minutes' walk to the beach and the center of Waikiki). It's like a Hawaii-style motel, built around a pool, with charming touches such as double-pitched roofs, shoji doors to the lanai, and tropical landscaping. All of the rooms come with a kitchenette, though the appliances look like they're from the '70s. Sure, the decor is dated and worn, but it's clean.

250 Beach Walk (btw. Kalakaua Ave. and Kalia Rd.), Honolulu. www.breakers-hawaii. com. © **800/426-0494** or 808/923-3181. 64 units, all with shower only. $160–$180 double (extra person $20 per day); $235 garden suite double. Limited free parking (just 6 stalls); additional parking across the street $16 per day. Bus: 19 or 20. **Amenities:** Restaurant; grill; outdoor pool; Wi-Fi (free, in lobby).

Coconut Waikiki Hotel ★   Rooms at this family-friendly hotel are spacious and immaculate and come with a small lanai and wet bar. The tiny pool is kind of wedged between the hotel and a fence—better to grab the free beach-towel rental and head to the ocean sands. Its sister hotel, **Shoreline Hotel Waikiki** (shorelinehotelwaikiki.com; © **808/931-2444**), is a few blocks away, with similar amenities and a midcentury modern vibe. Check out **Heavenly,** inside the Shoreline, with its surfer-chic decor and delicious brunch fare, including the French toast and loco moco.

450 Lewers St. (at Ala Wai Blvd.), Honolulu. coconutwaikikihotel.com. © **808/923-8828.** 81 units. $169–$219 double; from $249 suite. Valet parking only (no self-parking) $26. Bus: 19 or 20. **Amenities:** Tiny outdoor pool w/sun deck; free Wi-Fi.

Vive Hotel ★   The good: a stylish lobby, clean rooms, free continental breakfast with lots of fresh fruit, and no resort fee. The bad: small, bordering on cramped quarters. But you can always take advantage of the free beach mats, chairs, and umbrellas and escape to the beach just minutes away. With a generous and friendly staff, this is a great value option.

2426 Kuhio Ave., Honolulu. vivehotelwaikiki.com. © **808/687-2000.** 119 units. $159–$337 double. Valet parking only (no self-parking) $25. Bus: 19 or 20. **Amenities:** Free Wi-Fi.

DIAMOND HEAD WAIKIKI

You'll find all these hotels between Ala Wai Boulevard and the ocean, and between Kaiulani Street and world-famous Diamond Head itself.

Moderate

Hotel Renew ★★   This is a stylish boutique hotel just a block from the beach. Like its lobby bar, rooms at Hotel Renew are small but well edited and well designed. You get a minimalist, Japanese aesthetic, mood lighting, and plush beds with a down featherbed and down comforter. The crowd that stays here are 20- and 30-somethings who don't need hibiscus and tropical prints to tell them they're vacationing in Hawaii.

129 Paoakalani Ave. (at Lemon Rd.), Honolulu. www.hotelrenew.com. ℂ **888/485-7639** or 808/687-7700. 72 units. $190–$350 double. Amenity fee $25 per day (includes continental breakfast). Valet parking $25. Bus: 19 or 20. **Amenities:** Lounge; concierge; Wi-Fi (included in amenity fee).

Lotus Honolulu at Diamond Head ★★   Here on the quiet side of Waikiki, between Kapiolani Park and Diamond Head, you can sleep with the windows open. A former W Hotel property, the Lotus was updated with dark hardwood floors, platform beds, granite-tiled bathrooms, and—in the corner units—a lanai and window that frame Diamond Head beautifully. Little touches like morning yoga classes in the park make for a welcoming boutique experience.

2885 Kalakaua Ave., Waikiki. www.lotushonolulu.com. ℂ **808/922-1700.** 51 units. $239–$512 double. Extra person $30. Amenity fee $25 (includes parking). Bus: 2 or 14. **Amenities:** Restaurant; concierge; shuttle to Waikiki and Ala Moana; Wi-Fi (included in amenity fee).

New Otani Kaimana Beach Hotel ★   It's almost a different world here, with Kapiolani Park providing a buffer from the frenzy of Waikiki. The hotel's best feature is its location right on Kaimana Beach, where the crowds are thinner and the water cleaner. The rooms can be a bit tight, but the pricier ones face the ocean straight on, with no obstructions, and have lanai where you can lose yourself to the aquamarine blues stretching all the way to the horizon. In 2017, the hotel finally finished a three-year update to the décor, putting the "new" back into the New Otani. Start your day with breakfast at the **Hau Tree Lānai** restaurant, under the canopy of the age-old tree.

2863 Kalakaua Ave. (ocean side of the street just before Diamond Head and just past the Waikiki Aquarium, across from Kapiolani Park), Waikiki. www.kaimana.com. ℂ **800/356-8264** or 808/923-1555. 124 units. $175–$350 double; from $176 studio; from $255 1-bedroom; from $400 suite. Extra person $50. Children 12 and under stay free in parent's room using existing bedding. Check website for special packages. Valet parking $23. Bus: 2 or 14. **Amenities:** 2 restaurants; beachfront bar; babysitting; concierge; room service; free Wi-Fi.

HONOLULU BEYOND WAIKIKI

To the East: Kahala

Kahala Hotel & Resort ★★★   Hotel magnate Conrad Hilton opened the Kahala in 1964 as a secluded and exclusive retreat away from Waikiki. Fifty years and a different owner later, the hotel retains that feeling of peacefulness and exclusivity. Its rooms convey a unique island luxury, aka "Kahala chic." In your private quarters, you'll get a plush bed and enormous bathroom with a soaking tub and separate shower. On the property, you have access to a small beach with a private feel (in Hawaii, all beaches are public, but few people come here). There's a pool, too, but what makes the Kahala unique is the Dolphin Quest, which allows you to get up close and personal with the dolphins in the lagoon. The hotel's restaurants offer experiences such as a beachfront brunch buffet, afternoon tea on the veranda, and an upscale Pacific Rim dinner, all of which make the Kahala a worthy escape from the bustle of Waikiki.

5000 Kahala Ave. (next to the Waialae Country Club), Honolulu. www.kahalaresort. com. ℂ **800/367-2525** or 808/739-8888. 343 units. From $450 double; from $1,095 suite. Extra person $100. Children 17 and under stay free in parent's room. Check online for packages and discounts. Parking $32. **Amenities:** 5 restaurants; 4 bars; babysitting; year-round children's program (for a fee); concierge; nearby golf course; fitness center; large outdoor pool; room service; watersports equipment rentals; free Wi-Fi.

THE WINDWARD COAST

For the Windward side, your best bet is VRBO.com and Airbnb.com (mentioned earlier in "Vacation Rentals"), where beachy bungalows start at $149 (plus cleaning fees) a night. *Note:* Windward Coast accommodations are located on the "Eastern Oahu & the Windward Coast" map (p. 97).

Kailua

Lanikai Beach Rentals ★   Lanikai clings tenaciously to its laidback, beachy vibe, even in the face of a growing number of visitors. Spend the night in an old-style, homey, and comfortable Lanikai house just across the street from the beach to feel a part of the neighborhood. Lanikai Beach Rentals offers a range of units, from a garden studio decorated in Hawaiiana print and rattan furniture to the beachfront house once the residence of John Walker, who built the Bishop Museum and Honolulu Hale. The properties are furnished with cooking utensils and beach equipment—all you need to make it home.

1277 Mokulua Dr. (btw. Onekea and Aala drives in Lanikai), Kailua. www.lanikai beachrentals.com. ℂ **808/261-7895.** Rentals range from a $249 studio or 1-bedroom double to $1,400 for a 5-bedroom house. Cleaning fee $131. 5-night minimum. Free parking. Bus: 56. **Amenities:** Free Wi-Fi.

4

OAHU | Where to Stay on Oahu

137

Sheffield House ★   Kailua is a small beach town, with restaurants, shops, and a business center anchored by Whole Foods. Staying with long-time Kailua residents Paul and Rachel Sheffield (they live in a separate, adjacent house on the property) puts you right in the middle of everything—it's just a few minutes' walk to the beach but also a short stroll to Whole Foods, the Sunday farmer's market, and "town" for groceries and entertainment. (Convenience does have its drawbacks, though—the house is on one of Kailua's busy streets, which means traffic sounds.) There are two vacation rentals here—a one-bedroom and a studio, each with its own private entry and kitchenette.

131 Kuulei Rd. (at Kalaheo Dr.), Kailua. www.hawaiisheffieldhouse.com. ℰ **808/262-0721**. 2 units. $144–$164 studio double; $164–$184 1-bedroom. Extra person $20. Cleaning fee $65–$75. Rates include 1st day's continental breakfast. Free parking. Bus: 56. **Amenities:** Free Wi-Fi.

THE NORTH SHORE

The North Shore has few tourist accommodations—some say that's its charm. VRBO.com and Airbnb.com (mentioned earlier in "Vacation Rentals") offer a good range of places to stay, such as a Haleiwa studio on the first floor of a two-story home for $85 a night, a North Shore loft with three beds from $159, and a three-bedroom house steps away from Sunset Beach for $410 a night. Cleaning fees vary.

Note: North Shore accommodations are located on the "Oahu's North Shore" map (p. 105).

Very Expensive

Turtle Bay Resort ★★★   The North Shore's only resort possesses a beachy, laidback, but luxurious style befitting the less-developed, unhurried North Shore. The lobby and gym open up with ocean views, the spa is amply sized, the restaurants' menus highlight locally grown ingredients, and rooms have ocean views, calming, neutral palettes and walk-in stone showers. Turtle Bay has also embraced its role as a surf-scene hub, especially in the wintertime, when the surfing season is in full swing. All the pros come to **Lei Lei's Bar and Grill** for a drink, and **Surfer, The Bar**—a collaboration between the resort and *Surfer* magazine—offers Surf Talk Story nights, bringing in pro surfers and watermen to share their tales. The resort really feels like a part of the North Shore landscape. Of all the resorts outside of Waikiki (including Kahala and Aulani), this would be my pick, for the vibe, the value, and the surroundings.

57-091 Kamehameha Hwy. (Hwy. 83), Kahuku. www.turtlebayresort.com. ℰ **800/203-3650** or 808/293-6000. 477 units. $290–$389 double; from $599 cottage; from $499 suite; from $1,169 villa. Daily $40 resort fee (includes self-parking and Internet access). Extra person $50. Children 17 and under stay free in parent's room. **Amenities:** 5 restaurants; 2 bars; concierge; 36-hole golf course; stable w/horseback riding; 2 outdoor heated pools (with 80-ft. water slide); room service; spa w/fitness center; 4 tennis courts; watersports equipment rentals; Wi-Fi (included in resort fee).

Inexpensive

Ke Iki Beach Bungalows ★ These bungalows are right on a beautiful, wide, and uncrowded beach, between Sharks Cove (great for snorkeling in the summer) and Pipeline (for the best pro-surfer wave-watching come winter). Ranging from basic studios to two-bedroom accommodations, each unit comes with bamboo furniture, a TV, and a full kitchen, plus its own grill. Stock up on groceries at the nearby Foodland (part of the largest locally owned supermarket chain in Hawaii). Be aware that units have no air-conditioning, but ceiling fans and North Shore breezes are usually enough to keep the air cool. Settle into one of the hammocks strung up between the palm trees overlooking the beach—this is island living.

59-579 Ke Iki Rd. (off Kamehameha Hwy.), Haleiwa. www.keikibeach.com. ☎ **866/638-8229** or 808/638-8229. 11 units with garden or ocean views, ranging from studios to 1 or 2 bedrooms. $135 (gardenview studio)–$230 (beachfront 2-bedroom). Extra person stays free. Cleaning fee $55–$100. Free parking. Bus: 52. **Amenities:** Free use of bikes and watersports equipment; free Wi-Fi.

LEEWARD OAHU: THE WAIANAE COAST

Ko Olina is growing as the luxury hotel hub of the Leeward coast. The Aulani opened in 2011, the Four Seasons in late 2016, and an Atlantis resort will be complete by 2019. The new resorts are in sharp contrast to the rest of the coast, which is Oahu's poorest.

Aulani, a Disney Resort & Spa, Ko Olina, Hawaii ★★★ Aulani offers plenty of fun from Mickey and friends to entertain the kids, such as a character breakfast with photo ops, but it's also a celebration of Hawaiian culture. Disney's "imagineers" worked with locals to get many of the details just right, from murals and woodcarvings throughout the property that tell the story of Hawaii. At the **Olelo Room,** one of the resort bars, common objects are labeled with their Hawaiian names (everyone learns a new language better when they're drinking, right?) and there's live Hawaiian music every night. A 900-foot-long lazy river threads the resort, which—along with children's programs like storytelling nights under the stars, Hawaiian crafts classes, and Disney movies on the lawn—makes the Aulani, perhaps unsurprisingly, one of the best lodging choices for families. Even I, by now a cynical adult, am always delighted when I set foot on this property.

92-1185 Aliinui Dr., Kapolei. http://resorts.disney.go.com/aulani-hawaii-resort. ☎ **714/520-7001** (reservations) or 808/674-6200 (hotel). 359 units in hotel, $449–$670 hotel room, from $1,340 suite. Parking $37. No bus service. Take H-1 west toward Pearl City/Ewa Beach; stay on H-1 until it becomes Hwy. 93 (Farrington Hwy.); look for the exit sign for Ko Olina Resort; turn left on Aliinui Dr. **Amenities:** 3 restaurants; 3 bars; babysitting; championship 18-hole golf course; numerous outdoor pools and water features; room service; spa; watersports equipment rentals; free Wi-Fi.

Camping & Wilderness Cabins

If you plan to camp, you'll need to bring your own gear; there aren't places on the island to rent equipment.

The best places to camp on Oahu are listed below. TheBus's Circle Island route can get you to or near all these sites, but remember: On TheBus, you're allowed only one bag, which has to fit under the seat. If you have more gear, you're going to have to drive or take a cab.

THE WINDWARD COAST

Hoomaluhia Botanical Garden ★

This little-known windward campground outside Kaneohe is a real treasure. It's hard to believe that it's just half an hour from downtown Honolulu. The name Hoomaluhia, or "peace and tranquility," accurately describes this 400-acre botanical garden at the foot of the jagged Ko'olau Range. In this lush setting, gardens are devoted to plants specific to tropical America, native Hawaii, Polynesia, India, Sri Lanka, and Africa. A 32-acre lake sits in the middle of the scenic park (no swimming or boating allowed), and there are numerous hiking trails. The visitor center offers free guided walks Saturday at 10am and Sunday at 1pm (call ✆ **808/233-7323** to register).

Facilities for this tent-camp area include restrooms, cold showers, dishwashing stations, picnic tables, and water. Shopping and gas are available in Kaneohe, 2 miles away. Stays are limited to 3 nights, from 9am Friday to 4pm Monday only. Reserve a campsite up to 2 weeks in advance at **camping.honolulu.gov.** Permits are $32, valid for the entire weekend (Fri–Sun). To get here from Waikiki, take H-1 to the Pali Highway (Hwy. 61); turn left on Kamehameha Highway (Hwy. 83); and at the fourth light, turn left on Luluku Road. TheBus nos. 55 and 65 stop nearby on Kamehameha Highway; from here, you'll have to walk 2 miles to the visitor center.

Kahana Bay Beach Park ★

Lying under Tahiti-like cliffs, with a beautiful gold-sand crescent beach framed by pine-needle casuarina trees, Kahana Bay Beach Park is a place of serene beauty. You can swim, bodysurf, fish, hike, and picnic or just sit and listen to the trade winds whistle through the beach pines (and sometimes, cars—the campsite is along Kamehameha Highway).

Facilities include restrooms, outdoor showers, picnic tables, and drinking water. *Note:* The restrooms are located at the north end of the beach, far away from the camping area.

Permits can be obtained at **camping.ehawaii.gov** for $18 a night. Camping is only allowed from Friday through Wednesday.

Kahana Bay Beach Park is set in the 52-222 block of Kamehameha Highway (Hwy. 83) in Kahana. From Waikiki, take the H-1 west to the Likelike Highway (Hwy. 63). Continue north on the Likelike, through the

Wilson Tunnel, turning left on Hwy. 83; Kahana Bay is 13 miles down the road on the right. You can also get here via TheBus no. 55.

THE NORTH SHORE

Mālaekahana Bay State Recreation Area ★★

This is one of the most beautiful beach-camping areas in the state, with a mile-long, gold-sand beach on Oahu's North Shore. During low tide, you can wade/swim out to Goat Island, a sanctuary for seabirds and turtles. There are two areas for tent camping. Facilities include picnic tables, restrooms, showers, sinks, and drinking water. For your safety, the park gate is closed between 6:45pm and 7am; vehicles cannot enter or exit during those hours. Groceries and gas are available in Laie and Kahuku, each less than a mile away.

Permits are $18 a night and available at **camping.ehawaii.gov**. Camping is limited to Friday through Wednesday.

The recreation area is located on Kamehameha Highway (Hwy. 83) between Laie and Kahuku. Take the H-2 to Hwy. 99 to Hwy. 83 (both roads are called Kamehameha Hwy.); continue on Hwy. 83, just past Kahuku. You can also get here via TheBus no. 55.

WHERE TO EAT ON OAHU

Hawaii offers food experiences that exist nowhere else in the world, from dishes based on foods eaten by ancient Native Hawaiians to plate lunches in which you can see the history of Hawaii, from postwar-era holes-in-the-wall (where the only thing that's changed is the prices) to fancy dining rooms that spawned the birth of Hawaii Regional Cuisine. Asian food dominates, thanks to the state's demographics (as of 2012, Hawaii was the country's only majority-Asian state, comprising 56.9% of the total population). On Oahu, the most promising places to eat are often found in the most unexpected places. For the adventurous, eating here is like a treasure hunt.

Honolulu: Waikiki

Thanks to an influx of Japanese tourists, Waikiki now has some of the best Japanese food outside of Japan. It also has some of Honolulu's most luxurious dining rooms with ocean views—at a price.

EXPENSIVE

Herringbone Waikiki ★ MODERN AMERICAN/SEAFOOD   Herringbone's whimsical dining room and open-air lanai feels part tropical terrarium, part natural-history museum, part New England crab shack thanks to the hanging foliage, repurposed lobster traps, and pufferfish ornaments that make up the décor. The seafood-focused menu is as interesting as the ambiance, with octopus dunked in a buffalo sauce (as in buffalo wings), whole fish ceviche, and onaga (a local snapper) in a citrus miso glaze. Tip: Come during happy hour for drink and pupu specials, as well as $2 oysters.

At the International Marketplace, 2330 Kalakaua Ave., Waikiki, Honolulu. www.herringboneeats.com. *©* **808/797-2435.** Main courses $34–$45. Brunch Fri–Sun 10:30am–2:30pm; happy hour daily 4–6pm; dinner Sun–Thurs 5–10pm, Fri–Sat 5–11pm.

La Mer ★★ NEOCLASSICAL FRENCH   La Belle Époque meets Pacific teak and rattan against heart-achingly romantic views of the ocean and Diamond Head. Sometimes it's all a little over the top, like when a red rose the size of your fist is perched on your cocktail, but those into haute French cuisine with a touch of the theatrical will love La Mer. Choose from three- or four-course tasting menus, or the *menu dégustation,* seven courses featuring luxe ingredients such as foie gras tiled with shiitake mushrooms, abalone *meunière,* lobster tail bathed in butter and lobster consommé, and a filet of beef with truffle. Luxe indeed. La Mer is one of the few restaurants on Oahu that requires men to wear a jacket or long-sleeved shirt.

At the Halekulani, 2199 Kalia Rd., Waikiki, Honolulu. www.halekulani.com. *©* **808/923-2311.** Reservations recommended. Jackets or long-sleeved shirts required for men. Tasting menus start at $110, *menu dégustation* $195, $95 for wine pairing. Daily 6–10pm.

MODERATE

Bills Sydney ★ AUSTRALIAN   Bill Granger is an Australian restaurateur whose claim to fame is his ricotta pancakes and scrambled eggs. Yup, scrambled eggs. They're that good. Come for breakfast or brunch for the light and moist pancakes or the full Aussie breakfast. The burger is excellent, too.

280 Beach Walk Ave., Waikiki, Honolulu. www.billshawaii.com. *©* **808/922-1500.** Main courses $8–$28. Mon–Sun 7am–10pm.

Ginza Bairin ★★ JAPANESE   The Japanese take their *tonkatsu*—fried pork cutlets—very, very seriously. Here, a kurobota pork loin katsu can run you $36, but, oh, there's such joy in the crispy, greaseless panko crust and the juicy pork within. Grind some sesame seeds into the plummy tonkatsu sauce, and dip your pork in. The tonkatsu is served on a wire pedestal (to keep the bottom from steaming and going soggy) and a bottomless chiffonade of cabbage salad. *Tip:* Just as good, and only $10, is the pork tenderloin katsu sandwich—a thinner cut of pork, expertly fried, between two slices of white bread with the crusts cut off.

255 Beach Walk, Waikiki, Honolulu. www.ginzabairin.com. *©* **808/926-8082.** Main courses $12–$32. Sun–Wed 11am–10:30pm; Thurs–Fri 11am–11:30pm.

Goofy Café and Dine ★ HEALTHY   Named not after the Disney character but the right-foot-forward surfing stance, this charming spot has a cozy, beachy vibe, lined with reclaimed wood and decorated with surfboards that, from the looks of it, are waxed and ready to go. (The popular

Waikiki Restaurants

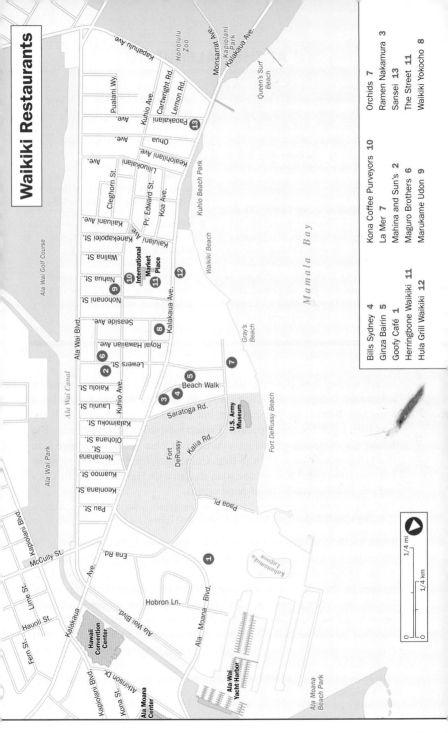

Bills Sydney **4**
Ginza Bairin **5**
Goofy Café **1**
Herringbone Waikiki **11**
Hula Grill Waikiki **12**

Kona Coffee Purveyors **10**
La Mer **7**
Mahina and Sun's **2**
Maguro Brothers **6**
Marukame Udon **9**

Orchids **7**
Ramen Nakamura **3**
Sansei **13**
The Street **11**
Waikiki Yokocho **8**

dining out **AT THE HALEKULANI**

Sure, dining in Waikiki's high-end hotels is often an overpriced affair, but sometimes the occasion warrants everything that comes with it—including ocean views and upscale service. My pick for special events is the **Halekulani** ★ ★ ★ (p. 130). Here are my favorite ways to soak up the Halekulani's rarefied restaurant experiences:

○ The **Sunday brunch buffet** at **Orchids** is a must—it's the best in Hawaii, with everything from a roast-suckling-pig carving station to a sashimi and poke bar. Leave room for the ice cream sundae bar, the Halekulani's signature fluffy coconut cake, and lots of dainty desserts. (**Note:** Reserve a spot weeks in advance.) Love afternoon tea?

Orchids also serves my favorite **afternoon tea** service on the island, with an array of sandwiches and sweets, as well as an excellent selection of premium teas.

○ Come sunset, head to **House Without a Key** for a mai tai and the lovely hula of five former Miss Hawaiis, including the legendary Kanoe Miller.

○ If the occasion calls for something more romantic and intimate, I go to **L'Aperitif,** the bar inside La Mer, where drinks are inspired by 19th-century French cocktail culture and each glass is accompanied by a delightful amuse bouche.

locals' surfing spot, Bowls, is nearby.) It's a surfer's cafe as envisioned by a Japanese company that also runs Aloha Table in Waikiki. Goofy has a breakfast, lunch, and dinner menu, but breakfast (served all day) is the best part: Look for eggs Benedict, French toast drizzled with creamy Big Island honey, green smoothies poured over chia seeds, and huge acai bowls mounded over with fresh fruit. Come later, for dinner or to sit at the bar, and you can get a sugarcane sour, shaken with Hawaiian Shochu Co.'s unique, Haleiwa-made sweet-potato spirit.

1831 Ala Moana Blvd., Suite 201., Waikiki, Honolulu. www.goofy-honolulu.com. © **808/943-0077.** Breakfast $10–$14. Daily 7am–11pm.

Hula Grill Waikiki ★ AMERICAN   The night before, you might be slamming back tiki drinks and making new friends at the ever-popular and rowdy Duke's down below. For the morning after, head to Hula Grill (owned by the same restaurant group as Duke's), where the ocean views, banana-and-macnut pancakes and chewy strawberry mochi waffle will smooth out any hangover. Not so adventurous in the morning? There's standard omelet breakfast fare, too. Breakfast and brunch are the most reasonably priced meals; dinner gets into the $30 range and isn't worth it.

At the Outrigger Waikiki on the Beach, 2335 Kalakaua Ave., Waikiki, Honolulu. www. hulagrillwaikiki.com. © **808/923-HULA** [4852]. Reservations recommended for dinner. Breakfast $7–$14; main courses $21–$35. Daily 6:30am–10pm, 2–6pm (aloha hour with light menu).

Kona Coffee Purveyors ★ CAFE/BAKERY   Don't go anywhere else for coffee and pastries in Waikiki. One of Hawaii's best coffee companies teamed up with one of San Francisco's best pastry chefs, Belinda Leong, and the result is a perfect cup of coffee paired with perfect baked goods. Don't miss the kouign amann, flaky croissant dough crusted with caramelized sugar and layered with flavors such as black sesame or chocolate.

At International Marketplace, 2330 Kalakaua Ave, Waikiki, Honolulu. www.konacoffee purveyors.com. ☎ **808/845-1700.** Pastries $4–$7. Daily 7am–10pm.

Mahina and Sun's ★★ MODERN HAWAIIAN   Local fish is the star at Ed Kenney's latest restaurant (his others, Mud Hen Water (p. 156) and Town (p. 157) are also worth checking out). The sad truth is that in Waikiki, it's hard to find good local seafood. Most of the stuff on menus, from shellfish to salmon, is imported. But you won't find any of that here. Order the Family Feast for the best Mahina and Sun's experience—a whole, mochiko fried local fish arrives to the table, surrounded by fixin's: roasted roots with ogo (seaweed), pohole (fiddlehead fern) salad, buttered ulu (breadfruit), plus oysters, raised on the windward side of Oahu, and to finish, a salted mac nut pavlova.

At Surfjack Hotel, 412 Lewers Street, Waikiki, Honolulu. www.surfjack.com. ☎ **808/924-5810.** Reservations recommended for dinner. Breakfast and lunch $9–$16; dinner entrees $17–$40. Breakfast and lunch daily 6:30am–4:30pm; Dinner Sun–Thurs 5:30–10pm; Fri–Sat until midnight.

Sansei Seafood Restaurant & Sushi Bar ★ SUSHI/PACIFIC RIM   Sushi purists and sticklers for rice/fish ratios need not come. But those looking for creativity in their sushi should make their way to restaurateur D. K. Kodama's most popular spot. The best rolls here don't even have rice, like the moi sashimi wrapped around sweet Maui onions in a pool of ponzu, or the panko-crusted ahi in a soy mustard sauce. Don't miss the crab truffle ramen. *Tip:* Sushi is half off from 10pm to 1am Friday and Saturday, although you might have to put up with some very loud karaoke. Just hope your fellow diners are good singers.

At the Waikiki Beach Marriott Resort, 2552 Kalakaua Ave., 3rd floor, Waikiki, Honolulu. www.sanseihawaii.com. ☎ **808/931-6286.** Reservations recommended. Sushi $3–$18; main courses $16–$35. Sat–Wed 5:30–10pm; Thurs–Fri 5:30pm–1am.

INEXPENSIVE

Maguro Brothers ★★★ SEAFOOD   Poke bowls have swept the continental U.S., but the best one you'll ever have is in Hawaii at this little takeout window. You'll find pristine ahi (tuna) in a variety of poke seasonings, from the classic shoyu (soy sauce and sesame oil) to the bright ume shiso (an herby, pickled plum concoction). If you need a break from poke (though I can't imagine why), don't miss the chirashi donburi featuring a variety of super-fresh sashimi. Better yet, get both. (There's also a Chinatown location inside Kekaulike Market, open for lunch.)

421 Lewers St., Waikiki, Honolulu. ☎ **808/230-3470.** Bowls $9–$14. Mon–Sat 5:30pm–9pm.

going local: **UNIQUELY HAWAIIAN EATS**

Talk to locals who move away from Hawaii, and these are the foods they miss. Everyone's got their own go-to place and go-to dishes—people here could spend hours arguing over the best. Here are some of my favorites:

Poke   Ruby-red cubes of fresh 'ahi (tuna), tossed with limu (seaweed), kukui nut, and Hawaiian chili pepper: Ahi poke (pronounced "po-kay") doesn't get better than the Hawaiian-style version at **Ono Seafood ★★** (p. 147) or any variety at **Maguro Brothers ★★** (p. 145).

Saimin   An only-in-Hawaii mashup of Chinese-style noodles in a Japanese dashi broth. Join the regulars at the communal table at **Palace Saimin,** 1256 N. King St. (☏ **808/841-9983**), where the interior is as simple as this bowl of noodles. Palace Saimin has been around since 1946, and it looks like it. (I mean that in the nicest way possible.)

Loco moco   Two sunny-side up eggs over a hamburger patty and rice, all doused in brown gravy. I love it at **Liliha Bakery ★★** (p. 155).

Spam musubi   Ah yes, Spam. Hawaii eats more Spam per capita than any other state. A dubious distinction to some, but don't knock it before you try it. Spam *musubi* (think of it as a giant sushi topped with Spam) is so ubiquitous you can find it at 7-Elevens and convenience stores (where it's pretty good). But for an even finer product, **Mana Bu,** 1618 S. King St. (☏ **808/358-0287**), is the tops. Get there early; the musubi, made fresh daily, are often sold out by 9am.

Hawaiian plate   *Laulau* (pork wrapped in taro leaves), kālua pig (shredded, roasted pork), poi (milled taro), and *haupia* (like coconut Jell-O): It's Hawaiian lū'au food, based on what native Hawaiians used to eat. Find it at **Helena's Hawaiian Food ★★** (p. 154) and **Highway Inn ★★** (p. 150).

Malasadas   Hole-less doughnuts, rolled in sugar, by way of Portugal. **Leonard's Bakery,** 933 Kapahulu Ave. (☏ **808/737-5571**), opened in 1946 by the descendants of Portuguese contract laborers brought to work in Hawaii's sugarcane fields. I love Leonard's *malasadas* dusted with *li hing mui* powder (made from dried, sweet-tart plums).

Shave ice   Nothing cools better on a hot day than powdery-soft ice drenched in tropical fruit syrups. I go to **Waiola Shave Ice,** 3113 Mokihana St. (☏ **808/735-8886**), for the nostalgia factor, but since you'll probably need more than one shave ice while you're in town, also hit up **Uncle Clay's House of Pure Aloha,** 820 W. Hind Dr. #116 (☏ **808/373-5111**) and at Ala Moana Center, which offers a variety of homemade syrups from real fruit (a rarity).

Marukame Udon ★★ JAPANESE/UDON   There's always a massive line out the door at this cafeteria-style noodle joint, but it moves quickly. Pass the time by watching the cooks roll out and cut the dough for udon right in front of you. Bowls of udon, hot or cold, with toppings such as a soft poached egg or Japanese curry, are all under $7.

2310 Kuhio Ave., Waikiki, Honolulu. www.toridollusa.com. ☏ **808/931-6000.** Noodles $4–$7. Daily 11am–10pm.

Ramen Nakamura ★ JAPANESE/RAMEN   Squeeze into this narrow ramen bar, grab a seat at the U-shaped counter, and get ready to slurp some noodles. It's famous for its oxtail ramen (think of oxtail like ribs—meaty chunks eaten off the bone—but from the tail), served with a side of fresh grated ginger and soy sauce for dipping. The spicy ramen is also a winner.
2141 Kalakaua Ave., Waikiki, Honolulu. ⟨ **808/922-7960.** Noodles $10–$22. Daily 11am–11:30pm.

The Street ★ FOOD HALL   Chef and restaurateur Michael Mina has more than 30 restaurants across the U.S. (and Dubai); this, though not strictly a restaurant, but a lively, upscale food court, is his most fun concept. It brings together seven chefs, each serving a distinct cuisine. Standouts include Mina's own Little Lafa, with Mediterranean flavors on flatbread; barbecue from International Smoke; and shave ice, made from real fruit, at Aloha Ice.
2330 Kalakaua Ave., Waikiki, Honolulu. www.thestreetsocialhouse.com. ⟨ **808/377-4402.** Entrees $11–$30. Daily 11am–9pm.

Waikiki Yokocho ★ JAPANESE FOOD HALL   What used to be a nondescript basement food court has been reimagined as *yokocho*—literally, alleyways off a main street, but often referring to the small bars and eateries in these narrow lanes. Here, you'll find tiny restaurants—some with just a few tables—dishing out tempura, sushi, and ramen, as well as a Japanese whiskey and cocktail bar in the center. For dessert, finish off with a matcha parfait or soft serve at Nana's Green Tea.
At the Waikiki Shopping Plaza, 2250 Kalākaua Ave., Waikiki, Honolulu. www.waikiki-yokocho.com. ⟨ **808/926-8093.** Items from $10. Daily 11am–10pm.

Honolulu Beyond Waikiki

KAPAHULU

Moderate

Side Street Inn on Da Strip ★ LOCAL   This newer and bigger version of Side Street Inn opened in 2010. You can still go to the original one near Ala Moana for the divey, locals-only atmosphere, but I've found that the food is better prepared at this location, even though it's pretty much the same menu of fried pork chops and kimchi fried rice with bacon, Portuguese sausage, and *char siu*. Portion sizes are as big as ever.
614 Kapahulu Ave., Honolulu. www.sidestreetinn.com. ⟨ **808/739-3939.** Starters $8–$14; main courses $13–$23. Mon–Fri 3–11:30pm; Sat–Sun 1–11:30pm.

Inexpensive

Ono Seafood ★★ LOCAL   This little seafood counter serves some of Honolulu's freshest and best poke—cubes of ruby-red ahi (tuna) seasoned to order with soy sauce and onions for the shoyu poke or *limu* (seaweed) and Hawaiian salt for Hawaiian-style poke.
747 Kapahulu Ave., Apt. 4, Honolulu. ⟨ **808/732-4806.** Poke bowls around $8. Mon and Wed–Sat 8am–6pm; Sun 10am–3pm.

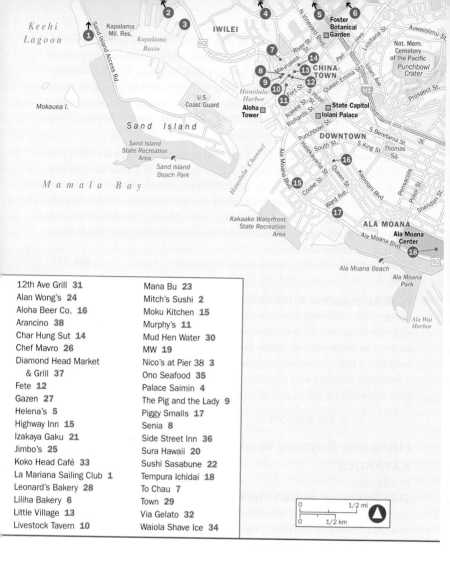

12th Ave Grill 31	Mana Bu 23
Alan Wong's 24	Mitch's Sushi 2
Aloha Beer Co. 16	Moku Kitchen 15
Arancino 38	Murphy's 11
Char Hung Sut 14	Mud Hen Water 30
Chef Mavro 26	MW 19
Diamond Head Market	Nico's at Pier 38 3
& Grill 37	Ono Seafood 35
Fete 12	Palace Saimin 4
Gazen 27	The Pig and the Lady 9
Helena's 5	Piggy Smalls 17
Highway Inn 15	Senia 8
Izakaya Gaku 21	Side Street Inn 36
Jimbo's 25	Sura Hawaii 20
Koko Head Café 33	Sushi Sasabune 22
La Mariana Sailing Club 1	Tempura Ichidai 18
Leonard's Bakery 28	To Chau 7
Liliha Bakery 6	Town 29
Little Village 13	Via Gelato 32
Livestock Tavern 10	Waiola Shave Ice 34

ALA MOANA & KAKAAKO

Expensive

MW ★★ HAWAII REGIONAL CUISINE   Michelle Karr-Ueoka and
Wade Ueoka, the wife-and-husband team in the kitchen, are Alan Wong
alums, and here they give their own take on Hawaii Regional Cuisine.
What that means at MW is local comfort food re-envisioned for fine dining. An ahi poke dish turns the familiar staple into something unexpected,
with spicy tuna, ikura, 'ahi, and uni topped with crispy rice crackers.
Oxtail soup becomes oxtail, deboned and stuffed with more meat, and set
on beef-stew risotto. Desserts outshine the entrees, though, such as a

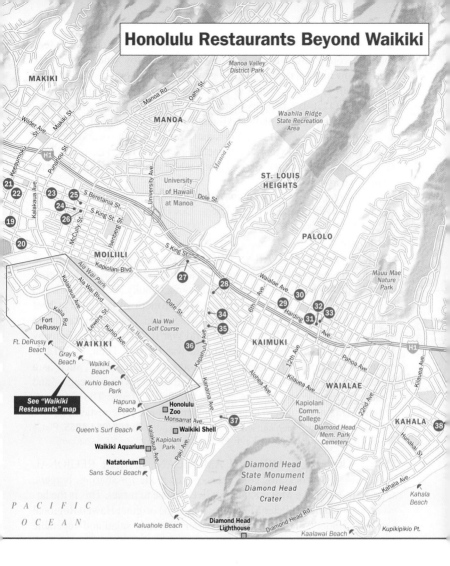

chocolate banana cream pie layered into a jar or a lemon meringue brûlée, full of custard, chewy jellies, and lemon sorbet and sealed with a torched sugar crust. You've never had anything like it.

1538 Kapiolani Blvd., #107, Honolulu. www.mwrestaurant.com. ℰ **808/955-6505.** Reservations recommended. Lunch $14–$26; dinner main courses $24–$36; desserts $9. Mon–Sat 10:30am–10pm; Sun 10:30am–9pm.

Sushi Sasabune ★★ SUSHI   This formerly austere restaurant has been updated with faux maple trees that reflect the progression of seasons. But if you think that means that Seiji Kumagawa, aka the "Sushi Nazi," has also softened up, you'd be mistaken. Sitting at his sushi bar and submitting to the *omakase* menu means you'll eat what he decides to feed you, and you've given up all control of your own soy sauce and wasabi dish. Follow his orders (dip gently in soy sauce only when instructed), and your reward is gorgeous orbs of house-cured *ikura,* scallop dusted with *yuzu kosho* (a citrusy, peppery condiment), mackerel topped with a translucent sheet of seaweed, and fish you may have never heard of. The rice is just as important—watch how Kumagawa molds it, just so, and then feel it break apart softly in your mouth, melding with the fish. This is sushi art. **Tip:** For sushi without the stress, sit at a table, where you're free to order sushi a la carte.

1417 S. King St., Honolulu. © **808/947-3800.** Reservations recommended. Sushi $5–$50; *omakase* $80–$100 per person. Tues–Fri noon–2pm and Tues–Sat 5:30–10pm.

Moderate

Highway Inn ★ HAWAIIAN/LOCAL   The original Highway Inn in Waipahu opened in 1947, serving Hawaiian food such as *laulau* (pork wrapped in taro leaves and steamed), kalua pig (smoky, roasted pork), and poi (mashed taro). Also on the menu: classic American fare such as beef stew and hamburgers, recipes that founder Seiichi Toguchi picked up in internment-camp mess halls during World War II. For decades, Highway Inn remained a snapshot of food in post-war Hawaii. Then, in 2012, it opened a location in Honolulu and introduced a few twists, such as a Smokin' Moco—smoked meat over rice and topped with two eggs—and a hoio salad, made with locally gathered fiddlehead ferns. The old favorites still remain, though, in the newer plantation-era-style restaurant.

680 Ala Moana Blvd., Honolulu. www.myhighwayinn.com. © **808/954-4955.** Plates $10–$14. Mon–Thurs 8:30am–8:30pm; Fri–Sat 8:30am–9pm; Sun 9am–2:30pm.

Moku Kitchen ★ MODERN AMERICAN/ HAWAII REGIONAL CUISINE   Fun cocktails, cold beers, plates made for sharing, burgers, and live music make Moku Kitchen a lively place to refuel. This is the latest concept from chef Peter Merriman, one of the original Hawaii Regional Cuisine founders, and it's a crowd pleaser. The kale salad and vegetable roasted plate are winners for vegetarians, while the prime rib and duck that come out of the rotisserie oven satisfy the carnivores.

660 Ala Moana Blvd., Honolulu. www.mokukitchen.com. © **808/591-6658.** Plates $10–$31. Daily 11am–11pm.

Piggy Smalls ★★ MODERN VIETNAMESE   Don't miss the phostrami at The Pig and the Lady's sibling restaurant; with this being the edgier little brother. The sandwich pairs a pho-spiced beef pastrami with pickled mustard seeds and a side of broth for dipping. Save room for dessert, including a slushy float with flavors that change weekly.

1200 Ala Moana Blvd. Suite 665, Honolulu. www.thepigandthelady.com/piggysmalls. © **808/777-3589.** Plates $14–$20. Mon–Sat 11am–3pm and 5:30–9:30pm; Sun 11am–4pm.

Sura Hawaii ★★ KOREAN This is Honolulu's hippest Korean barbecue restaurant, where different cuts of high-quality pork and beef sizzle on the tabletop grill in front of you. The atmosphere draws young and old alike, with everyone reaching over for bits of meat to dip into the moat of corn cheese and egg custard warmed by the grill. Servers are quick and cheerful—call them by pressing a button on the table—and happy to replenish the *banchan,* or little side dishes, until you can't eat anymore. If only all eating experiences were this fun!

1726 Kapiolani Blvd., Honolulu. www.sura-hawaii.com. © **808/941-6678.** Reservations recommended. Combo meal for 2–3 people $44–$55. Sun–Thurs 11am–1am; Fri–Sat 11am–2am.

Tempura Ichidai ★ JAPANESE This is the tempura version of a cocktail bar, serving the best tempura on the island. Sit at the counter and watch the chefs fry each piece right in front of you and place it on the rack on your plate in stages (so it doesn't get soggy from the steam). The tempura is light, crisp, and practically greaseless. The impeccably fresh sashimi is terrific, too.

At Ala Moana Shopping Center, third floor. 1450 Ala Moana Blvd., Honolulu. www.tempuraichidai.com. © **808/955-8899.** Entrees $15–$29. Daily 11am–10pm.

Inexpensive

Aloha Beer Co. ★ BREWERY Drinking in carports, like the poor man's lanai, is a Hawaii thing. You can approximate it at this craft brewery's warehouse digs, where the atmosphere is casual and the tables communal. Choose from about a dozen beers, some seasonal and experimental, which range from light session beers to extra-hoppy IPAs. Pair them with any of the hearty sandwiches or the excellent bratwurst.

700 Queen St., Honolulu. www.alohabeer.com. © **808/544-1605.** Sandwiches and small plates $9–$16. Mon–Sat 4pm–11pm.

DOWNTOWN/CHINATOWN

Moderate

Fête ★ MODERN AMERICAN In a space that's come to define the new modern Chinatown aesthetic—lofty ceilings and redbrick walls—chef Robynne Maii serves the food she craves. What that means: polished comfort food with no boundaries. You'll find a carbonara with Portuguese sausage, a textbook-perfect burger, and a kalbi-marinated bavette steak. This is also one of my favorite places for a cocktail, from the classics to those with subtle hints of the Pacific.

2 N. Hotel St., Honolulu. www.fetehawaii.com. © **808/369-1390.** Entrees $18–$55. Mon–Thurs 11am–10pm; Fri–Sat 11am–11pm.

Little Village Noodle House ★ CHINESE For almost every year it's been open, Little Village has been awarded Best Chinese Restaurant by readers of local publications. It's Chinese food geared toward local tastes, but that doesn't mean it's not tasty. Added plus: a clean, charming interior decorated with Christmas lights and bamboo, a nice change from the sometimes harsh spaces of Chinatown's other restaurants. I like the Shanghai mochi stir fry, honey walnut shrimp, dried green beans, and beef chow fun. 1113 Smith St., Honolulu. www.littlevillagehawaii.com. © **808/545-3008.** Most items under $17. Sun–Thurs 10:30am–10pm; Fri–Sat 10:30am–midnight.

Livestock Tavern ★★ AMERICAN   For the past 2 decades, restaurateurs and artists have been trying to revitalize Chinatown, which, in the second half of the 20th century, became more well known as a red-light district than a place to eat and hang out. Restaurateurs Jesse Cruz and Dusty Grable have helped make Chinatown a destination with their eateries—**Lucky Belly,** which serves modern Asian comfort food; **Tchin Tchin!,** a bar and lounge with an incomparable wine list; and **Livestock Tavern.** All are great, but Livestock Tavern is my favorite, serving modern American food at its finest, with an excellent cocktail menu to boot. The menu changes seasonally (yes, even Hawaii has seasons, however subtle), with heartier dishes like a mushroom bread pudding in the winter and lighter options such as the grilled catch of the day in the summer. The hamburger is a staple on the menu, and it's one of Honolulu's best. 49 N. Hotel St., Honolulu. www.livestocktavern.com. © **808/537-2577.** Reservations recommended. Main courses $16–$32. Mon–Sat 11am–2pm and 5–10pm.

Murphy's Bar and Grill ★ IRISH   Maybe you didn't come to Honolulu to hang out in an Irish bar. But if you did, Murphy's is the place to be. At lunch, it's packed with downtown businessmen tucking into Blarney Burgers (a hamburger with Guinness cheese) or open-face turkey sandwiches. After work, this is one of Honolulu's favorite *pau hana* (afterwork) spots with great wings, local beers on draft (get anything from Maui Brewing Co.), and some of the friendliest bartenders in town. You would expect nothing less from an Irish bar. 2 Merchant St., Honolulu. www.murphyshawaii.com. © **808/531-0422.** Main courses $12–$23. Lunch daily 11:30am–2:30pm; dinner Sun–Wed 5:30–9pm; Thurs–Sat 5:30–10pm.

The Pig and the Lady ★★★ MODERN VIETNAMESE   It's one of Chinatown's liveliest dining rooms, with brick walls, long communal tables hewed from single slabs of mango wood, benches reupholstered with burlap rice bags, and a rotating display of fun, bright prints by local, young artists. The Pig and the Lady introduces you to a world of Vietnamese noodle soups beyond pho—such as one with oxtail, another with crab and tomato. But Chef Andrew Le also applies creative twists to Southeast Asian food for unique eats like a pho French dip banh mi—an absolute must with its melting slices of braised brisket, smeared with a bright Thai basil chimichurri and served with a side of pho broth for dipping. Everything is en pointe here, from the cocktails to the dessert. 83 N. King St., Honolulu. www.thepigandthelady.com. © **808/383-2152.** Reservations recommended. Main courses $11–$30. Mon–Fri 10:30am–2pm; Sat 10:30am–3pm; Tues–Sat 5:30–10pm.

Senia ★★★ MODERN AMERICAN   This is one of Honolulu's newest and most exciting restaurants, where something as ordinary as cabbage can surprise and delight. Senia, deriving from "xenia," the Greek word for hospitality, is a rare mesh of the fine dining and comfort food worlds. The food is fancy—bone marrow custard, foie gras terrine, and pretty presentations of smoked salmon with date and cauliflower—but the flavors are accessible, the setting leans casual, and the prices are moderate. The menu changes frequently, but will always be a combination of surprise and comfort.
75 N. King St., Honolulu. www.restaurantsenia.com ℂ **808/200-5412.** Reservations recommended. Small plates $12–$22. Mon–Sat 5:30–10pm.

Inexpensive

Char Hung Sut ★ LOCAL CHINESE   For locals, this 60-year-old Chinatown institution is synonymous with *manapua,* Hawaii's version of Chinese *char siu bao.* At Char Hung Sut, they're big, fluffy steamed buns stuffed with slightly sweet, shredded pork. Go early and watch them being made right in front of you. It's takeout only here—the shop is more factory than restaurant. Also try the pork hash (also known as *siu mai* on the Mainland)—juicy ground pork steamed in wonton-style wrappers.
64 N. Pauahi St., Honolulu. ℂ **808/538-3335.** Under $10. Cash only. Mon and Wed–Sat 5:30am–2pm; Sun 5:30am–1pm.

To Chau ★ VIETNAMESE PHO   Is there anything on the menu other than pho? I couldn't even tell you. I just walk in, order a medium number 9, meat outside, and iced coffee with milk. What arrives: strong, black coffee percolating into a mug and a cup of ice and condensed milk. When the coffee is finished brewing, dump it into the cup and stir. By that time, you'll have a plate mounded with bean sprouts, Thai basil, sawtooth coriander, jalapeños, and lemon wedges. Soon after, the bowl of pho arrives, with flank, tendon, and tripe, as well as slices of rare steak on the side to dip into the hot brothlike fondue. You can also get your pho with all the meat in and just steak if you want; there are 14 possible combinations.

4

OAHU | Where to Eat on Oahu

That's the only hard choice in this Chinatown eatery. Getting the pho and Vietnamese coffee shouldn't be one.

1007 River St., Honolulu. © **808/533-4549.** Reservations not accepted. All items under $10. Cash only. Mon–Fri 8:30am–2:30pm.

KALIHI/LILIHA/SAND ISLAND
Moderate
La Mariana Sailing Club ★ AMERICAN   Only one authentic vintage tiki bar remains in Honolulu, and it's in the industrial wasteland near the airport (which makes it awfully convenient to have your last drink here before getting on the plane). But once you enter, you'll feel as if you've stepped back into 1955, the year La Mariana opened. It's pure kitsch, with glass floats and puffer fish lamps hanging from the ceiling. Come for a mai tai or a Zombie and watch the sunset over the docked sailboats. Stay for the live piano entertainment nightly, when regulars croon their favorite Hawaiian and American songs. You're here more for the ambience and entertainment than for the forgettable food.

50 Sand Island Rd., Honolulu. www.lamarianasailingclub.com. © **808/848-2800.** Reservations recommended, especially Sat–Sun. Main courses $8–$16 lunch, $15–$29 dinner. Daily 11am–9pm. Turn *makai* (toward the ocean) on Sand Island Rd. from Nimitz Hwy.; immediately after the first light on Sand Island, take a right and drive toward the ocean; it's not far from the airport.

Mitch's Sushi ★★ SUSHI   The family that owns Mitch's Sushi also owns a seafood import business, which is why Mitch's has some of the freshest fish around. It's one of Honolulu's most expensive sushi bars, as well as its most casual, a place where slippers (local lingo for flip-flops) and T-shirts are the norm, along with a cooler of beer (Mitch's is BYOB). Here you'll find New Zealand salmon, as luxurious as fatty tuna belly, and Mitch's famous lobster sashimi, which you inspect as it's brought to your table, alive and kicking, and then sample in the form of sashimi and lobster miso soup.

524 Ohohia St., Honolulu. www.mitchssushi.com. © **808/837-7774.** Reservations recommended. Sushi $4–$30. Daily 11:30am–8:30pm.

Inexpensive
Helena's Hawaiian Food ★★ HAWAIIAN   Definitely seek out this humble little restaurant, winner of the James Beard Regional Classics award in 2000. When first-generation-Chinese Helen Chock started Helena's in 1946 (she added an "a" at the end to make it sound more "Hawaiian"), she served Chinese and Hawaiian food. Eventually, she pared down the menu to the most popular items—Hawaiian food such as *laulau*, kalua pig, and poi. Sixty years later, her grandson runs the place, and it's as popular as ever. What makes Helena's stand out among other Hawaiian food restaurants? The *pipikaula:* marinated, bone-in short ribs hung above the stove to dry and fried right before they land on your table.

1240 N. School St., Honolulu. www.helenashawaiianfood.com. © **808/845-8044.** Full meals $9–$20. Cash only. Tues–Fri 10am–7:30pm.

Liliha Bakery ★ AMERICAN/LOCAL   It's a bakery, well known for its Coco Puffs (similar to cream puffs), but it's also one of Oahu's favorite old-school diners, beloved by young and old alike. Sit at the counter and watch the ladies expertly man the flattop and grill, turning out light and fluffy pancakes, crisp and seriously buttery waffles, loaded country-style omelets, and satisfying hamburgers and hamburger steaks. There's a newer location on Nimitz, but I prefer the ambience of the original.

515 N. Kuakini St., Honolulu. www.lilihabakeryhawaii.com. ℂ **808/531-1651.** Most items under $10. Open 24 hr. from Tues at 6am to Sun at 8pm.

Nico's at Pier 38 ★ FRESH FISH   Nico's has expanded from a hole-in-the-wall to a gleaming, open-air restaurant almost four times its original size. The food isn't quite as good as it used to be, but it's still one of the best places around to get fresh fish plates for under $20. I also love its setting along the industrial waterfront, where Hawaii's commercial fishing fleet resides—this isn't a fake fisherman's wharf but the real deal. Popular dishes here are the furikake pan-seared 'ahi and the catch-of-the-day special—perhaps opah sauced with tomato beurre blanc or swordfish topped with crab bisque (the chef, Nico Chaize, is French born). As part of the expansion, there's also a fish market next door where you can take out fresh poke and smoked swordfish to eat on the tables outside. Renting a place with a kitchen? Pick up fresh fish filets to take home and cook. (There's also a new location in Kailua.)

Pier 38, 1129 N. Nimitz Hwy., Honolulu. www.nicospier38.com. ℂ **808/540-1377.** Takeout orders accepted by phone. Lunch $8–$13; dinner $14–$26. Mon–Sat 6:30am–9pm; Sun 10am–9pm.

MANOA VALLEY/MOILIILI/MAKIKI
Expensive
Alan Wong's Restaurant ★ HAWAII REGIONAL CUISINE   Alan Wong was one of the founders of Hawaii Regional Cuisine, which championed Hawaii farmers and local flavors back in the '90s when most restaurants were of the Continental variety and flying in frozen seafood and meat. Wong brought uniquely local flavors to the fine-dining table, in dishes such as a ginger-crusted onaga, soy-braised short ribs, and *li hing mui* tomato salad. To this day, Alan Wong's remains one of Honolulu's best restaurants. The menu retains many of the classics, but for newer dishes, try the chef's tasting menu, which features the kitchen's latest, creative dishes, such as a pan-seared *opakapaka* on kimchi risotto or Maui Cattle Co. rib steak with a beef and foie gras "burger."

1857 S. King St., 3rd floor, Honolulu. www.alanwongs.com. ℂ **808/949-2526.** Reservations highly recommended. Main courses $28–$55; tasting menu $85 ($125 with wine). Daily 5–10pm.

Chef Mavro Restaurant ★★ HAWAII REGIONAL CUISINE   James Beard Award–winner George Mavrothalassitis melds his French background with pristine Hawaiian ingredients for one of Hawaii's top fine-dining experiences. The menu changes quarterly to reflect the seasons. A recent menu featured onaga baked in a Hawaiian salt crust, lamb loin with a vadouvan curry, and liliko'i malasadas. Four- and six-course menus are offered. Wine is only available as pairings for each course, which elevates the experience to divine.

1969 S. King St., Honolulu. www.chefmavro.com. ℂ **808/944-4714.** Reservations recommended. Prix-fixe menu $105–$148 ($162–$211 with wine pairings). Tues–Sun 6–9pm.

Sushi Izakaya Gaku ★★★ JAPANESE   There is life beyond maguro and hamachi nigiri, and the best place to experience it is at Izakaya Gaku. The Izakaya restaurants embrace small plates as the best way to eat and drink with friends; although Honolulu offers many of them, Izakaya Gaku is the best. Here you can get uncommon seasonal sushi and seafood, such as wild yellowtail and grilled ray. One of the best dishes here is a hamachi tartare, with hamachi scraped off the bones and topped with tobiko and raw quail egg, served with sheets of crisp nori. But you're not likely to be disappointed with any dish.

1329 S. King St., Honolulu. ℂ **808/589-1329.** Reservations highly recommended. Sashimi $12–$40; small plates $4–$13. Mon–Sat 5–11pm.

Moderate
Gazen ★★ JAPANESE/SUSHI   This spot, perpetually packed with locals, is the best of the mid-range *izakaya,* a Japanese pub with snacks made for sharing. Don't miss the fresh, homemade tofu sampler (it will change your opinion of tofu forever); mochi agedashi (fried sticky rice balls in dashi); daikon salad, an explosion of textures; and the fresh fish carpaccio. Finish off with the fried sweet potato mochi.

2840 Kapiolani Blvd., Honolulu. www.e-k-c.co.jp/gazen/honolulu. ℂ **808/737-0230.** Reservations recommended. Plates $7–$50. Thurs–Tue 4:30–11pm.

Inexpensive
Jimbo's Restaurant ★ JAPANESE   Jimbo's offers fresh noodles made by hand—or should we say foot? To give the udon noodles their characteristic chew, Jimbo's cooks stomp on the noodle dough (wrapped, of course) before rolling it out. Enjoy it cold with a dipping sauce or hot in a shoyu and dashi-based broth. For sumo-sized appetites, get the *nabeyaki* udon, brought to the table in a heavy pot and filled with udon, vegetable and shrimp tempura, chicken, and an egg.

1936 S. King St., Honolulu. ℂ **808/947-2211.** Main courses $10–$14. Daily 11am–2:30pm and 5–9:45pm (Fri–Sat until 10:30pm).

KAIMUKI
Moderate
Mud Hen Water ★ MODERN HAWAIIAN   This is the sister restaurant to Town (see below). Whereas Town is Italian in its flavors, Mud Hen Water draws inspiration from all of the cultures influencing Hawaii. What that translates into: mapo tofu gravy and biscuits for brunch and *ia lawalu,*

fish wrapped in a banana leaf and grilled over an open fire. You won't find dishes like this anywhere else. Plates are small and made for sharing.

3452 Waialae Ave. (at 9th St.), Honolulu. www.mudhenwater.com. © **808/737-6000.** Reservations highly recommended for dinner. Small plates $8–$28. Tues–Sat 5:30–10pm (Fri–Sat until midnight).

Town ★ CONTEMPORARY ITALIAN   Town's motto is "Local first, organic whenever possible, with Aloha always." Chef/owner Ed Kenney lovingly showcases local ingredients: in a pork sugo on the lightest gnocchi you may ever have, or as the seasonal produce tossed with hand-cut pasta. Kenney definitely has a way with pork: If you see it on the menu—as charcuterie, porchetta, or roasted shoulder—get it. I also love the mussels in a fennel and Cinzano broth. Order it with a side of fries, and use them to soak up all the goodness. Also worth checking out: **Kaimuki Superette** across the street, Chef Kenney's casual breakfast and lunch spot specializing in sandwiches.

3435 Waialae Ave. (at 9th St.), Honolulu. www.townkaimuki.com. © **808/735-5900.** Reservations highly recommended for dinner. Main courses $9–$16 lunch, $16–$26 dinner. Mon–Sat 7am–2:30pm and 5:30–9:30pm (Fri–Sat until 10pm).

12th Ave Grill ★ CONTEMPORARY AMERICAN   Outside of Waikiki and the Keeaumoku region, Honolulu lacks dense, walkable neighborhoods—it's more like L.A. than San Francisco. One of the few urban neighborhoods is Kaimuki, with a cluster of some of Honolulu's best restaurants. This is one of them, with a menu leaning towards comfort food, like baked mac 'n' cheese, and locally raised meat, such as pork chops with potato pancakes and rib eye on fresh pappardelle. Another reason why I love this place? It's the rare restaurant that serves good food *and* good cocktails. *Tip:* Sit in the bar area during opening or closing hours, when the bar serves a special menu of extremely satisfying hamburgers and meatloaf sandwiches, and nothing costs more than $10.

1120 12th Ave., Honolulu. www.12thavegrill.com. © **808/732-9469.** Reservations recommended. Small plates $7–$13; large plates $23–$36. Daily 5:30–11pm.

Inexpensive

Koko Head Café ★ BREAKFAST/BRUNCH   This "island-style brunch house" offers inspired takes on breakfast favorites. There's the cornflake French toast, extra crunchy on the outside and custardy on the inside, crowned with frosted flake gelato, and the Don Buri Chen, a rice bowl for carnivores, with miso-smoked pork, five-spice pork belly, and eggs.

1145c 12th Ave., Honolulu. www.kokoheadcafe.com. © **808/732-8920.** Main courses $9–$16. Daily 7am–2:30pm.

Via Gelato ★ DESSERT   When you've had your fill of shave ice, come here for gelato churned daily in island-inspired flavors such as guava, lychee, strawberry, and *ume* (salted plum). It's a tough decision, though, choosing between those and other favorites such as green tea

Oreo and black sesame. The flavors change daily. Be sure to get here early on weekend nights before they run out.

1142 12th Ave., Honolulu. www.viagelatohawaii.com. ℂ **808/732-2800.** Scoops starting at $3. Tues–Sun 11am–10pm (Fri–Sat until 11pm).

TO THE EAST: DIAMOND HEAD & KāHALA

Expensive

Arancino at the Kahala ★★ MODERN ITALIAN   This, Arancino's third location (the other two are in Waikiki), opened in 2013. Befitting its new digs, it isn't a casual trattoria; it's meant to be a fine-dining destination with a dress code (pants and shoes required for men). Menu standouts include a *bagna cauda,* with the vegetables planted in a pot of cremini mushroom "dirt"; grilled calamari, shrimp, and seafood over housemade squid-ink chitarra; and a decadent uni spaghetti. For a town surprisingly short on alfresco dining, especially outside of Waikiki, Arancino at the Kahala is a breath of fresh air (even if it is facing the Kahala Resort's valet).

At the Kahala Hotel Resort, 5000 Kahala Ave., Honolulu. www.kahalaresort.com. ℂ **808/380-4400.** Reservations recommended. Collared shirts and long pants required for men. Main courses $18–$32 lunch; $18–$80 dinner. Daily 11:30am–2:30pm and 5–9:30pm.

Inexpensive

Diamond Head Market & Grill ★ AMERICAN/LOCAL   Here you'll find some of our favorite plate lunches, near the base of Diamond Head. For breakfast, the pancakes with mac nuts or pineapple are a winner, or start the morning with a savory plate like the kimchi fried rice. Lunch and dinner offer tasty ahi steaks and kalbi (Korean-marinated short ribs). Don't miss dessert: The lemon crunch cake is the perfect capper to a Diamond Head hike.

3158 Monsarrat Ave., Honolulu. www.diamondheadmarket.com. ℂ **808/732-0077.** Plates $6–$17. Daily 6:30am–9pm.

East Oahu

Expensive

Roy's Restaurant ★ HAWAII REGIONAL CUISINE   This is the original Roy's, the one that launched more than 30 Roy's restaurants around the world (6 of them in Hawaii). One of Hawaii Regional Cuisine's most famous founders, Roy Yamaguchi started fusing local flavors and ingredients with European techniques some 20 years ago. The original menu items are still here, such as blackened island ahi with spicy soy mustard and Roy's famous melting-hot chocolate soufflé. Sit on the lanai to watch the sunset over Maunalua Bay.

6600 Kalanianaole Hwy., Hawaii Kai. www.roysrestaurant.com. ℂ **808/396-7697.** Reservations recommended. Main courses $20–$40; 3-course prix-fixe $42. Mon–Thurs 5:30–9pm; Fri 5:30–9:30pm; Sat 5–9:30pm; Sun 5–9pm.

The Shrimp Trucks

Shrimp farming took hold in Kahuku in the '90s and, before long, the first shrimp truck set up, serving fresh shrimp from a lunch wagon window. Now you can smell the garlic cooking before you see all the trucks and shrimp shacks—at least five, by last count. **Giovanni's Original White Shrimp Truck,** 56-505 Kamehameha Hwy. (© **808/293-1839**), is the most popular—so popular that a makeshift food court with picnic tables, shade, and a handful of other businesses has sprung up around the beat-up old white truck scrawled with tourists' signatures. Even though the shrimp are now imported and previously frozen, Giovanni's knows how to cook them perfectly. Scampi style is my favorite—shell-on shrimp coated in lots of butter and garlic. Twelve bucks gets you a dozen, plus two scoops of rice. Head north from Giovanni's about a mile, and you'll hit **Romy's,** 56-781 Kamehameha Hwy. (© **808/232-2202**), a shrimp shack instead of a truck. Here the shrimp actually come from the farm behind it. Romy's is my favorite for the sauce—tons of sautéed and fried garlic over a half-pound of head-on shrimp, plus a container of spicy soy sauce for dipping. The shrimp, however, are inconsistent—sometimes firm and sweet, sometimes mealy.

The Windward Coast

Note: The following restaurants are located on the "Eastern Oahu & the Windward Coast" map (p. 97).

Moderate

Prima ★ ITALIAN Oahu's best Neopolitan-style pizzas come out of the wood-burning oven at Prima. What that translates into: a thin crust that gives way to puffy edges, spare toppings, fresh-pulled mozzarella, and a bright, San Marzano tomato sauce. Sample a classic margherita pizza or my favorite, the Five P, with pickled piquillo pepper, pepperoncini, and pepperoni.
108 Hekili St. #107, Kailua. www.primahawaii.com. © **808/888-8933.** Pizzas $16–$22. Sun–Thurs 10am–9pm; Fri–Sat 10am–9:30pm.

Inexpensive

Ai Love Nalo ★ LOCAL/VEGAN This roadside gem offers a plant-based take on local favorites, such as the *laulau,* here a package of *kalo* (taro, a staple in the Hawaiian diet), *ulu* (breadfruit), Okinawan sweet potato, and carrot, all bundled in a *luau* leaf (taro leaf) and slow-cooked in coconut milk. Everything is lovely and full of flavor. Try the poi parfait or the soft serve, both topped with fresh, seasonal fruit and toasted cacao coconut flakes.
41-1025 Kalanianaole Hwy., Waimanalo. www.ailovenalo.com. © **808/888-9102.** Everything under $11. Wed–Mon 9am–5pm.

Hale Kealoha Restaurant ★ LOCAL Eating here feels like hanging out at a friend's backyard lū 'au, complete with foldout picnic tables and chairs and Christmas lights. On Saturday nights, there's even live Hawaiian music. Order the Pa Paina plate for the full experience, a Hawaiian

LUAU!

The sun is setting, the tiki torches are lit, the pig is taken from the *imu* (an oven in the earth), the *pu* (conch) sounds—it's luau time! Few experiences say "Hawaii" to visitors as the luau. In ancient times, the luau was called *aha aina* (*aha* means means gathering and *aina*, land); these were celebrations with family and friends to mark important occasions, such as a victory at war or a baby surviving its first year. Luau are still a part of life in Hawaii; in particular, the legacy of the baby's first luau lives on.

For visitors, luau are a way to experience a feast of food and entertainment, Hawaiian style. The luau at the **Royal Hawaiian,** 2259 Kalakaua Ave. (www.royal-hawaiian.com; ✆ **888/808-4668**), is the priciest of all the options, but it's the only beachfront one in Waikiki and it

offers the best food, an open bar, and quality entertainment. It takes place every Monday from 5:30 to 9pm and costs $179 for adults, $101 for children 5 to 12.

About an hour outside of Waikiki on the Leeward coast, **Paradise Cove Luau,** 92-1089 Alii Nui Dr., Kapolei (www.paradisecovehawaii.com; ✆ **808/842-5911**), is a popular option. It has a lovely setting, perfect for sunset photos, and the evening starts with arts and crafts and activities for kids. As for the buffet, you'll find better food at the Hawaiian restaurants listed on p. 141. Waikiki bus pickup and return is included in the package prices: Paradise Cove's luau is nightly at 6pm and costs $85 to $156 for adults, $75 to $137 for teens 13 to 18, $65 to $123 for children 4 to 12, and free for children 3 and under.

plate lunch with all the fixin's—kalua pig, chicken long rice, squid luau, lomi salmon, poke, rice, poi, haupia, uala (sweet potato), and mamaki tea.

120 Hekili St., Kailua. www.halekealoharestaurant.com. ℂ **808/262-1100.** Plates $10–$28. Wed–Thurs 10am–8pm, Fri–Sat 10am–10pm.

Moke's Bread and Breakfast ★ BREAKFAST/BRUNCH Of all the pancake joints in Kailua, Moke's is my pick—their *lilikoi* pancakes are unparalleled. A light passion fruit cream sauce cascades over tender, fluffy pancakes, a perfect blend of tart and sweet, simple and decadent. Other staples, such as the loco moco and omelets, are also spot-on.

27 Hoolai St., Kailua. www.mokeskailua.com. ℂ **808/261-5565.** Entrees $8–$14. Wed–Mon 6:30am–2pm.

Over Easy ★ BREAKFAST/BRUNCH There's stiff competition in the brunch market in Kailua, so when Over Easy opened up we wondered, Do we really need another breakfast spot? Judging from the lines, yes, we do. There's a lot of care put into the short menu, from the light, crisp-edged pancakes to the kalua pig hash, brightened with a green goddess dressing.

418 Kuulei Rd. Kailua. www.overeasyhi.com. ℂ **808/260-1732.** Entrees $8–$14. Tues–Fri 7am–1pm, Sat–Sun 7am–1:30pm.

Waiahole Poi Factory ★ LOCAL On your way up the Windward side, stop by this ramshackle, roadside spot (one side is a gallery for Native Hawaiian arts). You'll find the classic Hawaiian plate lunch, with smoky kalua pig, succulent laulau, and fresh poi made onsite. Linger a little longer over the kulolo (a sticky dessert made with taro and coconut), served warm and topped with a scoop of coconut ice cream.

48-140 Kamehameha Hwy., Waiahole. www.waiaholepoifactory.com. ℂ **808/239-2222.** Plates $7.50–$12. Daily 10am–6pm.

The North Shore

Note: The following are on the "Oahu's North Shore" map (p. 105).

Moderate

Haleiwa Beach House ★ AMERICAN/LOCAL When you tire of the North Shore food trucks, come here. This newly renovated restaurant opens up to a fabulous view of Haleiwa beach park; come during *pau hana* (happy hour) when you can watch the sun set. Menu highlights include whole fried fish, kalua pig grilled cheese, and Beach House fries—thick, spiral-cut fries tossed with garlic and furikake.

62-540 Kamehameha Hwy., Haleiwa. ℂ **808/637-3435.** Lunch $12–$29; dinner $26–$36. Daily 11am–11pm.

Inexpensive

Beet Box Café ★ VEGETARIAN For me, a perfect day on the North Shore involves waves and a stop at Beet Box. Warm wood paneling (upcycled, of course) welcomes you into the space. Veggie-forward fare comes in the form of satisfying sandwiches with portobello and feta or avocado and local greens. The breakfast burritos and smoothies are popular, too.

66-437 Kamehameha Hwy., Haleʻiwa. www.thebeetboxcafe.com. © **808/637-3000.** Breakfast and lunch $8–$12. Daily 7am–4pm.

The Elephant Shack ★ THAI From truck to shack, this formerly roving mobile operation now has a cheerful, permanent spot with lots of outside seating that's particularly charming at night, when the tabletop lanterns cast a warm glow. It serves up simple and fresh Thai food such as fish tossed in a tangy chili and lime vinaigrette or bamboo and chicken stir-fried with slightly chewy glass noodles. Staples such as green curry and pad thai are solid. Extra bonus: the menu is vegan-friendly, too.

66-145 Kamehameha Hwy., Haleiwa. www.808elephant.com © **808/638-1854.** Dishes $11–$19. Daily noon–9pm.

Kahuku Farms ★ SANDWICHES & SNACKS Not a fan of shrimp? Then stop by Kahuku Farms' Farm Café, where you can get a simple grilled veggie panini made with veggies all grown right here on the farm, and a smoothie with papaya and banana, also grown here. If I'm driving up this way, I always try to stop for the grilled banana bread topped with caramel and *haupia* (coconut) sauce and a scoop of ice cream. Yup, so decadent and so good.

56-800 Kamehameha Hwy., Kahuku. www.kahukufarms.com. © **808/293-8159.** Items $8–$10. Wed–Mon 11am–4pm.

Leeward Oahu: The Waianae Coast

Moderate

Monkeypod Kitchen ★ AMERICAN This is the best dining option at Ko Olina Station, a strip mall of casual eateries servicing Ko Olina Resort. One of the latest ventures from Peter Merriman, who pioneered farm-to-table fine dining on the Big Island in the '80s, Monkeypod is a larger, more casual restaurant (with another location on Maui). The vibe in this two-story space is welcoming and friendly, with live music on the lānai and a long bar with 36 (!) beers on tap. Expect fresh salads and entrees like fish and chips and burgers. I always go for the saimin, which is nothing like the traditional version you'll find elsewhere; here it comes with kalua pork and fresh vegetables. To drink: the bracingly zingy house-made ginger beer. *Tip:* Want a more intimate bar experience? Head upstairs, where the bartenders spend a little more time making your cocktails, which include fresh takes on the mai tai (topped with a honey *lilikoi* foam) and the Makawao Ave., made with rye and that terrific ginger beer.

At Ko Olina Station, 92-1048 Olani St., Suite 4-107, Kapolei. www.monkeypodkitchen. com. © **808/380-4086.** Reservations recommended. Main courses $12–$35. Daily 11am–11pm.

Inexpensive

Kahumana Café ★ FARM   The fare here is simple but fresh and tasty; the setting is right on an organic farm. Enjoy a salad or fresh veggie stir-fry while overlooking the herbs and vegetables grown right there. There aren't a lot of eating options on the west side, which makes Kahumana Café even more welcome.

86-660 Lualualei Homestead Rd., Waianae. www.kahumana.org. ✆ **808/696-2655.** Main courses $10–$15. Tues–Sat 11:30am–2:30pm and 6–8pm. Head up Farrington Hwy. and turn right on Mailiili Rd. Go straight for 2 miles, past Puhawai Rd. Continue until you reach the Kahumana gate. The cafe is the blue building at the end of the driveway.

OAHU SHOPPING

The trend in Honolulu shopping of late has been toward luxury brands, catering to Japanese (and increasingly, Chinese) tourists and leading to the demise, at the end of 2013, of the International Marketplace. Truthfully, the open-air Waikiki marketplace had become a maze of kitschy junk, but it had a 56-year run, long enough for many people to feel sentimental about it. In its place the high-end **International Marketplace mall** anchored by Saks Fifth Avenue opened in 2016.

You can also find plenty of luxury goods at the new **Ala Moana Center** wing. But just as the luxury market is growing, so is Honolulu's boutique culture and the vitality of the local crafts scene, as artisans endeavor to capture what makes Hawaii so unique. You'll find the best boutique shopping in Chinatown and Haleiwa, but you'll find gems even at the malls.

Shopping in & Around Honolulu & Waikiki
CLOTHING

The **aloha shirt** is alive and well, thanks to a revival of vintage aloha wear and the modern take, which features more subdued prints and slimmer silhouettes.

Vintage 1930s to 1950s Hawaiian wear is still beautiful, found in collectibles shops, such as the packed-to-the-rafters **Bailey's Antiques and Aloha Shirts,** 517 Kapahulu Ave. (✆ **808/734-7628**). Of the contemporary aloha-wear designers, one of the best Oahu-based ones is **Tori Richard,** who creates tasteful tropical prints in the form of linen and silk shirts for men and flowy dresses for women. **Reyn Spooner,** Ala Moana Center (www.reynspooner.com; ✆ **808/949-5929;** with four other Oahu locations), is another source of attractive aloha shirts in traditional and contemporary styles; the new Modern Collection appeals to younger tastes, combining more fitted sleeves and a 1960s preppy look with some of Reyn Spooner's classic prints. Also check out **Kahala Sportswear,** Ala Moana Center (www.kahala.com; ✆ **808/941-2444;** with two other Oahu

World's largest aloha shirt

locations in Waikiki and Haleiwa), which has been designing aloha shirts since 1936 and remains an island favorite.

The hippest guys and gals go to **Roberta Oaks,** 19 N. Pauahi St. (www.robertaoaks.com; ℭ **808/428-1214**), in Chinatown, where a slew of trendy boutiques has opened in recent years. Roberta Oaks ditches the too-big aloha shirt for a more stylish, fitted look, but keeps the vintage designs. Plus, she even has super-cute, tailored aloha shirts for the ladies. New to Chinatown, but a fixture in Hilo on Hawaii Island and in politicians' closets are Sig Zane aloha shirts. At the Honolulu outpost, **Sig on Smith,** 1020 Smith St. (www.sigzanedesigns.com), you'll find Zane's designs inspired by native Hawaiian culture, such as plants significant to hula and patterns based off of Hawaiian legends. The Chinatown location also features limited-release capsule collections: visit the shop's Instagram (www.instagram.com/sigonsmith) to see the latest.

Just 2 years after its launch, **Manaola,** Ala Moana Center (www.manaolahawaii.com; ℭ **808/944-8011**) debuted to an international audience with its own runway show at New York Fashion Week. Native Hawaiian designer Manaola Yap creates clothing for both men and women, with prints that rely on repetition and symmetry to convey Hawaii's natural beauty and oral stories.

EDIBLES

Nisshodo Candy Store ★   Mochi (Japanese rice cake) is so essential to locals' lives that even the drugstores sell it. But for the freshest and widest variety, go straight to the source: Nisshodo, an almost century-old business. Choose among pink-and-white *chichi dango* (or milk mochi), mochi filled with smooth azuki bean, *monaka* (delicate rice wafers sandwiching sweetened lima-bean paste), and much more. 1095 Dillingham Blvd. www.nisshodomochicandy.com. ☏ **808/847-1244.**

Padovani's Chocolates ★   Brothers Philippe and Pierre Padovani are two of Hawaii's best chefs, involved with the Hawaii Regional Cuisine movement. In recent years, they've been devoting their attention to choco-late truffles. Their edible gems come in delightful flavors such as a cala-mansi (a small Filipino lime) and pirie mango ganache, flavored with fragrant, local mangoes picked at the height of the season. Other favorites incorporate ginger, Manoa honey, and *lilikoi* (passion fruit). You could pick up some of these to bring home, but I'm guessing they'll never make it. 650 Iwilei Rd., #280. ☏ **808/536-4567.**

Whole Foods ★   Whole Foods does a great job of sourcing local, both in produce and in specialty items such as honey, jams, hot sauces, coffee, and chocolate. It's also got one of the best selections of locally made soaps, great for gifts to take home. 4211 Waialae Ave at Kahala Mall. ☏ **808/738-0820.** Two other locations on Oahu at Ward and Kailua.

FLOWERS & LEIS

The best place to shop for leis is in Chinatown, where lei vendors line Beretania and Maunakea streets and the fragrances of their wares mix with the earthy scents of incense and ethnic foods. My top picks are **Lita's Leis,** 59 N. Beretania St. (☏ **808/521-9065**), which has fresh *puakenikeni,* gardenias that last, and a supply of fresh and reasonable leis; **Lin's Lei Shop,** 1017-A Mau-nakea St. (☏ **808/537-4112**), with creatively fashioned, unusual leis; and **Cindy's Lei Shoppe,** 1034 Maunakea St. (☏ **808/536-6538**), with terrific sources for unusual leis such as feather dendrobiums and firecracker combinations, as well as everyday favorites like ginger, tube-rose, orchid, and *pikake.*

Plumeria leis

HAWAIIANA & GIFT ITEMS

Visit the **Museum Shop** at the Honolulu Museum of Art, 900 S. Beretania St. (☏ **808/532-8703**), for crafts, jewelry, and prints, including Georgia O'Keefe's illustrations from her time in Hawaii. You'll find gifts to bring home, such as lauhala clutches, macadamia nut oil soaps, and color-satu-rated screenprints. I'm a fan of the local artists' limited-edition T-shirts and collection of beautiful ceramics.

SHOPPING IN chinatown

In the 1840s, Honolulu's Chinatown began to take shape as many Chinese brought in to work on the sugar plantations opted not to renew their contracts and instead moved to Chinatown to open businesses. Fronting Honolulu harbor, Chinatown catered to whalers and sailors. It reached its zenith in the 1920s, with restaurants and markets flourishing by day, and prostitutes and opium dens doing brisk business at night. As its reputation as a red-light district began to eclipse everything else the neighborhood slowly declined. That is, until recent decades. Fresh boutiques and restaurants are filling in previously abandoned storefronts—which retain much of their original architectural details from the 1900s—as Chinatown once again attracts the entrepreneurial.

At the original location of **Fighting Eel,** 1133 Bethel St. (www.fightingeel. com; © **808/738-9300,** multiple locations on Oahu), you'll find bright, easy-to-wear dresses and shirts with island prints that are in every local fashionista's closet—perfect for Honolulu weather, but chic enough to wear back home. **Owens and Co.,** 1152 Nuuanu Ave. (www.owens andcompany.com; © **808/531-4300**), offers a colorful selection of housewares and accessories, including candles, stationery, jewelry, and totes, many of which are locally made or island inspired. Go treasure-hunting at **Tin Can Mailman** (p. 167) and the funky **Hound & Quail,** 1156 Nuuanu Ave. (www.houndandquail. com; © **808/779-8436**), where a collection of antiques and curiosities, from a taxidermied ostrich to old medical texts, make for a fascinating perusal. Find nostalgia in a 1950s tiki print dress or red silk kimono at **Barrio Vintage,** 1161 Nuuanu Ave. (www.barriovintage.com; © **808/674-7156**), one of the island's best shops for vintage clothing. At **Ginger13,** 22 S. Pauahi St. (www.ginger13. com; © **808/531-5311**), local jewelry designer Cindy Yokoyama offers a refreshing change from the delicate jewelry found all over Hawaii by creating asymmetrical styles with chunky stones such as agate and opal.

Na Mea Hawaii ★ A one-stop shop and resource for all things local and Hawaiian, you'll find hula stones and *ipu* (gourds); Niihau shell lei; prints, crafts, and jewelry from local artists; local jams and coffee; and shelves of Hawaiian history and culture books. Regular classes in lauhala weaving, Hawaiian featherwork, ukulele, the Hawaiian language, and more are also held here. Call for the schedule. At the Ward Village Shops, 1200 Ala Moana Blvd. © **808/596-8885.**

Nohea Gallery ★ Since its inception in 1990 Nohea Gallery has carried the work of more than 2,100 artists, almost all local. Here you'll find original *gyotaku*, or prints using real fish such as ono and opelu by Naoki Hayashi, and woodwork, including beautiful bowls made of mango wood and koa. I love that you can buy everything from trinkets such as koa wood magnets to ki*ele's beachy, delicate jewelry using sea glass and shells to a Russell Lowrey original (painting) of Pounder's Beach for $7,500. At the Hyatt Waikiki, 2424 Kalakaua Ave. #128. www.noheagallery.com. © **808/596-0074.**

Tin Can Mailman ★ What, not looking for a 1950s oil hula lamp? Check out this shop anyway. It's packed with vintage Hawaiiana to emulate old-school general stores. The emphasis is on ephemera, such as pin-ups, postcards, old sheet music and advertisements, and the elusive Betty Boop hula girl bobblehead. 1026 Nuuanu Ave. www.tincanmailman.net. ℭ **808/524-3009.**

SHOPPING CENTERS

Ala Moana Center ★★ Hawaii's largest mall includes luxury brands and mainstream chains. But it also offers a selection of local stores. Make sure to browse **Manaola** and stop by **Tori Richard** and **Reyn Spooner** (see "Clothing," above, for all three); for surf-and-skate wear, check out **Hawaiian Island Creations** or **T&C Surf Designs.** Local boutique **Cinnamon Girl** is a perennial favorite for ultra-feminine dresses and mother-and-daughter matching outfits. For presents to bring home, stop in **Blue Hawaii Lifestyle,** which offers locally made food gifts such as chocolate and honey, as well as Hawaii-made soaps and beauty products. Pick up beautifully packaged, chocolate-dipped mac nut shortbread at **Big Island Candies** and only-in-Hawaii treats such as *manju* (resembling a filled cookie) and ume-shiso chocolates. Hungry? There are plenty of options: **The Lanai** is a new food court with all-natural shave ice at **Uncle Clay's House of Pure Aloha,** fresh poke bowls at **Ahi and Vegetable,** and soft rolls and mochi bread at the Japanese **Brug Bakery.** Get lost browsing all the ramen and bento stalls at the **Shirokiya Japan Village Walk,** and then head to **Takoyaki Yama Chan** for hot, doughy balls studded with octopus. Treat yourself to a slice of cake and a plantation iced-tea jelly at the Japanese/French patisserie **Palme D'Or.** The center is open Monday to Saturday 9:30am to 9pm, and Sunday 10am to 7pm. 1450 Ala Moana Blvd. www.alamoanacenter.com. ℭ **808/955-9517.** Bus: 8, 19, or 20. Various shuttle services also stop here. For Waikiki Trolley information, see "Getting Around" (p. 70).

Salt at Kakaako ★ There are grand plans for Kakaako, the neighborhood between Waikiki and downtown. Mostly, it's a lot of new, hi-rise luxury condos, but developers are also trying to create an interesting mix of restaurants and retailers. Here, you'll find **Milo,** a hip surf shop that also carries accessories for the home; **Paiko,** an adorable tropical botanical boutique, and **Treehouse,** a must for any photography lover, especially those with a penchant for vintage and film. Sample local chocolate at **Lonohana Estate Chocolate,** a company that grows its own cacao and turns it into smooth bars, from milk chocolate to extra dark. 660 Ala Moana Blvd. www.saltatkakaako.com.

Ward Village Shops ★ Gems here include **Na Mea Hawaii** (see "Hawaiiana & Gift Items," above). Find unique gifts at **Red Pineapple,** such as Sumadra clutches printed with silhouettes of the Mokulua Islands off Kailua, and Saffron James' scents, which capture the exoticism of Hawaii's flowers. Don't miss the Everything Is Jake! retro-styled travel posters of Oahu's Haleiwa town and other iconic Hawaii landscapes. You'll find a lot of young Hawaii fashion designers at the **South Shore Market,** the building that houses the breezy designs of **Kealopiko** and **Salvage Public**'s menswear for surfers in and out of the water. Ward Village Shops is open Monday through Saturday 10am to 9pm, Sunday 10am to 6pm. *Note:* This area is currently being redeveloped, and the intent is to find new spaces for many of the current tenants while bringing in new stores for the mixed-use condo and retail development, dubbed Ward Village. To find the most up-to-date store directory, visit the Ward Village website. 1200 Ala Moana Blvd. www.wardvillageshops.com. ✆ **808/591-8411.**

Shopping in Kailua

Befitting Oahu's favorite beach town, many of the boutiques in Kailua offer plenty of swimsuits, breezy styles for men and women, and T-shirts from homegrown brands. In addition to the shops below, also make sure to stop by Manoa Chocolate (see "Specialty Tours," p. 125).

Aloha Beach Club ★   One of Kailua's newer boutiques, Aloha Beach Club also designs and makes its own aloha shirts and board shorts in Hawaii. The style is updated retro. You'll also find tasteful Aloha Beach Club logo wear. Make sure to grab a shave ice in the shop-within-a-shop, **The Local Hawaii,** made with locally grown fruit (a rarity in the artificially flavored shave ice world). 131 Hekili St., Suite 108, Kailua. www.alohabeachclub.com.

Island Bungalow ★   Come here to furnish the beachy bohemian house of your dreams. Don't have one? Pretend you do while browsing indigo dipped pillowcases, gauzy cotton canopies, tea glasses from Morocco, and intricately patterned textiles and caftans from India . . . because if you don't have that beach house, at least you can dress like you're going to one. 131 Hekili St., Kailua. www.islandbungalowhawaii.com. ✆ **808/536-4543.**

Madre Chocolate ★   Honolulu's first bean-to-bar maker pays homage to chocolate's origins—no surprise, considering owner Nat Bletter's career as an ethnobotanist. The Triple Cacao bar blends cacao in all its forms: cacao pulp from Brazil, and nibs and chocolate from Mexico, reflecting the origin of the cacao trees in South America and chocolate's invention in Central America. Other chocolate-bar flavors include *lilikoi* (passion fruit) and coconut milk with candied ginger. 20A Kainehe St., Kailua. www.madrechocolate.com. ✆ **808/262-6789.**

Oliver ★   This tiny, quirky shop for stylish men sells aloha shirts from local brand Salvage Public, pocket knives for the urban explorer, and soaps to clean up with when you're done exploring. Browse the shop's collection of vinyl records for some great vintage surf-band finds. Next door, **Olive** is for women, offering beach blankets, über-stylish swimsuits

farmer's MARKETS

Farmer's markets have proliferated on Oahu—there's now one for every neighborhood for every day of the week. Unfortunately, the number of farmers has not kept up. In fact, some of the markets have vendors that sell repackaged Mainland produce. The best farmer's markets are those run by the **Hawaii Farm Bureau Federation** (**HFBF**; www.hfbf. org/markets) and **FarmLovers** (www. farmloversmarkets.com), which mandate locally grown meats, fruits, and veggies. Check their websites for detailed information. Here are my favorites:

○ **Kapiolani Community College:** The original and still the biggest and best. Unfortunately, you'll have to deal with crowds—busloads of tourists get dropped off here. But you'll find items unavailable at any other market—endless varieties of bananas and mangoes,

tropical fruit you've never seen before, persimmons, and local duck eggs. Pick up cut, chilled pineapple or jackfruit to snack on, yogurt from Oahu's one remaining dairy, perhaps some grilled abalone from Kona, and corn from Kahuku. And with a healthy dose of prepared-food vendors serving everything from fresh tomato pizzas to raw and vegan snacks, you won't go hungry (4355 Diamond Head Rd.; ℂ **808/848-2074;** Sat 7:30–11am; TheBus: 23 or 24).

○ **Honolulu Farmer's Market:** This HFBF market is less crowded and has more locals stopping by to pick up groceries after work, plus some of the same vendors as the Kapiolani Community College market (777 Ward Ave.; ℂ **808/848-2074;** Wed 4–7pm; TheBus: 13).

(to match Oliver's über-stylish man), and beachy, well-made dresses. 49 Kihapai St., Kailua. www.oliverhawaii.com. ℂ **808/261-6587.**

Shopping on the North Shore

The newly developed **Haleiwa Store Lots,** 66-087 Kamehameha Hwy. (www.haleiwastorelots.com), replaces some of the old, dusty buildings (some would say charming) in Haleiwa with an open-air, plantation-style shopping center. You'll also find the **Clark Little Gallery,** showcasing the photographer's shorebreak photos, which capture the fluidity, beauty, and power of a wave just as it's about to hit the shoreline. Don't miss **Polu Gallery** featuring local artists' work, including Heather Brown's bold and bright surf art and Kris Goto's quirky drawings combining manga sensibilities with Hawaii surf culture. **Guava Shop** is Haleiwa's quintessential clothing boutique. Its beachy, bohemian styles capture the aesthetic of a North Shore surfer girl.

Farther south into Haleiwa is **Coffee Gallery,** 66-250 Kamehameha Hwy., Suite C106 (www.roastmaster.com; ℂ **808/637-5571**), the best cafe in town, with a great selection of locally grown coffee beans to take home. **Tini Manini,** 66-250 Kamehameha Hwy., Suite C101 (www.tinimanini. com; ℂ **808/637-8464**), is an adorable children's shop with everything from bathing suits to baby blankets for your little one. North Shore residents are relentlessly active, keeping in shape through running, surfing, stand-up paddling, and yoga. **Mahiku,** 66-165 Kamehameha Hwy. (www.mahiku.com; ✆ **808/888-6857**), keeps them stylish, with fun and bright activewear that can go straight from the yoga mat into the ocean.

Over in Waialua, a collection of surfboard shapers and small businesses have turned the **Waialua Sugar Mill,** which stopped producing sugar in 1996, into a low-key retail and industrial space. Stop at **North Shore Soap Factory,** 67-106 Kealohanui St. (www.northshoresoap factory.com; ✆ **808/637-8400**), to watch all-natural and fragrant soaps being made. You can even stamp your bar of soap with a shaka or the silhouette of the sugar mill. It also has a line of bath and body care, with scrubs, lotions, and moisturizing kukui-nut oil.

OAHU NIGHTLIFE

Nightlife in Hawaii begins at sunset, when all eyes turn westward to see how the day will end. Sunset viewers always seem to bond in the mutual enjoyment of a natural spectacle.

Enjoy hula dancing and a torch-lighting ceremony on Tuesday, Thursday, Saturday, and Sunday from 6:30 to 7:30pm (6–7pm Nov–Jan), as the sun casts its golden glow on the beach at the **Kuhio Beach Hula Mound,** close to Duke Kahanamoku's statue (Ulunui and Kalakaua sts.). This is a thoroughly

Performers at House Without a Key

get down with ARTAFTERDARK

On the last Friday of every month (except Nov–Dec), the place to be after the sun goes down is **ARTafterDARK,** a *pau hana* (after-work) mixer in the **Honolulu Academy of Arts,** 900 S. Beretania St. (www.artafterdark.org; ✆ **808/532-8700**), that brings residents and visitors together around a theme combining art with food, music, and dancing. In addition to the exhibits in the gallery, ARTafterDARK features visual and live performances. Previous themes have ranged from "Plant Rice"—with rice and sake tastings, rice dishes, Asian beers, live Asian fusion music, and a tour of the "Art of Rice" exhibit—to "'80s Night," "Turkish Delights," "Cool Nights, Hot Jazz and Blues," and "Havana Heat." The entrance fee is $10. The party gets going around 6 and lasts till 9pm. The crowd ranges from 20s to 50s, and the dress is everything from jeans and T-shirts to cocktail-party attire.

delightful free offering of hula and music by some of the Hawaii's finest performers. Start off early with a picnic basket and walk along the ocean-side path fronting Queen's Beach near the Waikiki Aquarium. (You can park along Kapiolani Park or near the zoo.) There are few more pleasing spots in Waikiki than the benches at water's edge at this Diamond Head end of Kalakaua Avenue. It's a short walk to where the seawall and daring boogie boarders attract hordes of spectators. To check the schedule, go to www.waikikiimprovement.com/waikiki-calendar-of-events/kuhio-beach-hula-show.

The Bar Scene

ON THE BEACH Waikiki's beachfront bars offer many possibilities, from the **Mai Tai Bar** (✆ **808/923-7311**) at the Royal Hawaiian (p. 133) a few feet from the sand, to the **Beach Bar** (✆ **808/921-4600**) under the banyan tree at the Moana Surfrider (p. 131), to the unfailingly enchanting **House Without a Key** (✆ **808/923-2311**) at the Halekulani (p. 130) where a lovely hula dancer sways to the riffs of Hawaiian steel-pedal guitar with the sunset and ocean glowing behind her—a romantic, evocative, nostalgic scene. (It doesn't hurt, either, that the Halekulani happens to make the best mai tais in the world.) The Halekulani has the after-dinner hours covered, too, with light jazz by local artists in the Lewers Lounge from 9pm to 2am nightly (see "Live Blues, R&B, Jazz & Pop," below).

Another great bar for watching the sun sink into the Pacific is **Duke's Waikiki** (www.dukeswaikiki.com; ✆ **808/922-2268**) in the Outrigger Waikiki Beach Resort. The outside Barefoot Bar is perfect for sipping a tropical drink, watching the waves and sunset, and listening to music. It can get crowded, so get here early. Hawaii sunset music is usually from 4 to 6pm daily, with live entertainment nightly from 9:30pm to midnight.

DOWNTOWN/CHINATOWN **First Fridays,** which originally started as an art gallery walk on the first Friday of the month, has now evolved into a club and bar crawl that can sometimes turn Chinatown into a frat party on the streets. Go on a non–First Friday weekend for a mellower scene. The activity is concentrated on Hotel Street, on the block between Smith and Nuunau. That's where you'll find **Tchin Tchin!** (p. 152) and **Manifest,** 32 N. Hotel St., with a great selection of whiskey and gin. The bartenders here are happy to whip up complex whiskey drinks or simple, classic cocktails. After 10pm, DJs and live music make the laid-back bar more clubby. Across the street is **Bar 35,** 35 N. Hotel St. (© **808/537-3535**), whose claim to fame is its 110 beers available, plus wine, cocktails, and even pizza. You must be 21 to enter (strictly enforced).

Hanks Cafe, around the corner on Nu'unau Avenue between Hotel and King streets (http://hankscafehawaii.com; © **808/526-1410**), is a tiny, kitschy, friendly pub with live music nightly, open-mic nights, and special events that attract great talent and a supportive crowd. On some nights, the music spills out into the streets and it's so packed you have to press your nose against the window to see what you're missing. Upstairs at the **Dragon Upstairs,** there's more live music Tuesday through Sunday nights (http://thedragonupstairs.com; © **808/526-1411**). At the *makai* end of Nuunau, toward the pier, **Murphy's Bar and Grill ★** (p. 152) is a popular downtown alehouse and media haunt.

Hawaiian Music

Oahu has several key spots for Hawaiian music. **House Without a Key** (see "The Bar Scene," above) is one of my favorite places to listen to Hawaiian music, both for the quality and the ambience.

Kana ka pila means to make music, so it makes sense then that the **Kana Ka Pila Grille** (© **808/924-4994**) at the Outrigger Reef on the Beach has one of the city's best Hawaiian-music lineups, including slack key guitarists Cyril Pahinui (son of famed guitarist Gabby Pahinui).

The Willows, 901 Hausten St. (www.willowshawaii.com; © **808/952-9200**) was once the garden home of Emma McGuire Hausten and her family in the 1920s. Its tropical setting, full of lush greenery, waterfalls and ponds, and restaurant is now where generations gather for graduation parties, birthdays, and weddings. Every Thursday, it hosts **Pakele Live,** a 2-hour concert featuring island entertainers.

Every year, halau (hula schools) and Hawaiian musicians from around the state gather for **Ola Ka Ha,** to honor Iolani Palace through song and dance. It's a free event; find this year's date at www.olakaha.com.

Live Blues, R&B, Jazz & Pop

Blue Note Hawaii, inside the Outrigger Waikiki, 2335 Kalakaua Ave. (www.bluenotehawaii.com; ⓒ **808/777-4890**), from the owner of the Blue Note jazz club in New York City, is the state's newest venue for jazz, blues, and favorite local entertainers. It has a great, old-school jazzy vibe, and the restaurant offers hearty plates like a hamburger and braised short ribs. Past performers have included Dee Dee Bridgewater and ukulele virtuoso Jake Shimabukuro.

Tops in taste and ambience is the perennially alluring **Lewers Lounge** in the Halekulani, 2199 Kalia Rd. (www.halekulani.com; ⓒ **808/923-2311**). Comfy intimate seating around the pillars makes this a great spot for contemporary jazz nightly from 8:30pm to midnight.

Outside Waikiki, the **Veranda,** at the Kahala Hotel & Resort, 5000 Kahala Ave. (www.kahalaresort.com; ⓒ **808/739-8888**), is a popular spot for the over-40 crowd, with nightly jazz music and a dance floor.

Off the beaten path (yes, that's a strip club in the neighborhood), you'll find the intimate bar and club **Jazz Minds** (www.honolulujazzclub.com; ⓒ **808/945-0800**) dedicated to jazz and jazz-fusion.

Check www.honolulujazzscene.com for daily listings.

Showroom Acts & Revues

Te Moana Nui, at the Sheraton Princess Kaiulani, is a theatrical journey of fire dancing, special effects, illusions, hula, and dances from Hawaii and the South Pacific. Shows are Sunday, Wednesday, and Friday (dinner show starts at $105 adults, $79 children 5–12; cocktail show $60 adults).

Also worth experiencing, even if you don't spend the day at the Polynesian Cultural Center, is *Ha: Breath of Life* (p. 100).

The Performing Arts

"Aloha shirt to Armani" is how I describe the night scene in Honolulu—mostly casual, but with ample opportunity to part with your flip-flops and dress up.

Audiences have grooved to the beat of the Hawaii International Jazz Festival, the American Repertory Dance Company, barbershop quartets, and John Kaimikaua's *halau*—all at the **Hawaii Theatre,** 1130 Bethel St., Downtown (www.hawaiitheatre.com; ⓒ **808/528-0506**). The theater is basking in its renaissance as a leading multipurpose center for the performing arts. The neoclassical Beaux-Arts landmark features a dome from 1922, 1,400 plush seats, a hydraulically elevated organ, breathtaking murals, and gilt galore.

In 2011, a new symphony orchestra was reborn from the disbanded century-old Honolulu Symphony Orchestra: **Hawaii Symphony** (http://hawaiisymphonyorchestra.org; ⓒ **808/593-2468**). Meanwhile, the **Hawaii**

Opera Theatre (www.hawaiiopera.org; © **808/596-7372** or 800/836-7372), celebrating more than 50 seasons, still draws fans to the **Neal S. Blaisdell Center** (www.blaisdellcenter.com; © **808/591-2211**), as does **Ballet Hawaii** (www.ballethawaii.org). Contemporary performances by **Iona** (www.iona360.com), a strikingly creative group whose dance evolved out of Butoh (a contemporary dance form that originated in Japan), are worth tracking down if you love the avant-garde.

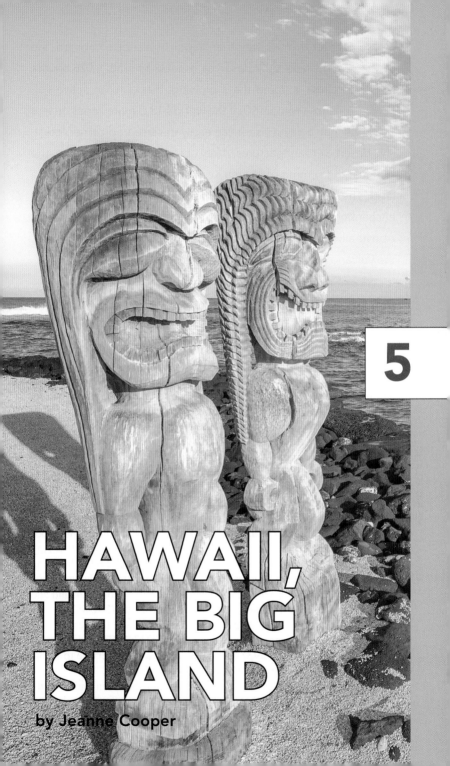

HAWAII, THE BIG ISLAND

by Jeanne Cooper

Larger than all the other Hawaiian Islands combined, the Big Island truly deserves its nickname. Its 4,028 square miles—a figure that's growing, thanks to an active volcano—contain 10 of the world's 13 climate zones. In less than a day, a visitor can easily traverse tropical rainforest, lava desert, verdant pastures, misty uplands, and chilly tundra, the last near the summit of Mauna Kea, almost 14,000 feet above sea level. The shoreline also boasts diversity, from golden beaches to enchanting coves with black, salt-and-pepper, even olivine sand. Above all, the island home of Kamehameha the Great and Pele, the volcano goddess, is big in *mana:* power and spirituality.

ESSENTIALS

Arriving

The Big Island has two major airports for interisland and trans-Pacific jet traffic: Kona and Hilo.

Most people arrive at **Kona International Airport** (**KOA;** http://hawaii.gov/koa) in Keahole, the island's westernmost point, and can be forgiven for wondering if there's really a runway among all the crinkly black lava and golden fountain grass. Leaving the airport, the ritzy Kohala Coast is to the left (north) and the town of Kailua-Kona—often just called "Kona," as is the airport—is to the right (south).

U.S. carriers offering nonstop service to Kona, in alphabetical order, are **Alaska Airlines** (www.alaskaair.com; ✆ **800/252-7522**), with flights from the Pacific Northwest hubs of Seattle, Portland, and Anchorage (plus Nov–Apr from Bellingham, Washington) and from San Diego, San Jose, and Oakland, California; **American Airlines** (www.aa.com; ✆ **800/433-7300**), departing from Los Angeles and Phoenix (also June—late Aug from Dallas); **Delta Air Lines** (www.delta.com; ✆ **800/221-1212**), flying from Los Angeles and Seattle; **Hawaiian Airlines** (www.hawaiianairlines.com; ✆ **800/367-5320**), offering summer service from Oakland and Los Angeles; **United Airlines** (www.united.com; ✆ **800/241-6522**), with year-round flights from Los Angeles, San Francisco, and Denver.

Air Canada (www.aircanada.com; ✆ **888/247-2267**) and **WestJet** (www.westjet.com; ✆ **888/937-8358**) also offer nonstop service to Kona, with frequency changing seasonally, from Vancouver.

United offers weekly nonstop service from the mainland to **Hilo International Airport** (**ITO;** http://hawaii.gov/ito), via Los Angeles.

Kona coast

For connecting flights or island-hopping, Hawaiian (see above) is the only carrier offering interisland jet service, available from Honolulu and Kahului, Maui, to both Kona and Hilo airports; it also flies daily nonstop between Kauai and Kona. Hawaiian's **Ohana by Hawaiian** subsidiary also flies from Kona and Hilo to Kahului on 48-passenger, twin-engine turboprops. **Mokulele Airlines** (www.mokuleleairlines.com; © **866/260-4040**) flies nine-passenger, single-engine turboprops to Kona from Molokai (Hoolehua) and Maui's Kahului and Kapalua airports, and to Waimea from Kahului. *Note:* Mokulele weighs passengers and their carry-ons to determine seats; those totaling 350 lbs. or more are not allowed to board.

Visitor Information

The **Big Island Visitors Bureau** (www.gohawaii.com/big-island; © **800/648-2441**) has two offices: one in the Shops at Mauna Lani, 68-1330 Mauna Lani Dr., Suite 109B, in the Mauna Lani Resort (© **808/885-1655**); the other at 101 Aupuni St., Suite 238, Hilo (© **808/961-5797**).

This Week (www.thisweekhawaii.com/big-island) and *101 Things to Do: Big Island* (www.101thingstodo.com/big-island) are free publications that offer good, useful information amid the advertisements, as well as discount coupons for a variety of island adventures. Copies are easy to find all around the island.

Konaweb.com has an extensive event calendar and handy links to sites and services around the island, not just the Kona side. Those fascinated by the island's active volcanoes—including Kilauea, which saw dramatic eruptions at its summit and in lower Puna beginning in May 2018—should check out the detailed daily lava reports, maps, photos, videos, and webcams on the U.S. Geological Survey's **Hawaiian Volcano Observatory** website (http://hvo.wr.usgs.gov), which also tracks the island's frequent but usually minor earthquake activity.

The national historic park at Honaunau

The Island in Brief

THE KONA COAST

Kona means "leeward side" in Hawaiian—and that means hot, dry weather virtually every day of the year on the 70-mile stretch of black lava shoreline encompassing the North and South Kona districts.

NORTH KONA   With the exception of the sumptuous but serenely low-key **Four Seasons Resort Hualalai ★★★** north of the airport, most of what everyone just calls "Kona" is an affordable vacation spot. An ample selection of midpriced condo units, timeshares, and several recently upgraded hotels lies between the bustling commercial district of **Kailua-Kona ★★★**, a one-time fishing village and royal compound now renowned as the start and finish of the Ironman World Championship, and Keauhou, an equally historic area about 6 miles south that boasts upscale condominiums, a shopping center, and golf-course homes.

The rightly named Alii ("Royalty") Drive begins in Kailua-Kona near King Kamehameha's royal compound at **Kamakahonu Bay,** which includes the off-limits temple complex of **Ahuena Heiau,** and continues past **Hulihee Palace ★★★,** an elegant retreat for later royals that sits across from the oldest church in the islands. Heading south, the road passes by the snorkelers' haven of **Kahaluu Beach ★★**, as well as sacred and royal sites on the former Keauhou Beach Resort, before the intersection with King Kamehameha III Road, which leads to that monarch's birthplace by Keauhou Bay. Several kayak excursions and snorkel boats leave from Keauhou, but Kailua Pier sees the most traffic—from cruise-ship tenders to fishing and dive boats, dinner cruises, and other sightseeing excursions.

Beaches between Kailua-Kona and Keauhou tend to be pocket coves, but heading north toward South Kohala (which begins near the entrance to the Waikoloa Beach Resort), beautiful, uncrowded sands lie out of sight from the highway, often reached by unpaved roads across vast lava fields. Among the steep coffee fields in North Kona's cooler upcountry, you'll find the rustic, artsy village of **Holualoa.**

SOUTH KONA   The rural, serrated coastline here is indented with numerous bays, from **Kealakekua,** a marine life and cultural preserve that's the island's best diving spot, down to **Honaunau,** where a national historical park recalls the days of old Hawaii. This is a great place to stay, in modest plantation-era inns or bed-and-breakfasts, if you want to get away from crowds but still be within driving distance of beaches and Kailua-Kona— you may hear the all-night cheeping of coqui frogs, though. The higher, cooler elevation of the main road means you'll pass many coffee, macadamia nut, and tropical fruit farms, some with tours or roadside stands.

THE KOHALA COAST

Also on the island's "Kona side," sunny and dry Kohala is divided into two distinctively different districts, although the resorts are more glamorous and the rural area that much less developed.

SOUTH KOHALA   Pleasure domes rise like palaces no Hawaiian king ever imagined along the sandy beaches carved into the craggy shores here, from the more moderately priced **Waikoloa Beach Resort** at Anaehoomalu Bay to the posher **Mauna Lani** and **Mauna Kea** resorts to the north. Mauna Kea is where Laurance Rockefeller opened the area's first resort in 1965, a virtual mirage of opulence and tropical greenery rising from bleak, black lava fields, framed by the white sands of Kaunaoa Beach and views of the eponymous mountain. But you don't have to be a billionaire to enjoy South Kohala's fabulous beaches and historic sites (such as petroglyph fields); all are open to the public, with parking and other facilities (including restaurants and shopping) provided by the resorts.

Several of the region's attractions are also located off the resorts, including the white sands of **Ohaiula Beach** at **Spencer Park ★★**; the massive **Puukohola Heiau ★★★**, a lava rock temple commissioned by King Kamehameha the Great; and the excellent restaurants and handful of stores in **Kawaihae,** the commercial harbor just after the turnoff for upcountry Waimea. *Note:* The golf course community of **Waikoloa Village** is not in the Waikoloa Beach Resort, but instead lies 5½ miles uphill from the coastal highway.

WAIMEA (KAMUELA) & MAUNA KEA   Officially part of South Kohala, the old upcountry cow town of Waimea on the northern road between the coasts is a world unto itself, with rolling green pastures, wide-open spaces dotted by *puu* (cindercone hills, pronounced *"pooh-ooh"*) and real cowpokes who work mammoth **Parker Ranch,** the state's largest working ranch. The postal service gave it the name Kamuela, after ranch founder Samuel (Kamuela) Parker, to distinguish it from another cowboy town, Waimea, Kauai. It's split between a "dry side" (closer to the Kohala Coast) and a "wet side" (closer to the Hamakua Coast), but both sides can be cooler than sea level. It's also headquarters for the **Keck Observatory,** whose twin telescopes atop the nearly 14,000-foot **Mauna Kea ★★★,** some 35 miles away, are the largest and most powerful in the world. Waimea is home to shopping centers and affordable B&Bs, while the expanded **Merriman's ★★★** remains a popular foodie outpost at Opelo Plaza.

NORTH KOHALA   Locals may remember when sugar was king here, but for visitors, little-developed North Kohala is most famous for another king, Kamehameha the Great. His birthplace is a short walk from one of the Hawaiian Islands' largest and most important temples, **Mookini Heiau ★,** which dates to a.d. 480; you'll want a four-wheel-drive (4WD) for the rugged road there. Much easier to find: the yellow-cloaked bronze statue of the warrior-king in front of the community center in **Kapaau,** a small plantation-era town. The road ends at the breathtaking **Pololu Valley Overlook ★★★.**

   Once the center of the Big Island's sugarcane industry, **Hawi** remains a regional hub, with a 3-block-long strip of sun-faded, false-fronted buildings holding a few shops and restaurants of interest to visitors. Eight miles south, **Lapakahi State Historical Park ★★** merits a stop to explore how less-exalted Hawaiians than Kamehameha lived in a simple village by the

Keck Observatory

sea. Beaches are less appealing here, with the northernmost coves subject to strong winds blowing across the Alenuihaha Channel from Maui, 26 miles away and visible on clear days.

THE HAMAKUA COAST

This emerald coast, a 52-mile stretch from Honokaa to Hilo on the island's windward northeast side, was once planted with sugarcane; it now blooms with macadamia nuts, papayas, vanilla orchids, and mushrooms. Resort-free and virtually without beaches, the Hamakua Coast includes the districts of Hamakua and North Hilo, with two unmissable destinations. Picture-perfect **Waipio Valley ★★★** has impossibly steep sides, taro patches, a green riot of wild plants, and a winding stream leading to a broad, black-sand beach, while **Akaka Falls State Park ★★★** offers views of two lovely waterfalls amid lush foliage. Also worth checking out: **Laupahoehoe Point ★**, with its mournful memorial to young victims of a 1946 tsunami; and the quirky assortment of shops in the plantation town of **Honokaa.**

HILO

The largest metropolis in Hawaii after Honolulu is a quaint, misty, flower-filled city of Victorian houses overlooking a half-moon bay, with a restored historic downtown and a clear view of Mauna Kea, often snow-capped in winter. However, it rains a lot in Hilo—about 128 inches a year—which tends to dampen visitors' enthusiasm for longer stays. It's ideal for growing ferns, orchids, and anthuriums, but not for catching constant rays.

Yet there's a lot to see and do in Hilo and the surrounding South Hilo district, both indoors and out—including visiting the bayfront Japanese-style **Liliuokalani Gardens ★★**, the **Pacific Tsunami Museum ★**, the **Mokupapapa Discovery Center ★★**, and **Rainbow Falls (Waian-ueanue) ★**—so grab your umbrella. The rain is warm (the temperature seldom dips below 70°F/21°C), and there's usually a rainbow afterward.

The town also holds the island's best bargains for budget travelers, with plenty of hotel rooms—most of the year, that is. Hilo's magic moment comes in spring, the week after Easter, when hula *hālau* (schools) arrive for the annual **Merrie Monarch Hula Festival** hula competition (www.merriemonarch.com). Plan ahead if you want to go: Tickets are sold out by the first week in January, and hotels within 30 miles are usually booked solid. Hilo is also the gateway to **Hawaii Volcanoes National Park ★★★**, where hula troupes have traditionally performed chants and dances before the Merrie Monarch festival; the park is 30 miles away, or about an hour's drive up-slope.

PUNA DISTRICT

PAHOA, KAPOHO & KALAPANA
Between Hilo and Hawaii Volcanoes National Park lies the "Wild Wild East," which gained international and

Rainbow Falls

viral social media fame in May 2018 with the onset of devastating, dramatic lava flows that at press time were expected to continue for months. It was already home to geothermal wonders such as the ghostly hollowed trunks of **Lava Tree State Monument ★★**, the volcanically heated waters of **Ahalanui Park ★★** and the **Kapoho warm ponds,** and the acres of lava from a 1986 flow that rolled through the Hawaiian hamlet of Kalapana and covered a popular black-sand beach. Closed indefinitely at press time, the areas were expected to reopen if air conditions and road access allowed; vacation rentals were also closed indefinitely for safety reasons. The destroyed residential neighborhoods built atop Kilauea's Lower East Rift Zone, however, are unlikely to be restored. In 2014, lava also threatened the part-Hawaiian, part-hippie plantation town of **Pahoa,** the region's funky gateway, consuming miles of forest before stopping just short of Hwy. 130, the only road in and out of lower Puna; in 2018, it was unclear if Pele would be so obliging.

HAWAII VOLCANOES NATIONAL PARK ★★★   This is America's most exciting national park, where a live volcano called Kilauea has been continuously erupting since 1983—stunningly so in 2018. Massive, steam-driven eruptions of ash at the summit began in May after its lava lake drained, leading most of the park ito close indefinitely; it was expected to reopen later in 2018 once conditions permitted. While you may not be able to witness molten lava, there's always something else impressive to see, whether it's the vast Halemaumau Crater, Nahuku (Thurston) Lava Tube, or the steam vents that have been belching sulphurous odors since long before Mark Twain visited in 1866. Ideally, plan to spend 3 days at the park exploring its many trails, watching the volcano, visiting the rainforest, and just enjoying this spectacular place. But even if you have only a day, it's worth the trip. Bring your sweats or jacket (honest!); it's cool up there.

VOLCANO VILLAGE If you're not camping or staying at the historic, 33-room **Volcano House ★★** inside the park (temporarily closed in 2018 during the eruption), you'll want to overnight in this quiet hamlet, just outside the national park entrance. Several cozy inns and B&Bs, some with fireplaces, reside under tree ferns in this cool mountain hideaway. The tiny highland community (elevation 4,000 ft.), first settled by Japanese immigrants, is now inhabited by artists, soul-searchers, and others who like the crisp high-country air, although in 2018 many faced hard times caused by the park's extended closure and ash fall.

KAU DISTRICT

Pronounced *"kah-oo,"* this windswept, often barren district between Puna and South Kona is one visitors are most likely to just drive through on their way to and from the national park. Nevertheless, it contains several noteworthy sites.

KA LAE (SOUTH POINT) This is the Plymouth Rock of Hawaii. The first Polynesians are thought to have arrived in seagoing canoes, probably from the Marquesas Islands, around a.d. 500 at this rocky promontory 500 feet above the sea. To the west is the old fishing village of Waiahukini, populated from a.d. 750 until the 1860s; ancient canoe moorings, shelter caves, and *heiau* (temples) poke through windblown pili grass today. The east coast curves inland to reveal **Papakolea (Green Sand) Beach ★★**, a world-famous anomaly that's best accessed on foot. Along the point, the southernmost spot in the 50 states, trees grow sideways due to the relentless gusts that also power wind turbines. It's a slow, nearly 12-mile drive from the highway to the tip of Ka Lae, so many visitors simply stop at the marked overlook on Highway 11, west of South Point Road.

NAALEHU, WAIOHINU & PAHALA Nearly every business in Naalehu and Waiohinu, the two wide spots on the main road near South Point, claims to be the southernmost this or that. But except for delicious *malasadas* (doughnut holes) or another pick-me-up from the **Punaluu Bake Shop ★** or **Hana Hou Restaurant ★**, there's no reason to linger before heading to **Punaluu Beach ★★★**, between Naalehu and Pahala. Protected green sea turtles bask on the fine black-sand beach when they're not bobbing in the clear waters, chilly from fresh springs bubbling from the ocean floor. Pahala is the center of the burgeoning Kau coffee-growing scene ("industry" might be overstated), so caffeine fans should also allot at least 45 minutes for a visit to the **Kau Coffee Mill ★**.

GETTING AROUND

The Hawaiian directions of *makai* (toward the ocean) and *mauka* (toward the mountains) come in handy when looking for unfamiliar sites, especially since numbered address signs may be invisible or nonexistent. They're used with addresses below as needed.

Papakolea (Green Sand) Beach

BY TAXI AND RIDESHARE Ride-sharing Uber and Lyft came to the island in 2017, although at press time coverage was sparse outside of Kailua-Kona and Hilo, and drivers were not allowed to make airport pickups yet. Taxis are readily available at both Kona and Hilo airports, although renting a car (see below) is a more likely option. Rates set by the county start at $3, plus $3.20 each additional mile—about $25 to $30 from the Kona airport to Kailua-Kona and $50 to $60 to the Waikoloa Beach Resort. On the Kona side, call **Kona Taxicab** (www.konataxicab.com; ℃ **808/324-4444**), which can also be booked in advance for airport pickups; drivers will check on your flight's arrival. On the Hilo side, call **Kwiki Taxi** (www.kwikitaxi.wordpress.com; ℃ **808/498-0308**).

BY CAR You'll want a rental car on the Big Island; not having one will really limit you. All major car-rental agencies have airport pickups in Kona and Hilo; some even offer cars at Kohala and Kona resorts. For tips on insurance and driving rules, see "Getting Around Hawaii" (p. 601).

The Big Island has more than 480 miles of paved road. The highway that circles the island is called the **Hawaii Belt Road.** From North Kona to South Kohala and Waimea, you have two driving choices: the scenic "upper" road, **Mamalahoa Highway** (Hwy. 190), or the speedier "lower" road, **Queen Kaahumanu Highway** (Hwy. 19). South of Kailua-Kona, the Hawaii Belt Road continues on Mamalahoa Highway (Hwy. 11) all the way to downtown Hilo, where it becomes Highway 19 again and follows the Hamakua Coast before heading up to Waimea.

North Kohala also has upper and lower highways. In Kawaihae, you can follow **Kawaihae Road** (Hwy. 19) uphill to the left turn onto the often-misty **Kohala Mountain Road** (Hwy. 250), which eventually drops down into Hawi. The **Akoni Pule Highway** (Hwy. 270) hugs the coast from Kawaihae to pavement's end at the Pololu Valley Lookout.

Note: **Saddle Road** (Hwy. 200) snakes between Mauna Kea and Mauna Loa en route from Hilo to Mamalahoa Highway (Hwy. 190). Despite improvements to its once-rough pavement and narrow shoulders, it's still frequented by large military vehicles and plagued by bad weather; as a result, most rental-car agencies forbid you from driving on it. I've found the 29 miles from Hilo to the Mauna Kea Access Road to be very easy to navigate in good conditions, but be careful not to speed, especially close to Hilo.

BY BUS & SHUTTLE SpeediShuttle (www.speedishuttle.com; ☏ **808/329-5433**) and **Roberts Hawaii** (www.robertshawaii.com; ☏ **866/570-2536** or 808/954-8640) offer door-to-door airport transfers to hotels and other lodgings. Sample round-trip, shared-ride rates from the Kona airport are $26 per person to Kailua-Kona, and $60 per person to the Mauna Lani Resort; Roberts agents meet you outside security and provide porter service in baggage claim, but be aware there may be up to five stops before your destination.

The islandwide bus system, the **Hele-On Bus** (www.heleonbus.org; ☏ **808/961-8744**), offers a great flat rate for riders: $2 general; $1 for students, seniors, and people with disabilities; and free for children under 5. Yet most routes have limited value for visitors, other than the Intra-Kona line between Kailua-Kona's big-box stores (Wal-Mart, Costco) and the Keauhou Shopping Center, which also stops at the Old Kona Airport Beach. Fares are cash only.

Travelers staying in Kailua-Kona and the Keauhou Resort can hop on the open-air, 44-seat **Keauhou Resort Trolley** operated by Roberts Hawaii (☏ **808/329-1688**), running from 9am to 9:15pm daily along Alii Drive. It makes six stops a day at 29 locations from the Sheraton Kona Resort and Keauhou Shopping Center to Kahaluu Beach, Kailua Pier, and the shops of downtown Kailua-Kona. The fare is $2, free for those with vouchers from their hotel (such as the Sheraton) or stores in the Kona Commons Shopping Center, which give them to customers who spend $25 or more.

The **Waikoloa Beach Resort shopping trolley** runs from 10am to 10pm daily from Hilton Waikoloa Village and the Waikoloa Beach Marriott to the Kings' Shops and Queens' MarketPlace; it costs $2 adults, $1 ages 5 to 12 (younger free). Guests at Kings' Land by Hilton Grand Vacations can catch a free van shuttle to Hilton Waikoloa Village and pick up the trolley from there. Hilton Waikoloa Village also runs beach and golf shuttles for guests.

BY BIKE Due to elevation changes, narrow shoulders (with the notable exception of the Queen Kaahumanu Highway between Kailua-Kona and Kawaihae), and high traffic speeds, point-to-point bike travel without a tour guide isn't recommended. However, several areas are ideal for recreational cycling and sightseeing. See "Biking" under "Other Outdoor Activities" for rental shops and routes.

BY MOTORCYCLE & SCOOTER The sunny Kohala and Kona coasts are ideal for tooling around on a motorcycle, while those sticking to one resort or Kailua-Kona can easily get around by scooter. In Kailua-Kona,

Hawaiian Adventure Rentals, 75-5669 Alii Dr. (www.hiadv.com; © **808/445-6722**), rents new and vintage Yamahas from $70 to $170 a day, including helmets and jackets, with discounts for longer bookings. Choose from a variety of heavier hogs at **Big Island Harley-Davidson,** 75-5633 Palani Rd. (www.bigislandharley.com; © **888/904-3155** or 808/217-8560), with rates starting at $99 daily ($639 weekly), including gear and unlimited mileage, for qualified drivers. **Big Island Mopeds** (www.konamopedrentals.com; © **808/443-6625**) will deliver mopeds to your door for $40 day ($200 weekly; note prices rise to $100 daily/$500 weekly during Ironman week in mid-Oct).

[FastFACTS] THE BIG ISLAND

ATMs/Banks ATMs are located everywhere on the Big Island, at banks, supermarkets, Long's Drugs, and at some shopping malls. The major banks on the Big Island are First Hawaiian, Bank of Hawaii, American Savings, and Central Pacific, all with branches in both Kona and Hilo.

Business Hours Most businesses on the island are open from 8 or 9am to 5 or 6pm.

Dentists In Kohala, contact **Dr. Craig C. Kimura** at Kamuela Office Center, 65-1230 Mamalahoa Hwy., Waimea (© **808/885-5947**). In Kailua-Kona, call **Dr. Christopher Bays** at **Kona Coast Dental Care,** 75-5591 Palani Rd., above the KBXtreme Bowling Center (www.konacoastdental.com; © **808/329-8067**). In Hilo, **Island Ohana Dental,** 519 E. Lanikaula St. (www.islandohanadental.com; © **808/935-4800**), is open Mon–Sat, with three siblings—**Drs. Germaine, Garrett,** and **Jill Uehara**—on staff.

Doctors For drop-in visits, head to **Urgent Care of Kona,** 77-311 Sunset Dr., Kailua-Kona (www.urgentcareofkona.com; © **808/327-4357**). It's open 8am–5pm weekdays and 9am–5pm on Sat. Kaiser Permanente has an affiliated **Urgent Care Center** at 45 Mohouli St., Hilo (© **808/969-3051**), open 8:30am–8:30pm weekdays and 8:30am–4:30pm weekends.

Emergencies For ambulance, fire, or rescue services, dial © **911.**

Hospitals Hospitals offering 24-hour, urgent-care facilities include the **Kona Community Hospital,** 79-1019 Haukapila St., off Highway 11, Kealakekua (www.kch.hhsc.org; © **808/322-9311**); **Hilo Medical Center,** 1190 Waianuenue Ave., Hilo (www.hilomedicalcenter.org; © **808/932-3000**); **North Hawaii Community Hospital,** 67-1125 Mamalahoa Hwy., Waimea (www.nhch.com; © **808/885-4444**); and the tiny **Kau Hospital,**

1 Kamani St., Pahala (www.kauhospital.org; © **808/932-4200**).

Internet Access Pretty much every lodging on the island has Wi-Fi; resorts typically include it in their exorbitant resort fees, but some hotels offer it for a daily charge. All **Starbucks** and **McDonald's** locations, plus numerous local coffee shops also offer free Wi-Fi.

Pharmacies The only 24-hour pharmacy is in Hilo at **Longs Drugs,** 555 Kilauea Ave., one of 12 around the island (www.cvs.com; © **808/935-9075**). The rest open as early as 7am and close as late as 9pm Monday through Saturday; some are closed Sunday. Kona and Hilo's national chain stores such as **Kmart, Safeway, Target, Wal-Mart,** and **Costco** (Kailua-Kona only) also have pharmacies with varying hours.

Police Dial © **911** in case of emergency; otherwise, call the **Hawaii Police Department** at © **808/935-3311** islandwide.

Post Office   The **U.S. Postal Service** (www.usps. com; ☎ **800/275-8777**) has 28 branches around the island, including in Kailua-Kona at 74-5577 Palani Rd., in Waimea (Kamuela) at 67-1197 Mamalahoa Hwy., and in Hilo at 1299 Kekuanaoa St. All are open weekdays; some are also open Saturday morning.

Volcanic Activity
Before you visit **Hawaii Volcanoes National Park,** learn if lava is flowing and check for road closures and other conditions at www. nps.gov/havo/planyourvisit/ index.htm. For daily **air-quality reports,** based on sulfur dioxide and particulates measured at eight sites around the island, visit http://hiso2index.info.

EXPLORING THE BIG ISLAND
Attractions & Points of Interest

Although parks are open year-round, some of the other attractions below may be closed on major holidays such as Christmas, New Year's, or Thanksgiving Day. Admission is often reduced for Hawaii residents (*kamaaina*) with state ID.

NORTH KONA

Hulihee Palace ★★★ HISTORIC SITE   John Adams Kuakini, royal governor of the island, built this stately, two-story New England–style mansion overlooking Kailua Bay in 1838. It later became a summer home for King Kalakaua and Queen Kapiolani and, like Queen Emma's Summer Palace and Iolani Palace on Oahu, is now lovingly maintained by the Daughters of Hawaii as a showcase for royal furnishings and Native Hawaiian artifacts, from hat boxes to koa furniture and a 22-foot spear. You can take a self-guided tour of its six spacious rooms, but it's worth arriving in time for a guided tour, at 10am and 1pm daily, to learn more of the monarchs' history and cultural context; guided tours are also the only ones permitted on the oceanfront lanai. A sign directs you to remove shoes before entering, with free booties provided upon request.

Hulihee Palace

The palace lawn hosts 12 free events a year honoring a different member of Hawaiian royalty, with performances by local hula schools and musicians. Called **Afternoon at the Palace,** they're generally held at 4pm on the third Sunday of the month (except June and Dec, when the performances are held in conjunction with King Kamehameha Day and Christmas). Check the Daughters of Hawaii website for dates.

75-5718 Alii Dr., Kailua-Kona. http://daughtersofhawaii.org. © **808/329-1877.** $10 adults, $8 seniors, $1 ages 5–17. Mon–Sat 9am–4pm, Sun 10am–3pm.

Kaloko-Honokoha National Historical Park ★★ HISTORIC SITE/NATURAL ATTRACTION   With no erupting volcano, impressive tikis, or massive temples, this 1,160-acre oceanfront site just north of Honokohau Harbor tends to get overlooked by visitors in favor of its showier siblings in the national park system. That's a shame for several reasons, among them it's a microcosm of ancient Hawaii, from fish ponds (one with an 800-ft.-long rock wall), house platforms, petroglyphs, and trails through barren lava to marshlands with native waterfowl, reefs teeming with fish, and a tranquil beach where green sea turtles bask in the shadow of Puuoina Heiau. Plus, it's rarely crowded, and admission is free. Stop by the small visitor center to pick up a brochure and ask about ocean conditions (if you're planning to snorkel), and then backtrack to Honokohau Harbor, a half-mile south, to park closer to the beach.

Ocean side of Hwy. 19, 3 miles south of Kona airport. www.nps.gov/kaho. © **808/326-9057.** Visitor center and parking lot ½-mile north of Honokohau Harbor daily 8:30am–4pm. Kaloko Rd. gate daily 8am–5pm. No time restrictions on parking at Honokohau Harbor; from Hwy.19, take Kealakehe Pkwy. west into harbor, then take 1st right, and follow to parking lot near Kona Sailing Club, a short walk to beach.

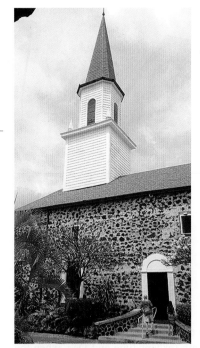

Mokuaikaua Church

Mokuaikaua Church ★ RELIGIOUS/HISTORIC SITE   In 1820, just a few months after King Kamehameha II and Queen Regent Kaahumanu had broken the *kapu* system (taboos) at Ahuena Heiau, the first missionaries to land in Hawaii arrived on the brig *Thaddeus* and received the royals' permission to preach. Within a few years a thatched-roof structure had risen on this site, on land donated by Gov. Kuakini, owner of Hulihee Palace across the road. But after several fires, Rev. Asa Thurston had this massive, New England–style structure erected, using lava rocks from a nearby *heiau* (temple) held together by coral mortar, with gleaming koa for the lofty interior; the 112-foot steeple is still the tallest structure in Kailua-Kona. Visitors are welcome to view the sanctuary, open daily,

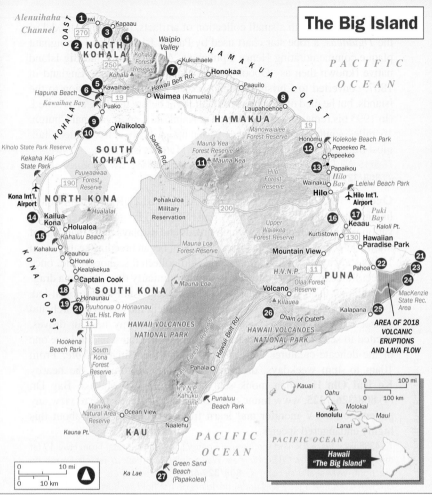

The Big Island

and a rear room with a small collection of artifacts, including a model of the *Thaddeus,* a rope star chart used by Pacific Islanders, and a poignant plaque commemorating Henry Opukahaia. As a teenager, the Big Island native (known then as "Obookiah") boarded a ship to New England in 1807, converted to Christianity, and helped plan the first mission to the islands, but he died of a fever in 1818, the year before the *Thaddeus* sailed. (In 1993 his remains were reinterred at Kahikolu Congregational Church, 16 miles south of Mokuaikaua.) Mokuaikaua hosts a free history talk most Sundays at 12:15pm, following the 11am service.

75-5713 Alii Dr., Kailua-Kona, across from Hulihee Palace. www.mokuaikaua.org. 🕐 **808/329-0655.** Daily 7:30am–5:30pm.

Ocean Rider Seahorse Farm ★★ AQUACULTURE   On the coastline just behind the Natural Energy Lab (NELHA) lies this 3-acre, conservation-oriented "aqua-farm," which breeds and displays more than half of the world's 36 species of seahorses. The farm began breeding seahorses in 1998 as a way of ending demand for wild-collected seahorses and, once successful, expanded its interests to include similarly threatened sea dragons and reef fish. Although the $41 online ticket cost of the biologist-led, 1-hour tour may seem excessive, proceeds benefit the farm's research and conservation. In any case, people still find their way here in droves, excited to see pregnant male seahorses and their babies, and to have one of the delicate creatures wrap its tail around their fingers. ***Note:*** From 10am to 4pm weekdays, drop-in visitors are welcome at the nearby **Ke Kai Ola** Hawaiian monk seal hospital, 73-731 Makako Bay Dr. (🕐 **808/326-7325,** www.tmmc.org/monkseal), where it's free to view any patients on a TV monitor and learn from interpretive signs about this highly endangered species.

73-4388 Ilikai Place (behind the Natural Energy Lab), Kailua-Kona. From Hwy. 19 (at mile marker 94), follow OTEC Rd. past Wawalaloli Beach Park to 1st left; farm is on the right. www.seahorse.com. 🕐 **808/329-6840.** Online tickets: $41 adults, $31 children 4–12, free ages 3 and under (toddlers do not hold seahorses). At the door: $43 adults, $33 ages 4–12. Tours Mon–Fri 10am, noon and 2pm; reservations recommended. Gift shop Mon–Fri 9:30am–3:30pm.

SOUTH KONA

Kealakekua Bay State Historical Park ★★ NATURAL ATTRACTION   The island's largest natural sheltered bay, a marine life conservation district, is not only one of the best places to snorkel on Hawaii Island, it's also an area of deep cultural and historical significance. On the southern Napoopoo *("nah-poh-oh-poh-oh")* side stands the large stacked-rock platform of **Hikiau Heiau,** a temple once used for human sacrifice and still considered sacred. A rocky beach park here includes picnic tables, barbecues, and restrooms. On the north side, a steep but relatively broad 2-mile trail leads down to Kaawaloa, where *Alii* (royalty) once lived; when they died, their bodies were taken to **Puhina O Lono Heiau** on the

CRAZY FOR KONA coffee

More than 600 farms grow coffee in the Kona Coffee Belt on the slopes of Hualalai, from Kailua-Kona and Holualoa in North Kona to Captain Cook and Honaunau in South Kona. The prettiest time to visit is between January and May, when the rainy season brings white blossoms known as "Kona snow." Harvesting is by hand—one reason Kona coffee is so costly—from July through January. At least 40 farms offer regular **tours with tastings,** and many more provide samples. You can make impromptu stops along Mamalahoa Highway (Hwy. 11 and Hwy. 180) or find more obscure farms and those requiring reservations via the **Kona Coffee Farmers Association** (www.konacoffeefarmers.org). Some highlights, heading north to south:

○ **Kona Blue Sky Coffee Company,** 76-973 Hualalai Rd., Holualoa (www.konablueskycoffee.com; ✆ **877/322-1700** or 808/322-1700): The Christian Twigg-Smith family and staff grows and sells its coffee on a 400-acre estate, with free, 15-minute guided walking tours (about half of which is watching a video) and tastings Tuesday to Friday, on the hour from 9am to 4pm.

○ **Holualoa Kona Coffee Company,** 77-6261 Mamalahoa Hwy. (Hwy. 180), Holulaloa (www.konalea.com; ✆ **800/334-0348** or 808/322-9937): Owned by Desmond and Lisen Twigg-Smith, this organic farm and mill sells its own and others' premium Kona coffee. Tour the orchards (mowed and fertilized by a flock of about 50 geese) and witness all phases of processing, weekdays from 8am to 4pm.

○ **Kona Joe Coffee,** 79-7346 Mamalahoa Hwy. (Hwy. 11 between mile markers 113 and 114), Kainaliu; www.konajoe.com; ✆ **808/322-2100**): The home of the world's first trellised coffee farm offers a free, self-guided tour with 8-minute video, as well as guided tours by request ($15 adults, free for kids 12 and under), daily from 8am to 4pm. Guided tours of the 20-acre estate include a mug, coffee, and chocolate, with reservations recommended for groups of six or more; coffee-loving couples should book the 1-hr., in-depth VIP tour ($170 per two adults.)

○ **Greenwell Farms,** 81-6581 Mamalahoa Hwy. (*makai* side of Hwy. 11, south of mile marker 112), Kealakekua (www.greenwellfarms.com; ✆ **808/323-2295**): If any farm can claim to be the granddaddy of Kona coffee, this would be it. Englishman Henry Nicholas Greenwell began growing coffee in the region in 1850. Now operated by his great-grandson and agricultural innovator Tom Greenwell, the farm offers free tours daily from 8:30am to 4pm. On Thursday, join volunteers baking Portuguese sweet bread in a stone oven from 10am to 1pm at the **Greenwell Store Museum** ★ just south of the farm; bread sales ($8) start at 12:30pm and sell out quickly.

slope above, prepared for burial, and hidden in caves on the 600-foot-cliff above the central bay. The **Captain Cook Monument** is an obelisk on Kaawaloa Flat, near where the British explorer was slain in 1779, after misunderstandings between Hawaiians and Cook's crew led to armed conflict. The Hawaiians then showed respect by taking Cook's body to Puhina O Lono before returning some of his remains to his crew. Please do not tread on the reef or cultural sites; to protect the area, only hikers and three guided kayak tour companies have access to Kaawaloa Flat (see "Kayaking" on p. 236).

From Hwy. 11 in Captain Cook heading south, take right fork onto Napoopoo Rd. (Hwy. 160). Kaawaloa trailhead is about 500 ft. on right. By car, continue on Napoopoo Rd. 4¼-mile to left on Puuhonua Rd.; go ⅕-mile to right on Manini Beach Rd. http://dlnr.hawaii.gov/dsp/parks/hawaii. Free. Daily during daylight hours.

The Painted Church (St. Benedict's) ★★ RELIGIOUS SITE

Beginning in 1899, Father John Berchman Velghe (a member of the same order as St. Damien of Molokai) painted biblical scenes and images of saints inside quaint St. Benedict's Catholic Church, built in 1842 and restored in 2002. As with stained-glass windows of yore, his pictures, created with simple house paint, were a way of sharing stories with illiterate parishioners. It's a wonderfully trippy experience to look up at arching palm fronds and shiny stars on the ceiling. Health issues forced the priest to return to Belgium in 1904 before finishing all the pictures. The ocean-view church is typically open during the day, but keep in mind it's an active parish, with Mass celebrated five times a week.

84-5140 Painted Church Rd., Captain Cook. ✆ **808/328-2227.** From Kailua-Kona, take Hwy. 11 south 20 miles to a right on Rte. 160. Go 1 mile to the 1st turnoff on the right, opposite from a King Kamehameha sign. Follow the narrow, winding road about ¼-mile to church sign and turn right. Free admission.

The Painted Church

Puuhonua O Honaunau National Historical Park ★★★

HISTORIC SITE With its fierce, haunting carved idols known as *ki'i*—the Hawaiian word for tiki—this sacred, 420-acre site on the black-lava Kona Coast certainly looks forbidding. To ancient Hawaiians, it served as a 16th-century place of refuge (*pu'uhonua*), providing sanctuary for defeated warriors and *kapu* (taboo) violators. A great rock wall—1,000 feet long, 10 feet high, and 17 feet thick—defines the refuge where Hawaiians found safety. On the wall's north end is **Hale O Keawe Heiau,** which holds the bones of 23 Hawaiian chiefs. Other archaeological finds include a royal compound, burial sites, old trails, and a portion of an ancient village. You can learn about reconstructed thatched huts, canoes, and idols on a self-guided tour, but try to make one of the free daily ranger talks, 10:30am and 2:30pm in a covered amphitheater. *Note:* Only bottled water is sold in the park, but there are picnic tables on the sandy stretch of the south side.

Puuhonua O Honaunau National Historical Park

Hwy. 160, Honaunau. From Kailua-Kona, take Hwy. 11 south 20 miles to a right on Hwy. 160. Head 3½ miles and turn left at park sign. www.nps.gov/puho. ℂ **808/328-2288.** $15 per vehicle; $10 per motorcycle; $7 per person on foot or bicycle; good for 7 days. Visitor center daily 8:30am–4:30pm; park daily 7am–sunset.

SOUTH KOHALA

Hamakua Macadamia Nut Factory ★ FACTORY TOUR

The self-guided tour of shelling, roasting, and other processing that results in flavored macadamia nuts and confections is not that compelling if production has stopped for the day, so go before 3pm or plan to watch a video to get caught up. But who are we kidding—it's really all about the free tastings here, generous samples of big, fresh nuts in island flavors such as chili "peppah," Spam, and Kona-coffee glazed. Outside the hilltop factory warehouse are picnic tables with an ocean view.

61-3251 Maluokalani St., Kawaihae. www.hawnnut.com. ℂ **888/643-6688** or 808/882-1690. Free. Daily 9am–5:30pm. From Kawaihae Harbor, take Hwy. 270 north ¾-mile, turn right on Maluokalani St., and drive ⅕-mile uphill; factory is on right.

Kohala Petrogylph Fields ★★★ ROCK CARVINGS

The Hawaiian petroglyphs are a great enigma of the Pacific—no one knows who made them or why. They appear at 135 different sites on six inhabited islands, but most are found on the Big Island, and include images of dancers and paddlers, fishermen and chiefs, and tools of daily life such as fish hooks and canoes. The most common representations are family groups, while some petroglyphs depict post–European contact objects such as ships, anchors, horses, and guns. Simple circles with dots were used to mark the *puka,* or holes, where parents would place their child's umbilical cord (*piko*).

The largest concentration of these stone symbols in the Pacific lies in the 233-acre **Puako Petroglyph Archaeological Preserve** next to the Fairmont Orchid, Hawaii, at the Mauna Lani Resort. Some 3,000 designs have been identified. The 1.5-mile **Malama Trail** through a kiawe field to the large, reddish lava field starts north of the hotel, *makai* side. Take Highway 19 to the resort turnoff and drive toward the coast on North Kaniku Drive, which ends at the Holoholokai Beach parking lot; the trailhead on your right is marked by a sign and interpretive kiosk. Go in the early morning or late afternoon when it's cooler; bring water, wear shoes with sturdy soles (to avoid kiawe thorns), and stay on the trail.

Local expert Kalei'ula Kaneau leads a **free 1-hour tour** of the petroglyphs near the Kings' Shops in the Waikoloa Beach Resort Thursdays and Fridays at 9:30am; meet lakeside by Island Fish & Chips. You can also follow the signs to the trail through the petroglyph field on your own, but be aware that the trail is exposed, uneven, and rough; wear closed-toe shoes, a hat, and sunscreen.

Note: The petroglyphs are thousands of years old and easily destroyed. Do not walk on them or take rubbings (the Puako preserve has a replica petroglyph you may use instead). The best way to capture a petroglyph is with a photo in the late afternoon when the shadows are long.

Puukohola Heiau National Historic Site ★★★ HISTORIC SITE   This seacoast temple, called "the hill of the whale," is the single most imposing and dramatic structure of the early Hawaiians, built by

Kamehameha I from 1790 to 1791. The *heiau* stands 224 feet long by 100 feet wide, with three narrow terraces on the seaside and an amphitheater to view canoes. Kamehameha built this temple to Ku, the war god, after a prophet told him he would conquer and unite the islands if he did so. He also slayed his cousin on the site, and 4 years later fulfilled his kingly goal. The site includes an interactive visitor center; a smaller *heiau*-turned-fort; the homestead of John Young (a trusted advisor of Kamehameha); and, offshore, the submerged ruins of what is believed to be **Hale O Kapuni,** a shrine dedicated to the shark gods or guardian spirits called *'aumakua.* (You can't see the temple, but shark fins are often spotted slicing through the waters.) Paved trails lead around the complex, with restricted access to the *heiau.*

62-3601 Kawaihae Rd. (Hwy. 270, *makai* side, south of Kawaihae Harbor). www.nps. gov/puhe. © **808/882-7218.** Free. Daily 8am–4:45pm.

NORTH KOHALA

It takes some effort to reach the **Kohala Historical Sites State Monument ★,** but for those with 4WD vehicles or the ability to hike 3 miles round-trip, visiting the windswept, culturally important site on the on the island's northern tip may be worth it. The 1,500-year-old **Mookini Heiau,** once used by kings to pray and offer human sacrifices, is among the oldest, largest (the size of a football field), and most significant shrines in Hawaii. It's off a coastal dirt road, 1½ miles southwest of 'Upolu Airport (http://dlnr.hawaii.gov/dsp/parks/hawaii; Thurs–Tues 9am–8pm; free admission).

King Kamehameha Statue ★★ MONUMENT   Here stands King Kamehameha the Great, right arm outstretched, left arm holding a spear, as if guarding the seniors who have turned a century-old, New England–style courthouse into an airy civic center. There's one just like it in Honolulu, across the street from Iolani Palace, and another in the U.S. Capitol, but this is the original: an 8-foot, 6-inch bronze by Thomas R. Gould, a Boston sculptor. Cast in Europe in 1880, it was lost at sea on its way to Hawaii. After a sea captain recovered the statue, it was placed here, near Kamehameha's Kohala birthplace, in 1912. The unifier of the islands, Kamehameha is believed to have been born in 1758 under Halley's Comet and became ruler of Hawaii in 1810. He died in Kailua-Kona in 1819, but his burial site remains a mystery.

In front of North Kohala Civic Center, *mauka* side of Hwy. 270, Kapaau, just north of Kapaau Rd.

Lapakahi State Historical Park ★★ HISTORIC SITE   This 14th-century fishing village on a hot, dry, dusty stretch of coast offers a glimpse into the lifestyle of the ancients. Lapakahi is the best-preserved fishing village in Hawaii. Take the self-guided, 1-mile loop trail past stone platforms, fish shrines, rock shelters, salt pans, and restored *hale* (houses) to a coral-sand beach and the deep-blue sea of Koai'e Cove, a marine life

Pololu Valley

conservation district. Wear good walking shoes and a hat, go early in the morning or late in the afternoon to beat the heat, and bring your own water. Facilities include portable toilets and picnic tables.

Makai side of Hwy. 270, Mahukona, 12.4 miles north of Kawaihae. http://dlnr.hawaii. gov/dsp/parks/hawaii. © **808/327-4958.** Free. Daily 8am–4pm.

Pololu Valley Lookout ★★★ NATURAL ATTRACTION   At this end-of-the-road scenic lookout, you can gaze at the vertical dark-green cliffs of the Hamakua Coast and two islets offshore or peer back into the often-misty uplands. The view may look familiar once you get here—it often appears on travel posters. Adventurous travelers should take the switchback trail (a good 45-min. hike) to a secluded black-sand beach at the mouth of a wild valley once planted in taro. Bring water and bug spray, avoid the surf (subject to strong currents), and refrain from creating new stacks of rocks, which disrupt the beach ecology.

At the northern end of Hwy. 270, 5½ miles east of Kapaau.

WAIMEA & MAUNA KEA

Mauna Kea ★★★ NATURAL ATTRACTION   The 13,796-foot summit of Mauna Kea, the world's tallest mountain if measured from its base on the ocean floor, is one of the best places on earth for astronomical observations, thanks to pollution-free skies, pitch-black nights, and a tropical location. Here are the world's largest telescopes—and at press time, some environmentalists and Native Hawaiians who still worship here were fighting construction of an even larger one—but the stargazing is fantastic even with the naked eye. *Note:* Some spell it Maunakea, a contraction of *Mauna a Wakea,* or "the mountain of Wakea" (said to be the sky father and ancestor of all Hawaiians), in lieu of Mauna Kea, or "white mountain."

SAFETY TIPS   Before heading out, make sure you have four-wheel drive and a full gas tank, and check current weather and road conditions (http://mkwc.ifa.hawaii.edu/current/road-conditions; ✆ **808/935-6268**). The drive via Saddle Road (Hwy. 200) to the visitor center takes about an hour from Hilo and 90 minutes from Kailua-Kona; stay at least 30 minutes to acclimate before ascending to the summit, a half-hour further on a steep, largely unpaved road. Dress warmly: It's chilly and windy by day, and after dark, temperatures drop into the 30s (from 3°C to -1°C). To avoid the bends, don't go within 24 hours of scuba diving; pregnant women, children under 16, and those with heart or lung conditions should also skip this trip. At night, bring a flashlight, with a red filter to reduce glare. *Note:* Many rental-car agencies ban driving on remote Saddle Road, so a private tour, while pricey, is probably the safest and easiest bet (see "Seeing Stars While Others Drive," below).

VISITOR CENTER   Named for Ellison Onizuka, the Big Island astronaut aboard the ill-fated *Challenger,* the **Onizuka Center for International Astronomy Visitor Information Station** (www.ifa.hawaii.edu/info/vis; ✆ **808/961-2180**) is 6¼ miles up Summit Road and at 9,200 feet elevation. It's open daily noon to 10pm, with interactive exhibits, 24-hour restrooms, and a bookstore with food, drink, gloves, and other gear for sale. Day visitors can peer through a solar telescope. From 6 to 10pm Tuesday, Wednesday, Friday, and Saturday (weather dependent), a guide leads a free **stargazing** program that starts with a screening of *First Light,* a documentary about the cultural and astronomical significance of Mauna Kea. *Note:* In peak seasons the parking lot can fill up quickly, with long lines for

On the way to Mauna Kea

seeing stars WHILE OTHERS DRIVE

Two excellent companies offer Mauna Kea tour packages that provide cold-weather gear, dinner, hot drinks, guided stargazing, and, best of all, someone else to worry about maneuvering the narrow, unpaved road to the summit. All tours are offered weather permitting, but most nights are clear—that's why the observatories are here, after all—with pickups from several locations. Read the fine print on health and age restrictions before booking, and don't forget to tip your guide ($10–$20 per person).

○ **Hawaii Forest & Trail** (www.hawaii-forest.com; ☎ **800/464-1993** or 808/331-8505), the island's premier outfitter, operates a daily **Maunakea Summit & Stars Adventure,** which includes a late-afternoon picnic dinner, sunset at the summit, and stargazing at the visitor center, for $221. The company uses two customized off-road buses (14 passengers max each) for the 7- to 8-hour tour. Early risers can take advantage of jet lag for the exclusive

Maunakea Sunrise Experience ($197), which departs at 3:15am and includes breakfast, allows you to see the night sky on the slope of the mountain and sunrise at the top. A daytime option from Hilo, **Maunakea Voyage** ($179) offers lunch and a private tour of the Imiloa Astronomy Center, with a peek inside a summit observatory. Like all of Hawaii Forest & Trail's tours, these are exceptional, with well-informed guides.

○ **Monty "Pat" Wright** was the first to run a Mauna Kea stargazing tour when he launched **Mauna Kea Summit Adventures** (www.maunakea.com; ☎ **888/322-2366** or 808/322-2366) in 1983. Guests now ride in a large-windowed, four-wheel-drive (4WD) van instead of a Land Cruiser and don parkas instead of old sweaters; otherwise, it's much the same, with veggie lasagna for dinner at the visitor center before a spectacular sunset and stargazing. The 7½- to 8-hour tour costs $216.

Observatories at Maunakea

telescopes. Check the website for special cultural or science programs at 6pm Saturday, preceding the stargazing.

AT THE SUMMIT   It's another steep 6 miles, most of them unpaved, to the summit from the visitor center. If you're driving, make sure your 4WD vehicle has plenty of gas and is in good condition before continuing on. Up here, 11 nations have set up 13 peerless infrared telescopes to look into deep space, making this the world's largest astronomical observatory. The **W. M. Keck Observatory** has a visitor gallery, open weekdays 10am–4pm, with informational panels, restrooms, and a viewing area of the eight-story-high telescope and dome (you can also visit its Waimea headquarters; see www.keckobservatory.org for details). For cultural reasons, visitors are discouraged from hiking the footpath across the road to the actual, unmarked summit where ancient astronomers and priests came to study the skies and where Native Hawaiians still worship today. No matter: From the summit parking lot you have an unparalleled view of other peaks, such as Mauna Loa and Haleakala, and the bright Pacific.

Another sacred site is **Lake Waiau,** which, at 13,020 feet above sea level, is one of the highest in the world. Although it shrinks drastically in time of drought, it has never dried up. It's named for one of the sisters of Poliahu, the snow goddess said to make her home atop Mauna Kea. To see it, you must take a brief hike: At Park 3, the first intersection on the road to the summit above the visitor center, follow the trail to the south for .5-mile, then take branch to the right that leads to the top of a crater and

Lake Waiau, inside the cinder cone just below the summit of Mauna Kea

the small, greenish lake. *Note:* Please respect cultural traditions by not drinking or entering the water, and leave all rocks undisturbed.

THE HAMAKUA COAST

Don't forget bug spray when exploring this warm, moist region, beloved by mosquitoes, and be ready for passing showers—you're in rainbow territory here. *Note:* Some sights below are in the North Hilo district, just south of the official Hamakua district, which shares its rural character.

Akaka Falls State Park ★★★ NATURAL ATTRACTION   See one of the most scenic waterfalls in Hawaii via a relatively easy .4-mile paved loop through a rainforest, past bamboo and flowering ginger, and down to an observation point. You'll have a perfect view of 442-foot Akaka Falls, plunging down a horseshoe-shaped green cliff, and nearby Kahuna Falls, a mere 100-footer. Keep your eyes peeled for rainbows; your ears are likely to pick up the two-note chirp of coqui frogs (see below). Facilities include restrooms and drinking water.

End of Akaka Falls Rd. (Hwy. 220), Honomu. http://dlnr.hawaii.gov/dsp/parks/hawaii. From Hilo, drive north 8 miles on Hwy. 19 to left at Akaka Falls Rd. Follow 3½ miles to parking lot. $5 per car, $1 per person on foot or bicycle. Walk-ins sunrise to sunset, parking lot 8:30am–6pm daily.

Akaka Falls

Co-key, Co-key: What Is That Noise?

That loud, chirping noise you hear after dark, especially on the eastern side of the Big Island, is the cry of the male coqui frog looking for a mate. A native of Puerto Rico, where the frogs are kept in check by snakes, the coqui frog came to Hawaii in some plant material, found no natural enemies, and spread quickly across the Big Island, concentrated on the Hilo side. (A handful have made it to Oahu, Maui, and Kauai, where they've been swiftly captured by state agriculture teams devoted to eradicating the invasive species.) A few frogs will sound like singing birds; a chorus of thousands can be deafening—and on Hawaii Island,

they can reach densities of up to 10,000 an acre. Coqui frogs don't like the cool weather of Waimea and Volcano as much, but anywhere else that's lush and rural is likely to have large populations. Pack earplugs if you're a light sleeper.

Botanical World Adventures ★ WATERFALL/GARDEN Just north of Hilo is one of the largest botanical gardens in Hawaii, with some 5,000 species. Although it no longer offers a vista of spectacular, triple-stacked Umauma Falls (see below), it still lays claim to a huge children's maze (second in size only to Dole Plantation's on Oahu), a tropical fruit arboretum, ethnobotanical and wellness gardens, and flower-lined walks. Waterfall lovers will be heartened to note that the owners have also created a road and trail leading to viewing areas above and below the previously hidden 100-foot **Kamaee Falls** ($6 if you want to go there only), as well as a trail leading past a series of shorter, bubbling cascades in **Hanapueo Stream.** If that's just too peaceful for you, opt for one of the **Segway tours,** ranging from 30 minutes to 3 hours ($57–$187) or a **zipline tour** ($167), which like guided walks should be reserved in advance. All tour rates include garden admission.

31-240 Old Mamalahoa Hwy., Hakalau. www.worldbotanicalgardens.com. ℂ **888/947-4753** or 808/963-5427. $15 adults, $7 teens 13–17, $3 children 5–12, free for children 4 and under. Guided 2-hr. garden tours $57 adults, $33 children 5–12, free for children 4 and under; guided rainforest/waterfall tours $129. Guided tours require 24-hr. advance reservations. Daily 9am–5:30pm. From Hilo, take Hwy. 19 north past mile marker 16, turn left on Leopolino Rd., and then right on Old Mamalahoa Hwy.; entrance is ¹⁄₁₀-mile on right.

Hawaii Tropical Botanical Garden ★★ GARDEN More than 2,000 species of tropical plants thrive in this little-known Eden by the sea. The 40-acre valley garden, nestled between the crashing surf and a thundering waterfall, includes torch gingers (which tower on 12-ft. stalks), a banyan canyon, an orchid garden, a banana grove, a bromeliad hill, an

A TASTE OF THE Hamakua coast

When the Hamakua Sugar Company—the Big Island's last sugar plantation—closed in 1996, it left a huge void in the local economy, transforming already shrinking villages into near ghost towns. But some residents turned to specialty crops that are now sought after by chefs throughout the islands. Hidden in the tall eucalyptus trees outside the old plantation community of Paauilo, the **Hawaiian Vanilla Company** ★★ (www.hawaiian vanilla.com; ✆ **808/776-1771**) is the first U.S. farm to grow vanilla. Before you even enter the huge Vanilla Gallery, you will be embraced by the heavenly scent of vanilla. The farm hosts one of the most sensuous experiences on the island, the four-course **Hawaiian Vanilla Luncheon** ($42 for age 12 and up; $28 for kids 4–11), served weekdays from 12:30 to 2:30pm. The 45-minute **Farm Tour** ($25 for age 4 and up; free for kids 3 and under), including dessert and tastings, takes place weekdays at 1pm. Reservations required for luncheon or tour; the gallery and gift shop are open 10am to 3pm Monday through Saturday.

anthurium corner, and a golden bamboo grove, which rattles like a jungle drum in the trade winds. Some endangered Hawaiian specimens, such as the rare *Gardenia remyi*, flourish in this habitat. The self-guided tour takes about 90 minutes, but you're welcome to linger. Pick up a loaner umbrella in the visitor center, where you register, so that passing showers don't curtail your visit. *Note:* You enter and exit the garden via a 500-foot-long boardwalk that descends along a verdant ravine. Free golf-cart assistance is provided for wheelchair users to reach the wheelchair-accessible path below; for those without wheelchairs but with limited physical ability, the cost to ride the cart there and back is $5.

27-717 Old Mamalahoa Hwy. (4-Mile Scenic Route), Papaikou. www.htbg.com. ✆ **808/964-5233.** $20 adults, $5 children 6–16, free for children 5 and under. Daily 9am–5pm (last entry 4pm). From Hilo, take Hwy. 19 north 7 miles to right turn on Scenic Route; visitor center is 2 miles on the left.

Laupahoehoe Point ★ HISTORIC SITE/NATURAL ATTRACTION
This idyllic place holds a grim reminder of nature's fury. On April 1, 1946, a tsunami swept across the schoolhouse that once stood on this peninsula of leaf-shaped lava (*laupāhoehoe*) and claimed the lives of 24 students, teachers, and residents. Their names are engraved on a stone memorial in this pretty little beach park, and a display holds newspaper stories on the tragedy. The land here ends in black sea stacks that resemble tombstones; when high surf crashes on them, it's positively spooky (and dangerous if you stand too close). The unprotected shoreline is not a place to swim, but the views are spectacular. Facilities include restrooms, picnic tables, and drinking water.

Laupahoehoe. From Hilo, take Hwy. 19 north 25 miles to Laupahoehoe Point exit, *makai* side; the exit is 31 miles south of Waimea.

Umauma Falls ★★ WATERFALL/GARDEN Formerly accessed through Botanical World Adventures (above), the triple-tiered, cascading pools of Umauma Falls are now the exclusive province of visitors to the neighboring Umauma Experience, which offers an array of ziplining, rappelling, swimming, and kayaking excursions on its lush 90 acres. The less adventurous can also just pay $10 to drive the paved road to the waterfall lookout, and then take a self-guided garden hike with several more overlooks; it's worth it. Pick up a map at the visitor center, which also sells snacks and drinks. You can enjoy your repast at the river walk's observation area, under guava trees (feel free to sample their fruit when ripe), or on the visitor center's back lanai, which overlooks the river, a giant swing for daredevils ($20 per ride), and the last line on the zip course (see "Ziplining" on p. 254). *Note:* Book online for best rates. Also, the swim in a waterfall pool allows a peek in one of the only petroglyphs on the island's east side.

31-313 Old Mamalahoa Hwy., Hakalau. http://umaumaexperience.com. ⓒ **808/930-9477.** $10 adults, free for children 11 and under; includes waterfall viewing, garden, and river walk. Daily 8am–5pm. Various times: Zipline tours $189–$239; waterfall rappelling $285; kayak/swim/picnic $49. On demand: Giant swing, $20. From Hilo, take Hwy. 19 north past mile marker 16, turn left on Leopolino Rd., then right on Old Mamalahoa Hwy., and follow ½-mile to entrance.

Waipio Valley ★★★ NATURAL ATTRACTION/HISTORIC SITE This breathtakingly beautiful valley has long been a source of fascination, inspiring song and story. From the black-sand bay at its mouth, Waipio ("curving water") sweeps 6 miles between sheer, cathedral-like walls some 2,000 feet high. The tallest waterfall in Hawaii, Hiilawe, tumbles

Saddle up for a horseback ride in lush Waipio Valley

1,300 feet from its rear cliffs. Called "the valley of kings" for the royal burial caves dotting forbiddingly steep walls, this was Kamehameha's boyhood residence; up to 10,000 Hawaiians are thought to have lived here before Westerners arrived. Chinese immigrants later joined them and a modest town arose, but it was destroyed in 1946 by the same tsunami that devastated Hilo and Laupahoehoe, though luckily without fatalities. The town was never rebuilt; only about 50 people live here today, most with no electricity or phones, although others come down on weekends to tend taro patches, camp, and fish.

To get to Waipio Valley, take Highway 19 from Waimea or Hilo to Highway 240 in Honokaa, and follow the highway almost 10 miles to Kukuihaele Road and the **Waipio Valley Lookout ★★★**, a grassy park and picnic area on the edge of Waipio Valley's sheer cliffs, with splendid views of the wild oasis below.

To explore the valley itself, a guided tour is best, for reasons of safety and access. The steep road has a grade of nearly 40% in places and is narrow and potholed; by law, you must use a 4WD vehicle, but even then rental-car agencies ban their vehicles from it, to avoid pricey tow jobs. Hiking down the 900-foot-road is hard on the knees going down and the lungs coming up, and requires dodging cars in both directions. Most of the valley floor is privately owned, with trespassing actively discouraged. Note that unmarked burial sites lie just behind the black-sand beach, which is not good for swimming or snorkeling and has no facilities.

Instead, book a ride on the **Waipio Valley Shuttle ★★** (www.waipio valleyshuttle.com; ✆ **808/775-7121**) for a 90- to 120-minute guided tour that begins with an exciting (and bumpy) drive down in an open-door van. Once on the valley floor, you'll be rewarded with breathtaking views of Hiilawe, plus a narrated tour of the taro patches *(lo'i)* and ruins from the 1946 tsunami. The tour is offered Monday through Saturday at 9am, 11am, 1pm, and 3pm; tickets are $59 for adults and $32 for kids 10 and under (minimum two adult fares); reservations recommended. Check-in is less than a mile from the lookout at **Waipio Valley Artworks** (www. waipiovalleyartworks.com; ✆ **808/775-0958**), on Kukuihaele Road. Waipio Valley Artworks is also the pickup point for Naalapa Stables' **Waipio Valley Horseback Adventure ★★** (www.naalapastables.com; ✆ **808/755-0419**), a 2½-hour guided ride ($94) for ages 8 and up; see "Horseback Riding" (p. 252) for details.

All ages may ride the mule-drawn surrey of **Waipio Valley Wagon Tours ★** (www.waipiovalleywagontours.com; ✆ **808/775-9518**), on a narrated, 90-minute excursion that starts with a van trip to the valley stables. Tours run Monday through Saturday at 10:30am, 12:30pm, and 2:30pm; cost is $60 adults, $55 seniors 65 and older, $30 children 3 to 11, and free for 2 and younger. Reservations are a must; weight distribution is a factor. Check-in is at **Neptune's Gardens Gallery** on Kukuihaele Road (www.neptunesgarden.net; ✆ **808/775-1343**).

HILO

Pick up the map to a self-guided walking tour of Hilo, which focuses on 21 historic sites dating from the 1870s to the present, at the information kiosk of the **Downtown Hilo Improvement Association** (www.down townhilo.com; © 808/935-8850) in the Mooheau Bus Depot, 329 Kamehameha Ave.—the first stop on the tour.

Hilo Bay ★★★ NATURAL ATTRACTION   Old banyan trees shade **Banyan Drive** ★, the lane that curves along the waterfront from Kamehameha Avenue (Hwy. 19) to the Hilo Bay hotels. Most of the trees were planted in the mid-1930s by visitors like Cecil B. DeMille (here in 1933 filming *Four Frightened People*), Babe Ruth (his tree is in front of the Hilo Hawaiian Hotel), King George V, Amelia Earhart, and celebs whose fleeting fame didn't last as long as the trees themselves.

It's worth a stop along Banyan Drive—especially if the coast is clear and the summit of Mauna Kea is free of clouds—to make the short walk across the concrete-arch bridge to **Moku Ola (Coconut Island)** ★, if only to gain a panoramic sense of Hilo Bay and its surroundings.

Continuing on Banyan Drive, just south of Coconut Island, are **Liliuokalani Gardens** ★★, the largest formal Japanese garden this side of Tokyo. The 30-acre park, named for the last monarch of Hawaii, Queen Liliuokalani, and dedicated in 1917 to the islands' first Japanese immigrants, is as pretty as a postcard (if occasionally a little unkempt), with stone lanterns, koi ponds, pagodas, rock gardens, bonsai, and a moon-gate bridge. Admission is free; it's open 24 hours.

Kaumana Caves Park ★★ NATURAL ATTRACTION   Pick up an inexpensive flashlight or headlight ($5–$15) at Walmart in Hilo or Kona before visiting this wilder, longer sibling to the more famous **Nahuku** (Thurston) lava tube (p. 215) in Hawaii Volcanoes National Park. As the sign warns, there are "no lights, no walkway" in this eerily fascinating set of caves formed by an 1881 lava flow that threatened downtown Hilo. Princess Ruth Keelikolani is credited with saving the town by praying to Pele to halt the lava. You can thank the county for maintaining the steep concrete stairs leading into the lava tube's fern-lined "skylight," where the larger right entrance offers a short loop trail and the left entrance leads to a more challenging (that is, watch your head) out-and-back path. Your flashlight will help you spot the lava that cooled fast enough to keep its red cover, and help you avoid stumbling over protruding roots. Wear long sleeves, since it can be cool and dripping, and sturdy shoes, to avoid slipping on the often-slick cave floor.

Kaumana Dr. (Hwy. 200), west of Akala Road (4-mile marker), Hilo. Driving from Hilo, caves are on right and parking lot is on left; cross road carefully. Free.

Lyman Museum & Mission House ★★ MUSEUM/HISTORIC SITE   Yankee missionaries Rev. David and Sarah Lyman had been married for just 24 days before they set sail for Hawaii in 1832, arriving 6 months later in a beautiful but utterly foreign land. Seven years later, they built this two-story home for their growing family (eventually seven children) in a blend of Hawaiian and New England design, with plastered walls, koa floors, and lanais on both floors. It's now the **Mission House,** a museum of 19th-century missionary life. You can only visit the house as part of a guided tour, offered twice daily except Sunday.

The larger, modern **Lyman Museum** next door gives a broader perspective of Hawaiian history and culture. Walk through a lava tube and make your way through multiple climate zones in the **Earth Heritage Gallery**'s "Habitats of Hawaii" exhibit, with recorded bird sounds and full-scale replicas of sea life; mineral and shell enthusiasts can pore over an extensive collection. The **Island Heritage Gallery** examines the life of early Hawaiians, with artifacts such as stone poi pounders, wooden bowls, and *kapa,* the delicate bark cloth; other displays showcase clothing and other artifacts of plantation-era immigrant cultures.

276 Haili St. (at Kapiolani St.). www.lymanmuseum.org. ℂ **808/935-5021.** $10 adults, $8 seniors 60 and over, $5 college students, $3 children 6–17; $21 per family. Mon–Sat 10am–4:30pm; guided house tours at 11am and 2pm (call to reserve).

Maunaloa Macadamia Nut Factory ★ FACTORY TOUR   It's a 3-mile drive through macadamia nut orchards before you reach the visitor center of this factory, where you can learn how the islands' favorite nut is grown and processed. (It's best to visit weekdays, when the actual husking, drying, roasting, and candy-making takes place; otherwise, you can watch short videos at each station.) The gift shop—mobbed when tour buses are in the parking lot—offers free samples and predictable souvenirs; a few items, such as Maunaloa chocolate-dipped macadamia nut shortbread, appear to be exclusive.

16-701 Macadamia Nut Rd., Keaau (5 miles from Hilo, 20 miles from Hawaii Volcanoes National Park). www.maunaloa.com/visitor-center. ℂ **888/628-6256** or 808/966-8618. Free; self-guided factory tours. Daily 8:30am–5pm (factory closed weekdays and holidays). Heading south from Hilo on Hwy. 11, turn left on Macadamia Nut Rd., and head 3 miles to factory; it's 20 miles north of Volcano.

Mokupapapa Discovery Center ★★ MUSEUM   You may never get to the vast coral-reef system that is the Northwest Hawaiian Islands— the protected chain of islets and atolls spanning 1,200 nautical miles is remote (stretching from Nihoa, 155 miles northwest of Kauai, to Kure Atoll, 56 miles west of Midway), and visitation is severely limited. But if you're in downtown Hilo, you can explore the wonders of the region that President George W. Bush protected as Papahanaumokuakea Marine National Monument in 2008 (and President Barack Obama expanded in 2016). Inside a handsomely renovated, century-old building, the Mokupapapa Discovery Center reveals the beauties and mysteries of the World Heritage Site's ecosystem and its relationship with Hawaiian culture. Exhibits include a 3,500-gallon saltwater aquarium with brilliant coral

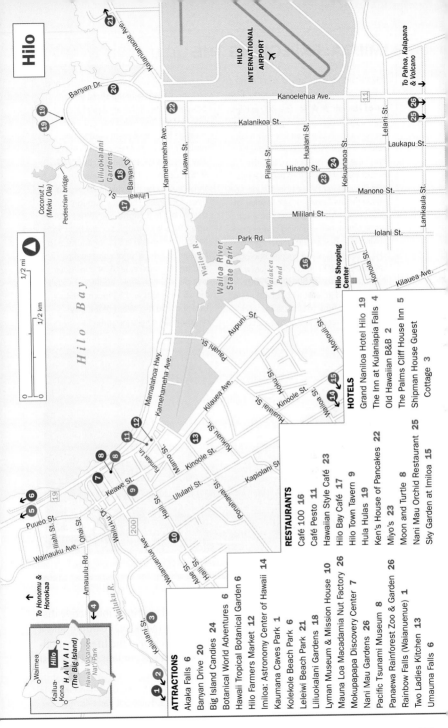

Hilo

Hilo Bay

To Honomu & Honokaa

To Pahoa, Kalapana & Volcano

HILO INTERNATIONAL AIRPORT

Coconut I. (Moku Ola)

Pedestrian bridge

Liliuokalani Gardens

Wailoa River State Park

Waiakea Pond

Hilo Shopping Center

Kanoelehua Ave.
Kalanikoa St.
Kamehameha Ave.
Kuawa St.
Hualani St.
Pilani St.
Hinano St.
Laukapu St.
Kekuanaoa St.
Lelani St.
Manono St.
Mililani St.
Lanikaula St.
Iolani St.
Kilauea Ave.
Kohola St.
Park Rd.
Aupuni St.
Piopio St.
Kinoole St.
Mohouli St.
Hualalai St.
Kapiolani Ave.
Ululani St.
Ponahawai St.
Kinoole St.
Kumau St.
Keawe St.
Furneax Ln.
Mano St.
Hali St.
Puueo St.
Wainaku Ave.
Wainuenue Ave.
Mamalahoa Hwy.
Kamehameha Ave.
Waianuenue Ave.
Amauulu Rd.
Kauilani St.
Aae St.
Hali St.
Ohai St.
Banyan Dr.
Kalanianaole Ave.
Liliuokalani St.
Banyan Dr.

HAWAII (The Big Island)
Waimea
Hilo
Kailua-Kona
Hawaii Volcanoes Nat'l Park

ATTRACTIONS

Akaka Falls **6**
Banyan Drive **20**
Big Island Candies **24**
Botanical World Adventures **6**
Hawaii Tropical Botanical Garden **6**
Hilo Farmers Market **12**
Imiloa: Astronomy Center of Hawaii **14**
Kaumana Caves Park **1**
Kolekole Beach Park **6**
Leleiwi Beach Park **21**
Liliuokalani Gardens **18**
Lyman Museum & Mission House **10**
Mauna Loa Macadamia Nut Factory **26**
Mokupapapa Discovery Center **7**
Nani Mau Gardens **26**
Pacific Tsunami Museum **8**
Panaewa Rainforest Zoo & Garden **26**
Rainbow Falls (Waianuenue) **1**
Two Ladies Kitchen **13**
Umauma Falls **6**

RESTAURANTS

Café 100 **16**
Café Pesto **11**
Hawaiian Style Café **23**
Hilo Bay Café **17**
Hilo Town Tavern **9**
Hula Hulas **19**
Ken's House of Pancakes **22**
Miyo's **23**
Moon and Turtle **8**
Nani Mau Orchid Restaurant **25**
Sky Garden at Imiloa **15**

HOTELS

Grand Naniloa Hotel Hilo **19**
The Inn at Kulaniapia Falls **4**
Old Hawaiian B&B **2**
The Palms Cliff House Inn **5**
Shipman House Guest Cottage **3**

207

IMILOA: EXPLORING THE unknown

The star attraction, literally and figuratively, of Hilo is **Imiloa: Astronomy Center of Hawaii ★★★**. The 300 exhibits in the 12,000-square-foot gallery make the connection between the Hawaiian culture and its explorers, who "discovered" the Hawaiian Islands, and the astronomers who explore the heavens from the observatories atop Mauna Kea. '*Imiloa* means "explorer" or "seeker of profound truth," the perfect name for this architecturally stunning center overlooking Hilo Bay on the University of Hawaii at Hilo Science and Technology Park campus, 600 Imiloa Place (www.imiloahawaii.org; © **808/969-9700**). Plan to spend at least a couple of hours here to allow time to browse the excellent, family-friendly interactive exhibits on astronomy and Hawaiian culture, and to take in a planetarium show, which boasts a state-of-the-art digital projection system. You'll also want to stroll through the native plant garden, and grab a power breakfast or lunch in the **Sky Garden Restaurant** (© **808/969-9753**), open 7am to 4pm Tuesday through Sunday; the restaurant is also open for dinner Thursday through Sunday from 5 to 8:30pm. The center itself is open Tuesday through Sunday from 9am to 5pm; admission is $18 for adults, $16 for seniors, and $10 for children 4 to 12, and free for kids under 4, and includes one planetarium show; additional shows are $5 for adults and $3 for children. Check online for "Word of the Day" discount ($2 off per person).

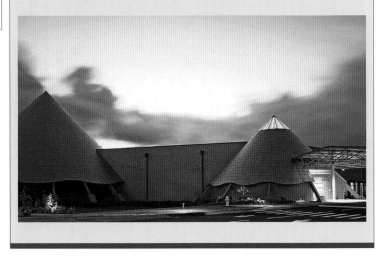

and reef fish; the sounds of Hawaiian chants and seabirds; interactive displays on each of the islets; a life-size Hawaiian monk seal exhibit; and a giant mural by Hilo artist Layne Luna, who also created the life-size models of giant fish, sharks, and the manta ray. Both the content and the cost of admission—free—are great for families.

76 Kamehameha Ave. (at the corner of Waianuenue Ave.) www.papahanaumokuakea.gov/education/center.html. © **808/933-8180.** Free. Tues–Sat 9am–4pm.

Nani Mau Gardens ★ GARDEN In 1972 Makato Nitahara turned a 20-acre papaya patch just outside Hilo into a tropical garden. Today Nani Mau ("forever beautiful") holds more than 2,000 varieties of plants, from fragile hibiscus, whose blooms last only a day, to durable red anthuriums imported from South America. It also has rare palms, a fruit orchard, Japanese gardens (with a bell tower built without nails), an orchid walkway, and a ginger garden. In 2012 Los Angeles tour operator Helen Koo bought the then-neglected property, restoring the gardens with the help of four full-time gardeners. She also opened a **garden restaurant** that's popular with tour companies; the buffet lunch, served daily from 10:30am to 2pm, is $18 and includes garden admission.

421 Makalika St. www.nanimaugardens.com. ✆ **808/959-3500.** $10 adults, $5 seniors and children 4–10; with lunch, $18 adults, $15 seniors and children 4–10. Daily 10am–3pm. From Hilo Airport, take Hwy. 11 south 2 miles to second left turn at Makalika St., and continue ¾ mile.

Pacific Tsunami Museum ★ MUSEUM Poignant exhibits on Japan's 2011 tsunami (which caused significant property damage on the Big Island) and the 2004 Indian Ocean tragedy have broadened the international perspective in this compact museum in a former bank, where displays explain the science of the deadly phenomenon. Still, the stories and artifacts related to Hilo's two most recent catastrophic tsunamis are impressive, including a parking meter nearly bent in two by the force of the 1960 killer waves, and accounts from survivors of the 1946 tsunami that washed away the school at Laupahoehoe. Many of the volunteers have hair-raising stories of their own to share—but you'll feel better after reading about the warning systems now in place.

130 Kamehameha Ave. (at the corner of Kalakaua Ave.). www.tsunami.org. ✆ **808/935-0926.** $8 adults, $7 seniors, $4 children 6–17, free for children 5 and under. Tues–Sat 10am–4pm.

Panaewa Rainforest Zoo & Gardens ★ ZOO/GARDEN This 12-acre zoo, in the heart of the Panaewa Forest Reserve south of Hilo, is the only outdoor rainforest zoo in the U.S. Some 80 species of animals from rainforests around the globe call Panaewa home, including tigers Tzatziki and Sriracha, as do a couple of "Kona nightingales"—donkeys that escaped decades ago from coffee farms. (Though highway signs still warn of them, virtually all were relocated to California in 2011 during a prolonged drought.) The Panaewa residents enjoy fairly natural, sometimes overgrown settings. Look for cute pygmy goats, capuchin monkeys, and giant anteaters, among other critters. This free attraction includes a covered playground popular with local families.

800 Stainback Hwy., Keaau (off Hwy. 11, 5 miles south of its intersection with Hwy. 19 in downtown Hilo). www.hilozoo.org. ✆ **808/959-7224.** Free. Daily 9am–4pm. Petting zoo Sat 1:30–2:30pm.

Wailuku River State Park ★ WATERFALL   Go in the morning, around 9 or 10am, just as the sun comes over the mango trees, to see **Rainbow Falls ★**, or Waianuenue, at its best. Part of the 16-acre Wailuku River State Park, the 80-foot falls (which can be slender in times of drought) spill into a big round natural pool surrounded by wild ginger. If you're lucky, you'll catch a rainbow created in the falls' mist. According to legend, Hina, the mother of demigod Maui, once lived in the cave behind the falls. Swimming in the pool is not allowed, but you can follow a trail left through the trees to the top of the falls (watch your step). Swimming in **Boiling Pots** (*Pe'epe'e* in Hawaiian), a series of cascading pools 1½ miles west, is extremely risky due to flash floods, but the view from an overlook located near the parking lot is impressive.

Rainbow Falls area: Rainbow Dr., just past the intersection of Waianuenue Ave. (Hwy. 200) and Puuhina St. Boiling Pots area: end of Pe'epe'e Falls Dr., off Waianuenue Ave. http://dlnr.hawaii.gov/dsp/parks/hawaii. Free. Daily during daylight hours.

PUNA

Most visitors understandably want to head straight to **Hawaii Volcanoes National Park ★★★** (p. 213) when exploring this region, where Pele still consumes the land and creates even more. But the celebrated national park is far from the only place where you can experience Puna's geothermal wonders, or see the destruction the volcano has wrought—provided it's safe to do so. *Note:* The following itinerary became inaccessible to visitors in May 2018, when Kilauea's Lower East Rift Zone sent lava into two neighborhoods and across Highway 137. Only Pahoa remained open

Kilauea volcano lava flow

to visitors at press time, but historical precedent indicates the massive new lava flow will eventually be accessible, too.

To explore the **Pahoa-Kapoho-Kalapana** triangle, start with a 5-minute detour from central Pahoa to the town's transfer station (i.e., landfill and recycling center) on Cemetery Road. There you'll see the ominous edge of the thick but slow-moving lava flow (2014–2015) that halted only after many in its predicted path had relocated. Leilani Estates and Lanipuna Gardens residents were not so lucky in 2018, nor were the residents of Kalapana, a town covered by lava in 1990.

Along the 9-mile drive to Kalapana from the intersection of highways 130 and 132, you may spot **steam vents** on the *makai* side of the two-lane highway in the Keauohana Forest Reserve, near mile marker 15 (but do not enter them). **Star of the Sea Painted Church ★** will also be on your left, shortly before Highway 130 meets Highway 137. Built in 1930, the quaint, pale-green wooden church features an elaborately painted interior similar to St. Benedict's in Captain Cook (p. 192). It was moved here in advance of the 1990 Kalapana lava flow. The church is open daily 9am to 4pm; visitor donations help pay for upkeep.

When lava is pouring into the sea west of Kalapan, the county has a **lava viewing area ★★** (www.hawaiicounty.gov/lava-viewing) where Highway 130 meets the emergency gravel road heading into the national park. (The eruption that began in May 2018 to the east of Kalapana had created two ocean entries at press time, but they were only viewable from helicopter and lava boat tours.)

It's much easier to visit Kalapana's **new black-sand beach,** reached by walking carefully along a short red-cinder trail, past fascinating fissures and dramatically craggy rocks, where ohia lehua and coconut palms are growing rapidly. They're used to rugged conditions, as are the people of Puna, who gather in great numbers at the open-air **Uncle Robert's Awa Club** for its two weekly evening events: the vibrant Wednesday-night food and crafts market and Hawaiian music on Fridays. The rest of the week, the club sells snacks and drinks during the day "by donation" for permit purposes (be aware the staff will let you know *exactly* how much to donate).

From Kalapana/Kaimu, you'll pick up Highway 137 (the Kapoho-Kalapana Rd.), and follow it east to Kapoho along 15 miles of nearly pristine coastline, past parks, forests, rugged beaches, and tide pools, some geothermally heated. The rolling, two-lane avenue is nicknamed the **Red Road,** for the rosy-hued cinders that once paved it.

Adventurers (or exhibitionists) may want to make the tricky hike down to unmarked **Kehena Black Sand Beach ★,** off Highway 137 about 3½ miles east of Kalapana. Here the law against public nudity is widely ignored, although the view of the ocean is usually more entrancing. (Clothed or not, avoid going into the water—currents are dangerous.) It's easier to take a brief detour to see the waves pounding the base of ironwood-shaded cliffs in the **MacKenzie State Recreation Area ★,**

9 miles northeast of Kalapana. Another 3 miles east leads to the scenic "hot pond" at **Ahalanui Park** ★★ (see below); both MacKenzie and Ahalanui have picnic and restroom facilities.

From Ahalanui, Highway 137 veers inland; drive 1¾ miles to a right turn on Kapoho Kai Road and follow it about a half-mile to a marked parking area for the **Waiopae Tidepools** ★★, a state marine-life conservation district (http://dlnr.hawaii.gov/dar). From there, it's about a half-mile walk to the craggy, coral-lined pools, the delight of snorkelers. With proper footwear, you can also walk along the edges of numerous tide pools, many very shallow and teeming with juvenile fish, while the breakers crash in the distance.

Back on Highway 137, head 1 mile north to Kapoho Beach Road. On your left is the **Green Lake Fruit Stand,** named for the unusual, freshwater **Green Lake,** inside nearby **Kapoho Crater** ★. The lake is actually a crater within the 360-foot-tall Kapoho Crater, formed 200 to 400 years ago. If she's not at the stand, call caretaker Smiley Burrows (☎ **808/965-5500**) to arrange a scenic hike or drive up the crater for $5. (You can also swim in the lake, one of only two on the island, but no one knows its depths, and algae sometimes obscure the water.)

Just east of the Green Lake Fruit Stand, Highway 137 intersects Highway 132 (Kapoho Rd.). A right turn onto unpaved Kapoho Road leads to the island's easternmost point and **Cape Kumukahi Lighthouse** ★, which miraculously survived the 1960 lava flow that destroyed the original village of Kapoho. Who cares if its modern steel frame isn't all that quaint? The fact that it's standing at all is impressive—the molten lava parted in two and flowed around it—while its bright-white trusses provide a striking contrast to the black lava.

A left turn onto a paved Highway 132 takes you back 9 miles to the funky, somewhat ramshackle village of Pahoa; you pass eerie **Lava Tree State Monument** ★★ (see below) and the towering monkeypod and invasive albizia trees of **Nanawale Forest Reserve** as you go.

Ahalanui Park (Hot Pond) ★★ PARK   Warmed by one of the area's many volcanically heated springs, this balmy, shallow pool lined with lava rocks and shady trees is protected from the surging ocean by a concrete wall, although very high surf can crash over it and cool the pond. It's not a snorkeling site per se, but silver fish use inlets to dart around the pool's usually clear waters, while a few eels hide in the rocks; if you don't bother the eels, they won't bother you. Shaded by tall palms, it's a pretty setting even if you don't plan to go into the water (which you shouldn't if you have any open cuts, due to possible bacteria, although the county does perform regular tests). Facilities include a lifeguard station, picnic tables, shower, and Porta-Potties—wear your bathing suit under your clothes so you don't have to change in one.

Makai side of Hwy. 137, between mile markers 10 and 11, Pahoa (9 miles southeast of town). Free. Daily 7am–7pm (closed until 1pm 2nd Wed each month for maintenance).

Lava Tree State Monument ★★ NATURAL ATTRACTION   In 1790, a fast-moving lava flow raced through a grove of ohia lehua trees here, cooling quickly and creating lava rock molds of their trunks. Today the ghostly sentinels punctuate a well-shaded, paved .7-mile loop trail through the rich foliage of the 17-acre park. Facilities include restrooms and a few spots for picnicking (or ducking out of the rain during one of the area's frequent showers). Some areas with deep fissures are fenced off, but keep to the trail regardless for safe footing.

Makai side of Hwy. 132 (Pahoa–Pohoiki Rd.), 2¾ miles southeast of Pahoa. http://dlnr.hawaii.gov/dsp/parks/hawaii. Free. Daily during daylight hours.

HAWAII VOLCANOES NATIONAL PARK ★★★

Before tourism became the islands' middle name, their singular attraction for visitors wasn't the beach, but the volcano. From the world over, curious spectators gathered on the rim of Kilauea's Halemaumau crater to see one of the greatest wonders of the globe. A century after it was named a national park in 1916, **Hawaii Volcanoes National Park** (www.nps.gov/havo; ✆ **808/985-6000**) remains the state's premier natural attraction, home to two active volcanoes and one of only two World Heritage Sites in the islands.

Note: In May 2018, Halemaumau was rattled by earthquakes and its lava lake started to drain. At the same time lava started coursing through fissures in Puna, the crater began expelling ash and rocks in a manner not seen since a two-week period in 1924, when boulders landed a half-mile away due to steam explosions caused by magma sinking into the water table. The summit area closed for safety reasons, but was expected to reopen in 2018 after the seismic activity and explosions ended.

Sadly, after driving about 100 miles from Kailua-Kona or 29 miles from Hilo, many visitors pause only briefly by the highlights along **Crater Rim Drive** ★★★ before heading back to their hotels. To allow the majesty and *mana* (spiritual energy) of this special place to sink in, you

Hawaii Volcanoes National Park

should really take at least 3 days—and certainly 1 night—to explore the park, including its miles of trails.

Fortunately, the admission fee ($25 per vehicle, $12 per bicyclist or hiker) is good for 7 days. Be prepared for rain and bring a jacket, especially in winter, when it can be downright chilly at night, in the 40s or 50s (single digits to midteens Celsius). *Note:* For details on hiking and camping in the park, see "Hiking" (p. 249) and "Camping" (p. 271).

Crater Rim Drive Tour

Stop by the **Kilauea Visitor Center** (daily 9am–5pm) to get the latest updates on lava flows and the day's free ranger-led tours and to watch an informative 25-minute film, shown on the hour from 9am to 4pm. Just beyond the center lies vast **Kilauea Caldera ★★★**, a circular depression nearly 2 miles by 3 miles and 540 feet deep. It's easy to imagine Mark Twain marveling over the sights here in 1866, when a wide, molten lava lake bubbled within view in the caldera's **Halemaumau Crater ★★★**, itself 3,000 feet across and 300 feet deep.

Though different today, the caldera's panorama is still compelling. Since 2008, a plume of ash, often visible from miles away, has billowed from Halemaumau, the legendary home of Pele. The sulfurous smoke has forced the ongoing closure of nearly half of Crater Rim Drive, now just a 6-mile crescent. The fumes normally drift northwest, where they often create vog (see "Vog & Other Volcanic Vocabulary" on p. 212), to the dismay of Kona residents. (Scientists monitor the park's air quality closely, just in case the plume changes direction, with rangers ready to evacuate the park quickly if needed.) However, the plume may disappear, along with the lava lake that once caused it to glow in the evening, once the eruption that began May 2018 has ended. **Volcano House ★★** (p. 270), the only public lodge and restaurant in the park, has an impressive view regardless.

Less than a mile from the visitor center, several **steam vents ★★★** line the rim of the caldera, puffing out moist warm air. Across the road, a boardwalk leads through the stinky, smoking **sulphur banks ★★★**, home to ohia lehua trees and unfazed native birds. (As with all trails here, stay on the path to avoid possible serious injury, or worse.)

The **observation deck ★★★** at **Thomas A. Jaggar Museum ★★** offers a prime spot for viewing the crater, especially at night. By day you can also see the vast, barren Kau Desert and the massive sloping flank of Mauna Loa. The museum itself is open daily 10am to 8pm, and admission is free; watch videos from the days when the volcano was really spewing, learn about the cultural significance of Pele, and track earthquakes (a precursor of eruptions) on a seismograph.

Heading southeast from the visitor center, Crater Rim Drive passes by the smaller but still impressive **Kilauea Iki Crater ★★**, which in 1959 was a roiling lava lake flinging lava 1,900 feet into the air. From here, you can walk or drive to **Thurston Lava Tube ★★★**, a 500-year-old lava cave in a pit of giant tree ferns. Also called Nahuku, it's partly illuminated, but take a flashlight and wear sturdy shoes so you can explore the unlit area for another half-mile or so.

Continuing on Crater Rim Drive leads to the **Puu Puai Overlook ★** of Kilauea Iki, where you find the upper trailhead of the aptly named half-mile **Devastation Trail ★★**, an easy walk through a cinder field that ends where Crater Rim Drive meets **Chain of Craters Road ★★★**.

Pedestrians and cyclists only can continue on Crater Rim Drive for the next .8 mile of road, closed to vehicular traffic since the 2008 eruption. The little-traveled pavement leads to **Keanakakoi Crater ★★**, scene of several eruptions in the 19th and 20th centuries. It provides yet another dazzling perspective on the Kilauea Caldera; turn your gaze north for an impressive view of Mauna Loa and Mauna Kea, the world's two highest mountains when measured from the sea floor.

Please Brake for Nene

Nene, the endangered native Hawaiian goose and state bird, are making a comeback in Hawaii Volcanoes National Park and other high-altitude areas in the islands, where they feast on the cranberry-like ohelo berries that grow at upper elevations. Unfortunately, these uplands are often misty, and the birds' feathers blend easily with the pavement, making it hard for inattentive drivers to see them. Drive carefully, and to discourage nene from approaching cars, don't feed them.

Chain of Craters Road

Chain of Craters Road ★★★

It's natural to drive slowly down the 19-mile **Chain of Craters Road,** which descends 3,700 feet to the sea and ends in a thick black mass of rock from a 2003 lava flow. You feel like you're driving on the moon, if the lunar horizon were a brilliant blue sea. Pack food and water for the journey, since there are officially no concessions after you pass the Volcano House; the nearest fuel lies outside the park, in Volcano Village.

Two miles down, before the road really starts twisting, the one-lane, 8½-mile **Hilina Pali Road ★★** veers off to the west, crossing windy scrublands and old lava flows. The payoff is at the end, where you stand nearly 2,300 feet above the coast along the rugged 12-mile *pali* (cliff). Some of the most challenging trails in the park, across the Kau Desert and down to the coast, start here.

Back on Chain of Craters Road, 10 miles below the Crater Rim Drive junction, the picnic shelter at **Kealakomo ★** provides another sweeping coastal vista. At mile marker 16.5, you'll see the parking lot for **Puu Loa ★★★**, an enormous field of some 23,000 petroglyphs—the largest in the islands. A three-quarter-mile, gently rolling lava trail leads to a boardwalk where you can view the stone carvings, 85% of which are *puka,* or holes (aka cupules); Hawaiians often placed their infants' umbilical cords in them. At the end of the paved Chain of Craters Road, a lookout area allows a glimpse of 90-foot **Holei Sea Arch ★★**, one of several striking formations carved in the oceanside cliffs. Stop by the ranger station before treading carefully across the 21st-century lava, "some of the youngest land on Earth," as the park calls it, or heading out on foot or mountain bike across the gravel emergency road. Bear in mind it's a slow drive back up in the dark.

KAU

At the end of 11 miles of bad road that peters out at Kaulana Bay, in the lee of a jagged, black-lava point, is *Ka Lae* ("The Point")—the tail end of the United States, often called South Point. From the tip, the nearest continental landfall is Antarctica, 7,500 miles away. It's a rugged 2-mile hike down a cliff from Ka Lae to the anomaly known as **Papakolea (Green Sand) Beach ★★**, described on p. 229. In May, the 10-day **Kau Coffee Festival** (www.kaucoffeefestival.com) in Pahala includes hikes, music, hula, and farm tours.

Kahuku Unit, Hawaii Volcanoes National Park ★ NATURAL ATTRACTION Few visitors are familiar with this 116,000-acre portion of the national park, some 24 miles from the Kilauea Visitor Center and accessible only since 2009. It's typically open just 3 days a week, although in May 2018 it temporarily expanded hours after eruptions forced the Kilauea summit area to close. You can hike through forest and fields that include a cinder cone, tree molds from an 1866 lava flow, and ranch-era relics. Rangers also frequently lead free hikes; check the online schedule. *Note:* There are restrooms but no drinking water.

Mauka side of Hwy. 11, btw mile markers 70 and 71, Pahala. www.nps.gov/havo/planyourvisit/kahuku-hikes.htm. ✆ **808/985-6000.** Free. Fri–Sun 9am–3pm.

Kau Coffee Mill ★★ FACTORY TOUR In the former sugarcane fields on the slopes of Mauna Loa, a number of small farmers are growing coffee beans whose quality equals—some say surpasses—Kona's. More and more tasting competitions seem to agree; in any case, this farm and mill in tiny Pahala provides an excellent excuse to break up the long drive to the main entrance of Hawaii Volcanoes National Park, 23 miles northeast. Free 45-minute tours are offered daily; enjoy tastings of coffee and macadamia nuts throughout the day in the pleasant visitor center and gift shop, which also has smoothies and sandwiches for sale.

96-2694 Wood Valley Rd., Pahala. http://kaucoffeemill.com. ✆ **808/928-0550.** Free. Daily 9am–4:30pm. Guided tours 10am, noon, and 2pm, weather permitting. From Kailua-Kona, take Hwy. 11 71 miles to a left on Kamani St., take 3rd right at Pikake St., which becomes Wood Valley Rd., and follow uphill 2½ miles to farm on left.

Kula Kai Caverns ★★ NATURAL ATTRACTION Ric Elhard and Rose Herrera have explored and mapped out the labyrinth of lava tubes and caves, carved out over the past 1,000 years or so, that crisscross their property near Ka Lae. Their "expeditions" range from the Lighted Trail tour, an easy, half-hour walk suitable for families, to longer (up to 2 hr.), more adventurous caving trips, where you crawl through tunnels and wind through labyrinthine passages (some restricted to kids 8 and older). Wear sturdy shoes.

92-8864 Lauhala Dr., Ocean View (46 miles south of Kailua-Kona). www.kulakaicaverns.com. ✆ **808/929-9725.** Lighted Trail tour $20 adults, $10 children 6–12, free for children 5 and under; longer tours $60–$95 adults ($60–$65 children 8–12). By reservation only; gate security code provided at booking.

THE BRUTE FORCE OF THE volcano

Volcanologists refer to Hawaiian volcanic eruptions as "quiet" eruptions because gases escape slowly instead of building up and exploding violently all at once. The Big Island's eruptions produce slow-moving, oozing lava that generally provide excellent, safe viewing when they're not in remote areas. Even so, **Kilauea** has still caused its share of destruction. Since the current eruption began on January 3, 1983, lava has covered more than 50 square miles of lowland and rainforest, ruining 300 homes and businesses, wiping out the pretty, black-sand beach of Kaimu, and burying other landmarks. Kilauea has also added more than 500 acres of new land on its southeastern shore. (Such land occasionally collapses under its own weight into the ocean—26 recently formed oceanfront acres slowly gave way on New Year's Eve, 2016.) Now drained of lava, the most prominent vent of the eruption has been Puu Oo, a 760-foot-high cinder-and-spatter cone 10 miles east of Kilauea's summit, in an off-limits natural reserve. Scientists are also keeping an eye on the active volcanoes of **Mauna Loa,** which has been swelling since its last eruption in 1984, and **Hualalai,** which hovers above Kailua-Kona and last erupted in 1801.

Organized Tours

Farms, gardens, and historic houses that may be open only to guided tours are listed under "Attractions & Points of Interest" on p. 187. For boat, kayak, bicycle, and similar tours, see listings under "Outdoor Activities."

HELICOPTER TOURS ★★

Don't believe the brochures with pictures of fountains of lava and "liquid hot magma," as Dr. Evil would say. Although there are no guarantees you'll see red-hot lava (and for safety reasons, you're not going to fly all that close to it), a helicopter ride offers a unique perspective on the island's thousands of acres of hardened black lava, Kilauea's enormous caldera, and the remote, now eerily drained Puu Oo vent. If you're pressed for time, a helicopter ride beats driving to the volcano and back from Kohala and Kona resorts.

Blue Hawaiian Helicopters ★★ (www.bluehawaiian.com; © **800/786-2583** or 808/886-1768), a professionally run, locally based company with comfortable, top-of-the-line copters and pilots who are extremely knowledgeable about everything from volcanology to Hawaii lore, flies three different tours out of Waikoloa, at Highway 19 and Waikoloa Road. The 2-hour **Big Island Spectacular ★★** stars the volcano, tropical valleys, the Hamakua Coast waterfalls, and the Kohala Mountains, and costs $589 per person ($739 with 20-minute landing at remote 1,200-foot Punalulu waterfall on the Hamakua Coast). If time is money for you, and you've got all that money, it's an impressive trip, If you just want to admire waterfalls, green mountains, and the deep valleys, including

Waipio, of North Kohala and the Hamakua Coast, the 50-minute **Kohala Coast Adventure** ★ is a less exorbitant but reliably picturesque outing, costing $279. Both tours use the somewhat quieter Eco-Star helicopters with panoramic views from the large cockpit.

Blue Hawaiian also operates out of the Hilo airport (✆ **808/961-5600**), flying the 50-minute **Circle of Fire Plus Waterfalls** ★★ tour, which is significantly cheaper—$259 to $309—because it's closer to the volcano and waterfalls. *Note:* If you're willing to drive to Hilo, you really should continue on to the national park.

The similarly professional **Sunshine Helicopters** ★★ (www.sunshinehelicopters.com; ✆ **866/501-7738** or 808/270-3999) offers a **Volcano Deluxe Tour** ★, a 105-minute ride out of the Hapuna heliport, which includes Kohala Mountains/Hamakua waterfalls. It's also pricey: $530 for open seating, $614 reserved seating next to the pilot on the six-passenger Whisper Star choppers. Less of a splurge—and less dependent on the ooh factor of oozing lava—is Sunshine's 30- to 40-minute **Kohala/Hamakua Coast Tour** ★★, which hovers above waterfall-lined sea cliffs and the Pololu, Waimanu, and Waipio valleys, for $209.

Note: Book online for best rates; ask about AAA discounts if booking in person. On all rides, your weight may determine where you sit in the helicopter. Wear dark shades to prevent glare, and dress in light layers.

VAN & BUS TOURS

Intrigued by the island lifestyle? Take a delectable peek inside private residences and gardens on one of the culinary home tours of **Home Tours Hawaii** ★★★ (www.hometourshawaii.com; ✆ 808/325-5772). Groups of 6 to 20 (maximum) travel in vans from Kona to unique properties, dining on either an island brunch on the 5-hour tour ($189) or a decadent, multicourse chocolate tasting on a 3-hour, cacao-themed tour ($99). The latter visits Kokoleka Lani ("Heavenly Chocolate") Farm, where affable host **Greg Colden** also runs Kona Natural Soap Company.

Many of the outdoor-oriented, but not especially physically taxing, excursions of **Hawaii Forest & Trail** ★★★ (www.hawaii-forest.com; ✆ **800/464-1993** or 808/331-8505) include a significant time in comfy vans heading to and from remote areas, with well-briefed guides providing narration along the way. Thus, they're ideal for seeing a large chunk of the island without having to drive yourself. The island's premier outfitter, this eco-friendly company also has exclusive access to many sites, including the waterfalls on its **Kohala Waterfalls Adventure** ($178 adults, $154 children 12 and under). Most of its dozen tours depart daily from several locations on the Kona side ($89–$249 adults, $79–$179 children). **Bird watchers** can choose from two exceptional tours, which include 2 to 4 miles of hiking over 4 hours ($197–$225 adults only). Tours from Hilo—exploring volcano country, Mauna Kea, or Hilo's waterfalls ($129–$179 adults, $99–$139 children)—are perfect for cruise

PLANTING A koa legacy tree

One of the most inspiring and memorable experiences I've had in Hawaii has been with **Hawaiian Legacy Tours** ★★★ (www.hawaiianlegacytours.com; ✆ 877/707-8733), which allows visitors to help restore the native koa forest high above the Hamakua Coast. More koa means more native birds and less runoff, which can harm the reefs far below. Over its lifetime, the tree can also offset the carbon impact of a week's vacation on this beautiful island. The freshly baked scones that await in the welcome center are pretty awesome, too.

After you check in at the handsomely restored ranch house in the tiny village of Umikoa (at 3,200 ft. elevation), guides in ATVs, or a Pinzgauer six-wheeler for larger groups, drive you even higher up the misty slopes of Mauna Kea, to the former personal forest of King Kamehameha the Great. Amid the new groves growing on the mountainside, where the *mana* (spiritual power) and beauty of your surroundings are spine-tingling, you'll be shown how to plant a seedling. You can dedicate it to a loved one on a special commemorative certificate, and you'll also receive its GPS coordinates, allowing you to monitor its growth via Google Earth.

The 2-hour **Planters Tour,** including one tree for planting, costs $140 for adults and $55 for kids 5 to 18, while the 3½-hour **Grand Tour,** which spends more time in the nurseries and on the Umikoa Trail, costs $210 for adults and $90 for kids 5 to 18. (Children's rates exclude a tree for planting, but additional trees may be purchased for $90 each.) Private tours and shuttles (from the Kona and Hilo airports, Four Seasons Resort Hualalai, and Hilo cruise terminal) are available for additional fees. **Note:** If you can't take a tour, you can pay to have a koa ($90) or an even rarer sandalwood tree ($110) planted for you; see www.legacy-trees.org for details.

passengers or anyone else on the Hilo side. *Note:* Mauna Kea tours are restricted to ages 16 and older, due to the high elevation.

From Kailua-Kona, it's easy to book other all-day volcano and "circle" tours, which include the black-sand **Punaluu Beach** ★★★ (p. 230), the national park, Hilo, and Waimea. I recommend the environmentally conscious, community-oriented **KapohoKine Adventures** ★★ (www.kapohokine.com; ✆ 808/964-1000), which offers a variety of tours from Kona and Hilo ($109–$229 adults, $99–$219 children 12 and under). Its 11-hour **Waipio Valley Explorer** tour, offered Monday and Wednesday through Saturday ($229 adults, $219 children, including lunch), departs from Waikoloa, with sightseeing at Rainbow Falls, Hilo Farmer's Market, Hawaii Tropical Botanical Garden, and Akaka Falls before the descent into Waipio Valley. Its rugged, but exhilarating **Lava Expedition** ($129 from Hilo, $209 from Waikoloa) brings you close to flowing lava on foot when conditions permit.

Note: Tipping the tour guide/driver $10 to $20 per person, depending on length and cost of the tour, is customary.

BEACHES

Too young geologically to have many great beaches, the Big Island instead has more colorful ones: brand-new black-sand beaches, salt-and-pepper beaches, and even a green-sand beach. If you know where to look, you'll also find some gorgeous pockets of golden sand off the main roads here and there, plus a few longer stretches, often hidden from view by either acres of lava or high-end resorts. Thankfully, by law all beaches are public, so even the toniest hotel must provide access (including free parking) to its sandy shores. *Note:* Never leave valuables in your trunk, particularly in remote areas, and please respect the privacy of residents with homes on the beach. For details on shoreline access around the island, see the maps and descriptions at **www.hawaiicounty.gov/pl-shoreline-access-big-island**. For more information on state beach parks and reserves, visit **http://dlnr.hawaii.gov/dsp/parks/hawaii**.

Note: You'll find relevant sites on the "Big Island" map on p. 189.

North Kona

KAHALUU BEACH ★★

The most popular beach on the Kona Coast has reef-protected lagoons and county park facilities that draw more than 400,000 people a year. Coconut trees line a narrow salt-and-pepper-sand shore that gently slopes to turquoise pools, home to schools of brilliantly colored tropical fish. In summer, it's an ideal spot for children and beginning snorkelers; the water is so shallow you can just stand up if you feel uncomfortable—but please, not on the living coral, which can take years to recover. In winter, there's a rip current when the high surf rolls in; look for any lifeguard warnings.

Kua Bay

Kahaluu isn't the biggest beach on the island, but it's one of the best equipped, with off-road parking, beach-gear rentals, a covered pavilion, restrooms, barbecue pits, and a food concession. Come early to stake out a spot. If you have to park on Alii Drive, be sure to poke your head into tiny, blue-roofed **St. Peter's by the Sea,** a Catholic chapel next to an old lava rock *heiau* where surfers once prayed for waves. Note: The park is closed until 10am the first or second Tuesday of each month for maintenance.

KEKAHA KAI STATE PARK ★★

Brilliant white sand offsets even more brilliant turquoise water at this beach park with several sandy bays and coves well hidden from the highway and two official entrances. About 4½ miles north of the airport off Highway 19 (across from West Hawaii Veterans Cemetery) is the turnoff for Maniniowali Beach, better known as **Kua Bay.** A thankfully paved road crosses acres of craggy lava, leading to the parking lot and a short, paved walkway to an even shorter, sandy scramble down a few rocks to the beach. It has restrooms and showers, but absolutely no shade or drinking water. Locals flock here to sunbathe, swim, bodyboard, and bodysurf, especially on weekends, so go during the week, and in mornings, when it's cooler; exercise caution since serious injuries have occurred in the strong shorebreak. If you have 4WD, you can take the marked turnoff 2½ miles north of the airport off Highway 19 and drive 1½ bumpy miles over a rough lava road to the parking area for sandy **Mahaiula Beach,** reached by another short trail. Sloping more steeply than Kua Bay, this sandy beach has stronger currents too, although if you're fit you can still swim or snorkel in calm conditions. You can also just laze under the shade—you're likely to see a snoozing green sea turtle or two—or follow the rugged path north through the lava about a mile to the white sandy coves of **Makalawena Beach.** The park is open 8am to 7pm daily.

KIHOLO STATE PARK RESERVE ★★★

To give yourself a preview of why you want to visit here, pull over at the marked Scenic Overlook on Highway 19 north of Kekaha Kai State Park, between mile markers 82 and 83. You'll see a shimmering pale blue lagoon, created by the remains of an ancient fish pond, and the bright cerulean **Kiholo Bay,** jewels in a crown of black lava. Now take the unmarked lava-gravel road (much smoother than Kekaha Kai's road to Mahaiula Beach) just south of the overlook and drive carefully to the even bumpier day-lot parking area. An unpaved road to the left leads to the campground parking lot; both lots have portable toilets and are a short walk to the shore. The "beach" here is black sand, lava pebbles, and coral, but it's fine for sunbathing or spotting dolphins and seasonal humpback whales. Keep your sturdy-soled shoes on, though, because you'll want to keep walking north to **Keanalele** (also called "Queen's Bath"), a collapsed lava tube found amid kiawe trees with steps leading into its fresh

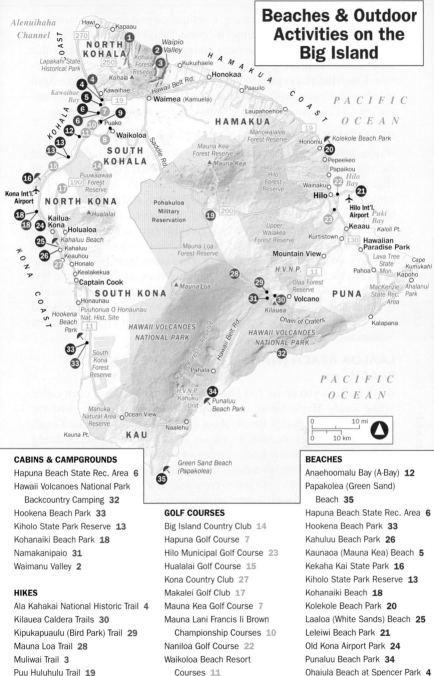

Beaches & Outdoor Activities on the Big Island

water pool, great for a cooling dip. Continue on past several mansions to the turquoise waters of the former fishpond, cut off by a lava flow, and the darker bay, clouded by freshwater springs. Green sea turtles love this area—as do scampering wild goats. The park opens at 7am daily year-round, with the access gate off the highway locked promptly at 7pm April to Labor Day (early Sept), and then at 6pm through March 31. See "Camping" (p. 271) for details on reserving campsites, open Friday–Sunday.

KOHANAIKI BEACH (PINE TREES) ★★

Hidden behind the Kohanaiki golf course development, 2 miles north of the main entrance to Kaloko-Honokohau National Historical Park off Highway 19, the 1½ miles of shoreline here include anchialine ponds, white-sand beaches, and a reef- and rock-lined bay that's home to a popular surf break called Pine Trees. Paddlers, snorkelers, and fishermen also flock to the rugged coastline, where a county park offers parking, restrooms, showers, water fountain, campsites, and a covered pavilion for cultural practices; there's also a well-marked petroglyph. From the Kohanaiki entrance on Highway 19 (at Hulikoa Drive), turn right at the first fork and follow nearly 1 mile to the first parking lot for beach access; facilities and more parking are farther south along the one-lane paved road, but you can also explore the shore to the north. It's open daily from 5:30am to 9pm (no camping Tues–Wed).

LAALOA BEACH (WHITE SANDS/MAGIC SANDS BEACH) ★★

Don't blink as you cruise Alii Drive, or you'll miss Laaloa, often called White Sands, Magic Sands, or Disappearing Beach. That's because the sand at this small pocket beach, about 4½ miles south of Kailua-Kona's historic center, does occasionally vanish, especially at high tide or during storms. On calm summer days, you can swim here, next to bodyboarders and bodysurfers taking advantage of the gentle shorebreak; you can also snorkel in a little rocky cove just to the south. In winter, though, a dangerous rip develops and waves swell, attracting expert surfers and spectators; stay out of the water then, but enjoy the gawking. The palm-tree-lined county beach park includes restrooms, showers, a lifeguard station, and a small parking lot off Alii Drive.

OLD KONA AIRPORT PARK ★

Yes, this used to be the airport for the Kona side of the island—hence the copious parking on the former runway at the end of Kuakini Highway about a half-mile north of Palani Road in Kailua-Kona. Now it's a park jointly managed by the county and state, which in 1992 designated its waters a marine life conservation district. It's easy to get distracted by all the other free amenities: two Olympic-size pools in the **Kona Community Aquatic Center** (✆ **808/327-3500**), a gym, tennis courts, ball fields. Yet there's a mile of sandy beach here, fronting tide pools perfect for families with small children, and Pawai Bay, whose reefs draw turtles and rays, and thus snorkelers and divers. The beach area also has covered picnic tables and grills, restrooms, and showers.

South Kona

HOOKENA BEACH PARK ★

A community group known as **Friends of Hookena** (www.hookena.org) have managed facilities and concessions at this secluded, taupe-colored sandy beach (technically a county park) since 2007. Visitors can rent kayaks and snorkel gear here to explore Kauhako Bay's populous reefs (avoid during high surf) or camping gear to enjoy the view—sometimes including wild spinner dolphins—from the shore. Reservations for gear and campgrounds can be made online; the welcome concession stand at this remote spot even accepts credit cards. Facilities include showers, restrooms, water fountains, picnic tables, pavilions, and parking. From Kailua-Kona, take Highway 11 south 22 miles to the Hookena Beach Road exit (just past Hookena Elementary School), between mile markers 101 and 102. Follow it downhill 2 miles to the end, and turn left on the one-lane road to the parking area.

The Kohala Coast

ANAEHOOMALU BAY ★★★

The Big Island makes up for its dearth of beaches with a few spectacular ones, like Anaehoomalu, or A-Bay, as many call it. This popular

Anaehoomalu Bay

gold-sand beach, fringed by a grove of palms and backed by royal fish-ponds still full of mullet, is one of the most beautiful in Hawaii. It fronts Marriott's Waikoloa Beach complex and is enjoyed by guests and locals alike (it's busier in summer, but doesn't ever get truly crowded). The beach slopes gently from shallow to deep water; swimming, snorkeling, diving, kayaking, and windsurfing are all excellent here. At the northern edge of the bay, snorkelers and divers can watch endangered green sea turtles line up and wait their turn to have small fish clean them. Equipment rental and snorkeling, scuba, and windsurfing instruction are available at the north end of the beach. Facilities include restrooms, showers, picnic tables, and plenty of parking; look for access signs off Waikoloa Beach Road, about 1 mile west of Highway 19. No lifeguards.

HAPUNA BEACH ★★★

Just off Queen Kaahumanu Highway, below the Westin Hapuna Beach Resort, lies this crescent of gold sand—a half-mile long and up to 200 feet wide. In summer, when the beach is widest, the ocean calmest, and the crowds biggest, this is a terrific place for swimming, bodysurfing, and snorkeling. But beware of Hapuna in winter or stormy weather, when its thundering waves and strong rip currents should only be plied by local experts. Facilities at Hapuna Beach, part of the **Hapuna Beach State Recreation Area,** include A-frame cabins (for camping by permit), picnic tables, restrooms, showers, snack bar, water fountains, a lifeguard station, and parking. You can also pick up the coastal **Ala Kahakai National Historic Trail** (p. 249) here to Spencer or Holoholokai parks to the north and south, respectively.

KAUNAOA BEACH (MAUNA KEA BEACH) ★★★

Nearly everyone refers to this gold-sand beach at the foot of Mauna Kea Beach Hotel by its hotel nickname, but its real name is Hawaiian for "native dodder," a lacy, yellow-orange vine that once thrived on the shore. A coconut grove sweeps around this golden arc, where the water is calm and protected by two black-lava points. The sandy bottom slopes gently into the bay, which often fills with tropical fish, sea turtles, and manta rays, especially at night, when lights shine down from a viewing promontory. Swimming is excellent year-round, except in rare winter storms. Snorkelers prefer the rocky points, where fish thrive in the surge. Facilities include restrooms, showers, and public-access parking (go early). No lifeguards.

SPENCER PARK (OHAIULA BEACH) ★★

Virtually in the shadow of the massive Puukohola Heiau (p. 194) to the north, this is a great place to stop when heading to or from the scenic and historic sites in North Kohala. The gently sloping, white-yellow sand beach is **Ohaiula,** though most just call it "Spencer," since it's part of **Samuel M. Spencer County Park.** Protected by both a long reef and Kawaihae Harbor, the beach has relatively safe swimming year-round.

Mauna Kea Beach

Parking is plentiful, but it may fill up on weekends and holidays. From the intersection of highways 19 and 270, take Highway 270 a half-mile north to a left turn at the sign for the park and Puukohola Heiau, and follow this to either of two parking areas at the end of the road. Facilities include picnic tables, restrooms, showers, grassy lawns, and shade trees; lifeguards are on duty weekends and holidays. Campsites at either end of the beach often serve the area's homeless population. (It's safe during daylight hours, but I'd avoid walking through the tents section.) *Note:* The park is typically closed all day the second Wednesday and Thursday of each month September through May.

WAIALEA BAY (BEACH 69) ★★

Once a hidden oasis, this light-golden sandy beach in Puako, between the Mauna Lani and Mauna Kea resorts, earned its nickname from the number on a former telephone pole off Old Puako Road, which signaled one of the public-access points. Still tucked behind private homes, it's now a proper beach park, with a paved parking lot, a trail to the beach, restrooms, and water fountains—but no lifeguards. The bay is generally calm in summer, good for swimming and snorkeling; waves can get big in winter, when surfers and bodyboarders tend to show up. From Kailua-Kona, take Highway 19 north to a left on Puako Road, and then a right on Old Puako Road; the access road to the parking area is on your left, near telephone pole No. 71 (the nickname has not caught up with the times).

Hilo

LELEIWI BEACH PARK ★★

This string of palm-fringed, black-lava tide pools fed by freshwater springs and rippled by gentle waves is a photographer's delight—and the perfect place to take a plunge. In winter, big waves can splash these ponds, but the shallow pools are generally free of currents and ideal for families

Leleiwi Beach

with children, especially in the protected inlets at the center of the park. Leleiwi often attracts endangered sea turtles, making this one of the island's most popular snorkeling spots. Open 7am to 7pm, the beach park is 4 miles east of town on Kalaniana'ole Avenue. Facilities include a lifeguard station (staffed weekends, holidays, and summer), picnic tables, pavilions, and parking. A second section of the park, known as **Richardson's Ocean Park,** includes showers, restrooms, daily lifeguards, and the marine life exhibits of Richardson Ocean Center. *Tip:* If the area is crowded, check out the tide pools and/or small sandy coves in the five other beach parks along Kalanianaole Avenue between Banyan Drive and Leleiwi, especially the protected white-sand lagoon of **Carlsmith Beach Park ★,** just a 2-minute drive west. It has lifeguard service in summer and on weekends and holidays, as does the rocky but kid-friendly **Onekahaha Beach Park ★,** at the end of Onekahakaha Road off Kalanianaole Avenue, just under a mile west from Carlsmith.

KOLEKOLE BEACH PARK ★

Not a place to enter the rough water, this streamside park is nonetheless an unusually picturesque spot for a picnic. The lush greenery around you contrasts with the black rock beach, aquamarine sea, and white sea foam where waves meet Kolekole Stream, several miles below **Akaka Falls ★★★** (p. 200) in Honomu. You may see local kids jumping from a rope swing into the stream, which also has a small waterfall. Facilities include picnic pavilions, grills, restrooms, and parking. It's open 6am to 11pm. From Hilo, take Highway 19 north 11 miles to a left turn on Old Mamalahoa Highway, and take the first (sharp) right, which descends a quarter-mile down to the park. No lifeguard.

Puna District

Access to the oceanfront was restricted to area residents during eruptions that began May 2018. Most of the shoreline is craggy, with rough waters and dangerous currents, although the oceanfront thermal pond at **Ahalanui ★★** (p. 182) and the **Waiopae Tidepools ★★** (p. 212) are certainly worth seeking out if accessible. Pounding waves have reclaimed much of the newest black-sand beach near **Kalapana,** born in the 1990 lava flow that buried Kaimu Beach. It's best viewed from the cliff above it, since rogue waves may suddenly break high on the beach. *Note:* Although nudism is common at secluded, unmarked **Kehena Beach** (p. 211), it is illegal.

Kau District

PAPAKOLEA (GREEN SAND) BEACH ★★

The island's famous green-sand beach is located at the base of Puu o Mahana, an old cinder cone spilling into the sea. It's difficult to reach; the open bay is often rough; there are no facilities, fresh water, or shade; and howling winds scour the point. Nevertheless, each year the unusual olive-brown sands—made of crushed olivine, a semiprecious green mineral found in eruptive rocks and meteorites—attract thousands of oglers. From Highway 11, between mile markers 69 and 70, take South Point Road about 8 miles south to a left fork for the Papakolea parking lot; be aware much of it is one lane. Driving from there to the top of the cinder cone is no longer permitted by the Department of Hawaiian Homelands, although enterprising locals now offer a round-trip shuttle for $10 to $20 (cash only); that's preferable to the windy, challenging hike along the remaining 2½ miles across unshaded dirt roads and lava rock (wear closed-toe shoes,

Hawaiian green turtles relaxing at Punaluu Black Sand Beach

sunglasses, and a hat, and bring lots of water). In either case, you'll still need to clamber carefully down the steep eroded cinder cone to the sand. If the surf's up, check out the beach from the cliff's edge; if the water's calm, you can go closer, but keep an eye on the ocean at all times (there are strong rip currents here).

PUNALUU BEACH ★★★

Green sea turtles love to bask on this remote, black-sand beach, beautifully framed by palm trees and easily photographed from the bluff above. The deep-blue waters can be choppy; swim only in very calm conditions, as there's no lifeguard present. You're welcome to admire the turtles, but at a respectful distance; the law against touching or harassing them is enforced here (if not by authorities, then by locals who also like to congregate in the park). Park facilities include camping, restrooms, showers, picnic tables, pavilions, water fountains, a concession stand, and parking. There are two access roads from Highway 11, at 7¾ and 8 miles northeast of Naalehu. The first, Ninole Loop Road, leads past the rather unkempt Sea Mountain golf course to a turnoff for a paved parking lot by the bluff. The second access from Highway 11, Punaluu Road, has a turnoff for a smaller, unpaved parking area.

WATERSPORTS

Boat, Raft & Submarine Tours

The relatively calm waters of the Kona and Kohala coasts are home to inquisitive reef fish, frolicking spinner dolphins, tranquil green sea turtles, spiraling manta rays, and spouting whales and their calves in season (Dec–Mar). A wide variety of vessels offer sightseeing and snorkel/dive tours (gear provided), while cocktail and dinner cruises take advantage of the region's predictably eye-popping sunsets. On the wild Puna side of the island, boat rides pass green clefts and coastal waterfalls. Thanks to Capt. Kiko Johnston-Kitazawa's **Waakaulua Sailing Excursions** (www.waakaula.com; ✆ **808/895-3743**), you can also experience the traditional **double-hulled sailing canoe,** or *wa'akaula,* used by Hawaiian voyagers; charter a three-hour sailing trip out of Hilo's Wailoa Harbor for $100 per person for up to six people, with a minimum of $400 per trip. For fishing charters, see p. 241.

Note: Prices below reflect discounts for online bookings, where applicable; book well in advance whenever possible.

KONA COAST

Atlantis Submarines ★ If you have what it takes (namely, no claustrophobia), head 100 feet below the sea in a 65-foot **submarine,** with a large porthole for each of the 48 passengers. During the 45 minutes underwater, the sub glides slowly through an 18,000-year-old, 25-acre coral reef in **Kailua Bay,** teeming with fish (including, unfortunately, invasive goatfish and *taape*) and two shipwrecks encrusted in coral. You'll take a 5-minute boat shuttle from Kailua Pier, across from the ticket office, to the air-conditioned submarine. *Note:* Children are allowed, but all passengers must be at least 3 feet tall.

75-5669 Alii Dr. (across the street from Kailua Pier), Kailua-Kona. © **800/548-6262.** www.atlantisadventures.com/kona. Tours leave at 9am, 10am, 11:30am, 1pm, and 2:30pm (check-in 30 min. before departure time). $109 ages 13 and older, $38 under 13; $119 special includes one adult with one child.

Body Glove Cruises ★★ Body Glove's *Kanoa II,* a 65-foot, solar-powered catamaran carrying up to 100 passengers, runs an environmentally friendly, 4½-hour **Snorkel & Dolphin Adventure** morning cruise, along with shorter dinner excursions and seasonal whale-watching trips; all depart from Kailua Pier. In the morning, you'll be greeted with fresh Kona coffee, fruit, and breakfast pastries before heading north to **Pawai Bay,** a marine preserve where you can snorkel, scuba dive, swim, or just hang out on the deck. (Spinner dolphin sightings are guaranteed, but for their health and your safety, you do not swim with them.) Before chowing down on the deli lunch buffet, take the plunge off the boat's 20-foot water slide or 15-foot-high diving board. The only thing you need to bring is a towel; all gear is provided, along with "reef safe" sunscreen. Dinner and lunch cruises feature a historian who points out significant sites on the 12-mile trip from Kailua Pier to **Kealakekua Bay,** where passengers feast on a buffet spread and enjoy live Hawaiian music. All cruises are free for children 5 and under, and the boat, including restrooms, is wheelchair accessible.

Kailua Pier, Kailua-Kona. www.bodyglovehawaii.com. © **800/551-8911** or 808/326-7122. Snorkel cruises (daily 8am) $132 adults, $88 children 6–17; see website for additional scuba charges. Dinner cruise (Thurs–Tues 4pm) $128 adults, $88 children 6–17. Whale-watching cruises (Dec–Apr only; Thurs–Tues 1pm) $98 adults, $78 children 6–17.

Captain Dan McSweeney's Whale Watch Learning Adventures ★★★ The islands' most impressive visitors—45-foot humpback whales—return each winter to warm Hawaiian waters. Capt. Dan McSweeney, who founded the Wild Whale Research Foundation in 1979, has no problem finding them. During the 3-hour **whale-watching tours,** typically offered December through April, he drops a hydrophone (an underwater microphone) into the water so you can listen to their songs, and sometimes uses an underwater video camera to show you what's going on. Cruises are aboard the *Lady Ann,* which has restrooms and a choice of sunny or shaded decks; cold drinks and snacks are provided. Trips depart from Honokohau Harbor, where parking is ample and free.

Honokohau Harbor, 74-380 Kealakehe Pkwy. (off Hwy. 19), Kailua-Kona. www.ilovewhales.com. © **888/942-5376** or 808/322-0028. Departures 7 and 11am Mon–Tues and Thurs–Fri Dec–Apr; arrive 15 min. early. $120 adults, $110 children 11 and under who also weigh under 90 lb.

Captain Zodiac ★   It's a wild, 14-mile ride to **Kealakekua Bay** aboard one of Captain Zodiac's 16-passenger, 24-foot **rigid-hull inflatable rafts,** or Zodiacs. There you'll spend about an hour snorkeling in the bay, perhaps with spinner dolphins, and enjoy snacks and beverages at the site. The small size of the craft mean no restrooms, but it also means you can explore sea caves on this craggy coast. Four-hour **snorkel trips** take place twice daily, while the 5-hour midday tour ingeniously arrives at Kealakekua when most other boats have left, leaving extra time for a second snorkel site, seasonal **whale-watching,** or other experiences at the captain's discretion, plus a deli lunch. Be prepared to get wet regardless (that includes your camera). There's also a 3-hour **swim with wild dolphins**—an activity I typically don't recommend, due to the disruption it causes to the pods of dolphins who need to rest during the day and feed at night. But Captain Zodiac claims to follow federal guidelines in these encounters and briefs passengers on proper protocol for letting the marine mammals approach them, rather than vice versa.

In Gentry's Kona Marina, Honokohau Harbor, 74-425 Kealakehe Pkwy. (off Hwy. 19), Kailua-Kona. www.captainzodiac.com. ℰ **808/329-3199.** 4-hr. snorkel cruise (Wed–Thurs and Sat–Sun 8am and 12:30pm) $100 adults, $79 children 5–12; 5-hr. snorkel cruise (Mon–Tues and Fri 9:45am), $115 adults, $89 children 5–12. Dolphin swim (Tues, Thurs, Sun 8am), $100 adults, $75 children 8–12. Whale-watching cruises (Jan–Apr only; Tues, Thurs, Sat 8:45am; Tues 3:30pm) $74 adults, $54 children 5–12.

Fair Wind Snorkeling & Diving Adventures ★★★   I love Fair Wind for several reasons, starting with its home in Keauhou Bay, 8 miles south of Kailua Pier and so that much closer to **Kealakekua Bay,** where its two very different but impressively equipped boats head for **snorkel/ dive tours:**

FAIR WIND II   When traveling with kids, I book a cruise on the *Fair Wind II,* a 60-foot catamaran that includes two 15-foot water slides, a high-dive jump, playpens, and child-friendly flotation devices with viewfinders, so even toddlers can peek at Kealakekua's glorious sea life. Year-round, the *Fair Wind II* offers a 4½-hour morning snorkel cruise that includes breakfast and barbecue lunch; most of the year it also sails a 3½-hour afternoon snorkel cruise that provides snacks, which in summer becomes a deluxe 4½-hour excursion with barbecue dinner. Swimmers age 8 and up can also try **SNUBA**—kind of a beginner's version of scuba—for an optional $69, with an in-water guide.

HULA KAI   When traveling with teens or adults, I prefer the *Hula Kai,* the Fair Wind's 55-foot foil-assist catamaran, open only to ages 7 and up. The boat provides a plusher experience (such as comfy seating with headrests) and, on its 5-hour morning snorkel cruise, a faster, smoother ride to two uncrowded Kona Coast snorkeling sites (usually neither is Kealakekua Bay), based on conditions. Guests have the option to try **stand-up**

Snorkeling the Big Island seas

paddleboarding, SNUBA (see above), or the propulsive **"Sea Rocket"** ($25 per half-hour) to cover even more ground underwater. The *Hula Kai* also offers a fascinating night snorkel with **manta rays,** a 1½-hour tour that doesn't have to voyage far from **Keauhou Bay** to find them. At night these gentle giants (no stingers!) are lured closer to the ocean's surface by the plankton that also rise there. Like other tour companies, Fair Wind uses dive lights to attract even more plankton; on the off chance you don't get to see a manta ray, you're welcome back for another evening or an afternoon snorkel tour. Wetsuits, warm soup, and hot drinks are provided to ward off chills; non-snorkelers can join for a $45 "ride-along" fee.

Keauhou Bay Pier, 78-7130 Kaleiopapa St., Kailua-Kona. www.fair-wind.com. ℂ **800/677-9461** or 808/322-2788. *Fair Wind II* morning snorkel cruise (daily 9am) $145 adults, $89 children 4–12, $29 children 3 and under. Afternoon snack snorkel cruise (Tues, Thurs, Sat 2pm) $89 adults, $49 children 4–12, free for children 3 and under. *Hula Kai* deluxe morning snorkel/dive cruise (Mon–Thurs and Sat 9:30am, daily in summer) $159 age 7 and up (younger not permitted). Manta ray snorkel/dive (daily; time varies by sunset) $129 age 7 and up (younger not permitted); snorkeling experience required. Parking is on opposite side of Keauhou Bay, at end of King Kamehameha III Rd.

Kamanu Charters ★★ The *Kamanu*, a sleek, 38-foot sailing catamaran, provides laidback **sail-and-snorkel cruises** from Honokohau Harbor to the marine preserve of **Pawai Bay.** The 3½-hour trip includes lunch (deli sandwiches, chips, fresh fruit, and drinks), snorkeling gear, and instruction for first-time snorkelers; weather permitting, it sails twice daily. The boat can hold up to 24 people but often has fewer, making it even more relaxed. The *Kamanu* also sails at sunset to snorkel with manta rays, and afternoon whale-watching excursions are offered in season. *Kamanu Elua*, a 31-foot, rigid-hull inflatable with seating, offers similar morning tours, but heads to **Kealakekua Bay**. *Note:* This Zodiac-style *Kamanu Elua* is not advised for children under 7, pregnant women, or those with back or neck injuries.

Honokohau Harbor, 74-7380 Kealakehe Pkwy. (off Hwy. 19), Kailua-Kona. www.kamanu.com. ℂ **800/348-3091** or 808/329-2021. Snorkel cruises 9am Thurs–Tues, $95 adults, $50 children 12 and under; 1pm, $85 adults, $55 children. Dolphin swim and snorkel (9am Thurs–Tues) $99 all ages. Sunset manta ray snorkel (daily; times vary) $95. Whale-watching Dec 15–Apr 15 (Thurs–Tues 1pm) $80 adults, $55 children 7 and older.

KOHALA COAST

Kohala Sail & Sea ★★★ It took 2 decades of waiting before Capt. Steve Turner finally realized his dream of sailing from the small-boat harbor in Kawaihae, which finally opened in 2015. But it was a dream worth waiting for. Passengers (no more than six at a time) board his gleaming white, 34-foot Islander sloop, *Riva*, on the sunny, sparsely developed coast next to Puukohola Heiau, a short drive from the Mauna Lani and Mauna Kea resorts. Turner and his knowledgeable crew share a deep respect for the ocean and local culture, easy to impart on these intimate cruises. In humpback-whale-watching season (Dec–Apr), they make three 2¼-hour trips daily ($106), including the year-round **sunset cruise** departing at 4pm. The 3½-hour **morning snorkel tours** ($139) take advantage of the Kohala Coast's brilliantly clear waters with dazzling sea life, especially in the reef off Puako, and include all gear, snacks, and drinks; they're also available by charter.

Kawaihae South Harbor, Slip No. 8, 61-3527 Kawaihae Rd., Kawaihae. www.kohala-sailandsea.com. ℂ **808/895-1781.** Whale-watching (daily 8:30am, 1pm, 4pm Dec–Apr) and sunset cruises (daily 4:15pm May–Nov) $106. Morning snorkel trips (on demand, daily 8am) $155 per person; 5-person minimum. Private charters also available.

HILO, THE HAMAKUA COAST & PUNA DISTRICT

Note: During whale-watching season, Hilo visitors may spot whales on one of the culturally focused **Waakaulua Sailing Excursions** (p. 230) out of Wailoa Harbor or during the 2-hour **Hilo Bay and River Falls Adventure** afternoon cruises ($69) offered up to twice daily by **Hilo Ocean Adventures** (www.hilooceanadventures.com; ℂ **808/934-8344**). The latter also operates a 4.5-hour morning snorkel/dive cruise at 8:30am daily ($135 per diver, $79 per snorkeler) and high-adrenaline, high-speed **banana boat rides** in Hilo Bay at 11am and 1pm daily ($39).

Lava Ocean Tours ★★ The unpredictability of Pele means there may or may not be lava-viewing tours. When molten rock collides with the ocean, Capt. Shane Turpin's **Volcano Boat Tours** depart several times a day from Hilo or Pohoiki Harbor near Pahoa to a daringly close (some would say too close) vantage point. The 49-passenger, 42-foot-long Lava-One catamaran provides the smoothest ride, relatively speaking; his smaller LavaKai and LavaKat craft offer bouncier voyages that thrill-seekers may appreciate. When lava isn't spouting (check before you book), Turpin may offer 3-hour **Hilo waterfall cruises** ($145 adults, $100 ages 4 to 12) and **whale-watching cruises** Dec–May ($99 adults, $50 ages 4 to 12) from Hilo's Wailoa Harbor.

Pohoiki Harbor, Isaac Hale Beach Park, Pahoa. www.seelava.com. ℂ **808/966-4200.** Volcano boat tours $180–$190 adults, $145 children 4–12.

Bodyboarding (Boogie Boarding) & Bodysurfing

As with other watersports, it's important to stay out of rough surf in winter or during storms that bring big surf. In normal conditions, the best beaches for bodyboarding and bodysurfing on the Kona side of the island are **Hapuna Beach** at the Mauna Kea Resort, **Laaloa Beach (White Sand/Magic Sands Beach)** ★★ in Kailua-Kona, and **Kua Bay** (Maniniowali Beach) in **Kekaha Kai State Park,** north of the airport. Experienced bodysurfers may want to check out South Kona's **Hookena Beach Park;** on the Hilo side, try **Leleiwi Beach Park.** See "Beaches" (p. 221) for details.

Hotel beach concessions and most surf shops (see "Surfing" on p. 242) rent bodyboards, but you can also find inexpensive rentals at **Snorkel Bob's** in the parking lot of Huggo's restaurant, 75-5831 Kahakai St. at Alii Drive, Kailua-Kona (www.snorkelbob.com; ℂ **808/329-0770**), and on the Kohala Coast in the Shops at Mauna Lani, 68-1330 Mauna Lani Dr., facing the road on the Mauna Lani Resort (ℂ **808/885-9499**). Both stores are open 8am to 5pm daily.

Kayaking

Imagine sitting at sea level, eye to eye with a turtle, a dolphin, even a whale—it's possible in an ocean kayak. After a few minutes of instruction and a little practice in a calm area (like **Kamakahonu Cove** in front of the Courtyard King Kamehameha Kona Beach Hotel), you'll be ready to explore. Beginners can practice their skills in **Kailua Bay,** intermediate kayakers might try paddling from **Honokohau Harbor** to **Kekaha Kai State Park,** and the more advanced can tackle the 5 miles from **Keauhou Bay** to **Kealakekua Bay** or the scenic but challenging **Hamakua Coast.**

You'll find rentals at nearly every beachfront Kona and Kohala resort, as well as the Grand Naniloa Doubletree by Hilton on **Hilo Bay;** hourly rates typically start at $20-$25. At **Hookena Beach Park** (p. 225), kayak rentals include a clear "peekaboo" version that allows you to view sea life and run $40 to $50 a day.

KEALAKEKUA BAY GUIDED TOURS & RENTALS   Although technically you can rent kayaks for exploring Kealakekua Bay on your own, it's best to go with a guided tour. Only three kayak companies are allowed to offer guided tours in Kealakekua Bay that land at the Cook monument (Kaawaloa), all launching from Napoopoo Wharf. These tours include equipment, snorkeling gear, snacks or lunch, and drinks, and they should be booked in advance, due to the 12-guest limit per tour. Note that Napoopoo is a residential area, where parking can be difficult if you're not on a tour.

Kona Boys ★★ (www.konaboys.com; © **808/328-1234**) was the first outfit to offer kayak rentals in Kona and is still widely regarded as the best. Its 5-hour Kealakekua Bay kayak snorkel tours, held daily by reservation, meet at the shop at 79-7539 Mamalahoa Hwy. (Hwy. 11), Kealakekua, at 7:15am; tours cost $189 for adults, $169 for ages 18 and under. The 4-hour "midday meander" tours ($139 adults, $119 children) depart at 12:15. You can also rent gear from Kona Boys' **beach shack** at Kamakahonu Bay (© **808/329-2345**), the only one of its two sites to offer kayaks by the hour, not just by the day or week. Rentals include kayak, paddles, backrests, cooler, life jackets, dry bag, and a soft rack to carry kayaks on top of your car (including convertibles). Hourly rates are $19 single kayak, $29 double, with daily rates $54 and $74, respectively (weekly $174/$249).

Owned by a Native Hawaiian family, **Aloha Kayak** ★★ (www.aloha kayak.com; © **877/322-1444** or 808/322-2868) offers two tours of different lengths to Kealakekua Bay and Kaawaloa Flat, where the memorial to Captain Cook stands. The 3½-hour tour (add an hour for check-in/check-out) departs at 8am and noon Monday, Wednesday, Friday, and Saturday; it's $99 for adults and $55 for children 11 and under. The 5-hour tour, which allows more time for snorkeling and exploring Kaawaloa (where a deli lunch is served), departs at 7:15am Sunday, Tuesday, and Thursday;

it's $129 for adults and $70 for children (check website for $20-off coupon). Aloha Kayak also offers morning tours of Keauhou Bay sea caves ($99 adults, $55 children) 4 days a week and nightly manta ray tours with snorkeling ($99 adults, $55 children ages 5 to 11). Half-day rental-only rates are $25 for a single and $45 for a double; full-day rates are $35 for a single and $60 for a double, with triple kayaks and discounts for longer periods. Aloha Kayak's original shop is in Honalo, about 8½ miles south of Kailua-Kona, at 79-7248 Mamalahoa Hwy. (Hwy. 11), just south of its intersection with Highway 180. A second site, with shave ice stand and other beach gear rentals, is on Napoopoo Road just below the Kona Pacific Farmers Cooperative mill.

The environmentally conscious **Adventures in Paradise ★★** (www. bigislandkayak.com; © **888/210-5365** or 808/447-0080) has a small office at 82-6020 Mamalahoa Hwy. (Hwy. 11) in Captain Cook, but generally meets clients at Napoopoo for its 3½-hour Kealakekua tours ($100 for ages 6 and up), departing at 7 and 11:30am daily. (*Tip:* Book the early tour for the least crowded snorkeling.)

Parasailing

Get a bird's-eye view of the Big Island's pristine waters with **UFO Parasail** (www.ufoparasail.net; © **800/FLY-4-UFO** or 808/325-5836), which offers parasail rides daily between 8am and 5:30pm from Kailua Pier. The cost is $85 for the standard flight of 8 minutes of air time at 800 feet, and $95 for a deluxe 10-minute ride at 1,200 feet. You can go up alone or with a friend (or two) ages 3 and older; single riders must weigh at least 160 pounds, and groups no more than 450 pounds. The boat may carry up to eight passengers (observers pay just $39), and the total time in the boat, around an hour, varies on the rides they've booked. *Tip:* Save $4 to $10 per rider by booking online.

Scuba Diving

The Big Island's leeward coast offers some of the best diving and snorkeling in the world; the water is calm, warm, and clear. Want to swim with fast-moving game fish? Try **Ulua Cave,** at the north end of the Kohala Coast, from 25 to 90 feet deep; dolphins, rays, and the occasional Hawaiian monk seal swim by. And don't forget to book a night dive to see the majestic **manta rays,** regularly seen in greater numbers here than anywhere else in Hawaii (or most of the world, for that matter). More than 2 dozen dive operators on island offer everything from scuba-certification courses to guided dives to snorkeling cruises.

Founded in 1984, **Kohala Divers ★★★** (www.kohaladivers.com; © **808/882-7774**) offers morning and evening one-tank ($109–$139) and two-tank dives ($149–$159) to spectacular sites off North and South Kohala, including a 30-foot-high lava dome covered in plate and knob coral that attracts huge schools of fish, and several spots off Puako frequented by green sea turtles. This is a great outfit for beginners as well as experienced divers, with friendly, well-versed guides. Snorkelers (gear included) and ride-alongs pay $90 to join these and other charters aboard the pristine 42-foot dive boat, which books just 15 of its 24-passenger capacity. You can also rent scuba and snorkel gear at its well-stocked shop in Kawaihae Harbor Shopping Center, 61-3665 Akoni Pule Hwy. (Hwy. 270), about a mile north of its intersection with Highway 19. It's open daily 8am to 6pm.

Farther south, **Kona Diving Company ★★,** 74-5467 Luhia St. (at Eho St.), Kailua-Kona (www.konadivingcompany.com; ✆ **808/331-1858**), prides itself on heading to uncommon dive sites in a 34-foot catamaran complete with showers, TV, and restrooms. It also offers introductory two-dive packages ($230), two-tank morning dives ($135), and one- and two-tank manta ray night dives from Honokohau Harbor ($125–$150). Snorkelers and ride-alongs pay $80 to $115, gear included, depending on the trip; scuba gear costs $35 a day ($60 for shore dive gear).

One of Kona's oldest and most eco-friendly dive shops, **Jack's Diving Locker ★★,** in the Coconut Marketplace, 75-5813 Alii Dr., Kailua-Kona (www.jacksdivinglocker.com; ✆ **800/345-4807** or 808/329-7585), boasts an 8,000-square-foot dive center with solar-heated swimming pool classrooms, full-service rentals, and sports-diving and technical-diving facilities. It offers the classic two-tank dive for $135 ($65 snorkelers) daily and a two-tank manta ray night dive for $155 ($125 snorkelers) five nights a week; Jack's four roomy boats take 10 to 18 divers (split into groups of 6). **Pelagic Magic,** a one-tank descent that reveals iridescent jellies and evanescent zooplankton ($175), is offered Tuesday and Thursday nights.

On the island's east side, Hilo's **Puhi Bay** and the waters of **Leleiwi Point** teem with turtles, octopus, goatfish and other sights for divers. Bill De Rooy of **Nautilus Dive Center ★★,** 382 Kamehameha Ave. at Nawahi Lane (next to the Shell gas station) in Hilo (www.nautilusdivehilo.com; ✆ **808/935-6939**), has been leading guided beach dive tours ($75–$150) and classes for more than 30 years. **Hilo Ocean Adventures ★★,** 1717 Kamehameha Ave. at Banyan Drive (www.hilooceanadventures.com; ✆ **808/934-8344**), offers daily beach dives in the morning ($80) and night ($109) and morning two-tank boat dives ($135 divers, $80 snorkelers).

Snorkeling

If you come to Hawaii and don't snorkel, you'll miss half the sights. The clear waters along the dry Kona and Kohala coasts, in particular, are home to spectacular marine life, including spinner dolphins by day and giant manta rays by night. You'll want to take an evening **boat tour** (p. 230) or **kayak tour** (p. 236) to see the latter; please heed instructions to just watch the mantas and not touch them, which harms their skin. For dolphins and reef denizens, go in the mornings, before afternoon clouds and winds lessen visibility. Please be very careful not to stand on, kick, or touch the live coral, which takes years to grow.

GEAR RENTALS If you're staying at a Kona or Kohala resort, the hotel concession should have basic gear for hourly rental. If you're thinking of exploring more than the beach outside your room, an inexpensive place to get basic rental equipment ($9 per week) is **Snorkel Bob's,** in the parking lot of Huggo's restaurant, 75-5831 Kahakai St. at Alii Drive, Kailua-Kona (www.snorkelbob.com; ✆ **808/329-0770**), and on the Kohala Coast in the Shops at Mauna Lani, 68-1330 Mauna Lani Dr., facing the road on the Mauna Lani Resort (✆ **808/885-9499**). Higher-quality gear costs $38 a week for adults, $24 for children; prescription masks are also available. Both stores are open 8am to 5pm daily.

You can also rent high-quality gear from **Jack's Diving Locker,** Coconut Grove Shopping Center (next to Outback Steak House), 75-5813 Alii Dr., Kailua-Kona (www.jacksdivinglocker.com; ✆ **800/345-4807** or 808/329-7585); it's open 8am to 8pm Monday to Saturday, until 6pm Sunday. Snorkel sets cost $9 a day. On the Kohala Coast, visit **Kohala Divers** (www.kohaladivers.com; ✆ **808/882-7774**) in the Kawaihae Shopping Center, 61-3665 Akoni Pule Highway (Hwy. 270), in Kawaihae, a mile north of the intersection with Highway 19. It's open 8am to 6pm daily, with snorkel sets starting at $10 a day.

In Hilo, **Nautilus Dive Center,** 382 Kamehameha Ave. at Nawahi Lane (www.nautilusdivehilo.com; ✆ **808/935-6939**), rents snorkel packages for $6 a day; it's open 9am to 5pm Monday through Saturday. Beach snorkel tours ($59) are offered twice daily by **Hilo Ocean Adventures,**

Spinner dolphins

1717 Kamehameha Ave. at Banyan Drive (www.hilooceanadventures. com; © **808/934-8344**); quality snorkel sets are $10 a day, $40 per week.

TOP SNORKEL SITES If you've never snorkeled before, **Kahaluu Beach** ★★ (p. 221) is the best place to start, as long as the crowds don't throw you off. Just wade in on one of the small, sandy paths through the lava-rock tide pools and you'll see colorful fish. Even better, swim out to the center of the shallow, well-protected bay to see schools of surgeonfish, Moorish idols, butterflyfish, and even green sea turtles. The friendly and knowledgeable volunteers of the **Kahaluu Bay Education Center** (**KBEC;** www.kahaluubay.org; © **808/640-1166**) are on-site daily from 9:30am to 4pm to explain reef etiquette—essentially: "Look, but don't touch"—and answer questions about its marine life. The KBEC also rents snorkel gear ($14) from Jack's Diving Locker and boogie boards with viewing windows ($10) if you don't want to put your face underwater; proceeds benefit conservation at this popular spot visited annually by some 400,000 snorkelers, swimmers, and surfers.

Kealakekua Bay ★★★ may offer the island's best overall snorkeling (coral heads, lava tubes, calm waters, underwater caves, and more), but because it's a marine life conservation district and state historical park (p. 190), access is restricted to preserve its treasures. The best way to snorkel here is via permitted **boat tours** (p. 230), generally departing from Kailua Pier or Keauhou Bay, or **kayak tours** (p. 236) with permits to launch from Napoopoo Wharf and land near the Captain Cook Monument. You can paddle a rental kayak, canoe, or stand-up paddleboard from Napoopoo on your own if the company has acquired a special permit; otherwise, it's about a 10-mile round-trip paddle from Keauhou. Carrying your snorkel gear down and up the steep 5-mile trail from the highway is possible but not recommended. Watch out for spiny urchins as well as fragile coral when entering the water from lava rocks along the shore.

Much more easily accessible snorkeling, with a terrific display of aquatic diversity, can be found at **Honaunau Bay,** nicknamed "Two Step" for the easy entry off flat lava rocks into the crystalline waters just before **Puuhonua O Honaunau National Historical Park** (p. 193). Snorkeling is not permitted in the park (and using bathrooms for changing in and out of swimsuits is discouraged), but you can pay the entrance fee to use the parking lot and walk to the bay if the 25 or so spaces on the waterfront road (look for the coastal access sign off Highway 160) are taken.

Beyond the beaches of the Kohala resorts, the well-protected waters of **Ohaiula Beach** at **Spencer Park** (p. 226) are a great site for families to snorkel, with convenient facilities (restrooms, showers, picnic tables), not to mention a lifeguard on weekends and holidays, and a reputation for attracting green sea turtles (let them come to you, but don't touch or approach them). It can get windy, so mornings are your best bet here. Puako's **Waialea Bay** (p. 227), home to coral colonies, reef fish and turtles, provides good snorkeling in calm waters, typically in summer.

Sport Fishing: The Hunt for Granders ★★

Big-game fish, including gigantic blue marlin and other Pacific billfish, tuna, sailfish, swordfish, ono (wahoo), and giant trevallies *(ulua),* roam the waters of the Kona Coast, known as the marlin capital of the world. When anglers catch marlin weighing 1,000 pounds or more, they call them "granders"; there's even a "wall of fame" in Kailua-Kona's Waterfront Row shopping mall honoring those who've nailed more than 20 tons of fighting fish. Nearby photos show celebrities such as Sylvester Stallone posing with their slightly less impressive catches. The celebrities of the fishing world descend on Kailua-Kona in August for the 5-day **Hawaiian International Billfish Tournament** (www.hibtfishing.com), founded in 1959. Note that it's not all carnage out there: Teams that tag and release marlin under 300 pounds get bonus points.

Nearly 100 charter boats with professional captains and crew offer fishing charters out of **Keauhou, Kawaihae, Honokohau,** and **Kailua Bay** harbors. If you're not an expert angler, the best way to arrange a charter is through a booking agency such as the **Charter Desk at Honokohau Marina** (www.charterdesk.com; ✆ **888/566-2487** or 808/326-1800), which can sort through the more than 60 different types of vessels and fishing specialties to match you with the right boat. Prices range from $750 to $3,500 or so for a full-day exclusive charter (you and up to five friends have an entire boat to yourselves) or $450 to $600 for a half-day. One or two people may be able to book a "share" on boats that hold four to eight anglers, who take turns fishing—generally for smaller catch—to increase everyone's chances of hooking something. Shares start at $95 to $150 per person for half-day trips, $250 for a full day.

Note: Most big-game charter boats carry six passengers max, and the boats supply all equipment, bait, tackle, and lures. No license is required. Many captains now tag and release marlins; other fish caught belong to the boat, not to you—that's island style. If you want to eat your catch or have your trophy mounted, arrange it with the captain before you go.

Stand-Up Paddleboarding (SUP)

Anywhere the water is calm is a fine place to learn stand-up paddleboarding (SUP), which takes much less finesse than traditional surfing but offers a fun alternative to kayaking for exploring the coast. Numerous hotel concessions offer rentals and lessons, as do traditional surf shops.

Kona Boys ★★ (www.konaboys.com; ✆ **808/328-1234**) has the best locale in Kailua-Kona to try your hand at SUP: **Kamakahonu Cove,** next to Kailua Pier and King Kamehameha's royal (and sacred) compound. The spring water in the well-protected cove is a little too cool and murky for snorkeling, but just right for getting your bearings. The 90-minute lessons costs $99 in a group setting, $149 private; once you've got the hang of it, you can also reserve one of Kona Boys' 90-minute tours ($99 group/$149 private) or just pick up a rental ($29 hourly, $74 daily). It also offers lessons and rentals at its Kealakekua location, 79-7539 Mamalahoa Hwy. (Hwy. 11), 1¼ miles south of its intersection with Highway 180. Both sites are open daily until 5pm; the Kamakahonu beach shack opens at 8am, Kealakekua at 7:30am.

Another good option in North Kona is at Keauhou Bay where **Ocean Safaris** (www.oceansafariskayaks.com; ⓒ **808/326-4699**) offers 2-hour lessons and tours, each $79; rentals are $25 for 2 hours, but paddlers must stay within Keauhou Bay.

On the Kohala Coast, the smooth crescents of **Anaehoomalu Bay** and **Puako Bay** are also well suited to exploring via SUP. **Ocean Sports** (www.hawaiioceansports.com) rents boards for $30 a half-hour ($50 hourly) from its kiosk on the sand in front of the Waikoloa Beach Marriott; see website for details on its other Kohala locations. **Hulakai** rents all kinds of beach gear from its outlet in the Shops at Mauna Lani (http://hulakai.com; ⓒ **808/896-3141**). Open 10am–4pm daily, it offers 1-hour SUP lessons ($68) and 90-minute "adventures" ($98), plus rentals for $69 a day, $249 a week.

In Hilo, **KapohoKine Adventures** rents boards for $25 an hour from its base inside the Grand Naniloa Doubletree by Hilton (p. 268), providing an easy launch into Hilo Bay (ⓒ **808/964-1000**).

Surfing

Most surfing off the Big Island is for the experienced only, thanks to rocks, coral reef, and rip currents at many of the reliable breaks. As a general rule, the beaches on the North and West Shores of the island get northern swells in winter, while those on the South and East shores get southern swells in summer. You'll also need to radiate courtesy and expertise in the lineup with local surfers, understandably territorial about their challenging breaks.

In Kailua-Kona, experienced surfers should check out the two breaks in **Holualoa Bay** off Alii Drive between downtown Kailua-Kona and Keauhou: **Banyans** near the northern point and **Lyman's** near the southern point, once home to a surfers' temple. If you don't have the chops, don't go in the water; just enjoy the show. Another surfing shrine, its black-lava rock walls still visible today, stands near **Kahaluu Beach ★★** (p. 221), where the waves are manageable most of the year and there's also a lifeguard. Less-experienced surfers can also try **Pine Trees,** north of town at **Kohanaiki Beach ★★** (p. 224), where it's best to avoid the busy weekends.

Surf breaks on the east side of the island are also generally best left to skilled or local surfers. They include **Honolii Point,** north of Hilo; **Richardson's Point** at **Leleiwi Beach Park** (p. 227); **Hilo Bay Front Park;** and **Pohoiki Bay,** home to **Isaac Hale Beach Park** near Pahoa.

PRIVATE & GROUP LESSONS   You can have a grand time taking a surf lesson, especially with instructors who know where the breaks are best for beginners and who genuinely enjoy being out in the waves with you. The Native Hawaiian–owned **Hawaii Lifeguard Surf Instructors** (HLSI; www.surflessonshawaii.com; ✆ **808/324-0442**), which gives lessons at Kahaluu Beach, has an especially good touch with kids and teens. For $125, adults and children as young as 3 can take a 90-minute private lesson (little ones under 55 pounds ride on the same board as their lifeguard/ teacher). Lessons for ages 11 and up cost $75 per person for small groups (no more than four students per instructor), or $190 for a class with just two people (who split the cost). On days when the waves are tame, HLSI offers the same lessons with stand-up paddleboards. Classes are offered three times a day, Monday through Saturday.

BOARD RENTALS You're never going to rent a board as good as your own, but you'll enjoy the local vibe at the appropriately named **Pacific Vibrations,** 75-5702 Likana Lane, tucked off Alii Drive just north of Mokuaikaua Church (✆ **808/329-4140**) and founded in 1978 by the McMichaels, a Native Hawaiian family with deep ties to surfing and the Ironman triathlon. It's a trip just to visit the densely stocked surf shop in downtown Kailua-Kona. Surfboards rent for $10 to $20 a day, and bodyboards for just $5. Stand-up paddleboards go for $15 an hour. The staff is happy to help steer you to waves to match your skills.

In the Shops at Mauna Lani, surfboard shaper **Hulakai** (www. hulakai.com; (✆ **808/896-3141**) rents soft-top surfboards for $20 a day ($70 a week) and offers 90-minute private or semiprivate surfing lessons ($150 or $125, respectively).

OTHER OUTDOOR ACTIVITIES
Biking
Note: In addition to the rental fees mentioned below, expect to put down a deposit on a credit card or leave your credit card number on file.

KONA & KOHALA COASTS
When you're planning to spend a fair amount of time in Kailua-Kona, where parking can be at a premium, consider renting a bicycle for easy riding and sightseeing along flat, often oceanview Alii Drive. A cruiser can also be handy if you're staying at a Kohala Coast resort and want an easy way to shuttle around shops, beaches, and condos without having to jump in the car. Experienced cyclists may also want to trace part of the Ironman course (112 miles round-trip) along the wide-shouldered "Queen K" and Akoni Pule highways from Kailua-Kona to Hawi, or join in one of several weekly group rides of the **Hawaii Cycling Club** (www.hawaii cyclingclub.com).

For simple cruisers, head to **Kona Beach & Sports,** in Kona Inn Shopping Village, 75-5744 Alii Dr., Kailua-Kona (www.konabeachand-sports.com; ✆ **808/329-2294**), which rents 24-speed hybrid bikes for $30

Other Outdoor Activities

Former U.S. pro cyclist Alex Candelario's **Big Island Bike Tours ★★★** (http://bigislandbiketours.com; ☎ **800/331-0159**) boasts experienced guides, elite-level mountain and road bikes, and, in several cases, exclusive access to scenery well worth the pedal. Based in a quaint, remodeled shed at Waimea's picturesque **Anna Ranch,** 65-1480 Kawaihae Rd. (Hwy. 11), the company offers a variety of day trips and longer tours for varying abilities. Ride a mountain bike (with electronically assisted bikes for the less hardy) to waterfalls above Anna Ranch, by the rolling pastures along Waimea's unpaved Mana Road, or across rugged terrain to Papakolea (Green Sand Beach); experts can take a shuttle ($35) to ride 46 miles around Mauna Kea on Mana Road. Road cyclists can cruise downhill to Honokaa and head either to the Waipio Valley Overlook or the Hawaiian Vanilla Company, do a 16-mile loop through Holualoa with a lunch break at Holuakoa Cafe, or explore back roads of Kau. Most tours last 2 to 3 hours and cost $189; multiday tours can also be arranged.

---

a day, $112 a week. Pros and amateurs alike flock to its sister store, **Bike Works,** in Hale Hana Centre, 74-5583 Luhia St., Kailua-Kona (www.bikeworkskona.com; ☎ **808/326-2453**) for an even bigger selection of bikes, including mountain bikes, road bikes, and triathlon bikes ($55-$65 daily), with big discounts for longer bookings. Bike Works also has a shop in Queens' MarketPlace, Waikoloa Beach Resort (www.bikeworkshawaii.com; ☎ **808/886-5000**), with road and city bike rentals ($30–$85 daily). Both stores offer weekly group rides.

Note: Reserve rentals well in advance for the first 2 weeks of October, during the lead-up to the Ironman World Championship.

HAWAII VOLCANOES NATIONAL PARK

The national park has miles of paved roads and trails open to cyclists, from easy, flat rides to challenging ascents, but you'll need to watch out for cars and buses on the often winding, narrow roads, and make sure you carry plenty of water and sunscreen. Download a cycling guide on the park's website (www.nps.gov/havo/planyourvisit/bike.htm) or pick one up at the Kilauea Visitor Center. The closest bike-rental shops are in Hilo, including **Mid-Pacific Wheels,** 1133 Manono St. (www.midpacific-wheelsllc.com; ☎ **808/935-6211**), which rents mountain and road bikes for $35 a day, including a helmet; bike racks are $10 a day. Or leave the planning to **Volcano Bike Tours** (www.bikevolcano.com; ☎ **888/934-9199** or 808/934-9199), which offers fully supported half- and full-day guided tours ($115–$150) in the national park that include some off-road riding and, on the longer tour, a van trip to the end of Chain of Craters Road. That's where a 1.25-mile stretch of pavement closed to cars connects with the 8-mile **emergency access gravel road** to Kalapana; it's suitable for hikers or mountain bikers, but was overrun midway by the

July 2016 lava flow. The first few miles feature interpretive signs and great coastal views, but if the flow is still active, flumes may discourage exploration.

Golf

Greens fees below are for visitors and include carts, unless noted; those with Hawaii state ID may receive substantial discounts.

THE KONA COAST

The fabulous **Hualalai Golf Course** ★★★ at the Four Seasons Resort Hualalai (p. 260) is open only to members and resort guests—but for committed golfers, this Jack Nicklaus–designed championship course is reason enough to book a room and pay the sky-high greens fee of $295 ($175 for kids 13–18, free for children 12 and under with paying guest).

Big Island Country Club ★★ Designed by Perry Dye, this par-72, 18-hole course offers sweeping views of towering Mauna Kea and the bright blue coastline from its perch 2,000 feet above sea level. Although it's not on the ocean, water features wind around nine of the holes, including the spectacular par-3 No. 17. Waterfalls, tall palms, and other lush greenery add to the tropical feel; look for native birds such as the nene (Hawaiian goose), hawks, stilts, and black-crowned night herons. The wide fairways and gently rolling terrain make it appropriate for players of every level. Facilities include club rentals, driving range, pro shop, lounge, and snack bar.
71-1420 Mamalahoa Hwy. (Hwy. 190), Kailua-Kona. www.bigislandcountryclub.com. © **808/325-5044.** Greens fees $135; 7-day vacation membership, $240 plus $30 cart fee per round.

Kona Country Club ★★ Although the 18-hole Mountain Course has permanently closed, the popular Keauhou club reopened its William Bell–designed Ocean Course in 2015 with expanded greens, new cart paths and bunkers, and a new irrigation system. The views of pounding waves on lava rock—also visible from the well-stocked pro shop—remain impressive. Other facilities include club rentals, driving range, pro shop, locker rooms, and putting and chipping greens.
78-7000 Alii Dr., Kailua-Kona. www.konagolf.com. © **808/322-3431.** Greens fees $180, $110 after 1 p.m., $45 juniors (8–17); 9 holes after 3pm, $90.

Makalei Golf Club ★ This par-72, 18-hole upcountry course—some 1,800 to 2,850 feet in elevation—goes up and down through native forests, cinder cones, and lava tubes over its championship length of 7,091 yards. The signature hole is the par-3 No. 15, offering a distant view of Maui and the best chance for a hole-in-one. A local favorite, Makalei is visited by wild peacocks, pheasants, and turkeys. Facilities include a golf shop, driving range, putting greens, club rentals (drop-off and pickup available), and the Peacock Grille restaurant, offering a full bar and a menu of burgers, salads, and snacks from 10am to 3pm.

72-3890 Hawaii Belt Rd. (Mamalahoa Hwy./Hwy. 190), Kailua-Kona. www.makalei. com. ✆ **808/325-6625.** Greens fees $109 before noon; $89 noon–2pm. From the intersection of Palani Rd. and Hwy. 11 in Kailua-Kona, take Palani Rd. (which becomes Hwy. 190) east 7¼ miles, and look for green gates and a small white sign on right.

THE KOHALA COAST

Hapuna Golf Course ★★★ Since its opening in 1992, this 18-hole championship course has been named the most environmentally sensitive course by *Golf* magazine, as well as "Course of the Future" by the U.S. Golf Association. Designed by Arnold Palmer and Ed Seay, the links-style course extends nearly 6,900 yards from the shoreline to 700 feet above sea level, with views of the pastoral Kohala Mountains and the coastline; look for Maui across the channel from the signature 12th hole. The elevation changes on the course keep it challenging (and windy the higher you go). There are a few elevated tee boxes and only 40 bunkers. Facilities include putting and chipping greens, driving range, practice bunker, lockers, showers, a pro shop, rental clubs, fitness center, and spa.

At the Westin Hapuna Beach Hotel, Mauna Kea Resort, off Hwy. 19 (near mile marker 69). www.westinhapunabeach.com. ✆ **808/880-3000.** Greens fees for hotel guests: $140–$150 before 1pm; $90–$100 after 1pm. Nonguests: $160–$175 before 1pm; $100–$125 after 1pm. All juniors (18 and younger) $55–$60.

Mauna Kea's famous 3rd hole

Other Outdoor Activities

HAWAII, THE BIG ISLAND

Mauna Kea Golf Course ★★★ This breathtakingly beautiful, par-72, 7,114-yard championship course designed by Robert Trent Jones, Jr., and later updated by son Rees Jones, is consistently rated one of the top golf courses in the United States. The signature 3rd hole is 175 yards long; the Pacific Ocean and shoreline cliffs stand between the tee and the green, giving every golfer, from beginner to pro, a real challenge. Another par-3 that confounds duffers is the 11th hole, which drops 100 feet from tee to green and plays down to the ocean, into the steady trade winds. When the trades are blowing, 181 yards might as well be 1,000 yards. Book ahead; the course is very popular, especially for early weekend tee times. Facilities include a pro shop and clubhouse with restaurant, named Number 3 for the hole that Jones, Sr., once called "the most beautiful in the world."

At the Mauna Kea Beach Hotel, Mauna Kea Resort, off Hwy. 19 (near mile marker 68). https://maunakeabeachhotel.com. ℂ **808/882-5400.** Greens fees $285 ($245 hotel guests) 7am–1pm; $195 after 1pm ($180 hotel guests). Afternoon 9 holes $135. All kids under age 18 play for $95.

Mauna Lani Francis H. Ii Brown Championship Courses ★★★ Carefully wrapped around ancient trails, fish ponds, and petroglyphs, the two 18-hole courses here have won *Golf* magazine's Gold Medal Award every year since the honor's inception in 1988. The **South Course,** a 7,029-yard, par-72, has two unforgettable ocean holes: the over-the-water 15th hole and the downhill, 221-yard, par-3 No. 7, which is bordered by the sea, a salt-and-pepper sand dune, and lush kiawe trees. The **sunset golf cart tour** ($45 for two people in one cart) visits both, among other beautiful stops. The **North Course** may not have the drama of the ocean-front holes, but because it was built on older lava flows, the more extensive indigenous vegetation gives the course a Scottish feel. The hole that's cursed the most is the 140-yard, par-3 17th: It's beautiful but plays right into the surrounding lava field. Facilities include two driving ranges, a golf shop (with teaching pros), a restaurant, and putting greens. Mauna Lani also has the island's only *keiki* (children's) course, the 9-hole Wiki-Wiki walking course for juniors, beginners, and families (golfers under 14 must be with an adult).

At the Mauna Lani Resort, Mauna Lani Dr., off Hwy. 19 (20 miles north of Kona Airport). www.maunalani.com. ℂ **808/885-6655.** Greens fees $235 ($175 for Mauna Lani or Fairmont Orchid guests) before 1pm; $155 ($130 hotel guests) after 1pm. WikiWiki course: $25 children, including clubs; $35 adults ($15 for three clubs).

Waikoloa Beach Resort Courses ★★ Two 18-hole courses beckon here. The pristine 18-hole, par-70 **Beach Course** certainly reflects the motto of designer Robert Trent Jones, Jr.: "Hard par, easy bogey." Most golfers remember the par-5, 505-yard 12th hole, a sharp dogleg left with bunkers in the corner and an elevated tee surrounded by lava. The **Kings' Course,** designed by Tom Weiskopf and Jay Morrish, is about 500 yards longer. Its links-style tract has a double green at the 3rd and 6th holes, and carefully placed bunkers see a lot of play, courtesy of the ever-present trade winds. Facilities include a golf shop, 15-acre practice range (with free clubs and unlimited balls for just $15), and chef Allen Hess' excellent **Mai Grille ★★** restaurant, serving gourmet comfort food (see p. 279); call for a free shuttle within the resort. *Tip:* Check online for multi-round discounts and afternoon family packages.

At the Waikoloa Beach Resort, 600 Waikoloa Beach Dr., Waikoloa. www.waikoloa-beachgolf.com. ℭ **808/886-7888.** Greens fees $125–$185 ($113–$148 for resort guests) before 12:30pm; $75–$98 after 12:30 pm; 9 holes after 8am, $69; $60 juniors 6–17. Second round same day, $55.

Waikoloa Village Golf Course ★   This semiprivate 18-hole course, with a par-72 for each of the three sets of tees, is hidden in the town of Waikoloa, next to the Paniolo Greens timeshare resort. Overshadowed by the glamorous resort courses of the Kohala Coast, it's nevertheless a beautiful course with terrific views and some great golfing. The wind can play havoc with your game here (like most Hawaii golf courses). Robert Trent Jones, Jr., in designing this challenging course, inserted his trademark sand traps, slick greens, and great fairways. The par-5, 490-yard 18th hole is a thriller: It doglegs to the left, and the last 75 yards up to the green are water, water, water. Enjoy the fabulous views of Mauna Kea and Mauna Loa, and—on a very clear day—Maui's Haleakala in the distance.

In Waikoloa Village, 68-1793 Melia St., Waikoloa. www.waikoloavillagegolf.com. ℭ **808/883-9621.** Greens fees $100 ($85 Paniolo Greens guests) before 1:30pm; $66 after. Children ages 7–17 $45 before 1:30pm; $41 after 2pm. From the airport, turn left on Hwy. 19; head 18 miles to stoplight at Waikoloa Rd. Turn right, drive uphill 6½ miles to left on Paniolo Ave. Take 1st right onto Lua Kula St. and follow ½-mile to Melia St.

HILO

Hilo Municipal Golf Course ★   This 146-acre course is great for the casual golfer: It's flat, scenic, and often fun. Just don't go after a heavy rain (especially in winter); the fairways can get really soggy and play can slow way down. The rain does keep the 18-hole course green and beautiful, though. Wonderful trees (monkeypods, coconuts, eucalyptus, and banyans) dot the grounds, and the views—of Mauna Kea on one side and Hilo Bay on the other—are breathtaking. There are four sets of tees, with a par-71 from all; the back tees give you 6,325 yards of play. It's the only municipal course on the island, so getting a tee time can be a challenge; weekdays are the best bet. Facilities include a driving range, pro shop, club rentals, restaurant, and snack bar.

340 Haihai St. (btw. Kinoole and Iwalani sts.), Hilo. www.hawaiicounty.gov/pr-golf. ℭ **808/959-7711.** Greens fees $35 Mon–Fri, $40 Sat–Sun and holidays; carts $20.

Naniloa Golf Course ★   At first glance, this semiprivate 9-hole course just off Hilo Bay looks pretty flat and short, but once you get beyond the 1st hole—a wide, straightforward 330-yard par-4—things get challenging. The tree-lined fairways require straight drives, and the huge lake on the 2nd and 5th holes is sure to haunt you. This course is very popular with locals and visitors alike. Facilities include a driving range, putting green, pro shop, and club rentals.

120 Banyan Dr. (at the intersection of hwys. 11 and 19), Hilo. © **808/935-3000.** Greens fees 9 holes, $12 adults ($9 seniors 62 and over, $5 kids under 17); carts $12.

Hiking

Trails on the Big Island wind through fields of coastal lava rock, deserts, rainforests, and mountain tundra, sometimes covered with snow. It's important to wear sturdy shoes, sunscreen, and a hat, and take plenty of water; for longer hikes, particularly in remote areas, it may also be essential to bring food, a flashlight, and a trail map—not one that requires a cellphone signal to access (coverage may be nonexistent). Hunting may be permitted in rural, upcountry, or remote areas, so stay on the trails and wear bright clothing.

The island has 16 trails in the state's **Na Ala Hele Trail & Access System** (www.hawaiitrails.org; © **808/974-4382**), highlights of which are included below; see the website for more information. For an even greater number of trails on a variety of public lands, see the detailed descriptions on **www.bigislandhikes.com**.

KONA & KOHALA COASTS

The **Ala Kahakai National Historic Trail** (www.nps.gov/alka; © **808/326-6012,** ext. 101) is the designation for an ancient, 175-mile series of paths through coastal lava rock, from Upolu Point in North Kohala along the island's west coast to Ka Lae (South Point) and east to Puna's Wahaula Heiau, an extensive temple complex. Some were created as long-distance trails, others for fishing and gathering, while a few were reserved for royal or chiefly use. There's unofficial access through the four national park sites—Puukohola Heiau, Kaloko-Honokohau, Puuhonua O Honaunau, and Hawaii Volcanoes (see "Attractions & Points of Interest" on p. 187)—but it's easy, free, and fun to walk a portion of the 15.4-mile stretch between Kawaihae and Anaehoomalu Bay, part of the state's **Na Ala Hele** trails system (www.hawaiitrails.org; © **808/974-4382**). Signs mark only the 8-mile portion of Ala Kahakai between the northern terminus of **Ohaiula Beach** at **Spencer Park** (p. 226) through Puako to **Holoholokai Beach Park,** near the petroglyph field on the Mauna Lani Resort, but it's fairly simple to follow farther south by hugging the shoreline, past resort hotels and multimillion-dollar homes, anchialine ponds, and jagged lava formations.

For those not satisfied with the view from the **Pololu Valley Lookout** (p. 196), the steep, 1-mile **Pololu Valley Trail** will lead you just behind the black-sand beach (beware of high surf and riptides). In addition to a 420-foot elevation change, the trail's challenges can include slippery mud and tricky footing over ancient cobblestones. As with all windward areas, be prepared for pesky mosquitos and/or cool mist.

If you're willing to venture on Saddle Road (Hwy. 200), which some rental-car companies still forbid, the **Puu Huluhulu Trail** is an easy, .6-mile hike that gradually loops around both crests of this forested cinder cone, with panoramic views of Mauna Kea and Mauna Loa between the trees. There's a parking lot in front of the hunter check-in station at the junction of the Mauna Loa observatory access road and Saddle Road.

THE HAMAKUA COAST

The 25% grade on the 1-mile "hike" down the road to **Waipio Valley** (p. 203) is a killer on the knees, and no picnic coming back up, but that's just the start of the epic, 18-mile round-trip adventure involving the **Muliwai Trail,** a very strenuous hike to primeval, waterfall-laced **Waimanu Valley.** This trail is the island's closest rival to Kauai's **Kalalau Trail** (p. 511), and so is only worth attempting by very physically fit and well-prepared hikers. Once in Waipio Valley, you must follow the beach to Wailoa Stream, ford it, and cross the dunes to the west side of the valley. There the zigzag Muliwai Trail officially begins, carving its way some 1,300 feet up the cliff; the reward at the third switchback is a wonderful view of Hiilawe Falls. Ahead lie 5 miles of 12 smaller, tree-covered gulches to cross before your first view of pristine Waimanu Valley, which has nine campsites (see "Camping" on p. 271) and two outhouses, but no drinking water. The trail is eroded in places and slippery when wet—which is often, due to the 100-plus inches of rain, which can also flood streams. This explains why the vast majority of those who see Waimanu Valley do so via helicopter (p. 218).

HAWAII VOLCANOES NATIONAL PARK

This magnificent national treasure and Hawaiian cultural icon (p. 182) has more than 150 miles of trails, including many day hikes, most of which are well maintained and well marked; a few are paved or have boardwalks, permitting strollers and wheelchairs. *Warning:* If you have heart or respiratory problems or if you're pregnant, don't attempt any hike in the park; the fumes could bother you. Also: Stacked rocks known as *ahu* mark trails crossing lava; please do not disturb or create your own.

Plan ahead by downloading maps and brochures on the park website (www.nps.gov/havo), which also lists areas closed due to current eruptions. Always check conditions with the rangers at the Kilauea Visitor Center, where you can pick up detailed trail guides. *Note:* All overnight backcountry hiking or camping requires a $10 permit, available only the day of or the day before your hike, from the park's **Backcountry Office** (© **808/985-6178**).

In addition to sights described on the **Crater Rim Drive** tour (p. 213) and **Chain of Craters Road** tour (p. 216), here are some of the more accessible highlights for hikers, all demonstrating the power of Pele:

Devastation Trail hiking path

KILAUEA IKI TRAIL ★★★   The 4-mile loop trail begins 2 miles from the visitor center on Crater Rim Road, descends through a forest of ferns into still-fuming Kilauea Iki Crater, and then crosses the crater floor past the vent where a 1959 lava blast shot a fountain of fire 1,900 feet into the air for 36 days. Allow 2 hours for this fair-to-moderate hike, and look for white-tailed tropicbirds and Hawaiian hawks above you.

DEVASTATION TRAIL ★★★   Up on the rim of Kilauea Iki Crater, you can see what an erupting volcano did to a once-flourishing ohia forest. The scorched earth with its ghostly tree skeletons stands in sharp contrast to the rest of the lush forest. Everyone can take this 1-mile round-trip hike on a paved path across the eerie bed of black cinders. The trailhead is on Crater Rim Road at Puu Puai Overlook.

KIPUKA PUAULU (BIRD PARK) TRAIL ★   This easy 1.2-mile round-trip hike lets you see native Hawaiian flora and fauna in a little oasis of living nature in a field of lava, known as a *kīpuka*. For some reason, the once red-hot lava skirted this mini-forest and let it survive. Go early in the morning or in the evening (or, even better, just after a rain) to see native birds like the *'apapane* (a small, bright-red bird with black wings and tail) and the *'i'iwi* (larger and orange-vermilion colored, with a curved salmon-hued bill). Native trees along the trail include giant ohia, koa, soapberry, kolea, and mamane.

PUU HULUHULU ★★★   This moderate 3-mile round-trip to the summit of a cinder cone (which shares its name with the one on Saddle Road, described above) crosses lava flows from 1973 and 1974, lava tree molds, and *kīpuka*. At the top is a panoramic vista of Mauna Loa, Mauna Kea, the coastline, and the often steaming vent of Puu Oo. The trailhead is in the Mauna Ulu parking area on Chain of Craters Road, 8 miles from the visitor center. (Sulfur fumes can be stronger here than on other trails.)

At the end of Chain of Craters Road, a 1.25 mile stretch of pavement leads to the 8-mile **emergency access gravel road ★★** to Kalapana, overrun midway by a 2016 lava flow; the first few miles have interpretive signs but it may have to reopen to vehicles if the May 2018 eruption cuts off other roads. For avid trekkers, several long, steep, unshaded hikes lead to the beaches and rocky bays on the park's remote shoreline; they're all considered overnight backcountry hikes and thus require a permit. Only hiking diehards should consider attempting the **Mauna Loa Trail,** perhaps the most challenging hike in all of Hawaii. Many hikers have had to be rescued over the years due to high-altitude sickness or exposure after becoming lost in snowy or foggy conditions. From the trailhead at the end of scenic but narrow Mauna Loa Road, about an hour's drive from the visitor center, it's a 7.5-mile trek to the Puu Ulaula ("Red Hill") cabin at 10,035 feet, and then 12 more miles up to the primitive Mauna Loa summit cabin at 13,250 feet, where the climate is subarctic and overnight temperatures are below freezing year-round. In addition to backcountry permits (see above), this 4-day round-trip requires special gear, great physical condition, and careful planning.

Horseback Riding

Although vast Parker Ranch, the historic center of Hawaiian ranching, no longer offers horseback tours, several other ranches in upcountry Waimea provide opportunities for riding with sweeping views of land and sea. Picturesque Waipio Valley is also another focus of equestrian excursions. *Note:* Most stables require riders to be at least 8 years old and weigh no more than 230 pounds; confirm before booking.

The 11,000-acre Ponoholo Ranch, whose herd of cattle (varying between 6,000 and 8,000) is second only to Parker Ranch's, is the scenic home base for **Paniolo Adventures** (www.panioloadventures.com; ✆ **808/889-5354**). Most of its five rides are open-range style and include brief stretches of trotting and cantering, although the gorgeous scenery outweighs the equine excitement—all but the 4-hour Wrangler Ride ($175) are suitable for beginners. The tamest option is the 1-hour City Slicker ride ($69), but the 1½-hour Sunset Ride ($89) appears to be the most popular. Boots, light jackets, Australian dusters, chaps, helmets, hats, drinks, and even sunscreen are provided. Look for Paniolo Adventures' red barn on Kohala Mountain Road (Hwy. 250), just north of mile marker 13.

Naalapa Stables (www.naalapastables.com; ✆ **808/889-0022**) operates rides at Kahua Ranch, which also has an entrance on Kohala Mountain Road, north of mile marker 11. Riding open-range style, you'll pass ancient Hawaiian ruins, through lush pastures with grazing sheep and cows, and along mountaintops with panoramic coastal views. The horses and various riding areas are suited to everyone from first-timers to experienced equestrians. There are several trips a day: a 2½-hour tour at 9am and 1pm for $94, and a 1½-hour tour at 10am and 1:30pm for $73; check-in is a half-hour earlier.

Naalapa has another stable in Waipio Valley (☏ **808/775-0419**), which offers the more rugged **Waipio Valley Horseback Adventure ★★**, a 2½-hour ride that starts with a four-wheel-drive (4WD) van ride down to this little-inhabited but widely revered valley (p. 203). The horses are sure-footed in the rocky streams and muddy trails, while the guides, who are well versed in Hawaiian history, provide running commentary. The cost is $94 for adults, with tours at 9:30am and 1pm Monday to Saturday. Don't forget your camera or bug spray; check in a half-hour earlier at **Waipio Valley Artworks,** 48-5415 Kukuihaele Rd., off Highway 240, about 8 miles northwest of Honokaa.

Waipio Valley Artworks (see above) is also the check-in point for **Waipio Ridge Stables** (www.waipioridgestables.com; ☏ **877/757-1414**), which leads riders on a 2½-hour **Valley Rim Ride** ($90), including views of the beach below and Hiilawe waterfall at the rear of the deep valley. The 5-hour **Hidden Waterfalls Ride** ($175) includes the sights along the rim ride and then follows the stream that feeds Hiilawe through the rain-forest to a picnic and swim in a bracingly cool waterfall pool, but it's rather long if you're not into riding. *Note:* Fog sometimes obscures views of Waipio Valley from the rim.

Tennis

Although some resorts only allow guests to use their tennis facilities, the Kohala Coast has several delightful exceptions. The 11-court **Seaside Tennis Club** (☏ **808/882-5420**) at the Mauna Kea Beach Hotel (p. 264) is frequently ranked among the world's finest for good reason: Three of the courts ($25 per person) are right on the ocean and all enjoy beautiful land-scaping. The club also boasts luxurious locker rooms, a pro shop with racket and ball machine rentals, daily clinics, round robins, and lessons for ages 4 and up. Those not staying at the hotel just need to make a reservation for a court (open daily 8am–5pm) or lesson.

Just as highly ranked, the **Hawaii Tennis Center** ☏ **808/887-7532**) at the Fairmont Orchid, Hawaii (p. 263) offers 10 courts (including one stadium court), with evening play available until 9pm by reservation. It has a pro shop, rents rackets and ball machines, and offers lessons. Fees are $30 per court; check in at pro shop. The **Pa Lea Lea Ocean Sports Tennis** program (www.hawaiioceansports.com; ☏ **808/886-6666,** ext. 108) at Hilton Waikoloa Village (p. 263) provides five cushioned courts and one stadium court, plus lessons, clinics, and racket and ball-machine rentals. Court fees are $20 per hour ($30 per day if available).

You can also play for free at any Hawaii County tennis court; the easiest way to find one nearest you is to visit **www.tennisinhawaii.com**. For those in Kailua-Kona, the four courts at **Old Kona Airport Park** (p. 224) offer the best experience.

Ziplining

Ziplining gives Big Island visitors an exhilarating way to view dramatic gulches, thick forests, gushing waterfalls, and other inspiring scenery—without significantly altering the landscape. Typically, the pulley-and-harness systems have redundant safety mechanisms, with lines and gear inspected daily and multiple checks of your equipment during the tour; your biggest worry may be losing your cellphone or anything not in a zipped pocket. Most outfitters also rent GoPro video cameras that attach to your helmets, so you can relive your whizzing rides at home.

Note: For safety reasons, tours have minimum ages (listed below) and/or minimum and maximum weights; read the fine print carefully before booking. Prices reflect online booking discounts.

NORTH KOHALA   The Australian eucalyptus and native kukui trees on **Kohala Zipline's Canopy Tour** ★★ (www.kohalazipline.com; ✆ **800/464-1993** or 808/331-3620) might not provide the most colorful panoramas, but this nine-line adventure ($178 adults, $154 kids 8–12) emphasizes environmental awareness and cultural history in a compelling way—and the extra-quiet ziplines and multiple suspension bridges are a hoot, too. You'll fly from platform to platform in a sylvan setting that includes ancient taro terraces believed to have been farmed by Kamehameha before he became king. Tours depart from the zip station on Highway 270 between Hawi and Kapaau up to 16 times daily. For a very special splurge, take the outfitter's 8-hour **Kohala Zip & Dip** ★★★, which combines the Canopy Tour with Hawaii Forest & Trail's fascinating Kohala Waterfalls Adventure (p. 219), including a waterfall swim and picnic overlooking beautiful Pololu Valley. The Zip & Dip tours ($264 adults, $236 for ages 8–12, with lunch) depart from Queens' MarketPlace in Waikoloa Beach Resort and Hawaii Forest & Trail headquarters on Highway 19 in Kailua-Kona, 74-5035 Queen Kaahumanu Hwy. (north of Kealakehe Parkway).

HILO & THE HAMAKUA COAST   A few miles north of Hilo, **Kapoho-Kine Adventures** ★★★ (https://kapohokine.com; ✆ **808/964-1000**) has 2 miles of dual (side-by-side) ziplines, eight in all, soaring over rainforest, waterfalls, and farmland on its **Zipline Through Paradise** tour ($189 adults, $169 ages 5 to 11, walk-along $49); the **Zip 'n Swim** version pairs zipping with a swim in a waterfall and deli lunch ($238). Other options include transport from Kona, barbecue, helicopter ride, and/or a guided tour of Hawaii Volcanoes National Park. For an unrivaled emphasis on Hawaiian culture, ask about the **Nohona Hawaii Tour** ($299 adults, $289 children), which combines zipping with a workshop in traditional herbal medicine, crafts, and legends. Tours depart from KapohoKine's store at the Grand Naniloa Hotel, 93 Banyan Dr., Hilo.

The name is misleading, but the thrills are real on the **Skyline Akaka Falls Adventure** ★★ (www.zipline.com/bigisland; ✆ **888/864-6947**), which actually zips past the nearly 250-foot-tall **Kolekole Falls,** downstream from more famous **Akaka Falls** (p. 200) in Honomu, 12 miles north of Hilo. The seven-line course builds in length and speed, while the well-informed guides share insights on local flora and fauna—including banana, taro, and wild pigs—and the area's history as a sugar plantation. The 2½- to 3-hour tour costs $170 (ages 10 and older); a 5-hour **Zip n' Dip** tour adds time at a waterfall swimming hole ($220).

The **Umauma Falls Zipline Tour ★★★** (www.ziplinehawaii.com; ✆ **808/930-9477**) lives up to its name, where you see the captivating, three-tiered falls (p. 203) and 13 other smaller cascades as you zip along its 2-mile, 9-line course ($189 ages 4 and older) in Hakalau, about 16 miles north of Hilo. The **Zip & Dip** option ($239 ages 4 and older) includes an hour of kayaking and swimming under a waterfall, next to the region's only known petroglyph. For a quicker thrill, try the three-person giant swing ($20, ages 4 and older), which soars 150 feet over the falls. The new **Umauma Waterfall Rappel and River Experience** skips the zips but combines rappelling down two waterfalls, hiking, and swimming ($285, ages 8 and older).

WHERE TO STAY ON THE BIG ISLAND

For additional **bed-and-breakfasts**, visit the website of the **Hawaii Island B&B Association** (www.stayhawaii.com), which only allows licensed, inspected properties to become members; only eight are currently listed, reflecting the impact of more casual Airbnb and vacation rentals. You'll find numerous listings of condos and houses on sites such as VRBO.com and Airbnb.com, which have been less of a hot-button issue here than on other islands. To help you compare units and complexes, as well as guarantee rapid assistance should issues arise during your stay, though, consider booking vacation rentals that have professional management, or go through an island-based company, such as those listed for specific regions below.

All rooms listed below come with a private bathroom and free parking unless otherwise noted; all pools are outdoors. Rates do not include the state's 13.41% tax, while cleaning fees refer to one-time charges, not daily service.

The Kona Coast

Many of the lodgings in Kailua-Kona and Keauhou are timeshares or individually owned condos; rates, decor, and amenities in the latter may vary widely by unit. For a broad selection of well-managed condos and a smaller selection of homes (most with pools), contact **Kona Rentals** (www.konarentals.com; ✆ **800/799-5662**) or **Kona Hawaii Vacation Rentals** (www.konahawaii.com; ✆ **809/244-4752** or 808/329-3333).

Note: Prices and minimum-stay requirements may be significantly higher during the week before and after the Ironman World Championship (usually the second Sat in Oct), as well as during holidays.

CENTRAL KAILUA-KONA

In addition to the lodgings below, consider booking a condo at the **Royal Sea Cliff** ★★, on the ocean side of Alii Drive about 2 miles south of the Kailua Pier. There's no beach, but it has two oceanfront pools, often the site of free entertainment, and a tennis court. **Outrigger Hotels & Resorts** (www.outrigger.com; ℂ **800/688-7444** or 808/329-8021) manages 62 of the 148 large air-conditioned units, ranging from studios (650 sq. ft.) up to two-bedroom, two-bathroom units (1,100–1,300 sq. ft.), all with full kitchens and washer/dryers. Outrigger charges $125 to $269 (two-night minimum), plus cleaning fees of $125 to $225, for its well-appointed accommodations, with free parking and Wi-Fi.

Moderate

Courtyard King Kamehameha's Kona Beach Hotel ★★★   This
Courtyard Marriott–managed hotel lives up to its premium setting in front of King Kamehameha's royal compound on Kailua Bay. Rooms boast not only flatscreen TVs, updated bathrooms, and modern furnishings, but also a sense of history and place. Subtle patterns in the stylish guest rooms reflect lava, native plants, and traditional tattoo designs, while colors suggest sand, coffee, and rainforest ferns. The high-ceilinged, bright lobby is home to a gallery of royal portraits and Hawaiian cultural scenes by the late Herb Kawainui Kane. More recently, the hotel restored its two tennis courts and pro shop, added a yoga studio, and expanded the offerings at **Honu's on the Beach** ★★, its popular indoor/outdoor restaurant. *Note:* In early October, this is Ironman central, full of buff bodies and international triathletes, all abuzz about the world championship that starts and ends just outside the hotel's front door.

75-5660 Palani Rd., Kailua-Kona. www.konabeachhotel.com. ℂ **800/367-2111** or 808/329-2911. 452 units. $199–$329 up to 4 people; from $399 one-bedroom suite. Check for online discounts and packages. Self-parking $18, valet $26. **Amenities:** 2 restaurants; bar; convenience store; fitness center; luau; infinity pool; hot tub; rental cars; room service; spa; 2 lighted tennis courts and pro shop; watersports equipment rentals; yoga studio; free Wi-Fi.

Holiday Inn Express Kailua-Kona ★   Its neutral-toned, modern
"chain hotel" decor may seem out of place in Hawaii, but this 75-room hotel is nevertheless a hidden gem. Tucked on a one-way street between Alii Drive and Kuakini Highway, the three-story building offers surprisingly quiet rooms, some with a glimpse of the ocean, including suites with a sofa sleeper. All have 42-inch flatpanel TVs, ample desk space, and gleaming bathrooms; the pool, hot tub, and fitness center are compact but also immaculate. The hot breakfast buffet may lack tropical touches, but it's free. The only downside: The hotel has just 55 parking spaces ($10) in

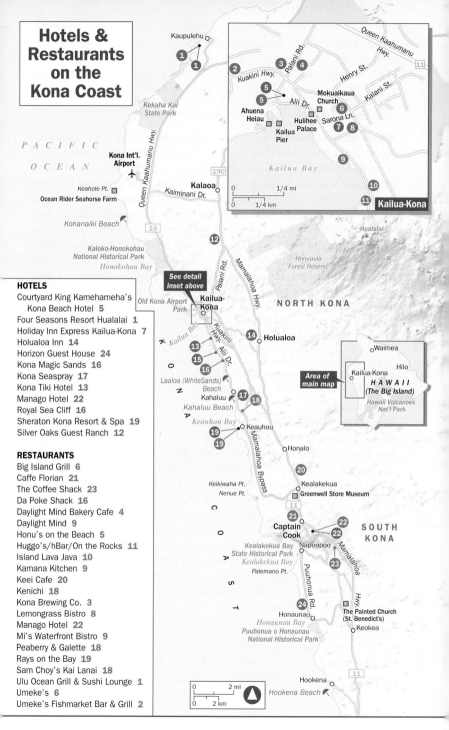

Hotels & Restaurants on the Kona Coast

Kaupulehu

Kona Int'l. Airport

Keahole Pt.
Ocean Rider Seahorse Farm

Kohanaiki Beach

Kaloko-Honokohau National Historical Park
Honokohau Bay

PACIFIC OCEAN

Kekaha Kai State Park

Kaloa
Kaiminani Dr.

Kailua-Kona (inset detail)

Kuakini Hwy.
Palani Rd.
Queen Kaahumanu Hwy.
Henry St.
Kalani St.
Mokuaikaua Church
Alii Dr.
Ahuena Heiau
Hulihee Palace
Sarona Ln.
Kailua Pier
Kailua Bay

Old Kona Airport Park
Kailua-Kona
See detail inset above

Palani Rd.
Mamalahoa Hwy.

Honuaula Forest Reserve
Hualalai

NORTH KONA

Kuakini Hwy.
Alii Dr.
Holualoa

Laaloa (WhiteSands) Beach
Kahalu
Kahaluu Beach
Keauhou Bay
Keauhou

Honalo

Waimea
Kailua-Kona
HAWAII (The Big Island)
Hilo
Hawaii Volcanoes Nat'l Park
Area of main map

Kealakekua
Greenwell Store Museum

Keikiwaha Pt.
Nenue Pt.

Captain Cook
Kealakekua Bay State Historical Park
Kealakekua Bay
Palemano Pt.
Napoopoo

SOUTH KONA

Mamalahoa Bypass
Mamalahoa Hwy.
Puuhonua Rd.

The Painted Church (St. Benedict's)
Keokea

Honaunau
Honaunau Bay
Puuhonua o Honaunau National Historical Park

Hookena
Hookena Beach

HOTELS

Courtyard King Kamehameha's Kona Beach Hotel **5**
Four Seasons Resort Hualalai **1**
Holiday Inn Express Kailua-Kona **7**
Holualoa Inn **14**
Horizon Guest House **24**
Kona Magic Sands **16**
Kona Seaspray **17**
Kona Tiki Hotel **13**
Manago Hotel **22**
Royal Sea Cliff **16**
Sheraton Kona Resort & Spa **19**
Silver Oaks Guest Ranch **12**

RESTAURANTS

Big Island Grill **6**
Caffe Florian **21**
The Coffee Shack **23**
Da Poke Shack **16**
Daylight Mind Bakery Cafe **4**
Daylight Mind **9**
Honu's on the Beach **5**
Huggo's/hBar/On the Rocks **11**
Island Lava Java **10**
Kamana Kitchen **9**
Keei Cafe **20**
Kenichi **18**
Kona Brewing Co. **3**
Lemongrass Bistro **8**
Manago Hotel **22**
Mi's Waterfront Bistro **9**
Peaberry & Galette **18**
Rays on the Bay **19**
Sam Choy's Kai Lanai **18**
Ulu Ocean Grill & Sushi Lounge **1**
Umeke's **6**
Umeke's Fishmarket Bar & Grill **2**

a shared lot. Luckily, the hospitable staff can advise you where to nab another spot.

77-146 Sarona Rd., Kailua-Kona. www.hiexpress.com/kailua-kona. ✆ **855/373-5450** or 808/329-2599. 75 units. $169 room, $179–$219 suite, $199–$239 oceanview suite; rates include up to 4 people per room. Parking $10. **Amenities:** Free breakfast buffet; business center; fitness center; hot tub; laundry; pool; free Wi-Fi.

Kona Magic Sands ★   With Kailua-Kona's largest (if somewhat fickle) sandy beach next door, and oceanfront lanais on every unit to soak in the sunsets and let in the sound of pounding waves, this location is ideal for couples who don't want to spend a bundle at a resort. All the units are studios, with the living/sleeping area bracketed by the lanai on one end and the kitchen on the other. Because they're individually owned (and some managed by other companies than the one listed below), furnishings vary greatly unit to unit. Try to book a corner unit, since those have larger lanais, or spring for the luxuriously remodeled No. 302, which comes with granite counters, travertine tile floors, and gorgeous hardwood cabinets, including one with a Murphy bed and Tempur-Pedic mattress. The pool is also right on the ocean.

77-6452 Alii Dr. (next to Laaloa/Magic Sands Beach Park), Kailua-Kona. Reservations c/o Hawaii Resort Management. www.konahawaii.com. ✆ **800/244-4752** or 808/329-3333. 37 units, all with shower only. Apr 15–Sept 30: $115–$189 corner. Oct 1–Apr 14: $185–$199. Higher rates for stays less than 3 nights; weekly and monthly discounts available. Cleaning fee $85 for 3-night or longer stays. **Amenities:** Pool; free Wi-Fi.

Inexpensive

Kona Tiki Hotel ★★   How close are you to the ocean here? Close enough that waves occasionally break on the seawall, sending sea spray into the oceanfront pool, and close enough that their constant crashing drowns out all or most of the traffic noise from nearby Alii Drive. The small, simply furnished rooms (no TV or phones) feature homey decor, such as pastel tropical print bedspreads. All come with oceanfront lanais, mini-fridges, and ceiling fans (you'll need them); upper-story units have kitchenettes so you can make light meals in addition to the basic continental breakfast (bagels, fruit, coffee) served by the pool. The warm, helpful staff members are quick to lend beach gear and give travel tips; they also make every sunset a special occasion, enlisting guests to help light the tiki torches and blow a conch shell. With no fees for parking, Wi-Fi, or cleaning, this is a true bargain.

75-5968 Alii Dr., Kailua-Kona (about a mile from downtown). www.konatikihotel.com. ✆ **808/329-1425.** 15 units. $99–$199, includes continental breakfast. 3-night minimum (4 for suite). Extra person $20 per adult ($27 in high season, Dec 15–Mar 31 and Ironman week), $10 per child 6–15. Futon $6 per night, crib $2 per night. Deposit required; credit cards accepted over $350; PayPal for lesser amounts. **Amenities:** Pool; free Wi-Fi.

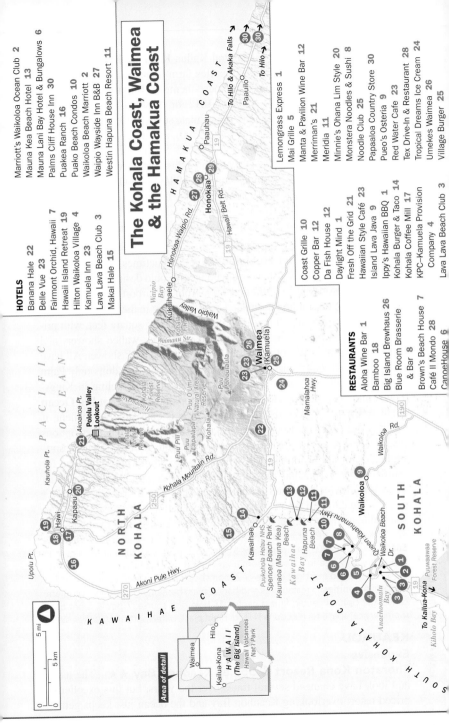

The Kohala Coast, Waimea & the Hamakua Coast

HOTELS

Banana Hale **22**
Belle Vue **23**
Fairmont Orchid, Hawaii **7**
Hawaii Island Retreat **19**
Hilton Waikoloa Village **4**
Kamuela Inn **23**
Lava Lava Beach Club **3**
Makai Hale **15**

Marriott's Waikoloa Ocean Club **2**
Mauna Kea Beach Hotel **13**
Mauna Lani Bay Hotel & Bungalows **6**
Palms Cliff House Inn **30**
Puakea Ranch **16**
Puako Beach Condos **10**
Waikoloa Beach Marriott **2**
Waipio Wayside Inn B&B **27**
Westin Hapuna Beach Resort **11**

RESTAURANTS

Aloha Wine Bar **1**
Bamboo **18**
Big Island Brewhaus **26**
Blue Room Brasserie & Bar **8**
Brown's Beach House **7**
Café Il Mondo **28**
CanoeHouse **6**
Coast Grille **10**
Copper Bar **12**
Da Fish House **12**
Daylight Mind **1**
Fresh Off the Grid **21**
Hawaiian Style Café **23**
Island Lava Java **9**
Ippy's Hawaiian BBQ **1**
Kohala Burger & Taco **14**
Kohala Coffee Mill **17**
KPC–Kamuela Provision Company **4**
Lava Lava Beach Club **3**

Lemongrass Express **1**
Mai Grille **5**
Manta & Pavilion Wine Bar **12**
Merriman's **21**
Meridia **11**
Minnie's Ohana Lim Style **20**
Monstera Noodles & Sushi **8**
Noodle Club **25**
Papaaloa Country Store **30**
Pueo's Osteria **9**
Red Water Cafe **23**
Tex Drive-In & Restaurant **28**
Tropical Dreams Ice Cream **24**
Umekes Waimea **26**
Village Burger **25**

259

NORTH KONA

The cool, rural uplands above central Kailua-Kona are home to two distinctive lodgings. Part of a 30-acre coffee farm in quaint Holualoa, owner Cassandra Hazen's gorgeous Balinese-themed **Holualoa Inn** ★★★ (www.holualoainn.com; © **800/392-1812** or 808/324-1121) offers an oceanview pool, lush gardens, six immaculate suites ($395–$495), a handsome cottage with a full kitchen ($560–$590), and the spacious, elegantly renovated Red Barn one-bedroom suite ($595–$650) at the top of the hillside property; rates include gourmet breakfast. At **Silver Oaks Guest Ranch** ★ (www.silveroaksranch.com; © **808/325-2000**), guests in two simply furnished cottages ($195 double) enjoy meeting miniature donkeys and other animals on the 10-acre working ranch, as well as sunsets from the pool and hot tub; groups may book additional suites in the main house.

Expensive

Four Seasons Resort Hualalai ★★★   Sometimes you do get what you pay for—and that's just about anything you could desire at this serenely welcoming resort, only a 15-minute drive from the airport but worlds away from anything resembling hustle and bustle. Rooms in the small clusters of two-story guest-room buildings and villa start at 635 square feet, with private lanais and large bathrooms outfitted with glass-walled showers and deep soaking tubs; ask for one with an outdoor lava-rock shower. All have views of the ocean or one of seven swimming pools; the adults-only Palm Grove Pool offers a swim-up bar and daybeds, but snorkeling in Kings' Pond amid rays and tropical fish remains a top draw. Dinner at **Ulu Ocean Grill** ★★★ (p. 276) or the **Beach Tree** ★★ is consistently excellent, if costly; it can be hard to tear yourself away in search of cheaper options nearly a half-hour away. Kudos to the Four Seasons for bucking the resort-fee trend, for not charging for its children's or cultural programs, and for numerous environmental measures, including support for the Hawaiian Legacy Hardwoods' koa reforestation (see "Planting a Koa Legacy Tree," p. 220). *Note:* The 18-hole Jack Nicklaus signature golf course, excellent spa and huge fitness center are open only to hotel guests and members.

72-100 Kaupulehu Dr., Kailua-Kona. www.fourseasons.com/hualalai. © **888/340-5662** or 808/325-8000. 243 units. $839–$1,504 double; from $1,739 suite. Children 18 and under stay free in parent's room (maximum 3 guests per room; couples with more than 1 child must get a suite or 2 rooms). Self-parking free; valet parking $25 per day. **Amenities:** 5 restaurants and bars; 2 bars; babysitting; children's program; concierge; cultural center; fitness center; 18-hole golf course; 7 pools; 5 hot tubs; room service; spa; 8 tennis courts (4 lit for night play); watersports rentals; free Wi-Fi.

KEAUHOU

Expensive

Sheraton Kona Resort & Spa at Keauhou Bay ★★   The name and look have changed several times over the years, but this excellently priced resort overlooking Keauhou Bay and the ocean just keeps getting better. Cultural expert and textile designer Sig Zane (see "Big Island

Shopping," p. 286) is behind the splashes of bright color and indigenous plant-inspired graphics, while signs and tours highlight the area's rich cultural history. In addition to the sandy-bottomed pool, water slide, and kid-pleasing fountain play area, there's a lounge just for teens, with Xbox, Wii, and table tennis. The vast majority of rooms have lanais, most with full or partial ocean views—all the better to ogle the manta rays that frequent this area. You can also spot rays from the lanai off **Rays on the Bay** ★★ (see p. 276), a vivacious restaurant/lounge with fire pits and tasty cocktails. *Note:* Check online for specials to offset the $30 daily resort fee and $15 parking. Upgrade to the Club Level to enjoy the breakfast buffet and evening pupus with cocktails at Kaiulu Club Lounge.

78-128 Ehukai St., Kailua-Kona. www.sheratonkona.com. ✆ **888/488-3535** or 808/930-4900. 509 units. $199–$432 double; suites from $499. Online specials available. Daily resort fee of $30 includes bottled water, local calls, Kona Trolley, yoga, cultural tours, Wi-Fi, and more. Self-parking $15, valet $22. Extra person or rollaway $65. Children 18 and under stay free in adult's room using existing bedding. **Amenities:** 3 restaurants; cafe; 2 bars; babysitting; rental bikes; concierge; fitness center; weekly luau (p. 292); multilevel pool w/water slide; room service; spa; 2 tennis courts, basketball and volleyball courts; whirlpool; free Wi-Fi.

Moderate

Kona Seaspray ★ Pay close attention to the details when booking a unit here, across Alii Drive from bustling Kahaluu Beach, because the eight, spacious two-bedroom/two-bathroom units in the three-story main building have varying bed types, views, and decor. All offer ocean views (best from the top two floors), full kitchens, and washer/dryers, but some have been remodeled with granite counters in the kitchen and slate tiles on the lanai. Two one-bedroom units in the adjacent, two-story Seaspray building share laundry facilities. A pretty blue-tiled wall provides privacy for the ground-floor pool, with lounges and a hammock next to a covered grill and dining area.

78-6671 Alii Dr., Kailua-Kona. www.konaseaspray.com. ✆ **808/322-2403.** 10 units. Main building: $175–$205 1-bedroom; $190–$215 2-bedroom. Seaspray building: $175–$205 double. 5% weekly discount, 10% discount May and Sept. Extra person $20. Bedroom air conditioning (some units) $10/day. Cleaning fee $110 2-bedroom, plus $20 per 5th or more person. 3-night minimum. **Amenities:** Barbecue; pool; whirlpool spa; free Wi-Fi.

SOUTH KONA

This rural region of steeply sloping hills, often dotted with coffee and macadamia nut farms, is home to many unassuming B&Bs that may appeal to budget travelers who don't mind being far from the beach.

At the higher end, in every sense, **Horizon Guest House** ★★ (www.horizonguesthouse.com; ✆ **808/938-7822**) offers four suites ($250–$350) with private entrances and lanais on a 40-acre property, including a spacious pool and whirlpool spa, at 1,100 feet of elevation in Honaunau, 21 miles south of Kailua-Kona. Rates include a gourmet breakfast by host Clem Classen; children 13 and under are not allowed.

Inexpensive

Manago Hotel ★   You can't beat the bargain rates at this plantation-era hotel, opened in 1917 and now run by the third generation of the friendly Manago family. Although clean, the 22 original rooms with shared bathrooms ($41 double) should be considered just above camping; they're ultra-spartan and subject to highway noise; children younger than 18 are not allowed. The 42 newer rooms in the three-story wing at the rear also have rather bare walls, but they come with private bathrooms and views of the coast that improve with each floor. Book the third-floor corner Japanese room for a *ryokan* experience, sleeping on a futon and soaking in the *ofuro* (hot tub). ***Note:*** There's no elevator. Walls are thin, and sound can carry through jalousie windows used to let cooling breezes in, but neighbors tend to be considerate. The lounge next to the **Manago Hotel Restaurant** ★★ (p. 277) has a TV.

82-6151 Mamalahoa Hwy., Captain Cook (Hwy. 11, *makai* side, btw. mile markers 109 and 110, 12 miles south of Kailua-Kona). www.managohotel.com. © **808/323-2642.** 64 units. $42 double with shared bathroom; $69–$74 double with private bathroom; $88 double Japanese room with private bathroom. Extra person $3. 4-person maximum. **Amenities:** Restaurant; bar; free Wi-Fi.

The Kohala Coast

SOUTH KOHALA

There's no way around it: The three resort areas here are very costly, but the beaches, weather, amenities, and services at their hotels are among the best in the state. Although you'll miss out on fabulous pools and other hotel perks, you can shave costs (and save money on dining) by booking a vacation rental. For the most affordable, rent one of the 38 **Puako Beach Condos** ★★ in Puako, a one-road, oceanfront town hidden between the Mauna Lani and Mauna Kea resorts. **Island Beach Rentals** (© **808/885-8856**; www.hawaiioceanfront.com) has some of the best units (including corner unit 101, offering three bedrooms, two baths, two lanais and air conditioning); rates start at $139, plus varying cleaning fees. Down the road is Bailey and Baki Wharton's spacious, ground-floor one-bedroom **Puako Beach rental** ★ with a large screened porch; it's below their unit, and averages $195 a night (www.vrbo.com/821534). **South Kohala Management** boasts the most listings (100-plus) of condos and homes in the Mauna Lani, Mauna Kea, and Waikoloa Beach resorts (www.southkohala.com; © **800/822-4252**). **Outrigger Hotels & Resorts** also manages well-maintained condos and townhomes in six complexes in the Mauna Lani and Waikoloa Beach resorts (www.outrigger.com; © **866/956-4262**).

Right on the sand at Anaehoomalu Bay, the lively **Lava Lava Beach Club** restaurant and bar (www.lavalavabeachclub.com/bigisland; © **808/769-5282**) also offers four luxurious **beach cottages** ★★ ($550–$675), with kitchenettes, king beds, day beds, and outdoor showers; keep in mind the bar is open until 10pm nightly, with live music until 9pm.

Expensive

Fairmont Orchid, Hawaii ★★★ The two guest wings at this polished but inviting sanctuary are set off the main lobby like two arms ready to embrace the well-manicured grounds and rugged shoreline; you may feel like hugging it, too, when you have to leave. Tucked among burbling waterfalls and lush greenery are 10 thatched-roof huts in the **Spa Without Walls,** which has another five oceanfront cabanas. Beyond the 10,000-square-foot swimming pool lies a cove of soft sand, where the Hui Holokai Beach Ambassadors make guests feel at home in the water and on shore, teaching all kinds of Hawaiiana and sharing their knowledge about the area's cultural treasures, such as the nearby Puako Petroglyph Archaeological Preserve (p. 194). The elegant, generously proportioned rooms (starting at 510 sq. ft.) with lanais offer subtle island accents such as rattan and carved wood, marble bathrooms and other luxurious fittings. Golf, tennis, and dining are also exceptional here, as befits the prices.

At the Mauna Lani Resort, 1 N. Kaniku Dr., Waimea. www.fairmont.com/orchid-hawaii. ⓒ **800/845-9905** or 808/885-2000. 540 units. $319–$769 double; $520–$820 Gold Floor double; from $869 suite. Check for online packages. Extra person $75. Children 17 and under stay free in parent's room. Daily resort fee $30, includes self-parking and Wi-Fi. Valet parking $10. **Amenities:** 6 restaurants; 3 bars; babysitting; bike rentals; children's program; concierge; 2 championship golf courses; fitness center; luau (p. 292); pool; room service; spa; theater; 10 tennis courts (7 lit for night play); watersports rentals; free Wi-Fi.

Westin Hapuna Beach Resort ★★★ Flying the Westin flag since summer 2018, this dramatically reshaped sister property to the Mauna Kea Beach Hotel has become a polished gem above the wide sands of **Hapuna Beach** ★★★. Its open-air entrance now cascades directly to its large, tropically landscaped pool complex that includes a new infinity pool just for adults, while all of its many cafes, bars, and restaurants have been reimagined. Although one wing has been converted to vacation condos, the refreshed rooms still start at 600 square feet, the largest standard rooms on the Kohala Coast, all with balconies and an ocean view. The sprawling, terraced grounds also host an 18-hole Arnold Palmer championship golf course (p. 246), fitness center, and spa.

At the Mauna Kea Resort, 62-100 Kaunaoa Dr., Waimea. ⓒ **800/882-6060** or 808/880-1111. www.westinhapunabeach.com. 249 units. $325–$465 double; from $765 suite. Children 17 and under stay free in parent's room using existing bedding. Adult rollaway $75, child rollaway $40. Daily resort fee $30, includes self-parking and Wi-Fi. Valet parking $20. **Amenities:** 3 restaurants; 2 bars; babysitting; cafe/gift shop; seasonal children's program; concierge; 18-hole championship golf course (p. 246); fitness center; pool; room service; spa; access to Mauna Kea Beach Hotel tennis center; watersports rentals; free Wi-Fi.

Hilton Waikoloa Village ★★★ It's up to you how to navigate this 62-acre oceanfront Disneyesque golf resort, laced with fantasy pools, lagoons, and a profusion of tropical plants in between three low-rise towers. If you're in a hurry, take the Swiss-made air-conditioned tram; for a more leisurely ride, handsome mahogany boats ply canals dotted with tropical fish. Or just walk a half-mile or so through galleries of Asian and Pacific art on your way to the ample-sized rooms designed for families. Among the best are the 161 rooms and eight suites in the Lagoon Tower's Makai section—all ocean view, with upgraded bathrooms (including dual vanities) and high-end bedding. Kids will want to head straight to the 175-foot water slide and 1-acre Kona Pool, and will pester you to pony up for the DolphinQuest encounter with Pacific bottlenose dolphins. The actual beach is rough, hence an enormous, sand-fronted swimming lagoon that's home to sea turtles and other marine life. You won't want for places to eat here either; its Kona Tap Room, a partnership with **Kona Brewing Co.** (p. 276) offers the brewer's full lineup on tap, including seasonal beers found only here and at the Kona brewery. *Note:* Self-parking ($27) is not included in the hefty $35 resort fee, so you may as well pay $10 more for valet parking to avoid a long, warm walk.

69-425 Waikoloa Beach Dr., Waikoloa. www.hiltonwaikoloavillage.com. (C) **800/445-8667** or 808/886-1234. 1,241 units. From $265 double with resort view ($325 ocean view) and from $815 suite. Daily resort fee $35 includes Wi-Fi, local/toll-free calls, cultural lessons, in-room PlayStation3 with movies and games, and more. Extra person $50. Children 18 and under stay free in parent's room. Self-parking $27; valet parking $37. **Amenities:** 9 restaurants; 5 bars; babysitting; bike rentals; children's program; concierge; fitness center; 2 18-hole golf courses; luau (p. 292); 3 pools (1 adults-only); Jacuzzis; room service; spa; 6 tennis courts; watersports rentals; free Wi-Fi.

Mauna Kea Beach Hotel ★★★ Old-money travelers have long embraced this golf-course resort, which began as a twinkle in Laurance Rockefeller's eye and in 1965 became the first hotel development on the rugged lava fields of the Kohala Coast. It still exudes upscale tranquility with an uncluttered, Asian-inspired aesthetic in spacious, modern rooms, while families relish the even larger lodgings in the Beachfront Wing and a new array of Hawaiian cultural activities, including throw-net fishing and hula lessons. At press time, plans were still afoot to expand the spa and add an adults-only pool. Dining, particularly at **Manta ★★★** (p. 278) and the gleaming **Copper Bar ★★★** (p. 292), remain top-notch, with glorious views from both the golf course (p. 247) and tennis center (p. 253). The pool is small by today's standards, but sandy **Kaunaoa Beach ★★★** (p. 226), where manta rays skim the north point, is just a few steps away. The true pearls are the gracious staff members, many of whom know several generations of guests by name. *Note:* The hotel is part of Marriott's Autograph Collection, but not owned by Marriott.

At the Mauna Kea Resort, 62-100 Mauna Kea Beach Dr., Waimea. https://mauna keabeachhotel.com. (C) **866/977-4589** or 808/882-7222. 252 units. $625–$1,275 double; from $1,450 suite. Extra person $80. 3-adult maximum. Valet parking $20; self-parking $15. **Amenities:** 4 restaurants; 3 bars; cafe; babysitting; seasonal children's program; concierge; 18-hole championship golf course (p. 247); fitness center; pool; hot tub; room service; 11 tennis courts; watersports rentals; basic free Wi-Fi; high-speed, $15 per day.

Mauna Lani Bay Hotel & Bungalows ★★ Under new ownership and management, the 32-acre oceanfront resort planned to close for a major redesign in October 2018. After a $100 million-plus in renovations, it is expected to reopen in late 2019 as **Mauna Lani, Auberge Resorts Collection.** Every public space and accommodation will be remodeled, leading to fewer rooms (previously 341) and more oceanview suites; the opulent two-bedroom bungalows (2,700 sq. ft.) will also be updated. **CanoeHouse** ★★★ (p. 278) will continue to offer sumptuous dining, with new three-meals-a-day service at Bay Terrace Restaurant. The new owners also plan to revamp the spa and 5,000-square-foot fitness center, create an adult infinity-edge pool with cabanas, update the family pool, add new beachfront services and children's programs, and enhance existing cultural programs on the resort, like the monthly "Twilight at Kalahuipuaa" (see p. 291).

At the Mauna Lani Resort, 68-1400 Mauna Lani Dr., Puako. maunalani.auberge resorts.com. ℂ **800/367-2323** or 808/885-6622. Number of units, rates not yet announced. **Expected amenities:** 3 restaurants; bar; concierge; children's program; 2 18-hole golf courses; fitness center with lap pool; 2 pools (adult and family); hot tub; room service; spa; access to tennis courts at the Fairmont Orchid; watersports rentals; free Wi-Fi.

Waikoloa Beach Marriott Resort & Spa ★★ Of all the lodgings in the Waikoloa Beach Resort, this hotel has the best location on **Anaehoomalu Bay** ★★ (nicknamed "A-Bay"; p. 225), with many rooms offering views of the crescent beach and historic fishponds; others look across the parking lot and gardens toward Mauna Kea. All were renovated in 2017; the luxury Cabana wing (closest to the water) debuted in 2018 with private outdoor showers on ground-floor lanais. Besides numerous beach watersports, kids enjoy the sandy-entrance children's pool, while adults delight in the heated infinity-edge pool, the open-air espresso bar/cocktail lounge **Akaula Lanai,** the two-level **Mandara Spa,** and the spacious, well-equipped fitness center. The light-hued rooms are also enticing, with glass-walled balconies and plush beds with down comforters in crisp white duvets. Families should book one of the spacious corner rooms, which include a king-size bed and a sofa bed. Despite the steep resort fee ($30 daily), this hotel typically offers the best prices of the Kohala Coast resorts, with easy access to nearby golf courses. *Note:* Even better values are found at **Marriott's Waikoloa Ocean Club** ★★★, handsome one- and two-bedroom timeshare suites with king beds, living rooms with sofa-beds, and kitchenettes, with starting rates of $324—plus free Wi-Fi, free parking, and no resort fee.

69-275 Waikoloa Beach Dr., Waikoloa. www.marriotthawaii.com. ℂ **888/236-2427** or 808/886-6789. 290 hotel units: $322–$4,097 double; $409 suite. Cabana wing: $729. Hotel's daily $30 resort fee includes cultural activities, Wi-Fi, fitness classes, and more. Self-parking $18, valet $28. Rollaway $45. Children 17 and under stay free in parent's room. 112 Ocean Club units: 1-bedroom from $327, 2-bedroom from $427. No resort fee; free self-parking, $10 valet parking. **Amenities:** Restaurant; 2

bars; babysitting; cafe; concierge; cultural activities; fitness center; Jacuzzi; luau; 3 pools; rental-car desk; room service; spa; watersports rentals; free Wi-Fi.

NORTH KOHALA

This rural area, steeped in Hawaiian history and legend, has few overnight visitors, given its distance from swimmable beaches and other attractions. But it does include two luxurious accommodations that reflect its heritage in unique ways. At eco-friendly **Puakea Ranch ★★★** (www.puakea ranch.com; ✆ **808/315-0805**), west of Hawi and 400 feet above the coast, three plantation-era bungalows and a former cowboy bunkhouse have been beautifully restored as vacation rentals ($289–$629; 3- to 7-night minimum, $150-$200 cleaning fee). Sizes vary, as do amenities such as soaking tubs and swimming pools, but all have access to the organic farm produce and eggs, plus fast Wi-Fi. On the ocean bluff between Hawi and Kapaau, hidden from the road, the "eco-boutique" **Hawaii Island Retreat ★★** (www.hawaiiislandretreat.com; ✆ **808/889-6336**) offers 10 posh guest rooms and three bungalows with large bathrooms and balconies ($425–$500 double, 4-night minimum). Clustered near the saltwater infinity pool are seven yurts (large tentlike structures) with private bathrooms and shared indoor/outdoor showers ($195 double). Rates include a sumptuous, homegrown organic breakfast.

For a more economical stay, consider **Makai Hale ★★**, a bed-and-breakfast in windy, higher-elevation Kohala Ranch, with panoramic ocean and Maui views. Jerry and Audrey Maluo offer one modern guest suite with queen bed, kitchenette, and bath ($165–$185, 2-night minimum), plus an optional queen bedroom with private bath ($110), both with access to the private pool and whirlpool spa and daily breakfast platters (www.makaihale.com; ✆ **808/880-1012**).

WAIMEA

Within a 15-minute drive or less of Hapuna Beach, the cowboy town can be a good alternative to pricey resorts. Attractively remodeled with rustic-chic touches, the 30-unit **Kamuela Inn ★★** sits in a quiet enclave off the main road, but still within walking distance of **Merriman's ★★★** (p. 281) and other dining and shopping, at 65-1300 Kawaihae Rd. (www. thekamuelainn.com; ✆ **800/555-8968**). Room rates ($139–$189) include continental breakfast; some units include kitchenettes and bedding for up to six. The original 1960s wing (rooms $129-$139) was slated for renovations at press time. Close to the center of town, the two-story, two-unit **Belle Vue ★** (www.hawaii-bellevue.com; ✆ **800/772-5044** or 808/885-7732) vacation rental has a penthouse apartment with high ceilings and views from the mountains to the distant sea, and a downstairs studio ($95–$175 double, $25 per extra person). Although decor is dated, both sleep four and come with breakfast fixings in kitchenettes. *Note:* Check VRBO.com and Airbnb.com for even more listings, such as the roomy **Banana Hale ★★** studio ($95), where bananas grow just outside your window;

owned by friendly local teachers, it's off Highway 19, a few miles west of downtown Waimea (www.airbnb.com/rooms/6392442).

The Hamakua Coast

This emerald-green, virtually empty coast is a far drive from resort-worthy beaches and Hawaii Volcanoes National Park and so is less frequented by overnight visitors (other than coqui frogs). Those who do choose to spend a night or more, though, will appreciate getting away from it all. Two miles north of Honokaa off Highway 240, the **Waipio Wayside Inn Bed & Breakfast** ★★ (www.waipiowayside.com; ✆ 800/833-8849 or 808/775-0275) perches on a sunny ocean bluff. A restored former plantation supervisor's residence, the inn has five antiques-decorated rooms with modern bathrooms ($130–$210 double) and a handsome living/dining room, where owner Jacqueline Horne serves hot organic breakfasts promptly at 8am.

Closer to Hilo, in rustic Honomu, the sprawling, Victorian-inspired **Palms Cliff House Inn** ★★ (www.palmscliffhouse.com; ✆ 866/963-6076 or 808/963-6076) serves a full breakfast on its lanai overlooking Pohakumanu Bay. Some of its eight large, quiet suites ($199–$449) have air-conditioning and jetted tubs; all offer king beds and an ocean view.

Note: You'll find these accommodations on "The Kohala Coast, Waimea & the Hamakua Coast" map on p. 259.

Hilo

Although several hotels line scenic Banyan Drive, most fall short of visitors' expectations, with the exception of the **Grand Naniloa Hotel Hilo—A Doubletree by Hilton** ★★★, described below. Be aware you may hear coqui frogs all night wherever windows are open in Hilo.

The owners of the Shipman House, a gracious Victorian mansion on Reed's Island formerly run as a bed-and-breakfast, now just rent out two rooms ($75) in its 1910 guest cottage on Airbnb. The mirror-image units in the **Shipman House Guest Cottage** come with queen bed, microwave, mini-fridge, desk, Wi-Fi, and a shared screened porch; the Mauka Room (www.airbnb.com/rooms/19664488) receives more cooling night breezes than the Makai Room (www.airbnb.com/rooms/19682128). The **Old Hawaiian Bed & Breakfast** ★ (www.thebigislandvacation.com; ✆ 877/961-2816 or 808/961-2816) provides easy access to Waianuenue (Rainbow Falls) from a quaint 1930s house with three rooms ($105–$150, with full breakfast); children under 12 not permitted.

On a hilltop 22-acre compound boasting its own waterfall swimming pool, the **Inn at Kulaniapia Falls** ★★★ (www.waterfall.net; ✆ 808/935-6789) offers a choice of 10 Asian- or Hawaiian-themed rooms ($169–$299, with full breakfast) or the Pagoda Cottage (from $339 for four, with kitchen stocked with breakfast supplies). Kayaks, paddleboards, yoga, and light lunches are also available.

Note: The lodgings in this section are on the "Hilo" map on p. 207.

MODERATE

Grand Naniloa Hotel Hilo—A DoubleTree by Hilton ★★★ This 12-story, thoroughly renovated oceanfront hotel with wonderful views of Hilo Bay has declared itself "the home of hula." Renowned photographer Kim Taylor Reese's images of hula dancers hang on virtually every wall, high-definition video of the "Merrie Monarch" hula competition plays in the new, open-air lobby, with a central bar. **Hula Hulas ★** poolside restaurant offers locally sourced dishes, live music, and hula. The refurbished rooms (most 312–330 sq. ft.) sport marble bathrooms and floors, flatscreen TVs, and triple-sheet white bedding; some suites (660 sq. feet) include kitchenettes, while corner rooms with wrap-around lanais offer sweeping vistas. Rent a kayak or paddleboard, or book a zipline, helicopter, or volcano excursion, at the KapohoKine Adventure Store, which includes a small market. Room rates include a free round at the 9-hole **Naniloa Golf Course** (p. 248).

93 Banyan Dr., Hilo. www.grandnaniloahilo.com. ✆ **808/969-3333.** 407 units. $134–$189 double; from $14 suite w/2 kings. **Amenities:** Activity desk; bar; fitness center; 9-hole golf course (free); pool; 2 restaurants; room service; free Wi-Fi.

Puna

Note: Access to these properties may be affected by the May 2018 eruptions. An unusual collection of more than 350 species of palm trees shelter the four luxurious yet off-the-grid Balinese-style bamboo cottages ($160–$220) of **Kipuka ★★** in Kapoho, all of which sleep two to six, and all have access to a saline pool (http://kipuka.co; ✆ **808/339-3027**). Yoga and nature lovers should investigate the variety of rustic lodgings ($95–$245) and classes at the bohemian, gay-friendly **Kalani Oceanside Retreat ★** on Highway 137 about halfway between Kapoho and Kalapana (www.kalani.com; ✆ **800/800-6886;** 808/965-7828). For an enchanted setting with its own thermal pond, a short walk to the Waiopae Tidepools, book **Lani Mai Honua Hale** ("Heaven on Earth"), a well-furnished 3-bedroom, 2-bath home in Kapoho Vacationland (from $195; www.vrbo.com/1054676). Throughout lower Puna, be prepared for humidity and the evening symphony of coqui frogs.

In **Volcano Village,** the frogs don't like the misty, cool nights at 3,700 feet; ask about heating when booking rentals in winter. Joey Gutierrez of **Hawaii Volcano Vacations** (www.hawaiivolcanovacations.com; ✆ **800/709-0907** or 808/967-7178) manages choice cottages and houses for $120 to $199 a night. **Mahinui Na Lani ★★★** (www.mahinui.com; ✆ **510/965-7367**) is a romantic, eco-friendly hideaway; the whimsical two-level treehouse studio offers a kitchenette and cedar hot tub for two, with a ship's ladder leading to a cozy sleeping loft ($295).

Note: You'll find Mahinui Na Lani and the following accommodations on the "Hotels & Restaurants in the Volcano Area" map (p. 269).

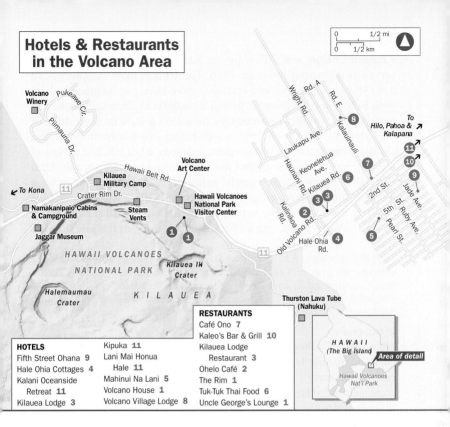

Hotels & Restaurants in the Volcano Area

Volcano Winery

Pukeawe Cir.

Piimauna Dr.

← To Kona

Hawaii Belt Rd.

Kilauea Military Camp

Volcano Art Center

Crater Rim Dr.

Namakanipaio Cabins & Campground

Steam Vents

Hawaii Volcanoes National Park Visitor Center

Jaggar Museum

HAWAII VOLCANOES NATIONAL PARK

Kilauea Iki Crater

K I L A U E A

Halemaumau Crater

Wright Rd.

Rd. A

Rd. E

Kalaunauili

To Hilo, Pahoa & Kalapana

Laukapu Ave.

Haunani Rd.

Keonelehua Ave.

Kilauea Rd.

Kalinikoa Rd.

Old Volcano Rd.

Hale Ohia Rd.

2nd St.

5th St.

Ruby Ave.

Pearl St.

Jade Ave.

Thurston Lava Tube (Nahuku)

RESTAURANTS
Café Ono **7**
Kaleo's Bar & Grill **10**
Kilauea Lodge
  Restaurant **3**
Ohelo Café **2**
The Rim **1**
Tuk-Tuk Thai Food **6**
Uncle George's Lounge **1**

H A W A I I
(The Big Island)

Area of detail

Hawaii Volcanoes Nat'l Park

HOTELS
Fifth Street Ohana **9**
Hale Ohia Cottages **4**
Kalani Oceanside
  Retreat **11**
Kilauea Lodge **3**

Kipuka **11**
Lani Mai Honua
  Hale **11**
Mahinui Na Lani **5**
Volcano House **1**
Volcano Village Lodge **8**

0   1/2 mi
0   1/2 km

VOLCANO VILLAGE

Expensive

Volcano Village Lodge ★★★   Built as an artists' retreat in 2004, the five romantic cottages in this leafy, 2-acre oasis offer gleaming hardwood floors and paneled walls, vaulted ceilings, fireplaces, kitchenettes, and endless walls of windows—the lush rainforest envelops the oh-so-peaceful lodge in privacy. Fixings for a full breakfast are left in your room each night. Enjoy the communal hot tub in the gardens after a day of hiking in the national park. For true sumptuousness or extra guests, book the two-room Mauna Loa cottage ($375), which includes a "meditation" loft under the eaves. *Note:* Families should also consider the lodge's **5th Street Ohana** (www.5thstohana.com; © **808/985-9500**). On the other side of Highway 11, this modern vacation rental offers a two-bedroom suite ($225) and a studio ($150), both with full kitchens, which can be combined as one unit ($375).

19-4183 Road E, Volcano. www.volcanovillagelodge.com. © **808/985-9500.** 5 units. $280–$375 double (up to 4 guests), includes full breakfast. From Hwy. 11, take Wright Rd. exit, and head .8 mile north to right on Laukapu St.; it ends at Road E. Turn left; lodge is first driveway on the left. **Amenities:** Hot tub; DVD library; free Wi-Fi.

Moderate

Kilauea Lodge ★★ This former YMCA camp, built in 1938, has served as a gracious inn since 1986. The 10-acre main campus has 12 units in two wings and two cottages; most have gas fireplaces, along with European-Hawaiian decor and thoughtful touches such as heated towel racks. Another four cottages lie within a walk or short drive of the lodge; my favorites are the two-bedroom, two-bathroom Pii Mauna ($280), which comes with two extra sofabeds, a hot tub, and a view of the Volcano Golf Course, and the two-bedroom, one-bathroom Olaa Plantation House, an elegantly restored 1935 home with a huge kitchen, breakfast room, and living room ($305). All rates include gourmet breakfast in the superb **Kilauea Lodge Restaurant** ★★★ (p. 284). *Note:* The lodge and restaurant were both for sale at press time.

19-3948 Old Volcano Rd., Volcano. www.kilauealodge.com. ℂ **808/967-7366.** 12 units on main property, 4 cottages nearby. $195–$225 double room; $240–$305 cottage. Extra person $20 (ages 2 and up), includes full breakfast. From Hwy. 11, take Wright Rd. exit to 1st left at Old Volcano Rd; lodge is .1 mile on right. **Amenities:** Restaurant; gift shop; hot tub; free Wi-Fi.

Inexpensive

Hale Ohia Cottages ★★ Kentucky native Michael Tuttle, a former chef and historic building renovator, came across this secluded garden estate in the early 1990s and happily made this "old Volcano home." The quiet main lodge has two units, with a connecting hallway to create a family suite if desired. I recommend one of the three unique guest cottages, each with one to three bedrooms and greater privacy. The circa-1920s Ihilani Cottage and Cottage 44, a transformed 1930s redwood water tank, have charming turret-shaped bedrooms and inviting nooks ($199). Families should consider the two-story, three-bedroom Hale Ohia, formerly the gardener's cottage, which has one queen and three twin beds (but only one bathroom; $295). Continental breakfast is included, except at the two off-site cottages.

11-3968 Hale Ohia Rd., Volcano. www.haleohia.com. ℂ **800/455-3803** or 808/967-7986. 12 units. $129–$199 double. Extra person $20. Most rates include continental breakfast. 2-night minimum in high season. **Amenities:** Free Wi-Fi at main property.

HAWAII VOLCANOES NATIONAL PARK

Expensive

Volcano House ★ This historic two-story wooden inn is extremely modest for its price, especially compared with Yosemite's Ahwahnee and the grand lodges of other national parks. Still, its location on the very rim of the Kilauea Caldera is nothing short of spectacular—to wake up to that view is very special indeed. Rooms are on the small and plain side and the vintage bathrooms downright tiny, so explore your surroundings during the day and then enjoy dinner and drinks at **The Rim** ★★ (p. 285) or **Uncle George's Lounge** downstairs, before falling into the comfy beds. Now that the crater-view rooms have risen to $335 and higher, this is a real splurge (note that ohia lehua trees may partially block the views). The hotel also manages 10 refurbished cabins and 16 campsites with rental tents inside the park; see "Camping," below. *Note:* If the park is closed, the hotel and campground close as well.

1 Crater Rim Dr., Hawaii Volcanoes National Park. www.hawaiivolcanohouse.com. ☏ **866/536-7972** or 808/756-9625. 33 units. $228–$365 double. Extra person $30. $25 park entrance fee, valid for 7 days. Check for online packages. **Amenities:** Restaurant; bar; bicycles; gift shops; free Wi-Fi.

Kau

As with the Hamakua Coast, few visitors overnight in this virtually undeveloped area, halfway between Kailua-Kona and Hawaii Volcanoes National Park, but there is one lodging that encourages guests to linger. In a tranquil setting above the road to Ka Lae (South Point), luxurious **Kalaekilohana** ★★ (www.kau-hawaii.com; ☏ **808/939-8052**) has four large guest suites ($369) in a modern plantation-style home. After one night in a plush bed, with a beautifully presented breakfast on the lanai, and true Hawaiian hospitality from hosts Kenny Joyce and Kilohano Domingo, many guests kick themselves for not having booked a second night or more—and multi-night discounts start at $40 off a 2-night stay. Kenny's delicious dinners ($25–$30 per person) are a nightly option.

Camping

Camping is available at 10 county beach parks, six state parks and reserves, a few private campgrounds, and Hawaii Volcanoes National Park. I don't recommend most county parks, because of noise at popular sites (such as **Spencer Park,** p. 226) and security concerns at more remote ones (such as **Punaluu Beach,** p. 230), but **Kohanaiki Beach Park** (p. 224) is zealously well maintained. County campsites require advance-purchase permits, which cost $20 a night per person for nonresidents (http://hawaiicounty.ehawaii.gov; ☏ **808/961-8311**).

State campsites also require permits that must be booked in advance (http://camping.ehawaii.gov; ☏ **808/961-9540**). The most desirable are at **Hapuna Beach** (p. 226), which offers six A-frame screened shelters with wooden sleeping platforms and a picnic table, plus communal restrooms and cold showers. Nonresidents pay $50 per shelter per night for permits; purchase at least a month in advance. Friday through Sunday nights, **Kiholo State Park Reserve** (p. 222) allows tent camping in a kiawe grove on a pebbly beach, with portable toilets but no water; nonresidents pay $18 per campsite per night. For hard-core backpackers, camping in the state preserve of remote **Waimanu Valley** is typically the reward for tackling the extremely arduous Muli-wai Trail (p. 250). Permits for nonresident campers cost $20 per site (for up to six people); you'll also need to pay $20 per night to leave your car at Waipio Valley Artworks, due to no overnight parking at the Waipio Valley Lookout.

At South Kona's **Hookena Beach Park** (p. 225), the privately run campground with local security is perfect for pitching a tent by the waves. Campsites for nonresidents cost $21 per person per night for ages 7 and older; reserve at last 72 hours in advance (www.hookena.org; ✆ **808/328-7321**). You can also rent tents, camping stoves, tables, and chairs for use on-site.

In **Hawaii Volcanoes National Park** (p. 213), two campgrounds are accessible by car. The easiest to reach and best supplied is **Namakanipaio Campground** ★★, which offers 10 cabins and 16 campsites. The updated one-room cabins sleep four, with bed linens and towels provided, grills, and a community restroom with hot showers; the cost is $80 a night. Tent campers have restrooms but not showers; sites cost $15 a night, on a first-come, first-served basis, with a 7-night maximum stay. Both cabins and campsites are managed by **Volcano House** (p. 270; www.hawaiivolcanohouse.com; ✆ **866/536-7972** or 808/441-7750). Call the hotel in advance to rent a tent set up for you with a comfy foam mattress, linens, cooler, lantern, and two chairs for $55 a night, including the site rental. Park entrance fee of $25 is additional. *Note:* It can be very cool and damp here, especially at night.

Kulanaokuaiki Campground, which has nine campsites with picnic tables but no running water, is a 5-mile drive down Hilina Pali Road. It's first-come, first-served; pay the $10 nightly fee (1-week maximum stay) at the self-registration station. Backpack camping is allowed at seven remote areas in the park (some with shelters, cabins, and water catchment tanks) but first you must register for a $10 permit, good for up to 12 people and 7 nights, at the **Backcountry Office** (www.nps.gov/havo; ✆ **808/985-6178**), no more than 1 day in advance.

Note: No island merchants rent camping gear, but you can buy some at the **Hilo Surplus Store,** 148 Mamo St., Hilo (www.hilosurplusstore.com; ✆ **808/935-6398**), or at a big-box store such as **Kmart,** 74-5456 Kamaka Eha Ave., Kailua-Kona (✆ **808/326-2331**). Another way to go, literally, is with a fully equipped rooftop tent in a pickup truck from **Huakai Campers** (www.huakaicampers.com; ✆ **808/896-3158**), $105 a night with 3-night minimum and pickup in Hilo. *Note:* Vehicle camping is allowed at county parks and the two national park campgrounds with standard camping permits.

WHERE TO EAT ON THE BIG ISLAND

Thanks to its deep waters, green pastures, and fertile fields, the Big Island provides local chefs with a cornucopia of fresh ingredients. The challenge for visitors is finding restaurants to match their budgets. Don't be afraid to nosh at a roadside stand or create a meal from a farmer's market (see "Big Island Shopping," p. 286), as locals do, but indulge at least once on an oceanfront sunset dinner for the best of all the Big Island has to offer. Reservations are advised during holidays and summer; OpenTable.com currently accepts bookings for 36 restaurants across the island.

The Kona Coast

CENTRAL KAILUA-KONA

With few exceptions, this is a no-man's-land for memorable, sensibly priced dining; chains abound, and service is often slow. One bright spot: **Honu's on the Beach** ★★ (daily 6–10:30am and 5:30–10pm), the indoor/outdoor restaurant at the Courtyard King Kamehameha Kona Beach Hotel (p. 256). Fresh sushi 5:30 to 8:30pm Sunday to Thursday attracts both locals and visitors; Chef Roy Basilio's well-prepared farm-to-table Hawaii Regional Cuisine is available nightly (main courses $15–$28), with a prime rib/seafood buffet ($50 adults, $26 ages 6–12) Friday and Saturday nights.

In a less scenic setting, duck into **Lemongrass Bistro** ★, 75-5742 Kuakini Hwy. (*makai* side, at Hualalai Rd) for fragrant curry and noodle dishes ($13–$25). It's open for lunch ($10 specials) and dinner till 9pm daily (www.lemongrassbistrokona.com; ☏ **808/331-2708**). Big appetites should head to the **Big Island Grill** ★, 75-5702 Kuakini Hwy. (*makai* side, south of Henry St.), for American fare and local favorites such as loco moco and chicken katsu ($5–$17 breakfast, $8–$20 lunch, $9–$24 dinner) in a strip mall, with parking. It's open daily 7am to 9pm except Sunday (www.facebook.com/BigIslandGrill; ☏ **808/326-1153**). **Kamana Kitchen** ★★, 75-5770 Alii Dr., serves classic South Indian dishes ($13-$21) in a pleasant Waterfront Row dining room (www.kamanakitchen.com; ☏ **808/326-7888**).

Gluten-free diners will want to go online to check the whereabouts of the **Lotus Cafe Fresh Express** food truck ★ (www.thelotuscafe.com), which serves pan-Asian fare like Malaysian laksa ($12) in Hawi, Kailua-Waimea, Kailua-Kona, and Keauhou on a rotating schedule.

Expensive

Daylight Mind ★★ HAWAII REGIONAL   Bakery, coffee bar, restaurant, coffee roaster, community center—this two-story complex with vaulted ceilings and a wraparound oceanfront lanai tries to be many things to many people, and mostly succeeds. Many of the ingredients are locally

TAKE YOUR PICK OF poke

With all the fishing boats plying Kona waters, it's no wonder places selling ahi poke—the finely diced raw tuna staple of the islands—and similar dishes pride themselves on just-caught ingredients. Fisherman Albert Vasconcelles' **Da Poke Shack ★★** (dapokeshack.com; ℂ **808/329-POKE** [7653]; daily 10am–6pm) built a loyal following for its ahi poke bowls and lunch plates ($14–$22, priced by the pound) in a hole in the wall in the Kona Bali Kai complex, at 76-6246 Alii Dr., Kailua-Kona. Taste the wares of award-winning chef Nakoa Pabre, from poke bombs (cone sushi topped with a variety of diced seafood; $8) to bowls with quinoa or native fiddlehead fern salad as side options ($10–$13), at two

sites in Kailua-Kona: the more spacious **Umekes Fishmarket Bar and Grill ★★★**, 74-5563 Kaiwi St. (www.umekes restaurants.com; ℂ **808/238-0571;** 11am–9pm Mon–Fri, 11am–5pm Sat), sports a handsome wood and aqua interior with plenty of seating and a full bar, while **Umekes ★★** in Alii Plaza, 75-143 Hualalai Rd. (www.umekesrestaurants. com; ℂ **808/329-3050**), is more of a to-go joint, open 10am to 5pm Mon to Sat. The newest location, **Umekes Waimea,** 64-1055 Mamalahoa Hwy., at Kamamalu St., Waimea, shares the latter's limited space and ambience, but still delicious poke; it's open 10am to 7pm Mon to Sat.

sourced, including coffee, of course. The coffee bar also serves kombucha, coffee cherry tisane, and other brews; check the bakery for fresh sourdough bread. In the restaurant, the eclectic brunch and dinner menu runs the gamut from trendily healthful (quinoa porridge with chia seed yogurt) to utterly rich (Keahole lobster BLT). A smaller branch in the Queens' MarketPlace in the Waikoloa Beach Resort has tasty food, but service seems slower. There's also a small bakery/deli in Kailua-Kona's Lanihau Center; try the scones or manapua.

At rear of Waterfront Row, 75-5770 Alii Dr., Kailua-Kona. www.daylightmind.com. ℂ **808/339-7824.** Coffee bar 7am–9pm daily, restaurant 8am–9pm. Also: 69-201 Waikoloa Beach Dr., Waikoloa. Coffee bar 6am–9:30pm; restaurant 7am–9:30pm. Main courses $10–$19 brunch, $15–$36 dinner. **Daylight Mind Bakery & Cafe,** Lanihau Center, 75-5595 Palani Rd., Kailua-Kona. 6am–5pm daily.

Huggo's ★★★ PACIFIC RIM/SEAFOOD   The setting doesn't get any better in Kailua-Kona than this, a covered wooden deck overlooking tide pools and the sweep of Kailua Bay. But executive chef Albert Asuncio, a Big Island native, makes sure what's on your plate is compelling, too, such as seared sesame ahi and chips with avocado fries, guava braised baby back rib, or ravioli of lobster, crab, and mascarpone. Huggo's lounge, **hBar ★★★,** has its own chic vibe and inventive small-plates menu, as well as an artisan cocktail menu. There's also a breakfast menu—pancakes, several varieties of eggs Benedict, breakfast pizzas, and a full bar (try the Bloody Mary)—called Huggo's Sunnyside Up. Next door is the more casual, moderately priced **On the Rocks** ★, which serves lunch and dinner; after sunset, it's a pulsating nightclub.

75-5828 Kahakai Rd., Kailua-Kona. www.huggos.com. *©* **808/329-1493.** Reservations recommended. Main courses $30–$40. Sun–Thurs 5–9pm, Fri–Sat 5–10pm. **hBar:** Mon–Thurs 4–10pm, Fri–Sat 4–midnight, Sun 5–10pm. Small plates $12–$28. **Huggo's Sunnyside Up:** Main courses $12–$22. Daily 7–11am. **On the Rocks:** https://huggosontherocks.com. *©* **808/329-9262.** Main courses $13–$20. Mon–Thurs 11:30am–11pm, Fri–Sat 11:30am–midnight, happy hour 3–5pm.

Moderate

Island Lava Java ★★ AMERICAN Although a branch opened in Waikoloa Village in 2012, there's no competing with the lively ambience and oceanview setting of the Kailua-Kona original. Founded in 1994, the former espresso bar blossomed into a full-service cafe for breakfast, lunch, and dinner, and now has a full bar in its new, ocean-view location in the Coconut Grove Marketplace. The coffee is 100% Kona; breads, pastries, and desserts are made in house; and organic salads, sandwiches, and pizzas feature mostly local ingredients. Compared with resorts, prices are almost reasonable for the Big Island grass-fed beef burger ($15), pizzas to share ($18–$20), and Nicoise salad with fresh ahi ($23); ribeye ($37) and other meat and fresh catch entrees can add up quickly.

75-5799 Alii Dr., Kailua-Kona. www.islandlavajava.com. *©* **808/327-2161.** Main courses $8–$20 breakfast; $13–$23 lunch; $14–$37 dinner. Daily breakfast 6:30am–11:30am, lunch 11:30am–5pm, dinner 5–9:30pm. Also in the Waikoloa Highlands Shopping Center, 68-1845 Waikoloa Rd., Waikoloa. *©* **808/769-5202.** Same hours and prices as Kailua-Kona location.

Mi's Waterfront Bistro ★★ ITALIAN Chef Morgan Starr, formerly at Four Seasons Resort Hualalai, is the "M" and wife Ingrid Chan is the "I" in Mi's, which relocated in 2016 from a drab South Kona strip center to a mostly outdoor, oceanfront site more worthy of the thoughtfully created Italian fare. The menu features fresh ingredients from Starr's own garden, local beef, handmade pasta, and off-the-hook ahi, with a well-priced menu and wine list. Porcini-crusted pork scaloppini ($27) with gnocchi comes with a velvety Hamakua mushroom sauce, while grilled rack of lamb in a Chianti demi-glaze ($39) is worth the splurge. Save some calories for a house-made dessert, such as Meyer lemon crème brûlée ($8) or white pineapple sorbet ($5). Gluten-free and vegetarian diners should note the baked polenta with sauteed vegetables and marinara on the lunch menu (served by request at dinner). Request an oceanfront table well in advance.

In Waterfront Row, 75-5770 Alii Dr., second floor, Kailua-Kona; park in underground lot. www.misitalianbistro.com. *©* **808/329-3880.** Main courses lunch $11–$16, dinner $15–$39. Lunch 12–4:30pm daily, dinner 5–9pm daily.

Father and son Cameron Healy and Spoon Khalsa opened microbrewery and pub **Kona Brewing Co.** ★★ (www. konabrewingco.com; ✆ **808/334-2739**) in an obscure warehouse in Kailua-Kona in 1998; now they also run a restaurant on Oahu and enjoy widespread Mainland distribution of their most popular brews, including Fire Rock Pale Ale and Longboard Lager, and a new brewery is due to open in 2019. The brewpub at 74-5612 Pawai Pl. offers affordable specials at lunch and happy hour (3 to 5pm weekdays), seasonal draft brews, a palm-fringed patio, and short free tours (for ages 15 and older) at 10:30am and 3pm weekdays, with additional tours at 2pm weekends and 4pm Saturday. Open daily 11am to 10pm.

NORTH KONA

Ulu Ocean Grill & Sushi Lounge ★★★ ISLAND FARM/SEAFOOD   With veteran Four Seasons executive chef Thomas Bellec at the helm, this beachfront destination restaurant remains a superb showcase for the wares of 160 local fishermen and farmers. Refined yet approachable dishes include miso-glazed kampachi with crispy bok choy and black pepper-crusted New York steak with kiawe-smoked potatoes. Jewel-like sashimi and artful sushi rolls can be ordered in the oceanview lounge (with fire pits) or the open-air dining room, behind roe-like curtains of glass balls. Ask the expert waitstaff for advice on the extensive wine list. On Saturday, sign up for the five-course, prix-fixe Oceanfront Harvest Dinner ($150) with wine pairings and a sushi reception; it's limited to 40 guests, who meet with the chef de cuisine and dine on a private lanai. *Note:* The breakfast menu is also locally sourced but seems more exorbitant. During peak holiday periods, only resort guests are allowed to make reservations (always a good idea here).

At the Four Seasons Resort Hualalai, 72-100 Kaupulehu Dr., Kailua-Kona (off Hwy. 19, 6 miles north of Kona airport). ✆ **808/325-8000.** www.uluoceangrill.com. Reservations recommended. Breakfast buffet $30–$44; dinner main courses $32–$55. Daily 6:30–11am (buffet 6:30–10:30am) and 5:30–9pm (sushi until 10pm).

KEAUHOU

The newly renovated **Rays on the Bay** ★★ (www.raysonthebay.com; ✆ 808/930-4900) at the **Sheraton Kona** (p. 260) is the only waterfront option, but it's a vibrant one, with nightly live music, great cocktails and slightly pricey but creative island cuisine (dinner mains $19-$39); valet parking is free. Keauhou Shopping Center has several more affordable options than **Kenichi** ★ (www.kenichipacific.com; ✆ 808/322-6400), a stylish Asian fusion/sushi dinner spot, open daily 5 to 9:30pm. The best is **Peaberry & Galette** ★ (www.peaberryandgalette.com; ✆ 808/322-6020), a small cafe with a wide selection of savory and sweet crepes ($9–$14), plus a few sandwiches, salads, and good, 100 percent Kona coffee; it's open 7am to 5pm Monday to Saturday, 8am to 5pm Sunday.

Sam Choy's Kai Lanai ★ HAWAII REGIONAL   The miles-long coastal views from this former Wendy's are spectacular—if only the service and food consistently measured up. When they're in top form, this aerie formerly run by renowned Honolulu chef Sam Choy is hard to beat. Breakfast and lunch offer hearty local dishes such as loco moco (grass-fed burger with fried egg, gravy, and rice) and beef stew. Dinner highlights include seafood *laulau* (i.e. in steamed ti leaves, $29) and Kona orange duck ($28). Go early for a happy-hour seat by the fire pit.

Above Keauhou Shopping Center, 78-6831 Alii Dr., Kailua-Kona. www.samchoyskai-lanai.com. *ⓒ* **808/333-3434.** Reservations recommended for dinner. Main courses: breakfast (available till 3pm) $10–$13; lunch $8–$15; dinner $16–$37. Weekdays 10am–9pm, weekends 8am–9pm, happy hour 3–5pm.

SOUTH KONA

For ocean views with your Kona coffee, consider two cafes on the makai side of Highway 11. **The Coffee Shack** ★, 83-5799 Mamalahoa Hwy. (between mile markers 108 and 109) in Captain Cook, serves egg dishes ($11–$16), plump sandwiches on fresh-baked bread ($13), and 8-inch pizzas ($13–$16); it's open daily 7:30am to 3pm (www.coffee-shack.com; *ⓒ* **808/328-9555**). Italian-themed **Caffe Florian** ★ serves panini ($10–$12) and other light fare; it's open 6:30am to 4pm weekdays, 7am to 2pm Saturday, and 8am to 1pm Sunday at 81-6637 Mamalahoa Hwy., Kealakekua (at Kee-Kee Rd.; www.caffefloriankona.com; *ⓒ* **808/238-0861**). Open for dinner only (Tues–Sat 5–9pm), the family-run **Keei Cafe** ★★, 79-7511 Mamalahoa Hwy. (mauka side), Kealakekua, includes pasta, fresh fish, steak and rack of lamb ($17–$31) on its compact but diverse menu, in a pleasant dining room featuring locally made art (www.keeicafe.net; *ⓒ* **808/322-9992**); reservations suggested.

Manago Hotel Restaurant ★★ AMERICAN   Like its clean but plain-spun hotel, the family-run dining room with Formica tabletops and vinyl-backed chairs has changed little over the years. Service is friendly and fairly swift, with family-style servings of rice, potato salad, and fresh vegetables accompanying hearty dishes such as the signature pork chops with gravy and grilled onions ($12), teriyaki chicken, and sautéed mahimahi, among other popular choices. Breakfast is a steal: papaya or juice, toast or rice, two eggs, breakfast meat, and coffee for $7.

At the Manago Hotel, 82-6151 Mamalahoa Hwy. (Hwy. 11), Captain Cook, btw. mile markers 109 and 110, *makai* side. www.managohotel.com/rest.html. *ⓒ* **808/323-2642.** Reservations recommended for dinner. Breakfast $5–$7, lunch and dinner $7–$19. Tues–Sun 7–9am, 11am–2pm, and 5–7:30pm.

SORTING OUT THE resorts

There's no getting around sticker shock when dining at the South Kohala resort hotels, especially at breakfast and lunch. Dazzling sunsets help soften the blow at dinner, when chefs at least show more ambition. Here's a quick guide to help you distinguish among the top dinner-only hotel restaurants, all serving excellent (for the most part) yet costly variations on farm-to-table Hawaii Regional Cuisine:

- **Mauna Lani: Brown's Beach House** ★★ at the Fairmont Orchid, Hawaii (p. 263) offers attentive service at tables on a lawn just a stone's throw from the water; main courses are $35 to $54. At **CanoeHouse** ★★★ in the Mauna Lani Bay Hotel (p. 265), Chef de Cuisine Allan Nagun presents each dish of his "Captain's Table" Blind Tasting Menu ($110; $160 with wine pairings), offered Thursday to Saturday by 24-hour reservation (ⓒ **808/881-7911;** main courses $36–$52).

- **Mauna Kea: Manta & Pavilion Wine Bar** ★★★ at the Mauna Kea Beach Hotel (p. 264) offers a sweeping ocean view, artful cuisine, and 48 high-end wines by the glass from the nifty Enomatic dispenser; main courses run $35 to $52. At press time, Westin Hapuna Beach Resort (p. 263) was revamping menus and decor at all its dining outlets, but Mediterranean-themed, hillside **Meridia** was expected to live up to the high standards of its previous incarnation, **Coast Grille.**

- **Waikoloa Beach: KPC–Kamuela Provision Company** ★ at the Hilton Waikoloa Village (p. 263) has the oceanfront setting to rival other resorts' restaurants, with culinary ambitions aiming as high as its prices (main courses $42–$83) and top service. Book an outdoor table for at least a half-hour before sunset.

The Kohala Coast

Note: You'll find the following restaurants on the "Kohala Coast, Waimea & the Hamakua Coast" map on p. 259.

SOUTH KOHALA

For convenient alternatives to pricey hotel dining, the Waikoloa Beach Resort offers several hidden treasures. The Queens' MarketPlace food court includes **Lemongrass Express** ★ (ⓒ **808/886-3400**), a compact version of Kailua-Kona's tasty Lemongrass Bistro (p. 273), with indoor-outdoor seating and seafood specials that rival those of resort chefs, and **Ippy's Hawaiian BBQ** ★ (ⓒ 808/886-8600), serving well-seasoned plate lunches with ribs, chicken, and fish, under the aegis of Food Network celebrity Philip "Ippy" Aiona. **Aloha Wine Bar** ★, inside Island Gourmet Markets, serves burgers, thin-crust pizzas, and sushi with good wine specials (ⓒ **808/886-3500;** daily 3–midnight); happy hour runs 3 to 6pm and 10 to 11:30pm

Views of Anaehoomalu Bay, especially at sunset, never fail to please at the open-air **Lava Lava Beach Club** ★★, which serves fresh American and island food from 11am to 9pm daily on the beach, with happy hour appetizer and drink specials 3 to 5pm. At lunch, main courses run $15 to $26; at dinner, they're $19 to $37. Owned by the team behind **Huggo's** (p. 274), it's at the end of Kuualii Place in the Waikoloa Beach Resort (www.lavalavabeachclub.com; ℂ 808/769-5282).

Chef Allen Hess, formerly of CanoeHouse, serves well-crafted, farm-to-table comfort food (that is, with plenty of housemade bacon) at **Mai Grille** ★★ (www.maigrille.com; ℂ **808/886-7600**). Overlooking the Kings' Golf Course, it's open for breakfast 7:30 to 10:45am Monday through Saturday, and brunch 8am to 1pm Sunday, plus lunch and *pupu* 11am to 6pm Monday through Saturday. Reservations are recommended for Hess' innovative, adult-oriented "supper club" menu ($12–$29), 5 to 7pm Thursday through Saturday.

The commercial port of Kawaihae also harbors several inexpensive, homespun eateries, including **Kohala Burger and Taco** ★★, upstairs in the Kawaihae Shopping Center (www.kohalaburgerandtaco.com; ℂ **808/880-1923**). Its juicy burgers ($7–$8) are made with local grass-fed beef, while buns and tortillas (used for fresh fish tacos, burritos, and quesadillas) are housemade. Run by former resort chefs, it opens daily at 11am; closing hours vary widely by season. The **lunch wagon** next to **Da Fish House** ★ fish market (p. 291) has fresh fish plates ($9–$12) but little seating; it's open weekdays 10:30am to 2:30pm and takes cash only.

Expensive
Monstera Noodles & Sushi ★★ JAPANESE Master sushi chef Norio Yamamoto left his namesake restaurant (still called Norio's) at the Fairmont Orchid, Hawaii to open this bright, less formal dining room in the Shops at Mauna Lani. His "sizzling plates" menu includes New York strip steak in a choice of sauces, boneless fried chicken in spicy garlic-sesame sauce, and pork loin stir-fried with kimchi. Although the bill adds up quickly here, it would be a shame to skip seafood specialties like his volcano roll (a combination of spicy tuna and shrimp tempura with local avocado) or ultra-fresh, silken sashimi such as Hawaiian fatty tuna (*chu toro*). Downstairs is Yamamoto and partner Wes Monty's **Blue Room Brasserie & Bar** ★★, a charming French/island-style bistro inspired by a room at Iolani Palace; it's open for lunch and dinner, notably with Belgian beers on tap, an oyster bar, excellent seafood entrees, and leafy patio seating.

Monstera: The Shops at Mauna Lani, 68-1330 Mauna Lani Dr., Waimea. www.monsterasushi.com. ℂ **808/887-2711.** Main courses $18–$30; sushi rolls $7–$22; sashimi $17–$20. Daily 5:30–9:30pm (last seating 9pm). **Blue Room:** http://theblueroomhi.com. ℂ **808/887-0999.** Lunch main courses $16–$20 ($42 bouillabaisse); dinner main courses, $17–$42. Daily 11:30am–10pm.

Moderate

Pueo's Osteria ★★★ ITALIAN   Upcountry residents and night owls flock to this rare bird of a great restaurant in Waikoloa Village, named for the native owl, but its appeal goes far beyond its location (just 8 minutes from the Waikoloa Beach Resort) and late hours. Executive chef-owner James Babian, who lined up more than 150 local food purveyors for Four Seasons Hualalai during his tenure there, still works his connections for the freshest seafood, meat, and produce, while importing only the finest of everything else (including olive oil and well-priced wines) to create a delicious Italian menu. Although some of the menu falls in the expensive category, bargains include "early owl" specials ($8, available 5–6pm) and bar menu items such as a Tuscan burger made with local beef, provolone, and bruschetta tomatoes, served with house-made fries for just $12, or build-your-own wood-fired pizzas starting at $13. Babian has a tender touch with fresh pasta, such as potato gnocchi with house fennel sausage and Hamakua mushrooms, but also adds zest to hearty dishes such as a Barolo-braised short rib and Niihau lamb osso buco. Gluten-free bread and pasta are also available.

In Waikoloa Village Highlands Center, 68-1845 Waikoloa Rd., Waikoloa. www.pueos osteria.com. *©* **808/339-7566.** Main courses $20–$39; pizza $18–$24; bar menu $9–$21. Reservations recommended. Dinner daily 5–9pm. Bar 5pm–1am Mon–Sat, Sun till 10pm; bar menu Mon–Sat 5pm–midnight, Sun till 10pm. Happy hour 9:30pm–midnight.

NORTH KOHALA

For a light meal or snack, stop at **Kohala Coffee Mill** ★, 55-3412 Akoni Pule Hwy. (*mauka* side, across from Bamboo, discussed below; *©* **808/889-5577**). Known best for scoops of Tropical Dreams ice cream (p. 282) and well-crafted coffee drinks, it's open weekdays 6am to 6pm, weekends 7am to 6pm. In Kapaau, homey **Minnie's Ohana Lim Style** ★, 54-3854 Akoni Pule Hwy. (*mauka* side, at Kamehameha Rd.), serves heaping portions of fresh fish, roast pork, Korean fried chicken, and local staples ($9–$15; *©* **808/889-5288;** Mon–Wed 11am–7pm, Thurs–Fri 11am–3pm, and Fri 6–8pm). Close to the Pololu Valley Overlook, the solar-powered **Fresh Off the Grid** food truck ★, 52-5088 Akoni Pule Hwy., Kapaau, offers refreshing shave ice, smoothies, tropical fruit, picnic tables, and a welcome portable toilet; it's open 11am–5pm Thursday through Tuesday.

Bamboo ★★ PACIFIC RIM   Dining here is a trip, literally and figuratively. A half-hour from the nearest resort, Bamboo adds an element of time travel, with vintage decor behind the screen doors of its pale-blue, plantation-era building; an art gallery and quirky gift shop provide great browsing if you have to wait for a table. The food is well worth the wait, from local lunch faves like barbecued baby-back ribs to a veggie stir-fry of soba noodles or grilled chicken with a kicky Thai-style coconut sauce. Dinner adds more fresh-catch preparations, including a grilled filet with a tangy passionfruit mustard sauce balanced by crispy goat cheese polenta. Friday and Saturday night often have live music.

55-3415 Akoni Pule Hwy. (Hwy. 270, just west of Hwy. 250/Hawi Rd.), Hawi. www. bamboorestaurant.info. © **808/889-5555.** Dinner reservations recommended. Main courses $10–$20 lunch, $15–$35 dinner (full- and half-size portions available at dinner). Tues–Sat 11:30am–2:30pm and 6–8pm; Sun brunch 11:30am–2:30pm. Happy hour Tues–Thurs 4–6pm.

WAIMEA

Daunted by high-priced Kohala resort menus? Visit the inexpensive **Hawaiian Style Café** ★, 65-1290 Kawaihae Rd. (Hwy. 19, 1 block east of Opelo Rd.; http://hawaiianstylecafe.us; © **808/885-4925**), which serves pancakes bigger than your head (try them with warm *haupia,* a coconut pudding), kalua pork hash, and other local favorites, along with burgers and sandwiches. It's cash only, and very crowded on weekends (Mon–Sat 7am–1:30pm; until noon Sun). Funky **Big Island Brewhaus** ★★, 64-1066 Mamalahoa Hwy. (http://bigislandbrewhaus.com; © **808/887-1717**), features master brewer Tom Kerns' wide-ranging taps with an equally diverse, locally sourced menu with burgers, Mexican, and Mediterranean fare. Its covered patio and smaller indoor dining area/bar are open Monday through Saturday 11am to 8:30pm and Sunday noon to 8pm. Locals also flock to **Red Water Cafe** ★★, 65-1299 Kawaihae Rd., for expert sushi ($14–$28), Waimea-grown salads ($11–$19), seafood and steak ($29–$45), and live jazz (Thurs–Sat night). It's open 3 to 11pm daily, with early-bird specials from 3 to 5pm (www.redwatercafe.com; © **808/885-9299**).

Expensive

Merriman's ★★★ HAWAII REGIONAL   This is where it all began in 1988 for Chef Peter Merriman, one of the founders of Hawaii Regional Cuisine and an early adopter of the farm-to-table trend. Now head of a culinary empire with various incarnations on four islands, the busy Merriman has entrusted Chef Vince McCarthy with maintaining his high standards and inventive flair. Lunch offers better values, such as the grilled fresh fish ($18), while weekend brunch includes a luscious eggs Benedict with jalapeño hollandaise. At dinner, you can order Merriman's famed wok-charred ahi, grass-fed steak, or molten chocolate purse with vanilla bean ice cream—but you'll also want to consider McCarthy's fresh-catch dish, or his family-style, four-course tasting menu for four or more ($75 per person). Cocktails show the same care in crafting.

In Opelo Plaza, 65-1227 Opelo Rd., off Hwy. 19, Waimea. www.merrimanshawaii. com. © **808/885-6822.** Reservations recommended. Main courses $13–$18 lunch, $28–$58 dinner (half-portions $23–$44). Lunch Mon–Fri 11:30am–1:30pm; dinner daily 5:30–9pm; Sat–Sun brunch 10am–1pm.

Moderate

Village Burger ★★ BURGERS Tucked into a cowboy-themed shopping center with a drafty food court (bring a jacket or sit by the fireplace), this burger stand run by former Four Seasons Lanai chef Edwin Goto has a compact menu: plump burgers made with local grass-fed beef, grilled ahi, taro, or Hamakua mushrooms; thick, sumptuous shakes made from Tropical Dreams ice cream (p. 282); and hand-cut, twice-cooked fries. Other than that, there's just a grilled ahi Niçoise salad featuring island greens—but it's also delicious. A few doors down is Goto's casual, sit-down **Noodle Club ★★,** serving artfully presented interpretations of local and Asian specialties such as saimin, pork belly bao buns, pho, and ramen; the yuzu pudding cake is a melt-away marvel.

Village Burger: In the Parker Ranch Center, 67-1185 Mamalahoa Hwy., Waimea. www. villageburgerwaimea.com. ⓒ **808/885-7319.** Burgers $8–$12. Mon–Sat 10:30am–8pm; Sun till 6pm. Noodle Club: In the Parker Ranch Center (same address). www.facebook.com/noodleclubwaimea. ⓒ **808/885-8825.** Main courses $10–$13. Tues–Sat 10:30am–8pm; Sun till 5pm.

The Hamakua Coast

Although dinner options are growing in Honokaa, it still pays to plan ahead, since restaurants often close early. In Honokaa, Italian bistro **Café Il Mondo ★**, 45-3880 Mamane St. (www.cafeilmondo.com; ⓒ **808/775-7711**), serves pizza ($13–$19), calzones ($14), and homey entrees such as roast chicken and beef lasagna at dinner ($17, including salad). It's open Monday to Saturday, from 11am to 2pm and 5 to 8pm, with live music Thursday through Saturday. Closer to Highway 19, the iconic, counter-service **Tex Drive-In & Restaurant ★**, 45-690 Pakalana St. (www.tex-driveinhawaii.com; ⓒ **808/775-0598**) is worth braving possible tour-bus crowds for its *malasadas*—large, chewy Portuguese sweet bread doughnut holes that are fried to order, dusted in sugar, and available with a filling, such as Bavarian cream, tropical jellies, or chocolate. Founded in 1969, Tex also serves breakfast, burgers, and Hawaiian plate lunches ($4–$11), but the *malasadas* are the real draw; open daily 6am to 8pm.

About 19 miles south, the **Papaaloa Country Store & Cafe**, 35-2032 Old Mamalahoa Hwy. (www.papaaloacountrystore.com; ⓒ **808/339-7614**),

---

Tropical Dreams: Ice Cream Reveries

Founded in North Kohala in 1983, ultra-rich **Tropical Dreams ★★★** ice cream is sold all over the island now, but you'll find the most flavors at the retail store next to its Waimea factory, 66-1250 Lalamilo Farm Rd. (off Hwy. 19; www.tropicaldreamsicecream.com;

ⓒ **888/888-8031**). Try the Tahitian vanilla, lychee, or poha, or sorbets like dragonfruit, passion-guava, or white pineapple ($3.50 for an 8 oz. cup—the smallest size). It's open weekdays 9am to 5pm.

offers wonderful browsing in the 1910 plantation-era store while you wait for a home-style breakfast, burger, or plate lunch; delicious tropical pastries await in the bakery. Restaurant and bar hours are 1 to 7pm Monday through Thursday, till 8pm Friday and Saturday (store opens at 7am). It's a short detour off Highway 11.

Note: You'll find the three restaurants above on "The Kohala Coast, Waimea & the Hamakua Coast" map on p. 259.

Hilo

The second largest city in Hawaii hosts a raft of unpretentious eateries that reflect East Hawaii's plantation heritage. A prime example of the former is **Ken's House of Pancakes ★**, 1730 Kamehameha Ave., at the corner of Hwys. 19 and 11 (www.kenshouseofpancakes.com; ℂ **808/935-8711**), which serves heaping helpings of local dishes, amazingly fluffy omelets, and American fare 24/7. The **Hawaiian Style Café ★**, 681 Manono St. (www.hawaiianstylecafe.com; ℂ **808/969-9265**), is an outpost of the Waimea favorite (p. 281) that also has dinner hours; it's open 7am to 2pm Tuesday through Sunday, 5 to 8:30pm Tuesday to Thursday, and 5 to 9pm Friday and Saturday. Food comes on paper plates at the venerable **Café 100 ★** (www.cafe100.com; ℂ **808/935-8683**), 969 Kilauea Ave., but the price is right for more than 30 varieties of "loco moco" (meat, eggs, rice, and gravy), starting at $4, and other hearty fare. It's open weekdays 6:45am to 8:30pm, and Saturday till 7:30pm. **Miyo's ★**, 564 Hinano St. (www.miyosrestaurant.com; ℂ **808/935-8825**), prides itself on "homestyle" Japanese cooking, with locally sourced ingredients. It's open Monday through Saturday for lunch (11am–2pm) and dinner (5:30–8:30pm), with main courses under $20.

Make reservations for tiny **Moon and Turtle ★★**, 51 Kalakaua St. (ℂ **808/961-0599**), where the fusion farm-to-table, shared-plate menu changes daily, 5:30 to 9pm Tuesday through Saturday. The new ocean-front, all-day restaurant in the **Grand Naniloa Hotel** (p. 268), **Hula Hulas** (http://hulahulashilo.com; ℂ **808/932-4545**) had some service issues in its infancy, but the kitchen was starting to live up to its spectacular setting with creative local fare such as *ulu* (breadfruit) fries.

Note: You'll find the following restaurants and the ones listed above on the "Hilo" map on p. 207.

Café Pesto ★★ PIZZA/PACIFIC RIM   The menu of wood-fired pizzas, pastas, risottos, fresh local seafood, and artfully prepared "creative island cuisine" such as mango-glazed chicken is much the same as it was at the now-closed, original Kawaihae location, and that's a good thing. Even better: The airy dining room in a restored 1912 building, with black-and-white tile floors and huge glass windows overlooking picturesque downtown Hilo. Service is attentive and swift, especially by island standards, but don't shy away from the two counters with high-backed chairs if tables are full.

At the S. Hata Bldg., 308 Kamehameha Ave., Hilo. www.cafepesto.com. © **808/969-6640.** Reservations recommended. Pizzas $10–$21; main courses $11–$17 lunch, $19–$30 dinner. Mon–Thurs 10:30am–9pm; Fri–Sat 11am–10pm; Sun 11am–9pm.

Hilo Bay Café ★★ PACIFIC RIM   Hilo's most ambitious restaurant overlooks Hilo Bay, next to Suisan Fish Market and the lovely Liliuokalani Gardens. Fittingly, sushi and seafood dishes are the most reliable pleasers, including horseradish panko-crusted ono and grilled asparagus salad with pan-roasted salmon, but fresh produce from the Hilo Farmer's Market also inspires several dishes. Vegetarians will appreciate thoughtful options such as the Hamakua mushroom curry pot-pie. The drink list is similarly wide-ranging, including locally sourced kombucha, superb cocktails, and craft beer. At lunch, ask for a seat with a bay view.

123 Lihiwai St., just north of Banyan Dr., Hilo. www.hilobaycafe.com. © **808/935-4939.** Reservations recommended for dinner. Main courses $14–$30 lunch, $14–$38 dinner. Mon–Sat lunch 11am–2:30pm, limited menu 2:30–5pm, dinner 5–9pm.

Puna District

Options are limited here, so plan meals carefully and stock up on supplies in Kailua-Kona or Hilo. *Note:* You'll find the following restaurants on the "Hotels & Restaurants in the Volcano Area" map (p. 269).

VOLCANO VILLAGE

In addition to the listings below, look for the **Tuk-Tuk Thai Food ★★** truck at the Cooper Center, 19-4030 Old Volcano Rd. (www.tuk-tukthai-food.com; © **808/747-3041**), from 11am to 6pm Tuesday to Saturday. You can even call ahead for its hearty curries and noodle dishes ($11–$14), a better value than the Thai restaurant down the road. Tiny **Ohelo Café ★★**, 19-4005 Haunani Rd. (www.ohelocafe.com; © **808/339-7865;** daily 11:30am–3pm and 5:30–9pm), may have a casual ambience but it aims high with wood-fired pizzas ($12–$14), fresh catch ($25), pastas, and salads; reservations are recommended.

Expensive

Kilauea Lodge Restaurant ★★ CONTINENTAL   Like his inn, owner-chef Albert Jeyte's woodsy restaurant radiates *Gemütlichkeit,* that ineffable German sense of warmth and cheer, symbolized by the "International Fireplace of Friendship" studded with stones from around the world. Although starters can be ho-hum, the European-style main courses showcase unique meats such as rabbit, antelope, buffalo, and duck, along with local grass-fed beef and lamb, plus the fresh catch (recommended). The wine list is well priced, while lilikoi margaritas are refreshing after a long day exploring the nearby national park. Dinner prices are steep, but entrees include soup or salad; lunch offers good values, including local grass-fed beef, buffalo and antelope burgers, and a curried chicken bowl.

Breakfast is another winner, especially the French toast made with Portuguese sweet bread.

19-3948 Old Volcano Rd., Volcano. www.kilauealodge.com. ℂ **808/967-7366.** Reservations recommended. Main courses $11–$14 breakfast, $12–$17 lunch, $26–$41 dinner. Daily breakfast 7:30–10am, lunch 10am–2pm, and dinner 5–9pm; Sun brunch 10am–2pm.

Moderate

Café Ono ★ VEGETARIAN When burgers and plate lunches start to pall, this cafe and tearoom hidden in Ira Ono's quirky art studio/gallery provides a delectably light alternative. The vegetarian/vegan menu is concise: a soup or two, chili, lasagna, crustless quiche (highly recommended), and sandwiches, most accompanied by a garden salad. Don't pass up the peanut butter and pumpkin soup ($9) if it's available, and allow time to explore the lush gardens outside.

In Volcano Garden Arts, 19-3834 Old Volcano Rd., Volcano. www.cafeono.net. ℂ **808/985-8979.** Reservations recommended for groups of 5 or more. Main courses $10–$15. Lunch Tues–Sun 11am–3pm, coffee/dessert menu 10am–4pm.

HAWAII VOLCANOES NATIONAL PARK

The Rim ★★ ISLAND FARM/SEAFOOD By no means is this your typical national park concession, as some hot dog–seeking visitors are discouraged to find. The Rim and the adjacent **Uncle George's Lounge ★★** try to match their premier views of Kilauea Caldera with a menu that's both artful and hyper-local. The bountiful breakfast buffet includes made-to-order eggs and waffles, tropical fruit smoothies, and housemade granola. Bento lunch boxes ($19, available 11am to 4pm) offer a choice of kalua pork, teriyaki chicken, an organic veggie/tofu stir-fry, or macadamia-nut mahimahi, plus four tasty sides, Hilo poi, and *haupia* pudding. Kalua pork pizza, a local grass-fed beef burger, and coconut-crusted fish and chips are also available. Culinary highlights include pan-seared Kona *kampachi,* and Hilo coffee-rubbed rack of lamb. The lounge serves burgers and *pupu* ($13–$18) such as chicken satay and avocado dip. ***Note:*** Diners must pay park admission ($25 a vehicle, good for 7 days) to access the restaurant or lounge. It's closed if the park is closed.

In Volcano House, 1 Crater Rim Dr., Volcano. www.hawaiivolcanohouse.com/dining. ℂ **808/930-6910.** Reservations recommended. Breakfast buffet $18 adults, $9 children. Main courses: lunch $12–$19, dinner $19–$39. Daily breakfast 7–10am, lunch 11am–2pm (bento boxes till 4pm), dinner 5:30–9pm, with live music 6–8:30pm Sun, Tues–Fri. Lounge daily 11am–10pm, with live music Sat–Sun (varying hours).

PAHOA

Kaleo's Bar & Grill ★★ ECLECTIC/LOCAL The best restaurant for miles around has a broad menu, ideal for multiple visits, and a welcoming, homey atmosphere. Local staples such as chicken katsu and spicy Korean kalbi ribs won't disappoint, but look for dishes with slight twists, such as tempura ahi roll or the blackened-ahi BLT with avocado and

A TASTE OF volcano wines

Volcano Winery (www.volcanowinery.com; ℂ 808/967-7772) has been a unique pit stop for visitors since 1993, when it began selling traditional grape wines, honey wines, and grape wines blended with tropical fruits in a location near Hawaii Volcanoes National Park. Del and Marie Bothof have owned the winery since 1999, planting Pinot Noir and Cayuga White grapes in 2000 and expanding into tea—a much better option, as recent awards show—in 2006. Wine tastings, for ages 21 and up, are $7 to $10; there's also a picnic area under cork and koa trees. The tasting room and store, 35 Pii Mauna Dr. in Volcano (just off Hwy. 11 near the 30-mile marker), are open 10am to 5:30pm daily.

mango mayo. Save room for the lilikoi cheesecake or banana spring rolls with vanilla ice cream. There's live music nightly, too.

15-2969 Pahoa Village Rd., Pahoa. www.kaleoshawaii.com. ℂ **808/965-5600.** Main courses $8–$18 lunch, $12–$32 dinner. Daily 11am–9pm.

Kau District

Driving from Kailua-Kona to Hawaii Volcanoes National Park, it's good to know about two places in Naalehu for a quick pick-me-up. The **Punaluu Bake Shop** ★ (www.bakeshophawaii.com; ℂ **866/366-3501** or 808/929-7343) is the busier tourist attraction, famed for its multihued varieties of sweet Portuguese bread now seen in stores across the islands; clean restrooms, a deli counter, and gift shop are also part of the appeal. It's open daily from 9am to 5pm. Across the highway, off a small lane, lies **Hana Hou Restaurant** ★ (www.hanahourestaurant.com; ℂ **808/929-9717**), which boasts a bakery counter with equally tempting sweets (try the macnut pie or passionfruit bar) and a retro dining room serving simple but fresh and filling plate lunches ($13–$17), burgers, sandwiches, and quesadillas; it's open Sunday through Thursday 8am to 7pm, Friday and Saturday until 8pm.

BIG ISLAND SHOPPING

This island is fertile ground, not just for coffee, tea, chocolate, macadamia nuts, honey, and other tasty souvenirs, but also for artists inspired by the volcanic cycle of destruction and creation, the boundless energy of the ocean, and the timeless beauty of native crafts. For those cooking meals or packing a picnic, see the "Edibles" listings.

Note: Stores are open daily unless otherwise stated.

The Kona Coast
KAILUA-KONA

For bargain shopping with an island flair, bypass the T-shirt and trinket shops and head 2 miles south from Kailua Pier to **Alii Gardens**

Marketplace, 75-6129 Alii Dr., a friendly, low-key combination farmer's market, flea market, and crafts fair, with plenty of parking and tent-covered stalls (open 10am–5pm Tues–Sun). You'll find fun items both handmade in Hawaii and manufactured in Chinese factories. Visit the **Kona Natural Soap Company** stand (www.konanaturalsoap.com) and learn about the ingredients grown on Greg Colden's Keauhou farm.

In Kailua-Kona's historic district, the funky, family-run **Pacific Vibrations** (✆ **808/329-4140**) has colorful surfwear; it's at 75-5702 Likana Lane, an alley off Alii Drive just north of Mokuaikaua Church. Across the street, the nonprofit **Hulihee Palace Gift Shop** stocks arts and crafts by local artists, including gorgeous feather lei, silk scarves, and woven lauhala hats (www.daughtersofhawaii.org; ✆ **808/329-6558**).

Keauhou Shopping Center, above Alii Drive at King Kamehameha III Road (www.keauhouvillageshops.com), has more restaurants and services than shops, but check out **Kona Stories** (www.konastories.com; ✆ **808/324-0350**) for thousands of books, especially Hawaiiana and children's titles, plus toys, cards, and gifts. Also in the mall, **Jams World** (www.jamsworld.com; ✆ **808/322-9361**) boasts colorful comfortable resort wear for men and women; the Hawaii company was founded in 1964. Hula troupes perform at 6pm Fridays on the Heritage Court Stage.

HOLUALOA

Charmingly rustic Holualoa, 1,400 feet and 10 minutes above Kailua-Kona at the top of Hualalai Road, is the perfect spot for visiting coffee farms (p. 191) and tasteful galleries, with a half-dozen or more within a short distance of each other on Mamalahoa Highway (Hwy. 180). Most galleries are closed Sunday and Monday; see **www.holualoahawaii.com** for listings. Among them, **Studio 7 Fine Arts** (www.studio7hawaii.com; ✆ **808/324-1335**) is a virtual Zen garden with pottery, wall hangings, and paper collages by Setsuko Morinoue, as well as paintings and prints by husband Hiroki.

Revel in the Hawaiian art of weaving leaves *(lau)* from the pandanus tree *(hala)* at **Kimura's Lauhala Shop,** farther south on the *makai* side of Mamalahoa Hwy., at 77-996 Hualalai Rd. (✆ **808/324-0053**). Founded in 1914, the store brims with locally woven mats, hats, handbags, and slippers, plus Kona coffee, koa wood bowls, and feather hatbands. It's closed Sunday.

SOUTH KONA

Many stores along Highway 11, the main road, are roadside fruit and/or coffee stands, well worth pulling over for, if only to "talk story" and pick up a snack. Fabric aficionados must stop at **Kimura Store,** a quaint general store and textile emporium with more than 10,000 bolts of aloha prints and other colorful cloth, at 79-7408 Mamalahoa Hwy. (*makai* side), Kainaliu (✆ **808/322-3771;** closed Sun).

The Kohala Coast

SOUTH KOHALA

Three open-air shopping malls claim the bulk of stores here, hosting a few island-only boutiques amid state and national chains. The real plus is the malls' free entertainment (check their websites for current calendars) and prices somewhat lower than those of shops in resort hotels.

The Waikoloa Beach Resort has two malls, both off its main drag, Waikoloa Beach Road. **Kings' Shops** (www.kingsshops.com) has a *keiki* (children's) hula performance at 6pm most Fridays and live music at 5 or 6pm Monday to Thursday. Along with luxury stores such as **Tiffany & Co.** and **Michael Kors,** you'll find affordable swimwear at **Making Waves** (℃ 808/886-1814) and batik-print fashions at **Noa Noa** (℃ 808/886-5449). Across the road, the shops at **Queens' MarketPlace** (http://queensmarket-place.net) include the **Hawaiian Quilt Collection** (℃ 808/886-0494), which also offers purses, placemats, and pottery with the distinctive quilt patterns of the islands; **Mahina** (http://shopmahina.com; ℃ 808/886-4000), known for casual chic women's apparel; and other island style-setters such as **Volcom, Reyn's,** and **Local Motion.** Free shows include hula and Polynesian dance 6pm Monday, Wednesday, and Friday.

In the **Shops at Mauna Lani** (www.shopsatmaunalani.com), on the main road of the Mauna Lani Resort, **Hawaiian Island Creations** (www.hicsurf.com; ℃ 808/881-1400) stands out for its diverse lineup of local, state, and national surfwear brands. Look for hula and Polynesian fire dancing at the shops on Monday and Thursday at 7pm.

In **Kawaihae,** an unassuming shopping strip on Highway 270, just north of Highway 19, hosts **Harbor Gallery** (www.harborgallery.biz; ℃ 808/882-1510). Browse the works of more than 150 Big Island artists, specializing in koa and other wood furniture, bowls, and sculpture; Sew Da Kine cork purses are an easy-to-pack item. Stock up on savory souvenirs at **Hamakua Macadamia Nut Factory** (p. 193).

NORTH KOHALA

When making the trek to the Pololu Valley Lookout, you'll pass a few stores of note along Highway 270. **As Hawi Turns,** 2 miles west of the Kohala Mountain Road (Hwy. 250), features eclectic women's clothing, locally made jewelry, home decor, and a consignment area cheekily called **As Hawi Returns** (℃ 808/889-5203). Across from the King Kamehameha Statue in Kapaau, **Ackerman Gallery** features Big Island arts and crafts (including paintings by owner Gary Ackerman), colorful clothing, and gifts (www.ackermanhawaii.com; ℃ 808/889-5138).

WAIMEA

The barn-red buildings of **Parker Square,** on the south side of Highway 19 east of Opelo Road, hold several pleasant surprises. The **Gallery of Great Things** (www.galleryofgreatthingshawaii.com; ℃ 808/885-7706) has high-quality Hawaiian artwork, including quilts and Niihau shell leis, as well as pieces from throughout the Pacific. **Bentley's Home & Garden Collection** (www.bentleyshomecollection.com; © **808/885-5565**) is chock-full of Western and country-inspired clothes, accessories, and cottage decor.

East Hawaii
HAMAKUA COAST

Park on Mamane Street (Hwy. 240) in "downtown" **Honokaa** and peruse the mom-and-pop shops, such as the **Green Chair** (© **808/747-4046;** closed Sun), which includes collectibles and thrift clothing among brightly hued vintage furnishings and small gifts. If you'd like something newer, head to **Big Island Grown,** selling edibles such as coffee, tea, and honey, plus locally made gifts and clothing (© **808/775-9777;** closed Sun), or **Taro Patch Gifts** (www.taropatchgifts.com; © **808/775-7228**), which adds books and international goodies to the mix. **Waipio Valley Artworks** (www.waipiovalleyartworks.com; © **808/775-0958**), on Kukuihaele Road near the overlook, offers handsome wood items, ceramics, prints, and more, plus a simple cafe.

HILO

The second-largest city in Hawaii has both mom-and-pop shops and big-box stores. The **Hilo Farmer's Market** is the prime attraction (see "A Feast for the Senses," below), but you should also hit the following for *omiyage,* or edible souvenirs: **Big Island Candies,** 585 Hinano St. (www.bigisland-candies.com; © **808/935-5510**), and **Two Ladies Kitchen,** 274 Kilauea Ave. (© **808/961-4766**). Big Island Candies is a busy tourist attraction that cranks out addictive macadamia-nut shortbread cookies. A cash-only, hole-in-the-wall that's closed Sunday and Monday, Two Ladies Kitchen makes delicious mochi, a sticky rice-flour treat with a filling of sweet bean paste, peanut butter or a giant strawberry, and *manju,* a kind of mini-turnover.

Visit **Sig Zane Designs,** 122 Kamehameha Ave. (www.sigzane.com; © **808/935-7077,** closed Sun), for apparel and home items with Zane's fabric designs, inspired by native Hawaiian plants and culture, including wife Nalani Kanakaole's hula lineage. **Basically Books,** 1672 Kamehameha Ave. (www.basicallybooks.com; © **808/961-0144**), has a wide assortment of maps and books emphasizing Hawaii and the Pacific.

PUNA DISTRICT

One of the prettiest places to visit in **Volcano Village** is **Volcano Garden Arts,** 19-3834 Old Volcano Rd. (www.volcanogardenarts.com; © **808/985-8979;** closed Mon), offering beautiful gardens with sculptures and open studios; delicious **Café Ono** (p. 285); and an airy gallery of artworks (some by owner Ira Ono), jewelry, and home decor by local artists. Look for Hawaiian quilts and fabrics, as well as island-made butters and jellies, at

A Feast for the Senses: Hilo Farmer's Market

You can't beat the **Hilo Farmer's Market** (www.hilofarmersmarket.com), considered by many the best in the state, from its dazzling display of tropical fruits and flowers (especially orchids) to savory prepared foods such as pad Thai and bento boxes, plus locally made crafts and baked goods, all in stalls pleasantly crammed around the corner of Kamehameha Avenue and Mamo Street. The full version with 200-plus farmers and artisans takes place 6am to 4pm Wednesday and Saturday; go early for the best selection. (About 30 vendors set up from 7am–4pm the rest of the week, but it's not quite the same experience.)

Kilauea Kreations, 19-3972 Old Volcano Rd. (www.kilaueakreations. com; *✆* **808/967-8090**).

In Hawaii Volcanoes National Park, the two **gift shops** at Volcano House (p. 270) stock tasteful gifts, many made on the Big Island, as well as attractive jackets for chilly nights. The original 1877 Volcano House, a short walk from the Kilauea Visitor Center, is home to the nonprofit **Volcano Art Center** (www.volcanoartcenter.org; *✆* **808/967-7565**), which sells locally made artworks, including the intricate, iconic prints of Dietrich Varez, who worked at the modern Volcano House in his youth.

Edibles

Since most visitors stay on the island's west side, the Hilo Farmer's Market isn't really an option to stock their larders. The **Keauhou Farmer's Market** (www.keauhoufarmersmarket.com), held from 8am to noon Saturday at the **Keauhou Shopping Center** (near Ace Hardware), can supply locally grown produce, fresh eggs, baked goods, coffee, and flowers. Pick up the rest of what you need at the center's **KTA Super Stores** (www.ktasuperstores.com; *✆* **808/323-2311**), a Big Island grocery chain, founded in 1916, at which you can find island-made specialties (poke, mochi) as well as national brands. Another **KTA** is in the Kona Coast Shopping Center, 74-5588 Palani Rd. (*✆* **808/329-1677**), open daily until 11pm. Wine aficionados will be amazed at the large and well-priced selection in **Kona Wine Market,** now near Home Depot at 73-5613 Olowalu St. (www.konawinemarket.com; *✆* **808/329-9400**). For **Costco** members, its local warehouse is at 73-4800 Maiau St., near Highway 19 and Hina Lani Street (*✆* **808/331-4800**).

On the Kohala Coast, the best prices are in **Waimea,** home to a **KTA** in Waimea Center, Highway 19 at Pulalani Road (*✆* **808/885-8866**). Buy smoked meat and fish, hot *malasadas* (doughnut holes), baked goods, and a cornucopia of produce at the **Waimea Homestead Farmer's Market,** Saturday 7am to noon behind the post office at 67-1229 Mamalahoa Hwy. (www.waimeafarmersmarket.com). The best deals for fresh fish are at **Da**

Fish House, 61-3665 Akoni Pule Hwy. (Hwy. 270) in Kawaihae (𝄢 **808/882-1052;** closed Sun). Among resort options, **Foodland Farms** in the Shops at Mauna Lani (www.foodland.com; 𝄢 **808/887-6101**), has top-quality local produce and seafood, while the Kings' Shops hosts a decent **farmer's market** Wednesday 8:30am to 3pm. **Island Gourmet Markets** (www.islandgourmethawaii.com; 𝄢 **808/886-3577**), centerpiece of the Queens' MarketPlace, has an almost overwhelming array of delicacies, including 200-plus kinds of cheese.

BIG ISLAND NIGHTLIFE

With few exceptions, the Big Island tucks in early, all the better to rise at daybreak, when the weather is cool and the roads (and waves) are open. But live Hawaiian music is everywhere, and it's easy to catch free, engaging hula shows, too, at several open-air resort malls (see "Big Island Shopping," p. 286).

Kailua-Kona

When the sun goes down, the scene heats up. Among the hot spots: **Gertrude's Jazz Bar**, 75-5699 Alii Dr., pairs tapas with live jazz, Hawaiian swing, Latin dance and more, 6 to 9pm Tuesday to Saturday and 4 to 7pm Sunday (https://gertrudesjazzbar.com; 𝄢 **808/327-5299**). **On the Rocks,** next to Huggo's restaurant (p. 274) at 75-5824 Kahakai Rd. (www.huggosontherocks.com; 𝄢 **808/329-1493**), has Hawaiian music and hula nightly, from 6 to 10pm (until 11pm Fri–Sat). Inside Huggo's, the stylish, oceanview **hBar** (www.huggos.com/hbar) offers the area's best artisanal cocktails; it's open till midnight Friday and Saturday, with live music 7:30 to 10:30pm.

Farther afield, **Rays on the Bay,** at the **Sheraton Kona Resort & Spa** (p. 260), lures locals and visitors to Keauhou with fire pits, a great happy hour, nightly live music, and free parking. The motto of the lively, gay-friendly **MyBar,** 74-5606 Luhia St., a block *makai* of Highway 19 (www.mybarkona.com; 𝄢 **808/331-8789**), is "We accept everyone as long as you want to have fun." It has darts, drag nights, and $6 cocktails.

Sharing Stories & Aloha Under the Stars

Twilight at Kalahuipuaa, a monthly Hawaiian-style celebration, takes place on the lawn in front of the oceanside Eva Parker Woods Cottage on the Mauna Lani Resort (www.maunalani.com/about/big-island-hawaii-events; 𝄢 **808/881-7911**). On the Saturday closest to the full moon, revered entertainers and local elders gather to "talk story," play music, and dance hula. The 3-hour show starts at 5:30pm, but the audience starts arriving an hour earlier, with picnic fare and beach mats. Bring yours, and plan to share food as well as the fun. Parking is free, too.

luaus' new taste **OF OLD HAWAII**

You may never have a truly great meal at a luau, but on the Big Island you can have a very good one, with a highly enjoyable—and educational—show to boot. Buffets offer more intriguing, tasty items such as pohole ferns and Molokai sweet potatoes, while shows feature more local history, from the first voyagers to *paniolo* days, plus spectacular fire knife and Polynesian dance. Try one of these oceanfront affairs:

o **Haleo** (www.haleoluau.com) at the **Sheraton Kona Resort & Spa** (p. 260) is simply the best in Kailua-Kona (Mon and Fri 4:30pm; $95 adults, $45 children 6–12).

o **Hawaii Loa** (www.gatheringofthe kings.com) at the **Fairmont Orchid, Hawaii** (p. 263), has the best selection of island-style food, including the taro leaf stew that gave lū'au its name (Sat 5:30pm; $115 adults, $79 children 6–12).

o **Legends of Hawaii** (www.hiltonwaiko-loavillage.com/resort-experiences) at **Hilton Waikoloa Village** (p. 263) is the most family-friendly, with pillow seating upfront for kids (Tues, Fri, and Sun 5:30pm; $128 adults, $70 children 5–12; free for children 4 and under). Add VIP options for $29 more per person.

The Kohala Coast

All the resorts have at least one lounge with nightly live music, usually Hawaiian, often with hula. Members of the renowned **Lim Family** perform at varying times and venues in the **Mauna Lani Bay Hotel & Bungalows** (p. 265), while award-winning singer **Darlene Ahuna** typically sings from 5 to 8pm Tuesday to Thursday at the **Westin Hapuna Beach** (p. 263). Enjoy creative cocktails and choice small plates with nightly music and hula at the chic **Copper Bar** at the **Mauna Kea Beach Hotel** (p. 264). The lively **Lava Lava Beach Club** (p. 262) offers nightly music and hula on the sands of Waikoloa Beach Resort, where the three-screen **Waikoloa Luxury Cinemas** includes a restaurant, bar, and leather loveseats (http://hawaiicinemas.com).

For a uniquely Big Island alternative to a luau, try **An Evening at Kahua Ranch** (www.kahuaranch.com; ✆ 808/882-7954), a barbecue with beer and wine, line dancing, rope tricks, live country music, campfire sing-along, and stargazing. The 3-hour event costs $139 for adults and $70 for kids 6 to 12 (5 and younger free) with shuttle to the ranch; drive yourself and it's $115 and $58, respectively. Festivities start at 6pm Wednesday in summer, 5:30pm in winter; call to check for additional evenings.

Hilo & the Hamakua Coast

Opened in 1925, the neoclassical **Palace Theater,** 38 Haili St., Hilo (www.hilopalace.com; ✆ 808/934-7010), screens first-run independent movies and hosts concerts, festivals, hula, and theater to pay for its ongoing restoration. **Hilo Town Tavern,** 168 Keawe St. (© **808/935-2171**), is a Cajun restaurant and dive bar open until 2am daily, with a pool room and live music ranging from hip-hop to Hawaiian. The **Grand Naniloa Hotel** (p. 268) offers nightly live music 6 to 8pm in either its Hula Lounge lobby bar or poolside restaurant Hula Hulas. Quaint Honokaa boasts the island's largest theater, the restored 1930 **People's Theatre,** 45-3574 Mamane St., seating 525 for first-run movies, concerts, and other events. The town also holds a festival the first Friday of each month, with sidewalk vendors and live music from 5 until 9pm.

Puna District

Although the revered founder of **Uncle Robert's Awa Club** (© **808/443-6913**) passed away in 2015, the bustling Wednesday-night marketplace (5–10pm) continues at Robert Keliihoomalu's Kalapana compound with live music from 6 to 9pm, provided lava isn't flowing nearby. Sample the mildly intoxicating *'awa* (the Hawaiian word for kava) at the tiki bar, or come back Friday at 6pm for more live music. In Pahoa, **Kaleo's Bar & Grill ★★** (p. 285) offers nightly live music, including jazz and slack key.

5

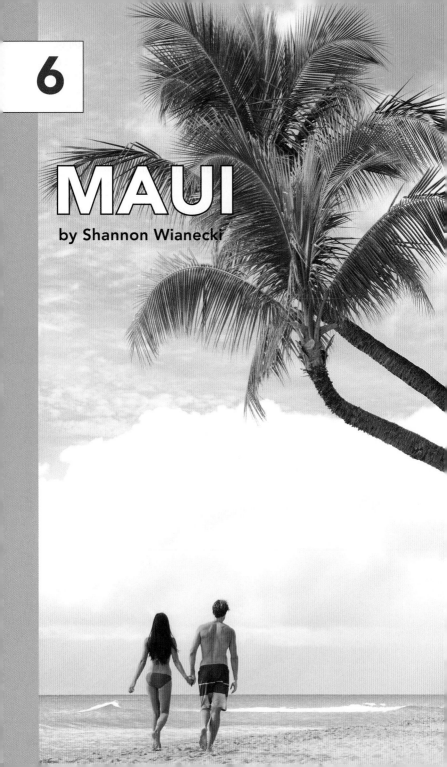

6

MAUI

by Shannon Wianecki

or many, Maui inhabits the sweet spot. Hawaii's second-largest island is a tangle of lovely contradictions, with a Gucci heel on one foot and a *puka*-shell anklet on the other. Culturally, it's a mix of farmers, *paniolo* (Hawaiian cowboys), aspiring chefs, artists, New Age healers, and big-wave riders. The landscape runs the gamut from sun-kissed golden beaches and fragrant rainforests to the frigid, windswept summit of Haleakala. Sure, more traffic lights sprout up around the island every year and spurts of development have turned cherished landmarks into mere memories. But even as Maui transforms, its allure remains.

ESSENTIALS
Arriving

BY PLANE   If you think of the island of Maui as the shape of a person's head and shoulders, you'll probably arrive near its neck, at **Kahului Airport** (OGG). Many airlines offer direct flights to Maui from the mainland U.S., including **Hawaiian Airlines** (www.hawaiianair.com; ℂ **800/367-5320**), **Alaska Airlines** (www.alaskaair.com; ℂ **800/252/7522**), **United Airlines** (www.united.com; ℂ **800/241-6522**), **Delta Air Lines** (www.delta.com; ℂ **800/221-1212**), **American Airlines** (www.aa.com; ℂ **800/882-8880**), and **Virgin America** (www.virginamerica.com; ℂ **877/359-8474**). The only international flights to Maui originate in Canada, via **Air Canada** (www.aircanada.com; ℂ **888/247-2262**) and **West Jet** (www.westjet.com; ℂ **888/937-8538**), both fly from Vancouver.

Other major carriers stop in Honolulu, where you'll catch an interisland flight to Maui on **Hawaiian.** A small commuter service, **Mokulele Airlines** (www.mokuleleairlines.com; ℂ **866/260-7070**), flies from Honolulu to Kahului Airport and Maui's two other airstrips. If you're staying in Lahaina or Kaanapali, you might consider flying in or out of **Kapalua–West Maui Airport** (JHM). From this tiny, one-pony airfield, it's only a 10- to 15-minute drive to most hotels in West Maui, as opposed to an hour or more from Kahului. Same story with **Hana Airport** (HNM): Flying directly here will save you a 3-hour drive.

Mokulele also flies between Maui, Molokai, the Big Island, and by charter to Lanai. Check-in is a breeze: no security lines (unless leaving from Honolulu). You'll be weighed, ushered onto the tarmac, and

FACING PAGE: **Kaanapali Beach, Maui**

welcomed aboard a nine-seat Cessna. The plane flies low, and the views between the islands are outstanding.

LANDING AT KAHULUI   If you're renting a car, proceed to the car-rental desks just beyond baggage claim. All of the major rental companies have branches at Kahului. Each rental agency has a shuttle that will deliver you to the car lot a half-mile away. For tips on insurance and driving rules in Hawaii, see "Getting Around Hawaii" (p. 601).

If you're not renting a car, the cheapest way to exit the airport is the **Maui Bus** (www.mauicounty.gov/bus; ✆ **808/871-4838**). For $2, it will deposit you at any one of the island's major towns. Simply cross the street at baggage claim and wait under the awning. Unfortunately, bus stops are far and few between, so you'll end up lugging your suitcase a long way to your destination. A much more convenient option is **Roberts Hawaii Express Shuttle** (www.airportshuttlehawaii.com/shuttles/maui; ✆ **866/ 898-2523** or 808/439-8800), which offers curb-to-curb service in a shared van or small bus and easy online booking. Plan to pay $24 (one-way) to Wailea and $34 to Kaanapali. Prices drop if you book round-trip. **Speedi-Shuttle Maui** (www.speedishuttle.com; ✆ **877/242-5777**). Prices (one-way, from the airport, for a shared van) range from $18 to Wailea to $31 to Kaanapali. You must book 24 hours in advance. **Bonus:** You can request a fresh flower lei greeting for an added fee.

Taxis usually cost 30% more than the shuttles—except when you're traveling with a large party, in which case they're a deal. **West Maui Taxi** (www.westmauitaxi.com; ✆ **888/661-4545**), for example, will drive up to six people from Kahului Airport to Kaanapali for $80.

Visitor Information

The website of the **Hawaii Tourism Authority** (www.gohawaii.com/ maui) is chock-full of helpful facts and tips. Visit the state-run **Visitor Information Center** at the Kahului Airport baggage claim for brochures and the latest issue of *This Week Maui,* which features great regional maps.

The Island in Brief

This medium-sized island lies in the center of the Hawaiian archipelago.

CENTRAL MAUI

Maui, the Valley Isle, is so named for the large isthmus between the island's two towering volcanoes: Haleakala and the West Maui Mountains. The flat landscape in between, Central Maui, is the heart of the island's business community and local government.

KAHULUI   Most Maui visitors fly over former sugarcane fields to land at Kahului Airport, just yards away from rolling surf. Sadly, your first sight out of the airport will likely be Target or Costco—hardly icons of Hawaiiana but always bustling with islanders and visitors alike. Beyond that,

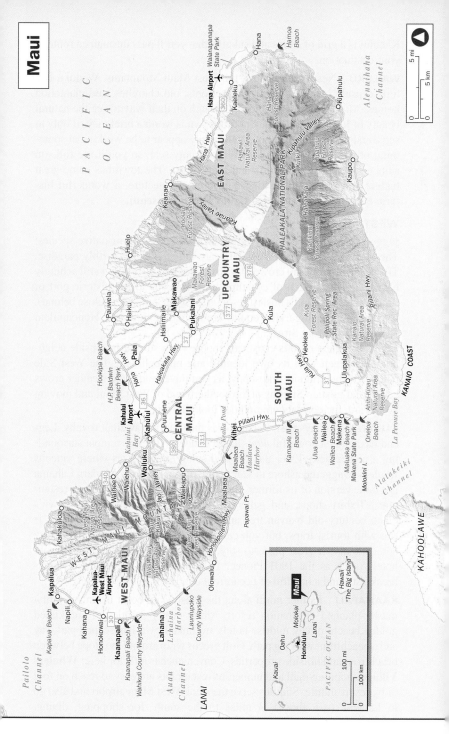

Maui

P A C I F I C
O C E A N

Hana
Hamoa Beach
Waianapanapa State Park
Hana Airport 360
Kaeleku

EAST MAUI

Alenuihaha Channel

Kipahulu

Hana Forest Reserve
Haleakala Hwy.
Hanawi Natural Area Reserve
Kipahulu Valley
Kuiki
Waihou Forest Reserve
Kaupo

Koolau Forest Reserve
Keanae Valley
Keanae

Huelo

HALEAKALA NATIONAL PARK
Haleakala

UPCOUNTRY MAUI

Makawao Forest Reserve

Pauwela
Haiku
Halliimaile
Makawao
Pukalani
377
Kula

Paia
Haleakala Hwy. 37
Kula
Polipoli Spring State Rec. Area
Kula Forest Reserve

Hookipa Beach
H.P. Baldwin Beach Park
Hana Hwy. 36
Keokea

Kahului Airport
Kahului
Kahului Bay
Puunene
378
Ulupalakua
Kanaio Natural Area Reserve
Piilani Hwy.

KANAIO COAST

CENTRAL MAUI
380
311
Kealia Pond
Piilani Hwy. 31

SOUTH MAUI

Wailuku
Waiehu
Waikapu
Kamaole III Beach
Ulua Beach
Wailea
Makena
Maluaka State Park
Ahihi-Kinau Natural Area Reserve
Oneloa Beach
La Perouse Bay

Maalaea Beach
Maalaea Harbor

Molokini I.

Alalakeiki Channel

Kahakuloa
340
West Maui Natural Area Reserve
Waihee
Iao Valley
Kukui
West Maui Natural Area Reserve
West Maui Forest Reserve

W E S T   M A U I   M O U N T A I N S

Honoapiilani Hwy.
Maalaea
Papawai Pt.

KAHOOLAWE

Kapalua
Kapalua–West Maui Airport
WEST MAUI
Napili
Kahana
Honokowai
Kaanapali
Kaanapali Beach
Wahikuli County Wayside
Lahaina
Lahaina Harbor
Launiupoko County Wayside
Olowalu

30

Kapalua Beach

Pailolo Channel

Auau Channel

LANAI

5 mi
5 km

Oahu
Molokai
Lanai
Maui
Kauai
Honolulu
Hawaii "The Big Island"
PACIFIC OCEAN
100 mi
100 km

297

Kahului is a grid of shops and suburbs that you'll pass through en route to your destination.

WAILUKU Nestled up against the West Maui Mountains, Wailuku is a time capsule of faded wooden storefronts, old churches, and plantation homes. Although most people zip through on their way to see the natural beauty of **Iao Valley,** this quaint little town is worth a brief visit, if only to see a real place where real people actually appear to be working at something other than a suntan. This is the county seat, so you'll see folks in suits (or at least aloha shirts and long pants). The town has some great budget restaurants, interesting bungalow architecture, a wonderful historic B&B, and the intriguing **Bailey House Museum.**

WEST MAUI

Jagged peaks, velvety green valleys, a wilderness full of native species: The majestic West Maui Mountains are the epitome of earthly paradise. The beaches below are crowded with condos and resorts, but still achingly beautiful. This stretch of coastline from Kapalua to the historic port of Lahaina, is the island's busiest resort area (with South Maui close behind). Expect slow-moving traffic on the two main thoroughfares: Honoapiilani Highway and Front Street.

Vacationers on this coast can choose from several beachside neighborhoods, each with its own identity and microclimate. The West Side tends to be hot, humid, and sunny; as you travel north, the weather grows cooler and mistier. Starting at the southern end of West Maui and moving northward, the coastal communities look like this:

LAHAINA In days past, Lahaina was the seat of Hawaiian royalty. Legend has it that a powerful *moo* (lizard goddess) dwelt in a moat surrounding a palace here. Later this hot and sunny seaport was where raucous whalers swaggered ashore in search of women and grog. Modern Lahaina is a tame version of its former self. Today Front Street teems with restaurants, T-shirt shops, and galleries. Action revolves around the town's giant, century-old banyan tree and busy recreational harbor. Lahaina is rife with tourist traps, but you can still find plenty of authentic history here. It's also a great place to stay; accommodations include a few old hotels (such as the 1901 Pioneer Inn on the harbor), quaint bed-and-breakfasts, and a handful of oceanfront condos.

KAANAPALI Farther north along the West Maui coast is Hawaii's first master-planned destination resort. Along nearly 3 miles of sun-kissed golden beach, pricey midrise hotels are linked by a landscaped parkway and a beachfront walking path. Golf greens wrap around the slope between beachfront and hillside properties. Convenience is a factor here: **Whalers Village** shopping mall and numerous restaurants are easy to reach on foot or by resort shuttle. Shuttles serve the small West Maui airport and also go to Lahaina (see above), 3 miles to the south, for shopping, dining,

Iao Needle, in the West Maui Mountains

entertainment, and boat tours. Kaanapali is popular with groups and families—and especially teenagers, who like all the action.

HONOKOWAI, KAHANA   In the building binge of the 1970s, condominiums sprouted along this gorgeous coastline like mushrooms after a rain. Today these older oceanside units offer excellent bargains for astute travelers. The great location—along sandy beaches, within minutes of both the Kapalua and Kaanapali resort areas, and close enough to the goings-on in Lahaina town—makes this a haven for the budget-minded.

In **Honokowai** and **Mahinahina,** you'll find mostly older, cheaper units. There's not much shopping here (mostly convenience stores), but you'll have easy access to the shops and restaurants of Kaanapali. **Kahana** is a little more upscale than Honokowai and Mahinahina, and most of its condos are big high-rise types, newer than those immediately to the south.

NAPILI   A quiet, tucked-away gem, with temperatures at least 5 degrees cooler than in Lahaina, this tiny neighborhood feels like a world unto itself. Wrapped around deliciously calm Napili Bay, Napili offers convenient activity desks and decent eateries and is close to the gourmet restaurants of Kapalua. Lodging is generally more expensive here—although I've found a few hidden jewels at affordable prices.

KAPALUA   Beyond the activity of Kaanapali and Kahana, the road starts to climb and the vista opens up to include unfettered views of Molokai across the channel. A country lane lined with Cook pines brings you to Kapalua. It's the exclusive domain of the luxurious Ritz-Carlton resort and expensive condos and villas, set above two sandy beaches. Just north are two jeweled bays: marine-life preserves and world-class surf spot in winter. Although rain is frequent here, it doesn't dampen the enjoyment of this wilder stretch of coast.

Anyone is welcome to visit Kapalua, guest of the resort or not. The Ritz-Carlton provides free public parking and beach access. The resort has swank restaurants, spas, golf courses, and hiking trails—all open to the public.

SOUTH MAUI

The hot, sunny South Maui coastline is popular with families and sun worshippers. Rain rarely falls here, and temperatures hover around 85°F (29°C) year-round. Cows once grazed and cacti grew wild on this former scrubland from Maalaea to Makena, now home to four distinct areas—**Maalaea, Kihei, Wailea,** and **Makena.** Maalaea is off on its own, at the mouth of an active small boat harbor, Kihei is the working-class, feeder community for well-heeled Wailea, and Makena is a luxurious wilderness at the road's end.

MAALAEA   If West Maui is the island's head, Maalaea is just under the chin. This windy, oceanfront village centers on a small-boat harbor (with a general store and a handful of restaurants) and the **Maui Ocean Center,** an aquarium/ocean complex. Visitors should be aware that tradewinds are near constant here, so a stroll on the beach often comes with a free sandblasting.

KIHEI   Less a proper town than a nearly continuous series of condos and mini-malls lining South Kihei Road, Kihei is Maui's best vacation bargain. Budget travelers swarm like sun-seeking geckos over the eight sandy beaches along this scalloped, 7-mile stretch of coast. Kihei is neither charming nor quaint; what it lacks in aesthetics, though, it more than makes up for in sunshine, affordability, and convenience. If you want the beach in the morning, shopping in the afternoon, and Hawaii Regional Cuisine in the evening—all at bargain prices—head to Kihei.

WAILEA   Just 4 decades ago, the road south of Kihei was a barely paved path through a tangle of *kiawe* trees. Now Wailea is a manicured oasis of multimillion-dollar resorts along 2 miles of palm-fringed gold coast. Wailea has warm, clear water full of tropical fish; year-round sunshine and clear blue skies; and hedonistic pleasure palaces on 1,500 acres of black-lava shore indented by five beautiful beaches, each one prettier than the next.

This is the playground of the stretch-limo set. The planned resort community has a shopping village, a plethora of award-winning restaurants, several prized golf courses, and a tennis complex. A growing number of large homes sprawl over the upper hillside, some offering excellent B&Bs at reasonable prices. The resorts along this fantasy coast are spectacular. Next door to the Four Seasons Resort Maui at Wailea, the most

A Makena beach at sunrise

elegant, is the Grand Wailea, built by Tokyo developer Takeshi Sekiguchi, who dropped $500 million in 1991 to create the most opulent Hawaiian resort to date. Stop in and take a look—sculptures by Botero and Léger populate its open-air art gallery and gardens. Stones imported from Mount Fuji line the resort's Japanese garden.

MAKENA Suddenly, the road enters raw wilderness. After Wailea's overdone density, the thorny landscape is a welcome relief. Although beautiful, this is an end-of-the-road kind of place: It's a long drive from Makena to anywhere on Maui. If you're looking for an activity-filled vacation, stay elsewhere, or you'll spend most of your vacation in the car. But if you want a quiet, relaxing respite, where the biggest trip of the day is from your bed to the beach, Makena is the place.

Puu Olai stands like Maui's Diamond Head near the southern tip of the island. The red-cinder cone shelters tropical fish and **Makena State Beach Park,** a vast stretch of golden sand spanked by feisty swells. Beyond Makena, you'll discover Haleakala's most recent lava flow; the bay famously visited by French explorer La Pérouse; and a sunbaked lava-rock trail known as the King's Highway, which threads around Maui's southernmost shore through the ruins of bygone fishing villages.

UPCOUNTRY MAUI

After a few days at the beach, you'll probably notice the 10,023-foot mountain towering over Maui. The leeward slopes of Haleakala (House of the Sun) are home to cowboys, farmers, and other rural folks who wave as you drive by. They're all up here enjoying the crisp air, emerald pastures, eucalyptus, and flower farms of this tropical Olympus.

The neighborhoods here are called "upcountry" because they're half-way up the mountain. You can see a thousand tropical sunsets reflected in the windows of houses old and new, strung along a road that runs like a loose hound from Makawao to Kula, leading up to the summit and **Hale-akala National Park.** If you head south on Kula Highway, beyond the tiny outpost of Kēokea, the road turns feral, undulating out toward the **MauiWine Vineyards,** where cattle, elk, and grapes flourish on Ulupal-akua Ranch. A stay upcountry is usually affordable and a nice contrast to the sizzling beaches and busy resorts below.

MAKAWAO   This small, two-street town has plenty of charm. It wasn't long ago that Hawaiian *paniolo* (cowboys) tied up their horses to the hitching posts outside the storefronts here; working ranchers still stroll through to pick up coffee and packages from the post office. The eclectic shops, galleries, and restaurants have a little something for everyone—from blocked Stetsons to wind chimes. Nearby, the **Hui Noeau Visual Arts Center,** Hawaii's premier arts collective, is definitely worth a detour. Makawao's only accommodations are reasonably priced B&Bs, ideal for those who love great views and don't mind slightly chilly nights.

KULA   A feeling of pastoral remoteness prevails in this upcountry com-munity of old flower farms, humble cottages, and new suburban ranch houses with million-dollar views that take in the ocean, the isthmus, the West Maui Mountains, and, at night, the lights that run along the gold coast like a string of pearls from Maalaea to Puu Olai. Everything flour-ishes at a cool 3,000 feet (bring a jacket), just below the cloud line, along a winding road on the way up to Haleakala National Park. Everyone here grows something—Maui onions, lavender, orchids, and proteas—and B&Bs cater to guests seeking cool tropical nights, panoramic views, and a rural upland escape. Here you'll find the true peace and quiet that only rural farming country can offer—yet you're still just 40 minutes away from the beach and a little more than an hour's drive from Lahaina.

Makawao town

ON THE ROAD TO HANA On Maui's North Shore, **Paia** was once a busy sugar plantation town with a railroad, two movie theaters, and a double-decker mercantile. As the sugar industry began to wane, the tuned-in, dropped-out hippies of the 1970s moved in, followed shortly by a cosmopolitan collection of windsurfers. When the international wave riders discovered **Hookipa Beach Park** just outside of town, their minds were blown; it's one of the best places on the planet to catch air. Today high-tech windsurf shops, trendy restaurants, bikini boutiques, and modern art galleries inhabit Paia's rainbow-colored vintage buildings. The Dalai Lama himself blessed the beautiful Tibetan stupa in the center of town. **Mama's Fish House** is located east of Paia in the tiny community of **Kuau,** 10 minutes farther east.

Once a pineapple plantation village, complete with two canneries (both now shopping complexes), Haiku offers vacation rentals and B&Bs in a pastoral setting. It's the perfect base for those who want to get off the beaten path and experience the quieter side of Maui.

HANA Set between an emerald rainforest and the blue Pacific is a Hawaiian village blissfully lacking in golf courses, shopping malls, and fast-food joints. Hana is more of a sensory overload than a destination; here you'll discover the simple joys of rain-misted flowers, the sweet taste of backyard bananas and papayas, and the easy calm and unabashed aloha spirit of old Hawaii. What saved "Heavenly" Hana from the inevitable march of progress? The 52-mile **Hana Highway,** which winds around 600 curves and crosses more than 50 one-lane bridges on its way from Kahului. You can go to Hana for the day—it's 3 hours (and a half-century) from Kihei and Lahaina—but 3 days are better.

GETTING AROUND

BY CAR The simplest way to see Maui is by rental car; public transit is still in its infancy here. All of the major car-rental firms—including Alamo, Avis, Budget, Dollar, Enterprise, Hertz, National, and Thrifty—have agencies on Maui. If you're on a budget or traveling with sports gear, you can rent an older vehicle by the week from **Aloha Rent-a-Car** (www.aloharentacar.com; ✆ **888/4562-5642** or 808/877-4477). For tips on insurance and driving rules in Hawaii, see "Getting Around Hawaii" (p. 601).

Maui has only a handful of major roads, and you can expect a traffic jam or two heading into Kihei, Lahaina, or Paia. In general, the roads hug the coastlines; one zigzags up to Haleakala's summit. When asking locals for directions don't bother using highway numbers; residents know the routes by name only.

Traffic advisory: Be alert on the Honoapiilani Highway (Hwy. 30) en route to Lahaina. Drivers ogling whales in the channel between Maui and Lanai often slam on the brakes and cause major tie-ups and accidents. This is the main road connecting the west side to the rest of the island; if an accident, rockslide, flooding, or other road hazard occurs, traffic can back up for 1 to 8 hours (no joke). So before you set off, check with Maui County for road closure advisories (www.co.maui.hi.us; © **808/986-1200**). The most up-to-date info can be found on its Twitter feed (@CountyofMaui) or that of a local news agency (@MauiNow).

BY MOTORCYCLE   Feel the wind on your face and smell the salt air as you tour the island on a Harley, available for rent from **Maui Motorcycle Co.,** 150 Dairy Rd., Kahului (www.mauimotorcycleco.com; © **808/877-7433**); rentals start at $139 a day.

BY TAXI   Because Maui's various destinations are so spread out, taxi service can be quite expensive and should be limited to travel within a neighborhood. **West Maui Taxi** (www.westmauitaxi.com; © **888/661-4545**) offers 24-hour service island-wide while **Kihei Wailea Taxi** (© **808/879-3000**) serves South Maui. The metered rate is $3 per mile.

BY BUS   The **Maui Bus** (www.mauicounty.gov/bus; © **808/871-4838**) is a public/private partnership that provides affordable but sadly inconsistent public transit to various communities across the island. Expect hour waits between rides. Air-conditioned buses service 13 routes, including several that stop at the airport. All routes operate daily, including holidays. Suitcases (one per passenger) and bikes are allowed; surfboards are not. Fares are $2.

[Fast FACTS] MAUI

Dentists   If you have dental problems, a nationwide referral service known as **1-800-DENTIST** (© 800/336-8478) will provide the name of a nearby dentist or clinic. Emergency dental care is available at **Hawaii Family Dental,** 1847 S. Kihei Rd., Kihei (www.hawaiifamilydental.com © **808/874-8401** and 95 Lono Av., Ste. 210, Kahului © **808/856-4626**), or at **Aloha Lahaina Dentists,** 134 Luakini St. (in the Maui Medical Group Bldg.), Lahaina (© **808/661-4005**).

Doctors   Urgent Care West Maui, located in the Fairway Shops, 2580 Kekaa Dr., Suite 111, Kaanapali (www.westmauidoctors.com; © **808/667-9721**), is open 365 days a year; no appointment necessary. In Kihei, call **Urgent Care Maui,** 1325 S. Kihei Rd., Suite 103 (at Lipoa St., across from Times Market), Kihei (© **808/879-7781**); it's open Monday to Saturday 7am to 9pm and Sunday 8am to 2pm.

Emergencies   Call © **911** for police, fire, and ambulance service. District stations are located in Lahaina (© **808/661-4441**) and in Hana (© **808/248-8311**). For the **Poison** **Control Center,** call © **800/222-1222.**

Hospitals   In Central Maui, **Maui Memorial Medical Center** is at 221 Mahalani, Wailuku (© **808/244-9056**). East Maui's **Hana Community Health Center** is open weekdays at 4590 Hana Hwy. (www.hanahealth.org; © **808/248-7515**). In upcountry Maui, **Kula Hospital** is at 100 Keokea Pl. (off of Kula Highway), Kula (© **808/878-1221**).

Internet Access   Many places offer free Wi-Fi. **Whole Foods** (www.wholefoodsmarket.com/stores/maui) has Wi-Fi at the Maui

Mall in Kahului, and **Star-bucks** (www.starbucks.com/store-locator) provides Internet service in its stores in Kahului, Pukalani, Lahaina, and Kihei. If you need a computer, visit a **public library** (to find the closest location, check www.publiclibraries.com/hawaii.htm). A library card gets you free access; you can purchase a 3-month visitor card for $10.

Post Office To find the nearest post office, call **📞 800/ASK-USPS.** In Lahaina, branches are located at the Lahaina Civic Center, 1760 Honoapiilani Hwy., and at the Lahaina Shopping Center, 132 Papalaua St. In Kahului, there's a branch at 138 S. Puunēnē

Ave., and in Kihei, there's one at 1254 S. Kihei Rd.

Weather For the current weather, the Haleakala National Park weather, or the marine and surf conditions, call the **National Weather Service's Maui forecast (📞 866/944-5025)** or visit www.prh.noaa.gov/hnl and click on the island of Maui.

EXPLORING MAUI
Attractions & Points of Interest

Tip: If you're a history buff, buy a "Passport to the Past" for $10 and gain admission to Maui's four best museums: the Baldwin Home and Wo Hing Museum in Lahaina, the Bailey House in Wailuku, and the A&B Sugar Museum in Puunene. The passport is sold at each of these locations.

CENTRAL MAUI
Kahului

Directly outside the Kahului Airport you can find an unlikely nature preserve: the **Kanaha Wildlife Sanctuary,** Haleakala Highway Extension and Hana Highway (📞 **808/984-8100**). Look for the parking area off the Haleakala Highway Extension (just past Krispy Kreme), and you'll find a 50-foot trail that meanders along the shore to a shade shelter and lookout. This wetland is the permanent home of the endangered black-neck Hawaiian stilt. It's also a good place to see endangered Hawaiian *koloa* (ducks), coots, and migrating shorebirds.

Maui Nui Botanical Garden ★ GARDEN   This garden is a living treasure box of native Hawaiian coastal species and plants brought here by Polynesian voyagers in their seafaring canoes. Stroll beneath the shade of the *hala* and breadfruit trees. Learn how the first Hawaiians made everything from medicine to musical instruments out of the plants they found growing in these islands. Ask to see the *hapai* (pregnant) banana tree—a variety with fruits that grow inside the trunk! Take a self-guided audio tour or take a do docent-led tour ($10) Tuesday through Thursday at 10am. If the garden happens to be hosting a lei-making or *kapa*-dyeing workshop while you're on the island, don't miss it.

150 Kanaloa Ave., Kahului. www.mnbg.org. 📞 **808/249-2798.** $5 adults, free for seniors and children 12 and under and on Sat; guided tours $10 per person.

Wailuku

Wailuku, the historic gateway to Iao Valley, is worth a visit for a little shopping and a stop at the small but fascinating Bailey House.

Bailey House Museum ★ HISTORIC SITE   Since 1957, the Maui Historical Society has welcomed visitors to the charming former home of Edward Bailey, a missionary, teacher, and accomplished artist. The 1833 building—a hybrid of Hawaiian stonework and Yankee-style architecture—is a trove of Hawaiiana. Inside you'll find pre-contact artifacts: precious feather lei, *kapa* (barkcloth) samples, a wooden spear so large it defies believability, and a collection of gemlike Hawaiian tree-snail shells. Bailey's exquisite landscapes decorate the rock walls, capturing on canvas a Maui that exists only in memory.

2375-A Main St., Wailuku. www.mauimuseum.org. © **808/244-3326.** $7 adults, $5 seniors/military, $2 children 7–12. Mon–Sat 10am–4pm.

Maui Tropical Plantation ★ GARDEN   About 3 miles south of Wailuku lies the tiny village of Waikapu, which has an attraction that's worth exploring. There's plenty to do here: shop for locally made souvenirs, learn how to husk a coconut, gawk at the longhorn cattle, and zoom on a zipline over the plantation's lush landscape. Relive Maui's past by taking a 40-minute narrated tram ride around fields of pineapple, sugarcane, and papaya trees at a working plantation. Tram tours start at 10am and leave about every 45 minutes. The grounds are fantastically landscaped with tropical plants and sculptures made from repurposed sugarcane-harvesting equipment. The **Mill House** restaurant offers exceptional, inventive cuisine for lunch and dinner (open 11am–9pm).

1670 Honoapiilani Hwy. www.mauitropicalplantation.com. © **808/270-0333.** Free admission. Tram tours $20 adults, $10 children 3–12. Daily 8am–9pm.

Iao Valley State Monument ★

A couple miles north of Wailuku, the houses grow less frequent and Maui's wild side begins to reveal itself. The transition from suburban sprawl to raw nature is so abrupt that most people who drive up into the valley don't realize they're suddenly in a rainforest. This is Iao Valley, a beautiful 6¼-acre state park whose verdant nature, waterfalls, swimming holes, and hiking trails have been enjoyed by millions of people from around the world for more than a century.

To get here from Wailuku, take Main Street to Iao Valley Road to the entrance to the state park. Two paved walkways loop into the massive green amphitheater, across the bridge of Iao Stream, and along the stream itself. This paved .35-mile loop is Maui's easiest hike—you can take your grandmother on this one. The leisurely walk will allow you to enjoy lovely views of Iao Needle and the lush vegetation.

The feature known as **Iao Needle** is an erosional remnant consisting of basalt dikes. This phallic rock juts an impressive 2,250 feet above sea level. Youngsters play in **Iao Stream,** a peaceful brook that belies its bloody history. In 1790, King Kamehameha the Great and his men engaged in the battle of Iao Valley to gain control of Maui. When the battle ended, so many bodies blocked Iao Stream that the battle site was named Kepaniwai, or "Damming of the Waters." An architectural heritage park of Hawaiian, Japanese, Chinese, Filipino, Korean, Portuguese, and New England–style houses stands in harmony by Iao Stream at **Kepaniwai Heritage Garden.** This is a good picnic spot, with plenty of tables and benches. You can see ferns, banana trees, and other native plants in the **Iao Valley Botanic Garden** along the stream.

WHEN TO GO   Park hours are 7am to 7pm daily and the entrance fee is $5 per car. Go early in the morning or late in the afternoon when the sun's rays slant into the valley and create a mystical mood. You can bring a picnic and spend the day, but be prepared at any time for one of the frequent tropical cloudbursts that soak the valley and swell both waterfalls and streams. For updated info, visit http://dlnr.hawaii.gov/dsp/parks/maui/iao-valley-state-monument or contact the State Parks Maui office at ✆ **808/984-8109.**

The Scenic Route to West Maui: The Kahekili Highway

The main route to West Maui is the Honoapiilani Highway, which sidles around the southern coastline along the *pali* (cliffs) to Lahaina. But those who relish adventures should consider exploring the backside of the West Maui Mountains.

From Wailuku, head north on the **Kahekili Highway** (Hwy. 340)—though "highway" is a bit of a misnomer for this paved but sometimes precarious road. It's named after a fierce 18th-century Maui king. The narrow and sometimes white-knuckle road weaves for 20 miles along an ancient Hawaiian coastal footpath to Honokohau Bay, at the island's northernmost tip, past blowholes, sea stacks, seabird rookeries, and the imposing 636-foot Kahakuloa headland. On the *mauka* (mountain) side, you'll pass high cliffs, deep valleys dotted with plantation houses, cattle grazing on green plateaus, old wooden churches, taro fields, and houses hung with fishing nets. It's slow going (you often have to inch past oncoming traffic on what feels like a one-lane track) but a spectacular drive. In Kahakuloa, between mile markers 12 and 13, stop in at the wooden roadside stand known as **Julia's Best Banana Bread** for world-famous warm, sweet loaves and coconut candy. *Note:* Check for road closures before heading out, especially if it's been raining heavily. Call Maui County at ✆ **808/270-7845.**

At Honokohau, pick up Highway 30 and continue on to the West Maui resorts; the first one you'll reach is Kapalua (see below).

WEST MAUI

For a map of attractions in Lahaina and Kaanapali, see p. 355.

Baldwin Home Museum ★ HISTORIC SITE   Step into this coral-and-rock house on Lahaina's Front Street and travel back in time. Built in 1835, it belonged to Rev. Dwight Baldwin, a missionary, naturalist, and self-trained physician who saved many Native Hawaiians from devastating influenza and smallpox epidemics. Baldwin's rudimentary medical

Baldwin Home Museum

tools (on display here) bear witness to the steep odds he faced. He was rewarded with 2,600 acres in Kapalua, where he grew pineapple—then an experimental crop. His children later became some of Hawaii's most powerful landholders and business owners. Tour the Baldwin family home and pick up a walking-tour map to Lahaina's most historic sites on your way out. On Friday night, docents dressed in period attire offer candlelit tours and serve free refreshments on the lanai.

120 Dickenson St. (at Front St.). www.lahainarestoration.org. (℃) **808/661-3262.** $7 adults, $5 seniors/military, free for children 12 and under (includes entry to Wo Hing Museum). Sat–Thurs 10am–4pm, Fri 10am–8:30pm.

Banyan Tree ★ NATURAL ATTRACTION   Of all the Indian banyan trees in Hawaii, this is the greatest—so big you can't fit it in your camera's viewfinder. It was 8 feet tall when planted in 1873. Today the arboreal octopus rises more than 50 feet high, has 12 major trunks, and shades artists and crafters selling their wares in Courthouse Square.

Plantation Museum ★ HISTORIC SITE   This tiny museum at the Wharf Cinema Center celebrates Maui's colorful plantation history. For 150-plus years sugar and pineapple plantations dominated island agriculture and fostered communities of diverse cultures. Learn about life in the camps: the festivals, traditions, innovations, and heroic athletes.

658 Front St. www.lahainarestoration.org. (℃) **808/661-3262.** Free. Daily 9am–6pm.

Wo Hing Museum & Cookhouse ★ HISTORIC SITE   Sandwiched between souvenir shops and restaurants on Front Street, this ornate building once served as a fraternal and social meeting hall for Lahaina's Chinese immigrants. Today it houses fascinating Asian artifacts, artwork, and a lovely shrine in the altar room upstairs. Beside the temple is a rustic cookhouse where you can watch some of Thomas Edison's first movies, filmed here in Hawaii. The footage of *paniolo* (cowboys) wrangling steer onto ships offshore and Honolulu circa 1898 is mesmerizing. Wo Hing hosts Lunar New Year and kite-making festivals that are catnip for kids.

858 Front St. www.lahainarestoration.org. © **808/661-3262.** $7 adults, $5 seniors/ military, free for children 12 and under (includes entry to Baldwin House Museum; see above). Daily 10am–4pm.

SOUTH MAUI

Maalaea

Maui Ocean Center ★★★ AQUARIUM   This 5-acre facility houses the largest aquarium in the state and features one of Hawaii's largest predators: the tiger shark. As you walk past the 3 dozen or so tanks and countless exhibits, you'll slowly descend from the tide pools to the pelagic zone—without ever getting wet. Start at the outdoor surge pool, where you'll see shallow-water spiny urchins and cauliflower coral; and then move on to the turtle pool and eagle-ray pools before heading indoors for the star of the show: a 100-foot-long, 600,000-gallon main tank featuring tiger, gray, and white-tip sharks, as well as feisty ulua, colorful surgeonfish, and numerous others. The walkway tunnels right through the tank, so you're surrounded on three sides by marine creatures. Check out the hammerhead exhibit, where juvenile scalloped hammerhead sharks are on display, and the Shark Dive Maui Program, where scuba divers plunge into the tank with sharks, stingrays, and tropical fish. You, too, can sign up to dive with sharks, and fish-loving kids can book a sleepover in the aquarium, staying up into the wee hours to watch glowing jellyfish and other nocturnal animals.

At the Maalaea Harbor Village, 192 Maalaea Rd. (the triangle btw. Honoapiilani Hwy. and Maalaea Rd.). www.mauioceancenter.com. © **808/270-7000.** $30 adults, $28 seniors, $20 children 3–12 (book online for a week pass upgrade). Daily 9am–5pm.

Maui Ocean Center

Wo Hing Museum & Cookhouse

Kihei

Kealia Pond National Wildlife Preserve ★ NATURE PRE-
SERVE Wedged between Mokulele Highway and Sugar Beach, this
700-acre wetland reserve provides habitat for endangered Hawaiian stilts,
coots, and ducks. The picturesque ponds work both as bird preserves and
as sedimentation basins that protect coral reefs from runoff. Check out the
new visitor center, then take a self-guided tour along a boardwalk dotted
with interpretive signs. Among the native waterfowl seen here are the black-
crowned high heron, Hawaiian coot, Hawaiian duck, and Hawaiian stilt.
From July to December, the hawksbill turtle comes ashore to lay its eggs.
Visitor Center entrance near mile marker 6 on Mokulele Hwy (Hwy. 311). Boardwalk
entrance near mile marker 2 on Piilani Hwy. www.fws.gov/kealiapond. ℭ **808/875-
1582.** Free. Visitor Center open Mon: 11am–3pm; Tues–Fri: 8am–3pm; Refuge open
Mon–Fri: 7:30am–4pm; Boardwalk open daily: 6am–7pm. Closed Federal Holidays.

Wailea

The best way to explore this golden resort coast is to head for Wailea's
1.5-mile **coastal nature trail** ★, stretching between the Fairmont Kea
Lani Maui and the *kiawe* thicket just beyond the Marriott Wailea Beach
Resort. The serpentine path meanders past an abundance of native plants
(on the *makai,* or ocean side), old Hawaiian habitats, and a billion dollars'
worth of luxury hotels. You can pick up the trail at any of the resorts or
from clearly marked shoreline access points along the coast. As the path
crosses several bold black-lava points, it affords new vistas of islands and
ocean; benches allow you to pause and contemplate the view across Alalakeiki Channel, where you may spy whales in season. It's nice in the cool

hours of the morning (though often clogged with joggers) and at sunset, when you can watch the burning sun sink into the Pacific.

Makena

A few miles south of Wailea, the manicured coast returns to wilderness; now you're in Makena. At one time cattle were driven down the slope from upland ranches, lashed to rafts, and sent into the water to swim to boats that waited to take them to market. Now **Makena Landing ★** is a great spot to launch kayaks and dive trips.

From the landing, go south on Makena Road; on the right is **Keawalai Congregational Church** (𝒞 **808/879-5557**), built in 1855, with walls 3 feet thick. Surrounded by *tī* leaves, which by Hawaiian custom provide protection, and built of lava rock with coral used as mortar, this church sits on its own cove with a gold-sand beach. It always attracts a Sunday crowd for its 7:30am and 10am Hawaiian-language services.

Farther south on the coast is **La Pérouse Monument,** a pyramid of lava rocks that marks the spot where French explorer Adm. Comte de la Pérouse set foot on Maui in 1789. He described the "burning climate" of the leeward coast, observed several fishing villages near Kihei, and sailed on into oblivion, never to be seen again. To get here, drive south to Ahihi Bay, where the road turns to gravel. Just beyond this is **Ahihi-Kinau Natural Reserve,** 1,238 acres of rare anchialine ponds and sunbaked lava fields from the last eruption of Haleakala between 200 and 500 years ago. Continue another 2 miles past Ahihi-Kinau to **La Pérouse Bay;** the monument sits amid a clearing in black lava at the end of the dirt road. If you've got plenty of water, sunblock, and sturdy shoes, you can embark on foot on the King's Trail, a rugged path built by ancient Hawaiian royals.

UPCOUNTRY MAUI

Makawao

Makawao is Hawaiian cowboy country—yup, the islands have a long-standing tradition of ranchers and rodeo masters, and this cool, misty upcountry town is its Maui epicenter. Modern-day *paniolo* come here to fuel up on cream puffs and stick donuts from **Komoda Store & Bakery,** 3674 Baldwin Ave. (𝒞 **808/572-7261**), a 100-year-old family grocery that seems frozen in time. Neighboring shops offer Tibetan jewelry, shabby-chic housewares, and marvelous paintings by local artists. A handful of decent restaurants crowd the intersection of Baldwin and Makawao avenues; take your pick of sushi, Maui cattle ribeye, or pasta.

Five minutes down Baldwin Avenue, the **Hui Noeau Visual Arts Center,** 2841 Baldwin Ave. (www.huinoeau.com; 𝒞 **808/572-6560**), occupies a two-story, Mediterranean-style stucco home designed in 1917 by C. W. Dickey, one of Hawaii's most prominent architects. The sprawling 9-acre estate, known as **Kaluanui,** hosts visiting artists for lectures and classes in basketry, jewelry making, ceramics, painting, and other media, all at reasonable prices. Call for details. The gallery's rotating exhibits include work by established and emerging artists, and the gift shop features many one-of-a-kind works, including ceramic seconds at a steal. Hours are Monday through Saturday 10am to 4pm.

Kula

While in the upcountry Kula region, visit one of the area's many farms (see "Maui Farms: Stop & Smell the Lavender," p. 326).

Kula Botanical Garden ★ GARDEN   You can take a self-guided, informative, leisurely stroll through this collection of more than 700 native and exotic plants—including three unique assemblages of orchids, proteas, and bromeliads—at this 5-acre garden. It offers a good overview of Hawaii's exotic flora in one small, cool place.

638 Kekaulike Ave, Kula. www.kulabotanicalgarden.com. ℭ **808/878-1715.** $10 adults, $3 children 6–12. Daily 9am–4pm.

MauiWine (Tedeschi Vineyards) ★★ VINEYARD/WINERY   On the southern shoulder of Haleakala is **Ulupalakua Ranch,** a 20,000-acre spread once owned by the legendary sea captain James Makee, celebrated in the Hawaiian song and dance "Hula O Makee." Wounded in a Honolulu waterfront brawl in 1843, Makee moved to Maui and bought Ulupalakua. He renamed it Rose Ranch, planted sugar as a cash crop, and grew rich. Still in operation, the ranch is now home to Maui's only winery, established in 1974 by Napa vintner Emil Tedeschi, who began growing California and European grapes here and produces serious still and sparkling wines, plus a silly wine made of pineapple juice. The grounds are the perfect place for a picnic. Settle under the sprawling camphor tree, pop the cork on a blanc de blanc, and toast your good fortune. Twice a week the staff offers historic tasting tours through the cellar, landscaped grounds, and old jail.

14815 Piilani Hwy., Kula. www.mauiwine.com. ℭ **808/878-6058.** Free. Tasting room open daily 10am–5:30pm. Tours at 10:30am and 1:30pm.

House of the Sun: Haleakala National Park ★★★

The summit of Haleakala, the House of the Sun, is a spectacular natural phenomenon. More than 1.3 million people a year ascend the 10,023-foot-high mountain to peer into the world's largest dormant volcano. Haleakala has not rumbled for at least 100 years, but it's still officially considered active. The lunarlike volcanic landscape is a national park, home to numerous rare and endangered plants, birds, and insects. Hardy adventurers hike and camp inside the crater's wilderness (see "Hiking," p. 347, and "Camping," p. 386). Those bound for the interior should bring survival gear, for the terrain is raw and rugged—not unlike the moon. Haleakala's interior is one of the world's quietest places—so silent that it exceeds the technical capacity of microphones.

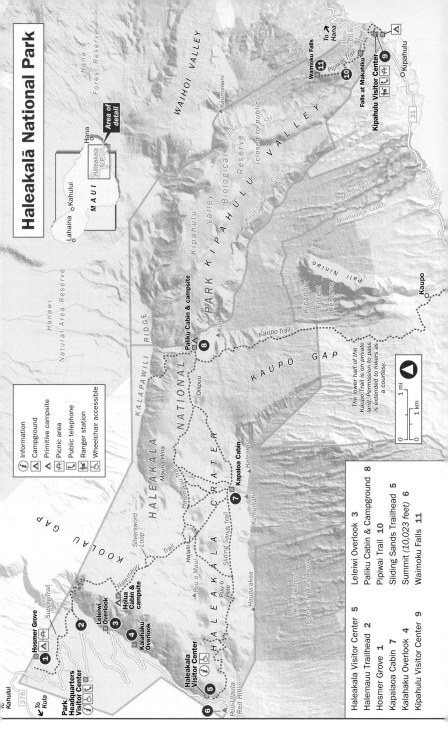

Haleakalā National Park

MAUI

Lahaina o ○ Kahului

Hana ○

Haleakala N.P.

Area of detail

Legend:
- (i) Information
- ⚠ Campground
- ▲ Primitive campsite
- ⛱ Picnic area
- ☎ Public telephone
- Ranger station
- ♿ Wheelchair accessible

Haleakala Visitor Center **5**
Halemauu Trailhead **2**
Hosmer Grove **1**
Kapalaoa Cabin **7**
Kalahaku Overlook **4**
Kipahulu Visitor Center **9**

Leleiwi Overlook **3**
Paliku Cabin & Campground **8**
Pipiwai Trail **10**
Sliding Sands Trailhead **5**
Summit (10,023 feet) **6**
Waimoku Falls **11**

313

BEFORE YOU go

You need reservations to view sunrise from the summit. The National Park Service now limits how many cars can access the summit between 3 and 7am. Book your spot up to 60 days in advance at **www.recreation.gov**. A fee of $1.50 (on top of the park entrance fee) applies. You'll need to show your reservation receipt and photo I.D. to enter the park.

Watching the sun's first golden rays break through the clouds *is* spectacular, though I recommend sunset instead. It's equally beautiful—and warmer! Plus, you're more likely to explore the rest of the park when you're not sleep-deprived and hungry for breakfast. Full-moon nights can be ethereal, too. No matter when you go, realize that weather is

extreme at the summit, ranging from blazing sun to sudden snow flurries. As you ascend the slopes, the temperature drops about 3 degrees every 1,000 feet (305m), so the top can be 30 degrees cooler than it was at sea level. But it's the alpine wind that really stings. Come prepared with warm layers and rain gear. For sunrise, bring every warm thing you can swaddle yourself with—blankets and sleeping bags included! And remember, glorious views aren't guaranteed; the summit may be misty or overcast at any time of day. Before you head up the mountain, get current weather conditions from the park (🕻 **808/572-4400**) or the **National Weather Service** (🕻 **866/944-5025,** option 4).

Haleakala National Park extends from the volcano's summit down its southeast flank to Maui's eastern coast, beyond Hana. There are actually two separate districts within the park: **Haleakala Summit** and **Kipahulu** (see "Tropical Haleakala: Oheo Gulch at Kipahulu," p. 323). No roads link the summit and the coast; you have to approach them separately, and you need at least a day to see each place.

THE DRIVE TO THE SUMMIT

Just driving up the mountain is an experience. **Haleakala Crater Road (Hwy. 378)** is one of the fastest-ascending roads in the world. Its 33 switchbacks travel through numerous climate zones, passing in and out of clouds to finally deliver a view that extends for more than 100 miles. The trip takes 1½ to 2 hours from Kahului. No matter where you start out, follow Highway 37 (Haleakala Hwy.) to Pukalani, where you'll pick up Highway 377 (also called Haleakala Hwy.), which you take to Highway 378. Fill up your gas tank before you go—Pukalani is the last stop for fuel. Along the way, expect fog, rain, and wind. Be on the lookout for downhill bicyclists, stray cattle, and naïve *nēnē,* the native Hawaiian geese.

Remember, you're entering a high-altitude wilderness area; some people get dizzy from lack of oxygen. Bring water, a jacket, and, if you go up for sunrise, every scrap of warmth you can find. There are no concessions in the park—not a coffee urn in sight. If you plan to hike, bring extra water and snacks.

At the **park entrance,** you'll pay a fee of $25 per car or $20 per motorcycle. It's good for 3 days and includes access to the Kipahulu district on the east side of the island. Immediately after the park entrance, take a left turn into **Hosmer's Grove.** A small campground abuts a beautiful evergreen forest. During Hawaii's territorial days, forester Ralph Hosmer planted experimental groves, hoping to launch a timber industry. It failed, but a few of his sweet-smelling cedars and pines remain. Birders should make a beeline here. A half-mile loop trail snakes from the parking lot through the evergreens to a picturesque gulch, where rare **Hawaiian honeycreepers** flit above native *'ōhi'a* and **sandalwood trees.** The charismatic birds are best spotted in the early morning hours.

One mile from the park entrance, at 7,000 feet, is **Haleakala National Park Headquarters** (© **808/572-4400**), open daily from 7am to 3:45pm. Stop here to pick up park information and camping permits, use the restroom, fill your water bottle, and purchase park swag. Keep an eye out for the native Hawaiian goose. With its black face, buff cheeks, and partially webbed feet, the gray-brown *nēnē* looks its cousin, the Canada goose; but the Hawaiian bird doesn't migrate and prefers lava beds to lakes. *Nēnē* once flourished throughout Hawaii, but habitat destruction and introduced predators (rats, cats, dogs, and mongooses) nearly caused their extinction. By 1951, there were only 30 left. The Boy Scouts helped reintroduce captive-raised birds into the park. The species remains endangered, but is now protected as Hawaii's state bird.

Beyond headquarters are **two scenic overlooks** on the way to the summit; stop at Leleiwi on the way up and Kalahaku on the way back down, if only to get out, stretch, and get accustomed to the heights. Take a deep breath, look around, and pop your ears. If you feel dizzy, or get a sudden headache, consider turning around and going back down.

The **Leleiwi Overlook** is just beyond mile marker 17. From the parking area, a short trail leads to a spectacular view of the colorful volcanic crater. When the clouds are low and the sun is in the right place (usually

GO WITH THE friends

The Friends of Haleakala National Park is a volunteer organization that leads three-day service trips into crater's wilderness. Backpack into the heart of Haleakala, spend a few hours pull weeds or painting cabins, and gain a deeper appreciation for this magnificent terrain in the company of likeminded volunteers.

Trip leaders take care of renting the cabins and supervising rides and meals—which can be hard to do from afar. The trip is free, though you will pitch in for shared meals. Be prepared for 4 to 10 miles of hiking in inclement weather. Sign up at ww.fhnp.org.

around sunset), you may witness the "Brocken Spectre"—a reflection of your shadow, ringed by a rainbow, in the clouds below. This optical illusion—caused by a rare combination of sun, shadow, and fog—occurs in just three places: Haleakala, Scotland, and Germany.

Continue on to the **Haleakala Visitor Center,** open daily at sunrise (5:45am–3pm). It offers panoramic views, with photos identifying the various features, and exhibits that explain the area's history, ecology, geology, and volcanology. Park staff members are often on hand to answer questions. Restrooms and water are available. The actual summit is a little farther on, at **Puu Ulaula Overlook** (also known as Red Hill), the volcano's highest point, where you'll see Haleakala Observatories' cluster of buildings—known unofficially as **Science City.** The Puu Ulaula Overlook, with its glass-enclosed windbreak, is a prime viewing spot, crowded with shivering folks at sunrise. It's also the best place to see a rare **silversword.** This botanical wonder is the punk of the plant world—like a spacey artichoke with attitude. Silverswords grow only in Hawaii, take from 4 to 30 years to bloom, and then, usually between May and October, send up a 1- to 6-foot stalk covered in multitudes of reddish, sunflower-like blooms. Don't walk too close to silversword plants, as footfalls can damage their roots.

On your way back down, stop at the **Kalahaku Overlook.** On a clear day you can see all the way across Alenuihaha Channel to the often snow-capped summit of Mauna Kea on the Big Island. *Tip:* Put your car in low gear when driving down the Haleakala Crater Road, so you don't destroy your brakes by riding them the whole way down.

Silversword

Haleakala National Park

East Maui & Heavenly Hana

Hana is about as close as you can get to paradise on Earth. In and around Hana, you'll find a lush tropical rainforest dotted with cascading waterfalls, trees spilling ripe fruits onto the grass, and the sparkling blue Pacific, skirted by red- and black-sand beaches.

THE ROAD TO HANA ★★★

Top down, sunscreen on, Hawaiian music playing on a breezy morning—it's time to head out along the Hana Highway (Hwy. 36), a wiggle of a road that runs along Maui's northeastern shore. The drive takes at least 3 hours from Lahaina or Kihei, but don't shortchange yourself—take all day. Going to Hana is about the journey, not the destination.

There are wilder, steeper, and more dangerous roads, but in all of Hawaii, no road is more celebrated than this one. It winds 50 miles past taro patches, magnificent seascapes, waterfall pools, botanical gardens, and verdant rainforests, and ends at one of Hawaii's most beautiful tropical places.

The outside world discovered the little village of Hana in 1926, when pickax-wielding convicts carved a narrow road out of the cliff's edge. Often subject to landslides and washouts, the mud-and-gravel track was paved in 1962, when tourist traffic began to increase; it now sees around 1,000 cars and dozens of vans a day. That translates into half a million people a year, which is way too many. Go at the wrong time, and you'll be stuck in a bumper-to-bumper rental-car parade—peak traffic hours are midmorning and midafternoon year-round, especially on weekends.

In the rush to "do" Hana in a day, most visitors spin around town in 10 minutes and wonder what all the fuss is about. It takes time to soak up the serene magic of Hana, play in the waterfalls, sniff the rain-misted gingers, hike through clattering bamboo forests, and merge with the tension-dissolving scenery. Stay overnight if you can, and meander back in a day or two. If you really must do the Hana Highway in a day, go just before sunrise and return after sunset.

Tips: Practice aloha. Yield at one-lane bridges, wave at oncoming motorists, let the big guys in 4×4s have the right of way—you're not in a hurry, after all! If the guy behind you blinks his lights, let him pass. Unless you're rounding a blind curve, don't honk your horn—in Hawaii, it's considered rude. *Safety note:* Be aware of the weather when hiking in streams. Flash floods happen frequently in this area. *Do not attempt to cross rising stream waters.* In the words of the Emergency Weather Forecast System: "Turn around. Don't drown."

THE JOURNEY BEGINS IN PAIA   Before you start out, fill up on fuel. Paia is the last place for gas until you get to Hana, some 50-plus bridges and 600-plus hairpin turns down the road. (It's fun to make a game out of counting the bridges.)

Paia ★★ was once a thriving sugar-mill town. The skeletal mill is still here, but in the 1950s the bulk of the population (10,000 in its heyday) shifted to Kahului. Like so many former plantation towns, Paia nearly foundered, but its beachfront charm lured hippies, followed by adrenaline-seeking windsurfers and, most recently, young families. The town has proven its adaptability. Now trendy boutiques and eateries occupy the old ma-and-pa establishments. Plan to get here early, around 7am, when **Charley's** ★, 142 Hana Hwy. (www.charleysmaui.com ✆ **808/579-8085**), opens. Enjoy a big, hearty breakfast for a reasonable price or continue down the road to the little town of **Kuau.** A rainbow fence made of surfboards announces **Kuau Store** (www.kuaustore.com ✆ **808/579-8844**), a great stop for smoothies and snacks.

WINDSURFING MECCA   Just before mile marker 9 is **Hookipa Beach Park** ★★★, where top-ranked windsurfers come to test themselves against thunderous surf and forceful wind. On nearly every windy day after noon (the board surfers have the waves in the morning), you can watch dozens of windsurfers twirling and dancing in the wind like colored butterflies. To watch them, do not stop on the highway, but go past the park and turn left at the entrance on the far side of the beach. Park on the high grassy bluff or drive down to the sandy beach and park alongside the pavilion. **Green sea turtles** haul out to rest on the east end of the beach. Go spy on them, but stay a respectful distance (15 ft.) away. Facilities include restrooms, a shower, picnic tables, and a barbecue area.

INTO THE COUNTRY   Past Hookipa Beach, the road winds down into **Maliko Gulch.** Big-wave surfers use the boat ramp here to launch jet skis and head out to **Jaws,** one of the world's biggest surf breaks a few coves over. Back on the Hana Highway, for the next few miles you'll pass through the rural area of **Haiku,** where banana patches and guava trees litter their sweet fruit onto the street.

At mile marker 16, the curves begin, one right after another. Slow down and enjoy the view of fern-covered hills and plunging valleys punctuated by mango and *kukui* trees. After mile marker 16, the road is still called the Hana Highway, but the number changes from Highway 36 to Highway 360, and the mile markers go back to 0.

TWIN FALLS   Not far beyond mile marker 2, you'll see a large fruit stand on the *mauka* (mountain) side of the road—most likely surrounded by lots of cars. This is **Twin Falls** (www.twinfallsmaui.net; ℰ **808/463-1275**), a privately owned piece of paradise with more waterfalls than anyone can count. A gravel footpath leads to the first waterfall pool. Continue up the mountain path to find many more. Swimming is safe as long as it's not raining and you don't have open wounds. (Bacterial infections aren't uncommon.) Be respectful of the residents and pack out your trash.

From here on out, there's a waterfall (and one-lane bridge) around nearly every turn in the road, so drive slowly and be prepared to stop and yield to oncoming cars.

WILD CURVES   About a half-mile after mile marker 6, there's a sharp U-curve in the road, going uphill. The road is super narrow here, with a brick wall on one side and virtually no maneuvering room. Sound your

The road to Hana

horn at the start of the U-curve to let approaching cars know you're coming. Take the curve slowly.

Just before mile marker 7, a forest of waving **bamboo** takes over the right-hand side of the road. To the left, you'll see a stand of **rainbow eucalyptus trees,** recognizable by their multicolored trunks. Drivers are often tempted to pull over here, but there isn't any shoulder. Continue on; you'll find many more beautiful trees to gawk at down the road.

AN EASY FAMILY HIKE   At mile marker 9, a small state wayside area has restrooms, picnic tables, and a barbecue area. The sign says Koolau Forest Reserve, but the real attraction here is the **Waikamoi Nature Trail,** an easy ¾-mile loop. The start of the trail is just behind the QUIET: TREES AT WORK sign. The well-marked trail meanders through eucalyptus, ferns, and hala trees.

CAN'T-MISS PHOTO OPS   Just past mile marker 12 is the **Kaumahina State Wayside Park ★**. This is a good pit stop and a great vista point. You can see all the way down the rugged coastline to the jutting Keanae Peninsula.

Another mile and a couple of bends in the road, and you'll enter the Honomanu Valley, with its beautiful bay. To get to the **Honomanu Bay,** look for the turnoff on your left, just after mile marker 14, as you begin your ascent up the other side of the valley. The rutted dirt-and-cinder road takes you down to the rocky black-sand beach. There are no facilities here. Because of the strong rip currents offshore, swimming is best in the stream inland from the ocean. You'll consider the detour worthwhile as

Windsurfers at Hookipa Beach Park

A church built in 1860 in Keanae

you stand on the beach, well away from the ocean, and turn to look back on the steep cliffs covered with vegetation.

KEANAE PENINSULA & ARBORETUM   At mile marker 17, the vintage Hawaiian village of **Keanae ★★** stands out against the Pacific like a place that time forgot. Here, on an old lava flow graced by an 1860 stone church and swaying palms, is one of the last coastal enclaves of native Hawaiians. They still grow taro in patches and pound it into poi, the staple of the old Hawaiian diet, and they still pluck *opihi* (limpets) from tide pools along the jagged coast and cast throw nets for fish. Pick up a loaf of still-warm banana bread from **Aunty Sandy's** (10 Keanae Rd.).

At nearby **Keanae Arboretum,** Hawaii's botanical world is divided into three parts: native forest, introduced forest, and traditional Hawaiian plants, food, and medicine. You can swim in the pools of Piinaau Stream or press on along a mile-long trail into Keanae Valley, where a lovely tropical rainforest waits at the end. Had enough foliage for one day? This is the prime spot to turn around.

PUAA KAA STATE WAYSIDE   Tourists and locals alike often overlook this convenient stop, a half-mile past mile marker 22. Park by the restrooms; then cross the street to explore a jade green waterfall pool. Break out your picnic lunch here at the shaded tables. Practice saying the park's name, pronounced pooh-*ahh*-ahh kahh-*ahh,* which means "rolling pig."

For the world's best dessert (only a slight exaggeration), continue on to **Nahiku,** near mile marker 27.5 (yes, half-mile markers come into play in this wild territory). You'll see the rainbow-splashed sign for **Coconut Glen's ★★** (www.coconutglens.com; ✆ **808/248-4876**). Pull over and indulge in some truly splendid ice cream—dairy-free and made with coconut milk. Scoops of chocolate chili, *lilikoi* (passion fruit), and honey macadamia nut ice cream are served in coconut bowls, with coconut chips as spoons. This whimsical stand oozes with aloha. From here, you're only 20 minutes from Hana.

KAHANU GARDENS & PIILANIHALE HEIAU ★★★ To see one of Hawaii's most impressive archaeological sites, take a detour off of Hana Highway down Ulaino Road. The National Tropical Botanical Garden maintains the world's largest breadfruit collection here—including novel varieties collected from every tropical corner of the globe. Ancient Hawaiian history comes alive when you walk through the manicured canoe garden and first glimpse the monumental 3-acre Piilanihale *heiau* (temple). Built 800 years ago from stacked rocks hand-carried from miles away, it is a testament to the great chiefdoms of the past. Gaze in wonder at the 50-foot retaining wall and thatched canoe *hale* (house). Imagine steering a war canoe onto the wave-swept shore. Take time to soak in the site's *mana* (spiritual power). Admission is $10; 2-hour guided tours are $25 (650 Ulaino Rd., Hana; www.ntbg.org; © **808/248-8912**).

WAIANAPANAPA STATE PARK ★★★ On the outskirts of Hana, the shiny black-sand beach appears like a vivid dream, with bright-green foliage on three sides and cobalt-blue water lapping at its shore. The 120-acre state park on an ancient lava flow includes sea cliffs, lava tubes, arches, and the beach—plus a dozen rustic cabins. See p. 387 for a review of the cabins. Also see "Beaches" and "Camping," below.

HANA ★★★

Green, tropical Hana, which some call heavenly, is a destination all its own, a small coastal village in a rainforest inhabited by 2,500 people, many with Native Hawaiian ancestry. Beautiful Hana enjoys more than 90 inches of rain a year—more than enough to keep the scenery lush. Banyans, bamboo, breadfruit trees—everything seems larger than life, especially the flowers, like wild ginger and plumeria. Several roadside stands offer exotic blooms for $5 a bunch. As the signs say, just Put Money in Box. It's the Hana honor system. The best farm stand of the bunch is **Hana Farms** ★★, 2910 Hana Hwy. (© **808/248-7371**; see p. 415 for details).

The last unspoiled Hawaiian town on Maui is, oddly enough, the home of Maui's first resort, which opened in 1946. Paul Fagan, then owner of the San Francisco Seals baseball team, bought an old inn and turned it into Hana's first and only resort, now called **Travaasa Hana.** Others have tried to open hotels and golf courses, but the Hana community always politely refuses. Several great inns are scattered around town, though; see p. 383 for reviews.

A wood-frame 1871 building that served as the old Hana District Police Station now holds the **Hana Cultural Center & Museum,** 4974 Uakea Rd. (www.hanaculturalcenter.org; © **808/248-8622**). The center tells the history of the area, with some excellent artifacts, memorabilia, and photographs. Also stop in at **Hasegawa General Store,** a Maui

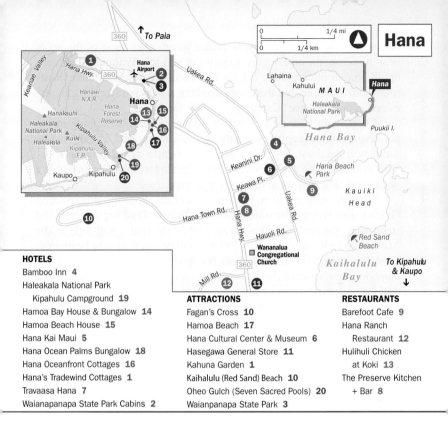

Hana

0   1/4 mi

0   1/4 km

↑ To Paia

Hana Airport

Lahaina   Kahului   **M A U I**

Haleakala National Park

Hana

Puukii I.

Hana Bay

Kauiki Head

Red Sand Beach

Wananalua Congregational Church

Kaihalulu Bay   To Kipahulu & Kaupo ↓

HOTELS

Bamboo Inn **4**

Haleakala National Park
Kipahulu Campground **19**

Hamoa Bay House & Bungalow **14**

Hamoa Beach House **15**

Hana Kai Maui **5**

Hana Ocean Palms Bungalow **18**

Hana Oceanfront Cottages **16**

Hana's Tradewind Cottages **1**

Travaasa Hana **7**

Waianapanapa State Park Cabins **2**

ATTRACTIONS

Fagan's Cross **10**

Hamoa Beach **17**

Hana Cultural Center & Museum **6**

Hasegawa General Store **11**

Kahuna Garden **1**

Kaihalulu (Red Sand) Beach **10**

Oheo Gulch (Seven Sacred Pools) **20**

Waianpanapa State Park **3**

RESTAURANTS

Barefoot Cafe **9**

Hana Ranch
Restaurant **12**

Huluhuli Chicken
at Koki **13**

The Preserve Kitchen
+ Bar **8**

institution. Buy a T-shirt or bumper sticker and check out the machete display above the office window.

On the green hills above Hana stands a 30-foot-high white cross made of lava rock. Citizens erected the cross in memory of Paul Fagan, who helped keep the town alive. The 3-mile hike up to **Fagan's Cross** provides a gorgeous view of the Hana coast, especially at sunset, when Fagan himself liked to climb this hill (see p. 351 for details).

Tropical Haleakala: Oheo Gulch at Kipahulu

If you're thinking about heading out to the so-called Seven Sacred Pools, past Hana in Kipahulu, let's clear this up right now: There are *more* than seven pools—and *all* water in Hawaii is considered sacred. **Oheo Gulch ★★★** (the rightful name of the pools) is in the Kipahulu district of Haleakala National Park (though you can't drive here from the summit). It's about 30 minutes beyond Hana town, along Highway 31. Expect rain showers on the Kipahulu coast.

The **Kipahulu Ranger Station** (© **808/248-7375**) is staffed from 8:30am to 5pm daily. Here you'll find park-safety information, exhibits, and books. Rangers offer a variety of walks and hikes year-round; check at the station for current activities. The fee to enter is $25 per car or $20 per motorcycle. The Highway 31 bridge passes over some of the pools near the ocean; the others, plus magnificent 400-foot **Waimoku Falls,** are uphill, via an often muddy but always rewarding hour-long hike. Restrooms are available, but there's no drinking water. Tent camping is permitted in the park; see "Camping" (p. 386) for details.

Check with park rangers before hiking up to or swimming in the pools, and always keep an eye on the water in the streams. The sky can be sunny near the coast, but floodwaters travel 6 miles down from the Kipahulu Valley, and the water level can rise 4 feet in less than 10 minutes. It's not a good idea to swim in the pools in winter.

From the ranger station, it's just a short hike above the famous Oheo Gulch to two spectacular **waterfalls.** The **Pipiwai Trail** begins across the street from the central parking area. Follow the trail a half-mile to the **Makahiku Falls** overlook. This 200-foot-tall beauty is just the beginning. Continue another 1½ miles, across two bridges and through a magical bamboo forest, to reach the dazzling 400-foot-tall **Waimoku Falls.** It's an uphill slog across slippery planks, but worth every step. Beware of falling rocks and never stand beneath the falls.

Beyond Oheo Gulch

A mile past Oheo Gulch on the ocean side of the road is **Lindbergh's Grave.** First to fly across the Atlantic Ocean, Charles A. Lindbergh found peace in the Pacific; he settled in Hana, where he died of cancer in 1974. The famous aviator is buried under river stones in a seaside graveyard behind the 1857 **Palapala Hoomau Congregational Church.**

Waimoku Falls trail

Adventurers can continue on around Haleakala, back toward civilization in Kula. Be warned that the route, Old Piilani Highway (Hwy. 31), is full of potholes and unpaved in parts. But it threads through ruggedly beautiful territory. Most rental-car companies warn you against traveling down this road, but it's really not so bad—just make sure a rockslide hasn't closed it before you go. If it's open, stop in for ice cream at **Kaupo General Store,** 34793 Piilani Hwy. (© **808/248-8054**). This remote outpost has a wonderful antique camera collection and many tempting souvenirs.

Organized Tours

Atlantis Submarine ★ TOUR   Descend more than 100 feet below the ocean's surface in air-conditioned comfort aboard this 48-passenger submarine. You'll see colorful fish, corals, and other marine creatures populating the waters off of Lahaina. Occasionally, eagle rays, white tip sharks, or a rare monk seal will swim past the submerged ship's windows. Whales have even been known to cruise alongside—filling the cabin with their otherworldly song. One guaranteed highlight is the sunken *Carthaginian,* a 19th-century replica supply boat that was scuttled to become an artificial reef.

At Pioneer Inn Hotel, 658 Wharf St., Lahaina. www.atlantisadventures.com/maui. © **808/667-2494.** 105-min. tours offered daily from 9am–2pm. $115 adults, $48 children 12 and under (book online for specials).

Blue Hawaiian Helicopters ★★ TOUR   Some of Maui's most spectacular scenery—3,000-foot-tall waterfalls thundering away in the chiseled heart of the West Maui Mountains, say, or Piilanihale, an impressive 3-acre heiau (temple) hidden away in Hana—can only be seen from the air. Blue Hawaiian can escort you there on one of their two types of helicopters: A-star or Eco-Star. Both are good, but the latter is worth the extra cash for its bucket seats (raised in the rear) and wraparound windows. Tours range from 30-minute flyovers to 2-hour excursions exploring Maui and Molokai or the Big Island. Be aware that if you visit another island, a good portion of the tour will be over ocean—not much to see. The 65-minute Complete Island Tour is the best value, especially if it's been raining and the waterfalls are gushing. After exploring West Maui, your pilot will flirt at the edges of Haleakala National Park so you can peer into the crater's paint-box colors, and then zip over Oprah's organic farm in Kula. Tip: Seats in the back can actually be better for photos, since you can press camera up to window. Wear plain, dark colors so your clothing doesn't reflect off the glass.

1 Kahului Airport Rd., Kahului. www.bluehawaiian.com. © **800/745-2583** or 808/871-8844. Flight times range 30–90 min. and cost $153–$510. Parking & flight video extra.

Maui Nei Native Expeditions ★★ TOUR   Discover the royal and supernatural history of Lahaina on this fascinating 2-hour walking tour. Your native Hawaiian *kumu,* or guide, will chant, tell stories, and reveal

MAUI FARMS: stop & smell the lavender

Idyllic farms abound across Maui. Many open their doors to visitors and have terrific island-grown products for purchase. To spend the day farm-hopping, join Marilyn Jansen Lopes and her husband, Rick. The sweet, knowledgeable guides of **Maui Country Farm Tours** ★★ (www.mauicountryfarmtours.com; ✆ 808/283-9131) offer an overview of Valley Isle agriculture and regale guests with anecdotes and extra treats along the way. They share their love of Maui plus historic background of the island's sugar mills, coffee plantations, family farms, and vineyards. Tours in eight-seat, air-conditioned buses start at $160 and include lunch. Their **Halfway to Hana** tour features tropical fruit tasting and waterfall dips when weather allows.

If you want to explore Maui's upcountry farms on your own, start by taking a detour on wild Omaopio Road to meet the frisky kids at the sweet, off-the-beaten-path **Surfing Goat Dairy** ★★ (3651 Omaopio Rd., Kula; www.surfinggoatdairy.com; ✆ **808/878-2870;** Mon–Sat 9am–5pm, Sun 9am–2pm). When you spot the surfboard nailed to the tree, you'll know you're close. Daily farm tours are $12 adults and $8 for kids. Book in advance if you want to help with evening

chores—milking mama goats (Mon–Sat 3:15pm; $17 adults, $14 children). Cheese aficionados will appreciate the **Grand Dairy Tours**: 2 hours of cheesemaking and sampling the farm's awardwinning chèvre, quarks, and truffles.

Never heard of a vodka farm? Neither had I until **Ocean Organic Vodka** ★★ (4051 Omaopio Rd., Kula; www.oceanvodka.com; ✆ **808/877-0009**) opened just below Surfing Goat Dairy. Sustainably harvested organic sugarcane is blended with deep ocean mineral water to make fine-quality liquor. See how it's done at this solar-powered distillery halfway up the leeward slope of Haleakala. (The views alone are worth the price of admission.) Fun and informative tours are $12 a person (ages 12 and up). Lunch ($27) can be added with 24-hour advance notice. Those 21 and over can sample various spirits (and vodka-filled truffles!) and take home a souvenir shot glass. It's open daily 9:30am to 5pm.

Stop and smell the **Alii Kula Lavender** ★★ (1100 Waipoli Rd., Kula; www.aliikulalavender.com; ✆ **808/878-3004**), at this gorgeous property set high up on the leeward slope of Haleakala. On the 30-minute walking tour (5 tours daily; $12 with advance reservation), you can sniff multiple varieties of lavender and

obscure sites of great import to the Hawaiian monarchy. If you haven't viewed the queen's birthing stone or visited the former home of a powerful lizard goddess, you haven't really seen Lahaina. Tours support the restoration of Mokuula, one of the most significant archaeological sites in all of Hawaii—currently hidden beneath an unused ball field. 505 Front St., Lahaina. www.mauinei.com. ✆ **808/283-4201.** 2-hour tour $50.

Temptation Tours ★ TOUR   If you'd rather leave the driving to someone else, this tour company will chauffeur you to Maui's top sites in a comfy deluxe van—much more luxurious than the large, crowded buses used by other agencies. Book a pre-dawn trip to the summit of Haleakala tropical flowers and leave with a fragrant bouquet. The store is chock-full of great culinary products (lavender seasonings, honey, jelly, and teas) and bath and body goodies (the salve is a lifesaver). General admission is $3; lunches and/or treasure hunts for kids can be arranged with 24-hour notice.

Also on Waipoli Road, **O'o Farm** ★★★ (651 Waipoli Rd., Kula; www.oofarm.com; *C* **808/667-4341**) hosts scrumptious seed-to-cup breakfast tours and gourmet lunches. It's pure delight to stroll through the 8½-acre citrus and coffee orchard and biodynamic farm, which was planted to supply the owners'

West side restaurants: Pacifico, Feast at Lele and Aina Gourmet Market. Pluck your own coffee beans, learn how ripe cherries become drinkable roasts, and then settle under the vine-covered canopy for a feast. Chef Daniel Eskelsen makes magic happen with his outdoor wood-burning oven, delivering dish after mouth-watering dish to the rustic table. The focaccia with Hawaiian sea salt is worth the price of admission all by itself. It's BYOB and costs $58—well worth it if you make this your main meal of the day. Bring sun protection, a light jacket, walking shoes, and your camera. The views from this elevation are stellar.

to witness the sunrise (followed by tasting tours at Surfing Goat Dairy and Ocean Organic Vodka; see below) or a picnic out in Hana. You'll pass numerous waterfalls and stop often, but don't expect to swim or get muddy hiking. The Hana Sky-Trek is actually a pretty great value; the 6-hour adventure starts with a drive (and swim stops) along the lush East Maui coast to Hana, where you board a helicopter for a scenic flight back home over hidden waterfalls and Haleakala National Park. The eight-person vans are safe and roomy, tour guides are generally knowledgeable, and the chicken wraps, seared ono, and brownies for lunch are tasty. www.temptationtours.com. *C* **800/817-1234** or 808/878-8888. All-day tours $225–$386. Free hotel pickup.

Unique Maui Tours ★★ TOUR If you want to see Maui from a local's perspective, hop into "Ella," your luxury chariot for a day of sweet, sweaty, muddy adventure. As you cruise around the island, you'll stop frequently to swim in waterfalls, hike up scenic ridges, and splash through secluded tide pools. Delphine Berbigier is an experienced guide who shares her enthusiasm with on small, personalized tours. For a memorable night, book a full moon hike!

www.uniquemauitours.com. ℂ **844/550-6284.** All-day tours $595 for 1–2 people, $79 per additional guest. Free hotel pickup.

BEACHES

West Maui

KAANAPALI BEACH ★★

Four-mile-long Kaanapali is one of Maui's most famous beaches. Recent storm events have shrunk its sugary golden expanse, though you'll still find somewhere to plunk down a towel. A paved walkway links hotels, open-air restaurants, and the Whalers Village shopping center. Summertime swimming is excellent. The best snorkeling is around Black Rock, in front of the Sheraton, where the water is clear, calm, and populated with clouds of tropical fish. Facilities include outdoor showers; you can also use the restrooms at the hotel pools. Various watersports outfitters and beach vendors line up in front of the hotels. Turn off Honoapiilani Highway into the Kaanapali Resort. Parking can be a problem—the free public access lots are small and hard to find. Look for the blue shoreline access signs at the Hyatt's southernmost lot, between Whalers Village and the Westin, and just before the Sheraton. Otherwise, park (for top dollar) at the mall or any resort.

KAHEKILI BEACH PARK ★★★

Off Puukolii Road in Kaanapali and often referred to as "North Kaanapali" or "Airport Beach," this park gets top marks for everything: grassy lawn with a pavilion and palm trees, plenty of soft sand, and a vibrant coral reef a few fin-kicks from shore. Herbivorous fish (surgeonfish and rainbow-colored parrotfish) are off-limits to fishermen here, so the snorkeling is truly excellent. Facilities include picnic tables, barbecues, showers, restrooms, and parking. On a stretch of coast where parking is often a problem, this park with its big shady lot is a gem.

KAPALUA BEACH ★★

This beach cove is the stuff of dreams: a golden crescent bordered by two palm-studded points. The sandy bottom slopes gently to deep water at the bay mouth; the water's so clear that you can see it turn to green and then deep blue. Protected from strong winds and currents by the lava-rock promontories, Kapalua's calm waters are ideal for swimmers of all

Beaches & Outdoor Activities on Maui

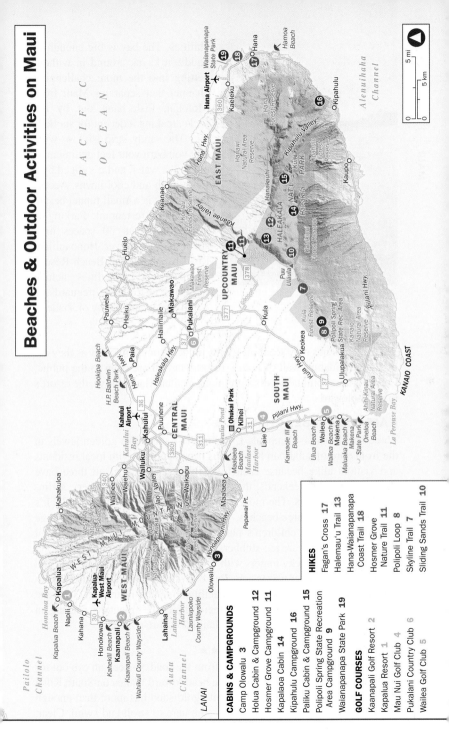

CABINS & CAMPGROUNDS

Camp Olowalu **3**
Holua Cabin & Campground **12**
Hosmer Grove Campground **11**
Kapalaoa Cabin **14**
Kipahulu Campground **16**
Paliku Cabin & Campground **15**
Polipoli Spring State Recreation
  Area Campground **9**
Waianapanapa State Park **19**

GOLF COURSES

Kaanapali Golf Resort **2**
Kapalua Resort **1**
Mau Nui Golf Club **4**
Pukalani Country Club **6**
Wailea Golf Club **5**

HIKES

Fagan's Cross **17**
Halemau'u Trail **13**
Hana-Waianapanapa
  Coast Trail **18**
Hosmer Grove
  Nature Trail **11**
Polipoli Loop **8**
Skyline Trail **7**
Sliding Sands Trail **10**

Bodysurfing

abilities. The bay is big enough to paddle a kayak around in without getting into the more challenging channel that separates Maui from Molokai. Fish hang out by the rocks, making it decent for snorkeling. The sandy strip isn't so wide that you burn your feet getting in or out of the water, and it's edged by a shady path and cool lawns. Access the beach via a small tunnel beside Merriman's restaurant. Parking is limited to about 30 spaces in a small lot off Lower Honoapiilani Road by Napili Kai Beach Resort, so arrive early. Facilities include showers, restrooms, lifeguards, a rental shack, and plenty of shade.

South Maui

Wailea's beaches may seem off limits, hidden from plain view as they are by an intimidating wall of luxury resorts, but all are open to the public. Look for the shoreline access signs along Wailea Alanui Drive, the resort's main boulevard.

KAMAOLE III BEACH PARK ★

Three beach parks—Kamaole I, II, and III—stand like golden jewels in the front yard of suburban Kihei. This trio is popular with local residents and visitors alike because each is easily accessible and all three have shady lawns. On weekends, they're jam-packed with picnickers, swimmers, and snorkelers. The most popular is Kamaole III, or "Kam-3." It's the biggest of the three beaches, with wide pockets of gold sand, a huge grassy lawn, and a children's playground. Swimming is safe here, but scattered lava rocks are toe-stubbers at the water line. Both the North and South Shores are rocky fingers with a surge big enough to attract fish and snorkelers; the winter waves appeal to bodysurfers. Kam-3 is also a wonderful place to watch the sunset. Facilities include restrooms, showers, picnic tables, barbecue grills, and lifeguards. There's plenty of parking on South Kihei Road across from the Maui Parkshore condos.

KEAWAKAPU BEACH PARK ★★

You can't see this mile-long beauty from the road, so keep an eye out for the blue shoreline-access signs as you head toward Wailea on South Kihei Road. The long expanse of soft, white-gold sand has more than enough room for the scores of people who come here to stroll and swim. Clear, aquamarine waves tumble to shore—just the right size for gentle riding, with or without a board. During winter, mama whales come in close to give birth and teach their calves the finer points of whale acrobatics. Dip your head underwater to eavesdrop on the humpbacks' songs. At any time of year, gorge yourself on phenomenal sunsets. The beach has three separate entrances: The first is an unpaved lot just past the Mana Kai Maui hotel, the second is a shady paved lot at the corner of South Kihei Road and Kilohana Drive (cross the street to the beach), and the third is a large lot at the terminus of South Kihei Road. Facilities include restrooms (at the third entrance only), showers, and parking.

ULUA BEACH ★★

Ulua's golden stretch of sand is popular with sunbathers, snorkelers, and scuba divers alike. Some of Wailea's best snorkeling is found on the adjoining reef. The ocean bottom is shallow and gently slopes down to deeper waters, making swimming generally safe. In high season (Christmas–Mar and June–Aug), it's carpeted with beach towels and packed with sunbathers like sardines in cocoa butter. Facilities include showers and restrooms. Beach equipment can be rented at the nearby Wailea Ocean Activity Center. Look for the blue shoreline access sign on Wailea Alanui Drive near the Wailea Beach Marriott Resort & Spa.

WAILEA BEACH ★

Brigades of resort umbrellas and beach chairs make it challenging to appreciate this beach's pristine beauty. It's the front yard of the Four Seasons and the Grand Wailea, and hotel staff makes plenty use of the deep sand. Still, the view out to sea is magnificent, framed by neighboring Kahoolawe, Lanai, and the tiny crescent of Molokini. From shore, you can see Pacific humpback whales in season (Dec–Mar) and unreal sunsets nightly. Facilities include restrooms, outdoor showers, and limited free parking at the blue shoreline access sign, just south of the Grand Wailea on Wailea Alanui Drive.

MALUAKA BEACH ★★★

For a less crowded beach experience, head south. Development falls off dramatically as you travel toward Makena and its wild, dry countryside of thorny *kiawe* trees. Maluaka Beach is notable for its serene beauty and its views of Molokini Crater, the offshore islet, and Kahoolawe, the so-called "target" island (it was used as a bombing target from 1945 until the early 1990s). This sandy, sun-kissed crescent is bound on one end by a grassy knoll and has little shade, so bring your own umbrella. Swimming is idyllic here, where the water is calm and sea turtles paddle by. Facilities include restrooms, showers, picnic tables, and parking. Along Makena Alanui, turn right on Makena Road, and head down to the shore.

MAKENA STATE BEACH PARK (BIG BEACH) ★★★

One of the most popular beaches on Maui, Makena is so vast it never feels crowded. Locals call it "Big Beach"—it's more than 100 feet wide and stretches out 3,300 feet from Puu Olai, the 360-foot cinder cone on its north end to its southern rocky point. The golden sand is luxuriant, deep, and soft, but the shorebreak is steep and powerful. Many a visitor has broken an arm in the surf here. If you're an inexperienced swimmer, better to watch the pros shred waves on skimboards. Facilities are limited to portable toilets, but there's plenty of parking and lifeguards at the first two entrances. Dolphins often frequent these waters, and nearly every afternoon a heavy cloud rolls in, providing welcome relief from the sun.

If you clamber up Puu Olai, you'll find **Little Beach** on the other side, a small crescent of sand where assorted nudists work on their all-over tans in defiance of the law. The shoreline doesn't drop off quite so steeply here, and bodysurfing is terrific—no pun intended.

Upcountry & East Maui

HOOKIPA BEACH PARK ★★★

Hookipa means "hospitality," and this sandy beach on Maui's north shore certainly rolls out the red carpet out for waveriders. Two miles past Paia on the Hana Highway, it's among the world's top spots for windsurfing and kiting—thanks to tradewinds that kick up whitecaps offshore. Hookipa offers no less than five surf breaks, and daring watermen and -women paddle out to carve waves up to 25 feet tall. Voyeurs are welcome as well; the cliff-top parking lot has a bird's-eye view. On flat days,

Makena Beach

Hookipa Beach Park

snorkelers explore the reef's treasure trove of marine life: Gentle garden eels wave below the surface. Sea turtles hunt for jellyfish and haul out by the dozens to nap on the sand. More than once, a rare Hawaiian monk seal has popped ashore during a surf contest. Facilities include restrooms, showers, pavilions, picnic tables, barbecue grills, and parking.

H. P. BALDWIN BEACH PARK ★★

This beach park draws lots of locals: dog walkers, yoga enthusiasts, boogie boarders, fishermen, and young families. The far ends of the beach are safest for swimming: "the cove" in the lee of the rocks at the north end, and "baby beach" at the south end, where an exposed reef creates a natural sandy swimming pool—often with a current that's fun to swim against. Facilities include a pavilion with picnic tables, barbecue grills, restrooms, showers, a semipaved parking area, a soccer field, and lifeguards. The park is busy on weekends and late afternoons; mornings and weekdays are much quieter. Heading east on Hana Highway, turn left at the soccer field just before reaching Paia.

WAIANAPANAPA STATE PARK ★★★

Jet-black sand, a cave pool, sea arches, blowholes, and historic *hala* groves: This dramatic 120-acre beach park offers many jewels. Listen to the lava boulders wash up in the foamy surf. Swim with caution; the sea here is churned by strong waves and rip currents. Watch the seabirds circle the offshore islet. Follow moss-covered stone steps through the tunnel of *hau* branches and dare yourself to plunge into the chilly freshwater cave. These are experiences that will make a deep impression on your psyche. Waianapanapa offers wonderful shoreline hikes and picnicking spots. You can follow the coastal trail for a long distance in both directions from the parking lot. Facilities include picnic tables, barbecue grills, restrooms, showers, tent sites, and 12 cabins (p. 387).

HAMOA BEACH ★★

James Michener called Hamoa "a beach so perfectly formed that I wonder at its comparative obscurity." Viewed from above, this half-moon-shaped, gray-sand beach is vision of paradise. The wide stretch of sand (a mix of coral and lava) is three football fields long and sits below 30-foot black-lava sea cliffs. Swells on this unprotected beach break offshore and roll in, making it a popular surfing and bodysurfing area. Hamoa is often swept by powerful rip currents, so take care. The calm left side is best for snorkeling in summer. Travaasa Hana resort has numerous facilities for guests, plus outdoor showers and restrooms for nonguests. Parking is limited. Look for the Hamoa Beach turnoff from Hana Highway.

WATERSPORTS

The watersports options on Maui are mind-boggling—from lazy snorkeling to high-energy kitesurfing and everything in between. Colorful, fish-filled reefs are easily accessible, often from a sandy beach.

You'll find rental gear and ocean toys all over the island. Most seaside hotels and resorts are stocked with watersports equipment (complimentary or rentals), from snorkels to kayaks to Hobies. **Snorkel Bob's** (www.snorkelbob.com) rents snorkel gear, boogie boards, wetsuits, and more at numerous locations: At Napili Bay, 5425 C Lower Honoapiilani Hwy., Lahaina (© **808/669-9603**); 1217 Front St. (behind Cannery Mall), Lahaina (© **808/661-4421**); 3350 Lower Honoapiilani Hwy. #201 (Near Times Supermarket), Honokowai (© **808/667-9999**); in Azeka's II Shopping Center, 1279 S. Kihei Rd., Kihei (© **808/875-6188**); 2411 S. Kihei Rd., Kihei (© **808/879-7449**); and 100 Wailea Ike Dr., Wailea (© **808/874-0011**). All locations are open daily from 8am to 5pm. If you're island-hopping, you can rent from a Snorkel Bob's location on one island and return to a branch on another.

Boss Frog's Dive, Surf, and Bike Shops (www.bossfrog.com) has eight locations for snorkel, boogie board, longboard, and stand-up paddleboard rentals and other gear, including these locations: 150 Lahainaluna Rd. in Lahaina (© **808/661-3333**); 3636 Lower Honoapiilani Rd. in Kaanapali (© **808/665-1200**); Napili Plaza, 5095 Napilihau St. in Napili (© **808/669-4949**); and 1215 S. Kihei Rd. (© **808/891-0077**), 1770 S. Kihei Rd. (© **808/874-5225**), and Dolphin Plaza, 2395 S. Kihei Rd. (© **808/875-4477**) in Kihei. Their $30 weekly snorkel rentals are the best deal.

Boating

You'll need a boat to visit the crescent-shaped islet **Molokini,** one of the best snorkel and scuba spots in Hawaii. Trips to the island of **Lanai** (see chapter 8) are also popular for a day of snorkeling. Bring a towel, a swimsuit, sunscreen, and a hat on a snorkel cruise; everything else is usually included. If you'd like to go a little deeper than snorkeling allows, consider trying **SNUBA,** a shallow-water diving system in which you are connected by a 20-foot air hose to an air tank that floats on a raft at the water's surface. Most of these snorkel boats offer it for an additional cost; it's usually around $60 for a half-hour or so. No certification is required for SNUBA. For fishing charters, see "Sport Fishing," below.

Maui Classic Charters ★ TOUR   Maui Classic Charters offers morning and afternoon **snorkel cruises to Molokini** on *Four Winds II*, a 55-foot glass-bottom catamaran. Rates for the morning sail are $105 for adults, $75 for children 3 to 12; continental breakfast and barbecue lunch are available for purchase. The afternoon sail is a steal at $49; though the captain usually only visits Coral Gardens, which is accessible from shore. All *Four Winds* trips include complimentary beer, wine, and soda; snorkeling gear and instruction; and sport fishing along the way. Those hoping to catch sight of dolphins should book a trip on the state-of-the-art catamaran *Maui Magic*. A 5-hour snorkel journey to both Molokini and Makena costs $120 for adults, $90 for children 5 to 12, and includes continental breakfast; a barbecue lunch; beer, wine, and soda; snorkel gear; and instruction.

Maalaea Harbor, slip 55 and slip 80. www.mauicharters.com. ✆ **800/736-5740** or 808/879-8188. Prices vary depending on cruise; check website for discounts.

Pacific Whale Foundation ★★ TOUR   This not-for-profit foundation supports its whale research, public education, and conservation programs by offering **whale-watch cruises, wild dolphin encounters,** and **snorkel tours,** some to Molokini, Honolua, and Lanai. Numerous daily trips are offered out of both Lahaina and Maalaea harbors. Two special tours include the **Island Rhythms Sunset Cruise** with Eric Gilliom (a honey-voiced local entertainer who woos whales with rollicking tunes) and **stargazing cruises** with Harriet Witt, a wonderful astronomer and storyteller.

300 Maalaea Rd., Suite 211, Wailuku. (Also: Lahaina Ocean Store, 612 Front St., Lahaina.) www.pacificwhale.org. ✆ **800/942-5311** or 808/249-8811. Trips from $33 adults, $20 children 7–12, free for 1 child 6 and under per adult; snorkeling cruises from $93 adults, $35 children. Book online for a 10% discount.

Scotch Mist Sailing Charters ★★ TOUR   This 50-foot Santa Cruz sailboat offers intimate, exhilarating 4-hour **snorkel-sail cruises,** limited to 25 passengers. You'll visit the glittering outer reefs at Olowalu. Rates ($109 ages 13 and up, $55 kids 5–12) include a fruit platter and beverages, gear, and instruction. The evening champagne sunset cruises ($70 13 and up; $35 children 5–12) are an elegant, gorgeous way to end the day, especially during winter when they double as a whale watch. *Note:* No children under 5 allowed unless the whole boat is chartered.

Lahaina Harbor, slip 2. www.scotchmistsailingcharters.com. ✆ **808/661-0386.** Prices vary depending on cruise, starting at $60.

Trilogy Excursions ★★★ TOUR   Trilogy offers my favorite **snorkel-sail trips.** The family-run company prioritizes environmental stewardship—along with ensuring you have a stellar marine adventure. Hop aboard one of Trilogy's fleet of custom-built catamarans, from 54 to 65 feet long, for a 9-mile **Maui-to-Lanai sail** from Lahaina Harbor to Hulopoe Marine Preserve and a fun-filled day of sailing and snorkeling. This is the only cruise that offers a personalized ground tour of the island and the only one with rights to take you to Hulopoe Beach. The full-day trip costs $205 for adults, $153 ages 13 to 18, and $100 for kids 3 to 12.

Trilogy also offers **snorkel-sail trips to Molokini.** This half-day trip leaves from Maalaea Harbor and costs $135 for adults, $101 for teens, and $68 for kids 3 to 12. These are the most expensive sail-snorkel cruises on Maui, but they're worth every penny. The crews are fun and knowledgeable, and the boats are comfortable and well equipped. All trips include breakfast (Mom's homemade cinnamon buns) and a very good barbecue lunch (onboard on the half-day trip; on land on the Lanai trip). During winter, 2-hour **whale watches** depart conveniently right from the sand on Kaanapali Beach ($59 adults, $44 teens, $30 children).

The **Captain's Sunset Dinner Sail** is a romantic adults-only adventure. Couples enjoy a four-course feast at private, candlelit tables, complete with handcrafted cocktails and cozy blankets ($129 per person). www.sailtrilogy.com. ✆ **888/225-MAUI** or 808/874-5649. Prices and departure points vary depending on cruise.

DAY CRUISES TO LANAI

You can visit the island of Lanai by booking a trip with **Trilogy** (see above) or by taking the passenger ferry.

Expeditions Lahaina/Lanai Passenger Ferry ★ FERRY The cheapest way to reach Lanai is via ferry, which runs five times a day, 365 days a year. It leaves Lahaina at 6:45 and 9:15am, and 12:45, 3:15, and 5:45pm; the return ferry from Lanai's Manele Bay leaves at 8 and 10:30am, and at 2, 4:30, and 6:45pm. The 9-mile channel crossing takes between 45 minutes and an hour, depending on sea conditions. Reservations are strongly recommended. During winter, the trip doubles as a whale watch. You can walk from the harbor to Hulopoe Beach, but if you want to explore the island further, you'll have to rent a car or book a tour. See p. 461 in chapter 8 for details.
Ferries depart from Lahaina Harbor; office: 658 Front St., Suite 127, Lahaina. www.go-lanai.com. ✆ **800/695-2624** or 808/661-3756. Round-trip fares from Maui to Lanai $60 adults, $40 children 2–11.

Ocean Kayaking

Numerous companies launch kayak tours from South and West Maui beaches. Some are definitely better than others—the difference being the personal attention from the guides and their level of experience. Kayaking can be a slog if you have to keep up with your guide, rather than paddle alongside someone who shares local knowledge. My favorite operator, **Hawaiian Paddle Sports ★★★** (www.hawaiianpaddlesports.com; ✆ **808/875-4848**) launches trips from Makena, Olowalu or Honolua Bay.

Ocean kayaking

The trips are pricy but private, starting at $149 per person for 2-4 guests. But you will get a wildlife adventure like no other, with a personal guide ready to point out snowflake eels hiding in the coral, guide you to hidden caverns, and shoot photos of you swimming with sea turtles.

Aloha Kayaks Maui ★★ (www.alohakayaksmaui.com; ☏ **808/270-3318**) is both excellent and more affordable, with trips starting at $95 for a max of eight people. Professional, informative, and eco-aware guides lead 3-hour trips that launch from Makena Landing (secluded coves with underwater arches and caves) or Olowalu (vibrant coral reefs and possible manta ray sightings). During whale season, guides can steer you towards the gentle giants for a once-in-a-lifetime encounter.

Outrigger Canoe

Outrigger canoes are much revered in Hawaiian culture, and several hotels—among them, the Fairmont Kea Lani Maui and the Andaz Maui—offer this wonderful cultural activity right off the beach. If you want to give paddling a try, expect to work as a team with five other paddlers. Your guide and steersman will show you how to haul the sleek boat into the water, properly enter and exit the boat, and paddle for maximum efficiency.

Hawaiian Paddle Sports ★★★ CANOE TOUR   For an intimate adventure on the great blue, book an outrigger canoe trip with Hawaiian Paddle Sports. Learn how to paddle in sync with your family or friends, just as the ancient Polynesians did when colonizing these islands. You'll visit some of Maui's very best snorkel spots: Makena Landing or the outer reef at Olowalu. The owner, Tim Lara, is one of the best in the business, brimming with knowledge about the island's culture, history, and marine life. When turtles, whales, manta rays, or monk seals surface alongside your canoe, you'll feel like a *National Geographic* explorer. And you'll have the pictures to prove it. Lara's guides are whizzes with a GoPro camera; after the trip they'll send you under- and above-water shots guaranteed to dazzle your friends. If you're feeling sporty, book a canoe surfing trip and race down the face of breaking waves. Hawaiian Paddle Sports also offers kayak tours, and surf and SUP instruction.

Departs from various locations. www.hawaiianpaddlesports.com. © **808/442-6436.** $149–$199 per person. Prices drop for groups.

Ocean Rafting

If you're semi-adventurous and looking for a wetter, wilder experience, try ocean rafting. The inflatable rafts hold 6 to 24 passengers. Tours usually include snorkeling and coastal cruising. Pregnant women and people with back problems are advised to avoid. During winter, these maneuverable boats offer exciting whale-watching tours.

Captain Steve's Rafting Excursions (www.captainsteves.com; © **808/667-5565**) offers 7-hour snorkel trips from **Mala Wharf** in Lahaina to the waters around **Lanai** (you don't actually land on the island). **Dolphin sightings** are almost guaranteed on these action-packed excursions. Discounted online rates of $135 for adults and $95 for children 5 to 12 include continental breakfast, deli-style lunch, snorkel gear, and wet suits.

One of the most reasonable outfitters is **Hawaii Ocean Rafting** (www.hawaiioceanrafting.com; © **808/661-7238**), which operates out of Lahaina Harbor and zips out towards **Lanai.** The best deal is the 4.5-hour morning tour ($85 adults, $72 children 5–12); it includes three snorkeling stops and time spent watching for dolphins, plus continental breakfast and midmorning snacks. Check the website for discounts.

Scuba Diving

Maui offers plenty of undersea attractions worth strapping on a tank for. Most divers start with **Molokini** (see "Snorkeling," below). In addition to the popular basin, experienced divers can explore the crater's dramatic **back wall** ★★★, which plunges 350 feet and is frequented by larger marine animals and schools of rare butterflyfish. Other top sites include **Mala Wharf,** the **St. Anthony** (a sunken longliner), and **Five Graves** at Makena Landing. Don't be scared off by the latter's ominous name—it's a magical spot with sea caves and arches.

Ed Robinson's Diving Adventures ★★ DIVE COMPANY   Ed Robinson, a widely published underwater photographer, offers specialized charters for small groups. Two-tank dives are $145 ($168 with all the gear). The check-in for the dive is at 165 Halekuai St. in Kihei, and the boat departs from the Kihei Boat Ramp.

165 Halekuai St., Kihei. www.mauiscuba.com. © **808/879-3584.**

Maui Dreams Dive Company ★★★ DIVE COMPANY   Run by husband-and-wife team Rachel and Don Domingo, this is the best full-service dive operation on the island. Stop in at their South Maui shop, and you might just end up scuba certified ($420 for a 3-day course). The skilled dive masters and instructors are so fun that they make every aspect of getting geared up to go underwater enjoyable. You don't need certification for an intro shore dive at Ulua Beach ($69), but you do for a two-tank adventure to **Molokini** aboard the *Maui Diamond II* ($159). Captain Don regales his passengers with jokes, snacks, and local trivia. Rachel has a knack for finding camouflaged **frogfish** on the reef. Even experienced divers will be dazzled by the **guided scooter dives** ($99–$129). The rideable rockets allow you to zip along the ocean's floor and visit sunken **World War II wrecks,** caves, and turtle-cleaning stations. The community-minded Domingos host regular reef cleanups, **pirate- and princess-themed dives,** and underwater Easter egg hunts.

1993 S. Kihei Rd. www.mauidreamsdiveco.com. ℂ **808/874-5332.**

Mike Severns Diving ★★★ DIVE COMPANY   For personalized diving tours on a 38-foot Munson/Hammerhead boat (with a freshwater shower), call Pauline Fiene at Mike Severns Diving. She and her fellow dive masters lead trips for a maximum of 12 people, divided into two groups of six. Exploring the underwater world is educational and fun with Fiene, a biologist who has authored several spectacular marine-photography books and leads dives during **coral spawning** events. She's particularly knowledgeable about nudibranchs, two of which have been named for her, *Hallaxa paulinae* and *Hypselodoris paulinae.* Two-tank dives are $145, including equipment rental, or $139 if you bring all your own equipment. Experienced divers can rent underwater cameras and tag along behind the pro photographers. Trips depart from Kihei Boat Ramp. www.mikeseversdiving.com. ℂ **808/879-6596.**

Hawaiian green sea turtles

Snorkeling

Snorkeling on Maui is easy—there are so many great spots where you can just wade in the water with a mask and look down and see tropical fish. If you haven't snorkeled before, or are a little rusty, practice breathing through your snorkel before you get out on the water. Mornings are best; blustery trade winds kick in around noon. Maui's best snorkeling spots include **Ulua** and **Mokapu Beaches** in Wailea; **Olowalu** along the Honoapiilani Highway; **Black Rock** at the north end of Kaanapali Beach; and, just beyond Black Rock, **Kahekili Beach ★★★**.

Three **truly terrific snorkel spots** are difficult to get to but rewarding—they're home to Hawaii's tropical marine life at its best:

Ahihi-Kinau Natural Preserve ★★ NATURAL ATTRACTION This 2,000-acre state natural area reserve in the lee of Cape Kinau, on Maui's rugged south coast, is home to bejeweled Ahihi Bay. It was here that Haleakala spilled its last red-hot lava into the sea, so the entrance to the ocean is sharp and rocky. Ease into the water to see brilliant corals and abundant fish. Fishing is strictly forbidden, and the fish know it; they're everywhere in this series of rocky coves and black-lava tide pools. To get here, drive south of Makena and watch for signs. A state naturalist is often on-site to offer advice. *Note:* The Hawaii Department of Land and Natural Resources has temporarily restricted access to portions of the popular and heavily used preserve. Visit www.hawaii.gov/dlnr/dofaw for details.

Honolua Bay ★★★ NATURAL ATTRACTION The snorkeling in this wide, secluded bay is worth the drive out to West Maui's far corner. Spectacular coral formations glitter beneath the surface. Turtles, rays, and a variety of snappers and goatfish cruise along beside you. In the crevices are eels, lobster, and rainbow-hued fish. Dolphins sometimes come here to rest. Follow Honoapiilani Highway past Kapalua to mile marker 32. Follow the dirt path through the dense forest to the sea.

Molokini ★★★ NATURAL ATTRACTION A sunken crater that sits like a crescent moon fallen from the sky, almost midway between Maui and the uninhabited island of Kahoolawe, Molokini stands like a scoop against the tide. This offshore site is very popular, thanks to astounding visibility (you can often peer down 100 ft.) and an abundance of marine life, from manta rays to clouds of yellow butterflyfish. On its concave side, Molokini serves as a natural sanctuary and preserve for tropical fish. Molokini is accessible only by boat, and snorkelers commute here daily in a fleet of dive boats. See "Boating," above, for outfitters that can take you here. Expect crowds in high season.

Sport Fishing

The best way to reserve a sport-fishing charter is through the experts; the top booking desk in the state is **Sportfish Hawaii ★** (www.sportfishhawaii.com; ✆ **877/388-1376**), which books boats on all the islands. These fishing vessels have been inspected and must meet rigorous criteria to guarantee that you'll have a great time. Prices start at $1,095 for a full-day exclusive charter (meaning you, plus five friends, get the entire boat to yourself); it's $699 for a half-day exclusive. **Bottom-fishing** trips for delicious snappers run $149 per adult; you'll share the boat with up to nine other anglers.

Stand-up Paddling (SUP) & Surfing

If you want to learn to surf, the best beginners' spots are **Charley Young Cove** in Kihei (the far north end of Kalama Beach Park), the break in front of **505 Front Street** in Lahaina, and several breaks along Honoapiilani Highway, including **Ukumehame.** The first two are the most convenient, with surf schools nearby. The breaks along Honoapiilani Highway tend to be longer, wider, and less crowded—perfect if you're confident enough to go solo.

During summer, gentle swells roll in long and slow along the South Shore. It's the best time to practice your stance on a longboard. During winter, the North Shore becomes the playground for adrenaline junkies who drop in on thundering waves 30 feet tall and higher. If you want to watch, head to **Hookipa** or **Honolua Bay,** where you can view the action from a cliff above.

Stand-up paddling (SUP) is one of Hawaii's oldest and newest ocean sports. Practiced by ancient Hawaiian kings, it's now back in fashion. You can SUP just about anywhere you can surf—and more, since you don't need a swell to get going, just a wide board and paddle, strong arms, and some balance. (And if you lack the latter two, willingness will make up for it.) Gliding over the fish-filled reefs with an unobstructed view of the islands on the horizon is a top-notch experience. Experienced watermen/women can rent a full range of surf, windsurf, and stand-up paddle boards from **Maui Windsurf Company,** 22 Hana Hwy., Kahului (www.maui windsurfcompany.com; ✆ **808/877-4816**).

Maui Surfer Girls ★★★ SURF INSTRUCTION   Despite its name, MSG offers coed surf and SUP instruction for groms and Betties alike. Owner Dustin Tester is a big-wave surf pioneer; she's among the first women to charge "Jaws," one of the planet's biggest breaks, and her commitment to helping others shred waves is inspirational. (She even coached her dog Luna to hang ten alongside her.) Personalized lessons at Ukumehame Beach Park with Tester or her teammates start at $89. But MSG's best offering is the **weeklong surf camp.** If you've got a teen girl who dreams of growing gills, sign her up for 7 saltwater-soaked days full of watersports, camaraderie, healthy food, island adventures, and campfire counsel. The Olowalu Campground serves as headquarters for a transformational experience. www.mauisurfergirls.com. ✆ **808/201-6879.**

Maui Stand Up Paddle Boarding ★★ SURF INSTRUCTION   Get up on a board and "walk on water" with a private SUP lesson or guided tour ($199 for one person, $139 for two or more). Adventures start out with an overview of paddling techniques on shore, then you'll launch into the water at Makena Landing or Olowalu for two salty hours. (Wear a water-friendly hat and sunglasses.) During whale season, you might be surprised by the exhalation of a mighty humpback nearby. Your instructor will snap action shots of you and deliver them by the day's end. The company also rents NAISH inflatable boards for $55 per day.

27-B Halekaui St. Kihei. www.mauistanduppaddleboarding.com. ✆ **808/568-0151.**

Maui Surf Clinics ★ SURF INSTRUCTION   One of Maui's oldest surf schools is just steps away from the reliable break at 505 Front Street. Paddle out to the swell and your instructor will cheer you on as you hang ten for the first time. It's $85 per person for a 2-hour group lesson; private classes are $170. All instructors are lifeguard certified.

505 Front St., Suite 224B, Lahaina. www.mauisurfclinics.com. ✆ **808/244-SURF [7873].**

Zack Howard Surf ★ SURF INSTRUCTION   Zack is a lifelong waterman who will help you stand up and surf—even on your very first wave. While most surf schools take newbies out into the crowded breaks at Charley Young in Kihei or the Lahaina Breakwall, Zack steers beginning students into the surf at Ukumehame, a gentle, consistent rolling break alongside Honoapiilani Highway. He also helps intermediate surfers sharpen their skills at world-famous Hookipa. In between swells, Zack offers tips on how to improve your stance and technique. Lessons start at $100 per person for 1½ hours.

www.zackhowardsurf.com. ✆ **808/214-7766.**

Whale-Watching

Maui is a favorite with Hawaiian humpback whales, who get downright frisky in the surrounding waters from about November to May (though Jan and Feb are the peak months). Seeing the massive marine mammals leap out of the sea or perfect their tail slap is mesmerizing. You can hear them sing underwater, too! Just duck your head a foot below the surface and listen for creaks, groans, and otherworldly serenades.

WHALE-WATCHING FROM SHORE   Just look out to sea anytime during the winter months. There's no best time of day, but it seems that when the sea is glassy and there's no wind, the whales appear. Others claim the opposite: that whales are most active when the water is pocked with whitecaps.

Good whale-watching spots on Maui include:

o **MCGREGOR POINT**   On the way to Lahaina, there's a scenic lookout at mile marker 9 (just before you get to the Lahaina Tunnel); it's a good viewpoint to scan for whales.

o **OLOWALU REEF** Along the straight part of Honoapiilani Highway, between McGregor Point and Olowalu, you'll sometimes see whales leap out of the water. Their appearance can bring traffic to a screeching halt: People abandon their cars and run down to the sea to watch, causing a major traffic jam. If you stop, pull off the road so others can pass.

o **WAILEA BEACH MARRIOTT RESORT & SPA** In the Wailea coastal walk, stop at this resort to look for whales through the telescope installed as a public service by the Hawaii Island Humpback Whale National Marine Sanctuary.

WHALE-WATCHING BY KAYAK & RAFT ★★ I recommend viewing humpback whales from a maneuverable, high-speed raft—you'll be close to the water and that much closer to the cetaceans. **Capt. Steve's Rafting Excursions** (www.captainsteves.com; ℅ **808/667-5565**) offers 2-hour whale-watching excursions out of Lahaina Harbor (from $55 adults, $45 children 5–12). *Tip:* Save $10 by booking the early-bird adventure, which leaves at 7:30am.

WHALE-WATCHING CRUISES Just about all of Hawaii's snorkel and dive boats become whale-watching boats in season; some of them even carry professional naturalists onboard so you'll know what you're seeing and drop hydrophones in the water so you can better hear the whales' song. For options, see "Boating," earlier in this section.

Windsurfing

Maui has Hawaii's best windsurfing beaches. In winter, windsurfers from around the world flock to the town of **Paia** to ride the waves; **Hookipa Beach ★★★**, known all over the globe for its brisk winds and excellent waves, is the site of several world championship contests. **Kanaha Beach,** west of Kahului Airport, also has dependable winds. When the winds turn northerly, **North Kihei** is the place to be (some days, you can even spot whales in the distance behind the windsurfers). **Ohukai Park,** the first beach as you enter South Kihei Road from the northern end, has good winds, plus parking, a long strip of grass to assemble your gear, and easy access to the water.

EQUIPMENT RENTALS & LESSONS **Hawaiian Sailboarding Techniques,** 425 Koloa St., Kahului (www.hstwindsurfing.com; ℅ **808/871-5423**), offers rentals and 2½-hour lessons from $99 at Kanaha Beach early in the morning before the breeze gets too strong for beginners. **Maui Windsurf Company,** 22 Hana Hwy., Kahului (www.mauiwindsurfcompany.com; ℅ **808/877-4816**), offers complete equipment rental (Goya boards, sails, rig harnesses, and roof racks) from $59, plus 2½-hour group lessons from $99 and private instruction at $99 per hour.

DAILY WIND & SURF CONDITIONS For reports on wind and surf conditions, call Hi-Tech's **Wind & Surf Report** at ℅ **808/877-3611,** ext. 2.

SURF VAN   Since most windsurf gear won't fit into a typical rental car, call **Aloha Rent-a-Car /Al West's Maui Vans** to rent a newish (or old) van by the week. Older vans start at $38 per day, four-day minimum. (www.mauivans.com; ℂ **808/877-0090**).

OTHER OUTDOOR ACTIVITIES
Biking
CRUISING HALEAKALA

Several companies offer the opportunity to coast down Haleakala, from near the summit to the shore, on basic cruiser bikes. It can be quite a thrilling experience—but one that should be approached with caution. Despite what various companies claim about their safety record, people have been injured and killed participating in this activity. If you do choose to go, pay close attention to the safety briefing. Bike tours aren't allowed in Haleakala National Park, so your van will take you to the summit first, and then drop you off just outside of the park. You'll descend through multiple climates and ecosystems, past eucalyptus groves and flower-filled gulches. But bear in mind: The roads are steep and curvy without designated bike lanes and little to no shoulder. During winter and the rainy season, conditions can be particularly harsh; you'll be saran-wrapped in rain gear. Temperatures at the summit can drop below freezing and 40-mph winds howl, so wear warm layers whatever the season.

Maui's oldest downhill company is **Maui Downhill** (www.maui downhill.com; ℂ **808/871-2155**), which offers sunrise bike tours, including breakfast and lunch stops (not hosted), starting at $189 (substantial discounts online). Be prepared for a 3am departure! **Mountain Riders Bike Tours** (www.mountainriders.com; ℂ **800/706-7700**) offers sunrise rides for $180 and midday trips for $160 (discounted if booked online). If you want to avoid the crowds and go down the mountain at your own pace (rather than in a choo-choo train of other bikers), call **Haleakala Bike Company** (www.bikemaui.com; ℂ **808/575-9575**). After assessing your skill, they'll outfit you with the latest gear and shuttle you up Haleakala. They also offer Haleakala sunrise tours sans bike—a decent option for folks who might feel too sleepy to pedal or drive.

RENTALS

Maui offers dynamic terrain for serious and amateur cyclists. If you've got the chops to pedal *up* Haleakala, the pros at **Maui Cyclery ★★★** (99 Hana Hwy., Paia; www.gocyclingmaui.com; ℂ **808/579-9009**) can outfit you and provide a support vehicle. Tour de France athletes launch their Maui training sessions from this full-service Paia bike shop, which rents top-of-the-line equipment and offers a range of guided tours. Shop owner Donny Arnoult hosts 6-day cycling camps and sponsors the annual Cycle to the Sun contest; riders travel from around the globe to tackle the 10,023-foot volcano on two wheels.

If **mountain biking** is more your style, hit up Moose at **Krank Cycles** ★★★ (1120 Makawao Ave., Makawao; www.krankmaui.com; ✆ **808/572-2299**) for a tricked-out bike and directions to the Makawao Forest trails.

Maui County has produced a **full-color map** of the island with various cycling routes, information on road suitability, climate, mileage, elevation changes, bike shops, and safety tips. It's available at most bike shops. You can also download it at **www.southmauibicycles.com**.

Golf

Golfers have many outstanding greens to choose from on Maui, from world championship courses to municipal parks with oceanfront views. Greens fees are pricey, but twilight tee times can be a giant deal. Be forewarned; the tradewinds pick up in the afternoon and can seriously alter your game. **Stand-by Golf** (www.hawaiistandbygolf.com; ✆ **888/645-2665**) rents clubs and offers savings off greens fees at Kaanapali, Wailea Golf Club's Gold and Emerald courses, and Pukalani golf courses. **Golf Club Rentals** (www.mauiclubrentals.com; ✆ **808/665-0800**) has custom-built clubs for men, women, and juniors (both right- and left-handed) that can be delivered island-wide; the rates are $25 a day for steel clubs, and a full graphite set is $30 a day.

WEST MAUI

Kaanapali Golf Resort ★   Both courses at Kaanapali will challenge golfers, from high-handicappers to near-pros. The par-72, 6,305-yard **Royal (North) Course** is a true Robert Trent Jones, Sr., design: It has an abundance of wide bunkers; several long, stretched-out tees; and the largest, most contoured greens on Maui. The tricky 18th hole (par-4, 435-yard) has a water hazard on the approach to the green. The par-72, 6,250-yard **Kai (South) Course** is an Arthur Jack Snyder design; although shorter than the North Course, it requires more accuracy on the narrow, hilly fairways. It also has a water hazard on its final hole, so don't tally up your scorecard until you sink the final putt. Facilities include a driving range and putting course. The clubhouse restaurant is run by celebrated chef Roy Yamaguchi.

Off Kaanapali Pkwy., Kaanapali (1st building on right). www.kaanapaligolfcourses.com. ✆ **808/661-3691.** Greens fees: Royal Course $255 ($179 for Kaanapali guests), twilight rates (starting at 1pm) $149, super twilight rates (starting at 3pm) $109; Kai Course $205 ($139 for Kaanapali guests), twilight rates (starting at 1pm) $99, super twilight rates (starting at 3pm) $79.

Kapalua Resort ★★★   The views from these two championship courses are worth the greens fees alone. The par-72, 6,761-yard **Bay Course** was designed by Arnold Palmer and Ed Seay. This course is a bit forgiving, with its wide fairways; the greens, however, are difficult to read. The oft-photographed 5th overlooks a small ocean cove; even the pros have trouble with this rocky par-3, 205-yard hole. The **Plantation**

Course, site of the Century Tournament of Champions, is a Ben Crenshaw/Bill Coore design. The 6,547-yard, par-73 course, set on a rolling hillside, is excellent for developing your low shots and precise chipping. Facilities for both courses include locker rooms, a driving range, and great dining. Sharpen your skills at the attached golf academy, which offers half-day golf school, private lessons, club fittings, and special clinics for beginners. Weekends are your best bet for tee times.

Off Hwy. 30, Kapalua. www.golfatkapalua.com. © **877/KAPALUA** or 808/669-8044. Greens fees: Bay Course $229 ($209 for resort guests), twilight rates (starting at 1pm) $169, super twilight (starting at 3pm) $129; Plantation Course $329 ($299 for guests), twilight rates $249, super twilight $199. Call for special packages.

SOUTH MAUI

Maui Nui Golf Club ★   The name has changed, but the Kihei course is the same forgiving, beautiful playground. Unspooling across the foothills of Haleakala, it's just high enough to afford spectacular ocean vistas from every hole. *One caveat:* Go in the morning. Not only is it cooler, but (more important) it's also less windy. In the afternoon, the winds bluster down Haleakala with gusto. It's a fun course to play, with some challenging holes; the par-5 2nd hole is a virtual minefield of bunkers, and the par-5 8th hole shoots over a swale and then uphill. Premium clubs rent for $50 with two sleeves of balls.

470 Lipoa Pkwy., Kihei. www.mauinuigolfclub.com. © **808/874-0777.** Greens fees $99 7:30–11am, $54–$89 before 7:30am and after 11am. Check website for specials and off-season rates.

Wailea Golf Club ★★   You'll have three courses to choose from at Wailea. The **Blue Course,** a par-72, 6,758-yard course designed by Arthur Jack Snyder and dotted with bunkers and water hazards, is for duffers and pros alike. The wide fairways appeal to beginners, while the undulating terrain makes it a course everyone can enjoy. More challenging is the par-72, 7,078-yard championship **Gold Course,** designed by Robert Trent Jones, Jr., with narrow fairways and several tricky dogleg holes, not to mention such natural hazards as lava-rock walls. The **Emerald Course,** also designed by Trent Jones, Jr., is Wailea's most scenic, with tropical landscaping and a player-friendly design. Sunday mornings are the least crowded. Facilities include a golf training facility, two pro shops, locker rooms, and two restaurants: **Gannon's,** by Chef Bev Gannon, and **Mulligan's,** a popular Irish pub.

Blue Course: 100 Wailea Ike Dr., Wailea. www.waileagolf.com. © **808/879-2530.** Emerald and Gold courses: 100 Wailea Golf Club Dr. © **888/328-MAUI** or 808/875-7450. Greens fees: Blue Course $190 ($175 for resort guests), $145 after noon, $115 after 2pm; Gold Course and Emerald Course $250 ($199 for resort guests), $170 after noon, $119 after 3:30pm. Check website for specials and unlimited passes.

UPCOUNTRY MAUI

Pukalani Country Club ★   This cool par-72, 6,962-yard course at 1,100 feet offers a break from the resorts' high greens fees, and it's really fun to play. The 3rd hole offers golfers two options: a tough (especially into the wind) iron shot from the tee, across a gully (yuck!) to the green, or a shot down the side of the gully across a second green into sand traps below. (Most people choose to shoot down the side of the gully; it's actually easier than shooting across a ravine.) High handicappers will love this course, and more experienced players can make it more challenging by playing from the back tees. Facilities include club and shoe rentals, practice areas, lockers, a pro shop, and a restaurant.

360 Pukalani St., Pukalani. www.pukalanigolf.com. © **808/572-1314.** Greens fees for 18 holes (including cart) $89, $69 11am–1pm, $39 1–2:30pm, $29 after 2:30pm. Take the Hana Hwy. (Hwy. 36) to Haleakala Hwy. (Hwy. 37) to the Pukalani exit; turn right onto Pukalani St. and go 2 blocks.

Hiking

Over a few brief decades, Maui transformed from a rural island to a fast-paced resort destination, but its natural beauty has remained largely inviolate. Many pristine places can be explored only on foot. Those interested in seeing the backcountry—complete with virgin waterfalls, remote wilderness trails, and quiet, meditative settings—should head to Haleakala or the tropical Hana Coast.

For details on Maui hiking trails and free maps, contact **Haleakala National Park** (www.nps.gov/hale; © **808/572-4400**), the **Hawaii State Department of Land and Natural Resources** (www.dlnr.hawaii.gov/dsp/hiking/maui; © **808/984-8109**) or the state's **Na Ala Hele program** (www.hawaiitrails.org; © **808/873-3508**). Choose different tabs on the Na Ala Hele website to download maps.

GUIDED HIKES   Maui's oldest hiking company is **Hike Maui ★★** (www.hikemaui.com; © **866/324-6284** or 808/879-5270), headed by Ken Schmitt, who pioneered guided treks on the Valley Isle. Hike Maui offers numerous treks island-wide, ranging from an easy 1-mile, 3-hour hike to a waterfall ($95) to a strenuous full-day hike in Haleakala Crater ($190). On the popular East Maui waterfall trips ($124), you can swim and jump from the rocks into rainforest pools. Guides share cultural and botanical knowledge along the trail. All prices include equipment and transportation. Hotel pickup costs an extra $25 per person.

If you'd like a knowledgeable guide to accompany you on a hike, call **Maui Hiking Safaris ★** (www.mauihikingsafaris.com; © **888/445-3963** or 808/573-0168). Owner Randy Warner takes eight or fewer adventurers on half- and full-day hikes into valleys, rainforests, and coastal areas. Randy's been hiking around Maui for more than 30 years and is wise in the ways of Hawaiian history, native flora and fauna, and volcanology. His rates range from $75 for a half-day to $169 for a full day, and hikes include daypacks, rain parkas, snacks, water, and, on full-day hikes, sandwiches. Private half-day tours are $150 per person ($125 per additional person).

The Maui chapter of the **Sierra Club ★★** offers the best deal by far: guided hikes for a $5 donation. Volunteer naturalists lead small groups along historic coastlines and up into forest waterfalls. Call ✆ **808/419-5143** or go to www.mauisierraclub.org.

HALEAKALA NATIONAL PARK ★★★

For complete coverage of the national park, see p. 312.

Wilderness Hikes: Sliding Sands & Halemauu Trails

Hiking into Maui's dormant volcano is an experience like no other. The terrain inside the wilderness area of the volcano, which ranges from burnt-red cinder cones to ebony-black lava flows, is astonishing. There are some 27 miles of hiking trails, two camping sites, and three cabins.

Entrance to Haleakala National Park is $25 per car. The rangers offer free guided hikes (usually Mon and Thurs), a great way to learn about the unusual flora and geological formations here. Wear sturdy shoes and be prepared for wind, rain, and intense sun. Bring water, snacks, and a hat. Additional options include full-moon hikes and star-program hikes. The hikes and briefing sessions may be canceled, so check first. Call ✆ **808/572-4400** or visit www.nps.gov/hale.

Avid hikers should plan to stay at least 1 night in the park; 2 or 3 nights will allow more time to explore the fascinating interior of the volcano (see below for details on the cabins and campgrounds in the wilderness area of the valley). If you want to venture out on your own, the best route takes in two trails: into the crater along **Sliding Sands Trail,** which begins on the rim at 9,800 feet and descends to the valley floor at 6,600 feet, and back out along **Halemauu Trail.** Before you set out, stop at park headquarters to get trail updates.

The trailhead for Sliding Sands is well marked and the trail easy to follow over lava flows and cinders. As you descend, look around: The view is breathtaking. In the afternoon, waves of clouds flow into the Kaupo and Koolau gaps. Vegetation is spare to nonexistent at the top, but the closer you get to the valley floor, the more growth you'll see: bracken ferns, pili grass, shrubs, even flowers. On the floor, the trail travels across rough lava flows, passing by rare silversword plants, volcanic vents, and multicolored cinder cones.

The Halemauu Trail goes over red and black lava and past native ohelo berries and *ohia* trees as it ascends up the valley wall. Occasionally, riders on horseback use this trail. The proper etiquette is to step aside and stand quietly next to the trail as the horses pass.

Some shorter and easier hiking options include the half-mile walk down the **Hosmer Grove Nature Trail,** or just the first mile or two down **Sliding Sands Trail.** (Even this short hike is exhausting at the high altitude.) A good day hike is **Halemauu Trail** to Holua Cabin and back, an 8-mile, half-day trip.

Haleakala Volcanic Crater

Kipahulu

All the way out in Hana, lush and rainy Kipahulu is one section of Haleakala National Park that is not accessible from the summit. From the ranger station just off of Hana Highway, it's a short hike above the famous **Oheo Gulch** (aka the Seven Sacred Pools) to two spectacular waterfalls. Check with rangers before heading out, to make sure that no flash floods are expected. (Streams can swell quickly, even when it appears sunny. Never attempt to cross flooding waters.) The **Pipiwai Trail** begins near the ranger station, across the street from the central parking area. Follow it 5 miles to the **Makahiku Falls** overlook. Continue on another 1.5 miles across two bridges and through a magical bamboo forest to **Waimoku Falls.** It's a challenging uphill trek, but mostly shaded and sweetened by the sounds of clattering bamboo canes.

POLIPOLI SPRINGS AREA ★

At this state recreation area, part of the 21,000-acre Kula and Kahikinui forest reserves on the slope of Haleakala, it's hard to believe that you're in Hawaii. First of all, it's cold, even in summer, because the elevation is 5,300 to 6,200 feet. Second, this former forest of native *koa, ohia,* and *mamane,* which was overlogged in the 1800s, was reforested in the 1930s with introduced species: pine, Monterey cypress, ash, sugi, red alder, redwood, and several varieties of eucalyptus. The result is a cool area, with muted sunlight filtered by towering trees.

Skyline Trail

This is some hike—strenuous but worth every step if you like seeing the big picture. It's 6.8 miles down, then back up again, with a dazzling 100-mile view of the islands dotting the blue Pacific, plus the West Maui Mountains, which seem like a separate island.

The trail is just outside Haleakala National Park at Polipoli Spring State Recreation Area; however, you access it by going through the

Oheo Gulch

national park to the summit. It starts just beyond the Puu Ulaula summit building on the south side of Science City and follows the southwest rift zone of Haleakala from its lunarlike cinder cones to a cool redwood grove. The trail drops 2,600 feet into the 12,000-acre Kahikinui Forest Reserve. Plan on 8 hours; bring water and extreme weather gear.

Polipoli Loop

Follow the Skyline trail to its terminus, and you'll reach the Polipoli Spring State Recreation Area. Alternately, you can drive straight there and embark on several cool weather hikes. (Four-wheel-drive vehicle recommended.) One of the most unusual hikes in the state is the easy 3.5-mile Polipoli Loop, which takes about 3 hours. Take the Haleakala Highway (Hwy. 37) to Kēokea and turn right onto Highway 337; after less than a half-mile, turn on Waipoli Road, which climbs swiftly. After 10 miles, Waipoli Road ends at the Polipoli Spring State Recreation Area campgrounds. The well-marked trailhead is next to the parking lot near a stand of Monterey cypress; the tree-lined trail offers the best view of the island. Dress warmly.

Polipoli Loop is really a network of three trails: **Haleakala Ridge, Plum Trail,** and **Redwood Trail.** After .5 miles of meandering through groves of eucalyptus, blackwood, swamp mahogany, and hybrid cypress, you'll join the Haleakala Ridge Trail, which, about a mile in, joins with the Plum Trail (named for the plums that ripen in June and July). This trail passes through massive redwoods and by an old Conservation Corps bunkhouse before joining up with the Redwood Trail, which climbs through Mexican pine, tropical ash, Port Orford cedar, and, of course, redwood.

WAIANAPANAPA STATE PARK ★★★

Tucked in a jungle on the outskirts of the little coastal town of Hana is this state park, a black-sand beach nestled against vine-strewn cliffs.

The **Hana-Waianapanapa Coast Trail** is an easy 6-mile hike that takes you back in time. Allow 4 hours to walk along this relatively flat trail, which parallels the sea, along lava cliffs and a forest of lauhala trees. The best time to take the hike is either early morning or late afternoon, when the light on the lava and surf makes for great photos. Midday is the worst time; not only is it hot (lava intensifies the heat), but there's also no shade or potable water available.

There's no formal trailhead; join the route at any point along the Waianapanapa Campground and go in either direction. Along the trail, you'll see remains of an ancient *heiau* (temple), stands of lauhala trees, caves, a blowhole, and a remarkable plant, the *naupaka*, which flourishes along the beach. Upon close inspection, you'll see that the naupaka have only half-blossoms; according to Hawaiian legend, a similar plant living in the mountains has the other half of the blossoms. Old myths say they are tragically separated lovers, one banished to the mountain and the other to the sea.

Hana: The Hike to Fagan's Cross

This 3-mile hike to the cross erected in memory of Paul Fagan, the founder of Hana Ranch and the former Hotel Hana-Maui (now the Travaasa Hana), offers spectacular views of the Hana Coast, particularly at sunset. The uphill trail starts across Hana Highway from the Hotel Hana-Maui. Enter the pastures at your own risk; they're often occupied by glaring bulls with sharp horns and cows with new calves. Watch your step as you ascend this steep hill on a jeep trail across open pastures to the cross and breathtaking views.

Horseback Riding

Maui offers spectacular horse rides through rugged ranchlands and into tropical forests. I recommend riding with **Mendes Ranch Trail Rides ★★**, 3530 Kahekili Hwy., 6¼ miles past Wailuku (www.mendesranch.com; ℂ **808/871-5222**). The 3,000-acre Mendes Ranch is a real-life working cowboy ranch with all the essential elements of an earthly paradise: rainbows, waterfalls, palm trees, coral-sand beaches, lagoons, tide pools, a rainforest, and its own volcanic peak (more than a mile high). Your guides, bona fide wranglers, will take you from the edge of the rainforest out to the sea and even teach you to lasso. They'll field questions and point out native flora, but generally just let you soak up Maui's natural splendor in golden silence. Experienced riders can run their horses. A 1½-hour morning or afternoon ride costs $110; add a barbecue lunch at the corral for an additional $30.

ESPECIALLY FOR kids

Take a Submarine Ride The **Atlantis Submarine** (p. 325 and pictured below) takes you and the kids down into the shallow coastal waters off Lahaina in a real sub, where you'll see plenty of fish (and maybe even a shark!). They'll love it, and you'll all stay dry the entire time. Allow about 2 hours for the trip.

Sleep with the Sharks What do fish do when the lights go out? Find out during one of the family sleepovers at the **Maui Ocean Center** (p. 309). The fun starts at 7pm, when kids help feed the turtles and rays, witness sharks and jacks on the prowl in the Open Ocean exhibit, and then snuggle into their sleeping bags. **Note:** Each child must be accompanied by an adult. The $75 per-person fee includes snacks, breakfast, a souvenir, and aquarium admission the following day.

Tour the Stars After sunset, the stars over Kaanapali shine big and bright: That's because the tropical sky is almost pollutant free and no big-city lights interfere with the cosmic view. Amateur astronomers can probe the Milky Way, see the rings of Saturn and Jupiter's moons, and scan the Sea of Tranquillity in a 60-minute star search on the world's first recreational computer-driven telescope. It takes place nightly at 8 and 9pm on the rooftop of the **Hyatt Regency Maui Resort** (p. 360). The cost is $30 for adults and $20 for children 12 and under. (There's also a 10pm tour for couples only; it's $45, and champagne and chocolate-covered strawberries are served.) Reservations are a must.

Another one of my favorites is **Piiholo Ranch Adventures ★★** in Makawao (www.piiholo.com; ☎ 808/740-0727). This working cattle ranch owned by the *kama'aina* (long-time resident) Baldwin family offers a variety of horseback adventures to suit your ability. Among them, the 2- to 3-hour private rides meander through the misty slopes of Haleakala with stops for picnic lunches (starting at $229). You can play "Cowboy for a Day" and learn how to round up cattle ($349). For a truly special occasion, book the **Heli Ranch Experience** ($3,335 for two people): A limo delivers you to the Kahului heliport, where you board an A-Star helicopter and fly to a private ranch cabin for breakfast and a 2-hour horseback ride. The ranch also has a zipline; check "Ziplining," below, for more details.

Tennis

Maui has excellent public tennis courts; all are free and available from daylight to sunset (a few are even lit until 10pm for night play). For a complete list of public courts, call **Maui County Parks and Recreation** (℅ 808/270-7383) or visit www.co.maui.hi.us/facilities.aspx. Courts are available on a first-come, first-served basis; when someone's waiting, limit your play to 45 minutes. Most public courts require a wait and aren't especially convenient for visitors. Exceptions include the courts in Kihei (in Kalama Park on South Kihei Rd. and in Waipualani Park on West Waipualani Rd. behind the Maui Sunset condo), in Lahaina (in Malu Ulu Olele Park at Front and Shaw sts.), and in Hana (in the Hana Ballpark just off of Hauoli Rd.).

Private tennis courts are available at most resorts and hotels on the island. The **Kapalua Tennis Garden and Village Tennis Center,** Kapalua Resort (www.golfatkapalua.com/tennis; ℅ 808/662-7730), is home to the Kapalua Open, which features the largest purse in the state, held on Labor Day weekend. Court rentals are $25 per person. Drop-in Doubles and Stroke of the Day clinics are offered most days at 8 and 9am. In Wailea, try the **Wailea Tennis Club,** 131 Wailea Ike Place (www.waileatennis.com; ℅ 808/879-1958), with 11 Plexipave courts. Court fees are $20 per player, with 2-day advance reservations required.

Ziplining

Piiholo Ranch Adventures ★ Explore this family ranch in the Makawao forest from above—flying through the eucalyptus canopy on one of six ziplines. Tour packages include access to the aerial bridge, tree platforms, ziplines (including side-by-side lines), and a trip to nearby waterfalls where you can take a refreshing dip.

799 Piiholo Rd., Makawao. www.piiholozipline.com. ℅ **808/572-1717.** Tours $99–$229.

Skyline EcoAdventures ★ Go on, let out a wild holler as you soar above a rainforested gulch in Kaanapali or down the slope of Haleakala. Pioneers of this internationally popular activity, the Skyline owners brought the first ziplines to the U.S. and launched them from their home, here on Maui. Skyline has two courses, one on the west side and the other halfway up Haleakala. Both are fast and fun, the guides are savvy and safety-conscious, and the scenery is breathtaking. In Kaanapali, you can even "zip and dip": drop off your line into a mountain pool. Beyond that, this eco-conscious company is carbon-neutral and donates thousands of dollars to local environmental agencies.

2½ miles up Haleakala Hwy., Makawao. www.zipline.com. © **808/878-8400.** Skyline EcoAdventures Kaanapali: 2580 Kekaa Dr. #122, Lahaina (meet at Fairway Shops). (© **808/662-1500**). Tours $109–$240.

WHERE TO STAY ON MAUI

Maui has accommodations to fit every kind of vacation, from deluxe oceanfront resorts to reasonably priced condos to historic bed-and-breakfasts. Be sure to reference "The Island in Brief," earlier in this chapter, to help you settle on a location.

Remember that Hawaii's 14.416% accommodations tax will be tacked on to your final bill. Also, if you're staying at an upscale hotel or resort, expect to pay a daily "resort fee" ($20–$35 a day) in addition to your room rate. Parking is free unless noted and all hotels are nonsmoking.

Central Maui

KAHULUI

Marriott Courtyard ★   Business travelers and vacationers looking to save on airport drive time will find a comfortable night's sleep here. Built in 2012, the hotel has soundproofed walls that adequately muffle noise from the neighboring airport. Spacious rooms are attractively furnished, featuring contemporary, island-inspired artwork. Suites come with full kitchens—super convenient considering the lobby has a 24-hour market, and several grocery stores are a 5-minute drive away. The palm-fringed pool deck is nice at night when it's lit by the glow of the fire pit.

532 Keolani Place, Kahului. www.marriott.com. © **808/871-1800.** 138 units. $329 double; $399 suite; $459 1-bedroom; $668 2-bedroom. Parking $10. Free airport shuttle. **Amenities:** Deli-style restaurant; fitness center; Jacuzzi; coin-operated laundry; 24-hr. market; pool; free Wi-Fi.

WAILUKU

Maui Seaside ★   As if frozen in time, this harborside hotel looks much the same as it might have in the 1970s: rattan furniture, aloha print bedspreads, and faux-leather booth seating in Tante's, the attached restaurant. The vintage decor has been updated and is now trendy. Rooms in the two-story building face the pool and Kahului Harbor with its sandy beach, where canoe clubs launch their paddling practice.

100 W. Kaahumanu Ave., Kahului. www.mauiseasidehotel.com. © **800/560-5552** or 808/877-3311. 180 units. Double from $169. Some rates include breakfast. Children under 12 stay free in parent's room using existing bedding. Extra person $15. Parking $7. **Amenities:** Restaurant; laundry room; pool; free Wi-Fi.

Old Wailuku Inn at Ulupono ★★   Innkeepers Janice and Thomas Fairbanks and their daughter Shelly offer genuine Hawaiian hospitality at this lovingly restored 1928 estate hidden down a sleepy side street in old

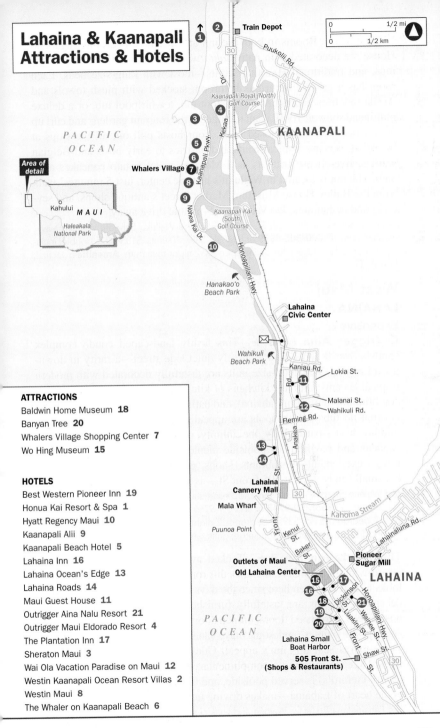

Lahaina & Kaanapali Attractions & Hotels

Train Depot

Puukolii Rd.

Kaanapali Royal (North) Golf Course

KAANAPALI

PACIFIC OCEAN

Whalers Village

Kaanapali Pkwy.

Kekaa Dr.

Nohea Kai Dr.

Kaanapali Kai (South) Golf Course

Honoapiilani Hwy.

Hanakao'o Beach Park

Lahaina Civic Center

Wahikuli Beach Park

Kaniau Rd. — Lokia St.

— Malanai St.

— Wahikuli Rd.

Fleming Rd.

Anakea St.

Lahaina Cannery Mall

Mala Wharf

Puunoa Point

Front St.

Kenui St.

Baker St.

Kahoma Stream

Lahainaluna Rd.

Pioneer Sugar Mill

LAHAINA

Outlets of Maui

Old Lahaina Center

Dickenson St.

Luakini St.

Waine'e St.

Honoapiilani Hwy.

PACIFIC OCEAN

Lahaina Small Boat Harbor

505 Front St. (Shops & Restaurants)

Shaw St.

Area of detail

Kahului *MAUI*

Haleakala National Park

0 ——— 1/2 mi
0 ——— 1/2 km

ATTRACTIONS
Baldwin Home Museum **18**
Banyan Tree **20**
Whalers Village Shopping Center **7**
Wo Hing Museum **15**

HOTELS
Best Western Pioneer Inn **19**
Honua Kai Resort & Spa **1**
Hyatt Regency Maui **10**
Kaanapali Alii **9**
Kaanapali Beach Hotel **5**
Lahaina Inn **16**
Lahaina Ocean's Edge **13**
Lahaina Roads **14**
Maui Guest House **11**
Outrigger Aina Nalu Resort **21**
Outrigger Maui Eldorado Resort **4**
The Plantation Inn **17**
Sheraton Maui **3**
Wai Ola Vacation Paradise on Maui **12**
Westin Kaanapali Ocean Resort Villas **2**
Westin Maui **8**
The Whaler on Kaanapali Beach **6**

Wailuku town. Rooms in both the inn and the three-bedroom Vagabond House are decorated with native *ohia*-wood or marble floors, high ceilings, and traditional Hawaiian quilts—most with king-size beds. Each room has a private, luxurious bathroom stocked with plush towels and Aveda toiletries and either a claw-foot tub, a whirlpool tub, or a deluxe multihead shower. You'll want to linger in the fragrant gardens and curl up with a book on the enclosed lanai. Your hosts pull out all the stops at breakfast, serving tropical fruits and pastries to early birds and Belgian waffles, five-cheese frittatas, and Molokai sweet potato pancakes after 8am. The inn is located in Wailuku's historic center, just 5 minutes' walk from the Bailey House Museum, Market Street's antique shops, and several good restaurants. Iao Valley is a 5-minute drive away.

2199 Kahookele St. (at High St., across from the Wailuku School), Wailuku. www. mauiinn.com. ✆ **800/305-4899** or 808/244-5897. 10 units. $185–$225 double, includes full breakfast. Check for online specials. 2-night minimum. **Amenities:** Jacuzzi; free Wi-Fi.

West Maui

LAHAINA

Expensive

Outrigger Aina Nalu ★ This lushly landscaped condo complex sprawls over 9 acres on a relatively quiet side street—a rarity in downtown Lahaina. The good-size units are tastefully decorated with modern tropical accents; all have kitchens or kitchenettes, laundry facilities, air-conditioning (a must in Lahaina), and bathrooms with large granite showers (but no tubs). Both pools are appealing places to retreat during the midday heat—particularly the infinity pool deck with its bright red cabanas and pavilion for poolside picnics. All of the historic whaling town's excitement—restaurants, shops, galleries, marine activities, and the small sandy cove at 505 Front St.—is within a 10-minute stroll.

660 Wainee St. (btw. Dickenson and Prison sts.), Lahaina. www.outriggerainanalu-condo.com. ✆ **866/253-9743** or 808/667-9766. 197 units. $139–$175 studio; $149–$315 1-bedroom; $199–$395 2-bedroom. 2-night minimum. Cleaning fee $125–$225. Parking $17.50. **Amenities:** Concierge; grills; whirlpool; 2 pools; free Wi-Fi.

The Plantation Inn ★★ Tucked away behind **Gerard's** (Maui's award-winning French restaurant), this romantic inn was built in 1987 but looks as if it has been here since the days of Hawaiian royalty—an artful deception. Rooms are tastefully furnished with vintage touches: four-poster beds, hardwood floors, French doors, and Hawaiian quilts. All units are blissfully quiet, and some have lanais overlooking Lahaina Town. Three extras seal this inn's appeal: Guests receive a $50 gift credit to Gerard's, each morning a complimentary gourmet breakfast (also courtesy of Gerard's) is served poolside, and the super-convenient location—in the heart of Lahaina—makes driving unnecessary.

174 Lahainaluna Rd. (btw. Wainee and Luakini sts., 1 block from Hwy. 30), Lahaina. www.theplantationinn.com. ✆ **800/433-6815** or 808/667-9225. 18 units. $178–$310

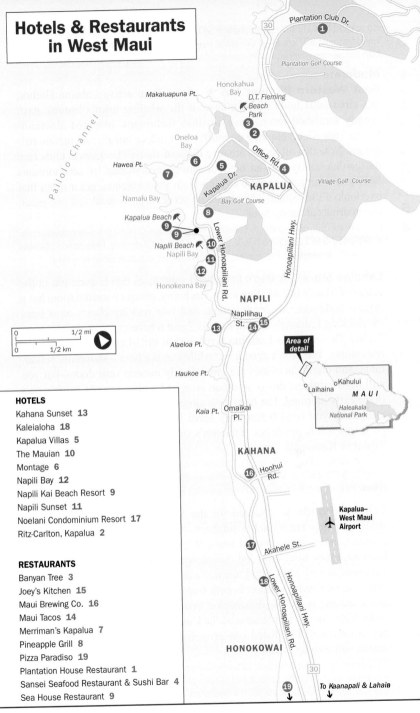

Hotels & Restaurants in West Maui

Plantation Club Dr. ❶
Plantation Golf Course

Honokahua Bay
Makaluapuna Pt.
D.T. Fleming Beach Park ❸
❷
Oneloa Bay
Office Rd. ❹
Hawea Pt. ❼
❻ ❺
Kapalua Dr.
KAPALUA
Village Golf Course
Namalu Bay
Bay Golf Course
Kapalua Beach ❽
❾
❾
Napili Beach ❿
Napili Bay ⓫
⓬
Honokeana Bay
Lower Honoapiilani Rd.
NAPILI
Napilihau St.
Honoapiilani Hwy.
⓭ ⓮ ⓯
Alaeloa Pt.

Pailolo Channel

Area of detail
○ Kahului
○ Laihaina
M A U I
Haleakala National Park

Haukoe Pt.

Kaia Pt. Omaikai Pl.

KAHANA
⓰ Hoohui Rd.

Kapalua–West Maui Airport ✈

⓱ Akahele St.
⓲
Lower Honoapiilani Rd.
Honoapiilani Hwy.

HONOKOWAI
30

⓳ To Kaanapali & Lahaia

0 | 1/2 mi
0 | 1/2 km

HOTELS
Kahana Sunset **13**
Kaleialoha **18**
Kapalua Villas **5**
The Mauian **10**
Montage **6**
Napili Bay **12**
Napili Kai Beach Resort **9**
Napili Sunset **11**
Noelani Condominium Resort **17**
Ritz-Carlton, Kapalua **2**

RESTAURANTS
Banyan Tree **3**
Joey's Kitchen **15**
Maui Brewing Co. **16**
Maui Tacos **14**
Merriman's Kapalua **7**
Pineapple Grill **8**
Pizza Paradiso **19**
Plantation House Restaurant **1**
Sansei Seafood Restaurant & Sushi Bar **4**
Sea House Restaurant **9**

double; $248–$313 suite. Extra person $40. Check website for deals. Rates include full breakfast and $50 credit at Gerard's; free self-parking. **Amenities:** Restaurant and bar; concierge; whirlpool; coin-operated laundry; large outdoor pool; free Wi-Fi.

Moderate

Best Western Pioneer Inn ★   Steps from active Lahaina Harbor, this circa-1901 hotel offers a taste of the whaling town's historic past. Simply furnished rooms have smallish bathrooms, mounted air-conditioners (not silent, but they do muffle the outdoor noise), and private balconies. Note that all rooms are up a flight of stairs. The quietest units face the garden courtyard—an outdoor dining area shaded by an enormous *hala* tree—but for people-watching from your veranda, get a room that overlooks Front Street. The restaurant serves a good breakfast and great, cheap drinks at happy hour.

658 Wharf St. (in front of Lahaina Pier), Lahaina. www.pioneerinnmaui.com. ℂ **800/457-5457** or 808/661-3636. 34 units. $187–$207 double. Free parking (across the street). **Amenities:** Restaurant; bar w/live music; outdoor pool; free Wi-Fi.

Lahaina Inn ★   A ship's figurehead announces this historic inn in the center of Maui's old whaling town. Each tiny, antiques-stuffed room has a private bathroom, air-conditioning, and two rocking chairs on a lanai overlooking Lahaina's action. Rooms 7 and 8 have views of the glittering Pacific. Downstairs is **Lahaina Grill,** one of the island's most celebrated restaurants. You won't need a car while staying here—shopping, restaurants, and marine activities are immediately outside your door—but you will need earplugs; this is an urban area, and garbage trucks rumble past in the early morning. The front desk closes at 7pm, so make sure you have everything you need before they leave for the day. Guests have beach, pool, and tennis privileges at the inn's sister property, the Royal Lahaina Resort in Kaanapali.

127 Lahainaluna Rd. (off Front St.), Lahaina. www.lahainainn.com. ℂ **808/661-0577.** 12 units. $119–$221 double; from $195 suite. Next-door parking $15 per day. **Amenities:** Restaurant; privileges at Royal Lahaina Resort; free Wi-Fi.

Lahaina Roads ★   Named for the Mala Wharf roadstead where a string of pretty boats anchor offshore, this older condo complex offers compact, individually owned units. It's located on the northern end of Lahaina, away from crowded downtown, but just down the street from Lahaina Cannery Mall, Old Lahaina Luau, and several terrific restaurants. One- and two-bedroom units benefit from full kitchens, oceanfront lanais, and a seaside pool. The drawbacks: Bedrooms face the road, which can make nights noisy, and some units lack air-conditioning (it can be boiling hot in Lahaina). I've listed one property manager, but a quick Internet search will turn up others.

1403 Front St. (1 block north of Lahaina Cannery Mall), Lahaina. Book with Chase'N Rainbows: www.westmauicondos.com/resorts/lahaina-roads. ℂ **877/661-6022** or 808/359-2636. 17 units. $140–$250 1-bedroom; $250–$405 2-bedroom. Cleaning fee from $200. 5-night minimum. **Amenities:** Oceanside pool; free Internet/Wi-Fi in some units.

Maui Guest House ★★   Tanna Swanson offers guests many extras at her charming B&B, tucked away in a residential Lahaina neighborhood. For starters, each private room has a full-size Jacuzzi (seriously!), noiseless air-conditioning, and gorgeous stained-glass windows depicting reef fish, flowers, and other Hawaiian scenes. Guests also have access to the saltwater pool; large, fully stocked kitchen; and a 30-foot sundeck for sunbathing, stargazing, and whale-watching. Tanna is a wealth of local information and an experienced scuba diver who takes good care of fellow aqua-holics. She also operates Trinity Tours, a discount activity agency. Her home is 1½ miles from either Lahaina's shopping and restaurants or Kaanapali's beaches.

1620 Ainakea Rd. (off Fleming Rd.), north of Lahaina town. www.mauiguesthouse. com. ⓒ **800/621-8942** or 808/661-8085. 5 rooms. $199 double, includes continental breakfast. Take Fleming Rd. off Hwy. 30; turn left on Ainakea; the B&B is 2 blocks down. **Amenities:** Concierge; saltwater pool; watersports equipment; free Wi-Fi.

Inexpensive

Lahaina Ocean's Edge ★   This funky 1964 hotel at the north end of Lahaina got a major makeover in late 2016. Thanks to its new owner, "The Edge" is now one of Maui's most affordable gems. Oceanfront units are on the small side (about 400 sq. ft.) and don't have phones or TVs, but they do have full kitchens with gas stoves and ocean views with Molokai in the distance. The largish unit on the southern corner has a private lanai that overlooks the Pacific on two sides. There's no beach access here, but the Lahaina Cannery Mall and several great restaurants are a short walk away.

1415 Front St., Lahaina. www.lahainaoceansedge.com. ⓒ **808/662-3200.** 18 units. $139–$199 double, $199 2-bedroom. Extra person $15. 3–5 night minimum. **Amenities:** Laundry room; free Wi-Fi.

KAANAPALI

Starwood's Maui properties (Sheraton Maui Resort & Spa, Westin Maui Resort & Spa, or the Westin Kaanapali Ocean Resort Villas) provide complimentary shuttle service to Lahaina and back.

Note: You'll find Kaanapali hotels on the "Lahaina & Kaanapali Attractions & Hotels" map (p. 355).

Expensive

Aston at the Whaler on Kaanapali Beach ★   Situated in the center of Kaanapali Beach next door to Whalers Village, this collection of condos feels more formal and sedate than its high-octane neighbors. Maybe it's the koi turning circles in the meditative lily pond, the manicured lawn between the two 12-story towers, or the lack of a water slide populated by stampeding kids. Decor in the individually owned units varies widely, but most boast full kitchens, upscale bathrooms, and private lanais with views of Kaanapali's gentle waves or the emerald peaks of the

West Maui Mountains. Unit no. 723, in the back corner of the north tower, is exquisite. The beachfront barbecue area is the envy of passersby on the Kaanapali Beach walkway.

2481 Kaanapali Pkwy. (next to Whalers Village), Lahaina. www.whalerkaanapali.com. © **888/671-5310** or 808/661-4861. 360 units. $306–$365 studio; $325–$589 1-bedroom; $535–$885 2-bedroom. Check for online specials. Daily $20 resort fee. **Amenities:** Concierge; fitness center; laundry; outdoor pool; salon; spa; tennis courts; free Wi-Fi.

Honua Kai Resort & Spa ★★

This North Kaanapali Beach resort is a favorite with residents and locals alike. The property sits on Kahekili Beach, immediately north of busier, flashier Kaanapali Beach, with a much better reef for snorkeling. The resort's upscale yet relaxed atmosphere takes a cue from its natural surroundings. Island-inspired artwork in the lobby gives way to colorful koi ponds, artfully landscaped grounds, and meandering swimming pools. Luxe accommodations range from huge 590-square-foot studios to vast 2,800-square-foot three-bedroom units, with top-of-the-line appliances, private lanais, and ocean views. The resort's sociable restaurant, **Duke's Maui Beach House,** offers an "ono-licious" breakfast and live music from 3 to 5pm. Stock up on organic snacks, gelato, and local coffee at **Aina Gourmet Market** in the lobby. **Hoola Spa** has the island's only therapeutic Himalayan salt room and uses organic, made-in-Hawaii products in its treatments.

130 Kai Malina Pkwy., North Kaanapali Beach. www.honuakai.com. © **855/718-5789** or 808/662-2800. 600 units. Studio from $379; 1-bedroom from $349; 2-bedroom from $470; 3-bedroom from $1083. Daily $29 resort fee. **Amenities:** Restaurant; deli; bar; fitness center; nearby 36-hole golf course; 5 whirlpools; 5 pools; spa w/therapeutic salt room; nearby tennis courts; watersports equipment rentals; free Wi-Fi.

Hyatt Regency Maui Resort & Spa ★★

You'll feel like royalty when you walk into this palatial resort with exotic parrots and South African penguins in the lobby. The southernmost property on Kaanapali Beach, it covers some 40 acres with 9 manmade waterfalls, abundant Asian and Pacific artwork, and a waterpark pool with a swim-up grotto bar, rope bridge, and 150-foot lava-tube slide that keeps kids occupied for hours. Spread out among three towers, the resort's ample rooms have huge marble bathrooms, feather-soft platform beds, and private lanais with eye-popping views of the Pacific or the West Maui Mountains. Two Regency Club floors offer a private concierge, complimentary breakfast, sunset cocktails, and snacks—not a bad choice for families looking to save on meals. Daily activities range from sushi-making classes at **Japengo,** the resort's superb Japanese restaurant, to stargazing on the rooftop. Camp Hyatt offers pint-size guests weekly scavenger hunts, penguin-feeding opportunities, and access to a game room. The oceanfront **Kamaha'o, Marilyn Monroe Spa,** a 20,000-square-foot wellness retreat, boasts 15 treatment rooms, sauna and steam rooms, and a huge menu of celebrity-inspired body treatments.

200 Nohea Kai Dr., Lahaina. https://maui.regency.hyatt.com. © **808/661-1234.** 806 rooms; 31 suites. Double from $323; Regency Club double from $493; Suite from $723. Daily $32 resort fee. Extra person $75 ($125 in Regency Club rooms). Children 18 and under stay free in parent's room using existing bedding. Packages available. Valet parking $28; self-parking $18. **Amenities:** 5 restaurants; 3 bars; luaus; babysitting; children's program; wildlife and star-gazing tours; concierge; club floor; 36-hole golf course; health club and classes; whirlpool; half-acre outdoor pool; room service; state-of-the-art spa; 6 tennis courts; watersports equipment rentals; free Wi-Fi.

Kaanapali Alii ★ This luxurious oceanfront condo complex sits on 8 landscaped acres in the center of Kaanapali Beach. Units are individually owned and decorated—some are considerably fancier than others. Both one- (1,500-sq.-ft.) and two-bedroom (1,900-sq.-ft.) units come with the comforts of home: spacious living areas, gourmet kitchens, washer/dryers, lanais, and two full bathrooms. Resortlike extras include bell service, daily housekeeping, and a complimentary kids' club (summer only). Views from each unit vary dramatically; if watching the sun sink into the ocean is important to you, request a central unit on floor six or higher. Mountain View units shouldn't be disregarded, though. They're cooler throughout the day, and the West Maui Mountains are arrestingly beautiful—particularly on full-moon nights. Other amenities include a swimming pool, a kiddie pool, barbecues and picnic areas, and tennis courts. You can even take yoga classes on the lawn.

50 Nohea Kai Dr., Lahaina. www.kaanapalialii.com. © **866/664-6410** or 808/667-1400. 264 units. $465–$695 1-bedroom; $680–$1,050 2-bedroom. 5-night minimum. Check for online specials. Free parking. **Amenities:** Babysitting; concierge; fitness center; fitness and yoga classes; 36-hole golf course; kids' club (June–Aug); 2 outdoor pools; 3 lighted tennis courts; watersports equipment; free Wi-Fi.

Sheraton Maui Resort & Spa ★★★ The Sheraton occupies the nicest spot on Kaanapali Beach, built into the side of Puu Kekaa, the dramatic lava rock point at the beach's north end. The sand has been disappearing as of late, but the snorkeling is still great around the base of the point, also known as Black Rock. At sunset, cliff divers swan dive into the sea from the torch-lit cliff. The resort's prime location, ample amenities, and great service make this an ideal place to stay. Rooms feature Hawaiian-inspired decor, private lanais, and trademark Sweet Sleeper beds, which live up to their name. The *ohana* (family) suites accommodate all ages with two double beds plus a *puneʻe* (sleeping chaise). The lagoonlike pool is refreshing but doesn't beat the sea full of actual fish and turtles just steps away. Activities ranging from outrigger canoe to hula and ukulele lessons will immerse you in Hawaiian culture; at night the Maui Nui Luau has an exciting fire-knife dance finale. Treatments at the elegant **Spa at Black Rock**—especially those catering to couples—are exquisite. Fans of **Hank's Haute Dogs** on Oahu will find their favorite gourmet dogs here, and DJs spin tunes from 10pm to midnight on weekends at the **Black Rock Lounge.** Rooms perched on the point include access to the Na Hoku club lounge with free breakfast and evening appetizers.

2605 Kaanapali Pkwy., Lahaina. www.sheraton-maui.com. © **866/627-8114** or 808/661-0031. 508 units. Double from $351; suites from $617. Extra person $89. Children 17 and under stay free in parent's room using existing bedding. Daily $26 resort fee. Valet parking $31 (free 1st day); self-parking $22. **Amenities:** 5 restaurants; poolside bar; weekly luau; club lounge; babysitting; children's program (at Westin Maui Resort & Spa); lobby and poolside concierge; 36-hole golf course; fitness center; whirlpool; lagoon-style pool; room service; shuttle service; day spa; 3 tennis courts; watersports equipment/rentals; free Wi-Fi.

The Westin Ka'anapali Ocean Resort Villas ★★
In contrast to the hotel-style Westin (see below), this elegant condo complex is so enormous it has two separate lobbies. The 26 acres fronting serene **Kahekili Beach** function as a small town with two grocery stores, three pools (yes, that's a life-size pirate ship in the kids' pool), three restaurants (hit the sports bar **Pailolo Bar & Grill** during a game), a Hawaiian cultural advisor, the luxurious **Spa Helani** (the 80-min. Polynesian ritual is unforgettable), and a high-energy gym with its own steam rooms, saunas, and lockers. Managed by Westin, the individually owned units (ranging from studios to two-bedrooms) are outfitted with trademark Heavenly beds, huge soaking tubs with jets, and upscale kitchens. Despite its seemingly massive footprint, the resort has accrued awards for its eco-friendly practices. One fun example: On July 4th, the resort ditches the usual fireworks display (which spreads ash on the fragile coral reefs) and opts instead to celebrate with "flower-works," dropping 60,000 orchids on the property. The lucky guest who finds the rose amid the orchids gets a free spa treatment or snorkel cruise. *Tip:* Ask for some leeway with the 4pm check-in and 10am checkout times.

6 Kai Ala Dr., Kaanapali Resort. www.westinkaanapali.com. © **866/716-8112** or 808/667-3200. 1,021 units. Studio from $399; 1-bedroom from $559; 2-bedroom from $829. Extra person $89. Valet $20, self-parking $15. **Amenities:** 3 restaurants; 2 bars; babysitting; children's program; concierge; 36-hole golf course; 2 fitness centers; 6 outdoor pools (including children's pool w/pirate ship); 4 whirlpools; room service; shuttle service; spa; tennis courts; free Wi-Fi.

The Westin Maui Resort & Spa ★★
The fantasy begins in the lobby, where waterfalls spill into pools stocked with flamingos and black swans. The lavish grounds wind around an 87,000-square-foot water wonderland with five pools and an extra-speedy 128-foot-long water slide. (I screamed the first time I flew down it.) After enjoying the pool action (waterfalls, aquatic basketball, volleyball), hit the beach for snorkeling, stand-up paddling, kayaking, or parasailing . . . the sky truly is the limit. Recharge at **Relish Burger Bistro,** the poolside restaurant, but save your appetite for **Wailele,** the resort's 3-hour luau experience. (Kids can get an all-day dining pass for $20.) Stroll two doors down to shop 'til you

drop at Whalers Village. Return to your room to sink into your fabulous Heavenly Bed, a Westin trademark, with no fewer than five different pillows. If you need further refreshment, hit the **Heavenly Spa** for a Hualani fruit scrub and lomilomi massage—I highly recommend it. There's also a "mind and body" studio for yoga and meditation classes, as well as a 2,000-square-foot fitness center. Forgot your workout clothes? No problem. You can borrow a set provided by New Balance.

2365 Kaanapali Pkwy., Lahaina. www.westinmaui.com. © **866/627-8413** or 808/667-2525. 759 units. Double from $359; suite from $842. Children 18 and under stay free in parent's room. Extra person $89. Packages available. Daily $30 resort fee. Valet parking $15, self-parking free. **Amenities:** 3 restaurants; 3 bars; babysitting; bike rental; children's program; concierge; fitness center; yoga; 36-hole golf course; 5 pools; room service; shuttle; salon; spa; tennis courts; watersports rentals; free Wi-Fi.

Moderate

Kaanapali Beach Hotel ★   A relic from a bygone era, Kaanapali Beach Hotel has humble charm and authentic Hawaiian warmth. Depending on your taste, you'll find this property's giant carved tikis, whale-shaped pool, and somewhat dated decor kitschy or refreshingly unpretentious. Instead of African parrots and Asian artwork, the lobby is adorned with traditional Hawaiian hula implements and weapons—many created by the staff during their annual Makahiki celebration. Three low-rise buildings border Kaanapali Beach; the beachfront units are mere steps from the water. The large-ish, motel-like rooms are decorated with wicker and rattan furniture, historic photos, and Hawaiian-style bedspreads. Hula and live music create a festive atmosphere every night in the courtyard. During the day, the expert watermen and women at Hale Huaka'i (the resort's water activity center) will teach you surf or paddle. Dry off and head to Hale Ho'okipa, the new cultural center, to practice throwing a fish net or playing the bamboo nose flute. The staff serenades you during a morning welcome reception and a farewell lei ceremony.

2525 Kaanapali Pkwy., Lahaina. www.kbhmaui.com. © **800/262-8450** or 808/661-0011. 430 units. Double from $207; suite from $311. Extra person $40. Packages available, as well as senior discounts. Valet parking $13; self-parking $11. **Amenities:** 2 restaurants; pool bar; babysitting; family activities; concierge; 36-hole golf course nearby; cultural center; pool; spa and salon services; access to tennis courts; watersports equipment rentals; free Wi-Fi.

Outrigger Maui Eldorado ★   It may have been one of Kaanapali's first properties in the late 1960s, but this 10-acre condo complex still manages to feel new. Developed in an era when real estate was abundant and contractors built to last, each spacious, individually owned unit has a full kitchen, washer/dryer, central air-conditioning, and outstanding ocean and mountain views. This is a great choice for active families. It's set on Kaanapali Golf Course, not on the beach, but guests have exclusive use of a beachfront pavilion on North Kaanapali, aka Kahekili Beach. It's a quick trip by car or golf cart. You're also within walking distance of the

Fairway Shops' excellent and affordable restaurants—a real bonus in otherwise pricey Kaanapali. *Note:* It's a two-level walkup without elevators. Grocery service and daily housekeeping are optional.

2661 Kekaa Dr., Lahaina. www.outrigger.com. © **888/339-8585** or 808/661-0021. 204 units, 87 managed by Outrigger. Studio from $145; 1-bedroom from $169; 2-bedroom from $239. 2-night minimum. Packages available. Daily $15 resort fee; $125–$225 mandatory cleaning charge. **Amenities:** Beach pavilion; concierge; 36-hole golf course; 3 outdoor pools; free Wi-Fi.

HONOKOWAI, KAHANA & NAPILI
Expensive
Napili Kai Beach Resort ★★★   This small resort nestled on Napili's white sandy cove feels like a well-kept secret. For 50-plus years, the staff here has been welcoming return guests for a taste of unspoiled paradise. The weekly mai tai and golf putting parties are blasts from the past, but the modern conveniences in each unit and startling ocean views will focus you on the splendid here and now. From the three buildings on the point (Puna, Puna 2, and Lani), you can gaze from your bed at the ocean, which looks like an infinity pool starting at the edge of your lanai. All units (aside from eight hotel rooms) have full kitchens, washer/dryers, flatscreen TVs, ultra-comfortable king-size beds, and private lanais separated by attractive shoji screens. Hawaiian cultural activities include *poi* pounding and *lauhala* weaving workshops, authentic *keiki* (children's) hula shows, and twice-weekly slack key guitar concerts led by Grammy award–winning musician George Kahumoku. Kids 12 and under eat for free at the resort's **Sea House** restaurant. As cozy as the rooms are, you'll probably spend most of your time on the beach or in the protected bay paddling past lazy sea turtles. *Bonus:* No resort fee.

5900 Honoapiilani Rd. (at north end of Napili, next to Kapalua), Lahaina. www.napili-kai.com. © **800/367-5030** or 808/669-6271. 162 units. Hotel room double from $335; studio from $475; 1-bedroom from $780; 2-bedroom from $1,050; 3-bedroom from $1,250. Packages available. **Amenities:** Restaurant; bar; babysitting; children's activities at holidays; concierge; 24-hr. fitness room; 2 18-hole putting greens; discounted rates at nearby golf courses; 4 pools; free Kapalua shuttle; tennis courts nearby (and free use of rackets); free use of watersports equipment; free Wi-Fi.

Moderate
Kahana Sunset ★   Set in the crook of a sharp bend on Lower Honoapiilani Road is a series of three-story wooden condos, stair-stepping down a hill to a private Keonenui beach—a strip of golden sand all but unknown, even to locals. Decor varies dramatically in the individually owned units, many of which feature master and children's bedrooms up a short flight of stairs. All units have full kitchens with dishwashers, washer/dryers, cable TV, and expansive lanais with marvelous views. Some rooms have air-conditioning, while most rely on ceiling fans—suitable on this cooler end of the coastline. The center of the property features a small heated pool,

whirlpool, and barbecue grills. This complex is ideal for families: The units are roomy and the adjoining beach is safe for swimming.

4909 Lower Honoapiilani Hwy. (at the northern end of Kahana), Lahaina. www.kahana sunset.com. ☎ **800/669-1488** or 808/669-8700. 79 units. 1-bedroom from $180; 2-bedroom from $250. 3- to 5-night minimum. **Amenities:** Private beach; barbecues; concierge; 2 pools (including kiddie pool); free high-speed Internet.

The Mauian Hotel ★★   Perched above beautiful Napili Bay, this vintage property offers a blend of old-time hospitality and modern flair. The verdant grounds burst with tropical color; the pool deck is shaded by umbrellas by day and lit with tiki torches at night. Rooms feature Indonesian-style furniture and lanais overlooking the grassy lawn and glittering Pacific. Studios have full kitchens. They don't have phones or TVs—encouraging you to unplug—though you'll find a TV and an extensive DVD library in the *ohana* (family) room. Guests gather there each morning for coffee, fresh fruit, and pastries before heading out to snorkel or try their luck at stand-up paddling in the supremely calm bay. Live music and free mai tais attract guests to the weekly "aloha party" by the pool, where they share *pupu* (appetizers) and travel tales. Nightly sunsets off the beach are spectacular—particularly during winter when whale spouts dot the horizon.

5441 Lower Honoapiilani Rd. (in Napili), Lahaina. www.mauian.com. ☎ **808/669-6205.** 44 units. Double from $219; Studio from $239. Extra person $13. Children 4 and under stay free in parent's room. **Amenities:** Coin-operated laundry; continental breakfast, outdoor pool; shuffleboard courts; free limited Wi-Fi.

Napili Sunset ★   This humble property hidden down a side street consists of three buildings, two facing spectacular Napili Bay and one across the street. At first glance, they don't look like much, but the prime location, low prices, and friendly staff make up for the plain-Jane exterior. The one- and two-bedroom units are beachfront. Upstairs units have bathtubs, while those downstairs have direct access to the sand. Across the street, overlooking a kidney-shaped pool and gardens, the economical studios feature expansive showers and Murphy beds. All units benefit from daily maid service, full kitchens, and ceiling fans (studios have air-conditioning). Unfortunately, bedrooms in the beachfront buildings face the road, but the ocean views from the lanais are outstanding. The strip of grassy lawn adjoining the beach is an added perk—especially when the sandy real estate is crowded. Several good restaurants are within walking distance, along with Kapalua's tennis courts and golf courses.

46 Hui Rd. (in Napili), Lahaina. www.napilisunset.com. ☎ **808/669-8083.** 43 units. $219 studio; 1-bedroom from $379; $599 2-bedroom. **Amenities:** Daily maid service; barbecues; coin-operated laundry; small outdoor pool; free Wi-Fi.

Inexpensive

Kaleialoha ★   This four-story condo complex is conveniently located near Honokowai's grocery shopping, budget restaurants, and public beach park. Each one-bedroom unit has a kitchen with marble countertops and dishwashers; a sofa bed in the living room; stacked washer/dryers; outdoor barbecues; and a view of Lanai and Molokai across the turquoise expanse of the Pacific. Top-floor units have the best views; ground-floor units open onto the lawn and oceanfront pool. There's decent snorkeling beyond the rock retaining wall, but you'll have to walk a block down the road for a sandy beach. *Tip:* You can inspect each unit on the website, plus view other nearby properties.

3785 Lower Honoapiilani Rd. (in Honokowai), Lahaina. www.mauicondosoceanfront. com. ✆ **800/222-8688** or 808/669-8197. 18 units. $149–$245 1-bedroom. Extra person $10. Children 3 and under stay free in parent's room. Cleaning fee $145. **Amenities:** Concierge; pool; free Wi-Fi.

Napili Bay ★   This small two-story condo complex sits on the southern edge of picturesque Napili Bay. Fall asleep to the sound of the surf and wake to birdsong. Individually owned studio apartments are compact, with king- or queen-size beds in the oceanfront living room (rather than facing the road like so many on this strip). You'll find a stocked kitchen, beach and snorkeling equipment, and a lanai with front-row seats for the sunset. You won't find a pool on the property or air-conditioning in the rooms, but louvered windows and ceiling fans keep the units fairly cool—and why waste time in a pool when you're steps away from one of the island's calmest and prettiest bays?

33 Hui Dr. (off Lower Honoapiilani Hwy., in Napili), Lahaina. www.alohacondos.com. ✆ **877/877-5758.** 28 units. $119–$329 double. Cleaning fees and minimum stays may apply. **Amenities:** Barbecue; laundry facility; free Wi-Fi.

Noelani Condominium Resort ★★   This Kahana condo is a real gem. Whether you book a studio or a three-bedroom unit, everything from the furnishings to the oceanfront pool is first class for budget prices. The only caveat: There's no sandy beach attached. Pohaku Beach Park (good for surfing, not as great for swimming) is next door; better beaches are a 5-minute drive away. All units feature full kitchens, daily maid service, panoramic views of passing whales during winter, and sunsets year-round; one-, two-, and three-bedrooms have washer/dryers. My favorites are the Orchid building's deluxe studios, where you can see the ocean from your bed. Units in the Anthurium Building boast oceanfront lanais just 20 feet from the water (the nicest are on the ground floor), but the bedrooms face the road. Guests are invited to lei-making and mai tai parties in the poolside cabana and have access to a teeny-tiny gym with a million-dollar view. With no cleaning fee, this place is a real deal.

4095 Lower Honoapiilani Rd. (in Kahana), Lahaina. www.noelani-condo-resort.com. ✆ **800/367-6030** or 808/669-8374. 40 units. Studio from $165; 1-bedroom from $210; 2-bedroom from $330; 3-bedroom from $365. Extra person $20. Children under 18 stay free in parent's room. Packages available. Rates include continental breakfast on 1st morning. 3-night minimum. **Amenities:** Concierge; fitness center; oceanfront whirlpool; laundry center (for studios); 2 pools (1 heated); DVD library; free Wi-Fi.

KAPALUA

Note: You'll find the following hotels on the "Hotels & Restaurants in West Maui" map (p. 357).

Expensive

Montage ★★★ From the dramatic entry to its freestanding spa, Montage is a full-service resort that invites families to feel luxuriously at home. Enormous residences range from 1,250 to 4,050 square feet—each with gourmet kitchens, deep soaking tubs, walk-in closets, washer/dryers, and expansive lanais. Rooms overlook gardens, pools, and the island of Molokai on the horizon. An elevator delivers you to your private floor, where you can store the gear you will almost certainly use at nearby Kapalua and Oneloa beaches. The open-air restaurant, **Cane and Canoe,** is great day or night, and the **Kapalua Beach Club** is a chic hangout spot with its own pool, hot tub, and comparatively cheap drinks. Kids will love the outdoor movies and games of capture the flag. Adults will adore the royal treatment in the cabanas, the convenience of everything being close at hand, and the museum-quality artwork exhibited throughout the property. Guests have free use of **Spa Montage**—a wellness wonderland with outdoor rain showers, cedar saunas, waterfall hot tubs, an oceanview yoga studio, and (best of all) a coed serenity pool where couples can lounge sipping organic juices before or after their spa treatments. Wedding parties should book the dreamy **Cliff House,** a private event venue hanging over the jeweled bay.
1 Bay Dr., Kapalua. www.montagekapaluabay.com. © **808/662-6600.** 56 units. 1-bedroom from $825; 2-bedroom from $1,125; 3-bedroom from $1,425; 4-bedroom from $2,570. Wedding/honeymoon, golf, and other packages available. Daily resort fee $30; valet parking $20. **Amenities:** 3 restaurants; 1 bar; babysitting; children's and teens programs; concierge; cultural classes; fitness classes; 3 pools; room service; shuttle service; luxury spa; golf and tennis privileges at Kapalua Villas; free Wi-Fi.

Ritz-Carlton, Kapalua ★★★ Perched on a knoll above D. T. Fleming Beach, this resort is a complete universe. The property's intimate relationship to Hawaiian culture began during construction: When the remains of hundreds of ancient Hawaiians were unearthed, the owners agreed to shift the hotel inland to avoid disrupting the graves. Today, Hawaiian cultural advisor Clifford Nae'ole helps guide resort developments and hosts the Ritz's signature events, such as the Celebration of the Arts—a weeklong, indigenous arts and cultural festival. The resplendent accommodations feature dark wood floors, plush beds, marble bathrooms, and private lanais overlooking the landscaped grounds and mostly undeveloped coast. The Ritz offers one of the best club lounges in the state, serving gourmet coffee and pastries, a lunch buffet, cookies in the afternoon, and hot appetizers and drinks at sunset. Additional amenities include several superior restaurants; a 10,000-square-foot, three-tiered pool; and the 17,500-square-foot **Waihua Spa,** with steam rooms, saunas, and whirlpools surrounded by lava-rock walls. Make sure to visit **Jean-Michel Cousteau's Ambassadors of the Environment center** and explore the captivating activities for adults and kids. (You can even feed the resident pot-bellied pigs.) A bit of a hike from the resort proper, **D. T. Fleming Beach** is beautiful but tends to be windier and rougher than the bays immediately south; a 5-minute shuttle ride delivers you to Oneloa or Kapalua.

1 Ritz-Carlton Dr., Kapalua. www.ritzcarlton.com/en/hotels/kapalua-maui. *©* **808/669-6200.** 463 units. Double from $489; club-level double from $799; suite from $967; 2-bedroom suite from $1367; club-level suite from $1,729. Extra person $50 (club level $100). Wedding/honeymoon, golf, and other packages available. Daily $35 resort fee. Valet parking $30; self-parking $22. **Amenities:** 4 restaurants; 4 bars; babysitting; basketball courts; bike rentals; children's program; club floor; concierge; cultural-history tours; fitness room with classes; 2 championship golf courses and golf academy; hiking trails; outdoor 3-tiered pool; room service; shuttle service; luxury spa; tennis complex; watersports equipment rentals; free Wi-Fi.

Moderate

Kapalua Villas ★★★   The stately townhouses populating the oceanfront cliffs and fairways of this idyllic coast are a (relative) bargain, particularly if you're traveling with a group. Several of the island's best restaurants (Sansei, Pineapple Grill, and Merriman's Kapalua) are within walking distance or a quick shuttle trip and you're granted signing privileges and a discount the nearby championship golf courses. Outrigger manages the individually owned one-, two-, and three-bedroom units, which feature full kitchens, upscale furnishings, queen-size sofa beds, and large private lanais. You'll enjoy the spaciousness—even the one-bedrooms exceed 1,200 square feet. Of the three complexes (Golf, Ridge, and Bay Villas), the Bay units are the nicest, positioned on the windswept bluff overlooking Molokai on the horizon. In the winter you can whale-watch without leaving your living room.

200 Village Rd., Kapalua. www.kapaluavillasmaui.com. *©* **800/367-2742** or 808/665-9170. 1-bedroom from $205; 2-bedroom from $285; 3-bedroom from $395. Daily $26 resort fee; $200–$275 cleaning fee. **Amenities:** Restaurants and beaches nearby; concierge; in-room laundry; golf; tennis; 9 outdoor pools; resort shuttle; free Wi-Fi.

South Maui

Two recommended booking agencies rent a host of condominiums and vacation homes throughout South Maui. **Condominium Rentals Hawaii** (www.crhmaui.com; *©* **800/367-5242**) offers affordable, quality properties in Kihei, Wailea, and Maalaea, plus a few in Lahaina. The online spreadsheet makes it easy to compare properties. **Destination Residences Hawaii,** 34 Wailea Gateway Place, #A102, Wailea (www.destination hotels.com; *©* **800/367-5246** or 808/495-4546), is the more upscale option, offering a wide selection of luxury rentals in Wailea and Makena. One-bedroom units start at $249 and include many extras: a hospitality desk to assist with activity planning, $160 in dining and spa credits, a discount grocery card, free Wi-Fi and parking, and, in some cases, a free rental car! *Tip:* The **Polo Beach** and **Makena Surf** units are a bit older, but nicer and closer to the beach.

Hotels & Restaurants in South Maui

KIHEI

Piilani Hwy.

Kulanihakoi St.

Kalepolepo Beach

Kulanihakoi Gulch

Kihei Rd.

Waipuilani Rd.

Keonoulu Beach

Lipoa St.

Lahaina

Kahului

MAUI

Area of detail

Haleakala National Park

Halama St.

Kalama Beach Park

Kamaole Beach Park

Kamaole Beach Park II

Kamaole Beach Park III

Kihei Rd.

Kilohana Dr.

Keawakapu Beach

WAILEA

MAUI MEADOWS

Piilani Hwy.

Mokapu Beach

The Shops at Wailea

Ulua Beach

Wailea Beach

Polo Beach

Palauea Beach

Makena Rd.

Poolenalena Beach

MAKENA

Maluaka Beach

Makena State Park

Makena Rd.

PACIFIC OCEAN

HOTELS

Andaz Maui **28**
Aston Maui Hill **17**
Dreams Come True on Maui **22**
Eva Villa **23**
The Fairmont Kea Lani Maui **38**
Four Seasons Resort Maui at Wailea **34**
Grand Wailea **33**
Hotel Wailea **37**
Kealia Resort **1**
Kohea Kai Resort **4**
Maalaea Surf Resort **2**
Mana Kai Maui Resort **18**
Maui Coast Hotel **13**
Maui Kamaole **16**
Nona Lani Cottages **3**
Pineapple Inn Maui **21**
Punahoa Beach Condominiums **12**
(Two) Mermaids on Maui B&B **19**
Wailea Beach Marriott Resort & Spa **31**
What a Wonderful World B&B **20**

RESTAURANTS

Cafe O' Lei Kihei **15**
Cow Pig Bun **9**
Fabiani's **8, 24**
Ferraro's Bar e Ristorante **35**
Gannon's **40**
Humble Market Kitchin **32**
Joy's Place **11**
Kaana Kitchen **29**
Ko **39**
Longhi's **27**
Maui Tacos **14**
Monkeypod Kitchen **26**
Monsoon India **5**
Morimoto Maui **30**
Nalu's South Shore Grill **6**
Pita Paradise **25**
Sansei Seafood Restaurant & Bar **10**
Spago **36**
Wow Wow Lemonade **7**

0   1 mi
0   1 km

KIHEI

Expensive

Kohea Kai Resort ★ Across the street from windswept Sugar Beach in North Kihei, this cheery, adults-only boutique property welcomes all, and caters especially to gay and lesbian travelers. When you book a standard room, studio, or suite, expect bright decor, comfy California king–size beds, air-conditioning (wall mount), and spacious ocean- or mountain-view lanais. Studios and suites have full kitchens or kitchenettes. The three penthouse suites are fabulous—especially #622, a gorgeous 3-bedroom retreat. Rates include a full hot breakfast. Chat with fellow guests over eggs and bagels or in the rooftop hot tub, where you can take in the panoramic view of Maalaea Bay and the West Maui Mountains. Maui's best beaches are a short drive away; the owners supply beach chairs and coolers.

551 S. Kihei Rd., Kihei. www.koheakai.com. ✆ **808/879-1261.** 26 units. Double from $369; studio from $389; suite from $489; Penthouse suite from $529. Extra person $45. No children allowed. **Amenities:** Concierge; 2 Jacuzzis (rooftop hot tub is clothing-optional); pool; free parking; no resort fee; free Wi-Fi.

Mana Kai Maui Resort ★ Even the views outside the elevator are astounding at this eight-story hotel/condo, which practically has its toes in the sand of beautiful Keawakapu Beach. Every unit in the 1973 building is oceanfront (though many lack views). Most, if not all, have been renovated with contemporary, island-inspired furnishings. The north-facing hotel rooms, which account for half of the units, have no lanais and are small enough to be filled by their king-size beds and kitchenettes. The one- and two-bedroom condos have full kitchens, sitting areas, and small lanais that overlook the glittering Pacific and several islands on the horizon. There's a surf shack on-site, along with a gourmet grocery/deli, oceanfront restaurant, and yoga studio. *Fun fact:* The lobby's iconic turtle mural appears in the film *Just Go With It.*

2960 S. Kihei Rd., Kihei. www.manakaimaui.com. ✆ **800/525-2025** or 808/879-1561. 98 units. $284 hotel room double; 1-bedroom from $357; 2-bedroom from $431. **Amenities:** Restaurant; bar; barbecues; concierge; coin-operated laundry; daily maid service; outdoor pool; watersports equipment rentals; free Wi-Fi.

Moderate

Aston Maui Hill ★ This condo complex with Mediterranean-style stucco buildings, red-tile roofs, and three-stories-tall arches marks the border between Kihei and Wailea—an excellent launching pad for your vacation. Managed by the respected Aston chain, Maui Hill combines the amenities of a hotel—24-hour front desk, concierge, pool, hot tub, tennis courts, putting green, and more—with the convenience of a condo. Units are spacious, with ample kitchens, air-conditioning (welcome in this climate), washer/dryers, queen-size sofa beds, and roomy lanais—most with ocean views. (For prime views, seek out units #35 and #36.) Two of South

Maui's best beaches are across the street; restaurants, shops, and golf courses are nearby. Check the website for significant discounts.

2881 S. Kihei Rd. (across from Kamaole Park III, btw. Keonekai St. and Kilohana Dr.), Kihei. www.astonmauihill.com. **855/945-4044** or 808/879-6321. 140 units. 1-bedroom from $229; 2-bedroom from $325; 3-bedroom from $510. Weekly rates discounted. **Amenities:** Concierge; putting green; outdoor pool; whirlpool; tennis courts; free Wi-Fi.

Eva Villa ★★

At the top of the Maui Meadows neighborhood above Wailea, Rick and Dale Pounds have done much to make their affordable B&B one of Maui's classiest. The hillside location offers respite from the shoreline's heat—and yet it's just a few minutes' drive to the beaches, shopping, and restaurants of both Kihei and Wailea. The tastefully designed cottage has a decent-size kitchen and living room, smallish bedroom, washer/dryer, and a sweet outdoor shower. The poolside studio is a single, long room with a huge kitchen and barstool seating. The suite next door has two bedrooms and a kitchenette. You aren't forced to be social here; continental breakfast (fresh fruit, juice, muffins, coffee) comes stocked in your kitchen. And with just three units, the luxurious pool deck is rarely ever crowded.

815 Kumulani Dr., Kihei. www.mauibnb.com. **808/874-6407.** 3 units. $155–$225 double, includes continental breakfast. Cleaning fee $75. Extra person $40. 5- to 7-night minimum. No credit cards. **Amenities:** Heated outdoor pool; free Wi-Fi.

Maalaea Surf Resort ★

Despite its name, this little-known beachfront retreat isn't in Maalaea, nor is it a resort. Rather, it's a collection of charming condos spread out across 5 acres at the far north end of Kihei. The four-unit townhouses with double-hipped roofs all have ocean views, big kitchens (with dishwashers), cable TV, and central air conditioning—a nice perk in summer. Sugar Beach, the adjacent salt-and-pepper stretch of sand, extends 3-plus miles to Maalaea. Often windy, it's not the best for swimming, but it's unmatched for sunsets (and whale-watching in winter). This is a decent headquarters for adventurers who want to explore the entire island. The property is nonsmoking.

12 S. Kihei Rd. (at N. Kihei Rd. and Mokulele Hwy. 311), Kihei. www.maalaeasurf resort.com. **800/423-7953** or 808/879-1267. 34 units. 1-bedroom from $245; 2-bedroom from $350; 5-night minimum. **Amenities:** Concierge; 2 outdoor pools; barbecues; shuffleboard; 2 tennis courts; free Wi-Fi.

Maui Coast Hotel ★

The chief advantage of Kihei's sole hotel is location, location, location. It's less than a block from sandy, sun-kissed Kamaole Beach Park I and within walking distance of South Kihei Road's bars, restaurants, and shopping. Another plus: nightly entertainment at the popular pool bar. Guest rooms are smallish, with sitting areas, huge flatscreen TVs, central air, and private garden lanais—no ocean views, though. Throughout the hotel, you'll find wonderful paintings by local artist Avi Kiriaty. Book the less-expensive "deluxe room" over the somewhat cramped "one-bedroom suite," unless you absolutely need the extra privacy. The **ami ami** restaurant serves reasonably priced local and organic dishes.

2259 S. Kihei Rd., Kihei. www.mauicoasthotel.com. $\mathcal{C}$ **808/874-6284.** 265 units. Double from $265; suite from $295; 1-bedroom from $335. Children 17 and under stay free in parent's room using existing bedding. Daily resort fee $25. Extra person charge $30. Packages available. **Amenities:** 2 restaurants; pool bar w/entertainment; free use of bicycles; concierge; rental car desk; fitness center; laundry facilities; outdoor pool (plus children's pool); 2 whirlpools; room service; 2 lighted tennis courts; free Wi-Fi.

Maui Kamaole ★   Directly opposite Kamaole Beach Park III's sandy beach, enormous lawn, and playground, this comfortable condo complex is ideal for families. Convenience is key here in the center of Kihei's beach and shopping zone. Each roomy, privately owned and furnished unit comes with an all-electric kitchen, central air, two bathrooms, and two private lanais. The one-bedroom units—which can easily accommodate four—are a terrific deal, especially during low season. Ground-floor units open onto a grassy lawn. The attractively landscaped property runs perpendicular to the shoreline, and some buildings (indicated by room numbers that start with E, F, K, L, and M) are quite a trek from the beach. Families with small children should seek out units beginning with A, B, G, or H, which are nearest to the beach but off the road. C units are close to both beach and pool.

2777 S. Kihei Rd., Kihei. www.mauikamaole.com. (Maui Condo and Home management site.) $\mathcal{C}$ **844/430-0606.** 316 units (not all in rental pool). 1-bedroom from $190; 2-bedroom from $246. $40 booking fee. **Amenities:** 2 outdoor pools; 2 whirlpools; 2 tennis courts; free Wi-Fi.

Inexpensive

Dreams Come True on Maui ★   After several years of vacationing on Maui, Tom Croly and Denise McKinnon moved here to open this dreamy B&B. They offer a stand-alone cottage and two private suites in their house, which is centrally located in the Maui Meadows neighborhood, just a 5- to 10-minute drive from the shopping, restaurants, golf courses, and beaches of Kihei and Wailea. Each colorfully decorated suite has a private entrance and lanai, kitchenette, 42-inch TV, air-conditioning, and use of laundry facilities. Continental breakfasts are offered room-service style: Choose from the menu of freshly baked pastries, mangoes right off the tree, and pop tarts. Hang your order on your door, and in the morning, it'll be delivered at your chosen time. Rooms are a bit tight, but you're free to use the oceanview deck, living room, and outdoor cooking area. The one-bedroom cottage has ocean views from several rooms, vaulted ceilings in the living room, wraparound decks, and marble in the kitchen and bathroom. Tom is on duty as a personal concierge, doling out beach equipment and suggestions for where to snorkel, shop, or eat dinner.

3259 Akala Dr., Kihei. www.dreamscometrueonmaui.com. $\mathcal{C}$ **877/782-9628** or 808/879-7099. 3 units. Suites (4-night minimum) from $125; cottage (6-night minimum) from $169. $125 cleaning fee; extra person $15. Continental breakfast included with suites. **Amenities:** Concierge; free Wi-Fi.

Kealia Resort ★   This oceanfront property at the northernmost end of Kihei isn't a resort, but it *is* worth a second look. From the outside, the older building might seem shabby, but on the inside the privately owned units shine—and rates are excellent. Avoid the lower-priced studios facing noisy Kihei Road. Instead, go for one of the oceanfront units (such as no. 203, which hangs over the pool). All have full kitchens, washer/dryers, and private lanais with truly spectacular views of 3-plus-mile-long Sugar Beach. Twice a week the management hosts social events for guests to mingle: Wednesday *pupu* parties and Friday morning coffee-and-doughnut get-togethers. *Tip:* Ask for some leeway with the 10am checkout time.

191 N. Kihei Rd., Kihei. www.kealiaresort.com. © **800/265-0686** or 808/879-0952 51 units. Studio from $130; 1-bedroom from $170; 2-bedroom from $225. Kids under 13 stay free in parent's room. Extra person $10. Cleaning fee $75–$125. Booking fee $25. 4- to 10-night minimum. **Amenities:** Outdoor pool; free Wi-Fi.

Nona Lani Cottages ★   Family-owned since the 1970s, this oceanside retreat is one of North Kihei's sweetest deals. Eight tiny vintage cottages are tucked among the coconut palms and plumeria trees, a stone's throw from Sugar Beach. Inside is everything you'll need: a compact kitchen, a separate bedroom with a queen-size bed, air-conditioning, and a cozy lanai—not to mention updated cabinetry and travertine tile floors. The three suites in the main house are stuffy; stick to the cottages. The charming grounds include a barbecue area and outdoor *hale* for weddings or parties—but no pool or spa. Your hosts, the Kong family, don't offer daily maid service, but they do make fresh flower leis—buy one and fill your cottage with fragrance. Wi-Fi is spotty here.

455 S. Kihei Rd. (just south of Hwy. 31), Kihei. www.nonalanicottages.com. © **808/879-2497.** 11 units. Double from $188; Cottage from $218. Extra person $25. 2- night minimum or $55 cleaning fee applies. Free parking. **Amenities:** On-site wedding coordinator; free Wi-Fi.

Pineapple Inn Maui ★★   Enjoy a resort vacation at a fraction of the price at this oasis in residential Maui Meadows, luxuriously landscaped with tall coconut palms, dinner-plate-sized pink hibiscus, a lily pond, and—best of all—a saltwater pool that's lit at night. The four guest rooms in the two-story "inn" are equally immaculate: Each has upscale furnishings, a private lanai with a serene ocean view, and a kitchenette that your hosts, Mark and Steve, stock with pastries, bagels, oatmeal, juice, and coffee upon arrival. The bright and airy cottage (two bedrooms, one bath) is one of the island's best deals. Landscaped for maximum privacy, it has a full kitchen, dark wood floors, central air, beautiful artwork, and a private barbecue area. Guests are invited to stargaze from the communal hot tub and make use of the fully equipped outdoor kitchen. Shopping, beaches, restaurants, and golf are minutes away and you can borrow snorkeling equipment, beach chairs, umbrellas, boogie boards, and a cooler to take on your outdoor adventures.

3170 Akala Dr., Kihei. www.pineappleinnmaui.com. ✆ **877/212-MAUI** (6284) or 808/298-4403. 5 units. Double from $169; Cottage from $235. 3-night minimum for rooms, 6-night minimum for cottage. Room rates include breakfast. No credit cards. **Amenities:** Saltwater pool; watersports equipment; free Wi-Fi.

Punahoa Beach Condominiums ★   This oceanfront condo sits on a large grassy lawn between the Charley Young surf break and Kamaole I Beach—an ideal headquarters for active sun-seekers. Each unit in the small four-story building boasts a lanai with a marvelous view of the Pacific and islands on the horizon. All are individually owned and decorated, so the aesthetic varies widely. (The website features photos of each.) Studios feature queen-size Murphy beds, full bathrooms, and compact, full-service kitchens. The three one-bedroom penthouses—the only units with air conditioning—are the sweetest option. Kihei's shops and restaurants are within walking distance.

2142 Iliili Rd. (off S. Kihei Rd., 300 ft. from Kamaole Beach I), Kihei. www.punahoa beach.com. ✆ **800/564-4380** or 808/879-2720. 15 units. Studio from $139; 1-bedroom from $239; 2-bedroom from $284; 1-bedroom penthouse from $264. $125–$150 cleaning fee. Extra person $15. 5-night minimum ($100 surcharge on shorter stays). **Amenities:** Free Wi-Fi.

Two Mermaids on Maui B&B ★   Your mermaid hosts, Juddee and Miranda, are both avid scuba divers, and the colorful decor throughout their charming B&B reflects their love of the sea. In the large, two-bedroom Ocean Ohana, the marine theme continues from the turquoise walls and dark stranded bamboo floors all the way to the kitchenette's fish-shaped cabinet knobs. This breezy, clean unit has air-conditioning, its own hot tub, and an adjoining "Surf Room" with bunk beds that's available for families. The equally stylish Poolside Suite opens up to the refreshing rock-lined pool. Every morning, Juddee places a deluxe continental breakfast (Greek yogurt, tropical fruits, and homemade banana bread) at your doorstep. Other amenities include Direct TV, barbecues, beach gear, and a tuned guitar in each unit for strumming island serenades. The house sits in a quiet residential cul-de-sac just a 3-minute drive (or 20-min. walk) from Kamaole III Beach. Juddee is a licensed minister and can perform weddings. She'll also help you book massages or childcare.

2840 Umalu Place, Kihei. www.twomermaids.com. ✆ **808/874-8687.** 2 units. Double from $135, includes continental breakfast. 3–5 night minimum. No credit cards. **Amenities:** Babysitting; barbecue; beach equipment; pool; free Wi-Fi.

What a Wonderful World B&B ★   Repeat guests here adore hostess Eva Tantillo, whose years of experience in the travel industry shows in thoughtful touches around her lovely property. Every unit is lovingly furnished with hardwood floors, Hawaiian quilts, and luxurious slate showers. The Guava Suite is smallest and a little dark for my taste. The Papaya

Suite, with its spacious living room, bathroom, and separate bedroom, is just right. Eva serves continental breakfast on the lanai, with views of the ocean, West Maui Mountains, and Haleakala. You're also welcome to use the full kitchen or barbecue. For movie nights, the common area has a gigantic TV and a fancy popcorn maker. This elegant B&B is centrally located in a residential Kihei neighborhood—next door to Two Mermaids, above—about a half-mile from Kamaole III Beach Park and 5 minutes from Wailea's golf courses, shopping, and restaurants. *Bonus:* No minimum stay or cleaning fee; cash discount.

2828 Umalu Place (off Keonakai St., near Hwy. 31), Kihei. www.amauibedand breakfast.com. © **808/879-9103.** 4 units. Double from $145, includes breakfast. Children under 12 stay free in parent's room. **Amenities:** Beach equipment; barbecue; laundry facilities; free international calls; free Wi-Fi.

WAILEA

Golfers should note that all Wailea resorts enjoy special privileges at the Wailea Golf Club's three 18-hole championship courses: Blue, Gold, and Emerald.

Note: You'll find the following hotels on the "Hotels & Restaurants in South Maui" map (p. 369).

Expensive

Andaz Maui at Wailea ★★★   The Andaz continues to garner rave reviews—small wonder, considering its prime beachfront locale, chic decor, apothecary-style spa, and two phenomenal restaurants, including one by superstar chef Masaharu Morimoto. Foodies should look no further: Not only is the **Morimoto Maui** sushi bar a must, but the resort's other restaurant, **Ka'ana Kitchen,** might be *even better.* Before you eat, though, you'll want to freshen up in your room. Accommodations here aren't the island's largest, but they ramp up the style quotient a notch with crisp white linens, warm wood furniture, and midcentury accents. Wrap yourself in a plush robe and nosh on the complimentary minibar snacks from the sanctuary of your private lanai. Wander past the tiered infinity pools (which look best at night, when lit in a shifting palette of colors). Then hit gorgeous **Mokapu Beach** out front to snorkel, kayak, or paddle outrigger canoe. This resort is a dynamic blend of modern and ancient values. Visit with the resident artist in the lobby gallery, or learn to braid *ti*-leaf leis and make coconut fiber cordage. Whatever you do, don't miss the **Awili Spa,** where you can mix your own massage oil and body scrubs. Fitness classes and outrigger canoe excursions are complimentary, and you even have a free GoPro to use for the duration of your stay. If you splurge on one of the resort's two-, three-, or four-bedroom villas—you'll have an entire wall that opens to the Pacific, a private plunge pool, and a Viking range to call your own.

3550 Wailea Alanui Dr., Wailea. https://maui.andaz.hyatt.com. © **808/573-1234.** 198 units. Double from $487; 1-bedroom suite from $694; call for villa prices. Resort fee $40. Valet parking $30. **Amenities:** 3 restaurants, 24-hr. market; 3 bars;

concierge; 24-hr. fitness center; use of Wailea Golf Club's 3 18-hole golf courses; 4 cascading infinity pools; 24-hr. room service; shuttle service; luxury spa and spa pool; watersports equipment rentals; free fitness classes and excursions; free minibar; free Wi-Fi.

The Fairmont Kea Lani Maui ★★★

At first blush, this blinding-white complex of Arabian turrets looks a tad out of place—but once you enter the orchid-filled lobby and see the big blue Pacific outside, there's no doubt you're in Hawaii. For the price of a regular room at the neighboring resorts, you get an entire suite here. Each unit in the all-suites hotel has a kitchenette with granite countertop, living room with sofa bed (great for kids), spacious bedroom, marble bathroom (head immediately for the deep soaking tub), and large lanai with views of the pools, lawns, and Pacific Ocean. The beachfront villas are perfect for families or couples traveling together. The two-story units each have two or three bedrooms, a gourmet kitchen, washer/dryer, and private plunge pool just steps from the white sand. **Polo Beach** is public, but feels private and secluded. Huge murals and artifacts decorate the resort's manicured property, which is home to several good restaurants, an excellent bakery and deli, and the **Willow Stream Spa.** Escape into this heavenly retreat to experience the rain showers, steam rooms, and warm lava-stone foot beds. Youngsters can build volcanoes in the kids' club, or practice swimming with a mono-fin in "Mermaid University," while the entire family can get into rhythm paddling a Hawaiian outrigger canoe.

4100 Wailea Alanui Dr., Wailea. www.fairmont.com/kealani. © **866/540-4456** or 808/875-4100. 450 units. Double from $409, suite from $553; villa from $1,775. $38 resort fee. Valet parking $27; free self-parking. **Amenities:** 4 restaurants, gourmet bakery & deli; 3 bars; babysitting; children's program; concierge; 24-hr. fitness center; use of Wailea Golf Club's 3 18-hole courses; 2 large pools; adults-only pool; 140-ft. water slide and swim-up bar, 24-hr. room service; luxury spa and salon; use of Wailea Tennis Center's 11 courts; watersports equipment rentals; free Wi-Fi.

Four Seasons Resort Maui at Wailea ★★★

Words fail to describe how luxurious you'll feel rubbing elbows with celebrities in this über-elegant yet relaxed atmosphere. Perched above Wailea Beach's golden sand, the Four Seasons inhabits its own world, where poolside attendants anticipate your needs: cucumber slices for your eyes? Mango smoothie sampler? Or perhaps your sunglasses need polishing? The adults-only infinity pool with underwater music and a swim-up bar is what all pools aspire to. The roughly 600-sq.-ft. guest rooms feature dream-inducing beds, deep marble bathtubs, walk-in showers big enough for two, and furnished lanais, most with superlative ocean views. If you get stuck with a North Tower room over the parking lot, ask politely to be moved. The sublime spa offers an incredible array of body treatments ranging from traditional Hawaiian to craniosacral and Ayurvedic massage. (As nice as the spa facility is, treatments in the oceanside thatched *hale* are even more idyllic.) The resort's restaurants, **Spago, Ferraro's,** and **DUO,** are great;

room service here is a must. Finally, this might be the island's most kid-friendly resort: Perks include milk and cookies on arrival, toddler-proofing for your room (everything from furniture bumpers to toilet-seat locks), *keiki* menus in all restaurants, a high-tech game room, and the unmatched, complimentary Kids for all Seasons program from 9am to 5pm. No resort fee. *Tip:* Wedding parties should book #798 or #301—stunning suites with room for entertaining.

3900 Wailea Alanui Dr., Wailea. www.fourseasons.com/maui. © **800/311-0630** or 808/874-8000. 380 units. Double from $599; club floor from $1,409; suite from $1,349. Children 17 and under stay free in parent's room. Packages available. Valet parking $29. **Amenities:** 3 restaurants, 4 bars w/nightly entertainment; babysitting; free use of bicycles; free children's program; concierge; concierge-level rooms; putting green; use of Wailea Golf Club's 3 18-hole courses; fitness center with classes; 3 outdoor pools; room service; luxury spa and salon; 2 on-site tennis courts; use of Wailea Tennis Center's 11 courts; watersports equipment rentals; free Wi-Fi ($20 for premium).

Grand Wailea ★★★   Built by a Japanese multimillionaire at the pinnacle of Hawaii's fling with fantasy megaresorts, the Grand Wailea is the grand prize in Hawaii vacation contests and the dream of many honeymooners. No expense was spared during construction: Some $30 million worth of original artwork decorates the grounds, much of it created expressly for the hotel by Hawaii artists and sculptors. More than 10,000 tropical plants beautify the lobby alone, and rocks hewn from the base of Mount Fuji adorn the Japanese garden. A Hawaiian-themed restaurant floats atop a man-made lagoon, and light filters majestically through the stained-glass walls of the wedding chapel. Guest rooms come with lavish, oversize bathrooms and plush bedding. But for kids, all that matters is the resort's unrivaled pool: an aquatic playground with nine separate swimming pools connected by slides, waterfalls, caves, rapids, a Tarzan swing, a swim-up bar, a baby beach, and a water elevator that shuttles swimmers back to the top. If this doesn't sate them, an actual beach made of real golden sand awaits just past the resort hammocks. The Grand is also home to Hawaii's largest and most resplendent spa: a 50,000-square-foot marble paradise with mineral soaking tubs, thundering waterfall showers, Japanese furo baths, Swiss jet showers, and many other luxurious features. Dining options include **Humuhumunukunukuapuaa,** the aforementioned floating restaurant where you can fish for your lobster straight from the lagoon. Minimalists may scoff, but the Grand Wailea's extravagance is worth experiencing even if you don't stay here.

3850 Wailea Alanui Dr., Wailea. www.grandwailea.com. © **800/888-6100** or 808/875-1234. 780 units. Double from $543; suite from $1,049; Napua Club Room from $599; Hoolei Villas from $1,036. Membership rates available. Extra person $50 ($100 in Napua Tower). Daily resort fee $30. Valet parking $30. **Amenities:** 6 restaurants; 4 bars; art and garden tours; babysitting; children's program; concierge; concierge-level rooms; use of Wailea Golf Club's 3 18-hole courses; fitness center and classes; 5 whirlpools (including one atop a man-made volcano); adults-only outdoor pool; 2,000-ft.-long pool with a swim/ride through grottoes; room service; scuba-diving clinics; shuttle service to Wailea; Hawaii's largest luxury spa and salon; racquetball court; use of Wailea Tennis Center's 11 courts; watersports equipment rentals; free Wi-Fi.

Hotel Wailea ★★★

This stylish boutique hotel is one of a kind in Wailea, the only Relais & Châteaux property in Hawaii. Compared with the flashier resorts at the coastline, it's small, secluded, and serene—an oasis for honeymooners. The pool and cabanas are swank, with free cocktails by the fire pit from 5 to 6pm and mixology classes every Sunday morning. The verdant grounds and koi ponds have been transformed into a meditative garden. Large suites are outfitted with modern luxuries: wide-planked wood floors, Hawaiian *kapa*-inspired prints on plush king-size platform beds, deep soaking tubs, and daybeds on the lanai. Tidy kitchenettes feature Nespresso machines, two-burner Wolf stoves and Sub-Zero refrigerators. Hotel staff will load up a free tote bag with towels and water and chauffeur you throughout Wailea in the resort's Mercedes SUV. It's a 3-minute shuttle to the beach, and the hotel's kiosk at Wailea Beach will supply you with umbrellas and chairs. Take advantage of the free outrigger canoe trip offered on Wednesdays. This isn't a place that nickel-and-dimes guests, and employees come to know you on a first-name basis. Definitely plan to indulge at the new restaurant, **Ondine**, run by the culinary masterminds from Senia on Oahu. ***Brides- and grooms-to-be, take note:*** The lawn and gazebo at the hotel's entrance is a fairy-tale venue for weddings and receptions.

555 Kaukahi St., Wailea. www.hotelwailea.com. ✆ **866/970-4167** or 808/874-0500. 72 units. Suite from $499. 2-person max occupancy. Daily $30 resort fee. Packages available. **Amenities:** Restaurant; 2 bars; concierge; fitness center; outdoor pool; room service; free shuttle service; free mixology classes and canoe trips; organic garden and orchard; signing privileges at nearby Grand Wailea; spa; free Wi-Fi.

Wailea Beach Marriott Resort & Spa ★★

Airy and comfortable, this recently renovated resort accentuates rather than overwhelms its sublime environment. Eight buildings, all low-rise except for an eight-story tower, unfold along 22 luxurious acres of lawns and gardens punctuated by coconut palms. You'll want to spend your entire vacation beneath the cabanas at the exquisite infinity pool. Unless you're age 12 or under—then your parents will have to drag you away from the adventure pool with its four slick slides and animal sculptures that spit water. The resort is positioned on a grassy slope between Wailea and Ulua beaches, so there's plenty of sandy real estate to explore, too. Rooms have tile or wood floors, modern furnishings, and lanais with views of the picturesque coastline. The small **Mandara Spa** offers an array of treatments (from massages to body wraps and rejuvenating facials) in a very Zen atmosphere. Just downstairs is Roy Yamaguchi's newest restaurant: **Humble Market Kitchin.** Kids can fuel up on shave ice and poke at the **Mo Bettah Food Truck.**

3700 Wailea Alanui Dr., Wailea. www.waileamarriott.com. © **808/879-1922.** 547 units. Doubles from $451; suite from $579; 2-bedroom from $679. Packages available. Extra person $40. Daily $35 resort fee. Valet parking $35, self-parking $25. **Amenities:** 2 restaurants; 2 bars; cafe; food truck; luau, babysitting; concierge; use of Wailea Golf Club's 3 18-hole golf courses; fitness center; outdoor pools (1 adults-only and 1 kids-only); room service; spa; use of Wailea Tennis Center's 11 courts; free watersports equipment and bike rentals; free Wi-Fi in lobby ($15–$19 in room).

Upcountry Maui

MAKAWAO

Here you'll be (relatively) close to Haleakala National Park; Makawao is approximately 90 minutes from the entrance to the park at the 7,000-foot level (from there it's another 3,000 ft. and 45 min. to get to the top). Temperatures are 5° to 10° cooler than at the coast, and misty rain is common.

Aloha Cottage ★★   If getting away from it all is your goal, this exotic retreat in the eucalyptus forest above Makawao might be your place. On 5 luxuriously landscaped acres sits the octagonal Aloha Cottage and Thai Tree House, both reminiscent of something you'd see in Southeast Asia. The 590-square-foot cottage's interior is lavishly furnished with vaulted ceilings, teak floors, Oriental rugs, and intricate Balinese carvings. (Whenever you glance at your reflection in the magnificent bathroom mirror, you'll feel like royalty.) Both the Cottage and Tree House feature granite counters, a gas stove, and teak cabinetry that makes cooking a pleasure. Olinda Road is a winding, narrow track that ascends through the trees above Makawao—coming and going from here is an adventure unto itself. After a day of exploring Maui, it's a sweet relief to enjoy a home-cooked dinner on the lanai, soak in the outdoor tub built for two, and retire to the king-size cherrywood bed where you can stare through the skylight at the stars.

1879 Olinda Rd., Makawao. www.alohacottage.com. © **808/573-8555.** 2 units. Cottage $259, tree house $239. $100 cleaning fee. Not suitable for children under 10. **Amenities:** Outdoor tub; barbecue; laundry facilities; free Wi-Fi.

Banyan Bed & Breakfast Retreat ★   Shaded by huge monkeypod trees, this upcountry estate on meandering Baldwin Avenue has a humble, old Hawaii ambience. Accommodations include 3 suites within a nicely restored 1927 plantation manager's house and 4 individual cottages. Each suite has a queen-size and a twin bed (perfect for families traveling with youngsters), a marble shower, a private entrance, a modest kitchenette, hardwood floors, and antique furniture. The cottages feature similar amenities; some (such as Gardenia) have full kitchens and bathtubs. Each morning, Marty, the retreat's proprietor, delivers a continental breakfast to your door. Fruit trees and flowers decorate the property; hammocks and swings hang from the branches of the massive shade trees. Guests have the use of a 50-foot-long saltwater swimming pool, Jacuzzi, and 700-square-foot yoga and meditation studio equipped with yoga props and a sophisticated audio/video system. This fully handicapped-accessible retreat is ideal for groups, and the house, decorated with vintage Hawaiian furniture, can be rented as a whole. Makawao's restaurants and shops are just minutes away, and Paia's beaches are less than a 15-minute drive from here.

3265 Baldwin Ave. (less than a mile below Makawao), Makawao. www.bed-breakfast-maui.com. ℭ **808/572-9021.** 7 units. Double from $185; Cottage from $185. Entire estate $1,300. Extra person $30, children 12 and under $15. Cleaning fee $30–$40. Rates include breakfast. **Amenities:** Babysitting; whirlpool; outdoor pool; free Wi-Fi.

Hale Hookipa Inn Makawao ★★

Cherie Attix restored this historic 1924 plantation-style home to its original charm, filling it with Hawaiian artwork, antique furniture (a giant oak armoire, wrought-iron bed frame, and vintage shutters repurposed as a headboard), and a generous dose of love. It's a 5-minute walk from the shops and restaurants of Makawao, 15-minute drive from beaches, and an hour's drive from the top of Haleakala. The pretty guest rooms have separate outside entrances and private bathrooms—two with claw-foot tubs. The Kona Wing is a two-bedroom suite with use of the kitchen. In addition to a daily continental breakfast, Cherie offers guests fresh eggs from her hens. Unlike many B&B operators, she allows 1-night stays—perfect for hikers wanting a head start on Haleakala in the morning. Best of all: She sponsors a terrific "volunteer on vacation" program. Lend a hand at one of the dozen local organizations listed on her website and she'll knock 5% off of your stay at Hale Ho'okipa. (And the experience will undoubtedly be the highlight of your vacation.)

32 Pakani Place, Makawao. www.maui-bed-and-breakfast.com. ℭ **877/572-6698** or 808/572-6698. 4 units. Double from $140, includes continental breakfast. $15 surcharge for 1-night stays. No children under 9. **Amenities:** Tropical fruit orchard; voluntourism program; free Wi-Fi.

Lumeria ★★

Halfway between Paia and Makawao on Maui's scenic North Shore, a historic women's college has been lovingly restored as a boutique resort. Nestled into six landscaped acres are two-dozen guest rooms, a resplendent lobby, yoga studio, spa, meditation garden, and farm-to-table restaurant. A small but dazzling pool overlooks a valley full of waving sugarcane as hammocks sway in the ironwood trees. The crystals, sacred artwork, and *objets d'art* tucked into every corner contribute to the charmed ambience of this serene retreat. Rooms are small—nearly filled by their plush four-poster beds—but luxuriously appointed with organic Italian linens, Japanese tansu cabinets, and showers with river-rock floors. A stay includes access to daily yoga, meditation, horticulture, and aromatherapy classes, as well as breakfast for two at the chic, semi-private restaurant, **Wooden Crate.** Baldwin Beach is only 2½ miles away; the staff will set you up with stand-up paddleboard equipment or pack a picnic for an excursion to Hana.

1813 Baldwin Ave., Makawao. www.lumeriamaui.com. ℭ **808/579-8877.** 25 units. Double from $279; suite from $325, includes organic breakfast. Resort fee $25 per person. **Amenities:** Restaurant; spa; concierge; 2 whirlpools (1 saltwater); outdoor pool; watersports equipment rental; yoga and aromatherapy class; free Wi-Fi.

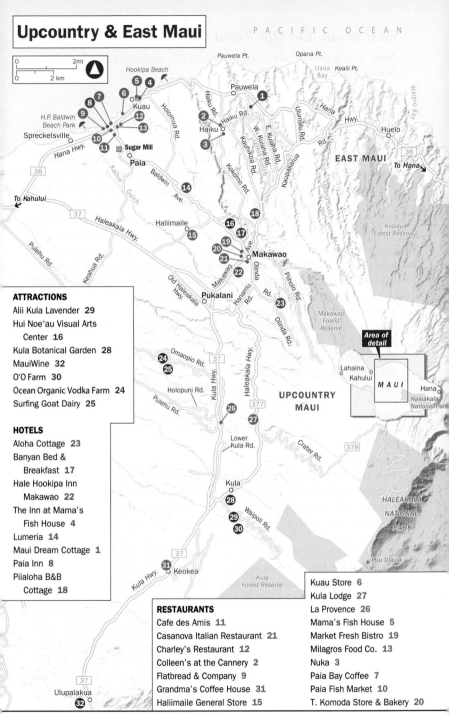

Upcountry & East Maui

PACIFIC OCEAN

Pauwela Pt.
Opana Pt.
Uaoa Kealii Pt.
Bay
Waipio Bay

0   2mi
0   2 km

Hookipa Beach

Pauwela

⑤ ④ ⑦ ⑥
⑧
⑨ Kuau
H.P. Baldwin ⑫
Beach Park ⑬
Spreckelsville ⑩
⑪ Sugar Mill
Paia

Haiku Rd.
Haiku Rd.
② Haiku
③

W. Kuiaha Rd.
E. Kuiaha Rd.
Opana Rd.
Kailua Gulch

Ulumalu Rd.
Hana Hwy.
Huelo
Kaupakalua Rd.

EAST MAUI

To Hana ⑯

Holomua Rd.

To Kahului

Hana Hwy.

Baldwin Ave.

Haleakala Hwy.

Haliimaile
⑭
⑯
⑮ ⑰
⑲
⑳ ㉑
㉒
Makawao
Olinda Rd.
Puohokamoa Rd.

Kokomo Rd.
Kaumahina Gulch

⑱

Koolau
Forest Reserve

Kula Gulch

Pulehu Rd.
Keahua Rd.

Old Haleakala Hwy.
Makawao Ave.
Hanamu Rd.
Pukalani

㉓
Makawao
Forest
Reserve

Area of
detail

Omaopio Rd.
㉔
㉕

Holopuni Rd.

Pulehu Rd.

Kula Hwy.

Haleakala Hwy.

Lahaina
Kahului

MAUI

Hana
Haleakala
National Park

UPCOUNTRY
MAUI

Lower
Kula Rd.

㉖
㉗

Crater Rd.

HALEAKALA
NATIONAL
PARK

Kula
㉘
㉙
㉚
Waipoli Rd.

Puu Ulaula

Kula Hwy.
㉛ Keokea

Kula
Forest Reserve

Ulupalakua
㉜

ATTRACTIONS
Alii Kula Lavender **29**
Hui Noeʻau Visual Arts
    Center **16**
Kula Botanical Garden **28**
MauiWine **32**
OʻO Farm **30**
Ocean Organic Vodka Farm **24**
Surfing Goat Dairy **25**

HOTELS
Aloha Cottage **23**
Banyan Bed &
    Breakfast **17**
Hale Hookipa Inn
    Makawao **22**
The Inn at Mamaʻs
    Fish House **4**
Lumeria **14**
Maui Dream Cottage **1**
Paia Inn **8**
Piialoha B&B
    Cottage **18**

RESTAURANTS
Cafe des Amis **11**
Casanova Italian Restaurant **21**
Charley's Restaurant **12**
Colleen's at the Cannery **2**
Flatbread & Company **9**
Grandma's Coffee House **31**
Haliimaile General Store **15**

Kuau Store **6**
Kula Lodge **27**
La Provence **26**
Mama's Fish House **5**
Market Fresh Bistro **19**
Milagros Food Co. **13**
Nuka **3**
Paia Bay Coffee **7**
Paia Fish Market **10**
T. Komoda Store & Bakery **20**

East Maui: On the Road to Hana

Note: You'll find the accommodations in this section on the "Upcountry & East Maui" map (p. 381).

PAIA-KUAU

Expensive

Paia Inn ★★   Embedded in colorful Paia town, this vibrant boutique inn offers a stylish introduction to Maui's North Shore. The inn comprises several vintage buildings that get progressively closer to the turquoise waters of Paia Bay. The owner's impeccable style seeps into every corner of the inn, from the organic Malie bath products in the travertine-tiled showers to the antique Balinese drawers repurposed as sink cabinets. The rooms in the main building hang right over Hana Highway's restaurants, surf shops, and cafes. The one- and two-bedroom suites in the next buildings are spacious, secluded retreats where you'll feel immediately at home. My favorite, #10, has a private outdoor shower and four-poster daybed. But it can't rival the three-bedroom beach house nestled up against the golden, sandy beach. Idyllic in every way, this miniature mansion is outfitted with a Viking stove, Jacuzzi, gorgeous artwork, and a huge outdoor living room. It's exclusive enough to attract celebrities, who've made it their Maui headquarters. In the courtyard behind the lobby, the Paia Inn Café serves outstanding brunch. Massages are available in the upstairs spa rooms.

93 Hana Hwy., Paia. www.paiainn.com. © **800/721-4000** or 808/579-6000. 17 units. Double from $189; 1-bedroom suite from $399; 2-bedroom suite from $499; 3-bedroom beach house from $1,000. **Amenities:** Restaurant, beach access; concierge; day spa; laundry services; free parking; free use of watersports equipment; free Wi-Fi.

Moderate

The Inn at Mama's Fish House ★★   The Gaudí-esque architect responsible for Mama's Fish House also works his magic on a handful of private suites and cottages next door. Amidst the coconuts on a pocket-sized beach, the Inn at Mama's features large private lanais with barbecues; imaginative Hawaiian artwork; fresh flowers tucked into large, fluffy bath towels; terrific toiletries; free laundry; and an easy stroll to Mama's Fish House, what many consider to be the finest restaurant on Maui. Each unit is unique; the luxury junior suites are especially classy, with deep soaking tubs and travertine showers. One- and two-bedroom cottages sit amid the tropical garden's red ginger, while a few two-bedroom units face the ocean. Restaurant guests stroll about the property until 10pm, but privacy is assured in your cottage's large enclosed lanai. In the morning, you'll be greeted with a tray of fresh fruit and banana bread. The inn sits on a small, sandy beach known simply as Mama's. It's better for exploring tide pools than for swimming—though Baldwin Beach is a short drive away and the thrills of Hookipa are right next-door. Keep in mind that this is the windward side of the island—it's often windy and rainy. You'll be perfectly situated here for a trip to Hana.

799 Poho Place (off the Hana Hwy. in Kuau), Paia. www.mamasfishhouse.com. ✆ **800/860-HULA** or 808/579-9764. 12 units. Garden studio from $275; 1-bedroom from $300; junior suite from $425; 2-bedroom cottage from $350. **Amenities:** Beach; barbecue; free laundry; free Wi-Fi.

HAIKU

Maui Dream Cottage ★ Danielle Chomel and her husband rent out a piece of their hidden paradise in Haiku. She's an expert orchid grower, and her blooms and bromeliads cover every inch of the property, from the entrance gate onwards. He's a classic car buff, and if you ask nicely he might show you his immaculate antique Porsche and Devins. Tucked in a corner of their fecund fruit orchard and garden, the two-bedroom cottage is comfortably furnished with a smallish kitchen, washer/dryer, a California king–size bed with Tempur-Pedic mattress in each of the cozy bedrooms, and a pullout futon in the living room. The off-the-beaten-path location is quiet and restful, offering a window into how real islanders live. It's a 3-minute walk to a great breakfast spot, but you'll have to drive 20 to 25 minutes to access Paia's restaurants, shopping, and beaches.

265 W. Kuiaha Rd., Haiku. www.mauidreamcottage.com. ✆ **808/575-9079.** 1 unit, shower only. $140 double. Extra person $15. 7-night minimum. **Amenities:** Free Wi-Fi.

Pilialoha B&B Cottage ★ In the heart of Haiku, this country cottage is set on a large lot with towering eucalyptus trees and some 200 varieties of roses blooming in the garden. Tastefully appointed in green and white, the cottage has warm wood floors and is private, clean, and spacious. The kitchen and closets are extremely well equipped—you'll find everything you need, from a rice cooker to beach towels, coolers, yoga mats, and fleece jackets for Haleakala sunrise trips. Your hosts, Machiko and Bill, live on-site and are happy to offer sightseeing suggestions. If you mention to Machiko that you're heading up the mountain, she'll likely send you off with a thermos of coffee and her homemade bread. The cottage is minutes from the restaurants and shopping of Haiku and Makawao and a short drive from Paia's beaches. In the winter months when Haiku weather can be cool and rainy, the gas fireplace is a welcome amenity.

2512 Kaupakalua Rd. (½-mile from Kokomo intersection), Haiku. www.pilialoha.com. ✆ **808/572-1440.** 1 unit. $165 double. Suitable for a couple only. 3-night minimum. **Amenities:** Watersports equipment; laundry facilities; free Wi-Fi.

At the End of the Road in East Maui: Hana

Note: You'll find Hana accommodations on the map on p. 323.

Expensive

Travaasa Hana ★★★ Ahhh . . . arriving at Travaasa (formerly the Hotel Hana Maui) is like letting out a deep sigh. The atmosphere is so relaxing you'll forget everything beyond this remote seaside sanctuary. Nestled in the center of quaint Hana town, the 66-acre resort wraps around

Kauiki Head, the dramatic point where Queen Kaahumanu was born. All of the accommodations here are wonderful, but the Ocean Bungalows (adults only, except over the holidays) are downright heavenly. These duplex cottages face the craggy shoreline, where horses graze above the rolling surf. Floor-to-ceiling sliding doors open to spacious lanais. Book your stay here a la carte or all-inclusive; the latter includes three meals, snacks, and a treatment in one of the planet's nicest spas. Whichever you choose, your room will be stocked with luxurious necessities: plush beds with organic linens, bamboo floors, giant soaking tubs, complimentary bottled water, Fair Trade coffee, homemade banana bread, and irresistibly scented bath products. You'll be far from shopping malls and sports bars, but exotic red-, black-, and white-sand beaches are just a short walk or shuttle ride away. The genuinely hospitable staff will set you up with numerous activities, many at no charge. Try stand-up paddling in Hana Bay, practice your archer's aim, take a tour of a nearby tropical fruit farm, or learn to throw a traditional Hawaiian fishing net. Rooms have no TVs (the Club Room has a giant one), but there are nightly talk-story sessions around the fire. This is luxury in its purest form. *Tip:* Stay 3 nights and fly for free from Kahului to Hana Airport.

5031 Hana Hwy., Hana. www.travaasa.com/hana. ℂ **888/820-1043.** 66 units. $450 single a la carte; $700 single inclusive; $500 double a la carte; $1000 double inclusive. Children stay free, can purchase $75 daily meal plan. **Amenities:** 2 restaurants (w/ Hawaiian entertainment Sun evenings); 2 bars (entertainment nightly); concierge; fitness center/fitness classes; complimentary clubs and use of the 3-hole practice golf courses; 2 outdoor pools; limited room service; luxury spa; tennis courts; free Wi-Fi.

Moderate

Bamboo Inn ★   This oceanfront, solar-powered "inn" is really just three exquisite suites, all with private lanais overlooking Waikaloa Beach's jet-black sand. The sumptuous accommodations include beds with ocean views, separate living rooms, and either a full kitchen or kitchenette. Naia, the largest unit, sleeps four and has a deep soaking tub on the lanai. The rooms and grounds are decorated with artifacts that your friendly and knowledgeable host, John Romain, collected during travels across Asia and Polynesia. Carved Balinese doors, Samoan tapa cloths, coconut wood floors, and a thatched-roof gazebo (where breakfast is served) add a rich and authentic elegance to a naturally lovely location. Waikaloa isn't great for swimming, but it's an incredible spot to watch the sunrise. All of Hana is within easy walking distance.

Uakea Rd. (between Waikaloa and Keanini rds.; look for the sign), Hana. www.bambooinn.com. ℂ **808/248-7718.** 3 units. $210–$285 double. Extra person $15. Rates include continental breakfast. 2-night minimum. **Amenities:** Beach, beach equipment; barbecue; free Wi-Fi (but only available in outdoor gazebo).

Hamoa Bay House & Bungalow ★★   This Eden-like property has two units: a bungalow and a house. Romance blooms in the 600-square-foot Balinese-style treetop bungalow, a gorgeous one-room studio with a beckoning bamboo bed, full kitchen, and a hot tub that hangs over the garden. The screened lanai and area downstairs function as separate rooms, giving you ample space. The house is just as spacious and lovingly decorated, with a large master bedroom and small second bedroom. Both the house and bungalow have private outdoor lava rock showers and access to tropical fruit trees and flowers. The property is on Hana Highway, just a 10-minute walk from Hamoa Beach.

Hana Hwy., between two entrances to Haneoo Rd., 2 miles south of Hana. www.vrbo.com/28451. *©* **808/248-7884.** 2 units. Bungalow $285–$310; house $325–$420. 3-night minimum. **Amenities:** Beach nearby; barbecue, hammock, beach equipment; barbecue; outdoor shower; whirlpool; free Wi-Fi.

Hamoa Beach House ★ Just around the bend from famed Hamoa Beach, this enormous 3-bedroom, 2-bathroom house is a great option for families or big parties. The rich woods, earthy tones, and rattan furnishings imbue the spacious interior of this '70s-era house with a cozy, nostalgic feeling. The living room has cathedral ceilings and two-story-tall windows that open up to the ocean. The upstairs bedrooms have vaulted ceilings, outdoor lanais, and a total of four king-size beds. A sweet little library is stocked with beach reading. Beneath the coconut palms outside, you'll find hammocks, a barbecue grill, a hot tub, and an outdoor shower—everything you need to enjoy Hana to the fullest.

487 Haneoo Rd., Hana. www.hamoabeachhouse.com. *©* **808/248-8277.** 1 unit. $525–$575 house (sleeps up to 8). 3-night minimum. **Amenities:** Beach nearby; beach equipment; barbecue; outdoor shower; whirlpool; free Wi-Fi.

Hana Kai Maui Resort ★★ "Condo complex" might not mesh with your idea of getting away from it all in Hana, but Hana Kai is truly special. Set on Hana Bay, the individually owned units are dotingly furnished and feature many hotel-like extras, such as organic bath products and fresh tropical bouquets. Studios and one- and two-bedroom units have kitchens and private lanais—but the corner units with wraparound ocean views are worth angling for. Gorgeously appointed Kaahumanu (#5) has a daybed on the lanai that you may never want to leave. For couples, Popolana (#2) is small but sweet, with woven bamboo walls and a Murphy bed that no one ever puts up. And why would you? You can lie in it and stare out to sea or, at daybreak, watch the sun rise straight out of the ocean. No air-conditioning or TVs—but they're not necessary here.

1533 Uakea Rd., Hana. www.hanakaimaui.com. *©* **800/346-2772** or 808/248-8426. 18 units. $210–$308 studio; $235–$325 1-bedroom; $425–$465 2-bedroom. Extra person $15. 2-night minimum for beachfront units. Children 6 and under stay free in parent's room. **Amenities:** Black-sand beach; beach equipment; barbecue; daily housekeeping; laundry facilities; breakfast service (for a charge); free Wi-Fi (free).

Hana Oceanfront Cottages ★ Serenity reigns at this plantation-style cottage and villa on the corner lot above beautiful Hamoa Bay. Your attentive hosts, Sandi and Dan Simoni, will stock your cottage with fresh flowers and arty postcards and light the tiki torches after sundown. The second-story villa has a Wolf stove and three sets of glass doors that open up to a 40-foot long lanai with a soul-soothing view. (The Simonis live below.) The freestanding, 600-square-foot cottage likewise has a gourmet kitchen, huge lanai, and an outdoor shower—exactly what you want after swimming at the beach next door.

522 Haneoo, Hana. www.hanabythesea.com. © **808/248-7558.** 2 units. $335–$375. 3-night minimum. $60 cleaning fee. **Amenities:** Barbecue; beach gear; free Wi-Fi.

Hana Ocean Palms Bungalow ★   This bungalow's location—opposite Waioka Pond (Venus Pool)—is perfect for adventurers who want to shed the trappings of modern life and dive deep into island culture. Spend your days relaxing in the hammock, jumping off the waterfall across the street, swimming at the black-sand beach, or exploring the nearby taro farm and national park trails. This rustic cabin is far from it all—stock up on groceries before heading here. Remember, this is country living: At night the rain might rattle against the tin roof, and if a gecko or two finds its way inside, consider it good luck.

Hana Hwy. btw. Waiohonu and St. Peter Church rds., Hana. www.hanapalmsbunga low.com. © **800/327-8097** or 808/248-8980. 1 unit. $245–$275 cottage (sleeps 4). Extra person $15. 2-night minimum. $50 cleaning fee for under 4 nights. **Amenities:** Barbecue; use of beach equipment; free Wi-Fi.

Hana's Tradewind Cottages ★   On a 5-acre flower farm, nestled amid pink gingers and scarlet heliconias, you have a choice of two rentals: the Hana Cabana or the Tradewinds Cottage. Each is sequestered in its own private corner of the farm and has a full kitchen, private hot tub, carport, and barbecue. Best for couples, the Cabana is a studio with vaulted ceilings and coconut palm–themed decor. The two-bedroom Tradewinds Cottage has a queen-size bed in one room and two twins in the other, one bathroom (with shower only), and a sizable living room and front porch. Days here are indescribably serene, and stars fill the sky at night. Guests are welcome to pick fruit from the surrounding banana and avocado trees, and you'll almost certainly want to take a box of tropical flowers home with you.

135 Alalele Place (the airport road), Hana. www.hanamaui.net. © **800/327-8097** or 808/248-8980. 2 units. $175–$195 double. Extra person $25. 2-night minimum. $50 cleaning fee for 3 nights or less. **Amenities:** Barbecue; whirlpool; free Wi-Fi (but spotty service).

Camping

Camping on Maui can be extreme (inside a volcano) or laid back (by the sea in Hana). It can be wet, cold, and rainy, or hot, dry, and windy—often all on the same day. If you're heading for Haleakala, remember that U.S. astronauts trained for the moon inside the volcano; pack survival gear. You'll need both a swimsuit and raincoat if you're bound for Waianapanapa. Bring your own equipment—Maui has no place that rents camping gear.

Camp Olowalu ★   Halfway to Lahaina on the Honoapiilani Highway, this campground abuts one of the island's best coral reefs. It's perfect for snorkeling and (during winter) whale watching. (You can hear the whales slap their fins against the sea's surface at night—a magical experience.) Tents sites are $20 with access to porta-potties and outdoor showers. Tentalows have twin or king beds with linens, private outdoor showers. They're close to the highway, but still cheap-ish at $80 per night ($95 during holiday season). Large groups can rent the six A-frame cabins with bathrooms, showers, and a kitchen. If you're tent camping, make sure a rowdy wedding party isn't booked that night. Either way, bring earplugs. You can rent kayaks here, too.

800 Olowalu Village Rd., Lahaina (off Honoapiilani Hwy.). www.campolowalu.com. ℂ **808/661-4303.** 6 cabins, 36 tent sites. Tent sites: $20 per night adults ($5 per night children 6–12). Tentalows: $80–$95 (2-night minimum). Cabins: $750–$1,100 for all 6 cabins (sleeps 36, 2-night minimum); contact camp for individual rates.

Haleakala National Park ★★★   This stunning national park offers a variety of options for campers throughout its diverse landscape: **car camping** at Hosmer's Grove halfway up the summit or at Oheo Gulch in Kipahulu; **pitching a tent** in the central Haleakala wilderness; or cozying up in one of the crater's **historic cabins.** The first three are free (aside from the $25 park entrance fee). No permit is required, but there's a 3-night limit. The cabins cost a flat $75, whether you rent them for 1 or 12 people.

Hosmer Grove, located at 6,800 feet, is a small, open grassy area surrounded by forest and frequented by native Hawaiian honeycreepers. Trees protect campers from the winds, but nights still get very cold; sometimes there's even ice on the ground up here. This is an ideal spot to spend the night if you want to see the Haleakala sunrise. Come up the day before, enjoy the park, take a day hike, and then turn in early. Facilities include a covered pavilion with picnic tables and grills, chemical toilets, and drinking water.

On the other side of the island, **Oheo Campground** is in the Kipahulu section of Haleakala National Park. You can set up your temporary home at a first-come, first-served drive-in campground with tent sites for 100 near the ocean. *Tip:* Get here early in the day to snag one of the secluded oceanfront sites under a shady *hala* tree. The campground has picnic tables, barbecue grills, and chemical toilets—but no potable water, so bring your own. Bring a tent as well—it rains 75 inches a year here. Call the **Kipahulu Ranger Station** (ℂ **808/248-7375**) for local weather.

Inside the volcano are two **wilderness tent-camping** areas: **Holua,** just off the Halemauu Trail and **Paliku,** 10 miles away, near the Kaupo Gap at the eastern end of the valley. Both are well over 6,000 feet in elevation and chilly at night. Facilities are limited to pit toilets and nonpotable catchment water. Water at Holua is limited, especially in summer. No open fires are allowed inside the volcano, so bring a stove if you plan to cook. Tent camping is restricted to the signed area and is not allowed in the horse pasture or the inviting grassy lawn in front of the cabins. Permits are issued at park headquarters daily from 8am to 3pm on a first-come, first-served basis on the day you plan to camp. Occupancy is limited to 25 people in each campground.

Also inside the volcano are three **wilderness cabins,** built in 1937 by the Civilian Conservation Corps. Each has 12 padded bunks (bring your own bedding), a table, chairs, cooking utensils, a two-burner propane stove, and a wood-burning stove with firewood. The cabins are spaced so that each one is a nice hike from the next: **Holua** cabin is 3.7 miles down the zigzagging Halemauu Trail, **Kapalaoa** cabin is 5.5 miles down the Sliding Sands Trail, and Paliku cabin is the farthest, at 9.3 miles down Sliding Sands and across the moonscape to the crater's eastern end. In spring and summer, the endangered 'ua'u (Hawaiian dark-rumped petrel) can be heard yipping and chortling on their way back home to their cliff-side burrows. Some campers and hikers exit through the Kaupo Gap—8.6 miles to the remote Piilani Highway. You can reserve cabins up to 6 months in advance on the park's reservation website (www.recreation. gov; ✆ **877/444-6777**). You're limited to 2 nights in 1 cabin and 3 nights total in the wilderness each month.

Note: All wilderness campers must watch a 10-minute orientation video at the park's visitor center.

Haleakala National Park, at top of Crater Rd., and at Kipahulu Visitor Center, 12 miles past Hana on Hana Hwy. www.nps.gov/hale. ✆ **808/572-4400.** 3 cabins, 100-plus tent sites. $75 flat rate for cabins; tent campers free (aside from $25 park entrance fee). Cabins by reservation only.

Polipoli State Park ★ High up on the slope of Haleakala, at 6,200 feet in elevation, this state park has extensive trails that wind through conifer forests reminiscent of the Pacific Northwest. It's frequently cold and foggy here—be prepared for extra-chilly nights! One eight-bunk cabin is available for $90; it has a cold shower and a gas stove but no electricity or drinking water (bring your own). Tent-campers can pitch on the grass nearby. Reserve on the website (the cabin must be reserved in person at the Wailuku office) and print out your permit, which must be displayed. *Note:* The park is only accessible by 4WD vehicles.

9¾ miles up Waipoli Rd., off Kekaulike (Hwy 377); 4WD vehicle recommended. By reservation only: c/o State Parks Division, 54 S. High St., Room 101, Wailuku. www. dlnr.hawaii.gov/dsp/camping-lodging/maui. ✆ **808/984-8109.** 1 cabin. $90 per night (sleeps 8). $18 for 1st tent-camper, $3 for additional campers. 5-night maximum.

Waianapanapa State Park ★★ The 12 rustic cabins tucked in the *hala* (pandanus) groves of Waianapanapa State Park are one of the best lodging deals on Maui. Each cabin has six twin bunks, a full kitchen (minus oven), and large lanai where you can wile away the hours watching rainstorms roll in from sea. Cabins #5 and #6 are closest to the water.

They've recently been spiffed up, but they're still frequented by geckos and are fairly Spartan. You can also pitch a tent above the black-sand beach on Pailoa Bay. Watch the sun rise out of the ocean and beat the crowds to the beach. There's an on-site caretaker, along with restrooms, showers, picnic tables, shoreline hiking trails, and historic sites. Bring rain gear and mosquito protection—this is the rainforest, after all. Reserve tent sites and cabins on the website (or in person at the Wailuku office) and print out your permit, which must be displayed.

End of Waianapanapa Rd., off Hana Hwy. By reservation only: c/o State Parks Division, 54 S. High St., Room 101, Wailuku. http://dlnr.hawaii.gov/dsp/parks/maui/waianapanapa-state-park. Ⓒ **808/984-8109.** 10 units. $90 per cabin per night (sleeps up to 6). $18 for 1st tent-camper, $3 for additional campers. 5-night maximum.

WHERE TO EAT ON MAUI

When it comes to dining in Maui, all I can say is: Come hungry and bring a fat wallet. Dining has never been better on the Valley Isle, home to numerous enterprising and imaginative chefs. The farm-to-table concept has finally taken root on this bountiful island, where in past years up to 90% of the food had been imported. Today chefs and farmers collaborate on menus, filling plates with tender micro-greens and heirloom tomatoes picked that morning. Fishers reel in glistening opakapaka (pink snapper), and ranchers offer up flavorful cuts of Maui-grown beef.

A new crop of inspired chefs is taking these ripe ingredients to new heights. At **Ka'ana Kitchen,** Chef Isaac Bancaco nearly outshines his celebrity neighbor, "Iron Chef" Masaharu Morimoto (who brought his high-octane Japanese fusion cuisine to Wailea). Both are outstanding; make time for each if you can swing it. On the other side of the island, at Chef Gerard Reversade continues to plate up perfect French cuisine at **Gerard's,** while Jojo Vasquez adds exciting Filipino accents to the gourmet dishes at the **Plantation House.** Stellar dining experiences all, with prices to match. You don't *have* to spend a fortune to eat well here—Maui does have a few budget eateries, noted below. Among the best is **Tin Roof,** by *Top Chef* star Sheldon Simeon. If you want to feast, there's never been a better time to do so on Maui.

Central Maui

Kahului and Wailuku have a few tasty finds. Minutes outside of the airport in a windy dirt lot across from Costco, you'll find an array of **food trucks** dishing out everything from pork belly sandwiches to poke (seasoned raw fish).

MODERATE

Bistro Casanova ★ MEDITERRANEAN   Hungry and marooned in Kahului? Head to this Mediterranean bistro for sweet and savory crepes, traditional Italian pastas, or a giant bowl of paella. The casual but classy restaurant fills with business lunchers at noon. It's more relaxed at dinner (unless there's a big show at the nearby Maui Arts & Cultural Center— then it will be hopping). It offers a private room for big parties and a full bar for *pau hana* (after work) drinks.

33 Lono Ave., Kahului. www.casanovamaui.com. © **808/873-3650.** Lunch main courses $9–$18; dinner main courses $14–$32. Mon–Sat 11am–2:30pm, 5–9pm.

Marco's Grill & Deli ★ ITALIAN   Located just outside the airport, Marco's offers decent Italian fare in an upscale diner with black-and-white booths and white linens on the tables. Portions tend to be huge, and everything is made in house, from the meatballs, sausages, and burgers to the sauces and salad dressing. Favorites include chicken Parmesan and vodka rigatoni.

395 Dairy Rd., Kahului. © **808/877-4446.** Breakfast $6–14; lunch and dinner main courses $12–$39. Daily 7:30am–9:30pm.

A Saigon Cafe ★★ VIETNAMESE   It's hard to say which is better at this beloved neighborhood restaurant—the delicious Vietnamese cuisine or the hilarious waiters who make wisecracks while taking your order. Whatever you order—the steamed opakapaka with ginger and garlic, one of a dozen soups, the catfish simmering in a clay pot, or the fragrant lemongrass curry—you'll notice the freshness of the flavors. Owner Jennifer Nguyen grows many of her own vegetables and herbs and even sprouts her own mung beans. My favorites are the Buddha rolls dunked in spicy peanut sauce and the Vietnamese "burritos." You make the latter tableside—tricky at first, but fun.

1792 Main St., Wailuku. www.asaigoncafe.com. © **808/243-9560.** Main courses $9–$27. Mon–Sat 10am–9:30pm, Sun 10am–8:30pm. Heading into Wailuku from Kahului, go over the bridge and take the 1st right onto Central Ave.; then take the 1st right on Nani St. At the next stop sign, look for the building with the neon sign that says open.

INEXPENSIVE

Down to Earth ★ ORGANIC HEALTH FOOD   Stop in here for a vegetarian snack or bag full of local organic produce. During mango season, this full-service natural-foods store carries as many as three different locally grown varieties of the fruit—worth their weight in gold. The deli includes creative salads, lasagna, chili, curries, and dozens of tasty dishes—including gluten-free and vegan options. Deli attendants can whip up a faux Reuben sandwich or tasty meatless burger for you. The upstairs dining area is plain but convenient.

305 Dairy Rd., Kahului. www.downtoearth.org. © **808/877-2661.** Self-serve hot buffet, salad bar, and deli; food sold by the pound; average $7–$12 for a plate; sandwiches $6–$11. Mon–Sat 6am–10pm, Sun 7am–9pm.

Poi by the Pound ★ HAWAIIAN/PLATE LUNCH   When in Hawaii, do as the Hawaiians and eat poi—steamed taro root pounded with water and slightly fermented. A small bowl of this traditional staple starch

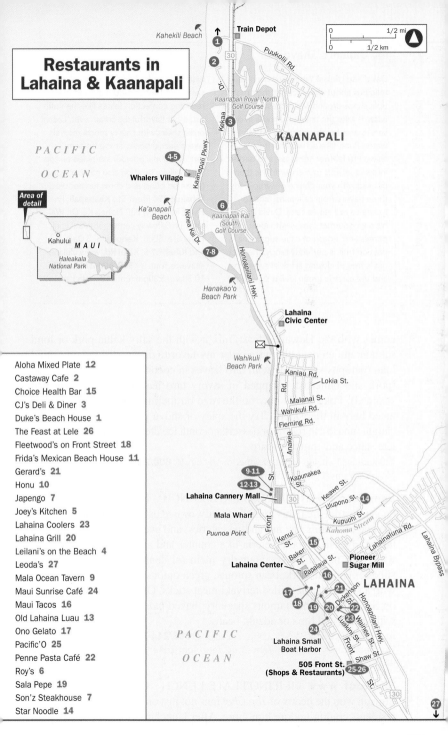

Restaurants in Lahaina & Kaanapali

Ululani's Shave Ice

David and Ululani Yamashiro are near-religious about shave ice. At their multiple shops around Maui, these shave-ice wizards take the uniquely Hawaiian dessert to new heights. It starts with the water: Pure, filtered water is frozen, shaved to feather lightness, and patted into shape. This mini-snowdrift is then doused with your choice of syrup—any three flavors from calamansi lime to lychee to red velvet cake. David makes his own gourmet syrups with local fruit purees and a dash of cane sugar. The passion fruit is perfectly tangy, the coconut is free of cloying artificial sweetness, and the electric green kiwi is studded with real seeds. Add a "snowcap" of sweetened condensed milk, and the resulting confection tastes like the fluffiest, most flavorful ice cream ever. Locals order theirs with chewy mochi morsels, sweet adzuki beans at the bottom, or tart *li hing mui* powder sprinkled on top. The Wailuku location also has *manapua* (steamed buns) and chow fun noodles. **Lahaina:** 790 Front St.; **Kaanapali:** [in Hyatt Regency] 200 Nohea Kai Dr. **Wailuku:** [in Safeway center] 58 Maui Lani Pkwy Ste. 5000; **Kahului:** 333 Dairy Rd.; and **Kihei:** 61 S. Kihei Rd. www.ululanisshaveice.com. ℂ **360/606-2745.** Daily 10:30am–6:30pm (until 10pm in Lahaina).

comes with the Hawaiian feast; mix it with the salty kalua pork or lomi salmon and enjoy. Otherwise order my favorite dishes: the creamy squid luau (octopus simmered with taro leaves in coconut milk) and the laulau (pork and butterfish wrapped in savory taro leaves like a present and steamed). Poke bowls may be the rage on the mainland, but they originated here in the islands. Try the spicy or shoyu poke made with locally caught tuna. Save room for dessert: coconut ice cream sundae with chocolate sauce and chunks of taro.

430 Kele St., Kahului. www.poibythepound.com. ℂ **808/283-9381.** Entrees $8–$24. Mon–Sat 9am–10pm; Sun 9am–5pm.

Sam Sato's ★ NOODLES/PLATE LUNCH   Hidden away in Wailuku's industrial area, this humble, family-owned eatery dates back to 1933. It's one of Maui's last ma-and-pa eateries, and everything on the menu is under $10. Sit at the cafeteria-like counter and strike up a conversation with your neighbor. Try your dry mein (al dente noodles served with slices of char siu pork, bean sprouts, green onions, and broth on the side) with a side order of grilled teriyaki meat sticks. On the way out, stock up on Sam Sato's other famous specialty: baked *manju,* flaky pastries filled with sweetened lima or adzuki beans.

At the Millyard, 1750 Wili Pa Loop, Wailuku. ℂ **808/244-7124.** Plate lunches $8–$9. No credit cards. Mon–Sat 7am–2pm; 7am–4pm bakery and preordered takeout items.

Tin Roof ★★★ FILIPINO/PLATE LUNCH   Celebrity chef Sheldon Simeon won the hearts of *Top Chef* fans not just once, but twice, and Maui residents couldn't adore him more. After launching Star Noodle (p. 396) into fame, he and his wife, Janice, opened their own business—a humble to-go spot in an industrial strip mall in Kahului. The menu, inspired by his Filipino roots, is so much fun: buy a 50-cent "dime bag" of house-made furikake to sprinkle on your mochiko chicken. Add a 6-minute egg to your pork belly bowl. You'll want to Instagram yourself eating the chocolate b'day cake bibingka, covered in party-colored sprinkles.

360 Papa Pl., Kahului. www.tinroofmaui.com. © **808/868-0753.** Everything under $9. Mon–Sat 10am–2pm.

West Maui

LAHAINA

Expensive

The Feast at Lele ★★★ POLYNESIAN   The Feast at Lele stands out from other luaus as the gourmand's choice. Although most luau seating is en masse, guests here sit at elegant tables in the sand facing a cirque-inspired stage. As the sun dips into the sea behind you, chanting dancers regale you with stories of Polynesia. You'll progress from Hawaii to New Zealand, Tahiti, and Samoa, feasting on each island nation's culinary specialties in turn. During the opening hula, you'll sample Hawaiian fish with mango sauce and *imu*-roasted kalua pig. While watching the exciting Maori *haka,* you'll eat New Zealand sea bean and duck salad. Pace yourself; each of the four savory courses includes three dishes—and then there's dessert, accompanied by a fantastic fire knife dance! The swish of *ti*-leaf skirts and the beat of the drums enhance the meal's flavors; it's a sensory experience even for the most jaded luau-goer.

505 Front St., Lahaina. www.feastatlele.com. © **866/244-5353** or 808/667-5353. Reservations required. Set 5-course menu (includes all beverages) $130 adults, $99 children 2–12. Apr 1–Sept 30 daily 6:30pm seating (to 9:30pm); Oct 1–Mar 31 daily 5:30pm seating (to 8:30pm).

Gerard's ★★★ FRENCH   Chef Gerard Reversade has called Hawaii home for nearly 4 decades, but his French accent hasn't lost one cédille. His charming residence-turned-restaurant beneath the Plantation Inn in Lahaina is equally authentic. I never would've imagined that a simple chilled cucumber soup could be transcendent—but this one is, its delicacy amplified by goat cheese and fresh dill. The roasted opakapaka served with fennel fondue and spiked with hints of orange and ginger is stellar, as is the grilled Hawaiian filet with salsify au gratin. Chef Reversade is every bit as much of a baker as a chef, and the savory dishes that incorporate pastry—such as the Hamakua mushroom appetizer—are delights. The dessert menu has a half-dozen excellent offerings, including a marvelous *millefeuille* and chocolate mousse with pistachio ice cream.

At the Plantation Inn, 174 Lahainaluna Rd., Lahaina. www.gerardsmaui.com. © **808/661-8939.** Reservations recommended. Main courses $39–$58. Daily 6–10pm.

Lahaina Grill ★★ NEW AMERICAN   For more than 2 decades, this classy restaurant has been collecting accolades for its perfectly executed island cuisine, gracious service, and great wine list. The striking decor—splashy artwork by local painter Jan Kasprzycki, pressed-tin ceilings, and warm lighting—creates an appealing atmosphere. The bar, despite lacking an ocean view, is among the busiest in town and often features special pricing. The menu hasn't strayed much over the years; fans will still find their favorites: the prawn-stuffed blue corn chile rellano, the aromatic Kona coffee–roasted rack of lamb, and memorable triple berry pie. If you're planning a special event or a large party, you can book a private room and design your own menu with the chef.

127 Lahainaluna Rd., Lahaina. www.lahainagrill.com. © **808/667-5117.** Reservations required. Main courses $35–$96. Daily 5:30–9 or 10pm. Bar daily 6–10pm (closing earlier on slow nights).

Pacific'O Restaurant ★★ SEAFOOD/CONTEMPORARY PACIFIC RIM   You can't get any closer to the ocean than these tables overlooking the beach at 505 Front Street. Start with flash-fried oysters and wakame seaweed salad or lobster ravioli. Move on to saffron beet risotto studded with seared shrimp and chunks of seafood. Vegetarians will delight in the Portobello mushrooms with quinoa and cilantro pesto. (The kitchen sources ingredients from its own O'o Farm up in Kula.) This is a superb and relatively affordable lunch spot. Indulge in ginger-crusted fish or Kalbi beef tacos and glass of spicy Syrah while watching the ships sail by.

505 Front St., Lahaina. www.pacificomaui.com. © **808/667-4341.** Reservations recommended. Main courses $14–$20 lunch, $27–$46 dinner. Daily 11:30am–3:30pm and 5:30–9:30pm.

Moderate

Fleetwood's on Front Street ★ AMERICAN   Rock and Roll Hall of Famer Mick Fleetwood ventured into the restaurant business with commendable results. His snazzy eatery occupies the top two floors of a lovingly restored three-story building on Front Street. For dinner, choose from locally grown salads, fresh fish entrees, or a Harley-Davidson Hog burger—hold the Harley. I find the food a little lackluster, but the atmosphere is outstanding. The dining room's cozy booths and wraparound bar evoke an older, more sophisticated era. But the real draw is the rooftop dining—plus the live entertainment. *Tip:* Nightly at 6pm, local musicians offer a short, free performance, ranging from bagpipes to Hawaiian chanting. Mick and his celebrity friends often pop in to play a set. When it rains, the upstairs seating is closed.

744 Front St., Lahaina. www.fleetwoodsonfrontst.com. © **808/669-6425.** Reservations recommended. Main courses $22–$48. Daily 5–10pm.

Frida's Mexican Beach House ★ MEXICAN   Mark Ellman owns three restaurants in a row on the beautiful seashore fronting Mala Wharf. Frida's, his latest, features Latin-inspired cuisine in a breezy dining room accented with pretty Mexican tiles and wrought-iron chandeliers. Sip one of 40 tequilas at the open-air bar. Rib-eye mojo de ajo and grilled Spanish octopus with tomatillo salsa and fresh guacamole are delicious, especially on the romantic oceanfront lanai.

1287 Front St., Lahaina. www.fridasmaui.com. ✆ **808/661-1287.** Reservations recommended. Main courses $16–$40. Daily 11am–9:30pm.

Honu ★★ PIZZA/SEAFOOD   Snag an oceanfront table where the gentle tide nearly tickles your toes and spy on the green sea turtles for whom this restaurant is named. Honu's diverse menu is guaranteed to please someone in your party, from the fried oyster sandwiches and authentic Neapolitan pizzas to the wok-fried Dungeness crab. The Middle Eastern kale salad will turn doubters into believers: Finely chopped kale is massaged with preserved lemon vinaigrette and tossed with bittersweet walnuts, rich and salty pecorino shavings, sweet slivers of chewy dates, and pomegranate seeds that burst on the tongue. Gluten-free and *keiki* (children's) menus are available, along with an extensive offering of draft beers, single malt scotches, and handcrafted cocktails.

1295 Front St., Lahaina. www.honumaui.com. ✆ **808/667-9390.** Reservations recommended. Main courses $17–$48. Daily 11am–9:30pm.

Lahaina Coolers ★ AMERICAN/INTERNATIONAL   The huge marlin hanging above the bar and persimmon-colored walls set a cheery tone at this casual indoor/outdoor restaurant. On Sunday, breakfast is served until 1pm. The huevos rancheros come in a sizzling cast-iron skillet heaped with kalua pork, and you have your choice of eggs Benedict: classic; Cajun, with seared fish and salsa; and the "Local" with kalua pork and sweetbreads. Spicy entrees dominate the lunch menu, such as Evil Jungle Pasta spiked with peppery Thai peanut sauce or whaler's stew—a poor man's cioppino. Prices increase at dinner but are still a fraction of what you'd pay at most Front Street establishments. Dinner is served until midnight.

180 Dickenson St., Lahaina. www.lahainacoolers.com. ✆ **808/661-7082.** Main courses $8–$15 breakfast, $11–$16 lunch, $17–$28 dinner. Daily 8am–1am.

Mala Ocean Tavern ★★ AMERICAN/INTERNATIONAL   This tiny tavern overlooking Mala Wharf in Lahaina is perfect. Brighter and classier than "tavern" suggests, the oceanfront seating lets diners peer down on sea turtles foraging in the surf. The bartenders know their business, and the complimentary edamame guacamole alerts your taste buds that something delicious is about to happen. The menu offers health-conscious and hedonistic options, from the *gado gado* (a vegan Indonesian rice dish heaped with sugar-snap peas and coconut peanut sauce) to the insanely rich and delicious adult mac and cheese (an oven-baked medley of three cheeses and Hamakua mushrooms). The weekend brunch is among Maui's tastiest, with local organic eggs served in Benedicts, chilaquiles, and huevos rancheros.

1307 Front St., Lahaina. www.malaoceantavern.com. ✆ **808/667-9394.** Main courses $12–$27 lunch, $17–$49 dinner; brunch $6–$32. Mon–Fri 11am–9:30pm; Sat–Sun 9am–9:30pm.

Star Noodle ★★ NOODLES/FUSION   This hip noodle house at the top of Lahaina's industrial park offers a deceivingly simple menu of noodles and share plates. The hapa ramen, with its smoky pork and spicy miso broth, is guaranteed to be unlike any you've had before. Each dish is a gourmet twist on a local favorite; the Lahaina fried soup isn't soup at all but thick and chewy house-made noodles tossed with ground pork and bean sprouts. The ahi avo is a divine mix of fresh red tuna and buttery avocado swimming in a pool of lemon-pressed olive oil and spiked with sambal. With its long communal table, Shepard Fairey artwork, and glamorous washrooms, this casual eatery has an urban feel. From the window seats you can catch a hint of an ocean view—just enough to remind you that you're still in Hawaii.

286 Kupuohi St., Lahaina. www.starnoodle.com. ℭ **808/667-5400.** Main courses $7–$30. Daily 10:30am–10pm.

Inexpensive

Aloha Mixed Plate ★ PLATE LUNCH/BEACHSIDE GRILL   This long-time local favorite just got a major makeover. You can still get the beachfront eatery's classics: fresh-made chow mein, Korean kalbi ribs and coconut prawns fried golden brown, but now you can also dig into kalo-flower mash (taro root mashed with cauliflower and butter) and a scrumptious chicken katsu "sammy" with slaw and tonkatsu sauce on a potato flour bun. A welcome novelty: some of the new ingredients have been roasted in the traditional Hawaiian *imu* (underground oven) at the luau grounds next door. *Imu*-roasted beets have a savory smokiness and the short ribs . . . are . . . mmm . . . meltingly good. The bar got an upgrade, too. Toss back a Maui Mule or try an adult shave ice: finely shaved ice doused with berry puree and SKYY Vodka.

1285 Front St., Lahaina. www.alohamixedplate.com. ℭ **808/661-3322.** Main courses $9–$22. Daily 8am–10pm.

Choice Health Bar ★★ GOURMET DELI/CAFE   This health-conscious juice bar and cafe is where the beautiful people in Lahaina come to fuel up. After a taxing morning of stand-up paddling past sea turtles, re-energize here with a sunrise acai bowl drizzled in honey and a "game changer"—iced cold brew coffee shaken with macadamia nut milk, vanilla, and maple syrup. Daily lunch specials include wholesome soups and savory rawviolis—a vegetarian reinvention of pasta. The plate lunches are an edible rainbow of scrumptious kale salad, coconut-garlic quinoa, and ruby red beet soup, with a bonus dessert.

1087 Limahana Place (off of Honoapiilani Hwy.), Lahaina. www.choicehealthbar.com. ℭ **808/661-7711.** Breakfast and lunch main courses $6–$12; dinner $12–$14. Mon–Sat 8am–6pm, Sun 9am–1pm.

Leoda's ★★ SANDWICHES/BAKERY   As you approach the counter, you'll see why the line stretches to the door: a glass case full of banana and coconut pies slathered in fresh whipped cream. The savory pies are just okay. But the sweet pies—especially the chocolate macadamia nut praline—are intergalactic. For breakfast, the outstanding seared ahi Benedict come with pesto, watercress, avocado, and local eggs. For lunch, the Ham'n sandwich is a hot and juicy mess of duroc ham, island pesto, melted Jarlsberg cheese, and apricot-tomato jam on buttered rye bread. Leoda's belongs to the Star Noodle, Old Lahaina Luau, and Aloha Mixed Plate restaurant family—a crew that knows how to please. The eatery's bright decor pays homage to Maui's bygone plantation days.

820 Olowalu Village Rd. (off of Honoapiilani Hwy), Lahaina. www.leodas.com. *©* **808/662-3600.** Breakfast items $3–$19; lunch/dinner items $4–$16. Daily 7am–8pm.

Maui Sunrise Café ★ CAFE   For a bargain lunch or breakfast, follow the surfers to this hole-in-the-wall located just off Front Street. (The address says Front St., but it's really off of Market, across from the library.) The kitchen turns out tasty breakfast burritos, a lox Benedict with home-fried potatoes, and decent sandwiches. Service can be slow, but the prices can't be beat in this neighborhood. Eat in the covered patio out back or take it to go and picnic in the adjoining park.

693A Front St., Lahaina. *©* **808/661-8558.** Breakfast items under $11; lunch items $7–$12. No credit cards. Daily 7am–4pm.

Ono Gelato Company ★★ CAFE/ICE CREAM   Who doesn't want to hang out on a picnic bench perched over the Lahaina surf while eating creamy gelato? This classy creamery uses locally sourced *lilikoi* (Hawaiian passion fruit), mango, and coffee to craft rich and flavorful scoops of gelato and sorbets. The coffee bar opens for breakfast, and the baristas make a mean *affogato*—gelato drowned in two shots of espresso. The back patio is the best spot to chill in town—and it has free Wi-Fi.

815 Front St., Lahaina. *©* **808/495-0203.** Most items under $7. Daily 8am–10pm.

Penne Pasta Café ★ ITALIAN/MEDITERRANEAN   With outdoor seating on a Lahaina side street, this casual spot features delicious Italian and Mediterranean cuisine. Order at the counter, and the manager delivers your pasta, pizza, or salad Niçoise to your table. It's a sit-down meal at takeout prices. The penne puttanesca, baked penne with braised beef, and lamb osso buco (Wed night special) are wonderful. Try the oven-roasted butternut squash simmered in almonds and sage.

180 Dickenson St., Lahaina. www.pennepastacafe.net *©* **808/661-6633.** Main courses $9–$18. Daily 11am–9:30pm.

Sala Pepe ★★ ITALIAN   The menu at this small Italian bistro changes to reflect what's in season, but the quality stays consistent. This husband and wife team (she's from Brooklyn, he's from Milan) puts a ton of love into their handcut pastas and pizza pies. Don't be surprised to see top chefs from nearby restaurants dining here on their day off. Daily specials include heavenly ravioli fatti in casa with short rib ragu, or sopprasata piccante pizza. Everything is written on the chalkboard in Italian—if you can't understand it, don't worry. It all translates as delicious.

In Old Lahaina Center, 878 Front St., Lahaina. www.salepepemaui.com. © **808/667-7667.** Main courses $8–$16 lunch, $10–$28 dinner. Mon–Sat 11am–2pm and 5–10pm.

KAANAPALI

Expensive

Japengo ★★ SUSHI/PACIFIC RIM   The open-air dining room hanging over the Hyatt pool is divided into multiple private nooks, evoking the feel of a Japanese teahouse. Meander inside for superb Japanese-influenced entrees and inspired sushi, sashimi, and hand rolls. Look around for signs of *tengu,* a long-nosed mythological trickster and the restaurant's mascot. Depending on what the fishermen reeled in that day, the *moriawase,* or chef's platter, may include achingly red tuna, translucent slivers of Big Island *hirame* (flounder), poached local abalone, creamy wedges of *uni* (sea urchin), or raw New Caledonia prawn. The sushi wizards at the bar beautifully garnish this bounty with nests of peppery daikon and aromatic shiso leaves. Delicious vegetable sides—kabocha pumpkin, asparagus in Thai chili sauce, and lavender-honey corn—originate on nearby Simpli-Fresh farm.

At the Hyatt Regency Maui Resort, 200 Nohea Kai Dr., Kaanapali. https://maui.regency.hyatt.com. © **808/661-1234.** Main courses $18–$69. Daily 5–10pm.

Roy's Kaanapali ★★ HAWAII REGIONAL CUISINE   Roy Yamaguchi, the James Beard award–winning chef and one of the pioneers of Hawaii Regional Cuisine, owns eponymous restaurants around the world. At his Maui kitchen, try mustard glazed short ribs or rich misoyaki butterfish. The restaurant serves lunch from 11am to 2pm and a bar menu from 2 to 5pm, which features the "canoe for two," an appetizer platter of ahi poke, pork lumpia, chicken pot stickers, Szechuan short ribs, and skewered shrimp. Hallelujah for the bartender who created the "Skinny Colada," a cocktail that delivers the flavor of a piña colada without the overwhelming milky cream. *Tip:* Two words: chocolate soufflé. It takes 20 minutes to prepare, so let your waiter know you want it in advance. And when it arrives, wait a moment for it to cool—don't burn your tongue on the hot lava chocolate!

2290 Kaanapali Pkwy., Kaanapali. www.royshawaii.com/roys-kaanapali. © **808/669-6999.** Lunch main courses $18–$32; dinner main courses $32–$64. Daily 11am–10pm.

Son'z Steakhouse ★ STEAKHOUSE   Descend a palatial staircase for dinner at Son'z, where tables overlook a lagoon with white and black swans swimming by. This is classy digs for a steakhouse; imagine Ruth's Chris with extra flavor and a fairy-tale atmosphere. Chef Geno Sarmiento knows how to prepare protein; his filet is on point with "Mauishire" sauce, as is the New Zealand rack of lamb with fig sauce and kohlrabi potato puree. Sides are generally sold separately; choose from grilled asparagus, truffle mac and cheese, or the loaded baked potato: a decadent spud cooked low and slow (200° for 4 hr.) and sinfully stuffed with mascarpone, bacon bits, truffle butter, chives, and Parmesan. Finish with Portuguese sweet-bread French toast, vanilla gelato, and sweetly tart local bananas set aflame, Foster's style.

At the Hyatt Regency Maui Resort, 200 Nohea Kai Dr., Kaanapali. www.sonz steakhouse.com. © **808/667-4506.** Main courses $30–$64. Daily 5:30–9:30pm.

Moderate

Duke's Beach House ★ PACIFIC RIM There are few more beautiful places to enjoy breakfast than here, facing Kahekili Beach. This restaurant mimics an open-air plantation home, decorated with memorabilia chronicling the life of world-famous Hawaiian surfer, Duke Kahanamoku. It's part of the TS Restaurants family, which includes Kimo's, Hula Grill, and Leilani's on Maui, Keoki's on Kauai, and Duke's in Waikiki—among others. The menu reflects much of what you'll find at the other locales: "onolicious" French toast made with Molokai sweet bread, omelets, and steel-cut oats for breakfast; coconut shrimp and burgers for lunch; macadamia-nut-crusted fish and steak for dinner; and the signature hula pie for dessert. What sets this restaurant apart is its gracious sea-breeze-kissed locale and the kitchen's commitment to serving locally raised beef, eggs, and vegetables. Add to that live music during dinner and the daily "aloha hour" (3–5pm).

At Honua Kai Resort & Spa, 130 Kai Malina Pkwy., North Kaanapali Beach. www. dukesmaui.com. © **808/662-2900.** Breakfast items $7–$18; lunch main courses $9–$21; dinner main courses $18–$46. Daily 7:30am–9:30pm.

Leilani's on the Beach ★★ STEAK/SEAFOOD With Chef Ryan Luckey running the kitchen at Leilani's, diners can expect creative upgrades to the generic surf-and-turf: filet mignon with black truffle butter and sesame-crusted ahi steak with coconut and citrus jasmine rise. The Surfing Goat cheese plate includes a trio of delectable local cheeses, served with taro crisps and lavosh. The **Beachside Grill**—with tables that bank right up to Kaanapali Beach—features a separate, more casual menu. Here you can people-watch while snacking on Cajun-rubbed fish tacos or a kalua pork Cuban and tossing back a Kaanapali cosmo. Leilani's belongs to the TS Restaurant family, so you can get the trademark Hula Pie, though I prefer the passion fruit Pono Pie made with breadfruit and without refined sugar.

At Whalers Village, 2435 Kaanapali Pkwy., Kaanapali. www.leilanis.com. © **808/661-4495.** Reservations suggested for dinner. Beachside Grill lunch and dinner main courses $12–$18; Leilani's dinner main courses $23–$33. Beachside Grill daily 11am–11pm. Leilani's daily 5–9:30pm.

Inexpensive

Castaway Café ★ AMERICAN   Hidden away in the Aston Maui Kaanapali Villas, this little cafe sits right on Kahekili Beach—privy to perfect views and salty breezes. Chef Lyndon Honda and the Cohn Restaurant group breathed new life into this local favorite, which has long been famous for its Saturday-night prime rib special. New menu items include a garden sandwich with edamame hummus and an array of burgers. Breakfast is extra-relaxing here. Avocado toast with two eggs and an ocean view? Yes, please!

In the Aston Maui Kaanapali Villas, 45 Kai Ala Dr., Kaanapali. www.castawaycafe.com. © 808/661-9091. Main courses: $10–$15 breakfast; $12–$17 lunch; $14–$29 dinner. Daily 7:30am–9pm.

CJ's Deli & Diner ★ AMERICAN/DELI   Need a break from resort prices? Head to this happening eatery just off of Honoapiilani Highway in Kaanapali. Prices are so low you won't believe you're still on Maui. The atmosphere is colorful and slightly chaotic, with a huge billboard menu that spans the back wall, shelves stuffed with souvenirs and brochures, and a . . . basketball hoop? Practice your free throws while debating over breakfast options: spinach-stuffed omelet, smoked salmon bagel, or French toast made with Hawaiian sweet bread. Lunch ranges from grilled panini sandwiches to fish and chips, mochiko chicken, and barbecue ribs. Kids can order happy-face pancakes and "squid-eyes" soup. If you're heading out to Hana or up to Haleakala, stop by for a box lunch. Toppings are packed separately so sandwiches don't get soggy. You can even order online for a to-go pickup.

At the Fairway Shops at Kaanapali, 2580 Kekaa Dr. (just off the Honoapiilani Hwy.), Kaanapali. www.cjsmaui.com. © 808/667-0968. Breakfast items $5–$10; lunch items $9–$17; Hana Lunch Box and Air Travel Lunch Box $14 each. Daily 7am–8pm.

Joey's Kitchen ★★ FILIPINO/PLATE LUNCH   Joey Macadangdang ran the kitchen at Roy's for many years, winning award after award for his inventive gourmet cuisine. Now he's got two restaurants of his own: an ultra-casual spot in the Whalers Village food court and this slightly fancier eatery in Napili, where Joey and his wife will personally take care of you. If you've never tried Filipino food before, this is your place. Get the savory pork adobo plate, or seafood sinigang—a hot and sour medley of fish, clams, and shrimp. You'll find familiar favorites, too: fried Brussels sprouts, and fish and chips.

5095 Napilihau St., Napili. © 808/214-5590. Open Tues–Sun 10am–2pm and 4–10pm. Also at Whalers Village, 2435 Kaanapali Pkwy., Kaanapali. Open 8am–9pm. www.joeyskitchenhimaui.com. © 808/868-4474. Entrees $9–$39.

HONOKOWAI, KAHANA & NAPILI

Note: You'll find the restaurants in this section on the "Hotels & Restaurants in West Maui" map (p. 357).

Moderate

Maui Brewing Co. ★ BREWPUB   Maui's uber popular microbrewery has expanded to Oahu, but the home is where the heart is. The Kahana brewpub offers beer flights at the bar and excellent pub fare—much of it beer-battered. You can try limited-release brews here, along with the company's standards: Bikini Blonde Ale, Big Swell IPA, Pineapple Mana, and a rich and chocolatey coconut porter. Note the cute lamps made from miniature kegs. This eco-friendly, community-minded business regularly donates a portion of its sales to the Maui Forest Bird Recovery Project. The Kihei tasting room features a rotation of food trucks: Teddy's Burgers and Aloha Thai Fusion are regulars.

At the Kahana Gateway Shopping Center, 4405 Honoapiilani Hwy. www.maui brewingco.com. ℭ **808/669-3474.** Also at 605 Lipoa Pkwy., Kihei. ℭ **808/213-3002 ext. 105**. Main courses $12–$25. Daily 11am–10pm.

Sea House Restaurant ★ PACIFIC RIM   Old-fashioned and a bit dated, this oceanfront restaurant at the Napili Kai Beach Resort is a throwback to earlier days. But the view here can't be beat. Breakfast is lovely under the umbrellas outside, overlooking serene Napili Bay. The oven-baked Crater pancake is a special treat, made with custard batter. Sunset is a good time to come, too. Sit at the **Whale Watcher's Bar** and order classic cocktails and poke nachos.

At the Napili Kai Beach Resort, 5900 Honoapiilani Hwy. www.napilikai.com. ℭ **808/669-1500.** Main courses $7–$12 breakfast, $10–$16 lunch, $21–$40 dinner, appetizer menu $6–$9 served 2–5pm. Daily 7am–10pm.

Inexpensive

Maui Tacos ★ MEXICAN   Many years ago, Mark Ellman launched this restaurant chain, dedicated to Mexican food with "Mauitude." Now it has locations as far away as Minnesota. Ellman has since moved on, but his successors healthful take on fast food will satisfy a hungry belly. Menu choices include fish tacos, chimichangas, and "surf burritos," loaded with charbroiled chicken or slow-cooked Hawaiian pork, black beans, rice, and salsa. Other locations are at Lahaina Square, Lahaina (ℭ **808/661-8883**); Kamaole Beach Center, Kihei (ℭ **808/879-5005**); Piilani Village, Kihei (ℭ **808/875-9340**); and Kaahumanu Center, Kahului (ℭ **808/871-7726**).

At Napili Plaza, 5095 Napili Hau St., Lahaina. ℭ **808/665-0222.** All items $5–$12. Mon–Sat 9am–9pm; Sun 9am–8pm.

Pizza Paradiso Mediterranean Grill ★ ITALIAN/MEDITERRANEAN   The pledge on the wall at this Honokowai hot spot—to use organic, local ingredients wherever possible and treat employees like family—gives a hint to the quality of food here. The large-ish menu includes gourmet and gluten-free pizzas with terrific toppings (barbecue chicken, smoked Gouda, cilantro), chicken shawarma, lamb gyros, kabobs, pastas, and more. The kitchen makes its own meatballs, out of grass-fed Maui Cattle Company beef, and its own sauces and dressings. But save room for dessert. The tiramisu is an award winner, and the locally made coconut gelato should be.

At the Honokowai Marketplace, 3350 Lower Honoapiilani Rd., Kaanapali. www.pizza paradiso.com. © **808/667-2929.** Pastas $9–$11; pizzas $16–$27. Daily 10am–9pm.

KAPALUA

Note: You'll find the restaurants in this section on the "Hotels & Restaurants in West Maui" map (p. 357).

Expensive

Banyan Tree ★★ PACIFIC RIM   This gorgeous dining room has an all new menu with a few standouts: grilled octopus with kale and macadamia nut pesto, breadfruit fondue, and a beautiful steamed snapper. The "garden to glass" cocktail menu is inspired, with muddled herbs and eclectic combinations. Try the Menehune Mule topped with a dollop of lilikoi (passionfruit) and Cointreau foam. During "Tiki Hour" from 5 to 6pm, glasses of Moet champagne and gourmet appetizers (including that tasty octopus) are half off.

At the Ritz-Carlton, Kapalua Resort 1 Ritz-Carlton Dr., Lahaina. www.ritzcarlton.com/ kapalua. © **808/665-7096.** Reservations recommended. Dinner main courses $29–$65. Daily 5–9pm.

Merriman's Kapalua ★★ PACIFIC RIM   Merriman's Kapalua sits on a picturesque rocky point jutting out into the Pacific. As you might have guessed, it belongs to Peter Merriman, a James Beard award–winning chef who helped launch the Hawaii Regional Cuisine movement in the 1990s and has restaurants on the Big Island and Kauai. He continues to champion the farm-to-table concept here, serving Keahole lobster with crispy pumpkin polenta and collards grown down the road. For the full Merriman's experience, order the "Pupu Taster," an entree sampler that includes the lobster, kalua pig quesadilla, crispy Hawaii Island goat cheese, and fresh ahi poke. Come before sunset to soak in the sensational scenery. If twilight tables are booked, come anyway and enjoy a hand-crafted mai tai with *lilikoi* foam on the large patio out on the point. It's an exceedingly romantic spot; don't be surprised if you see a "Just Maui'd" couple stroll by or witness a neighboring diner propose. Brunch is elegant; the spicy chili ramen with pork belly and a poached egg is a welcome hangover cure.

One Bay Club Place, Kapalua Resort, Kapalua. www.merrimanshawaii.com. © **808/ 669-6400.** Reservations recommended. Main courses brunch $10–$19, dinner $24–$62. Daily 5:30–9pm. Bar menu daily 3–9pm. Sunday brunch 9:30am–1:30pm.

Moderate

Pineapple Grill ★ AMERICAN   This gracious location on the Bay golf course offers views of the azure Pacific in one direction and the misty West Maui Mountains in the other. Sadly, the once dynamic dinner menu has returned to the shallow end of the pool, with safe dishes like baked mac and cheese, cobb salads, and pork chops with sage and fingerling potatoes. You'll be satisfied, if not wowed.

At the Kapalua Golf Club Bay Course, 200 Kapalua Dr., Kapalua. www.pineapple kapalua.com. © **808/669-9600.** Reservations recommended for dinner. Main courses $15–$32 lunch, $25–$40 dinner. Daily 11am–9pm.

Plantation House Restaurant ★★ PACIFIC RIM   A dramatic destination for breakfast, lunch, or dinner, the Plantation House sits amid lush golf greens. Arrive early enough to enjoy the panoramic ocean views. Chef Jojo Vasquez's menu features simple yet sophisticated preparations that draw on an international culinary vocabulary. His *kampachi* tartare, lightly dressed in dashi soy and decorated with a spicy nasturtium flower, is bright and fresh. The *monchong* (pomfret), served in tamarind coriander broth, is a perfect balance of sweet, sour, and salty flavors. At breakfast, enjoy a bowl of flawlessly ripe tropical fruit or choose from "Six Degrees of Benediction," a half-dozen Benedicts made with such delicacies as lox, roasted Maui vegetables (superb), or seared ahi. On Thursday nights, "chop house" steaks occupy the menu. On Fridays, the chef and his wife team up to present "Beats and Eats," specialty cocktails and appetizers served with DJ Eliza's smooth tunes.

At the Kapalua Golf Club Plantation Course, 2000 Plantation Club Dr., Kapalua. www.plantationhouse.com. © **808/669-6299.** Reservations recommended. Main courses $7–$18 breakfast, $11–$20 lunch, $29–$48 dinner. Daily 8am–9pm.

Sansei Seafood Restaurant & Sushi Bar ★★ PACIFIC RIM/ SUSHI   With its creative take on sushi (think foie gras nigiri and "Pink Cadillac" rolls with eel, shrimp, *tamago,* and veggies wrapped in light pink rice paper), Sansei's menu scores higher with adventurous diners than with purists. But expertly sliced sashimi platters and straightforward gobo rolls will accommodate even the pickiest sushi snobs. Small and big plates are meant for sharing, though you'll fight over the last bites of misoyaki butterfish. The Dungeness crab ramen is my favorite—I like to inhale the fragrant truffle broth flecked with cilantro, Thai basil, and jalapeños. For dessert, most people go for tempura-fried ice cream or the Granny Smith apple tart with homemade caramel sauce. *Tip:* Thursday and Friday nights, a rousing karaoke session erupts at the bar from 10pm to 1am and sushi is 50% off. At the second location in Kihei Town Center, Kihei (© **808/879-0004**), sushi is 50% off on Sunday and Monday from 5 to 6:30pm.

600 Office Rd., Kapalua Resort, Kapalua. www.sanseihawaii.com. © **808/669-6286.** Reservations recommended. Main courses $16–$43. Daily 5:30–10pm.

South Maui
KIHEI/MAALAEA
Note: You'll find the Kihei restaurants in this section on the "Hotels & Restaurants in South Maui" map (p. 369).

Moderate

Cafe O'Lei Kihei ★ STEAK/SEAFOOD

Over the years, chefs Michael and Dana Pastula have opened multiple Cafe O'Lei restaurants across Maui. Every one has been a winner, and this one is nicest of all. The open, airy dining room is inviting, with hardwood floors, tables separated by sheer curtains, a big circular bar in the center of the restaurant, and a sushi bar and brick oven in back. The food is delicious and a bargain to boot. Call ahead for a midday table—locals flood this place during their lunch break. For dinner, the Maui onion soup (baked in the wood-burning oven) is a savory treat with fresh thyme and brandy. The *togarashi* (chili) and sesame-seared ahi with ginger butter sauce and wasabi aioli over steamed rice is as good as you'll find at fancier restaurants, here for nearly half the price. This is a great place to bring a group—the diverse menu offers something for everyone, from prime rib to sushi and even pizza with gluten-free crusts.

2439 S. Kihei Rd., Kihei. www.cafeoleirestaurants.com. © **808/891-1368.** Reservations recommended. Main courses $7–$13 lunch, $15–$27 dinner. Daily 10:30am–3:30pm and 4:30–9:30pm.

Cow Pig Bun ★ AMERICAN

The anonymous entryway through the black glass building at the Maui Tech Park should tip you off: This is something different for Maui. For starters, it's open long after most island residents have knocked off for the day. This hole-in-the-wall hosts late-night "knife fights," during which local celebrity chefs battle for the CPB crown. It's crazy, decadent fun, worth postponing bedtime for. From lunchtime on, this eatery is a gluttonous celebration of pork, beef, bourbon, and beer. Burgers are served on brioche buns and topped with bacon jam, bourbon pickled veggies, or Sriracha aioli. The pork belly banh mi comes with foie gras butter. The Brussels sprouts and mac-and-cheese both have devout fans—maybe something to do with bacon?

In the Kihei Tech Park, 535 Lipoa Pkwy., Ste. 100, Kihei. www.cowpigbun.com. © **808/875-8100.** Main courses $15–$24. Mon–Sat noon–midnight.

Monsoon India ★ INDIAN

If there's one thing Maui could use more of, it's Indian flavors. Thank goodness for Monsoon India, a humble restaurant at the north edge of Kihei—without it, we'd have to board a plane to enjoy piping-hot naan bread and crisp papadum. The chicken korma here is creamy and fragrant, the chana masala spicy and satisfying. Even the simple dal curry is delightful. With tables that overlook Maalaea Bay, this serene spot is lovely just before sunset—particularly during winter when whales are jumping. *Note:* The open-air dining room is closed when it rains.

In the Menehune Shores Bldg., 760 S. Kihei Rd., Kihei. www.monsoonindiamaui. com. © **808/875-6666.** Main courses $15–$28. Daily 5–9pm; Wed–Sun 11:30am–2pm.

Pita Paradise ★ GREEK/MEDITERRANEAN   For fresh, flavorful Greek food cooked to order and served with creamy tzatziki sauce and rice pilaf, head to this oasis in Wailea. Owner Johnny Arabatzis, Jr., catches his own fish, which he prepares with dill scallionaise and roasted red peppers. The roasted lamb shank with gnocchi and fennel puree is a delight, if a bit heavy. A trickling fountain serenades the tables in the courtyard, which sometimes hosts musicians and belly dancers. The baklava ice cream cake is exquisite—though definitely enough to share.

34 Wailea Gateway Center. www.pitaparadisehawaii.com. *✆* **808/879-7177.** Lunch main courses $10–$21; dinner main courses $19–$32. Daily 11am–9:30pm.

Inexpensive

Joy's Place ★ HEALTHY DELI   Nourish yourself with nutritious, delicious meals at this small cafe, where the emphasis is on healthful living. For breakfast, rev your engine with an acai bowl or a still-warm spelt muffin. Soups are made daily, and sandwiches are huge, with thick slices of nitrate-free turkey piled onto sprouted grain bread—or, if you prefer, packed into a collard-green wrap. Most ingredients are organic.

In the Island Surf Bldg., 1993 S. Kihei Rd. (entrance on Auhana St.), Kihei. www.joysplacemauihawaii.com. *✆* **808/879-9258.** All items under $12. Mon–Sat 7:30am–4pm.

Nalu's South Shore Grill ★ AMERICAN   Casual, noisy, and a lot of fun, this restaurant fills an important niche in Kihei. Order at the counter, from a wide range of menu items—everything from chicken and waffles to a commendable Cubano sandwich. It's a great place to bring the family or big groups. Extra touches show that the owners care about customer satisfaction: friendly and attentive service, a choice of flavored waters, and terrific live music, including a Saturday dinner show with local rock stars Barry Flanagan and Eric Gilliom. (It's $25 for the show only and $55 for show plus a three-course meal. Reservations required.)

1280 S. Kihei Rd. (in Azeka's II), Kihei. www.nalusmaui.com. *✆* **808/891-8650.** Main courses $9–$18. Daily 8am–10pm.

WowWow Lemonade ★ CAFE/JUICE BAR   The cashiers at this permanent lemonade stand are a testament to their product: sweet, wholesome, and helpful. Choose from an array of fresh-squeezed lime- and lemonades made with local honey, strawberry, *lilikoi,* watermelon, mint, and basil. Purchase a custom Mason jar (complete with cozy and a reusable straw), and your future drinks are discounted. Trust us, you'll want to return as often as possible. The açai and pitaya bowls are enormous and generously loaded with goodies: coconut custard, cacao, bee pollen, taro, and apple bananas. Smoothies have similar ingredients, blended with sprouted almond or coconut milk.

1279 S. Kihei Rd. (in Azeka's II), Kihei. www.wowwowhawaiianlemonade.com. *✆* **808/344-0319.** All items under $12. Daily 7:30am–4pm.

WAILEA

Note: You'll find the restaurants in this section on the "Hotels & Restaurants in South Maui" map (p. 369).

Expensive

Ferraro's Bar e Ristorante ★★ ITALIAN   The stunning location—overlooking Wailea Beach with an unobstructed view of the West Maui Mountains—sets the stage for a romantic (if pricey) repast, whether you dine beneath sun-splashed umbrellas by day or the starry sky at night. For lunch, indulge your inner celebrity: Sip a Prosecco or pineapple mojito and snack on a lobster melt or tartufo pizza pulled from the wood-burning oven. As the sun sinks into the Pacific, the atmosphere transforms. Live classical music casts a spell over the terraced dining area. The breadbaskets are sumptuous, freshly baked with flecks of olive. You have your choice of two sea salts to season your meal, should you so desire. The entrees are not particularly adventurous—rack of lamb with chantrelles, and seared ahi with white beans—but they are flawless. The desserts, which change often, are creative and worth every calorie.

At the Four Seasons Resort Maui at Wailea, 3900 Wailea Alanui Dr., Wailea. www.fourseasons.com/maui. ℂ **808/874-8000.** Reservations recommended. Main courses $19–$28 lunch, $34–$52 dinner. Daily 11am–9pm.

Humble Market Kitchin ★★ HAWAII REGIONAL CUISINE   Celebrity chef Roy Yamaguchi pays tribute to summers spent volunteering in his grandfather's general store at Humble Market Kitchin, which opened in late 2016 as part of the Wailea Beach Marriott Resort's $100 million renovation. The menu features re-imagined Hawaiian comfort foods: poke (raw, seasoned fish), misoyaki butterfish with green tea soba noodles, and ramen loaded with pork belly, dumplings, a sous vide egg, and lip-smacking sesame broth. Wander around the menu sampling the signature pot stickers, unagi sushi, and Szechuan baby back ribs just as if you were a teen snacking at your favorite grandpa's counter—only in this instance, "grandpa" is one of Hawaii's greatest chefs. Breakfast is a lavish affair here, with Hawaiian sweet bread French toast slathered in whipped maple butter and *lilikoi* syrup—or, for the health conscious, avocado toast on Blue Door sourdough. For once, the ocean views live up to the food and not the other way around.

At the Wailea Beach Resort Marriott, 3700 Wailea Alanui Dr., Wailea. www.hmkmaui.com. ℂ **808/879-4655.** Reservations recommended. Main courses $12–$27 breakfast, $34 breakfast buffet, $20–$57 dinner. Daily 6:30–11am, 5–11pm.

Ka'ana Kitchen ★★★ HAWAII REGIONAL CUISINE   You can hardly tell where the dining room ends and the kitchen begins in this bright, open restaurant. Sit ringside where you can watch Chef Isaac Bancaco in action. Start off with a hand-mixed cocktail and the grilled octopus: fat chunks of tender meat tossed with frisée, watercress, and goat cheese. The ahi tataki is beautiful: ruby-red tuna, heirloom tomato, and fresh burratta decorated with black salt and nasturtium petals. Don't be thrown by Bancaco's grid menu. Treat it like a gourmet bingo card; every combo is a winner. Breakfasts here are among the island's best, with local poached eggs, Molokai sweet potatoes, and creative bento boxes packed with fried rice and pickled vegetables. The $47 buffet grants you access to the kitchen's novel chilled countertops, which are stocked with every delicacy and fresh juice you could imagine.

At the Andaz Maui, 3550 Wailea Alanui Dr., Wailea. www.maui.andaz.hyatt.com. ✆ **808/573-1234.** $47 breakfast buffet, main courses $19–$29, $17–$56 dinner. Daily 6:30–11am and 5:30–9pm.

Kō ★★ GOURMET PLANTATION CUISINE *Kō* is Hawaiian for sugarcane, and this restaurant revives the melting pot of Maui's bygone plantation days. Chef Tylun Pang takes the ethnic foods of the islands' Japanese, Filipino, Chinese, Portuguese, and Korean immigrants and presents them in gourmet fashion. The "ahi on the rock" appetizer is my favorite: large squares of seasoned ruby-red tuna delivered with a hot *ishiyaki* stone. Sear the ahi on the rock to your desired temperature, and then submerge it in an orange-ginger miso sauce. The paella, fat chunks of lobster, shrimp, scallops, and chorizo simmered in a rich saffron broth, is also fantastic. If dishes sound unfamiliar, let your waiter guide you. On Sunday, a special Hawaiian *laulau* is served: Fresh fish, shellfish, and bok choy are wrapped in *ti* leaves and steamed. Served with jasmine rice, it's a marvelous re-creation of a traditional island meal. Monthly winemakers' dinners here are special treats; check the website for dates. At lunchtime, you can order small portions of many of the dinner entrees, as well as ahi sandwiches and *paniolo* burgers.

At the Fairmont Kea Lani Maui, 4100 Wailea Alanui Dr., Wailea. www.korestaurant. com. ✆ **808/875-2210.** Reservations recommended. Main courses $14–$28 lunch, $28–$62 dinner. Lunch 11:30am–2:30pm, dinner 5–9pm.

Longhi's ★ ITALIAN After a tough day sunbathing or shopping, head to the bar at Longhi's for an elegant *pau hana* (finish work) martini. The breezy restaurant with its trademark black-and-white-checkered floor is a great backdrop for breakfast, too. Luxurious lobster eggs Benedict is certainly worth waking up for, served on thick slices of grilled Italian bread. If an omelet is more your style, you can get that with lobster too, along with spinach and fresh mozzarella. At lunch and dinner, standard Italian fare is served: eggplant Parmesan, pasta Bolognese, and fresh fish. The restaurant's most coveted item isn't even on the menu: the cheesy jalapeño pizza bread. It's served free with dinner, but you should ask for a few slices, even at breakfast.

At the Shops at Wailea, 3750 Wailea Alanui Dr., Wailea. www.longhis.com. ✆ **808/891-8883.** Breakfast items $10–$21; lunch items $11–$38; dinner main courses $29–$120. Mon–Fri 8am–10pm; Sat–Sun 7:30am–10pm.

Morimoto Maui ★★★ JAPANESE/PERUVIAN Iron Chef Masaharu Morimoto's poolside restaurant is sedate and spare, directing all of the attention to the culinary fireworks. The immaculate kitchen houses a space-age freezer full of fish bought at auction, and a rice polisher that ensures that every grain is perfect. The tasting menu starts with Morimoto-san's signature appetizer, the toro tartare. Balanced on ice, it's edible artwork. A tilted rectangle offers up a delectable smear of minced Kindai bluefin tuna, accented by colorful stripes of condiments: black nori paste, wasabi, crème fraîche, Maui onion, and tiny yellow rice crackers. A chilled Japanese mountain peach serves as a palate cleanser. The chef's tribute to Maui features locally caught opakapaka (pink snapper) in Thai curry with *pohole* fern, plump mussels, and sushi rice, topped with grilled bananas that balance the curry's heat. Everything is indulgent here: A *chawanmushi* (Japanese custard) is flavored with foie gras and topped with slivered duck breast; spicy Spanish octopus comes in Morimoto's angry sauce; and an amazing crispy, salty, fatty seared pork is amplified by sweet *poha* berry and applesauce. For dessert, the resourceful pastry chef uses leftover rice shavings to create an earthy panna cotta paired with miso butterscotch ice cream and crowned with a wee wasabi sprout. The decadent lunch features flatbreads, sushi, Asian-inspired sandwiches, and many of the items served at dinner.

At the Andaz Maui, 3550 Wailea Alanui Dr., Wailea. www.maui.andaz.hyatt.com. © **808/573-1234.** Main courses $18–$39 lunch, $36–$150 dinner. Daily 11:30am–9pm.

Spago ★★★ ASIAN FUSION/NEW AMERICAN At Wolfgang Puck's gorgeous restaurant tucked into the posh lobby of the Four Seasons, dishes are flavorful but light—not burdened by heavy sauces. If the chef tried to remove the ahi sesame-miso cones from the menu, fans would probably riot. This appetizer is perfection: bright red spicy ahi spooned into a crunchy, sweet, and nutty cone and topped with flying fish roe. The Thai coconut soup with kaffir lime and Keahole lobster is a gourmet version of the traditional staple—and it excels on every level. The Chinois lamb chops are worth the steep price tag. During truffle season, fragrant shavings of black or white truffles can be added to your dish. Seating hangs over the elegant pool with Pacific views, and the bartenders pour handcrafted libations with clever names: Pavlov's Dog, Tainted Love, and Rolling Fog Over Mount Fuji.

At the Four Seasons Resort Maui at Wailea, 3900 Wailea Alanui Dr., Wailea. www.fourseasons.com/maui. © **808/879-2999.** Reservations required. Main courses $39–$135. Daily 5:30–9:30pm. Bar with appetizers daily 6–11pm.

Moderate

Fabiani's ★ ITALIAN At the top of Wailea, this little bistro serves the most affordable breakfast, lunch, and dinner in the neighborhood. Come here early in your stay because you'll want to return. The Italian-born chef turns out tasty pastas and pizzas for literally half the price of spots down the road. Sate your hunger with Chef Lorenzo's meat lasagna—a rich medley of sausage, ground beef, pork, marinara, and béchamel. Make your own thin-crust Italian-style pizza with an array of gourmet toppings—a selection you won't find elsewhere on island—including mascarpone, Kalamata olives, shrimp, and pancetta. The bakery offers tempting French macaroons: pistachio and caramel sea salt, among others. A second location in Kihei (95 E. Lipoa St., #101; *©* **808/874-0888**) offers half-off pizza during happy hours, 3 to 5pm daily.

In the Wailea Gateway Plaza, 34 Wailea Gateway Place, #A101, Wailea. www.fabianis. com. *©* **808/874-1234.** Main courses $12–$29. Daily 8am–9pm.

Gannon's ★★ HAWAII REGIONAL CUISINE/AMERICAN   Set up above the Makena and Wailea coastline, this clubhouse on the Wailea Gold golf course has spectacular views in every direction. Award-winning chef Bev Gannon—the culinary force behind Haliimaile General Store (p. 410)—has brought her gourmet-style comfort food to Wailea. For lunch, linger over the Haiku caprese with pistachio pesto or the fish tacos with taro flour tortillas and mole sauce. At night, when the view isn't a lure, it's fun to sit at the sparkly **Red Bar.** Dig into ginger hoisin barbecue ribs or an ahi tempura roll. The raw bar features flash-cured ahi with honey yuzu vinaigrette and oysters with sambal. Handcrafted cocktails include the refreshing Wailea Spritz (Aperol and Prosecco with a dash of passion fruit puree) or the Road to Hana (Maui vodka with orchid guava liqueur and ginger syrup).

At the Wailea Gold Golf Course, 100 Wailea Golf Club Dr., Wailea. www.gannons restaurant.com. *©* **808/875-8080.** Reservations recommended for dinner. Main courses $14–$40 lunch, $26–$68 dinner. Daily 11am–9pm.

Monkeypod Kitchen ★★ AMERICAN/LOCAL CUISINE   Celebrated chef Peter Merriman's latest venture spotlights local, organic produce, pasture-raised beef, and sustainably caught fish—all of which contribute to better tasting food. Pull up a seat at the lively bar here and enjoy *saimin* (soup with locally made noodles), bulgogi pork tacos, or Waipoli greens with beet and chevre. The expansive drink menu is among the island's best—offering everything from fresh coconut water, kombucha, and "shrubs" (soda or juice with fresh muddled herbs) to award-winning handcrafted cocktails. The dessert menu is less inspired; the cream pies are only so-so. A second location at the Whalers Village shopping mall in Kaanapali serves the same fare.

In the Wailea Gateway Plaza, 10 Wailea Gateway Place, #B201, Wailea. *©* **808/891-2322.** Also in Whalers Village, 2435 Kaanapali Pkwy., Kaanapali. *©* **808/878-6763.** www.monkeypodkitchen.com. Main courses $17–$41. Daily 10:30am–11pm.

Upcountry Maui

Note: You'll find the restaurants in this section on the "Upcountry & East Maui" map (p. 381).

HALIIMAILE (ON THE WAY TO UPCOUNTRY MAUI)
Moderate
Haliimaile General Store ★★ HAWAII REGIONAL/AMERICAN
Three decades ago Bev Gannon, one of the pioneering chefs of Hawaii Regional Cuisine, brought her gourmet comfort food to this renovated plantation store in rural Haliimaile. It was a gamble then; now it's one of the island's most beloved restaurants. Menu items reflect island cuisine with hints of Texas, from which Gannon hails. The Asian duck tostada, for example, pairs shredded duck with ginger chili dressing, jicama, and toasted macadamia nuts in a crispy lumpia shell. The warm goat cheese tart comes with slivered poached pears, fennel, and pine nuts. Sauces can be rich, so it's best to stick to one or two items rather than ordering a bunch to share. That rule does not apply to the sashimi Napoleon, however. The creamy wasabi vinaigrette that the waiter pours atop your stack of ahi tartare, smoked salmon, and wonton chips *is* rich, but worth the indulgence. Sound ricochets in this vintage camp store, with its polished wooden floors, high ceilings, and open kitchen. It's quieter in the back room, which is worth exploring anyway for its rotating exhibit of paintings by top local artists. Vegetarians: Ask for the extensive veggie menu.
900 Haliimaile Rd., Haliimaile. www.hgsmaui.com. ℂ **808/572-2666.** Reservations recommended. Main courses $16–$26 lunch, $20–$46 dinner. Mon–Fri 11am–2:30pm; daily 5–9pm.

MAKAWAO & PUKALANI
Moderate
Market Fresh Bistro ★ HAWAIIAN/MEDITERRANEAN At this off-the-beaten-path bistro, Chef Justin Pardo steadfastly adheres to the locavore ethic: Nearly everything he serves is grown within a few miles of the kitchen. Because of this, the menu changes daily. Salads are exceptional here, with slivered rainbow radishes, heirloom carrots, and greens picked literally that morning. Past entrees have included Kupaa Farm taro-crusted fish with asparagus in fennel-saffron tomato jus, and lamb ragout atop 2-inch-wide pasta ribbons. Breakfasts in the shaded courtyard will transport you to the French countryside: Thick slices of wheat toast slathered in house-made *lilikoi* (passionfruit) jam accompany omelets stuffed with goat cheese, mushrooms, and pesto. The high-quality ingredients are fresh off the farm, and you can taste it. On Thursday night, the team serves prix-fixe farm dinners, seven courses for $75 (more with wine pairing).
3620 Baldwin Ave., Makawao. www.marketfreshbistro.com. ℂ **808/572-4877.** Reservations recommended for dinner. Breakfast $10–$13; lunch $10–$15; dinner $28–$34. Tues–Sat 9–11am and 11:30am–3pm; Sun 9am–2pm; Thurs prix-fixe 6–8:30pm.

Inexpensive
Casanova Italian Restaurant & Deli ★ ITALIAN   On the corner of Baldwin and Makawao avenues, this upcountry institution serves wonderful Italian fare at a sit-down restaurant and an attached cozy deli. The deli serves simple breakfasts (omelets with fresh mozzarella, and buttermilk muffins and bagels loaded with lox and capers) and terrific sandwiches for lunch. Try the New York meatball on a baguette, or the goat cheese and eggplant on focaccia. The deli's outdoor barstool seating makes a great perch for observing the Makawao traffic—always entertaining. The restaurant proper opens for lunch and serves a range of pastas and pizzas baked in a brick oven, and tables are set with white linens. At dinner, snack on freshly baked focaccia with olive oil and balsamic vinegar while waiting for your entree; the truffle ravioli with sage sauce is a favorite of mine. Pizza is served until at least 10pm, and on many nights of the week the dance floor erupts to the sounds of live salsa or reggae music or visiting DJs—dinner earns you free admission. Check the website for the entertainment calendar.

1188 Makawao Ave., Makawao. www.casanovamaui.com. ✆ **808/572-0220.** Reservations recommended for dinner. Lunch items $9–$18; dinner main courses $14–$44. Mon–Sat 11:30am–2pm; daily 5:30–9pm. Dancing Wed and Fri–Sat 10pm–1:30am. Deli Mon–Sat 7:30am–5:30pm; Sun 8:30am–5:30pm.

T. Komoda Store and Bakery ★ BAKERY   The coveted cream puffs (filled with vanilla or mocha cream) are just one of the temptations at this 100+-year-old family bakery. Stick donuts encrusted with macadamia nuts, Chantilly cakes, fruit pies, and butter rolls keep loyal customers coming back. Old-timers know to arrive before noon or miss out. Bring cash and note the odd business hours.

3674 Baldwin Ave., Makawao. ✆ **808/572-7261.** Mon, Tues, Thurs, Fri 7am–5pm; Sat 7am–2pm.

KULA
Moderate
Kula Lodge ★ HAWAII REGIONAL/AMERICAN   The lodge's restaurant is best at breakfast, when the prices are lower and the views through the picture windows have an eye-popping intensity. The million-dollar vista spans the flanks of Haleakala, all of Central Maui, the emerald-green West Maui Mountains, and the Pacific Ocean on two coasts. The kitchen turns out decent eggs Benedicts, including one topped with fresh fish and a veggie version crowned with spinach, tomatoes, and feta cheese. The buttermilk pancakes with macadamia nuts are tasty, but avoid the bland loco moco (hamburger, rice, and a fried egg slathered in listless brown gravy). For dinner, your best bet is pizza baked in the brick oven outdoors (if it's fired up). Try the upcountry vegetable pie with San Marzano tomato sauce, smoked mozzarella, and herb-roasted veggies.

15200 Haleakala Hwy. (Hwy. 377), Kula. www.kulalodge.com. ✆ **808/878-2517.** Main courses $12–$27 breakfast, $11–$28 lunch, $14–$42 dinner. Daily 7am–9pm.

Inexpensive

Grandma's Coffee House ★ COFFEEHOUSE/AMERICAN   Alfred Franco's grandmother started growing and roasting coffee in remote and charming Keokea back in 1918. Five generations later, this family-run cafe is still fueled by homegrown Haleakala beans and frequented by local *paniolo* (cowboys). Line up at the busy counter for espresso, home-baked pastries, hot oatmeal, scrambled eggs, or, on Sundays, eggs Benedict served on a cornmeal waffle. Rotating lunch specials include spinach lasagna, teriyaki chicken, and beef stew. Sit out on the scenic lanai where the air is always the perfect temperature and listen to a Hawaiian guitarist serenade his bygone sweethearts. Pick up a few lemon squares and a slice of pumpkin bread to go.

At the end of Hwy. 37, Keokea (about 6 miles before the Tedeschi Vineyards in Ulupalakua). www.grandmascoffee.com. ℭ **808/878-2140.** Most items under $10. Daily 7am–5pm.

La Provence ★★ BAKERY/FRENCH/PIZZA   Hidden away up in Kula is a family-owned French bakery that's worth driving across the island for. It's also worth overlooking the service, which can be slow, inconsistent, and even surly. Every item stashed in the bakery case is exquisite. Arrive well before noon or risk watching the last almond croissants and mango blueberry scones walk out the door without you. Dine in the garden courtyard beside cyclists who've worked up appetites circumnavigating the island. The crepes, filled with Kula vegetables and goat cheese or salmon and spinach, have a secret addictive ingredient: béchamel sauce. On Sunday, eggs Benedict is served with perfect roasted potatoes and wild greens drizzled in a transcendent *lilikoi* balsamic dressing. For lunch, try the marvelous duck confit salad or roast chicken sandwich with melted Brie cheese. They're still ironing out the kinks of dinner service in their space next door—but the filet mignon in puff pastry and lamb chops with peppercorn sauce are worth the gamble. Bring cash; there isn't an ATM for miles and they don't take credit cards.

3158 Lower Kula Hwy., Kula. www.laprovencekula.com. ℭ **808/878-1313.** Breakfast $12–$13; lunch $12–$17; dinner $26–$32. Cash or check only. Wed–Sun 7am–2pm. Dinner 6–9pm second and fourth Fri of the month.

East Maui

Note: You'll find the restaurants in this section on the "Upcountry & East Maui" map (p. 381).

PAIA

Moderate

Charley's Restaurant ★ AMERICAN   Named for Charley P. Woofer, a spotted Great Dane, this North Shore institution serves food and music to the masses. The downtown Paia hangout does double duty as a power-breakfast fuel station for windsurfers and an after-dark saloon with live music and DJs. It's a decent place to grab a bite before heading out to Hana. For breakfast, you'll find standards: omelets, pancakes, biscuits and gravy. Lunch is half-pound burgers (made from locally raised beef), fish and chicken sandwiches, salads, and pizza. Dinner is grilled fish and steak—hearty, but nothing exciting. The addition of a sushi bar (open 5–10pm Tues–Sat) is drawing fans.

142 Hana Hwy., Paia. www.charleysmaui.com. ⓒ **808/579-8085.** Breakfast items $10–$16; lunch items $11–$12; dinner main courses $11–$22. Daily 7am–10pm; food served at the bar until 10pm.

Flatbread & Company ★★ PIZZA   This family-friendly Paia outpost embraces a locavore philosophy. The hand-colored menus highlight the best Maui farmers have to offer, particularly where the inventive daily *carne* and veggie specials are concerned. You can watch the chefs hand-toss organic dough, dress it with high-quality toppings—local goat cheese, macadamia-nut pesto, slow-roasted kalua pork, or homemade, nitrate-free sausage—and shovel it into the wood-burning furnace that serves as the restaurant's magical hearth. Salads come sprinkled with grated green papaya and dressing so delicious that everyone clamors for the recipe. Tuesdays are charity night: $3.50 of each flatbread sold benefits a local cause.

71 Baldwin Ave., Paia. www.flatbreadcompany.com. ⓒ **808/579-9999.** Reservations recommended. Entrees $15–$28. Daily 11am–10pm.

Milagros Food Company ★ SOUTHWESTERN/SEAFOOD   You'll have a prime view of the Paia action from the lanai of this corner restaurant. The kitchen turns out Tex-Mex dishes with Maui flair, such as blackened mahimahi tacos with salsa, cheese, fresh guacamole, and sweet chili sauce (sounds strange perhaps, but tastes great). You can also order Anaheim chili enchiladas, fajitas with sautéed vegetables finished in achiote glaze, a variety of burgers, and giant salads. The bar pours an assortment of fine tequilas, offering several flights so that you can compare flavors and no fewer than 10 different margaritas. Don Julio Reposado in a classic margarita on the rocks, please! The restaurant is sometimes open for breakfast; call ahead.

3 Baldwin Ave., Paia. www.milagrosfoodcompany.com. ⓒ **808/579-8755.** Main courses $12–$29. Daily 8am–10pm.

Inexpensive

Cafe des Amis ★★ CREPES/MEDITERRANEAN/INDIAN   This sweet, eclectic restaurant serves crepes, curries, and Mediterranean platters that are fresh, tasty, and easy on the wallet. Crepes come with organic local greens and a dollop of sour cream. The breakfast crepe with Gruyère and ham is perfect any time of day, as is the Italian lentil crepe with pesto and mozzarella. The curries aren't exactly Indian, but they are delicious. Wraps come with cucumber raita; bowls with mango, tomato, and extra-hot habañero chutney on the side. The coconut shrimp curry is a fragrant blend of ginger, garlic, cinnamon, cilantro, and Bengal spices; the slow-cooked organic chicken curry has a creamy, tomato-y base. For dessert, sweet

GROCERIES & edible souvenirs

Consider the following shops, markets, and stands to offset some of your culinary splurges—or to stock up on tasty souvenirs to bring back home:

Immediately outside of Kahului Airport, the monolith of **Costco,** 540 Haleakala Hwy. (www.costco.com; **℃ 808/877-52451**), offers members numerous local items—including macadamia nuts, Kona coffee, and Maui pineapple. (The discount gas makes this a worthy stop at the end of your vacation.)

You can stock up on quality snacks (at steep prices) for your hotel room at **Whole Foods,** in the Maui Mall, 70 E. Kaahumanu Ave., Kahului (www.wholefoodsmarket.com/stores/maui; **℃ 808/872-3310**). The meat selection is superior and they have Bubbies mochi ice cream (multiple flavors) in bulk. Around the corner, **Down to Earth,** 305 Dairy Rd., Kahului (www.downtoearth. org; **℃ 808/877-2661**) dishes out vegetarian deli items and an assortment of natural foods.

True gourmands should prioritize a trip to **Mana Foods ★★★**, 49 Baldwin Ave., Paia (www.manafoodsmaui.com; **℃ 808/579-8078**). The state's best health-food store hides behind an unimposing dark-green facade in the center of the north shore town. Shopping here is an adventure, to be sure—parking can be a nuisance, and the narrow aisles inside are crammed with *nuevo* hippies and wild-haired children. Don't let this dissuade you. The compact store has a better natural-foods selection than you'll find in most big cities—at great prices, too. The deli turns out fresh-made sushi, soups, salads, hot entrees, and raw desserts. The produce shelves are worthy of worship, with ripe avocados, local asparagus, and more tropical fruits than you have names for. Ask to sample rambutan or rolinia and hit up the health and beauty room for locally made soaps and hard-to-find essential oils.

On Saturday, visit the **Maui Swap Meet** (see p. 419) or the **Upcountry**

crepes are stuffed with melted Nutella or bananas and chocolate. Excellent espresso is found here, along with some stiff *lilikoi* margaritas. Musicians often play beneath the twinkling lights in the courtyard seating area.
42 Baldwin Ave., Paia. www.cdamaui.com. **℃ 808/579-6323.** All-day menu items: crepes $9–$12; main courses $12–$28. Daily 8:30am–8:30pm.

Paia Bay Coffee ★★ CAFE   Tucked behind the San Lorenzo swimsuit shop, this garden coffee shop is Paia's best-kept secret. Pop in for an expertly brewed espresso and a fresh-baked croissant or slice of banana bread and you'll see locals networking in shady corners over cappuccinos. The menu is a bit more sophisticated than that of your typical cafe. In addition to the standard bagel and lox, the kitchen turns out organic scrambled eggs and sandwiches garnished with brie, sliced green apple, microgreens, tomato, and black-pepper herb mayo. The vegan bagel is delicious—topped with roasted red peppers, local avocado, tomato, and pesto. The baristas are genuinely friendly and make everything with care here.
115 Hana Hwy., Paia. www.paiabaycoffee.com. **℃ 808/579-9125.** All items under $11. Daily 7am–5:30pm.

Farmers Market ★★★. The market fills the Kulamalu Town Center parking lot in Pukalani (near Longs Drugs). You'll find local honey, fresh-shucked coconuts, pickled veggies, and heaps of bright, Maui-grown produce, plus ready-to-eat foods, flower bouquets, and gorgeous hand-carved cutting boards.

On the road to Hana, you'll pass many tempting fruit stands. The best of the bunch is **Hana Farms ★★**, 2190 Hana Hwy. (www.hanafarmsonline.com; *©* **808/248-7553**), a series of thatched huts just outside of Hana town that overflow with every variety of tropical fruit, Maui-grown coffee, and fresh-squeezed juices and ginger sodas that are just the ticket if the drive has made you queasy. Stock up on coconut candy, hot sauce, *lilikoi* jam, and banana butter to slather on top of your choice of six banana breads. Everything is grown nearby.

Elsewhere on the island, coffee lovers can get their fix at the

MauiGrown Coffee Company Store, 277 Lahainaluna Rd., Lahaina (www.mauigrowncoffee.com; *©* **808/661-2728**), which opens at 6:30am every day but Sunday. The Maui Mokka variety sold here is among the world's oldest and rarest coffees; the rich, chocolatey beans regularly win awards. **Maui Coffee Roasters,** 444 Hana Hwy., Kahului (www.mauicoffeeroasters.com; *©* **808/877-2877**) is another dependable caffeine source, with a huge assortment of Hawaiian grown coffees, conveniently located near the airport.

For a taste of plantation-era cuisine, head to **Takamiya Market,** 359 N. Market St., Wailuku (www.takamiyamarket.com; *©* **808/244-3404**). Unpretentious home-cooked dishes include shoyu chicken, fried squid, kalua pork, Chinese noodles, *pohole* (fiddlehead) ferns, and Western comfort foods such as cornbread and potato salad. The chilled-fish counter has fresh sashimi, poke, and *limu* (seaweed).

Paia Fish Market ★ SEAFOOD At the corner of Baldwin Avenue and Hana Highway in Paia, this busy fish market must maintain its own fleet of fishing boats. How else to explain how the cooks can dish out filet after giant fresh filet for little more than it would cost to buy the same at the grocery? There's only one thing to order here: a fish sandwich. A giant slab of perfectly grilled ahi, opah, or opakapaka laid out on a bun with coleslaw and grated cheese is extra satisfying after a briny day at the beach. Also in Lahaina at 632 Front St. *©* **808/662-3456** and in Kihei at 1913 S. Kihei Rd. *©* **808/874-8888.**

110 Hana Hwy., Paia. www.paiafishmarket.com. *©* **808/579-3111.** Lunch and dinner plates $10–$22. Daily 11am–9:30pm.

HAIKU

Moderate

Colleen's at the Cannery ★ ECLECTIC This go-to spot for Haiku residents serves an excellent breakfast, lunch, and dinner in a casual yet classy setting. Slide into a booth beside world-famous surfers, yoga teachers, and inspirational speakers: Maui's local celebrities. Wake up with an omelet stuffed with portobello mushroom and goat cheese, accompanied by organic chai or a spicy Bloody Mary, depending on your mood. For lunch, the roasted eggplant sandwich is served warm, with sun-dried tomatoes, carrots, and melted Muenster cheese. Hearty burgers are made from Maui Cattle Company beef, and pizzas are loaded with creative toppings. For dinner, the local fish specials are spot-on, rivaling some of the island's pricier restaurants—but service can be frustratingly inattentive here. The dessert case contains some treasures, including extra-rich espresso brownies and sweetly tart *lilikoi* (passion fruit) bars.

At the Haiku Cannery Marketplace, 810 Haiku Rd., Haiku. www.colleensinhaiku.com. ℂ **808/575-9211.** Reservations not accepted. Breakfast and lunch $8–$15; dinner main courses $9–$30. Daily 6am–9:30pm.

Nuka ★★ SUSHI   Sushi chef Hiro Takanashi smiles from behind the bar as he turns out beautiful specialty rolls loaded with sprouts, pea shoots, avocado, and glistening red tuna. The garden-fresh ingredients served at this compact sushi restaurant reflect its rural Haiku address, but its stylish decor suggests somewhere more cosmopolitan. Start with a side of house pickles or *kinpira gobo*—a salty, sweet, and sour mix of slivered burdock root. Then proceed to the sushi menu for excellent nigiri, sashimi, and rolls. Not up for sushi? The wonderful Nuka bowls—your choice of protein piled atop fresh herbs, crushed peanuts, sesame lime dressing, rice, and veggies—are deeply nourishing. For dessert, try the house-made black sesame ice cream. *Tip:* Nuka doesn't take reservations and is often packed; plan to eat early (before 6pm) or late (after 7:30pm) to avoid crowds.

780 Haiku Rd., Haiku. www.nukamaui.com. ℂ **808/575-2939.** Reservations not accepted. Dinner $8–$38. Daily 4:30–10pm.

ON THE ROAD TO HANA

Expensive

Mama's Fish House ★★★ SEAFOOD   Overlooking idyllic Kuau Cove on Maui's North Shore, this island institution is the realization of a South Pacific fantasy. Though pricey, a meal at Mama's is a complete experience. Recapture the grace of early Hawaii when feasts lasted for days beneath the swaying palms. Wander through the landscaped grounds down to the restaurant, where smiling servers wear Polynesian prints and flowers behind their ears. The dining room features curved *lauhala*-lined ceilings, lavish arrangements of tropical flowers, and windows open wide to let the ocean breeze in. Start your repast with the coconut ceviche or the marvelous beef Polynesian—a garlicky mix of seared-steak morsels, tomatoes, and onion served in a papaya half. The menu lists the names of the anglers who reeled in the day's catch; you can order ono "caught by Keith Nakamura along the 40-fathom ledge near Hana" or deepwater ahi seared with coconut and lime. As a finale, the Tahitian Pearl dessert is almost too stunning to eat: a shiny chocolate ganache sphere filled with *lilikoi* crème, set in an edible pastry clamshell. Everything is perfect, from the refreshing, umbrella-topped cocktails to the almond-scented hand towels passed out before dessert. As a parting shot, squares of creamy coconut *haupia* are delivered with your bill.

799 Poho Place, just off the Hana Hwy., Kuau. www.mamasfishhouse.com. © **808/579-8488.** Reservations recommended for lunch, required for dinner. Main courses: $26–$48 lunch; $28–$62 dinner. Daily 11am–3pm and 4:15–9pm (last seating).

Inexpensive

Kuau Store ★ DELI   Decorated with vintage maps of Maui, this is one of my favorite spots on the North Shore for breakfast or lunch to go. The handsome convenience store and deli offers gourmet breakfast paninis, smoothies with all kinds of extras, fresh juices, kombucha on tap, shoyu chicken plate lunches, and pulled pork sandwiches. Inside the deli case you'll find quinoa salads and four types of *poke*. The espresso counter is built out of repurposed wood from the mart that was here before. The logo hats behind the register make great souvenirs. For an easy entrance and exit, park on the side street under the bright mural featuring surfers, sharks, and owls.

701 Hana Hwy., Paia. www.kuaustore.com. © **808/579-8844.** Deli items $5–$12. Daily 6:30am–7pm.

HANA

Expensive

The Preserve Kitchen + Bar ★ AMERICAN/PACIFIC RIM   Hana's only fine-dining restaurant has always struggled to assert itself, and meals here are hit and miss for the price. Still, breakfasts on the lanai are luxurious—where else you can sip locally grown coffee while watching the *iwa* (frigate birds) circle Kauiki Hill? All day long the menu showcases Hana-grown ingredients: The baby beet salad is a lavish affair with crunchy green beans and creamy goat cheese, and blanched *pohole* ferns decorate the ahi and Kona kampachi sashimi. For dinner, the togarashi seared scallops and the chimichurri Hamakua mushrooms are irresistible. Specials change nightly.

At Travaasa Hana, 5031 Hana Hwy., Hana. www.travaasa.com/hana. © **808/248-8211.** Main courses: $12–$28 breakfast; $17–$32 lunch; $30–$50 dinner. Daily 7:30am–9pm.

Moderate

Hana Ranch Restaurant ★ AMERICAN   Dining options are slim in Hana after 3pm, so you might find yourself hungry with nowhere else to eat. The ranch restaurant serves diner fare for slightly more than you'd pay elsewhere on Maui; adjust your expectations accordingly and you'll be satisfied. The service is friendly (if slow) and the portions are large. The seared ahi and coconut shrimp are better bets than the pasta.

2 Mill St. (off Hana Hwy.), Hana. © **808/270-5280.** Lunch items $6–$17; dinner main courses $15–$35. Daily 11am–8:30pm.

Inexpensive

Barefoot Café ★ SNACK SHOP/CAFE   Place your order for simple homespun fare at the window and eat at picnic tables facing picturesque Hana Bay. This cash-only cafe is the spot for an unpretentious East Maui breakfast: Choose from Benedicts, fried rice, eggs, and fresh baked goods. Although lunch and dinner (kalbi beef, saimin) are less inspired, this is still an affordable alternative to the neighboring resort restaurants.

1632 Keawa Pl., Hana. 🕻 **808/446-5732.** Breakfast items $5–$10; lunch and dinner items $6–$16. Cash only. Daily 7–10am and 11am–8pm.

Hulihuli Chicken at Koki ★ PLATE LUNCH/BBQ   This roadside shack just past Koki Beach might be the best place to eat in Hana—but it's not really a restaurant and we can't vouch that it will be open when you arrive. Hulihuli chicken is a mouthwatering Hawaiian version of barbecue. "Huli" means "turn" as in, turn over the flame. Place your order for chicken, pork, ribs, or (my favorite) the enchilada special. Then park yourself at the picnic table facing scenic little Alau Island and count your blessings.

Just past Koki Beach Park on Haneoo Rd., Hana. Lunch courses under $18. Daily 10am–6pm.

MAUI SHOPPING

Maui's best shopping is found in the small, independent boutiques and galleries scattered around the island—particularly in Makawao and Paia. (If you're in the market for a bikini, there's no better spot than the intersection of Baldwin Ave. and Hana Hwy. on Maui's North Shore.) The two upscale resort shopping malls, the **Shops at Wailea** in South Maui and **Whalers Village** in Kaanapali, have everything from Louis Vuitton to Gap—plus a handful of local designers. If you're looking for that perfect souvenir, consider visiting one of Maui's farms (or farmer's markets), most of which offer fantastic value-added products. Take home Kaanapali coffee, Kula lavender spice rub, Ocean Vodka, Maui Gold pineapple, and other tasty treats that can be shipped worldwide.

Central Maui

KAHULUI

Kahului's shopping is concentrated in two malls. The **Maui Mall,** 70 E. Kaahumanu Ave. (www.mauimall.com; 🕻 **808/877-8952**), is home to **Whole Foods, Longs Drugs, T.J. Maxx,** and **Tasaka Guri Guri** (the decades-old purveyor of inimitable icy treats that are neither ice cream nor shave ice, but something in between), plus Kahului's largest movie theater, a 12-screen megaplex that features mainly current releases. **Queen Kaahumanu Center,** 275 Kaahumanu Ave. (www.queenkaahumanucenter.com; 🕻 **808/877-3369**), a 7-minute drive from the Kahului Airport, offers two levels of shops, restaurants, and theaters. It covers the

Whalers Village

bases, from arts and crafts to **Macy's** and everything in between: a thriving food court and mall standards like **Victoria's Secret, Sunglass Hut,** and **Local Motion** (surf and beach wear). The **Maui Friends of the Library** (www.mfol.org; © **808/877-2509**) runs a new and used bookstore that is an excellent source for Hawaii reading material. Like Tasaka Guri Guri, **Camellia Seed Shop** (© **808/877-5714**) is a throwback to plantation days when locals enjoyed strange sweet-and-sour treats made from pickled plum seeds. Give them a try!

Maui Swap Meet ★ For just 50¢, you're granted admission to a colorful maze of booths and tables occupying the Maui Community College's parking lot every Saturday from 7am to 1pm. Vendors come from across the island to lay out their treasures: fresh fruits and vegetables from Kula and Keanae, orchids, jewelry, ceramics, clothing, household items, homemade jams, and baked goods. It's fun to stroll around and "talk story" with the farmers, artists, and crafters. At Maui Community College in an area bounded by Kahului Beach Rd. and Wahine Pio Ave. (access via Wahine Pio Ave.). © **808/244-3100.**

WAILUKU

Wailuku's vintage architecture, antiques shops, and mom-and-pop eateries imbue the town with charm. You won't find any plastic aloha in Wailuku; in fact, this is the best place to buy authentic souvenirs.

Bailey House Museum Shop ★ The small gift shop at the entrance of this wonderful museum offers a trove of authoritative Hawaiiana, from hand-sewn feather hatbands to traditional Hawaiian games, music, and limited-edition books. Make sure to stroll through the gracious gardens and view Edward Bailey's paintings of early Maui. At the very least, take time to appreciate the massive koa outrigger canoe displayed outside. Bailey House Museum, 2375-A Main St. www.mauimuseum.org. © **808/244-3326.**

Bird of Paradise Unique Antiques ★   Come here for old Matson liner menus, vintage aloha shirts, silk kimonos, and anything nostalgic that happens to be Hawaiian. Owner Joe Myhand collects everything from 1940s rattan furniture to Depression-era glass and lilting Hawaiian music on vinyl or cassette. 56 N. Market St. © **808/242-7699.**

Native Intelligence ★★★   This wonderful shop feels like a museum or gallery—only you can take the marvelous artifacts home with you. From the rich monkeypod wood floors to the collection of finely woven *lauhala* hats, shopping here is a feast for the senses. The store's owners are committed to supporting indigenous Hawaiian artisans, who come here both to shop and stock the shelves with artwork of the highest craftsmanship. Browse the truly Hawaiian keepsakes and gifts: locally designed Kealopiko clothing silkscreened with Hawaiian proverbs, *kukui* nut spinning tops, soaps scented with native herbs, and *lei o manu*—fierce war clubs fringed with shark teeth. You can also buy bags of fresh poi and the island's most precious leis, made of feathers, shells, or fragrant flowers. 1980 Market St., #2. www.native-intel.com. © **808/242-2421.**

West Maui

LAHAINA

Lahaina's merchants and art galleries go all out from 7 to 10pm every Friday, when **Art Night ★** brings an extra measure of hospitality and community spirit. The Art Night openings are usually marked with live entertainment and refreshments, plus a livelier-than-usual street scene. A free walking map of participating galleries is available at the **Lahaina Visitor Center** in the Old Lahaina Courthouse, 648 Wharf St. #101, Lahaina (www.visitlahaina.com; © **808/667-9175**).

Across from the seawall on Front Street, you'll find the **Outlets of Maui,** 900 Front St. (www.theoutletsofmaui.com; © **808/667-9216**). There's plenty of free validated parking and easy access to more than two dozen outlet shops, including **Calvin Klein, Coach, Banana Republic, Adidas, Kay Jewelers,** and more.

At the northern end of Lahaina town, what was formerly a big, belching pineapple cannery is now a maze of shops and restaurants known as the **Lahaina Cannery Mall,** 1221 Honoapiilani Hwy. (www.lahainacannerymall.com; © **808/661-5304**). Inside the air-conditioned building there's a **Longs Drugs** and a 24-hour **Safeway** for groceries.

Honolua Surf ★   Gear up for a day on the water at this local franchise named for one of Maui's best surf breaks. You'll find cute beach coverups, rash guards, bikinis and surf trunks, sweatshirts, sandals, hats and even duffle bags to carry it all. www.honoluasurf.com. Lahaina: 845 Front St. © 808/661-18848. Kaanapali: At the Whalers Village, 2345 Kaanapali Pkwy., Kaanapali. © **808/661-1778.** Kihei: 2411 S. Kihei Rd. © **808/874-0999.** Paia: 115 Hana Hwy. © **808/579-9593.**

Lahaina Arts Society Galleries ★★   Since 1967, the Lahaina Arts Society has been promoting the excellent work of local artists. The society's two galleries inhabit the Old Lahaina Courthouse, the historic building that sits between Lahaina harbor and the giant banyan tree in the center of town. In addition to hosting changing monthly exhibits, the galleries are jam-packed with paintings, photography, ceramics, jewelry, and more. The artists host "Art in the Park" fairs several times each month in the shade of the sprawling banyan tree (check the website for dates). 648 Wharf St. www.lahaina-arts.com. © **808/661-0111.**

Lahaina Galleries ★   Sea creatures sculpted from bronze and wood greet you at the entrance of this Front Street haven for art. Whether you fancy Robert Bissell's whimsical portraits of elephants swarmed by monarch butterflies, Guy Buffet's Parisian cafe scenes, or Dario Campanile's provocative still lifes, this gallery has an artist and aesthetic for you. The knowledgeable staff is helpful and not prone to the high-pressured sales pitches of some nearby galleries. Also at the **Shops at Wailea** (3750 Wailea Alanui; © **808/874-8583**). 828 Front St. www.lahainagalleries.com. © **808/661-6284.**

Mahina ★★   Fashionable young ladies will beeline to Mahina for wardrobe staples: feminine mini and maxi dresses, strappy shoes, clutches with pineapple prints, and gold bangles decorated with puka shells. Reasonable prices make it easy to rock tropical glamour at the beach or bar. www.shopmahina.com. Lahaina: 335 Keawe St. © **808/661-0383.** Kaanapali: Kihei: 1913 S. Kihei Rd. © **808/879-3453.** Wailea: Shops at Wailea 3750 Wailea Alanui Dr. © **808/868-4717.** Paia: 23 Baldwin. © **808/579-9131.**

Maui Hands ★★   This artists' collective has several consignment shops/galleries around the island, each teeming with handcrafted treasures by local artisans. You'll find Niihau shell necklaces, vivid paintings of local beaches and tropical flowers, carved koa bowls and rocking chairs, screen-printed textiles, and one-of-a-kind souvenirs for every budget. The artists are on hand and happy to discuss their work. www.mauihands.com. Lahain: 612 Front St. © 808/677-9898. Paia: 84 Hana Hwy. © **808/579-9245.** Makawao: 1169 Makawao. © **808/572-2008.** Kaanapali: In the Hyatt Regency, 200 Nohea Kai Dr., Kaanapali. © **808/667-7997.**

KAANAPALI

WHALERS VILLAGE ★★   Right on Kaanapali Beach, this landmark mall offers everything from **Louis Vuitton** and **Kate Spade** to **Tommy Bahama** and **Sephora,** with a few local designers in the mix. Find classy aloha wear at **Tory Richard** (© **808/667-7762**) and matching mother-daughter batik clothing at **Blue Ginger** (*ⓒ* **808/667-5793**). The **Sandal Tree** (*ⓒ* **808/667-5330**) has one of the best summer shoe selections on the island—including fashionable Olukai sandals with arch support. The **Totally Hawaiian Gift Gallery** (www.totallyhawaiian.com; *ⓒ* **808/667-4070**) carries Niihau shell jewelry, Norfolk pine bowls, and Hawaiian quilt kits. **Na Hoku** jewelers (www.nahoku.com; *ⓒ* **808/667-5411**) offers stellar island-inspired sparkles and watches. In contrast to most Maui shops, stores here remain open until 10pm. Sate your hunger at **Monkeypod Kitchen** or **Joey's Kitchen,** hidden in the otherwise unimpressive food court. Parking is unfortunately expensive; be sure to get validation. 2435 Kaanapali Pkwy. www.whalersvillage.com. *ⓒ* **808/661-4567.**

HONOKOWAI, KAHANA & NAPILI

Those driving north of Kaanapali toward Kapalua will notice the **Honokowai Marketplace,** on Lower Honoapiilani Road, only minutes before the Kapalua Airport. It houses restaurants and coffee shops, a dry cleaner, the flagship **Times Supermarket,** and a few clothing stores.

KAPALUA

Village Galleries ★★   This well-regarded gallery showcases the finest regional artists in a small space inside the Ritz-Carlton lobby. View Pegge Hopper's iconic Hawaiian women, George Allan's luminous oil landscapes, and Betty Hay Freeland's colorful local scenes. Three-dimensional pieces include gemstone-quality Niihau shell leis, hand-blown glass sculptures, and delicately turned bowls of Norfolk pine. The Ritz-Carlton's monthly artist-in-residence program features the gallery's artists in hands-on workshops (free, including materials). It has two additional locations in Lahaina, one at 120 Dickenson St. (*ⓒ* **808/661-4402**) and another in the Baldwin House's Master Reading Room at the corner of Dickenson and Front St. (*ⓒ* **808/661-5199**). At the Ritz-Carlton Kapalua, 1 Ritz-Carlton Dr. www.villagegalleriesmaui.com. *ⓒ* **808/669-1800.**

South Maui

KIHEI

Kihei is one long stretch of strip malls. Most of the shopping is concentrated in the **Azeka Place Shopping Center** on South Kihei Road. Across the street, **Azeka Place II** houses several prominent attractions, including a cluster of specialty shops with everything from children's clothes to shoes, sunglasses, and swimwear.

WAILEA

Shops at Wailea ★★   This elegant high-end mall mainly features luxury brands (**Prada, Bottega Veneta, Tiffany & Co., Gucci**), but some unique gems are hidden amid the complex's 50-odd shops. **Martin & MacArthur** (*ⓒ* **808/891-8844**) sells luminous, curly koa bowls and

Maui's North Shore Is Bikini Central

Paia has a half-dozen boutiques dedicated to Maui's sun-kissed beach uniform, the bikini. And that's not all; many of the other shops lining Baldwin Avenue and Hana Highway also sell swimwear. Head to this north-shore beach town for everything from Brazilian thongs to full-figured, mix-and-match-your-own suits. The best of the bunch are **Maui Girl,** 12 Baldwin Ave. (www.maui-girl.com; ℂ 808/579-9266; daily 9am–6pm); **Le Tarte,** 24 Baldwin Ave. (www.letarteswimwear.com; ℂ 808/579-6022; daily 10am–6pm); **Pakaloha,** 120 Hana Hwy. (www.pakalohamaui.com; ℂ 808/579-8882; daily 10am–6pm); and **San Lorenzo,** 115 Hana Hwy. (www.sanlorenzobikinis.com; ℂ 808/873-7972; daily 9am–9pm).

keepsake boxes—or you could bring home a beautiful handmade Hawaiian musical instrument from **Mele Ukulele** (www.meleukulele.com; ℂ 808/879-6353). When Paris Hilton shops for bling on Maui, she heads to **Maui Enchantress** (www.mauienchantress.com; ℂ 808/891-6360), a pinker-than-thou boutique brimming with Swarovski crystal–studded slippers, glitter powder, fringed tank tops, and shell-encrusted silver mirrors. The mall is home to several good restaurants, and the **Island Gourmet Markets** offer affordable options for breakfast and lunch: everything from pastries to sushi, burgers, sandwiches, and gelato. 3750 Wailea Alanui. www.theshopsatwailea.com. ℂ 808/891-6770.

Upcountry Maui

Makawao has several gorgeous boutiques and galleries to browse, plus a small grocery. **Rodeo General Store,** 3661 Baldwin Ave. (ℂ 808/572-1868) offers ready-made items, dry goods, and a fine deli. A superior wine selection is housed in a temperature-controlled cave at the back of the store. Fuel up with stick donuts from one of Maui's oldest and most beloved mom-and-pop shops, **T. Komoda Store & Bakery** (see p. 411).

Altitude ★★   French shopowner Jeannine deRoode is every bit as stylish and charming as her boutique, which offers an array of classy, contemporary clothing, jewelry, and handbags. This is the place to find wardrobe staples that will last a lifetime. 3620 Baldwin Ave. ℂ 808/573-4733.

Driftwood ★★   One-stop shopping for a glamorous life: browse the shelves for baby-soft suede boots, booty-bearing bikinis, swoon-worthy photo books, and dangly crystal earrings that will draw second looks as you cross Makawao Avenue, a surprisingly fashionable address. 1152 Makawao Ave. www.driftwoodmaui.com. ℂ 808/573-1152.

Hot Island Glassblowing Studio & Gallery ★★   Watch glass blowers transform molten glass into artwork in this Makawao Courtyard studio. If you didn't witness it happening, you might not believe that the kaleidoscopic vases and charismatic marine animals were truly made out of the fragile, fiery-hot medium. Several artists show their work here; prices range from under $20 for pretty plumeria dishes to over $4,000 for sculptural pieces. In the middle range are luminescent jellyfish floating in glass. 3620 Baldwin Ave. www.hotislandglass.com. ℂ **808/572-4527.**

Hui Noeau Visual Arts Center ★★   This marvelous gallery's gift shop spills into the foyer and sunroom. The Hui is a hub for local art and education and many inspired artists contribute their work to the shop here. Browse the shelves for whimsical jewelry, paintings, wood block prints, children's toys, and much more. 2841 Baldwin Ave. www.huinoeau.com. ℂ **808/572-6560.**

The Mercantile ★★   Every texture in this boutique is sumptuous, from the cashmere sweaters to the tooled leather belts. In addition to upscale men's and women's clothing, you'll find Kiehl's cosmetics, Jurlique organic body products, eye-catching jewelry, and an assortment of French soaps and luxurious linens. 3673 Baldwin Ave. ℂ **808/572-1407.**

Viewpoints Gallery ★★   Tucked into in Makawao Courtyard, this small gallery features the museum-quality work of 40 established Maui artists. The front half is dedicated to revolving solo shows and invitational exhibits—always worth a look. The gallery's back half features works by collective artists: luminous oils by George Allan, breathtakingly realistic pastels by Kit Gentry, and ceramic tea sets brimming with personality by Christina Cowan. 3620 Baldwin Ave. www.viewpointsgallerymaui.com. ℂ **808/572-5979.**

FRESH FLOWERS IN KULA

Like anthuriums on the Big Island, proteas are a Maui trademark and an abundant crop on Haleakala's rich volcanic slopes. They also travel well, dry beautifully, and can be shipped worldwide with ease. **Proteas of Hawaii,** 15200 Haleakala Hwy., Kula (www.proteasofhawaii.com; ℂ **808/878-2533,** ext. 210), located next door to the Kula Lodge, is a reliable source of this exotic flower.

East Maui

PAIA

Maui Crafts Guild ★★   On the corner of Hana Highway and Baldwin Avenue, this artists' collective features distinctive, high-quality

King Protea

crafts. For over 3 decades, the guild's dozen or so artists have been fashioning exquisite works out of ceramic, glass, wood, mixed media, and natural fibers. The fluid, evocative stained-glass pieces by Joshua Lee Cox and the whimsical ceramics by Arabella Ark are particularly wonderful—and well worth the trouble of shipping home. 120 Hana Hwy. www.maui craftsguild.com. © **808/579-9697.**

Pearl ★★ This chic housewares shop has two locations in Paia, both which supply everything necessary for beach cottage living: Turkish spa towels, vintage hardware, embroidered cover-ups, and Indonesian furnishings. Stylish shop owner Malia Vandervoort collects treasures from around the globe that match her soulful, simple aesthetic. Among her best-selling items, Annie Fischer's handpainted, made-in-Maui pillows capture the hypnotic colors of Baldwin Beach just down the road. 285 Hana Hwy. and 71 Baldwin Ave. www.pearlbutik.com. © **808/579-8899.**

Wings ★ Local designers and seamstresses claim to craft clothing for "real life mermaids" here at Wings. You'll find one-of-a-kind pieces (boyfriend flannels with crochet patches and repurposed kimonos) and screen tees with clever logos—everything a young or young-at-heart lady needs to rule the beach like a queen. 69 Hana Hwy. www.wingshawaiishop.com. © **808/579-3110.**

HANA

Hana Coast Gallery ★★★ Hidden away in the posh Travaasa Hana resort, this critically acclaimed, 3,000-square-foot gallery is an cultural experience to savor. You won't find pandering sunsets or jumping dolphins here. Known for its quality curatorship and commitment to Hawaiian culture, this art haven is almost entirely devoted to Hawaii artists. Among the stellar Maui artists represented are *plein air* painter Michael Clements, master carver Keola Sequeira, and Melissa Chimera, whose massive botanical canvases feature endemic Hawaiian flowers. If you're considering buying a koa wood bowl or piece of furniture, look here first; you'd be hard-pressed to find a better selection under one roof. At the Travaasa Hana. www.hanacoast.com. © **808/248-8636.**

Hasegawa General Store ★ Since 1910, this family-run mercantile has been serving the Hana community. This humble, tin-roofed grocery store has just about anything you might need. (Check out the assortment of machetes above the office window.) Harkening back to the days when stores like these were islanders' sole shopping outlet, the aisles are packed with books and music, fishing poles, Hana-grown coffee, diapers, fridge magnets, garden tools, fresh vegetables, dry goods, and ice cream. Don't leave without a Hasegawa T-shirt or baseball cap to prove you were here. 5165 Hana Hwy. © **808/248-8231.**

luau, **MAUI STYLE**

Most of the larger hotels in Maui's major resorts offer luau on a regular basis. You'll pay about $80 to $120 to attend one, but don't expect it to be a homegrown affair prepared in the traditional Hawaiian way. There are, however, commercial luaus that capture the romance and spirit of the luau with quality food and entertainment.

Maui's best choice is indisputably the nightly **Old Lahaina Luau** ★★★ (www. oldlahainaluau.com; *✆* **800/248-5828** or 808/667-1998). Located just ocean-side of the Lahaina Cannery, the Old Lahaina Luau maintains its high standards in food and entertainment—and enjoys an oceanfront setting that is peerless. Local craftspeople display their wares only a few feet from the ocean. Seating is provided on *lauhala* mats for those who wish to dine as the traditional Hawaiians did, but there are tables for everyone else. There's no fire dancing in the 3-hour program, but you won't miss it (for that, go to the **Feast at Lele;** p. 393). This luau offers a healthy balance of entertainment, showmanship, authentic high-quality food, educational value, and sheer romantic beauty. (No watered-down mai tais either; these are the real thing.)

The luau begins at sunset and features Tahitian and Hawaiian entertainment, including powerful hula *kahiko* (ancient hula), hula *auana* (modern hula), and an intelligent narrative on the dance's rocky course of survival into modern times. The food, served from an open-air thatched structure, is as much Pacific Rim as authentically Hawaiian: *imu*-roasted kalua pig, baked mahi-mahi in Maui onion cream sauce, guava chicken, teriyaki sirloin steak, lomi salmon, poi, dried fish, poke, Hawaiian sweet potato, sautéed vegetables, seafood salad, and taro leaves with coconut milk. The cost is $125 for adults, $78 for children 12 and under.

For information on all of Maui's luau, go to **www.mauihawaiiluau.com**.

MAUI NIGHTLIFE

Maui tends to turn out the lights at 10pm; nightlife options on this island are limited, but you'll find a few gems listed below.

Many lobby lounges in the major hotels offer Hawaiian music, soft jazz, or hula shows beginning at sunset. If **Amy Hanaialii,** or **Kealii Reichel** are playing anywhere on their native island, don't miss them; they're among the finest Hawaiian musicians around today. Same with **Hapa,** a first-rate band composed of Barry Flanagan and rotating guests. Catch his dinner show on Tuesdays and Saturdays at **Nalu's South Shore Bar & Grill, in Azeka's I 1280** S. Kihei Rd., Kihei (www.nalusmaui. com; *✆* **808/891-8650**). Maui's answer to Jimi Hendrix, **Willie K** performs a weekly dinner show at **Mulligan's on the Blue,** 100 Kaukahi St., Wailea (www.mulligansontheblue.com; *✆* **808/874-1131** [restaurant] and *✆* **808/280-8288** [show reservations]) and during Sunday brunch at the **King Kamehameha Golf Club**, 2500 Honoapiilani Hwy., Waikapu (www.kamehamehagolf.com; *✆* **808/249-0033**).

West Maui

Make time to see **Ulalena ★★★**, Maui Theatre, 878 Front St., Lahaina (www.ulalena.com; ℭ 808/856-7900), a Cirque du Soleil–style entertainment that weaves Hawaiian mythology with drama, dance, and state-of-the-art multimedia capabilities in a multimillion-dollar theater. It's interactive; dancers stream down the aisles and musicians play from surprising corners. The story unfolds so seamlessly that at the end you'll be shocked to realize that not a single word of dialogue was spoken. Performances Tuesday through Saturday; tickets run $70 to $115 for adults, $30 to $115 for children 6 to 12.

A very different type of live entertainment, **Warren & Annabelle's ★★**, 900 Front St., Lahaina (www.warrenandannabelles.com; ℭ 808/667-6244), is a magic/comedy cocktail show with illusionist Warren Gibson and "Annabelle," an 1800s-era ghost who plays the grand piano (even taking requests from the audience) as Warren dazzles with his sleight-of-hand magic. Appetizers, desserts, and cocktails are available (as a package or a la carte). Two 4-hour shows, with check-in at 5 or 7:30pm. The show-only price is $69; the show plus gourmet appetizers and dessert costs $115. You must be 21 to attend.

Slack key guitar masters are showcased every Wednesday night at the Napili Kai Beach Resort's indoor amphitheater, thanks to the **Masters of Hawaiian Slack Key Guitar Series ★★★** (www.slackkey.com; ℭ 888/669-3858). The intimate shows present a side of Hawaii that few visitors get to see. Host George Kahumoku, Jr., introduces a different slack key master every week. Not only is there incredible Hawaiian music and singing, but George and his guest also "talk story" about old Hawaii, music, and local culture. Not to be missed. The show-only price is $38; the show plus dinner costs $95.

On the rooftop at **Fleetwood's on Front Street,** 744 Front St., Lahaina (www.fleetwoodsonfrontst.com; ℭ 808/669-6425), you can catch local rock stars jamming with superstar Mick Fleetwood and his friends.

Other venues for music in West Maui include the following:

- **Hula Grill,** in Whalers Village, Kaanapali (www.hulagrillkaanapali.com; ℭ 808/667-6636), has live music (usually Hawaiian) every day from 11am to 9pm.

- **Kimo's,** 845 Front St., Lahaina (www.kimosmaui.com; ℭ 808/661-4811), has live musicians every night at various times; call for details.

- **Pioneer Inn,** 658 Wharf St., Lahaina (www.pioneerinnmaui.com; ℭ 808/661-3636), offers a variety of live music Tuesday and Thursday nights 5:30 to 8pm.

- **Sansei Seafood Restaurant & Sushi Bar,** 600 Office Rd., Kapalua (www.sanseihawaii.com; ℭ 808/669-6286), has karaoke Thursday and

Get Rhythm

Climb aboard the Pacific Whale Foundation's **Island Rhythms Sunset Cocktail Cruise ★★★** (www.pacificwhale.org; ℂ **808/249-8811**) for a rocking good time. Local musician Eric Gilliom gets everybody up and dancing on the deck of the boat. During whale season, even the Hawaiian humpbacks swim over to show their appreciation for his sweet serenades. Enjoy hearty appetizers and mixed cocktails while watching the sun sink into the liquid horizon. Adults $71, children 3–12 $46. Book online for 10% discount and board at Maalaea Harbor.

Friday from 10pm to 1am—during which time you can enjoy 50% off sushi and appetizers.

o **Sea House Restaurant,** at the Napili Kai Beach Resort, Napili (www.napilikai.com; ℂ **808/669-1500**), has live music nightly from 7 to 9pm.

South Maui

The Kihei and Wailea in South Maui also feature music in a variety of locations:

o **Kahale's Beach Club,** 36 Keala Place, Kihei (ℂ **808/875-7711**), is a bit of a dive bar but has a potpourri of rock music nightly.

o **Haui's Life's a Beach,** 1913 S. Kihei Rd., Kihei (www.mauibars.com; ℂ **808/891-8010**), has live music nightly and karaoke; call for times.

o **Mulligan's on the Blue,** 100 Kaukahi St., Wailea (www.mulligansontheblue.com; ℂ **808/874-1131**), offers rollicking Irish music on Sunday, a Wednesday dinner show with local legend Willie K, and other entertainers during the week.

o **Sansei Seafood Restaurant & Sushi Bar,** in Kihei Town Center, 1881 South Kihei Rd., Kihei (www.sanseihawaii.com; ℂ **808/879-0004**), has karaoke Thursday through Saturday from 10pm to 1am—during which time you can enjoy 50% off sushi and appetizers.

o **South Shore Tiki Lounge,** 1913 S. Kihei Rd., Kihei (www.southshoretikilounge.com; ℂ **808/874-6444**), has dancing nightly from 10pm to 1:30am.

Central Maui, Paia & Upcountry

The island's most prestigious entertainment venue is the $32-million **Maui Arts & Cultural Center** in Kahului (www.mauiarts.org; ℂ **808/242-7469**). The center is as precious to Maui as the Met is to New York, with a visual arts gallery, outdoor amphitheater, rehearsal space, a 300-seat theater for experimental performances, and a 1,200-seat main theater. Check the website for schedules and buy your tickets in advance.

The **Kahului Ale House,** 355 E. Kamehameha Ave., Kahului (www.kahuluialehouse.com; ℂ **808/877-0001**), has live music or a DJ most nights. In Waikapu, the **Maui Tropical Plantation**, 1670 Honoapiilani Hwy. (www.mauitropicalplantation.com; © **808/270-0333**) is a dynamic venue for outdoor movies, parties, and live entertainment. Check the website for upcoming events.

In Paia, **Charley's Restaurant,** 142 Hana Hwy. (www.charleysmaui. com; © **808/579-8085**), features an eclectic selection of music, from country to reggae to rock 'n' roll Thursday through Saturday. Upcountry in Makawao, the party never ends at the popular Italian restaurant **Casanova,** 1188 Makawao Ave. (www.casanovamaui.com; © **808/572-0220**). If a big-name Mainland band is resting up on Maui following a sold-out concert on Oahu, you may find its members setting up for an impromptu night here. DJs take over on Wednesday (ladies' night); on Friday and Saturday, live music starts between 9 and 10pm and continues to 1:30am. Expect blues, rock 'n' roll, reggae, jazz, and Hawaiian. Elvin Bishop, the local duo Hapa, Los Lobos, and others have taken Casanova's stage. The cover is usually $10 to $20.

7 MOLOKAI

by Shannon Wianecki

"Don't try to change Molokai. Let Molokai change you." That's the mantra on this least developed of the major Hawaiian Islands. No luxury hotels, no stoplights, and "no rush" are points of pride for locals, nearly half of whom are of Native Hawaiian descent. The island welcomes adventure travelers, spiritual pilgrims, and all who appreciate its untrammeled beauty and unhurried ways.

Known as "the child of the moon" in Native Hawaiian lore, Molokai remains a place apart, luminous yet largely inaccessible to the casual visitor. Tourism, and modern conveniences in general, have only a small footprint here, and although the island is just 38 miles long by 10 miles wide, it takes time to see what it has to offer. As the sign at the airport reads: ALOHA, SLOW DOWN, THIS IS MOLOKAI.

Patience and planning reward travelers with a compass of superlatives. The world's tallest sea cliffs stand on the North Shore; on the South Shore, historic fishponds line the state's longest fringing reef. The island's most ancient settlement sits within gorgeous Halawa Valley on the East End, while the West End offers one of the most impressive stretches of golden sand in Hawaii, the more than 2-mile-long (and often empty) Papohaku.

The percentage of people of Native Hawaiian decent is also higher on Molokai than on the other major islands. Many have maintained or revived Hawaiian traditions such as growing taro, managing fishponds, and staging games for Makahiki, the winter festival. "Sustainability" isn't a buzzword here but a way of life, and one that eyes modern innovations with caution—many islanders are fiercely opposed to growth.

Residents and visitors alike take inspiration from the stories of Father Damien and others who cared for the suffering exiles of Kalaupapa. Once a natural prison for those diagnosed with leprosy, the remote North Shore peninsula is now a national historical park with very limited access but profound appeal—much like Molokai itself.

ESSENTIALS

Arriving

BY PLANE   Unless you're flying to the island as part of a Kalaupapa charter tour, you'll arrive in **Hoolehua** (airport code: MKK), which many just call the Molokai Airport. It's about 7½ miles from the center of Kaunakakai town. *Note:* Make sure to book your flight for daylight hours

FACING PAGE: **Molokai coastline**

and get a window seat. The views of Molokai from above are outstanding, no matter which way you approach the island.

Hawaiian Airlines (www.hawaiianairlines.com; ℂ **800/367-5320**) services Molokai with its subsidiary, Ohana by Hawaiian. The twin-engine turboprops feature splashy designs by Sig Zane and carry 48 passengers. Multiple direct flights travel daily to Hoolehua from Honolulu, Oahu and Kahului, Maui. A single direct flight leaves each morning from Lanai.

The visuals are doubly impressive from the single-engine, nine-seat aircraft of **Mokulele Airlines** (www.mokuleleairlines.com; ℂ **866/260-7070** or 808/270-8767 outside the U.S.), which provides nonstop service from Honolulu, with most flights on Wednesday and Saturday. Mokulele also flies to Molokai nonstop from three airports on Maui (Kahului, Kapalua, and Hana) and two airports on Hawaii Island (Kona and Kamuela). *Note:* At check-in, you'll be asked to stand on a scale with any carry-on luggage. Only the agent is able to see the results, but those who weigh more than 350 pounds are not allowed to fly. Keep your shoes on—there are no security screenings.

Makani Kai Air (www.makanikaiair.com; ℂ **808/834-1111**) also flies nine-seaters to Molokai from Oahu and Maui for a flat fee of $50. In addition, the small airline offers tour packages to Kalaupapa National Historical Park from Honolulu and Kahului. Flights are met by **Damien Tours**—the only way visitors, who must be at least 16 years old, are allowed inside the national historical park. Don't book Kalaupapa flights independently. See page 442.

Note: Important to consider if you're booking connecting flights: On Oahu, Makani Air departs from a private terminal on the perimeter of the Honolulu airport. Mokulele operates from the commuter terminal and Ohana by Hawaiian from the interisland terminal. On Maui and Hawaii Island, Makani Air and Mokulele both depart from small commuter terminals walking distance from the main airports. The Maui commuter terminal has its own convenient parking lot.

Visitor Information

Molokai Visitors Association (www.gohawaii.com/molokai; ℂ **800/800-6367** from the U.S. mainland and Canada, or 808/553-3876) offers a wealth of practical tips and cultural insights on its website, and encourages first-time visitors in particular to stop by its office in Kaunakakai for sightseeing advice tailored to current conditions as well as personal preferences. Open weekdays from 9am until noon, the bureau is in the Moore Center, 2 Kamoi St. (just off Hwy. 450), next to the office of the *Molokai Dispatch* (www.themolokaidispatch.com), the island's weekly newspaper. Browse the paper online before you arrive to familiarize yourself with local issues and special events, and pick up a free copy, published Wednesdays, for the island's current dining specials and entertainment. Some of the practical information on **VisitMolokai.com** (slogan: "EVERYTHING

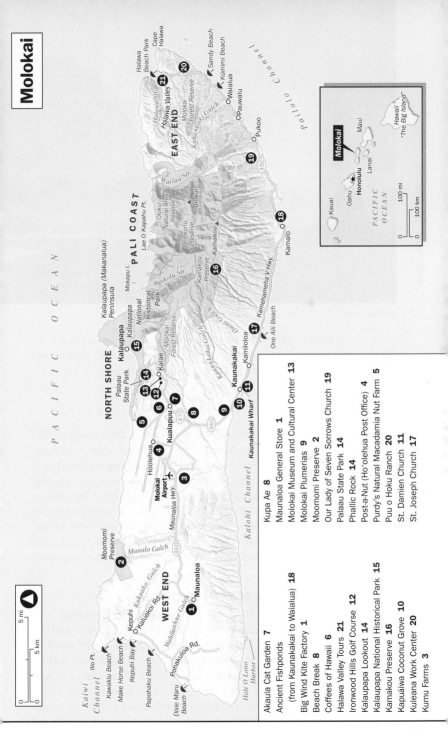

Molokai

PACIFIC OCEAN

Kaiwi Channel

WEST END

Ilio Pt.
Kawakiu Beach
Make Horse Beach
Kepuhi Bay
Kepuhi
Papohaku Beach
Dixie Maru Beach
Pohakuloa Rd.
Kaluakoi Rd.
Hale O Lono Harbor
Wahikuluhue Gulch
Kakaako Gulch

Moomomi Preserve
Manalo Gulch

1 Maunaloa

NORTH SHORE

Kalaupapa (Makanalua) Peninsula
Kalaupapa
Palaau State Park
Kalaupapa National Historical Park

PALI COAST

Mokapu I.
Lae O Kapahu Pt.
Okoku Natural Area Reserve
Wailau Str.
Olokui
Waikolu Str.
Pelekunu Preserve

EAST END

Halawa Str.
Halawa Valley
Halawa Beach Park
Cape Halawa
Sandy Beach
Kumimi Beach
Waialua
Pauwalu
Kumueli
Molokai Forest Reserve
Kalaupapa Gulch
Kamakou Preserve
Kamakou
Pukoo

Pailolo Channel

Kamalo
One Alii Beach
Kamehameha V Hwy.
Kamiloloa
Kaunakakai
Kaunakakai Wharf
Kalae
Okalae
Hoolehua
Kualapuu
Molokai HWY.
Maunaloa HWY.
Molokai Airport

Kalohi Channel

13 14 12 6 7
5
4
3
8
9
10 11
15
16
17
18
19
20 21

Akaula Cat Garden **7**
Ancient Fishponds (from Kaunakakai to Waialua) **18**
Big Wind Kite Factory **1**
Beach Break **8**
Coffees of Hawaii **6**
Halawa Valley Tours **21**
Ironwood Hills Golf Course **12**
Kalaupapa Lookout **14**
Kalaupapa National Historical Park **15**
Kamakou Preserve **16**
Kapuāiwa Coconut Grove **10**
Kuleana Work Center **20**
Kumu Farms **3**

Kupa Ae **8**
Maunaloa General Store **1**
Molokai Museum and Cultural Center **13**
Molokai Plumerias **9**
Moomomi Preserve **2**
Our Lady of Seven Sorrows Church **19**
Palaau State Park **14**
Phallic Rock **14**
Post-a-Nut (Ho'olehua Post Office) **4**
Purdy's Natural Macadamia Nut Farm **5**
Puu o Hoku Ranch **20**
St. Damien Church **11**
St. Joseph Church **17**

Inset map:
Kauai
Oahu
Honolulu
Molokai
Lanai
Maui
Hawaii "The Big Island"
PACIFIC OCEAN
100 mi
100 km

0 5 mi
0 5 km

Molokai coast

ABOUT MOLOKAI, BY FOLKS WHO LIVE ON MOLOKAI") is outdated, but the website still has a useful events calendar, sightseeing tips, photos, and insights. These sources all maintain Facebook pages, too.

The Island in Brief

KAUNAKAKAI ★

This central, usually sunny town on the south side is the island's closest approximation to a downtown. Nearly every restaurant, store, and community facility on the island lies within a few blocks of one another. You'll find a public library with a great Hawaiian history section, two gas stations, and Friendly's Market, where aloha spirit is required for entry—according to a note taped to the front door. The state's longest pier serves fishing boats, outrigger canoes, and kids enjoying a dip in the ocean. Other than Saturday mornings, when it seems as if the entire island (pop. 7,400) turns out for the farmer's market, it's easy to find a parking space among the pickup trucks.

CENTRAL UPLANDS & NORTH SHORE ★★

Upland from Kaunakakai, Hawaiian homesteaders in **Hoolehua** tend small plots near the state's largest producer of organic papaya and the main airport. In the nearby plantation town of **Kualapuu,** the smell of Coffees of Hawaii's roasting beans perks up hikers returning from **Kalaupapa National Historical Park ★★★** on the North Shore's isolated peninsula, where generations of people diagnosed with leprosy (now called Hansen's disease) were exiled. The forest grows denser and the air cooler as Kalae Highway (Hwy. 470) passes the island's lone golf course and ends at **Palaau State Park ★★**, known for its phallic rock and dramatic overlook of Kalaupapa, some 1,700 feet below. To the east stand the world's tallest sea cliffs, 3,600 to 3,900 feet, which bracket the North Shore's cascading waterfalls, lush valleys, and dramatic islets, all virtually inaccessible. Fishing charters, helicopter tours from Maui, and, in summer, a strenuous kayak trip can bring them within closer view.

THE WEST END ★

Molokai Ranch (www.molokairanch.com) owns most of the rugged, often arid West End of the island, famous for the nearly 3-mile-long **Papohaku Beach ★★★**—and not much else since the ranch shut down in 2008, closing its lodge, beach camp, movie theater, and golf course, among other facilities. The plantation-era village of **Maunaloa** at the end of the Maunaloa Highway (Hwy. 460) remains a virtual ghost town, and the decaying buildings of Kaluakoi Hotel (closed in 2001), above **Kepuhi Beach ★★**, look like a set from *Lost.* Summer is the best time to explore the shoreline here, although the crash of winter waves provides a convenient sleep aid for inhabitants of the three still-open condo developments on the overgrown **Kaluakoi** resort. Look out for axis deer when driving here at night; wild turkeys rule the roost by day.

THE EAST END ★★★

From Kaunakakai, the two-lane King Kamehameha V Highway (Hwy. 450) heads 27 miles east past coastal fishponds and sculpted hillsides to **Halawa Valley.** This stunning, culturally significant enclave is only accessible by guided tour, though anyone may drive to the road's end and explore **Halawa Beach Park ★★**. Before the road makes its final dip to the valley, pull over for a distant view of 500-foot **Hipuapua Falls** and 250-foot, two-tiered **Mooula Falls** (also known as Moaula Falls). Before you arrive, though, you'll pass pocket beaches, a mom-and-pop grocery/take-out counter, two churches built by Father Damien, and picturesque **Puu O Hoku,** a working cattle ranch and biodynamic farm that also serves as a reserve for nene, the endangered state bird. Stop here for local honey and fresh produce. This is the rainier half of the island, with more frequent showers January through March, but be careful: The sun still blazes here, too.

Halawa Valley

435

GETTING AROUND

Getting around Molokai isn't easy without a rental car, which you should reserve as early as possible. During special events and holiday weekends (see "When to Go" in chapter 3), rental agencies run out of vehicles. Stay alert to invasive axis deer darting onto the highway, especially at night.

BY CAR   The international chain **Alamo Rent a Car** (www.alamo.com; ℂ 888/826-6893) has both an office and cars at the airport in Hoolehua. The office of **Molokai Car Rental** (www.molokaicars.com; ℂ 808/336-0670) may be in Kaunakakai, where owner Amanda Schonely also sells her unique shell-decorated caps and island jewelry, but she's happy to leave a serviceable car (or minivan) for you at the airport or ferry dock, with the keys inside. If you're renting for a week or longer, consider reserving a lightly used but perfectly adequate car, van, or SUV from **Mobettah Car Rentals** (www.mobettahcarrentals.com; ℂ 808/308-9566). The company will drop vehicles at the airport, or you can pick up your rental at its office 2 miles west on the Maunaloa Highway.

BY TAXI   Per state law, taxis charge $3 a mile plus a "drop charge" of $3.50, or about $32 from the airport to the Hotel Molokai in Kaunakakai and $42 to a West End condo. Try to arrange rides a day or two in advance, either with the friendly folks at **Hele Mai Taxi** (www.molokaitaxi.com; ℂ 808/336-0967) or **Midnight Taxi** (ℂ 808/658-1410).

BY BUS   The nonprofit **Maui Economic Opportunity, Inc.** (www.meo inc.org; ℂ 808/877-7651) provides free daytime shuttle bus service between Kaunakakai and the East End, Hoolehua/Kualapuu, and Maunaloa/Kalua-koi, running six times daily Monday to Friday and once on Saturdays. It's designed for rural residents but open to all; if you're feeling adventurous, check out the online schedule (click "Programs & Services," and then follow the drop-down links, starting with "Transportation").

[FastFACTS] MOLOKAI

Note: All addresses are in Kaunakakai unless otherwise noted.

ATMs/Banks   Both **Bank of Hawaii,** 20 Ala Malama Ave. (www.boh. com; ℂ 808/553-3273), and **American Savings Bank,** 40 Ala Malama Ave. (www.asbhawaii.com; ℂ 808/553-8391), have 24-hour ATMs.

Cellphones   Good luck getting service here. The island has a few cellphone towers, but the signal is weak island-wide.

Dentists/Doctors   The **Molokai Community Health Center,** 30 Oki Place (www.molokaihc.org; ℂ 808/553-5038), provides dental and medical services from 8am to 5pm weekdays.

Emergencies   Call ℂ **911** in life-threatening circumstances. Otherwise, contact the **police** at ℂ 808/553-5355 or the **fire department** at ℂ 808/553-5601.

Hospital **Molokai General Hospital,** 280 Homeolu Place (www.molokaigeneralhospital.org; ☏ **808/553-5331**), has 15 beds, a 24-hour emergency room open daily, and an outpatient clinic open 7am to 6pm weekdays.

Internet Access **Molokai Public Library,** 15 Ala Malama Ave. (www.librarieshawaii.org; ☏ **808/553-1765**) offers free Wi-Fi and computers by reservation. **Hotel Molokai** and several restaurants also offer free, semi-reliable Wi-Fi.

Pharmacy The family-run **Molokai Drugs,** 28 Kamoi St. (www.molokaidrugs.com; ☏ **808/553-5790**), carries everything from greeting cards to hospital-grade equipment and is open 8:45am to 5:45pm Monday to Friday, 8am to 2pm Saturday.

Post Office The **central office** at 120 Ala Malama Ave. is open Monday to Friday 9am to 3:30pm and Saturday 9 to 11am. The **Hoolehua branch,** just off Farrington Avenue (Hwy. 480) at 69-2 Puupeelua Ave., offers the popular "Post-a-Nut" service (p. 439); it's open weekdays 8:30am to noon and 12:30 to 4pm.

EXPLORING MOLOKAI

Note: You'll find the following attractions on the "Molokai" map on p. 433.

Attractions & Points of Interest

Most of Molokai's attractions are of the natural variety, but a few man-made sights are worth adding to your itinerary. For the quaint churches related to St. Damien, see "The Saints of Molokai," p. 433.

KAUNAKAKAI

Molokai Plumerias ★★ FARM   Hundreds of plumeria trees produce fragrant yellow, pink and scarlet blooms virtually year-round here, just off the main highway between the airport and town. Drop in to purchase lei or make a weekday appointment for an informative blossom-gathering tour that ends with a lesson on how to string your own lei. The perfume is intoxicating.

1342 Maunaloa Hwy. (Hwy. 460), 2½ miles west of Kaunakakai. www.molokaiplumerias.com. ☏ **808/553-3391.** Tours $25 (Mon–Fri by appointment).

CENTRAL UPLANDS & NORTH SHORE

Akaula Cat Garden ★ ANIMAL SHELTER   You're bound to see homeless (not necessarily feral) cats on the island, but thanks to this indoor-outdoor shelter—the only animal sanctuary on the island, and welcoming to visitors—more of the island's felines stand a chance of finding homes. Founder Carol Gartland enlists the help of students at neighboring Akaula School to care for the cats, and will even pay the costs of flying a kitty home with you, should you be so smitten.

Next to Akaula School, 900 Kalae Hwy. (Hwy. 470), just south of Farrington Rd., Kualapuu. www.akaulacatgarden.com. ☏ **808/658-0398.** Open by appointment.

A HIKE BACK IN history

"There are things on Molokai, sacred things, that you may not be able to see or hear, but they are there," says Pilipo Solatorio, who was born and raised in **Halawa Valley.** "As Hawaiians, we respect these things."

Solatorio and his family are among the few who allow visitors into the emerald East End valley, offering **cultural waterfall tours ★★★** Monday to Saturday by reservation only. After welcoming visitors with traditional chants and the sharing of inhaled breath, foreheads pressed together, "Uncle" Pilipo relates the history of the area before son Greg guides the group along the rocky trail, which crosses two shallow streams. Greg also notes ancient sites, taro terraces, and native and invasive species along the path (1.7 miles each way). If conditions permit, visitors may swim in the pool below the 250-foot, double-tiered Mooula Falls, which the Solatorios

explain is named after its legendary resident *mo'o*, or lizard.

Uncle Pilipo, who can recall the 1946 tsunami that barreled into the ancient settlement when he was 6 years old, feels that learning about the history and culture of Molokai is part of the secret to appreciating the island. "To see the real Molokai, you need to understand and know things so that you are *pono*, you are right with the land, and don't disrespect the culture," he says.

Leave a phone message for the Solatorios (www.halawavalleymolokai.com; ✆ **808/542-1855**), giving your name, telephone number, the number of people in your party (minimum of two), and requested date of visit; the cash-only price is $60 adults, $35 children. Wear a swimsuit under your clothes and wear shoes that can get wet; bring a backpack with insect repellent, sunscreen, water, a rain poncho, a towel, lunch, and a camera.

Coffees of Hawaii ★ FARM   Molokai's main coffee farm features a gift shop where you can buy bags (and cups) of Muleskinner coffee, coffee-related souvenirs and upscale local art. But the real attraction? The twice-weekly morning jam sessions held on the building's wide front porch. Every Tuesday and Friday from 10am to noon, visiting musicians (some of the best in Hawaii) join *kū* puna (seniors) in unrehearsed but stellar performances.

1630 Farrington Ave. (Hwy. 480), off Hwy. 470, Kualapuu. www.coffeesofhawaii.com. ✆ **877/322-3276** or 808/567-9490.

Molokai Museum and Cultural Center ★ MUSEUM/HISTORIC SITE   Halfway between Coffees of Hawaii and the Kalaupapa Overlook, this small museum on the site of a restored sugar mill has a large gift shop of local arts and crafts (look for *lilikoi* butter) and eclectic exhibits from petroglyphs to plantation-era furnishings. Lining the walls are the poignant portraits of Kalaupapa residents, including a granddaughter of mill founder Rudolph W. Meyer, a German surveyor who married Kalama, a Hawaiian chiefess. Kalaupapa's historic buildings are the subject of one of two 10-minute videos shown on a TV; the other focuses on the ingenuity of the mill, built in 1878. Walk a few yards uphill from the museum (the Meyers' former home) to see the barnlike mill and outdoor pit where circling mules once powered cane-crushing machinery.

West side of Kalae Hwy. (Hwy. 470), near mile marker 4 (just past turnoff for the Ironwood Hills Golf Course), Kalae. $5 adults, $1 children and students. Mon–Sat 10am–2pm. ℭ **808/567-6436.**

Post-a-Nut ★ ICON   Molokai postmaster Gary Lam will help you say "Aloha" with a Molokai coconut. Just write a message on the coconut with a felt-tip pen, and he'll send it via U.S. mail. Coconuts are free, but postage averages $12 to $20 for a smaller, Mainland-bound coconut. Gary mails out about 3,000 per year, usually decorated with colorful stamps.

Hoolehua Post Office, 69-2 Puupeelua Ave. (Hwy. 480), near Maunaloa Hwy. (Hwy. 460). ℭ **808/567-6144.** Mon–Fri 8:30am–noon and 12:30–4:30pm.

Purdy's All-Natural Macadamia Nut Farm ★★ FARM   Hawaiian homesteaders Kammy and Tuddie Purdy offer free tours in the shade of their 100-year-old macadamia nut orchard. Tuddie is a wealth of information and aloha. After an educational spin around the family farm, he'll ply you with samples of delicious nuts—raw, salted, or air-dried—and macadamia blossom honey. Whatever you can't stuff in your suitcase can be shipped home.

4 Lihi Pali Ave., above Molokai High School, Hoolehua. www.molokai-aloha.com/macnuts. ℭ **808/567-6601.** Mon–Fri 9:30am–3:30pm and Sat 10am–2pm, Sun and holidays by appointment.

Post-a-Nut

Kapuaiwa Coconut Grove

EAST END

Ancient Fishponds ★ HISTORIC SITE   The rock walls of dozens of ancient fishponds—a pinnacle of Pacific aquaculture—can be seen for miles along the shoreline from the highway between Kaunakakai and the East End. The U-shaped lava rock and coral walls contain *mākaha* (sluice gates) that allowed smaller fish to enter, but trapped them as they grew larger. Some are still in use today; join volunteers with **Ka Honua Momona** (www.kahonuamomona.org; ✆ **808/553-8353**) in restoring the 15th-century **Alii Fishpond,** a half-mile west of One Alii Beach Park (p. 445) and once reserved for kings, and **Kalokoeli Pond,** another 3½ miles east, generally on the third Saturday of each month.

Parks & Preserves

For information on the relatively inaccessible Kamakou and Moomomi preserves, managed by the Nature Conservancy, see "Fragile Beauties," p. 450.

Kapuaiwa Coconut Grove ★ HISTORIC SITE   Planted in the 1860s by King Kamehameha V (born Prince of Kapuaiwa), this royal grove of 1,000 coconut trees (some sadly now frondless) on 10 oceanfront acres is off-limits to visitors, for safety and preservation reasons, but still presents a side-of-the-road photo op. Across the highway stands Church Row: seven churches, each of a different denomination—clear evidence of the missionary impact on Hawaii.

Ocean side of Maunaloa Hwy. (Hwy. 460), 1 mile west of Kaunakakai.

CENTRAL UPLANDS & NORTH SHORE

Kalaupapa National Historical Park ★★★ HISTORIC SITE   Only 100 people a day, age 16 and older, may visit this isolated peninsula below the North Shore's soaring sea cliffs, and then only by reservation with **Damien Tours** (see "Organized Tours" on p. 442). Visitors must arrive on foot or by plane—there's no road, and access by water is not allowed—

but the trek is well worth the effort. The area formally known as the Makanalua Peninsula was once home to the Native Hawaiian villages of Kalawao and Kalaupapa, on either side of 443-foot Kauhako Crater. Residents were evicted and the naturally isolated peninsula turned into a place of exile.

No More Mules

It was announced at press time that because of a dispute between the landowner and tour operators, the extremely popular Kalaupapa Guided Mule Tour has ceased operations and is not expected to reopen. So for now, at least, the only way to traverse the Kalaupapa Trail is on two feet--your own.

In 1865 King Kamehameha V signed the Act to Prevent the Spread of Leprosy, which ultimately sent some 8,000 people with the dreaded disease to live in Kalawao and Kalaupapa. The exiles' suffering was particularly acute before the arrival in 1873 of now-canonized Father Damien (see "The Saints of Molokai," p. 443), who worked tirelessly on their behalf until his death from the disease in 1889. Only a handful of elderly patients, free to come and go since the 1960s, still live on site, but many buildings and ruins remain from more populous times; the park service is kept busy restoring many of them. The Damien Tours bus picks up passengers from arriving prop planes at the tiny airstrip, near the Pacific's tallest lighthouse, before retrieving hikers near the beach at the trail's end. Kalaupapa. www.nps.gov/kala. ℂ **808/567-6802.** Access restricted to ages 16 and older on guided tours only, Mon–Sat. **Kalaupapa Trail** starts on the east side of Kalae Hwy. (behind gate marked No Trespassing). Hiking package with permit and tour, $60 from Damien Tours (www.damientoursllc.com ℂ **808/567-6171**). **Makani Kai** (www.makanikaiair.com; ℂ **808/834-1111**) offers air/tour/lunch packages from Hoolehua, $249 fly in/fly out, $149 hike in/fly out; from Honolulu, $315 and $249, respectively; from Kahului, Maui, $349 and $249, respectively.

Kalaupapa National Historical Park

Palaau State Park ★★ PARK   This 234-acre forest park literally puts visitors between a rock and a hard place. From the parking lot, go left on the short but steep dirt trail through an ironwood grove to the **Phallic Rock ★**; go right on the paved path, and the **Kalaupapa Lookout ★★★** offers a panoramic view of the peninsula that was once a place of exile (see "Kalaupapa National Historical Park," above). Interpretive signs identify the sights some 1,700 feet below and briefly relate the tragic history that also spawned inspirational stories. As for that unmistakably shaped 6-foot-tall boulder, one legend holds that it's the fertility demigod Nanahoa, turned to stone after he threw his wife over a cliff during an argument about his roving eye. It's also believed that a woman wishing to become pregnant need only spend the night nearby. (Treat this cultural site with respect, as signs urge.) *Note:* There are restrooms near the overlook and at a small pavilion on the left before the parking lot, but no potable water. Tent camping allowed with state permit (see "Camping," p. 454).

At the end of Kalae Hwy. (Hwy. 470), Palaau. www.hawaiistateparks.org. ⓒ **808/567-6923.** Free admission.

Organized Tours

Although Molokai attracts (and rewards) independent travelers, a few guided tours are essential—they're the only way to see the island's most awe-inspiring sights up close.

BIRDING TOURS   Arleone Dibben-Young will chauffer you to the island's unpredictably great birding spots: suburban wetlands, a wastewater treatment plant, mangrove-fringed mudflats, and a softball field, where a rare seabird likes to hang out in the diamond. Not only can Dibben-Young reliably call the rare kioea (bristle-thighed curlew), she has a permit to shelter endangered nene (Hawaiian geese) at her home. Even non-birders will get a kick out of her tremendous humor and passion for Hawaiian avifauna. Contact **Ahupuaa Natives ★★** (ⓒ **808/553-5992**) for early-morning excursions, typically at high tide. Tours cost $60 per hour, per person, with 1½ hours minimum.

DAMIEN TOURS   The only way to explore the spectacular, haunting Kalaupapa peninsula is with **Damien Tours ★★★** (www.damientoursllc.com; ⓒ **808/567-6171**). Whether you descend the treacherous sea cliffs by foot or air, you must meet the bus at 10am (Mon–Sat) for a 4-hour tour, designed to protect the privacy of the few remaining residents. Prepare to be deeply moved by the landscape and the stories of those exiled here. Stops include the original graves of Father Damien and Mother Marianne (see "The Saints of Molokai," p. 443); St. Philomena Church, where the Belgian priest carved holes in the floor so patients could discreetly spit during services; a snack shop and bookstore (bring cash; no large bills); and a small museum with heart-rending photos and artifacts, such as a spoon reshaped for a disfigured hand. Lunch is an oceanside picnic at Kalawao,

THE saints OF MOLOKAI

Tiny Molokai can claim two saints canonized by the Roman Catholic church in recent years, both revered for years of devotion to the outcasts of Kalaupapa (see "Kalaupapa National Historical Park," below). Born in Belgium as Joseph de Veuster, **Father Damien** moved to Hawai'i in 1864, building churches around the islands until 1873, when he answered a call to serve in the infamous leper colony (a now-discouraged term). He tended the sick, rebuilt St. Philomena's church, and pleaded with church and state officials for better care for the exiles, the earliest of whom had been thrown overboard and left to fend for themselves. Damien ultimately died of Hansen's disease, as leprosy is now known, in Kalaupapa in 1889. Caring for him at the end was **Mother Marianne,** who came to Hawaii with a group of nuns from New York in 1883. She spent 30 years serving the Kalaupapa community, before dying in 1918 at age 80, without contracting Hansen's disease. (It's only communicable to a small percentage of people.)

You'll see many images of both saints in Kalaupapa as well as "topside" (the exiles' nickname for the rest of Molokai). Three topside churches are worth peeking into: in Kaunakakai, the modernist, concrete **St. Damien Church** ★ (115 Ala Malama Ave.) features four lovely mosaics depicting scenes from Damien's life. Inside, you'll find a life-size wooden sculpture of the eponymous saint, canonized in 2009. Turn around to see the large banners bearing his photograph and one of Marianne, canonized in 2012. Next door, the parish office offers exhibits on both saints (open Tues–Fri 9am–noon).

Ten miles east of Kaunakakai, on the ocean side of Highway 450, **St. Joseph** ★★ is a diminutive wood-frame church built by Damien in 1876. A lava-rock statue of the sainted Belgian priest stands in the little cemetery by the newer, 7-foot marble sculpture of Brother Dutton, a Civil War veteran and former alcoholic inspired by Damien to serve at Kalaupapa for 45 years, until his death in 1931. Four miles east, set back from the large cross on the mountain side of the highway, is the larger but still picturesque **Our Lady of Seven Sorrows** ★, the first church Damien built outside Kalaupapa. Inside both East End churches hang colorful iconic portraits of the saints by local artist Linda Johnston.

one of the most scenic spots in all of Hawaii. Restricted to ages 16 and older, the tour costs $60, with limited spaces. *Note:* All tours must be booked in advance, which is easier to do through the "topside" outfitters listed in "Kalaupapa National Historical Park," p. 440.

HALAWA VALLEY TOURS On the East End, a guided tour or authorized escort is required to go beyond Halawa Beach Park into breathtakingly beautiful Halawa Valley, home to the island's earliest settlement and 250-foot Mooula Falls. **Pilipo Solatorio**'s 4-hour, culturally focused tours start with traditional Hawaiian protocol and are the most renowned (see "A Hike Back in History" on p. 438 for details). **Kalani Pruet** will pair Halawa Valley tours ($40 adults, $20 children) with a visit to his flower farm (www.molokaiflowers.com; Tues–Sat 10am–4pm, Sun by

Molokai Oo: Place of Powerful Prayer

Molokai emits a deep spirituality, earning it the nickname "place of powerful prayer." In ancient times, the island was an epicenter of religious practices and home to a school of sorcery. According to legend, powerful *kaula* (sorcerers) could pray away attacking armies, summon fish into nets, and control the weather at will. The modern population still puts a lot of stock into prayer. Churches of every denomination line the rural roads. You can count eight on the way from the airport into Kaunakakai, and a dozen more on the way to Halawa Valley.

appointment; e-mail him several days in advance at kuleanaworkcenter@yahoo.com). *Note:* The valley is privately owned—trespassers may be prosecuted, and almost certainly hassled, if caught.

WHALE-WATCHING TOURS If you're on island in winter (Dec–Mar), don't miss the chance to see humpback whales from Alaska frolic in island waters, often with clingy calves in tow, or boisterous pods of males competing for a female's attention. Though you may spot whales spouting or breaching from the shore, a whale-watching cruise from Kaunakakai skirts the fringing reef to provide front-row seats. Veteran outfitter **Molokai Fish & Dive** (www.molokaifishanddive.com; ✆ 808/553-5926) offers 2- to 3-hour tours for $79 on its comfortable 31-foot power catamaran or 38-foot, two-level dive boat. **Molokai Ocean Tours** (www.molokai-oceantours.com; ✆ 808/553-3290) also leads humpback-spotting hunts on its 30- and 40-foot power cats for $75.

VAN TOURS If your time on the island is tight—as in a day trip from Maui or Oahu—I also recommend a van tour with an affable local guide. For groups of four or more, **Molokai Outdoors** (www.molokai-outdoors.com; ✆ 877/553-4477 or 808/633-8700) offers the 7- to 8-hour **Island Tour** ($184), covering Halawa Valley Lookout on the East End to Papohaku Beach on the West End with lunch included. **Molokai Ocean Tours** (www.molokaioceantours.com; ✆ 808/553-3290) provides a rare glimpse of natural and historic sites in the nearly inaccessible upland

Halawa Falls in Halawa Valley

forest on its 6-hour **Mountain Cultural Tour.** The expert local guide uses a 4WD vehicle to explore Molokai Forest Reserve, home to the dramatic Waikolu Canyon Overlook and a massive ship-size pit dug during the early-19th-century sandalwood trade. Time permitting, he'll also show you petroglyph sites and sea cliffs. Four guests maximum: $155 each for the first two guests and $85 apiece for the additional two.

BEACHES

Because of the South Shore's extensive shallows, hemmed by a fringing reef and fishponds, and the general inaccessibility of the North Shore, the best Molokai beaches for visitors are on the East or West Ends. There are no lifeguards; on weekdays, you may even be the sole person on the sand. So enter the water only in calm conditions, and even then be cautious: If you get into trouble, help may take longer to arrive than you expect. *Note:* You'll find relevant sites on the "Molokai" map on p. 433.

Kaunakakai

Local kids swim off the wharf, but if you just want to dip your feet in the water, head 3 miles east along the Kamehameha V Highway to the sandy shore of **One Alii Beach Park ★**. Pronounced *"o-nay ah-lee-ee,"* it has a thin strip of golden *one* (sand) once reserved for the *ali'i* (high chiefs). Although the water is too shallow and murky for swimming, the spacious park is a picnic spot and draws many families on weekends. Facilities include outdoor showers, picnic areas, and restrooms; tent camping allowed with permit (see "Camping" on p. 454).

East End

At mile marker 20, palm-fringed **Kumimi Beach ★★**, also known as Murphy Beach or 20-Mile Beach, provides a small, shaded park with picnic tables, white sand, and good swimming, snorkeling, and diving in calm conditions. Look for **Sandy Beach ★★** between mile markers 21 and 22—the last beach before you head uphill en route to lush Halawa Valley. It has no facilities, just winsome views of Maui and Lanai and generally safe swimming; stay out of high surf.

At the narrow end of the winding highway, 28 miles east of Kaunakakai, lies **Halawa Beach Park ★★**. Tucked between sea cliffs, the wide rocky bay is beautiful but not safe for swimming. Behind it, the gray sand cove adjacent to the river is a serene option for those willing to ford the stream. Avoid this during winter or after heavy rains. Look back into Halawa Valley (accessible only via cultural tours; see p. 438) for distant waterfall views. A picnic pavilion has restrooms, a shower, and water tap; it's 100 yards from the shore, across from **Ierusalema Hou,** a tiny green church built in 1948.

West End

Much of the shoreline here is for sightseeing only, thanks to dangerous currents and fierce surf—especially in winter. But solitude, sunsets, and clear-day vistas of Diamond Head on Oahu across the 26-mile Kaiwi Channel make it worth the trek. From Kaunakakai, take Maunaloa Highway (Hwy. 460) almost 15 miles west, turn right on Kaluakoi Road, and drive 4½ miles until you see the sign on your right pointing to Ke Nani Kai; turn right for public beach access parking at the end of the road. Walk past the eerily decaying, closed hotel to gold-sand **Kepuhi Beach ★★**, and watch surfers navigate the rocky break. A 15-minute walk north along the bluff leads to the Pohaku Mauliuli cinder cone, which shares its name with two sandy coves better known as **Make Horse Beach ★**, pronounced *"mah-kay"* and meaning "dead horse" (don't ask). You can snorkel and explore the tide pools in calm conditions, but do keep an eye on the waves. Hiking several miles north on a rugged dirt road leads to the white crescent of **Kawakiu Beach ★**, the original launch site of the Molokai to Oahu outrigger canoe race. It's relatively safe in summer, but be wary whenever surf is up.

Continue on Kaluakoi Road 2 miles south from the resort to the parking lot for **Papohaku Beach Park ★★★**, where the light-blond sand is more than 2 miles long and 300 feet wide. Enjoy strolling the broad

Kumimi Beach

expanse, but beware the water's ferocious rip currents. County facilities—restrooms, water, picnic, and campsites (see "Camping" on p. 454)—are at the northern end, a third of a mile past the intersection with Pa Loa Loop Road (a shortcut back to upper Kaluakoi Rd.).

From Papohaku, follow Kaluakoi Road 1¾ miles south to the T at Pohakuloa Road; turn right and head another 1¾ miles. Just before the road ends, turn seaward at the beach access sign. Park in the small lot and follow a short downhill path to cozy **Dixie Maru Beach ★★★** (formerly Kapukahehu, but renamed after a Japanese shipwreck). Popular with families in summer, this sheltered cove is the island's best, safest spot to swim.

WATERSPORTS

The miles-long, untrammeled South Shore reef is home to curious turtles and Hawaiian monk seals, billowing eagle and manta rays, and giant bouquets of colorful fish, but because it lies a half-mile or more offshore, it's easiest to explore via watercraft of some kind. Surfers, stand-up paddleboarders, and boogie boarders can find waves to entertain themselves, just as sport fishers have numerous near-shore and deep-sea options; since conditions are variable by day as well as by season, consult one of the Kaunakakai-based outfitters below before venturing out.

Diving, Fishing & Snorkeling

Molokai Fish & Dive, 61 Ala Malama Ave. (www.molokaifishanddive. com; ✆ 808/553-5926), carefully selects the day's best sites for its **snorkel tours** ($79 standard) and two-tank **scuba dives** ($145). Owner, captain, and certified dive master Tim Forsberg runs tours from one of two Coast Guard–inspected boats: the comfy, 38-foot Delta dive boat *Coral Princess* and the twin-hulled, 31-foot power catamaran *Ama Lua.* When conditions permit, he also offers three-tank dives ($295) along the remote North Shore. Half-day **deep-sea fishing charters** start at $695, while groups of up to six may also charter the new 42-foot sailing cruiser, *Maka Pueo,* for 2- to 3-hour sunset cruises ($395). All kinds of dive and fishing gear, along with snacks and gifts, are for rent or sale at the downtown headquarters.

Among several other charter operators, Captain Tim Brunnert of **Captain's Gig Charters** (www.molokaifishingcharters.com; ✆ 808/552-0390 or 808/336-1055) books **sport-fishing, snorkel, sunset,** and **sightseeing cruises** on the biggest, most comfortable boat in the harbor. He lets sportfishers keep some of the catch. He's also a certified dive master. Call for current rates.

Molokai Ocean Tours, 40 Ala Malama Ave., above American Savings Bank (www.molokaioceantours.com; ✆ 808/553-3290), uses its six-passenger power catamaran to offer 3-hour **troll fishing** ($500 for the boat up six people) and a half-day **deep-sea fishing charter** ($625). Its snorkel tours ($75 adults, $60 children 10 and younger) include a **SNUBA** option that allows up to two people at a time to dive 30 feet, using hoses connected to a special mouthpiece.

For **whale-watching tours** (Dec–Mar), see "Organized Tours" on p. 442.

Paddling

Molokai Outdoors ★★ (www.molokai-outdoors.com; ☎ **877/553-4477** or 808/633-8700) leads fantastic downwind **kayak** and **stand-up-paddleboard reef tours** from 5 to 14 miles ($75 adults, less for children); owner and former world champion windsurfer Clare Seeger Mawae occasionally guides the tours. Her company also rents kayaks ($42), snorkel sets and boogie boards ($7), and stand-up paddleboards ($42); in summer, experienced paddlers can arrange a North Shore kayak excursion that starts in Halawa Valley, with pickup by boat.

If you want to experience the ancient sport of **outrigger canoe paddling,** visit the **Waakapaemua Canoe Club** (molokaiwaa@gmail.com; ☎ **808/553-8018**) at Kaunakakai Wharf on Thursday morning at 7:15am sharp. You can jump into a six-person boat and participate in the club's weekly practice. First come, first paddle! Bring a $25 cash donation to help support the youth teams. Custom bookings are available for parties of four or more.

Stand-up paddleboarder in Molokai

Surfing & Bodyboarding

Conveniently located between the airport and Kaunakakai at the corner of highways 460 and 470 (Holomua Junction), you'll spot **Beach Break** (www.bigwindkites.com/beachbreak; (C) **808/567-6091**) by its rainbow fence made of surfboards. Inside, owner, photographer, and avid surfer Zach Socher rents surfboards ($24–$30 daily/$120–$150 weekly), bodyboards ($10/$35), and fins ($5/$21), among other beach gear for rent or sale. Check out the bright array of bikinis, board shorts, "slippahs," T-shirts, and sarongs, too. Socher dispenses free coffee and advice on surf spots during store hours, Monday through Saturday 10am to 4pm.

OTHER OUTDOOR ACTIVITIES

Biking

Molokai is a great place to see by bicycle, with lightly used roads and, on the East End, inviting places to pull over for a quick dip. **Molokai Bicycle,** 80 Mohala St., Kaunakakai (www.mauimolokaibicycle.com; (C) **800/709-2453** or 808/553-5740), offers mountain, road, and hybrid bike rentals for $25 to $32 a day, or $95 to $130 a week, including helmet and lock; add a trailer for $12 a day, $60 a week. Because owner Phillip Kikukawa is a schoolteacher, the store is open only Wednesday (3–6pm) and Saturday (9am–2pm); call to set up an appointment for other hours. Drop-off and pickup in or near Kaunakakai is free, with charges for runs to the airport ($20 each way/$30 round-trip) or Kaluakoi Resort and Wavecrest condos ($25 each way).

Golf

Take a swing back into golf history at **Ironwood Hills Golf Course** ((C) **808/567-6000**). Built in 1929 by the Del Monte Plantation for its executives, the nine-hole, undulating course with uneven fairways lies a half-mile down an unpaved road off Highway 470 in Kalae, between Coffees of Hawaii in Kualapuu and the Kalaupapa Lookout. Gorgeous mountain and ocean views, some filtered by tree growth, also compensate for the challenging course. Greens fees are $36 for 9 holes, including cart; club rentals are $10. Pick up a logo cap in the pro shop trailer.

Hiking

With most land privately held, the only real hiking opportunities on Molokai are the Kalaupapa Trail (permit required; see p. 440), Halawa Valley by guided tour (see p. 438), or in two hard-to-access Nature Conservancy preserves (see "Fragile Beauties," below). Molokai Ocean Tours' 6-hour **Mountain Cultural Tour** (p. 445) includes some hiking in the Molokai Forest Reserve.

FRAGILE BEAUTIES: HIKING MOLOKAI'S
nature reserves

For spectacularly unique views of Molokai, the Nature Conservancy of Hawaii offers **monthly guided hikes** ★★★ March through October into two of the island's most fragile landscapes: the windswept dunes in the 920-acre **Moomomi Preserve** on the northwest shore, and the cloud-ringed forest of the island's highest mountain, part of the 2,774-acre **Kamakou Preserve** on the island's East End.

Just 8½ miles northwest of Hoolehua, Moomomi is the most intact beach and sand dune area in the main Hawaiian islands, harboring jewel-like endemic plants, nesting green sea turtles, and fossils of now-extinct flightless birds.

Towering over the island's eastern half, 4,970-foot Kamakou provides 60% of the fresh water on Molokai and shelter for rare native species, such happy-faced spiders and deep-throated lobelias. The Pepeopae Trail boardwalk (3 miles round-trip) meanders through a bog of miniature ohia trees and silver-leaved lilies that evolved over millennia; it leads to a view of pristine Pelekunu Valley on the North Shore.

Hikes are free (donations welcome), but the number of participants is limited. Book in advance; exact dates (usually Sat) are listed on the conservancy website (www.nature.org/hawaii). To check availability, e-mail hike_molokai@tnc.org, or call the field office (ⓒ **808/553-5236;** weekdays 8am–3pm).

It's possible to access the preserves on your own, but you'll need a rugged four-wheel-drive (4WD) vehicle, dry roads, and clear weather. Check in first at the field office, just north of Kaunakakai in Molokai Industrial Park, 23 Pueo Place, off Ulili Street near Highway 460. Ask for directions and current road conditions; in the case of Moomomi, you'll also need to get a pass for the locked gate. Clean your shoes and gear before visiting the preserves to avoid bringing in invasive species, and drive cautiously—a tow job from these remote areas can easily cost $1,000.

WHERE TO STAY ON MOLOKAI

With only one small hotel on the island, the majority of Molokai's approximately 58,000 annual visitors tend to stay in vacation rentals or condominiums. Individually owned and decorated condo units vary widely in taste and quality, leaning heavy on the rattan. Don't expect air-conditioning or elevators in the two- and three-story buildings, either.

Molokai Vacation Properties ★★ (www.molokai-vacation-rental. net; ⓒ **800/367-2984** or 808/553-8334) can help you navigate what's available. The agents represent only licensed and legal rentals, most of them oceanfront and all guaranteed to be clean and fully equipped. You can book online, but it's best to contact the office directly to identify the most suitable unit for your needs. Their customer service is excellent. You'll find more (though not necessarily licensed) properties online at VRBO.com, Airbnb.com, and other rental websites.

Note: Taxes of 13.416% are added to hotel and vacation rental bills. Parking is free. Unless noted, cleaning fees refer to one-time charges.

Hotels & Restaurants on Molokai

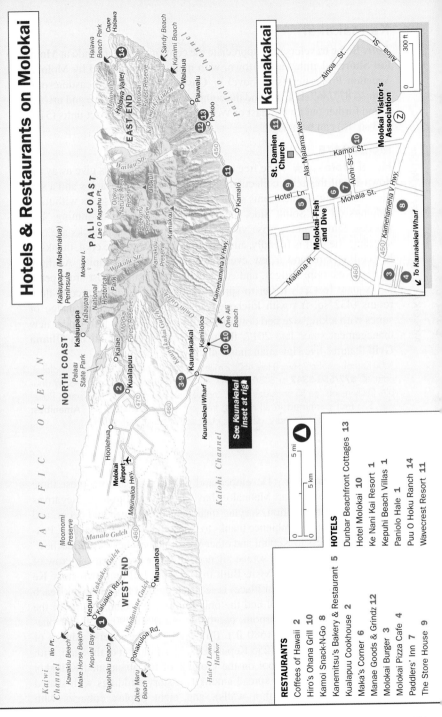

Kaunakakai

RESTAURANTS

Coffees of Hawaii 2
Hiro's Ohana Grill 10
Kamoi Snack-N-Go 8
Kanemitsu's Bakery & Restaurant 5
Kualapuu Cookhouse 2
Maka's Corner 6
Manae Goods & Grindz 12
Molokai Burger 3
Molokai Pizza Cafe 4
Paddlers' Inn 7
The Store House 9

HOTELS

Dunbar Beachfront Cottages 13
Hotel Molokai 10
Ke Nani Kai Resort 1
Kepuhi Beach Villas 1
Paniolo Hale 1
Puu O Hoku Ranch 14
Wavecrest Resort 11

Kaunakakai

Note: Some travelers may appreciate the convenience of a condo at **Molokai Shores,** 1 mile east of town, with many units managed by Molokai Vacation Properties (see above) or **Castle Resorts** (www.castleresorts. com; ℂ **877/367-1912**). I find the complex lacks the ambience and privacy found further out on the East or West End, while the compact units (510–663 sq. ft.) can be noisy.

MODERATE

Hotel Molokai ★   The free earplugs on the nightstands give away the downside of this retro collection of Polynesian-style A-frames and a single-story wing: Some rooms suffer from traffic noise. Also, as with most lodgings on the South Side, the beach isn't good for swimming. The upsides: Sunset and sunrise views from the pool or hammocks are outstanding, the staff is friendly, and the remodeled rooms are cool, thanks to big ceiling fans and a few even have air-conditioning units. All have microwaves, mini fridges, and coffeemakers, but since most are a petite 228 square feet, it's better to spring for one of the deluxe second-floor rooms (432 sq. ft.) with kitchenettes. Families can take advantage of suites with a king-size bed downstairs and twin beds in a loft. Under new management since late 2017, the oceanfront restaurant **Hiro's Ohana Grill** features live Hawaiian music nightly.

1300 Kamehameha V Hwy. (Hwy. 450), 2 miles east of Kaunakakai. www.hotelmolokai. com. ℂ **877/553-5347** or 808/553-5347. 40 units (14 timeshares). $179–$269 double. Daily resort fee $5 (includes Wi-Fi, snorkel and beach gear, DVD library). Rollaway $25 (not permitted in all rooms); free crib. Airport shuttle $25. **Amenities:** Restaurant, bar; coin laundry; gift shop; pool; activity desk; free Wi-Fi.

West End

MODERATE

Kaluakoi Resort ★   Developed and managed separately, these three condo complexes near Maunaloa have much in common. Negatives include a remote location, varying quality of furnishings and decor, and the slightly haunted ambience thanks to the shuttered hotel next door. Positives: easy access to Kepuhi and other West End beaches (see "Beaches," p. 446), large lanais, and serene silence—I didn't even hear the crow of wild roosters on my last visit. Built in 1983, the 120-unit, two-story **Ke Nani Kai ★★** (50 Kepuhi Place) is set back farthest from Kepuhi Beach but boasts the nicest pool and the only hot tub and tennis courts of the bunch; units are two-bedroom, two-bathroom (880–990 sq. ft.) or one-bedroom, one-bathroom (680 ft.). Built in 1978, the diverse condos of **Kepuhi Beach Villas ★** (255 Kepuhi Beach) are closest to the sand, with a generous oceanview pool on the grounds of the abandoned Kaluakoi Hotel. The 148 units are spread among two-story buildings with shared laundry facilities (and thin walls), and eight duplex cottages with

Dunbar Cottages

individual washer/dryers; the largest units have a ground floor (642 sq. ft.) with a master bedroom and bathroom, and a small loft with a second bedroom and bathroom. Nearly hidden in tropical foliage, the 78-unit **Paniolo Hale ★** (100 Lio Place) means "cowboy house," and the large screened lanais and wooden floors give it a hint of the Old West. Built in 1980, the 21 two-story buildings come in a host of floor plans, from studios (548 sq. ft.) to two-bedroom, two-bathroom units (1,398 sq. ft.), some with lofts and sleeping quarters in the living room.

Kaluakoi Resort, Maunaloa. 346 units. Reservations for select units c/o Molokai Vacation Properties: www.molokai-vacation-rental.com. © **800/367-2984** or 808/553-8334. $125–$250 condo; 10% discount for stays of a week or more. $75–$125 cleaning fee. 3- to 7-night minimum. **Amenities:** Barbecues; Jacuzzi; pools; tennis courts (Ke Nani Kai only); Wi-Fi (varies by unit).

East End

Note: Mailing addresses for these lodgings use Kaunakakai.

MODERATE

Dunbar Beachfront Cottages ★★★   These two attractive, green-and-white, plantation-style cottages sit on hidden beaches, with year-round swimming and snorkeling—your own slice of paradise. Each has two bedrooms (one with twin beds), one bathroom, a full kitchen, washer and dryer, and attractive furnishings. The family-friendly Pauwalu cottage is at ocean level, with a queen-size bed in the master and an ancient fish-pond out front. The Puunana cottage has a king-size bed in its master bedroom and sits one flight of stairs above the beach.

9750 Kamehameha V Hwy. (Hwy. 450), past mile marker 18, Kainalu. www.molokai-beachfront-cottages.com. © **800/673-0520** or 808/558-8153. 2 cottages (each sleeps 4). $190. $85 cleaning fee. 3-night minimum. No credit cards. **Amenities:** Free Wi-Fi.

Puu O Hoku Ranch ★★★   Its name means "hill of stars," which accurately describes this 14,000-acre retreat on a cloudless night. You'll stay in one of three 1930s-era cottages, thoughtfully decorated with Hawaiian and Balinese furnishings. Sitting well above the ocean, the four-bedroom, three-bathroom **Grove Cottage** is in a field closer to the ranch operations, while the two-bedroom, two-bathroom **Sunrise Cottage** has a more secluded feel and a panoramic view. The one-bedroom, one-bathroom **Sugar Mill Cottage,** named for the nearby remains of a mill, hides just above **Kumimi Beach** ★★ (p. 445). Only ranch guests have access to its numerous hiking trails, which pass ocean bluffs, an ancient grove, and a nursery for nene. *Note:* Groups (a minimum of 14 people) can also book the handsome 11-room **lodge,** which comes with a private pool, yoga deck, and fireplace as well as three meals a day featuring the ranch's organic meat and produce ($185 per person, 4-night minimum).

Main entrance off Kamehameha V Hwy. (Hwy. 450) at mile marker 25. www.puuohoku. com. © **808/558-8109.** 3 cottage units. $200–$300 double, 7th night free. Extra person $30. $100–$150 refundable cleaning fee (charged at check-in). 2-night minimum. **Amenities:** Store (9am–5pm Mon–Fri); Wi-Fi (free at select hotspots).

Wavecrest Resort ★★   Halfway to Halawa Valley from Kaunakakai, this three-story condo complex on 6 green acres is a convenient, clean home base. Your best bet is Building A, the closest to the ocean. Top floors offer the best views of Maui, Lanai, and uninhabited Kahoolawe, but keep in mind that the resort has no elevators (or air-conditioning). Bottom floor units aren't bad, as they open straight to the grass and plumeria trees. Bedroom windows face the parking lot, so you'll hear traffic. Units are individually owned and decorated; scrutinize photos and amenity lists closely. The gated pool and cabana with barbecues are well maintained, and the front desk has free tennis equipment to use on its two courts.

7148 Kamehameha V Hwy. (Hwy. 450), 13 miles east of Kaunakakai. 128 total units. Reservations for select units c/o Molokai Vacation Properties: www.molokai-vaca tion-rental.com. © **800/367-2984** or 808/553-8334. $105–$165 condo; 10% discount for stays of a week or more. $75–$100 cleaning fee. 3- to 7-night minimum. **Amenities:** Barbecues; coin laundry; pool; tennis courts; Wi-Fi (varies by unit).

Camping

All campgrounds are for tents only, and permits for county and state sites must be purchased in advance. You'll have to bring your own equipment or plan to buy it on the island, as there are no rentals.

County Campgrounds ★   The family-friendly **One Alii Beach Park** (p. 445) provides restrooms, barbecues, outdoor showers, drinking water, picnic tables, and electricity; **Papohaku Beach Park** ★★ (p. 446) has the same, minus electricity and plus plenty of sharp *kiawe* thorns. *Note:* The NO CAMPING signs near the Papohaku parking lot apply only to the lawn to the right of the restrooms.

Permits $10 adults, $6 minors Mon–Thurs, $20 adults, $12 minors Fri–Sun and holidays (discounts for state residents). 3-night maximum. Available in person 8am–1pm and 2:30–4pm weekdays at the Maui County parks office, Mitchell Pauole Community Center, 90 Ainoa St., Kaunakakai, 96748. ℂ **808/553-3204.** To purchase by mail, download the form at www.co.maui.hi.us and mail to the parks office with check and self-addressed, stamped envelope.

State Campgrounds ★★ The state manages two campgrounds at high, often misty elevations: **Palaau State Park ★★** (p. 442) and the remote **Waikolu Overlook** in the Molokai Forest Reserve. Both have restroom and picnic facilities, but no drinking water or barbecues. *Note:* Waikolu is spectacular, but requires a 4WD vehicle to drive 10 miles up mostly unpaved Maunahui Road starting from its unmarked intersection with Maunaloa Highway (Hwy. 460) near mile marker 4; do not attempt in muddy or rainy conditions. If the area is not covered in clouds, you'll be rewarded with views of the pristine Waikolu Valley and the Pacific, and be that much closer to the **Kamakou Preserve ★★★** (p. 450).

Permits $18 per campsite (up to 6 persons), $3 per additional person (kids 2 and under free). 5-night maximum. ℂ **808/984-8100.** Available online at https://camping.ehawaii.gov.

WHERE TO EAT ON MOLOKAI

Gourmands looking for fine dining will be disappointed on Molokai, but with a little strategizing you can eat well. Plan on cooking most of your meals if you are staying any distance from Kaunakakai. See p. 456 for where to stock up before heading out to your accommodations. *Note:* If you arrive on a Sunday, bring snacks! Most restaurants and groceries are only open Monday through Saturday. Find the restaurants noted below on the "Hotels & Restaurants on Molokai" map on p. 451.

Kaunakakai

The new restaurant at Hotel Molokai, **Hiro's Ohana Grill** (ℂ **808/660-3400**), is a family affair, with several generations stepping in to serve local dishes with a little flair. The locally sourced fish entrees, fresh pesto chicken sandwiches and the bananas lumpia Foster dessert have already won diners' devotion. **Paddlers' Inn ★** (see "Molokai Nightlife," below) is the only other restaurant in town that serves alcohol (including draft beer), which explains its popularity. It has an eclectic menu—beef noodle soup, kalua pork sliders, salads with local greens—and free Wi-Fi. At night, it's noisy and packed.

On the corner of Highway 450 and Ala Malama Avenue, **Molokai Burger ★** (www.molokaiburger.com; ℂ **808/553-3533**) offers burgers and dinner plates ($14) such as fried chicken or kalbi ribs. It's open Monday to Saturday until 9pm, with egg dishes and pancakes available 7 to 10:30am Saturday and free Wi-Fi. Next door, **Molokai Pizza Cafe ★**, 15 Kaunakakai Place, off Wharf Road (ℂ **808/553-3288**) serves standard pizza, salads, and burgers in a 1950s diner setting and is one of the few places that stays open late (until 11pm Fri–Sat, otherwise 10pm). Locals

GROCERIES, MARKETS & edibles

Nearly every storefront in Kaunakakai sells groceries of some sort and you'll want to visit several to stock up on specialty items. Start at **Friendly's Market,** 90 Ala Malama Ave. (✆ **808/553-5595**), which has a variety of dry goods and a small produce section. A few doors down, **Misaki's Store** (78 Ala Malama Ave.; ✆ **808/553-5505**) features fresh poke (seasoned, raw fish) and a few more vegetables. Across the street, tiny **C. Pascua Store,** 109 Ala Malama Ave. (✆ **808/553-5443**), often has ripe fruit and jumbo frozen prawns farm-raised on Oahu—perfect for pairing with a crisp Sauvignon Blanc from **Molokai Wines N Spirits,** 77 Ala Malama Ave. (✆ **808/553-5009**). Aside from an excellent array of adult beverages, you'll also find gourmet cheeses and crackers here. For organic and health-food brands, head to **The Planter Box,** 145 Puali St. (✆ **808/560-0010**). Nearly everything is shuttered on Sundays, with the exception of **Molokai Minimart,** 35 Mohala St. (✆ **808/553-4447**), helpfully open until 11pm daily.

If you can, try to coordinate your shopping with the **Saturday morning farmer's market** in Kaunakakai (8am–noon). Several vendors sell homegrown fruits and vegetables. Otherwise, head to **Kumu Farms** ★★, 9 Hua Ai Road, 1 mile south of Highway 460, near the airport (✆ **808/351-3326**). Famed for luscious papayas, the farm stand also sells organic herbs, vegetables, pesto, banana bread, and other treats. It's open Tuesday through Friday, 9am to 4pm.

Grocery shopping is very limited outside of Kaunakakai. On the West End, the **Maunaloa General Store** ★, 200 Maunaloa Hwy., Maunaloa (✆ **808/552-2346**), has staples and occasional plate lunches for sale; it's open Monday to Saturday 9am to 6pm, Sunday 9am to noon. Thirsty beachgoers will be glad to discover **A Touch of Molokai** (✆ **808/552-0133**), inside the otherwise-empty Kaluakoi Hotel. It's open 9am to 5pm daily, with snacks, sodas, and microwaveable fare. On the East End, the "Goods" (convenience store) half of **Manae Goods & Grindz,** 8615 Kamehameha V Hwy., Pukoo, near mile marker 16 (✆ **808/558-8498**), is open weekdays 8am to 6pm (until 5pm weekends). At mile marker 25, the **Puu O Hoku Ranch Store** ★★ (✆ **888/573-7775**) sells organic produce, honey, fresh herbs, frozen awa, and free-range organic beef—all produced at the ranch. In the central uplands, **Kualapuu Market,** 311 Farrington Rd. (Hwy. 480) at Uwao Street, Kualapuu (✆ **808/567-6243**), is handy for picking up a ready-to-grill steak (Mon–Sat 8:30am–6pm).

flock to **Maka's Korner** ★, 35 Mohala St. (✆ **808/553-8058**) for plate lunches (try the mahimahi) and more burgers. It has a handful of outdoor tables with counter service for breakfast, lunch, and dinner weekdays (breakfast and lunch only weekends). The quaint **Store House** ★, 145 Puali St. (✆ **808/553-5222**), has an array of tropical lemonades, smoothies, pastries, salads, and sandwiches (check the specials). It's a great place to stock up before heading out on an East End adventure. Open 7am to 5pm weekdays and 9am to 5pm on weekends.

Sweets lovers have many temptations. At **Kamoi Snack-n-Go** ★, 28 Kamoi St. (✆ **808/553-3742**), choose from more than 31 flavors of Dave's

Hawaiian Ice Cream from Honolulu, including local favorites such as *kulolo* (taro-coconut custard), *haupia* (coconut pudding), and *ube* (purple yam). You can't miss the lime green storefront of **Kanemitsu's Bakery ★** , 79 Ala Malama Ave. (℃ **808/553-5585**), a throwback to the 1960s that churns out pies, pastries, and cookies as well as sweet and savory breads. During breakfast and lunch hours, the attached restaurant serves typical American fare with local touches such as kimchi fried rice with eggs ($9) and local organic papaya (for just $1).

Elsewhere on the Island

Outside of Kaunakakai, the **Kualapuu Cookhouse ★**, 102 Farrington Road and Uwao Street, Kualapuu (℃ **808/567-9655**), serves gourmet diner fare, with entrees ($11–$33) such as spicy crusted ahi with lime cilantro sauce and a Thursday prime-rib special that's a local favorite. Breakfast and lunch menus are less ambitious but still tasty; sit amid cheery plantation-style decor inside or at covered picnic tables outside. On the East End, the takeout counter at **Manae Goods & Grindz,** 8615 Kamehameha V Hwy., Pukoo, near mile marker 16 (℃ **808/558-8498**), is the area's lone dining option. Smiling faces serve simple tuna sandwiches, burgers, and acai bowls for breakfast through the counter window. It's open from 6:30am to 6pm weekdays and 7:30am to 4:30pm on weekends. For food on the West End, see "Groceries, Markets & Edibles," above.

MOLOKAI SHOPPING
Gifts & Souvenirs
KAUNAKAKAI

The eclectic **Kalele Bookstore ★★★**, 64 Ala Malama Ave. (www.molokaispirit.com; ℃ **808/553-5112**) is a great place to start your Molokai vacation. Owner Teri Waros is a marvelous fount of local information and can orient you to the island. Ogle her curated selection of feather lei, shell necklaces, and earrings made with *kapa* (traditional bark fabric), then peruse the excellent collection of new and used books (including many rare Hawaiian titles), locally made artwork, and children's games.

The artist cooperative **Molokai Art From the Heart,** also at 64 Ala Malama Ave. (www.molokaigallery.com; ℃ **808/553-8018**), features

---

The Perfect Molokai Souvenir

Found in nearly every Molokai store, the dozen varieties of local sea salts from **Pacifica Hawaii** (www.pacificahawaii.com) make ideal gifts. Salt master Nancy Gove evaporates seawater in elevated pans at the front of her home in Kaunakakai and then infuses colors and flavors via ingredients such as local clay (*alaea*), Kauai-made rum, and Maui sugar. To see how she does it, call ℃ **808/553-8484** and book a free tour.

works by some 150 artists, virtually all from Molokai. **Something For Everybody,** 40 Ala Malama Ave. (www.allthingsmolokai.com; © 808/553-3299) will print custom T-shirts or trucker hats to commemorate your trip, in addition to selling locally designed goods. Decorated with vintage finds, the **Attic Boutique,** 145 Puali St. (© 808/553-5222), specializes in handmade jewelry and casual women's wear.

Make sure to hit the **Saturday morning farmer's market** (8am–noon) in downtown Kaunakakai; among the aunties sitting on the sidewalk with giant papaya and other produce, you'll find a dozen vendors of island arts and crafts, clothing, and specialty foods such as local vanilla extract.

ELSEWHERE ON THE ISLAND

Don't speed past **Holumua Junction** (the intersection of highways 460 and 470 on the way to Kualapuu). The entrepreneurial ladies at **Kupu Ae ★★★** (www.kupuaemolokai.com; © 808/646-1504) design and handcraft beautiful silkscreens and batiks—sarongs, pillows, wall hangings and more—each with deep Hawaiian meaning. You'll also find lovely jewelry, soaps, and art supplies. Next door, the **Beach Break ★★** sporting goods store (© 808/567-6091) sells everything you need for fun in the sun, plus top-quality ukuleles, cards, books, children's items, home decor, women's clothing in natural fabrics, and large-format prints of owner Zach Socher's impressive photos from around the island.

Two miles uphill, **Denise's Gifts,** inside Molokai Furniture at the intersection of Highway 470 and Farrington Road (Hwy. 480), offers bargain-priced *lauhala* (woven) boxes, straw fedoras, woven ornaments, shell and pearl jewelry, and children's aloha wear (www.molokaifurniture.com; © 808/567-6083).

Tucked behind Coffees of Hawaii, the **Molokai Arts Center** (© 808/567-9696) is an active hub for local ceramicists and you can buy beautiful handmade bowls, chimes, and mugs for decent prices. Park on Hula Street and follow the signs.

Zach Socher's parents, Jonathan and Daphne, own the colorful **Big Wind Kite Factory & Plantation Gallery ★★**, 120 Maunaloa Hwy., Maunaloa (www.bigwindkites.com; © 808/552-2364), chock-full of Balinese furnishings, stone and shell jewelry, Kalaupapa memoirs, and other books on Molokai. Test-fly one of the handmade Big Wind kites at the nearby park.

MOLOKAI NIGHTLIFE

The few choices for evening entertainment at least mean a lively crowd is guaranteed wherever you go. **Paddlers Restaurant and Bar,** on the ocean side of Highway 450 at Mohala Street (www.paddlersrestaurant.com; © 808/553-3300), is the island's primary watering hole. The spacious indoor-outdoor restaurant and bar hosts predominantly local acts onstage most nights and Sunday afternoons, when Na Ohana Aloha plays

ancient CELEBRATIONS

If possible, time your trip to coincide with **Ka Hula Piko** ★★★ (www.kahulapiko. com), an intimate celebration of the ancient art of hula. Over 3 days, hula practitioners offer powerful chants and dance, not as performance but as gifts to their ancestors. This hula is unlike anything you'll see elsewhere: dances mimicking mythological turtles, honoring the work of taro farmers, and proclaiming ancient prophesies. The island-wide festivities typically occur in the first week of June and wrap up with an all-day *ho'olaule'a* (festival) during which visiting hula troupes from as far as Japan and Europe share their skills.

The annual **Ka Molokai Makahiki** ★★★ (www.molokaievents.com) is another not-to-miss event. Islanders celebrate the rainy season—a time of peace and prosperity in ancient Hawaii—with traditional crafts, hula, chanting, games, and competitions. All of Molokai gathers for the daylong event, held on a Saturday in January at the Mitchell Pauole Center in Kaunakakai.

Hawaiian music at 3pm. For the later shows, you'll hear classic and contemporary Hawaiian music, country, even jazz, usually 6:30 to 8:30pm; some nights, a disco DJ or karaoke will keep the party going until midnight.

Most nights of the week, Hawaiian music enlivens **Hiro's Ohana Grill,** the oceanfront/poolside bar and restaurant at Hotel Molokai (p. 452). On Thursdays, live music (plus the prime rib) draws patrons to **Kualapuu Cookhouse** (p. 457). Finally, while it's not nightlife, per se, the twice-weekly **kanikapila** (jam session) at **Coffees of Hawaii,** 1630 Farrington Hwy. (www.coffeesofhawaii.com; ✆ **808/567-9490**) is definitely worth attending. A group of ukulele-strumming aunties and uncles fill the broad lanai, playing American and Hawaiian standards. The island's sweet-voiced kupuna (elders) dress up for the occasion and Hawaii's best musicians drop in whenever they're on island to croon alongside them. Don't miss it: Tuesday mornings 10am to 1pm and Friday afternoons 3pm to 6pm.

LANAI

by Shannon Wianecki

L anai is deliciously remote: The island's tiny airport doesn't accommodate direct flights from the Mainland and its closest neighbor is a 45-minute ferry ride away. It's almost as if this quiet, gentle oasis—known for both its small-town feel and celebrity appeal—demands that visitors go to great lengths to get here in order to better appreciate it.

ESSENTIALS

Arriving

BY PLANE   If you're coming from outside Hawaii, you'll have to make a connection on Oahu (Honolulu/HNL) or Maui (Kahului/OGG or Kapalua/JHM), where you can catch a blink-and-you'll-miss-it flight to Lanai's airport. You'll touch down in Palawai Basin, once the world's largest pineapple plantation; it's about 10 minutes by car to Lanai City and 25 minutes to Manele Bay.

Hawaiian Airlines (www.hawaiianairlines.com; ✆ **800/367-5320**) operates a fleet of pretty turboprop planes that fly direct from Honolulu to Lanai. **Mokulele Airlines** (www.mokuleleairlines.com; ✆ **866/260-7070**) offers charter flights to the island on nine-passenger Cessna Grand Caravan planes.

BY BOAT   A round-trip on **Expeditions Lahaina/Lanai Passenger Ferry** (http://go-lanai.com; ✆ **800/695-2624**) takes you between Maui and Lanai for $30 adults and $20 children each way. The ferry runs five times a day, 365 days a year, between Lahaina (on Maui) and Lanai's Manele Bay harbor. The 9-mile channel crossing takes 45 minutes to an hour, depending on sea conditions. Reservations are strongly recommended; call or book online. Baggage is limited to two checked bags and one carry-on. *Bonus:* During the winter months, taking the ferry amounts to a free whale-watch.

If you feel the need for speed (and have $1600 to spare), charter private passage with **Lanai Ocean Sports** (✆ **808/866-8256**) aboard *Kalulu.* The six-person 39' inflatable previously served as a chase boat for the Americas Cup and can zip along at 50mph. On a calm day you'll cross the channel separating Maui and Lanai in just 20 minutes.

Visitor Information

Lanai Visitors Bureau, 1727 Wili Pa Loop, Wailuku, Maui 96793 (www.gohawaii.com/lanai; ✆ **800/947-4774** or 808/565-7600), and the **Hawaii Visitors & Convention Bureau** (www.gohawaii.com; ✆ **800/GO-HAWAII** or 808/923-1811) provide brochures, maps, and island guides.

FACING PAGE: **Hulupoe Bay**

The Island in Brief

With barely 30 miles of paved road and not a single stoplight, Lanai (pronounced "lah-*nigh*-ee") is unspoiled by what passes for progress. It's a place of surreal juxtapositions. Much of the island is still untamed, except for a tiny 1920s-era plantation village and two luxury hotels.

Inhabited Lanai is divided into two regions: Lanai City, up on the mountain where the weather is cool and misty, and Manele, on the sunny southwestern coast where the weather is hot and dry.

Lanai City (pop. 3,200) sits at the heart of the island at 1,645 feet above sea level. It's the only place on Lanai that offers services (gas and groceries), and the airport is just outside of town. Built in 1924, this plantation village is a tidy grid of quaint tin-roofed cottages in bright pastels, with backyard gardens of banana, passion fruit, and papaya. Many of the residents are Filipino immigrants who once toiled in Lanai's pineapple fields. Their humble homes, now worth $500,000 or more (for a 1,500-sq.-ft. home, built in 1935, on a 6,000-sq.-ft. lot), are excellent examples of historic preservation; the whole town looks like it's been kept under a bell jar.

Around **Dole Park,** a charming village square lined with towering Norfolk and Cook pines, plantation buildings house general stores, a post office (where people stop to chat), two banks, a half-dozen restaurants, an art gallery, an art center, a few boutiques, and a coffee shop that easily outshines any Starbucks. The historic one-room police station displays a "jail" consisting of three padlocked, outhouse-size cells as a throwback to earlier times. The new station—a block away, with regulation-size jail cells—probably sees just as little action.

Just up the road from Dole Park is the **Lodge at Koele,** a stately resort owned by tech billionaire Larry Ellison and closed indefinitely. Year after year, plans to reopen the hotel have fallen through. Like a grand European manor, it stands alone on a knoll overlooking pastures and the sea at the edge of a pine forest.

Manele is directly downhill—comprising Manele Bay (with its small boat harbor), Hulopoe Beach, and the island's remaining bastion of extravagance, the **Four Seasons Resort Lanai.** You'll see more of "typical" Hawaii here—sandy beach, swaying palms, and superlative sunsets.

With such a small population, everybody knows everybody here. The minute you arrive on island, you'll feel the small-town coziness. People

THERE'S AN app FOR THAT

The Lanai Culture & Heritage Center partnered with Pulama Lanai to create a great new tool for exploring the island. The **Lanai Guide** is a GPS-enabled app that directs you to historic sites, replete with old photos, aerial videos, and chants. It's free on iTunes.

Lanai

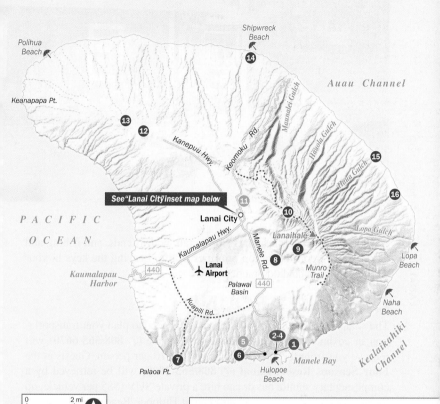

Plantation houses on Lanai

wave to passing cars, residents stop to talk with friends, and fishing and gardening are considered top priorities in life. Leaving the keys in your car's ignition is standard practice.

GETTING AROUND

The island has little infrastructure, so you'll need to plan your transportation in advance. **Rabaca's Limousine Service** (⌀ **808/565-6670**) will retrieve you from the airport or harbor for $10 per person. Guests at the **Four Seasons Resort Lanai** (⌀ **808/565-2000**) will be retrieved by a complimentary shuttle bus or can hire a private SUV ($85 per vehicle, up to four passengers). If you're camping at Hulopoe Beach, you can walk over from the harbor—a 5-minute stroll.

Once you've arrived at your lodging, it's entirely possible to enjoy Lanai without getting behind the wheel. Lanai City is easily walkable and if you're staying at the Four Seasons you'll hardly want to stray from the luxurious property. But if you plan to explore the island's remote shores or forested summit (which I highly recommend), you'll need a four-wheel-drive (4WD) vehicle for at least a day.

Reserve your ride far in advance; cars are in short supply here. On top of that, gas is expensive on Lanai—upward of $4 a gallon—and off-road vehicles get lousy mileage. Spending $40 to $50 per day on gas isn't unheard of. *Tip:* Rent only for the day (or days) you want to explore the island's hinterlands. Keep in mind that rainy weather makes many roads impassable. Check with your rental agent to see which roads are open—and whether renting that day is worth your money.

Dollar Rent A Car, 1036 Lanai Ave. (http://dollarlanai.com; ⌀ **800/533-7808 ext.1**) is the standard, no-frills stop for cars, minivans, and 4WD jeeps. Expect to pay $139 (plus taxes) per day and abide by

ghosts **TO GOLF COURSES**

Lanai hasn't always been so welcoming. Early Hawaiians believed the island was haunted by Pahulu (the god of nightmares) and spirits so wily and vicious that no human could survive here. But many have, for the past 1,000 years. Remnants of ancient Hawaiian villages, temples, fishponds, and petroglyphs decorate the Lanai landscape. King Kamehameha spent his summers here at a cliffside palace overlooking the sunny southern coast.

The island's arid terrain was once native forest—patches of which persist on the 3,379-foot summit of **Lanaihale**—along with native birds, insects, and jewel-like tree snails. But the 1800s brought foreign ambitions and foreign strife to Hawaii: Disease took more than half of her native people, and Western commerce supplanted the islanders' subsistence culture. Exotic pests such as rats, mosquitos, and feral goats and cattle decimated the native ecosystem and the island's watershed. Various entrepreneurs tried to make their fortune here, farming sugarcane, cotton, sisal, or sugar beets. All failed, mostly for lack of water.

Jim Dole was the first to have real commercial success here. In 1921, he bought the island for $1.1 million. He built Lanai City, blasted out a harbor, and turned the island into a fancy fruit plantation. For 70 years, the island was essentially one big pineapple patch. Acres of prickly fields surrounded a tiny grid of workers' homes. Life continued pretty much unchanged into the 1980s.

Ultimately, cheaper pineapple production in Asia brought an end to Lanai's heyday. In 1985, self-made billionaire David Murdock acquired the island in a merger (well, 98% of it anyway; the remaining 2% is owned by the government or longtime Lanai families). Murdock built two grand hotels, and almost overnight the plain, red-dirt pineapple plantation became one of the world's top travel destinations. Murdock's grand maneuver to replace agriculture with tourism never proved quite lucrative enough, however. In 2010, after years of six-figure losses, he sold his share of the island to the third-richest person in the United States, Larry Ellison.

The software tycoon made important moves to endear himself to the tiny, tight-knit community. He reopened the movie theater and the public swimming pool, closed for a decade. He built ball courts so that student athletes finally had somewhere to practice. He formed Pulama Lanai, a company tasked with directing the island's future, and hired a Lanai native to run its chief operating office. Ellison's ambitious plans include everything from sustainable agriculture to another über-exclusive resort at Halepalaoa on Lanai's pristine eastern shore. Longtime residents, who have lived through several island makeovers, remain optimistic but cautious.

Visitors will find an island still in flux. But Lanai has plenty of charms to capture a traveler's imagination, from wild dolphins jumping at Hulopoe Beach to hidden *heiau* (temples) that seem to vibrate with power.

their rather cautious recommendations regarding which roads you can access. **Lanai Adventure Club** (http://jeeplanai.net; ⓒ **800/565-7373**) tends to be more flexible with their Jeep Wranglers and where you can drive them; call for pricing. Alternately, check with Susan and Michael Hunter of **Dreams Come True** (www.dreamscometruelanai.com;

© 808/565-6961). They rent 4WD vehicles to their guests for $125 per day and might have an extra available.

If serious off-roading is your goal, consider renting an all-terrain vehicle (ATV) from **Lanai Jeep Rental** (www.lanaijeeprental.net; © **808/280-7092**) for $150 per day. John Price will give you a tour (see p. 476) or turn you loose, depending on your confidence. You can't drive the ATV on paved roads, but you can go wild exploring the island's red dirt tracks—which lead to its most pristine sites. Bonus: you don't have to refill the ATV's tank before returning. Price also rents Jeep Wranglers for $140 per day. He'll deliver yours to the harbor or wherever you are staying.

With all of that in mind, if you'd rather leave the driving to someone else, **Rabaca's Limousine Service** (see above) is a terrific option for a short romp around the island. Knowledgeable local drivers will navigate the rough roads for you, visiting Shipwreck Beach, Keahiakawelo, and even Keomoku Village in roomy Suburbans. Trips run 3½ hours and cost $80 per person (minimum two guests). If you've got a larger group, Rabaca's will chauffer the lot of you around in a six-person SUV for $110 per hour. Fifteen-passenger vans go for $150 per hour; they stay on paved roads.

Alternately, book the all-inclusive "4x4 Trekker Tour" package from **Expeditions** (www.go-lanai.com; © **808/695-2624;** from $181), which includes ferry travel to Lanai.

Whether or not you rent a car, sooner or later you'll find yourself at the **Lanai Plantation Store,** 1036 Lanai Ave. (© **808/565-7227 ext. 3**). Get directions, maps, and all the local gossip at this all-in-one grocery, gourmet deli, gas station, rental-car agency, and souvenir shop. It's also a good place to fill your water jugs: A reverse-osmosis water dispenser is just out front.

[FastFACTS] LANAI

Note: Lanai is part of Maui County.

Doctors & Dentists
For over-the-counter prescriptions and vaccines, head to **Rainbow Pharmacy** right in Dole Park (www.rainbowpharmacy.co; 431 7th St., Lanai City; © **808/565-9332**). If you need a doctor, contact the **Straub Lanai Family Health Center** (© **808/565-6423**) or the **Lanai Community**

Hospital (© **808/565-8450**). Next door to the Lanai Cultural & Heritage Center, **Hawaii Dental Clinic** (www.hawaiidental clinic.com; 730 Lanai Ave. Suite 101, Lanai City © **808/565-6418**) offers full services from 8am to 6pm.

Emergencies In case of **emergencies,** call the police, fire department, or

ambulance services at © **911,** or the **Poison Control Center** at © **800/ 222-1222.** For non-emergencies, call the **police** at © **808/565-6428.**

Weather For both land and sea conditions, visit the **National Weather Service** website (www.prh.noaa.gov) and type Lanai, Hawaii, in the search box.

EXPLORING LANAI

You'll need an off-road vehicle to reach the sights listed below. Four-wheel-drive rentals on Lanai are expensive—but worth it for a day or two of adventure. For details on vehicle rentals, see "Getting Around," above.

Your first stop on Lanai (perhaps after baptizing yourself at Hulopoe Beach) should be the **Lanai Culture & Heritage Center ★★**, 730 Lanai Ave. (www.lanaichc.org; © **808/565-7177**), located in the heart of town. Orient yourself to the island's cultural and natural history at this tiny, well-curated museum. Learn how indigenous Hawaiians navigated thousands of miles of Pacific Ocean, see relics of the Dole plantation years, and get directions to the island's petroglyph fields. Even better, ask the docents to recount local legends passed down in their families. A visit is guaranteed to make your explorations of Lanai that much richer.

Note: You'll find the following attractions on the "Lanai" map on p. 463.

Kanepuu Preserve

This ancient grove on Lanai's western plateau is the island's last remaining dryland forest, containing 48 native species. A self-guided hike allows visitors to see the rare trees and shrubs that once covered the dry lowlands of all the main Hawaiian Islands. Elsewhere these species have succumbed to axis deer, agriculture, or "progress." The botanical marvels growing within this protected reserve include *olopua* (Hawaiian olive), *lama* (Hawaiian ebony), *ma'o hau hele* (a Hawaiian hibiscus), and *nānū* (Hawaiian gardenia). Kanepuu is easily reached via 4WD. Head west from Koele Lodge on Polihua Road; in about 1¾ miles, you'll see the fenced area on the left.

Keahiakawelo (Garden of the Gods) ★★★

A four-wheel-drive dirt road leads out of Lanai City, through fallow pineapple fields, past the Kanepuu Preserve (see above) to Keahiakawelo. The rugged beauty of this place is punctuated by boulders strewn by volcanic forces and sculpted by the elements into varying shapes and colors—brilliant reds, oranges, ochers, and yellows.

Modern visitors nicknamed this otherworldly landscape "the Garden of the Gods," but its ancient Hawaiian name, Ke-ahi-a-kawelo, means "the fire of Kawelo." According to legend, it's the site of a sorcerers' battle. Kawelo, a powerful *kahuna* (priest) noticed that the people and animals of Lanai were falling ill. He traced their sickness to smoke coming from the neighboring island of Molokai. There, an ill-intentioned priest, Lanikaula, sat chanting over a fire. Kawelo started a fire of his own, here at Keahiakawelo, and tossed some of Lanikaula's excrement into the flames. The smoke turned purple, Lanikaula perished, and health and prosperity returned to Lanai.

Garden of the Gods

Take the dusty, bumpy drive out to Keahiakewalo early in the morning or just before sunset, when the light casts eerie shadows on the mysterious lava formations. Drive west from Koele Lodge on Polihua Road; in about 2 miles, you'll see a hand-painted sign pointing left down a one-lane, red-dirt road through a *kiawe* forest to the large stone sign. Don't stack rocks or otherwise disturb this interesting site; leave everything as you found it.

Luahiwa Petroglyph Field ★★

Lanai is second only to the Big Island in its wealth of prehistoric rock art, but you'll have to search a little to find it. Some of the best examples are on the outskirts of Lanai City, on a hillside site known as Luahiwa Petroglyph Field. The characters incised on 13 boulders in this grassy 3-acre knoll include a running man, a canoe, turtles, and curly-tailed dogs (a latter-day wag put a leash on one).

To get here, take Manele Road from Lanai City toward Hulopoe Beach. About 2 miles out of town, you'll see a pump house on the left. Look up on the hillside for a cluster of dark boulders—the petroglyphs are there, but you'll have to zigzag to get to them. Two dirt roads lead off of Manele Road, on either side of the pump house. Take the first one, which leads straight toward the hillside. After about 1 mile, you'll come to a fork. Head right. Drive for another ½ mile. At the first V in the road, take a sharp left and double back the way you came, this time on an upper road. After about ¼ mile; you'll come to the large cluster of boulders on the right. It's just a short walk up the cliffs (wear walking or hiking shoes) to the petroglyphs. Exit the same way you came. Go between 3pm and

off the tourist trail: **EASTSIDE LANAI**

If you've got good weather and a trusty 4×4 vehicle, go find adventure on Lanai's untamed east side. Bring snacks and extra water; there are no facilities out here and cell service is scarce. Follow Keomoku Road for 8 miles to the coast. Here the road turns to dirt, mud, or sand; proceed with caution. Head left to find **Shipwreck Beach** and the **Kukui Point petroglyphs** (p. 473).

Venture right to explore a string of empty beaches and abandoned villages, including **Keomoku**—about 5¾ miles down the rough-and-tumble dirt road. This former ranching and fishing community of 2,000 was home to the first non-Hawaiian settlement on Lanai. A ghost town since the mid-1950s, it dried up after droughts killed off the Maunalei Sugar Company. Check out **Ka Lanakila,**

the sweetly restored church that dates back to 1903.

Continue another 2 miles to the deserted remains of **Club Lanai.** A lonely pier stretches into the Pacific from a golden-sand beach populated by coconut palms, a few gazebos, and an empty bar floating in a lagoon. You can pretend you're on the set of *Gilligan's Island* here. This secluded area's Hawaiian name, **Halepaloa,** means "whale ivory house." Historians speculate that the teeth and bones of a sperm whale—rare in these waters—once washed ashore here. If you have time, press on to **Lopa Beach** (good for surfing, not for swimming). The road ends at **Naha Beach** with its ancient fishponds. Return the way you came and take any trash with you.

sunset for ideal viewing and photo ops. Don't touch the petroglyphs or climb on the rocks; these cultural resources are very fragile.

Munro Trail ★

In the first golden rays of dawn, when owls swoop silently over the abandoned pineapple fields, take a peek at **Mount Lanaihale,** the 3,370-foot summit of Lanai. If it's clear, hop into a 4×4 and head for the Munro Trail, the narrow, winding ridge trail that runs across Lanai's razorback spine to its peak. From here, you may get a rare treat: On a clear day, you can see most of the main islands in the Hawaiian chain.

But if it's raining, forget it. On rainy days, the Munro Trail becomes slick and boggy with major washouts. Rainy-day excursions often end with a rental jeep on the hook of the island's lone tow truck—and a $250 tow charge. You could even slide off into a major gulch and never be found, so don't try it. But in late August and September, when trade winds stop blowing and the air over the islands stalls in what's called a *kona* condition, Mount Lanaihale's suddenly visible summit becomes an irresistible attraction.

Look for a red-dirt road off Manele Road (Hwy. 440), about 5 miles south of Lanai City; turn left and head up the ridgeline. No sign marks the peak, so you'll have to keep an eye out. Look for a wide spot in the road and a clearing that falls sharply to the sea. From here you can also see

Kaunolu Village site

silver domes of Space City atop the summit of Haleakala on Maui; Puu Moaulanui, the tongue-twisting summit of Kahoolawe; the tiny crescent of Molokini; and, looming above the clouds, Mauna Kea on the Big Island. At another clearing farther along the thickly forested ridge, all of Molokai, including the 4,961-foot summit of Kamakou and the faint outline of Oahu (more than 30 miles across the sea), are visible. For details on hiking the trail, see "Hiking" on p. 470.

Kaunolu Village ★★

Out on Lanai's nearly vertical, Gibraltar-like sea cliffs is an old royal compound and fishing village. Now a national historic landmark and one of Hawaii's most treasured ruins, it's believed to have been inhabited by King Kamehameha the Great and hundreds of his closest followers about 200 years ago.

It's a hot, dry, 3-mile 4×4 drive from Lanai City to Kaunolu, but the mini-expedition is worth it. Take plenty of water, don a hat for protection against the sun, and wear sturdy shoes. Signs explain the sacred site's importance. Ruins of 86 house platforms and 35 stone shelters have been identified on both sides of Kaunolu Gulch. The residential complex also includes the **Halulu Heiau temple,** named after a mythical man-eating bird. The king's royal retreat is thought to have stood on the eastern edge of Kaunolu Gulch, overlooking the rocky shore facing **Kahekili's Leap.** Chiefs leapt from the 62-foot-high perch as a show of bravado. Nearby are **burial caves,** a **fishing shrine,** a **lookout tower,** and warrior-like stick figures—**petroglyphs**—carved on boulders. Just offshore stands the telltale fin of little **Shark Island,** a popular dive spot that teems with bright tropical fish and, frequently, sharks.

From Lanai City, take Kaumalapau Highway past the airport. Look for a carved boulder on the left side of the road. Turn left onto a dirt road (Kaupili Rd.) and drive east until you see another carved boulder. Turn right, toward the ocean. *Tip:* On your way out, turn right to continue on Kaupili Road. It meets with Hulopoe Drive, a shortcut to Manele Bay.

BEACHES

If you like big, wide, empty, gold-sand beaches and crystal-clear, cobalt-blue water full of bright tropical fish—and who doesn't?— Lanai is your place. With 18 miles of sandy shoreline, Lanai has some of Hawaii's least crowded and most interesting beaches.

Hulopoe Beach ★★★

Hulopoe is one of the loveliest beaches in all of Hawaii. Palm-fringed golden sand is bordered by black-lava fingers, which protect swimmers from ocean currents. The bay at the foot of the Four Seasons Resort Lanai is a protected marine preserve, with schools of colorful fish, spinner dolphins, and humpback whales that cruise by in winter and often stop to put on a show. The water is perfect for snorkeling, swimming, or just lolling about; the water temperature is usually in the mid-70s (mid-20s Celsius). Swells kick up slightly in winter. Hulopoe is also Lanai's premier beach

Ka Lanakila church in Keomoku

park, with a grassy lawn, picnic tables, barbecue grills, restrooms, showers, and ample parking. You can camp here, too.

HULOPOE'S TIDE POOLS ★★   Some of the best **tide pools** in Hawaii are found along the south shore of Hulopoe Bay. These submerged pockets of lava rock are full of strange creatures such as asteroids (sea stars) and holothurians (sea cucumbers), not to mention spaghetti worms, barber pole shrimp, and Hawaii's favorite local delicacy, the *opihi,* a tasty morsel also known as the limpet. Youngsters enjoy swimming in the enlarged tide pool at the eastern edge of the bay. *A few tips:* When you explore tide pools, do so at low tide. Never turn your back on the waves. Wear tennis shoes or reef walkers, as wet rocks are slippery. Collecting specimens in this marine preserve is forbidden, so don't take any souvenirs home.

Polihua Beach ★

According to legend, a mythical sea turtle once hauled herself out of the water to lay her eggs in the deep sand at Polihua, or "egg nest." This deserted beach lies at the end of Polihua Road, a 4-mile jeep trail. When it isn't windy, this huge, empty stretch on Lanai's northwestern shore is ideal for beachcombing, fishing, or indulging fantasies of being marooned on a desert island. When the wind *is* blowing, beware—you'll be sandblasted. Look for treasures in the flotsam and (during winter months) whales on the horizon. There are no facilities except fishermen's huts and driftwood shelters. Bring water and sunscreen. Strong currents and undertow make the water unsafe for swimming.

Shipwreck Beach ★★

This 8-mile-long windswept strand on Lanai's northeastern shore—named for the rusty ship *Liberty* stuck on the coral reef—is a sailor's nightmare and a beachcomber's dream. The strong currents yield all sorts of sea debris, from hand-blown glass fishing floats and paper nautilus shells to lots of junk. Shipwreck isn't good for swimming, but is a great place to spot whales from December to April, when Hawaiian humpbacks cruise in from Alaska. The road to the beach is paved most

Shipwreck Beach

Polihua Beach

of the way, but you really need a four-wheel-drive to get down here. At the end of the road, you'll find a trail that leads about 200 yards inland to the **Kukui Point petroglyphs;** follow the stacked rock *ahu* (altars) to the large boulders. Respect this historic site by not adding anything to it or taking anything away. Most important, *do not* touch the petroglyphs.

WATERSPORTS

Because Lanai lacks major development and experiences very little rainfall/runoff, it typically boasts Hawaii's best water clarity. The coast is washed clean daily by strong sea currents, which can wash you away, too, if you aren't careful where you jump in. Most of the aquatic adventures—swimming, snorkeling, scuba diving—are centered on the somewhat protected west coast, particularly around Hulopoe Bay. Spinner dolphins often cruise this coast, traveling in large pods and leaping from the water to twirl mid-air. Green sea turtles, humpback whales, and monk seals make appearances, too. For surf breaks, you'll head to the untamed east shore.

Boat trips—along with most island activities—can be booked at the Four Seasons' **Island Adventure Center** (1 Manele Bay Rd., Lanai City; ☏ **808/565-2072**). Their new vendor, **Lanai Ocean Sports** (www.lanai-oceansports.com ☏ **808/866-8256**), took over the Trilogy vessels and crew—so you can expect the same top-notch service. They offer sailing and snorkeling tours aboard a decked-out 49' catamaran and chartered adventures on *Kalulu*, a 39' rigid-hull inflatable. The six-person raft can plow through the sea at 50mph; it previously chased yachts in the Americas Cup. Keep in mind that during "festive season" (mid-December through the first week of January) the boats are fully committed to Four Seasons guests.

Kayaking

Lanai's south and west coastlines offer spectacular vistas: dramatic sea cliffs punctuated by hidden caves, quiet coves, and mysterious sea stacks. You can put kayaks in at **Manele** or **Kaumalapau Harbor**. Both are working harbors, but not very busy. From Kaumalapau, paddle roughly two-and-a-half miles north to reach **Nanahoa**, a cluster of needle-like sea stacks. It's a picturesque lunch stop, with a shady cave and rocky apron to pull up onto for a landing. The snorkeling around these islets can be magical. Check weather conditions and currents before you go. You can rent kayaks and gear from **Lanai Adventure Club** (http://jeeplanai.net; © **800/565-7373**). They also offer 4-hour guided tours from 8am to noon; call for pricing.

Sailing & Whale-Watching

Every evening, **Lanai Ocean Sports** (see above) offers a **two-hour sunset sail.** Cruise past sea cliffs and unspoiled coastline while spinner dolphins and flying fish dart ahead of the bow. You'll arrive at Puu Pehe, Sweetheart Rock, just in time for the best sunset shots. The trip costs $100, inclusive of snacks, beverages, and Dramamine for those suffering from seasickness.

During whale season (Dec–Mar), Hawaiian humpback whales put on impressive shows, breaching, slapping their pectoral fins, and singing complex melodies underwater. You can view them from just about any spot on Lanai, particularly on the eastside, looking toward Maui.

If you want to witness whales up close, hop aboard Lanai Ocean Sports' catamaran for **two-hour whale-spotting tour.** Scan the horizon for the massive marine mammals, which are almost guaranteed to surface nearby with gusty exhalations. The captain and crew are certified naturalists who make each trip educational. The cost and amenities are the same as the sunset sails.

Snorkeling Tours

To snorkel on your own, simply strap on a mask and head out from **Hulopoe Beach.** The marine-life conservation area is Lanai's best snorkeling spot; fish are abundant in the bay and marine mammals regularly swim by. Try the lava-rock points at either end of the beach and around the tide pools.

Venture further afield with **Lanai Ocean Sports** (see above) aboard their 49' sailing catamaran. The captains will steer you alongside the island's dramatic southern coast to a site near the Kaunolu lighthouse. The **3-hour snorkel trips** cost $150 and include sandwiches, cookies, cocktails and local microbrews. Help yourself to the stand-up paddleboards and organic Coola sunscreen.

Tropical fish

Scuba Diving

Two of Hawaii's best-known dive spots are found in Lanai's clear waters, just off the south shore: **Cathedrals I** and **II,** so named because the sun lights up an underwater grotto like a magnificent church. Sadly, the on-island scuba options have shrunk over the years. **Lanai Ocean Sports** (see above) is your best bet. You can charter *Kalulu* for a private two-tank dive, or tag along on a snorkel trip for a one-tank dive. Certified divers only; make sure you bring your PADI or NAU card.

Sport Fishing

Sportfishers can charter *Kalulu*, a 39' rigid-hull inflatable from **Lanai Ocean Sports** (see above). It's $1600 for several hours of trolling.

Surfing/Stand-Up Paddleboarding (SUP)

If you've ever wanted to learn how to surf, let instructor and surfing champion Nick Palumbo take you on a 4WD surfing safari to a secluded surf spot on the island's rugged eastside. He'll have you up and riding the waves in no time. His **Lanai Surf School & Surf Safari ★★** (www.lanaisurfsafari.com; ℂ **808/649-0739**) offers 5-hour surf safaris, which include four-wheel-drive transportation to Lopa Beach, refreshments, and "a really good time." The adventures cost $200 per person, minimum of two guests. He also offers stand-up paddleboarding (SUP) lessons at Hulopoe Beach, 2 hours for $100.

OTHER OUTDOOR ACTIVITIES

The **Four Seasons Resort Lanai** operates the **Island Adventure Center,** 1 Manele Bay Rd., Lanai City (*C* **808/565-2072**), where resort guests and the general public can book an assortment of activities: golf, sporting clays, off-road tours, horseback rides, sunset sails, and more. Located next door to the resort's tennis courts, it's open from 6am to 6pm.

ATV Tours

If you're feeling extra adventurous, call John Price at **Lanai Jeep Rental** (www.lanaijeeprental.net; *C* **808/280-7092**). He offers guided all-terrain vehicle (ATV) tours far afield—up the forested Munro Trail to the island's summit and out to the Garden of Gods. The ATVs can't travel on roads, but they can go many places cars can't—especially in wet and muddy weather. Wear clothes you're willing to sacrifice to Lanai's red dirt (long pants and closed-toe shoes) and bring a jacket (rain is frequent). Tours are $150 and the ATV is yours for 24 hours.

The Four Seasons' **Island Adventure Center** (1 Manele Bay Rd., Lanai City; *C* **808/565-2072**) offers the Cadillac version of this adventure. Slide on a sleek helmet, balaclava, and goggles, and mount your Polaris Razor 1000; the off-road suspension is so smooth you'll hardly notice the boulders. Local guides will chauffeur you into the forested uplands above Palawai Basin where you'll explore an ancient agricultural temple, view petroglyphs, and dodge spotted deer. Same as above, you'll need long pants, closed-toed shoes, a jacket, and clothes that can handle dirt. Two-hour tours leave twice daily at 9am and 1:30pm and cost $247.50 per person or $395 per couple.

Biking

Lanai Cycles (www.lanaicycles.com; *C* **808/563-0535**) offers terrific, 3½-hour guided bike tours of off-the-beaten-path locales. Start your adventure in the misty clouds above Lanai City. Hop on a specialized Sirrus multiuse bike and coast 7 miles down to the island's scenic east coast. A support vehicle will shuttle you back up to town, where you can fuel up on smoothies or coffee before taking off again, this time down to Kuamalapau Harbor or Shipwreck Beach. Tours cost $180 and are small and personalized.

Golf

Cavendish Golf Course ★ This quirky par-36, 9-hole public course lacks not only a clubhouse and club pros, but also tee times, scorecards, and club rentals. To play, just show up, put a donation into the little wooden box next to the first tee, and hit away. The 3,071-yard, E. B. Cavendish–designed course was built by the Dole plantation in 1947 for its employees. The greens are a bit bumpy, but the views of Lanai are great and the temperatures usually quite mild.

Off of Kaunaoa Dr., next to the Lodge at Koele, Lanai City. Greens fees by donation.

The Challenge at Manele ★★★   Designed by Jack Nicklaus, this target-style, desert-links course, is one of the most challenging courses in the state. Check out some of the course rules: no retrieving golf balls from the 150-foot cliffs on the ocean holes 12, 13, or 17, and all whales, axis deer, and other wild animals are considered immovable obstructions. That's just a hint of the unique experience you'll have on this starkly beautiful oceanfront course, which is routed among lava outcroppings, archaeological sites, and *kiawe* groves. The five sets of staggered tees pose a challenge to everyone from the casual golfer to the pro. The staff hands out complimentary Bloody Marys and screwdivers to those who partake, and new carts come with Bluetooth, so you can stream your own music. Facilities include a clubhouse, pro shop, rentals, practice area, lockers, and showers.

Next to the Four Seasons Resort Lanai. www.fourseasons.com/lanai. ⓒ **808/565-2222.** Greens fees $425 ($350 for guests). Club rentals $80 per day.

Horseback Riding

Get a taste of the *paniolo* (cowboy) life on a horseback tour. Sign up for an upland trail ride at the **Island Adventure Center,** 1 Manele Bay Rd., Lanai City (ⓒ **808/565-2072**), where you'll catch a shuttle up to Koele and meet your steed. On horseback, you'll meander through guava groves and past ironwood trees; catch glimpses of spotted deer, wild turkeys, and quail; and end with panoramic views of Maui and Lanai. The trails are dusty and rain is frequent; wear clothes you don't mind getting dirty and bring a light jacket. Long pants and closed-toe shoes are required. Daily tours start at 9am, 11am and 1pm, last 1½ hours, and cost $195 per person. Private rides are available for $225 per person per hour.

Even if you don't book a ride, you may want to visit the stables to "Meet the Minis." Visitors who drop by around lunchtime can help groom the twelve miniature horses and four donkeys.

Hiking

KAPIHAA TRAIL   An old fisherman's trail starts at Manele Bay and snakes along the scenic coastline. This easy hike will expose you to Lanai's unique geography and many unusual native Hawaiian coastal plants. The back-and-forth trek takes around 90 minutes. Venture out on your own or, if you're a Four Seasons hotel guest, arrange a complimentary guided hike through the concierge (www.fourseasons.com/lanai; ⓒ **808/565-2000**). You can also download an informative brochure from the **Lanai Visitor Center website** (www.lanaichc.org/kapihaa.html).

Maunalei Gulch

KOLOIKI RIDGE HIKE   The leisurely 2-hour self-guided hike starts by the reflecting pool in the backyard of the Lodge at Koele and takes you on a 5-mile loop through Norfolk Island pines, into Hulopoe Valley, past wild ginger, and up to Koloiki Ridge, with its panoramic view of Maunalei Valley and the islands of Molokai and Maui in the distance. Go in the morning; by afternoon, the clouds usually roll in, marring visibility at the top and increasing your chance of being caught in a downpour. The path isn't clearly marked, so ask the concierge at the Four Seasons (www.four seasons.com/lanai; ✆ 808/565-2000) for a free map, or sign up for a guided hike. It's considered moderate, with some uphill and downhill hiking.

MUNRO TRAIL   This tough, 11-mile (round-trip) uphill climb through groves of Norfolk pines is a lung-buster, but if you reach the top, you'll be rewarded with a breathtaking view of Molokai, Maui, Kahoolawe, and Hawaii Island. Figure on 7 hours. The trail begins at Lanai Cemetery (interesting in its own right) along Keomoku Road (Hwy. 44) and follows Lanai's ancient caldera rim, ending up at the island's highest point, **Lanai-hale.** Go in the morning for the best visibility. After 4 miles, you'll get a view of Lanai City. The weary retrace their steps from here, while the more determined go the last 1.25 miles to the top. Diehards head down Lanai's steep south-crater rim to join the highway to Manele Bay. For more details on the Munro Trail—including four-wheel-driving it to the top—see "Munro Trail" (p. 469).

PUU PEHE   Skirt along Hulopoe Bay to scale the cliff on its southern edge (it's a gentle slope, not a steep climb). This 20-minute hike leads above the turquoise-gray waters of Shark's Cove to the dramatic point overlooking Puu Pehe, or Sweetheart's Rock. The picturesque islet rises 80 feet from the sea and is home to nesting seabirds. Look closely and you'll see an *'ahu,* altar of rocks at the top. According to legend, a young Lanai warrior hid his beautiful wife in a sea cave at the base of the cliffs here. One day a storm flooded the cave and she drowned. Grief-stricken, her beloved climbed the sheer face of the islet, carrying her body. He buried her, then jumped to his death in the pounding surf below.

Sporting Clays

Go on, take a crack at the clay disk hurtling through the air . . . you might just surprise yourself by shattering it! Both sharpshooters and novices will enjoy this 14-station shooting clay course in the Lanai uplands. Zip from station to station beneath the whispering ironwood trees in your own golf cart. Each target mimics the movement of a different bird or rabbit; shots grow increasingly difficult as the course progresses. Private lessons start at $125 per person for 1 hour. Experienced shooters can do the course on their own. The complex includes an archery range and options for kids. Wear closed-toe shoes and bring a jacket. Book at the Four Seasons' **Island Adventure Center** (1 Manele Bay Rd., Lanai City; ✆ **808/565-2072**).

Tennis

Public courts, lit for night play, are available in Lanai City at no charge; call ✆ **808/565-6979** for reservations. If you're staying at the Four Seasons, you can take advantage of the upgraded "tennis garden," with its two Plexi-Pave cushion courts and Har-Tru green clay court—the same used by the pros. Court access comes with complimentary use of Prince rackets, balls, and bottled water—even shoes if you need them.

WHERE TO STAY ON LANAI

Accommodations on Lanai are limited: You can go for broke at the luxurious Four Seasons, book a plantation-style room at the Hotel Lanai, or camp under the stars at Hulopoe Beach Park. When you stay with the Four Seasons, you're greeted at the airport or ferry with chilled towels and shuttled off in style.

Expensive

Four Seasons Resort Lanai ★★★   A conch shell's trumpeting call announces your arrival at this oceanfront retreat, where everyone magically knows your name—even the computer screen in your bathroom mirror. Every inch of this opulent oasis reflects the latest in tech-savvy luxury, from the wristband room keys to the Toto toilets. Service is impeccable: The concierge texts you when dolphins or whales appear in the bay. Beach attendants set up umbrellas in the sand for you, spritz you with Evian, and deliver popsicles.

Guest rooms are large and luxurious, with blackout shades that you can control with a flick of your hand. Suites have Japanese cedar tubs and views that stretch on forever. The resort's two wings overlook Hulopoe Beach and are lushly landscaped with waterfalls, koi-filled lotus ponds, and artwork tucked into every corner. Rare Polynesian artifacts purchased from the Bishop Museum decorate the main lobby's lower level, which is home to two fantastic restaurants: **Nobu Lanai ★★★** and **One Forty ★★★**. Other amenities include a first-rate adventure center, shuffleboard tables in the chic sports bar, and an exercise room with a view so grand you'll forget you're burning calories on a stationary bike. Inspired by indigenous healing traditions, the resort's **Hawanawna Spa** offers traditional *lomi lomi* Hawaiian massages, seaweed body wraps, facials, and salon services in serene treatment rooms. Guests have free access to the spa facility's saunas and steam rooms. The "Kids for All Seasons" childcare programs activities are excellent, but you'll probably have trouble pulling your youngsters away from the beach and tide pools.

1 Manele Bay Rd., Lanai City. www.fourseasons.com/lanai. © **800/321-4666** or 808/565-2000. 168 rooms, 45 suites. Doubles from $1,075; suites from $2,200. **Amenities:** 5 restaurants; bar with live music; babysitting; children's program; concierge; fitness center w/classes; golf at Jack Nicklaus–designed Challenge at Manele; whirlpools; 2 pools; room service; full spa; tennis courts; watersports equipment; Wi-Fi (free or premium for $20/day).

Moderate

Hotel Lanai ★   This boutique hotel in the heart of town is perfect for families and other vacationers who can't afford to spend a small fortune but still want to experience Lanai. If you're looking for the old-time aloha that the island is famous for, this is your place. Built in the 1920s, it has retained its quaint, plantation-era character.

That character comes at a price: Guest rooms are small and noise travels. But the comfy beds come with Hawaiian quilts, and the ceiling fans do a more than adequate job in the cooler climate. The popular Lanai units are slightly larger and share a furnished deck that faces Dole Park. The one-bedroom cottage costs slightly more than those rooms and boasts the added amenities of a private yard, living room with TV, and a bathtub. All of Lanai City is within walking distance. The in-house restaurant, **Lanai City Bar & Grille,** is a social spot where visitors mingle with locals in the bar, talking or playing the ukulele long into the night. *Tip:* room rates are cheaper on weekdays.

828 Lanai Ave., Lanai City. www.hotellanai.com. © **800/795-7211** or 808/565-7211. 10 units, 1 cottage. $185–$310 double; $285–$310 cottage, $55 for child. Rates include continental breakfast. Free parking. **Amenities:** Restaurant; bar; access to golf courses; complimentary beach equipment; nearby tennis courts; free Wi-Fi.

Inexpensive

Dreams Come True ★   Susan and Michael Hunter have operated this bed-and-breakfast in the heart of Lanai City for 30-plus years. The nicely renovated 1925 plantation house is roomy and quaint, with four bedrooms, four bathrooms, and a backyard orchard of papaya, banana, and avocado trees. Among the many perks: marble bathrooms, fresh *lilikoi* juice served with the delicious breakfast each morning, and private four-wheel-drive rentals—a real bonus on this car-deficient island!

1168 Lanai Ave., Lanai City. https://dreamscometruelanai.com ℂ **808/565-6961** or 808/565-7211. 4 rooms, or entire house. Double $141–$160; $564 entire house, plus $100 cleaning fee. Rates include continental breakfast. **Amenities:** Car rental; concierge; laundry; barbecue; free Wi-Fi.

Camping at Hulopoe Beach Park ★★★

There is only one legal place to camp on Lanai, but it's a beauty. **Hulopoe Beach Park** (www.lanai96763.com/information; ℂ **808/215-1107**) has eight campsites on the shady grass lawn fronting this idyllic white-sand beach. Facilities include restrooms, showers, barbecues, and picnic tables. Email info@lanaibeachpark.com 72 hours in advance to request a permit. You'll pay an $80 permit fee, which covers four people for 3 nights. Payment is by credit card only. Permits are issued in person, first-come, first-served, major holidays excluded.

WHERE TO EAT ON LANAI

Lanai offers dining experiences on two ends of the spectrum, from humble ma-and-pa eateries to world-class culinary adventures. The posh resort restaurants require deep pockets, and Lanai City has only a handful of other options.

Note: You'll find the restaurants reviewed in this chapter on the "Lanai" map on p. 463.

Expensive

Nobu Lanai ★★★ JAPANESE   What does Lanai have in common with New York, Milan, Budapest, and Mexico City? All have a Nobu restaurant—a measure of how fun a place is, according to pop star Madonna. The best way to experience this epicurean phenomenon is to order the *omakase*—the chef's tasting menu—for $120. Every dish is as delicious as it is artful: the smoked Wagyu gyoza with jalapeño miso, the immaculate plates of nigiri sushi, and the ahi avocado salad with greens grown at Alberta's farm up the road. A new teppanyaki tasting menu—fifteen courses for $250—is available at one of the two teppan tables. The wine and cocktail list is top-notch, including exclusive Hokusetu sake and a sassy caipirinha with Pisco, fresh lime, ginger beer, and sprigs of shiso. Request a sake tasting, and the resident sake master will teach you the subtleties of a dry *onigorishi* and a dynamic *daiginjo*.

At the Four Seasons Resort Lanai, 1 Manele Bay Rd., Lanai City. www.fourseasons.com/lanai. ℂ **808/565-2832.** Main courses $12–$58; 15-course tasting menu $120. Daily 6–9pm.

One Forty ★★★ BREAKFAST/STEAK & SEAFOOD   This breakfast buffet is probably the best in the state. Weeks later I'm still fantasizing about my One Forty breakfast overlooking sparkling Manele Bay.

Imagine: a cornucopia of ripe tropical fruit, "make-your-own" omelet and smoothie stations, artisan cheese, charcuterie, four types of sausages, brioche French toast, eggs any which way, and a *malasada* machine. Not just lox, but house-cured *ono* with toasted bagels—now *that* is what I call breakfast. Dinner is also stellar. The pan-seared kampachi with forbidden rice, bok choy, and chimichurri sauce is perfectly on point, as is the 20-ounce bone-in ribeye (it should be, for a staggering $95). Order the chocolate soufflé early; it takes 20 minutes to bake and is worth every second of the wait.

At the Four Seasons Resort Lanai, 1 Manele Bay Rd., Lanai City. www.fourseasons.com/lanai. © **808/565-2290.** Breakfast main courses $12–$24; buffet $52; dinner $32–$95. Daily 6:30–10am and 6–9pm.

Moderate

Lanai City Bar & Grille ★ AMERICAN   This Lanai mainstay has three comfortable dining areas to choose from: the bright and lovely dining room, the bar with large-screen TVs and couchlike chairs, and the outdoor patio where Hawaiian musicians croon under the stars. Local venison is the star of the menu, which also features pasta, burgers, and specialty cocktails. The service is friendly if a tad slow. Bring a jacket if you want to sit outside by the fire pits and soak up the friendly Lanai ambience and fantastic live music.

At the Hotel Lanai, 828 Lanai Ave., Lanai City. www.lanaicitybarandgrille.com. © **808/565-7212.** Main courses $18–$34. Wed–Sat 5–9pm; Sun 8am–1pm.

Malibu Farms ★ AMERICAN   Lunch and dinner are glamorous affairs by the Four Seasons pool. After a midday swim, indulge in an acai bowl or skirt steak with quinoa. The emphasis here is on local, organic produce. At dusk, pull up a seat at the bar for a craft cocktail and watch the sun melt into the sea.

At the Four Seasons Resort Lanai, 1 Manele Bay Rd., Lanai City. www.fourseasons.com/lanai. © **808/565-2092.** Main courses $18–$34. Daily 11am–8:30pm.

Inexpensive

Blue Ginger Cafe ★ COFFEE SHOP   With its cheery curtains and oilcloth-covered tables, this humble eatery welcomes residents and locals alike in for eggs and Spam (a beloved breakfast meat in Hawaii), adequate bowls of saimin, epic plates of fried rice, fried chicken katsu, and decent egg/tuna/chicken salad sandwiches on homemade bread. The kitchen staff bakes all of its own breads and pastries, so burgers and sandwiches taste especially fresh. Hot out of the oven, the blueberry turnovers, cinnamon buns, and cookies are local favorites.

409 Seventh St. (at Ilima St.), Lanai City. www.bluegingercafelanai.com. © **808/565-6363.** Breakfast and lunch items under $17; dinner main courses under $18. Cash only. Thurs–Mon 6am–8pm; Tues–Wed 6am–2pm.

Coffee Works ★ COFFEEHOUSE   A biscuit's toss from Dole Park, this cozy coffeehouse churns out excellent espresso drinks, amply loaded lox and bagels, acai bowls, ice cream, crepes, and sandwiches. The renovated plantation home is the perfect place to fuel up in the morning. It's also Lanai City's local watering hole—expect to see your waiter from dinner last night chatting away with the shuttle driver on the wide wooden deck. As you wait for your cappuccino, browse the gift items opposite the counter: T-shirts to prove you were here, tea infusers and pots, and island coffee beans.

604 Ilima St., Lanai City. www.coffeeworkshawaii.com. © **808/565-6962.** Most items under $15. Mon–Fri 7am–4pm; Sat 8am–3pm.

Lanai City Service ★ DELI   The island's sole gas station now serves tasty deli sandwiches and a few hot items—more gourmet than you might expect. The paninis have upscale ingredients (the grilled cheese comes with Boursin, Swiss, provolone, and avocado) and you can build your own sandwich for just $7. If the bahn mi is on special, order that and head out for a picnic.

1036 Lanai Ave., Lanai City. © **808/565-7227.** Lunch items $4–$8. Daily 6am–6pm.

Pele's Other Garden ★ DELI/BISTRO   The checkered floor and vanity license plates decorating the walls set an upbeat tone at this casual bistro. For lunch, dig into an avocado and feta wrap or an Italian hoagie. Cheese lovers will swoon over the thin-crusted four-cheese pizza—a gooey medley of mozzarella, Parmesan, feta, and provolone. During happy hour, nosh on onion rings and coconut shrimp at one of Lanai City's only bars. Enjoy cocktails, wine by the glass, or one of the dozen brews on tap. The atmosphere grows slightly more romantic after sundown, with white linens on the tables and twinkle lights over the outdoor seating.

811 Houston St., Lanai City. www.pelesothergarden.com. © **808/565-9628.** Main courses $9–$13 lunch, $17–$20 dinner; pizza from $9. Mon–Fri 11am–2pm; Mon–Sat 5:30–8pm.

LANAI SHOPPING

Lanai has limited shopping, but you can find some gems here. A stroll around Dole Park will yield original artwork, clothing, and souvenirs, and the Four Seasons has excellent boutiques. Just remember that groceries are delivered only once a week (Wednesday is barge day)—so plan your shopping accordingly. Shops are typically open from 9 to 6pm Monday to Saturday, more limited hours on Sundays.

Art

Lanai Art Center ★★   Established in 1989, the Lanai Art Center showcases works by Lanai residents, including evocative watercolor paintings of local landmarks, silkscreened clothing, and necklaces made of polished shells and bone. Often, the artists are at work in back. Check out the center's reasonably priced workshops, where local and visiting artists offer instruction on everything from *raku* (Japanese pottery) to silk-printing, lei-making, and *gyotaku* (printing a real fish on your own T-shirt). 339 Seventh St., Lanai City. www.lanaiart.org. © **808/565-7503.**

Mike Carroll Gallery ★★★ Oil painter Mike Carroll left a successful 22-year career as a professional artist in Chicago for a distinctly slower pace on Lanai. His gorgeous, color-saturated interpretations of local life and landscapes fill the walls of his eponymous gallery, which also sells original work by top Maui and Lanai artists. 443 Seventh St., Lanai City. www.mikecarrollgallery.com. © **808/565-7122.**

Edibles & Grocery Staples

Pine Isle Market ★ The Honda family has operated this grocery for 6 decades. Three doors down from Richard's (below), it carries everything that its competition doesn't. A visit to both will net you a fine haul. Pine Isle specializes in locally caught fresh fish, but you can also find ice cream, canned goods, fresh herbs, toys, diapers, paint, and other essentials. Take a spin through the fishing section to ogle every imaginable lure. The market is open Monday to Saturday 8am to 7pm and Sunday 8am to 5pm. 356 Eighth St., Lanai City. © **808/565-6488.**

Richard's Market ★★ Since 1946, this family grocery has been the go-to for dry goods, frozen meats and vegetables, liquor, paper products, cosmetics, utensils, and other miscellany. It got a major makeover, courtesy of Larry Ellison and Pulama Lanai. Now the inside resembles a

The Local Gentry

miniature Whole Foods with an array of fancy chocolates and fine wines, mixed in with aloha shirts, and fold-up *lauhala* mats. Don't faint when you see that milk costs $9 a gallon; that's the price of paradise. The fish counter sells fantastic poke (raw seasoned fish). Open daily 6am to 10pm. 434 Eighth St., Lanai City. ☏ **808/565-3781.**

Saturday Market ★ From 8am to noon-ish each Saturday, the southeast corner of Dole Park turns into a farmer's market. Lanai residents bring their homegrown fruits and vegetables, freshly baked pastries, plate lunches, and handicrafts to sell. If you want one of Juanita's scrumptious pork flautas with a dollop of hot sauce, get here early. Other treats include fresh pressed juices from the bygone Anuenue Juice Bar and fantastic Thai summer rolls.

Gifts & Souvenirs

The Local Gentry ★★ Jenna (Gentry) Majkus manages to outfit her small but wonderful boutique with every wardrobe essential, from fancy lingerie to stylish chapeaux, for the whole family. If you need sunglasses, come here for polarized Maui Jims. 363 Seventh St., Lanai City. ☏ **808/565-9130.**

Makamae/Pilina ★★★ Just try to resist this resort shop's bona-fide (read: top-dollar) treasures, including delicately wrapped freshwater pearl and diamond bead necklaces by Jordan Alexander, the cutest-ever bikinis and beach cover-ups by Hawaii's own Letarte, and slinky dresses and housewares by Missoni (yes, you can fit that throw pillow in your suitcase). Four Seasons Resort Lanai, 1 Manele Bay Rd. ☏ **808/565-2093.**

Mua Loa ★★ Kids can't help but ogle the old-fashioned candy jars at the resort's extra-glam sundries shop. Come here for organic sunblock, colorful rash guards, and adorable, beach-y souvenirs. Four Seasons Resort Lanai, 1 Manele Bay Rd. ☏ **808/565-2000.**

Rainbow Pharmacy ★★ Like so many island institutions, this pharmacy plays dual roles. It's not just a place to fill your prescription or stock up on earplugs and sunburn gel; you'll also find quality locally made souvenirs here (including coin purses and clutches made with vintage Hawaiian fabric). From the counter in back, you can order an assortment of medicinal Chinese teas and—unpredictably—shave ice. 431 Seventh St., Lanai City. ☏ **808/565-9332.**

LANAI NIGHTLIFE

The Four Seasons and Hotel Lanai are the island's two mainstays for nightlife. Before sunset, head to **Malibu Farm** at the **Four Seasons Resort Lanai,** 1 Manele Bay Rd. (www.fourseasons.com/lanai; ☏ **808/565-2093**), for cocktails; after dark, you can shoot pool in the **Sports Bar & Grill.** Several nights a week, local musicians get together for jams at the **Lanai City Bar & Grille** ★ at the Hotel Lanai, 828 Lanai Ave. (www.lanaicitybarandgrille.com; ☏ **808/565-7212**). No trip to the island is complete without an evening spent here, enjoying Hawaiian harmonies under the stars alongside the locals and day-trip golfers. Bring a jacket if you plan to sit outside; the fire pits are cozy, but not quite enough to keep you warm.

Another fun option is the wonderfully renovated Lanai Theater, renamed **Hale Keaka** ★ (www.lanai96763.com/showtimes; 456 Seventh St., Lanai City). Built in 1926, this iconic landmark shared films, live plays, and musical performances with the community for 80 years. The $4-million renovation kept the vintage feel but added air-conditioning, digital sound, two stages and screens, cushy seats, and more. Two films—an adult and a children's selection—change weekly. The box office opens 1 hour prior to the start of each movie. And because it's Lanai, you'll find *furikake* and shoyu among the complimentary popcorn condiments.

KAUAI

by Jeanne Cooper

Time has been kind to Kauai, the oldest and northern-most of the Hawaiian Islands. Millions of years of erosion have carved fluted ridges, emerald valleys, and glistening waterfalls into the flanks of Waialeale, the extinct volcano at the center of this near-circular isle. Similar eons have created a ring of enticing sandy beaches and coral reefs. Its wild beauty sometimes translates to rough seas and slippery trails, but with a little prudence, anyone can safely revel in the natural grandeur of Kauai.

ESSENTIALS

Arriving

BY PLANE A number of North American airlines offer regularly sched-uled, nonstop service to Kauai's main airport in Lihue (airport code: LIH) from the Mainland, nearly all from the West Coast. (*Note:* From California, flights generally take about 5½ hours heading to Kauai, but only 4½ hours on the return, due to prevailing winds.)

United Airlines (www.united.com; © 800/225-5825) flies nonstop to Kauai daily from Los Angeles, San Francisco, and Denver; **Delta Air-lines** (www.delta.com; © 800/221-1212) also flies nonstop from Los Angeles and Seattle. **American Airlines** (www.aa.com; © 800/433-7300) has year-round nonstop services from Los Angeles and Phoenix, with nonstop flights from Dallas-Fort Worth December to March. **Alaska Airlines** (www.alaskaair.com) flies nonstop to Lihue several times a week from San Jose, Oakland, and San Diego in California, as well as Portland, Oregon, and Seattle. **Hawaiian Airlines** (www.hawaiianairlines.com; © 800/367-5320) flies nonstop daily to Lihue from Los Angeles and Oakland.

Other carriers' service varies by season. **WestJet** (www.westjet.com; © 888/937-8538) offers nonstop flights between Vancouver and Lihue from November through April, with most departures from December to March. **Southwest Airlines** (www.southwest.com; © 800/367-5320) is expected to begin service from the West Coast to Honolulu, with connec-tions to outer islands, by the end of 2018.

You can also travel to Lihue via Honolulu; Kahului, Maui; and Kona, on the Big Island. **Hawaiian Airlines** (see above) flies nonstop to Kauai 16 to 20 times a day from Honolulu, four times a day from Maui, and once from Kona. The Honolulu flight is about 35 minutes; the Maui route, about 45, and Kona, about 50, all using Boeing 717s that seat around 120.

PREVIOUS PAGE: **Wailua Falls, Kauai**

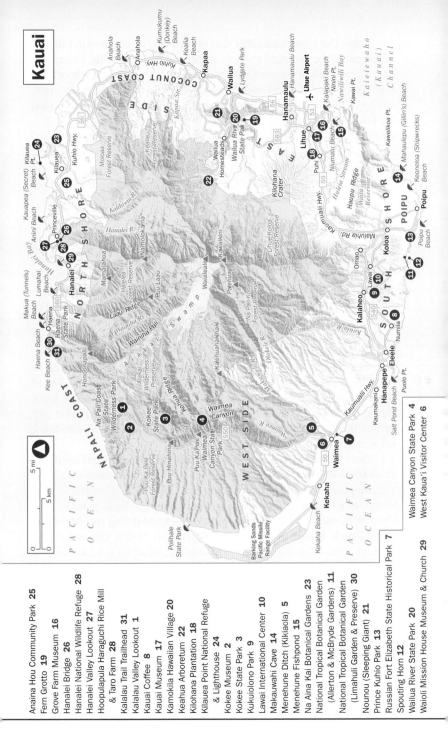

Kauai

Anaina Hou Community Park **25**
Fern Grotto **19**
Grove Farm Museum **16**
Hanalei Bridge **26**
Hanalei National Wildlife Refuge **28**
Hanalei Valley Lookout **27**
Hoopulapula Haraguchi Rice Mill
& Taro Farm **28**
Kalalau Trail Trailhead **31**
Kalalau Valley Lookout **1**
Kauai Coffee **8**
Kauai Museum **17**
Kamokila Hawaiian Village **20**
Keahua Arboretum **22**
Kilohana Plantation **18**
Kilauea Point National Refuge
& Lighthouse **24**
Kokee Museum **2**
Kokee State Park **3**
Kukuiolono Park **9**
Lawai International Center **10**
Makauwahi Cave **14**
Menehune Ditch (Kikiaola) **5**
Menehune Fishpond **15**
Na Aina Kai Botanical Gardens **23**
National Tropical Botanical Garden
(Allerton & McBryde Gardens) **11**
National Tropical Botanical Garden
(Limahuli Garden & Preserve) **30**
Nounou (Sleeping Giant) **21**
Prince Kuhio Park **13**
Russian Fort Elizabeth State Historical Park **7**
Spouting Horn **12**
Wailua River State Park **20**
Waioli Mission House Museum & Church **29**
Waimea Canyon State Park **4**
West Kaua'i Visitor Center **6**

Note: The view from either side of the plane as you land in Lihue, 2 miles east of the center of town, is arresting. On the left side, passengers have a close look at Haupu Ridge, separating the unspoiled beach of Kipu Kai (seen in *The Descendants*) from busy Nawiliwili Harbor; on the right, shades of green demarcate former sugarcane fields, coconut groves, and the ridgeline of Nounou ("Sleeping Giant") to the north.

BY CRUISE SHIP   Several cruise lines call in Kauai's main port of Nawili-wili, but **Norwegian Cruise Lines** (www.ncl.com; © **866/234-7350**) is unique in offering weekly Hawaii itineraries that include overnight stays on Kauai and Maui, allowing for multiple excursions (from $1,429 per person).

Visitor Information

Before your trip begins, visit www.gohawaii.com/kauai, the website of **Kauai Visitors Bureau** (© **800/262-1400**), and download or view the free "Kauai Official Travel Planner." (*Note:* The bureau's Lihue office in Watumull Plaza, 4334 Rice St., Suite 101, is not the most convenient area for drop-bys, but it's open 8am–4pm weekdays.) Before and during your trip, consult the authoritative **Kauai Explorer** website (www.kauaiex-plorer.com) for detailed descriptions of 18 of the island's most popular beaches (nine with lifeguards), plus a daily ocean report, surf forecasts, and safety tips. Hikers will also want to read Kauai Explorer's notes on 10 island trails, from easy to super-strenuous. Click on the "Visitors" link of **Kauai County**'s homepage (www.kauai.gov), for links to Kauai Explorer, the Visitors Bureau, bus schedules, camping information, park and golf facility listings, a festival and events calendar, farmers market schedules, recycling drop-off sites, and more.

The **Poipu Beach Resort Association** (www.poipubeach.org; © **888/744-0888** or 808/742-7444) highlights accommodations, activi-ties, shopping, and dining in the Poipu area; follow the "Contact Us" link to receive a free map of the Koloa and/or Mahaulepu heritage trails.

Check out the latest entertainment listings and dining specials online at **Midweek Kauai** (www.midweekkauai.com) before you arrive, and look for a free copy, distributed on Wednesday, once you're on Kauai. The **Garden Island** daily newspaper (www.thegardenisland.com) publicizes concerts and other events online under the "Entertainment" link.

First-time visitors with smartphones may enjoy the three **Shaka Guide** driving tour apps for Kauai (North Shore, Waimea/Na Pali, and Wailua Waterfalls), downloadable for $4.99 each at www.shakaguide.com.

The Island in Brief

EAST SIDE

Home to the airport, the main harbor, most of the civic and commercial buildings on the island, and the majority of its residents, the East Side of Kauai has nevertheless preserved much of its rural character, with green

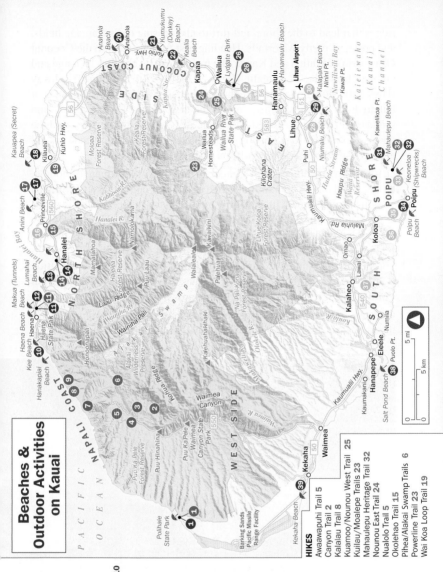

Beaches & Outdoor Activities on Kauai

BEACHES & BEACH PARKS
* Anahola Beach Park **20**
Anini Beach Park **17**
Brennecke's Beach **34**
* Haena Beach Park **11**
* Hanalei Bay Beach Parks **14**
Kalapaki Beach **29**
Kauapea (Secret) Beach **18**
* Kealia Beach Park **22**
* Kee Beach (Haena State Park) **10**
Kekaha Beach Park **39**
Keoneloa (Shipwrecks) Beach **32**
Kumukumu (Donkey) Beach **21**
Lumahai Beach **13**
* Lydgate Park **26**
Mahaulepu (Gillin's) Beach **31**
Makua (Tunnels) Beach **12**
* Poipu Beach Park **34**
Polihale State Park **1**
* Salt Pond Beach Park **38**

CABINS & CAMPGROUNDS
Anini Beach Park **17**
Haena Beach Park **11**
Hanakoa Valley **9**
Hanalei Blackpot Beach Park **14**
Kalalau Valley **7**
Kokee State Park **3**
Kokee Cabins **4**
Lydgate Park **26**
Polihale State Park **1**
YWCA of Kauai Camp Sloggett **3**

GOLF COURSES
Hokuala Golf Club **30**
Kiahuna Golf Club **35**
Kukuiolono Golf Course **37**
Kukuiula Golf Course **36**
Makai Golf Club **16**
Poipu Bay Golf Course **33**
Puakea Golf Course **28**
Wailua Golf Course **27**

HIKES
Awaawapuhi Trail **5**
Canyon Trail **2**
Kalalau Trail **8**
Kuamoo/Nounou West Trail **25**
Kuilau/Moalepe Trails **23**
Mahaulepu Heritage Trail **32**
Nounou East Trail **24**
Nualolo Trail **5**
Okolehao Trail **15**
Pihea/Alakai Swamp Trails **6**
Powerline Trail **23**
Wai Koa Loop Trail **19**

ridges that lead to the shore, red-dirt roads crossing old sugarcane fields, and postcard-pretty waterfalls. Heading east from Lihue into the Coconut Coast strip of Wailua and Kapaa, the main highway changes its name and number from the Kaumualii Highway (Hwy. 50) to Kuhio Highway (Hwy. 56). More noticeable are the steady trade winds that riffle fronds of hundreds of coconut palms, part of the area's royal legacy; a long and broad river (by Hawaii standards) and easily accessed waterfalls; and the chock-a-block low-rise condos, budget hotels, and shopping centers—all adding to the East Side's significant rush-hour traffic jams.

LIHUE   Bargain hunters will appreciate the county seat's many shopping, lodging, and dining options, but Lihue also boasts cultural assets, from the exhibits at the **Kauai Museum ★★** to hula shows, concerts, and festivals at the **Kauai War Memorial Convention Hall** and **Kauai Community College's Performing Arts Center.** Nearby outdoor attractions include **Kalapaki Beach ★★**, next to the cruise port of Nawiliwili; ATV, ziplining, hiking, and tubing excursions, the latter on old sugarcane irrigation flumes; and kayaking on Huleia River past the historic **Menehune Fish Pond ★**, an ancient feat of aquaculture, now privately owned.

WAILUA   **Wailua Falls ★** (seen in the opening credits of *Fantasy Island*), the twin cascades of **Opaekaa Falls ★★**, and a riverboat cruise to **Fern**

Aerial view of spectacular Na Pali coast

MOA BETTER: chickens & roosters

One of the first things visitors notice about Kauai is the unusually large number of wild chickens. Mostly rural, Kauai has always had plenty of poultry, including the colorful jungle fowl known as *moa*, but after Hurricane Iniki blew through the island in 1992, they soon were everywhere, reproducing quickly and, in the case of roosters, crowing night and day. Although resorts work tirelessly to trap or shoo them away, it's impossible to ensure you'll never be awakened by a rooster; if you're staying outside a resort, it's pretty much guaranteed you will be. Light sleepers should bring earplugs; some hotels provide them at the front desk or on demand.

Grotto ★★ are highlights of this former royal compound, which includes remains of stone-walled *heiau* (places of worship), birthstones, and other ancient sites. Kayakers flock to Wailua River, which also offers wakeboarding and water-skiing opportunities; the municipal **Wailua Golf Course** ★★ is routinely ranked as one of the top in the state; and hikers can choose from three trailheads to ascend Nounou (Sleeping Giant) mountain. Highway 56 also passes by the iconic Coco Palms resort, featured in Elvis Presley's *Blue Hawaii,* closed after being damaged by Hurricane Iniki in 1992; some restoration began in 2017 but has been delayed by permitting issues. The family-friendly destination of **Lydgate Park** ★ connects with one leg of the popular **Ke Ala Hele Makalae coastal path** ★★★.

KAPAA The modern condos, motels, and shopping strips of Wailua and Waipouli along the Kuhio Highway eventually segue into **Old Kapaa**

Town, where funky boutiques and cafes share plantation-era buildings with mom-and-pop groceries and restaurants. There are sandy beaches here, but they're hidden from the highway until the road rises past **Kealia Beach Park ★**, a boogie-boarding destination along the northern leg of the coastal bike path.

ANAHOLA Just before the East Side becomes the North Shore, the highway dips and passes through this predominantly Native Hawaiian community near Kalalea Mountain, more widely known as **King Kong Mountain,** or just Kong, for its famous profile. Farm stands, a convenience store with homemade goodies, and the roadside **Duane's Ono Char-Burger ★★** can supply provisions for a weekday picnic at **Anahola Beach Park ★**; weekends draw local crowds.

NORTH SHORE

On a sunny day, there may be no more beautiful place on earth than North Shore Kauai. It's not half-bad even on a rainy day (more frequent in winter) when waterfalls almost magically appear on verdant mountains; once the showers stop, rainbows soar over farms, taro patches, and long, curving beaches. The speed limit, and pace of life, slow down dramatically as the Kuhio Highway traverses a series of one-lane bridges, climaxing at a

suitably show-stopping beach and the trailhead for the breathtaking **Napali Coast.** (*Note:* The road was open only to residents after flood damage in April 2018 but was expected to reopen to all traffic by late summer.) The quaint towns of Hanalei and Kilauea—the latter home to a lighthouse and a seabird preserve—plus the island's most luxurious hotel provide ample lodging, dining, and shopping options to match the natural wonders. But it's far enough from the South Shore (minimum 1½ hrs. away) that day-trippers may wish they had relocated for a night or two.

KILAUEA A right turn going north on Kuhio Highway brings you to this village of quaint stone buildings and the plantation-vintage **Kong Lung**

Kilauea Lighthouse

Hanalei

Historic Market Center ★, a cozy den of cafes, crafts makers, and boutiques. Kilauea Road heads *makai* (seaward) to **Kilauea Point National Wildlife Refuge** ★★★, a sanctuary for nene (the gooselike state bird) and other endangered species, and home to the stubby, red-topped **Kilauea Lighthouse,** built in 1913. Shortly before the preserve is the turnoff for scenic but not-so-secret **Kauapea (Secret) Beach** ★★, a 15-minute hike from a dirt parking lot. Actor Ben Stiller owns a home on the cliffs here; numerous farms, the island's only mini-golf course, and the extensive **Na Aina Kai Botanical Gardens** ★★ are the immediate area's other claims to fame. Two miles north, a 5-minute detour off the highway leads to **Anini Beach** ★★★, where a 2-mile fringing reef—the longest on Kauai—creates a shallow, pondlike setting for swimmers, snorkelers, and (when conditions permit) windsurfers.

PRINCEVILLE This 11,000-acre resort and residential development is home to two 18-hole golf courses, steep trails to pocket beaches, and gorgeous views of crescent-shaped Hanalei Bay and iconic **Makana,** the mountain that portrayed Bali Hai in *South Pacific.* The **Princeville Shopping Center** holds a few bargain eateries as well as supplies for those staying in one of the many condo or timeshare units; money is generally no object for guests at the **St. Regis Princeville** ★★★, the island's most luxurious hotel, with elevator service to the beach below. Just before the highway drops into Hanalei Valley, a vista point offers a photo-worthy panorama of the Hanalei River winding through wetland taro patches under towering green peaks.

HANALEI   Waiting to cross the first of nine one-lane bridges on the northern stretch of the Kuhio Highway (now Hwy. 560) is a good introduction to the hang-loose ethos of the last real town before road's end. The fringing green mountains share their hue with the 1912 **Waioli Huiia Church** ★ and other vintage wooden buildings, some of which house unique shops and moderately priced restaurants. Nearby, the beaches along 2-mile-long, half-moon **Hanalei Bay** ★★★ attract surfers year-round; during the calmer summer conditions, children splash in the water while parents lounge on the sand. Three county beach parks offer various facilities and lifeguard stations. *Note:* the southernmost **Black Pot Beach Park** ★★, renowned for its 300-foot-long pier, was expected to reopen by 2019 after repairs to damages from flooding in April 2018.

HAENA   Homes modest and grand hide in the lush greenery of Haena on either side of the Kuhio Highway as it undulates past rugged coves, tranquil beaches, and immense caves. The road dead-ends at **Kee Beach** ★★★, gateway to the Napali Coast and a popular destination for snorkelers (when the surf permits) and campers, where parking has, alas, become very difficult. **Limahuli Garden and Preserve** ★★, the northern outpost of the National Tropical Botanical Garden, explains Haena's legends, rich cultural heritage, and ecological significance to visitors able to navigate its steep terraces in the shadow of Mount Makana. Food trucks at **Haena Beach Park** ★★★ supplement the meager if delicious dining options, such as Opakapaka at the **Hanalei Colony Resort** ★★ (p. 565), the only North Shore resort with rooms on the sand. (*Note:* This flood-damaged area was off-limits to visitors in spring 2018, but was expected to reopen by summer.)

NAPALI COAST ★★★   Often written as Na Pali ("the cliffs"), this dramatically crenellated region that bridges the North Shore and West Side begins not far from where the road ends. Hardy (and some foolhardy) hikers will cross five valleys as they follow the narrow, 11-mile Kalalau Trail to its end at beautiful **Kalalau Valley,** with tempting detours to waterfalls along the way. The less ambitious (or more sensible) will attempt shorter stretches, such as the 2-mile hike to Hanakapiai Beach. (*Note:* Heavily damaged by the April 2018 flood, the trail remained closed at press time for repairs.) In summer, physically fit kayakers can spend a day exploring Napali's pristine reefs, sea caves, and hidden coves, which also come into view on catamaran and motorized raft tours (almost all departing from the West Side); helicopter tours from Lihue, Port Allen, or Princeville offer the quickest if most expensive way to explore Napali's stunning topography (see "Organized Tours," p. 521).

SOUTH SHORE

After a short drive west from Lihue on Kaumualii Highway, a well-marked left turn leads to a mile-long **tree tunnel** of eucalyptus trees, planted in 1911. The well-shaded Maluhia Road is ironically the primary entrance to

Koloa eucalyptus tree tunnel

the sunniest of Kauai resort areas, Poipu. The South Shore also generally has the calmest ocean conditions in winter. Among outdoor attractions are the geyserlike **Spouting Horn ★★**, the restored **Kaneiolouma** cultural complex **★★**, multiple gardens at the **National Tropical Botanical Garden ★★**, family-friendly **Poipu Beach Park ★★★**, and other sandy beaches, including those in rugged **Mahaulepu ★★**, where **Makauwahi Cave Reserve ★★** reveals the island's fascinating prehistory. Pocket coves, surf breaks, and dive sites also make the area ideal for watersports. The only downside: The North Shore is at least 1½ hours away.

POIPU AND KUKUIULA Four of the best hotels on Kauai—the lavish **Grand Hyatt Kauai Resort & Spa ★★★**, the family-friendly **Sheraton Kauai Resort** and **Koloa Landing Resort ★★★**, and the luxury boutique **Koa Kea Hotel & Resort ★★★**—punctuate the many low-rise condos and vacation homes in **Poipu Beach Resort.** Landlubbers can enjoy tennis, 36 holes of golf, and numerous options for dining and shopping, including those at the **Shops at Kukuiula,** part of the nearby luxury Kukuiula development, which includes roomy rental bungalows.

KOLOA Before the Koloa Bypass Road (Ala Kinoiki) was built, nearly every South Shore beachgoer drove through Hawaii's oldest sugar plantation town, founded in 1835. It would be a shame not to visit at least once, to browse the shops and restaurants in quaint storefronts under towering monkeypod trees. Historical plaques on each building give glimpses into the lives of the predominantly Japanese-American families who created the first businesses there. Those staying in South Shore condos may find themselves making multiple trips, especially to stock up on produce at the "sunshine market" at noon Mondays, to buy fresh seafood from the **Koloa Fish Market ★**, or to purchase other groceries from two local supermarkets; several food trucks also hang out here.

KALAHEO & LAWAI These more residential communities on either side of the main highway are just a 15-minute drive from Poipu Beach Park. On the way, you'll pass through the green fields of rural Omao along Koloa Road (Hwy. 530); stop at Warehouse 3540 for shave ice and intriguing shops. Visitors en route to or from Waimea Canyon often refuel at the locally oriented restaurants here; others find lodgings in the relatively inexpensive (but often unlicensed) bed-and-breakfasts. (Keep in mind higher elevations are mistier, and have more wild chickens, than the beachfront resorts.) Savvy golfers savor the views and discount fees at upcountry **Kukuiolono Golf Course ★★**. Others find serenity amid the 88 Buddhist shrines and golden temple of the **Lawai International Center ★★**. On the west edge of Kalaheo, look for the turnoff for **Kauai Coffee ★★**, where the 3,100-acre farm yields a dizzying variety of coffees, with free samples at the visitor center.

WEST SIDE

This arid region may have the fewest lodgings, destination restaurants, or swimmable beaches, but the twin draws of **Waimea Canyon State Park ★★★** (rightly hailed as the "Grand Canyon of the Pacific") and the **Kalalau Overlook ★★★** in Kokee State Park make up for the long drive (80 min. to the latter from Poipu). Most Napali snorkel tours are also based here, not to mention two swinging bridges, a weekly art festival, and other good excuses to pull over. Those who can manage the bumpy, unpaved 5-mile road to **Polihale State Park ★★** are rewarded with views of Niihau and Napali, as well as a 17-mile stretch of sand (including the restricted-access **Barking Sands Beach** on the Pacific Missile Range Facility).

ELEELE & PORT ALLEN The main highway from Kalaheo passes by Eleele's plantation homes and several miles of coffee trees before the intersection with Waialo Road. Turn *makai* (seaward) and the road deadends a few blocks later at Port Allen, the island's second largest commercial harbor; nearly all boat tours launch from here. Although the area is fairly industrial—and its once-vaunted "Glass Beach" by the oil tanks no longer has enough polished sea glass left to recommend it—the affordable dining and shopping options in Port Allen and adjacent **Eleele Shopping Center** are worth exploring post-snorkel or pre-sunset cruise.

HANAPEPE An easy detour off Kaumualii Highway, Hanapepe looks like an Old West town, with more than 2 dozen art galleries and quaint stores, plus a couple of cafes, behind rustic wooden facades that inspired Disney's *Lilo & Stitch*. Musicians, food trucks, and other vendors truly animate the quiet town during the Friday night festival and artwalk from 6 to 9pm. The other daytime attraction is the **swinging footbridge ★** over Hanapepe River (rebuilt after 1992's Hurricane Iniki, and marked by a large sign off Hanapepe Rd.). Across the highway, family-friendly **Salt Pond Beach ★★** is named for the traditional Hawaiian salt pans in the

Hanapepe swinging footbridge

red dirt, which gives the salt its distinctive color and flavor.

WAIMEA Hawaii's modern history officially begins here with the landing of British explorer Capt. James Cook on Jan. 20, 1778, 2 days after his ships sailed past Oahu. Despite Cook's orders to the contrary, his sailors quickly mingled with native women, introducing venereal disease to a long-isolated population. Foreigners kept coming to this enclave at the mouth of the Waimea ("reddish-water") River, including a German doctor who tried to claim Kauai for Russia in 1815, and American missionaries in 1820. Today Waimea is attuned to its more recent history of plantation and *paniolo* (cowboy) culture, as well as its Native Hawaiian roots, all of which can be explored at the **West Kauai Visitor Center ★**. Waimea Canyon and Kokee State Park hikers flock to Waimea's shave ice stands and budget dining choices in the late afternoon, while locals seek out **Waimea Theater,** one of the island's few places to catch a movie or concert.

KEKAHA Travelers heading to or from Waimea Canyon may be tempted to go via Kokee Road (Hwy. 55) in Kekaha as a change of pace from Waimea Canyon Road. Don't bother. There's not much to see in this former sugar town, whose mill operated for 122 years before shutting down in 2000, other than **Kekaha Beach Park,** a long, narrow strand with often-rough waters. You do have to pass through Kekaha on the way to **Polihale State Park ★★★**; if the latter's access road is impassable, stop by Kekaha for a striking view of **Niihau,** 17 miles offshore.

NIIHAU Just 17 miles across the Kaulakahi Channel from the West Side of Kauai lies the arid island of Niihau (pronounced "nee-ee-how"), nick-named "The Forbidden Island." Casual visitors are not allowed on this privately owned isle, once a cattle and sheep ranch that now supports fewer than 200 full-time residents, all living in the single town of Puuwai, and nearly all Native Hawaiians. Nonresidents can visit on hunting safaris (starting at $1,950, for feral pig and sheep) and half-day helicopter tours including lunch and beach time ($440 per person, five-person minimum), departing from the West Side (www.niihau.us; ✆ **877/441-3500**). You're more likely to see the endangered Hawaiian monk seal than you are Niihauans, which is how they like it.

GETTING AROUND

Unless you're on a fairly leisurely schedule, you'll need a car or other motorized vehicle to see and do everything on Kauai, which has one major road—one lane in each direction in most places—that rings the island except along the Napali Coast. During rush hour, from about 6 to 9am and 3 to 6pm, the road between Lihue and Kapaa—the central business district—can turn into a giant parking lot, even with a third, "contra-flow" lane whose direction is determined by time of day. Bypass roads in Kipu (when heading north from Poipu) and Kapaa (when heading south) can alleviate some of the stress, but plan accordingly.

Note: The top speed is 50mph, with many slower sections in residential and business areas. Addresses in this chapter will use Kaumualii Highway for Highway 50 and Kuhio Highway for Highway 56/560, following local convention. Some addresses use a single number before a dash, which simply indicates one of five island divisions. Since highway addresses can be hard to spot (if marked at all), directions may be given with mile marker numbers, cross streets, and/or the descriptors *mauka* (toward the mountains) and *makai* (toward the sea).

The official mailing address of sites in and around Poipu Beach is Koloa, which GPS devices may require. This chapter lists them as "Poipu" to distinguish them from Old Koloa Town and environs.

BY CAR   All of the major car-rental agencies are represented on Kauai. At the airport baggage claim, cross the street to catch one of the frequent shuttle vans to the rental lots. **Avis** (www.avis.com; ✆ **800/230-4898**) also rents cars from the Grand Hyatt Kauai and Princeville Airport. Be sure to book early for peak periods. **Discount Hawaii Car Rental** (www. discounthawaiicarrental.com; ✆ **800/292-1939**) may have cheaper options for last-minute bookings; it also offers free pickup for cruise passengers.

BY MOTORCYCLE, MOPED, OR SCOOTER   Riders 21 and older with a heavyweight motorcycle license can rent a "hog" from **Kauai Harley-Davidson** (www.kauaiharley.com; ✆ **888/690-6233** or 808/212-9469) outside Lihue. Rates for a Sportster start at $99 for 24 hours, with unlimited mileage; bigger rides start at $179. **Kauai Mopeds** (www.kauai-mopeds.com; ✆ **808/652-7407**) in Lihue offers two-person scooters with similar age and license restrictions; daily rates start at $75 for models with a top speed of 52mph, and $110 for those reaching 75mph. For cruising back roads (directions provided), those 18 or older with a driver's license can rent a single-person moped with a top speed of 30mph for $65 a day.

BY TAXI, RIDESHARE OR SHUTTLE   Set by the county, taxi meter rates start at $3, with an additional $3 per mile; from the airport, it's about $65 to Poipu and $117 to Princeville, plus 40¢ per item of luggage, and $4 per bulky item. You can also arrange private tours by taxi starting at $120 for 2 hours. Call **Kauai Taxi Company** (www.kauaitaxico.com; ✆ **808/246-9554**) for taxi, limousine, or airport shuttle service. Ride-sharing app

Uber came to Kauai in 2017; pricing varies by demand, but a typical rate from the airport to Poipu is $34 and to Princeville, $63.

Solo travelers who don't use Uber will save money taking **Speedi-Shuttle** (www.speedishuttle.com; ☏ **877/242-5777**) from the airport ($42 to Poipu, $72 to Princeville), but be aware it may make multiple stops. **Pono Express** (www.ponoexpress.com; ☏ **800/258-6880**) offers airport cab service ($50 to Poipu) and sightseeing tours in vans accommodating one to 14 passengers; rate is by vehicle or by hour. Once in Poipu, book a free ride on the **Aloha Spirit Shuttle** (www.poipu-shuttle.com; ☏ **808/651-9945**); Doug Bean's 12-person open-air tram—a former Disneyland people-mover built in 1965—shuttles locals and visitors around resorts and restaurants from 6 to 10pm Sunday–Thursday; tips are appreciated. A 45-minute sunset "cruise" on Bean's newer 22-person trolley costs $25.

BY BUS **Kauai Bus** (www.kauai.gov/bus; ☏ **808/246-8110**) has daily service between Kekaha and Hanalei, including stops near several Poipu and Lihue hotels, the central Kapaa hotel corridor, the Princeville Shopping Center, and Hanalei. *Note:* There's also an airport stop, but suitcases, large backpacks, and surfboards are not allowed on the bus. The white-and-green buses, which have small bike racks in front, run more or less hourly from 5:30am to 10:30pm weekdays, and 6:30am to 6pm on weekends and holidays. The fare (exact change only) is $2 for adults and $1 for seniors, 60 and older, and children, 7 to 18.

BY BIKE Due to narrow (or nonexistent) shoulders along much of the main highway, relying on bicycles for transportation is generally unsafe. For recreational routes, including the **Ke Ala Hele Makalae** coastal path on the East Side, see "Biking," p. 544.

[Fast FACTS] KAUAI

Dentists Emergency dental care is available from **Dr. Mark A. Baird,** 4-9768 Kuhio Hwy. (at Keaka Rd.), Kapaa (☏ **808/822-9393**) and **Dr. Terry Allen,** 4366 Kukui Grove St., Ste. 24, Lihue (www.lihue-dental. com; ☏ **808/378-4754** weekdays 8:30am–5pm; after hours, ☏ **808/651-8404**).

Doctors Walk-ins are accepted from 8am to 7pm daily (except Jan. 1, Thanksgiving, and Dec. 25) at the **Kauai Urgent Care Clinic** (☏ **808/245-1532**), 4484 Pahee St., Lihue. The non-urgent-care **Kauai Medical Clinic** (☏ **808/245-1500**), part of the Wilcox Memorial Hospital complex at 3-3420 Kuhio Hwy., *makai* side (at Ehiku St.), Lihue, is open for appointments 8am to 5pm weekdays and 8am to noon Saturday. Kauai Medical Clinic also has branches, with varying hours, in **Koloa,** 5371 Koloa Rd. (☏ **808/742-1621**); **Kapaa,** 4-1105 Kuhio Hwy., *mauka* side, in the Kapaa Shopping Center (☏ **808/822-3431**); and **Eleele,** 4382 Waialo Rd. (☏ **808/335-0499**). **Hale Lea Medicine,** 2460 Oka St. (at Kilauea Rd.), in Kilauea (☏ **808/828-2885**), serves the North Shore, with urgent care and appoint-ments offered 8am to 7pm weekdays and 9am to 5pm weekends.

Emergencies Dial *©* **911** for police, fire, or ambulance service.

Hospitals **Wilcox Memorial Hospital,** 3-3420 Kuhio Hwy. *makai* side (at Ehiku St.), Lihue (*©* **808/ 245-1100**), has emergency services (*©* **808/245-1010**) available 24 hours a day, as do the smaller **Mahelona Memorial Hospital,** 4800 Kawaihau Rd., Kapaa (*©* **808/823-4166**), and **Kauai Veterans Memorial Hospital,** 4643 Waimea Canyon Dr., Waimea (*©* **808/338-9431**).

Internet Access
Numerous cafes (including three **Starbucks** outlets in Poipu, Lihue, and Kapaa; www.starbucks.com) offer free Wi-Fi hotspots; many hotels offer free Wi-Fi in public areas and, if not free, for a fee in rooms. All Hawaii public libraries have free Wi-Fi but require a library card ($10 nonresidents, good for 3 months). Local branches are in Hanapepe, Kapaa, Koloa, Lihue, Princeville, and Waimea; all are closed Sunday. For details on locations, hours, and reserving a personal computer with Wi-Fi, see www.librarieshawaii.org (click on "How Do I . . . ").

Police For non-emergencies, call *©* **808/241-1711.**

Post Office The **main** post office is at 4441 Rice St., Lihue, open 8am to 4pm weekdays and 9am to 1pm Saturday; hours vary at the 14 other offices across the island. To find the one nearest you, visit www.usps. com or call *©* **800/275-8777.**

Weather For current weather conditions and forecasts, call the National Weather Service at *©* **808/245-6001.** For the daily ocean report, including high surf advisories and other alerts, visit **www. kauaiexplorer.com/ ocean_report.**

EXPLORING KAUAI
Attractions & Points of Interest
EAST SIDE

Fern Grotto ★★ NATURAL ATTRACTION   The journey as much as the destination has kept this tourist attraction popular since 1946, when the Smith family first began offering boat trips 2 miles up the Wailua River to this lava-rock cave with lush ferns hanging from its roof. The open-air barge cruises past royal and sacred sites of antiquity, noted by a guide, until it arrives at a landing that's a short walk from the grotto. Ancient Hawaiians knew it as Maamaakualono, a site dedicated to the god Lono, who is associated with agriculture and healing. Although you can no longer enter the cave, an observation deck provides a decent view, as well as the stage for a musician and hula dancer to perform the "Hawaiian Wedding Song" (made famous by Elvis Presley's 1961 film *Blue Hawaii,* filmed nearby at the Coco Palms). The tour, a total of 80 minutes, includes music and hula on the return trip down the state's longest navigable river (see "Wailua River State Park," below). *Note:* Kayakers and other paddlers may visit Fern Grotto on their own, as long as their arrival or departure doesn't overlap with those of the tour boats; see "Kayaking" on p. 535 for rental information. **Kamokila Hawaiian Village** (see below), across the river from the grotto, also offers guided outrigger canoe tours and rentals.

2 miles inland from Wailua Marina State Park, south side of Wailua River off Kuhio Hwy. Smith's Motor Boats (www.smithskauai.com; *©* **808/821-6895**) tours depart at 9:30 and 11am, and 2 and 3:30pm. $25 adults, $12.50 children 3–12. Free shuttle from Wailua area.

Fern Grotto

Grove Farm Museum ★ HISTORIC SITE/MUSEUM AOL cofounder Steve Case may own Grove Farm now, but little else has changed at the 100-acre homestead of George N. Wilcox. The son of missionaries in Hanalei, Wilcox bought the original 900-acre Grove Farm from a German immigrant in 1864 and turned it into a successful sugar plantation. Two-hour guided tours start at the original plantation office and include the two-story main home, still furnished with vintage decor and Hawaiiana, plus extensive gardens and intriguing outbuildings, such as a Japanese teahouse built in 1898. *Note:* Tours may be canceled on rainy days. Contact the museum about its free rides on restored, plantation-era steam trains near the old Lihue Sugar Mill, usually offered the second Thursday of each month.

4050 Nawiliwili Rd. (Hwy. 58), at Pikaka St., Lihue. www.grovefarm.org. ☎ **808/245-3202.** $20 adults, $10 children 5–12. Open only for guided tours Mon and Wed–Thurs at 10am and 1pm; reservations required.

Kamokila Hawaiian Village ★ CULTURAL ATTRACTION This family-run 4-acre compound of thatched huts and other replica structures, opened in 1979 on the site of an ancient village, always looks in need of more upkeep. Nevertheless, it serves as a pleasantly low-key introduction to traditional Hawaiian culture, especially for families. Peacocks and wild chickens roam around huts designated for healing, sleeping, eating, birthing, and more, all part of a self-guided tour, with displays inside some huts. You're also welcome to sample fruit hanging from the many labeled trees, including mountain apple, guava, and mango. A stand-in for an African village in the 1995 movie *Outbreak,* Kamokila is known as having the fastest (and cheapest) access for paddling to **Uluwehi (Secret)**

Falls ★★, **Fern Grotto** ★★, and several swimming holes, just 10 to 15 minutes away.

Off Kuamoo Rd. (Hwy. 580), Kapaa. Look for sign across from Opaekaa Falls, 2 miles inland from Kuhio Hwy.; entrance road is steep. www.villagekauai.com.com. ℂ **808/823-0559.** $5 adults, $3 children 3–12. Daily canoe rentals $35 adults, $30 children 3–12. Guided outrigger canoe rides: **Secret Falls** $30 adults/$20 children 3–12; **Fern Grotto** $20 adults/$15 children; **swimming hole** $20 adults/$15 children. Daily 9am–5pm.

Kauai Museum ★★ MUSEUM   Though admission has jumped to $15, that fee allows you to return within a week—and you may well want to, in order to absorb more of the fascinating geological and cultural history of Kauai and Niihau. Visitors enter through the Wilcox Building, the former county library built in 1924 with a Greco-Roman facade on its lava rock exterior. Pass through the small gift shop with an extensive book selection into the Heritage Gallery, where koa wood-lined cases brim with exquisite Niihau shell lei, feather work, and other items that once belonged to royalty. Also on display are some of the hundreds of Western and Hawaiian artifacts recovered from *Haaheo O Hawaii* ("Pride of Hawaii"), King Kamehameha II's luxurious barge, which sank off the North Shore in 1824. Another room holds beautifully carved wooden bowls (*'umeke*) and other handsome koa pieces, while a theater has continuous screenings of *The Hawaiians,* a sobering (if somewhat dated) hour-long documentary on Hawaiian history.

The adjacent Rice Building, a two-story lava rock structure opened in 1960, tells "The Story of Kauai." The main floor's exhibits focus on the island's volcanic origins through the arrival of Polynesian voyagers and the beginning of Western contact, including the whalers and missionaries who quickly followed in Capt. Cook's wake. Rare artifacts include a torn piece of a Niihau *makaloa* mat, a highly prized bed covering and art form that was essentially abandoned in the late–19th century. On the second floor, the story shifts to that of the plantation era, when waves of immigrants fomented the complex stew known as "local" culture, and continues through World War II.

4428 Rice St., Lihue. www.kauaimuseum.org. ℂ **808/245-6931.** $15 adults, $12 seniors, $10 students 8–17, $3 children 7 and younger, free. Check "Events" listings online for crafts workshops and festivals. Mon–Sat 9am–4pm.

Keahua Arboretum ★ GARDEN   Part of the vast Lihue–Koloa Forest Reserve, this grove of rainbow eucalyptus (named for its colorful bark), monkeypod, and mango trees may not be well maintained from an arborist's standpoint, but it's a nifty, family-friendly place to picnic and dip in a cool stream, particularly after a hike on the nearby **Kuilau Trail** (p. 511). A short loop trail leads to a swimming hole with a rope swing; be sure to wear mosquito repellent. Facilities include picnic tables, pavilions, and composting toilets. Part of the fun is getting here: The main parking area and picnic tables are across a spillway at the paved end of Kuamoo

Road, about 5 miles inland from Opaekaa Falls. (Please use good judgment when deciding if it's safe to ford the stream.) This is also where adventurers will find the trailhead for the 13-mile **Powerline Trail** (p. 549), which ends near Princeville, and the extremely rugged, unpaved Wailua Forestry Management Road, the start of much more challenging treks to the *Jurassic Park* gates (just poles now) and the "Blue Hole" inside Waialeale.

End of Kuamoo Rd., Kapaa. 7 miles inland from intersection with Kuhio Hwy., Wailua. www.dlnr.hawaii.gov/forestry/frs/reserves/kauai/lihue-koloa. ✆ **808/274-3433.** Free admission. Daily during daylight hours.

Kilohana Plantation ★★ FARM/ATTRACTIONS   This 105-acre portion of a former sugar plantation has long been known for the unique shops tucked into a handsome 1930s mansion, its luau, and the courtyard Gaylord's restaurant, named for original owner Gaylord Wilcox. But more recent additions are also memorable. Beyond sampling the wares of the **Mahiko Lounge** in the mansion's former living room (see "Kauai Nightlife," p. 596), tipplers ages 21 and up can create their own mini mai tai around a gleaming wood bar in the **Koloa Rum Co.**'s tasting room (www.koloarum.com; ✆ **808/246-8900**). There's a 16-person maximum for the free half-hour tasting (see website for hours), while an all-ages store sells the locally made spirits and non-alcoholic gifts.

Kilohana Plantation

The **Kauai Plantation Railway** ★★ (www.kauaiplantationrailway. com; © **808/245-7245**) uses a restored diesel locomotive to pull open-sided cars with trolley-style bench seats around a 2½-mile track. The train passes by Kilohana's gardens growing 50 varieties of fruit and vegetables and through flowering fields and forest on a 40-minute narrated tour that includes a stop to feed goats, sheep, and wild pigs (watch your hands). It departs five times daily between 10am and 2pm, with a 5:30pm trip on Tuesday and Friday. Tickets are $18 for adults and $14 for kids 3 to 12. On weekdays, you can also combine a train ride that starts at 9:30am with an easy hike, lunch, and orchard tour that costs $75 for adults and $65 for kids 3 to 12.

On Tuesday and Friday, the railway offers an "express train" package with **Luau Kalamaku** ★★★ (www.luaukalamaku.com; © **808/833-3000**), a theatrical-style show with dinner buffet in a specially-built the-ater-in-the-round near the Wilcox mansion. The train-luau package is $122 for adults, $88 for teens 13 to 18, and $54 kids 3 to 12. For the luau only, it's $104 for adults, $70 for teens, and $40 for children.

3-2087 Kaumualii Hwy., Lihue, just north of Kauai Community College and a half-mile south of Kukui Grove Shopping Center. www.kilohanakauai.com. © **808/245-5608.** Mansion opens at 10:30am daily; restaurant, lounge, and shop hours vary.

Lydgate Park ★ PARK   This is one of the rare beach parks in Hawaii where the facilities almost outshine the beach. In front of the Hilton Gar-den Inn Kauai Wailua Bay, **Lydgate Beach** ★ (p. 526) offers two rock-walled ponds for safe swimming and snorkeling. But many families also gravitate to the 58-acre, half-mile-long park for the immense **Kamalani Playground,** a sprawling wooden fantasy fortress decorated with ocean-themed ceramics. Stroller pushers, joggers, and cyclists also pick up the 2.5-mile southern leg of the **Ke Ala Hele Makalae coastal path** here; Lydgate's northern end is next to **Hikinaakala Heiau,** part of Wailua River State Park (below). Facilities include picnic tables, restrooms, showers, pavilions, and campgrounds.

Leho Dr. at Nalu Rd., Wailua. From intersection of Kuhio Hwy. and Hwy. 51 outside of Lihue, head 2½ miles north to Leho Dr. and turn right. Turn right again on Nalu Rd. and follow to parking areas. Free admission. Daily during daylight hours.

Wailua River State Park ★★ PARK/HISTORIC SITE   Ancients called the Wailua River "the river of the great sacred spirit." Seven temples once stood along this 20-mile river, Hawaii's longest, fed by the some 450 inches of rain that fall annually on Waialeale at the island's center. The entire district from the river mouth to the summit of Waialeale was once royal land, originally claimed by Puna, a Tahitian priest said to have arrived in one of the first double-hulled voyaging canoes to come to Hawaii.

Cultural highlights include the remains of four major temples; royal birthing stones, used to support female royalty in labor; a stone bell used to announce such births; and the ancient stone carvings known as petroglyphs, found on boulders near the mouth of the Wailua River when currents wash away enough sand. Many sites have **Wailua Heritage Trail** markers; go to www.wailuaheritagetrail.org for map and details. The **Hawaii State Parks website** (http://dlnr.hawaii.gov/dsp) also has downloadable brochures on two *heiau* (temples) that each enclosed an acre of land: Just north of Lydgate Park, next to the mouth of the Wailua River, **Hikinaakala Heiau** once hosted sunrise ceremonies; its name means "rising of the sun." Now reduced to its foundation stones, it's part of a sacred oceanfront complex that also appears to have been a place of refuge (*pu'uhonua*). Two miles up Kuamoo Road (Hwy. 580) from the main highway, **Poliahu Heiau** shares its name with the goddess of snow (admittedly a weather phenomenon more common to the Big Island). The 5×5-feet lava rock walls—attributed to *menehune,* and most likely erected by the 1600s—may have surrounded a *luakini,* used for human sacrifice. (Please don't stand on the rock walls, enter the center of the heiau, or leave "offerings," all of which are considered disrespectful.)

Across the road from Poliahu is an ample parking lot and sidewalk leading to the overlook of 40-foot-wide, 151-foot-tall **Opaekaa Falls ★★**. Named for the "rolling shrimp" that were once abundant here, this twin cascade glistens under the Makaleha ridge—but don't be tempted to try to find a way to swim beneath it. The danger keep out signs and wire fencing are there because two hikers fell to their deaths from the steep, slippery hillside in 2006.

You're allowed to wade at the base of the 100-foot **Uluwehi Falls ★★,** widely known as Secret Falls, but first you'll need to paddle a kayak or canoe several miles to the narrow right fork of the Wailua River, and then hike about 30 to 45 minutes on a trail with a stream crossing. Many kayak rental companies offer guided tours here (see "Kayaking," p. 535), as does Kamokila Hawaiian Village (p. 503).

Also part of the state park, but at the end of Maalo Road (Hwy. 583), 4 miles inland from the main highway in Kapaia, is equally scenic **Wailua Falls ★**. Pictured in the opening credits of *Fantasy Island,* this double-barreled waterfall drops at least 80 feet (some say 113) into a large pool. Go early to avoid crowds and enjoy the morning light. *Note:* The state has also installed fencing here to block attempts at a hazardous descent—please don't risk your life trying to find a way around it.

Opaekaa Falls and **Poliahu Heiau:** Off Kuamoo Rd., 2 miles *mauka* of intersection with Kuhio Hwy. just north of Wailua River Bridge. **Hikinaakala Heiau:** South side of Wailua River mouth; access from Lydgate Park (p. 526). **Wailua Falls:** End of Maalo Rd. (Hwy. 583), 4 miles north (inland) of intersection with Kuhio Hwy. in Kapaia, near Lihue. http://dlnr.hawaii.gov/dsp/parks/kauai. ℭ **808/274-3444.** Free admission. Daily during daylight hours.

NORTH SHORE

Anaina Hou Community Park ★ ATTRACTION   Anywhere else, a mini-golf park might be easily dismissed as a tourist trap. On Kauai, it's a wonderful introduction for families to the Garden Island's tropical flora and cultural history, and just one of several visitor attractions in this inviting park. The well-landscaped, 18-hole **Anaina Hou Mini Golf & Gardens** showcases native species, Polynesian introductions, plantation crops, Japanese and Chinese gardens, and modern plantings; open daily, it's quite popular on weekends. Weekly 1-hour guided walking tours of the botanical gardens include tastings and refreshments. The park's 4.5-mile **Wai Koa Loop Trail** was closed "until further notice" after severe flood damage in April 2018, with hopes of reopening by 2019. This unpaved, rolling path starts in a forest of albizia and Cook Island pines and passes through a working farm and mahogany orchard before reaching the Kalihiwai Lagoon reservoirs and stone dam lookout. When open, it's free to access during daylight hours; you're asked to sign a waiver at the gift shop. Donated by the founder of E-Trade and his wife, Bill and Joan Porter, the 500-acre community park also offers a playground, skateboard ramps, dog park, dining pavilion with food trucks, and farmers markets (see p. 595). A lively night market takes place from 4 to 8pm the last Saturday of each month.

5-2723 Kuhio Hwy. (*mauka* side), Kilauea. Heading north from Lihue, pass the Shell station at the Kolo Rd. turnoff to Kilauea; entrance is 500 yards farther on the left at the Kauai Mini Golf sign. www.anainahou.org. © **808/828-2118. Anaina Hou Community Park:** Free admission. **Mini Golf:** Daily 8am–8pm (last start at 7pm); $19 adults, $15 ages 11–17, $10 children 5–11, free for children 4 and under. **Garden Tour:** 9am Mon; $35 adults, $20 ages 12–17. **Wai Koa Loop Trail:** Free admission.

Haena State Park ★★ NATURAL ATTRACTIONS   Besides snorkeling at pretty **Kee Beach** ★★★ (p. 528), in the shadow of jutting Makana (Bali Hai) mountain, or camping, the main allure of this state park is that it's at the end of the road, the perfect place to witness sunset after a leisurely drive to the North Shore. It's also the start of the 11-mile **Kalalau Trail** (p. 511), meaning its large parking area always fills up quickly—if so, just turn around and, if it's early enough in the day, you'll find overflow parking farther away (carpools recommended). At the western end of Kee Beach, an uphill path leads to an ancient hula platform and temple (*heiau*), where hula schools still conduct formal ceremonies; please be respectful by wearing a coverup over your bathing suit before hiking here, and leave any offerings undisturbed. Before the road's end, you'll also want to stop for a look at two **wet caves,** former sea caves left high but not dry when the ocean receded; chilly water percolates into them from a spring that's affected by the nearby tides. The larger **Waikanaloa** is just off the road, with parking in front. From there it's a short, uphill walk to the craggier **Waikapalae,** seen as the entrance to the Fountain of Youth in *Pirates of the Caribbean: On Stranger Tides.* Cave swimming is not allowed—nor considered safe. ***Note:*** The park and trail were closed for flood repairs at press time.

Hoopulapula Haraguchi Rice Mill & Taro Farm ★★ FARM/
MUSEUM   Many of the green taro patches seen from the Hanalei Valley Overlook belong to the 30-acre **Haraguchi Farm,** where fifth-generation farmer Lyndsey Haraguchi-Nakayama, family members, and other laborers tend Hawaii's revered staple by hand. When the Haraguchis bought the farm in 1924, the wetlands were rice paddies, planted by Chinese immigrants in the 1800s. With the purchase came a wooden rice mill that stayed in operation until 1960 and is the only such structure left in the state. Restored several times after fire and hurricanes, the **Hoopulapula Haraguchi Rice Mill** is now a nonprofit "agrarian museum" and, like the farm, is open to visitors only as part of a weekly guided tour. Adults will appreciate hearing Haraguchi-Nakayama's stories from the family's rice-growing days, when children would be tasked with keeping grain-hungry birds away; she'll also point out the endangered birds in this corner of the **Hanalei National Wildlife Refuge.** Once you've begun to appreciate the hard work of cultivating *kalo,* as the Hawaiians call taro, it's time to sample fluffy, freshly pounded taro rolled in coconut. The 3½-hour tour begins at the family's roadside stand in Hanalei with a taro smoothie and ends there with a tasty lunch; a small gift shop is nearby.

Check in at Hanalei Taro & Juice stand, 5-5070 Kuhio Hwy., *makai* side, Hanalei, 1¼ miles west of Hanalei Bridge. www.haraguchiricemill.org. *808/651-3399.* Tours $84 adults, $50 children 5–12; Wed. 9:45am by reservation only.

Kilauea Point National Wildlife Refuge & Lighthouse ★★★
NATURE PRESERVE/LIGHTHOUSE   Two miles north of the historic town of Kilauea is a 200-acre headland habitat—the island's only wildlife refuge open to the public—that includes cliffs, two rocky wave-lashed bays, and a tiny islet serving as a jumping-off spot for seabirds. You can easily spot red-footed boobies, which nest in trees and shrubs, and wedge-tailed shearwaters, which burrow in nests along the cliffs between March and November (they spend winters at sea). Scan the skies for the great frigatebird, which has a 7-foot wingspan, and the red-tailed tropicbird, which performs aerial acrobatics during the breeding season of March through August. Endangered nene, the native goose reintroduced to Kauai in 1982, often stroll close to visitors, but please don't feed them. Telescopes and loaner binoculars may bring into view the area's marine life, from spinner dolphins, Hawaiian monk seals, and green sea turtles year-round to humpback whales in winter. Still, the primary draw for many of the half-million annual visitors is the 52-foot-tall, red-capped **Daniel K. Inouye Kilauea Point Lighthouse** (www.kilauealpoint.org), built in 1913 and renamed in memory of the state's late senator. Listed on the National Register of Historic Places, the beacon boasts a 7,000-pound

Fresnel lens, whose beam could be seen from 20 miles away before it was deactivated in 1976. When available, docents offer free tours hourly from 10:30am to 2:30pm Wednesday and Saturday.

End of Kilauea Rd., Kilauea. www.fws.gov/refuge/kilauea_point. ℂ **808/828-1413.** $5 ages 16 and up (cash or traveler's checks only); free for ages 15 and under. Tues–Sat 10am–4pm. Heading north on Kuhio Hwy., turn right on Kolo Rd., just past mile marker 23, then left on Kilauea Rd., and follow 2 miles to entrance.

Limahuli Garden and Preserve ★★ GARDEN Beyond Hanalei and the last wooden bridge, there's a mighty cleft in the coastal range where ancestral Hawaiians lived in what can only be called paradise. Carved by a waterfall stream known as Limahuli, the lush valley sits at the foot of steepled cliffs that Hollywood portrayed as Bali Hai in *South Pacific*. This small, almost secret garden, part of the National Tropical Botanical Garden, is ecotourism at its best. Here botanists hope to save endangered native plants, some of which grow in the 1,000-acre Limahuli Preserve behind the garden, an area that is off-limits to visitors. The self-guided tour encourages visitors to walk slowly up and down the .75-mile loop trail (resting places provided) to view indigenous and "canoe" plants, which are identified in Hawaiian and English, as well as plantation-era imported flowers and fruits. From taro to sugarcane, the plants brought over in Polynesians' voyaging canoes (hence their nickname) tell the story of the people who cultivated them for food, medicine, clothing, shelter, and decoration. The tour booklet also shares some of the fascinating legends inspired by the area's dramatically perched rocks and Makana mountain, where men once hurled firebrands *('oahi)* that floated far out to sea. You'll learn even more on the daily 2½-hour guided tour, if you reserve well in advance; a weekly family tour, for parties with at least one child age 12 or younger, treats the garden as an outdoor classroom and lasts 1½ to 2 hours. *Note:* Limahuli closed due to flood damage and lack of road access in spring 2018, but was expected to reopen by 2019.

5-8291 Kuhio Hwy. (*mauka* side), Haena, ½-mile after mile marker 9. www.ntbg.org/gardens/limahuli.php. ℂ **808/826-1053.** Self-guided tour $20 adults, $10 college students with ID, free for children 17 and younger with adult; Tues–Sat 9:30am–4pm (grounds close at 5pm). Guided tour $40 adults, $20 college students with ID, $20 children 10–17 with adult (not recommended for kids under 10); Tues–Sat 10am by reservation only. Family guided tour $30 adults, $20 college students, $5 ages 5–17 with adult, free for 4 and under; Tues–Sat 9:30am by reservation only. Specialty and private guided tours ($75–$100) available by request. Credit card required to book guided tours.

Na Aina Kai Botanical Gardens & Sculpture Park ★★ GARDEN Off the North Shore's beaten path, this magical garden and hardwood plantation covers 240 acres, sprinkled with 70 life-size (some larger-than-life-size) whimsical bronze statues. It's the place for avid gardeners, as well as people who think they don't like botanical gardens. It has something for everyone: a poinciana maze, an orchid house, a lagoon with

Na Aina Kai Botanical Gardens

spouting fountains, a Japanese teahouse, a streamside path to a hidden beach—even re-creations of traditional Navajo and Hawaiian compounds. A host of different tours is available, from 1½ hours ($35) to 5 hours ($85) long, ranging from casual, guided strolls and rides in small covered trams to treks from one end of the gardens to the ocean; they're open only to ages 13 and older. Younger kids are invited on tours of the wonderful "Under the Rainbow" garden, featuring a gecko hedge maze, a tropical jungle gym, a pint-size railroad, a treehouse in a rubber tree, and a 16-foot-tall Jack-and-the-Beanstalk giant with a 33-foot wading pool below. The 2-hour family tour is $35 for adults and $20 for kids 13 and under, and includes the maze and koi pond in the formal gardens. *Tip:* Most tours are limited to eight or nine guests, and held just 4 days a week, so book well in advance. The last Saturday of the month (Jan–Nov) is Keiki (Children's) Day, when the children's garden is open from 9am to 1pm for just $10.

4101 Wailapa Rd., Kilauea. www.naainakai.org. © **808/828-0525.** Tours Tues–Fri; most tours start at 9 or 9:30am, with some repeated at 1 or 1:30pm; $35–$85. Dec–Apr bird-watching tours, 8:30am Wed; $60. Reservations strongly recommended. From Lihue, drive north on Kuhio Hwy. past mile marker 21 and turn right on Wailapa; from Princeville, drive south 6½ miles and take the 2nd left past mile marker 22 onto Wailapa. At road's end, drive through iron gates to visitor center on the right.

Napali Coast State Wilderness Park ★★★ PARK   This 15-mile-long crown of serrated ridges and lush valleys is the most impressive of Kauai's natural features—and also its most inaccessible. Only hardy, well-equipped hikers should attempt the full length of the 11-mile **Kalalau Trail,** which begins at Kee Beach and plunges up and down before ending at **Kalalau Valley.** The area's last Hawaiian community lived in this 3-mile-wide, 3-mile-deep valley until the early 1900s. The valley, which can also be viewed from an overlook in Kokee State Park ★★★

(p. 517), is the setting for Jack London's 1912 short story "Koolau the Leper," based on a true tale of a man who hid from authorities determined to exile him to Molokai. (Today, marijuana growers and squatters bedevil rangers and others determined to protect the valley's cultural treasures.) Most visitors just huff and puff 4 miles round-trip from Kee Beach to scenic but dangerously unswimmable **Hanakapiai Beach,** or make it a day-long adventure by adding a 4-mile, boulder-hopping slog to Hanakapiai Falls (see "Hiking," p. 548). (*Note:* Kalalau Trail and Valley closed indefinitely in spring 2018 for flood repairs.)

In late spring and summer, kayakers may explore the sea caves and oceanside waterfalls of Napali, but landing is only allowed at **Kalalau** and **Milolii beaches;** Kalalau requires a camping permit, while Milolii allows day use (see "Kayaking," p. 535). **Nualolo Kai,** the lower, seaside portion of another valley, has many archaeological sites, some under restoration, but only motorized raft (Zodiac) tours may land here (see "Boat & Raft [Zodiac] Tours," p. 533). The natural arch at **Honopu Beach** is a highlight of the snorkel cruises passing by, but may be examined closely only by the few capable of swimming here from Kalalau or a moored kayak—a dicey proposition much of the year.

The easiest, and most expensive, way to survey Napali's stunning land- and seascape is by helicopter (see "Helicopter Tours," p. 521). However you experience it, you'll understand why Napali remains the star of countless calendars, postcards, and screen savers.

Btw. Kee Beach and Polihale State Park. http://dlnr.hawaii.gov/dsp/parks/kauai/napali-coast-state-wilderness-park. ✆ **808/274-3444.**

Waioli Mission House Museum and Church ★ HISTORIC SITE/MUSEUM   Many visitors passing through Hanalei pull over for a photo of **Waioli Huiia Church** (www.hanaleichurch.org; ✆ **808/826-6253**), a 1912 American Gothic wooden church with a steep roof, forest-green walls, and belfry reflecting the shape and hues of the mountains behind it. Nearby is the timber-and-plaster **Mission Hall,** built in 1841 and the oldest surviving church building on Kauai. Hidden by a grove of trees behind it is the two-story **Mission House,** erected in 1837 by the area's first missionaries, who traveled from Waimea via outrigger canoe. Teachers Abner and Lucy Wilcox and their four sons moved to this two-story, surprisingly airy home in 1846; four more sons were born here while the Wilcoxes instructed native students in English and the newly transliterated Hawaiian language. The homespun Americana—well-thumbed Bibles, braided rugs, and a spinning wheel—is complemented by Hawaiian elements such as ohia wood floors, a lava rock chimney, and lanais. Restored in 1921, the house is open for drop-in, first-come, first-served guided tours 3 days a week; you'll leave your shoes on the lanai, and stay about 30 minutes.

5-5363 Kuhio Hwy., Hanalei. www.grovefarm.org/waiolimissionhouse. ✆ **808/245-3202.** Requested donation $10 adults, $5 children 5–12. Tours on demand Tues,

Waioli Huiia Church

Thurs, and Sat 9am–3pm. Heading north from Hanalei Bridge, pass Waioli Huiia Church and turn left on the dirt road just before Hanalei School. A dirt parking area is about 150 yards (137 meters) on the left, with a footpath to the house.

SOUTH SHORE

Kauai Coffee ★★ FARM Some 4 million coffee trees grow on 3,100 acres of former sugarcane fields from Lawai Valley to Eleele, making Kauai Coffee the largest producer of coffee in Hawaii—and the United States. Kona coffee fans might sniff at the fact that the beans are machine-harvested, but it's surprisingly sustainable for such massive production, with 2,500 miles of drip-irrigation tubes, water recycling, cherry-pulp mulching, and other practices. You can learn all about the coffee-growing and roasting process on a free short, self-guided or guided walking tour, on the personalized, hourlong "Coffee on the Brain" tour ($20), or from a video and displays in the free tasting area behind the gift shop on a covered porch. Everyone heads to the latter first: How better to determine the difference between coffee varietals such as Blue Mountain, yellow catuai, or red catuai beans in an equally wide array of roasts and blends? A small snack bar in the tasting room helps take the edge off all that caffeine.

870 Halewili Rd. (Hwy. 540), Kalaheo. www.kauaicoffee.com. © **808/335-0813.** Free. Daily 9am–5pm. Free guided tours daily 10am, noon, 2, and 4pm. Coffee on the Brain Tour, 8:30am Tues, Thurs, Sun; $20. From westbound Kaumualii Hwy., drive through Kalaheo and look for Hwy. 540 on left just outside of town. From that intersection, it's 2½ miles to the visitor center. Hwy. 540 rejoins Kaumualii Hwy. another 1½ miles west.

Ke Kahua O Kaneiolouma ★★ CULTURAL SITE It's impossible to miss the four towering tiki on a stone platform by the main turnoff for Poipu Beach Park, but you're doing yourself a disservice if you just drive by. Still under restoration, this rock-walled, centuries-old complex contains a navigation-themed *heiau* (temple), fishpond and taro patches, home sites and a large games arena used during the winter season of *Makahiki*. Entry isn't permitted, but well-designed signs explain the site's cultural and historical significance.

Poipu Rd., *makai* side (at Hoowili Rd.), Poipu. www.kaneiolouma.org. Free (do not enter rock-walled compound). Daily during daylight hours.

Kukuiolono Park ★ HISTORIC SITE/GARDEN   Hawaiians once lit signal fires atop this Kalaheo hillside, perhaps to aid seafarers or warn of invaders. Most visitors are still in the dark about this unusual park, created by pineapple magnate Walter McBryde and then bequeathed to the public after his death in 1930. A mile off the main highway it includes the 9-hole **Kukuiolono Golf Course ★★** (p. 547); the clubhouse sports bar and restaurant, **Paco's Tacos Cantina** (open 8am to 5:30pm daily); a Japanese garden; a collection of intriguing Hawaiian lava rock artifacts; and several miles of jogging paths. A meditation pavilion and stone benches also provide excuses to enjoy the views.

854 Puu Rd., Kalaheo. ℂ **808/332-9151.** Free. Gates open daily 7am–6pm. From Lihue, take Kaumualii Hwy. west into Kalaheo, turn left on Papalina Rd., and drive mostly uphill for about a mile; look for sign at right—entrance has huge iron gates and stone pillars—and continue uphill to park.

Lawai International Center ★★ BUDDHIST SHRINE/HISTORIC SITE   Although you'll hear some noise from the unseen highway, the serenity of this historic 32-acre valley, open only for free guided tours, is unshakable, especially once you ascend the former Hawaiian *heiau* (temple) to the new **Hall of Compassion,** a gleaming wooden structure in the style of a 13th-century Buddhist shrine. You're expected to keep silent there and on the hillside path marked by 88 diminutive Shingon Buddhist shrines, a replica of a 900-mile temple route in Shikoku, Japan. Built in 1904 by young plantation workers from Japan, the shrines beckoned pilgrims for decades until the local cannery closed, workers moved away, and the site became overgrown. An all-volunteer, nondenominational effort has led to their restoration; you'll hear that inspiring story over a cup of tea and cookies first before heading up the steep hill (walking staffs included).

End of Wawae Rd., off Kaumualii Hwy., *makai* side, Lawai. From Lihue, turn left onto Wawae just west of stoplight at Koloa Rd. www.lawaicenter.org. ℂ **808/639-4300.** Tours by reservation at 10am, noon, and 2pm the 2nd and last Sun of each month, and by appt. Free admission; donations welcomed.

Makauwahi Cave Reserve ★★ ARCHAEOLOGICAL SITE   The Pacific's greatest cache of fossils, including those of enormous, long-extinct waterfowl, may lie in the depths of the largest limestone cave in Hawaii. Exposed by a sinkhole thousands of years ago, the cave is

A prince OF A PRINCE

With his name gracing half of the main Kauai highway as well as a popular beach and busy avenue in Waikiki, you could say **Prince Jonah Kuhio Kalanianaole** is all over the map, just as he was in life. The nephew and adopted son of King David Kalakaua and Queen Kapiolani, Prince Kuhio studied in California and England before the American-backed overthrow of the monarchy in 1893. He spent a year in prison after being arrested in 1895 for plotting to restore the kingdom and later fought with the British in the Boer War. In 1903, he was elected as a territorial delegate to the U.S. Congress, where he served until his death in 1922, at age 50.

Along the way, Prince Kuhio founded the first Hawaiian Civic Club, restored the Royal Order of Kamehameha, created the Hawaiian Home Lands Commission (which awards long-term leases to Native Hawaiians), established national parks on Maui and the island of Hawaii, opened his Waikiki beachfront to the public, and popularized outrigger canoe racing—just to name a few of the reasons "the people's prince" is so revered. His March 26 birthday is a state holiday, which his home island of Kauai marks with various **festivities** (see www.kauaifestivals.com).

His birthplace in Poipu is part of **Prince Kuhio Park**, a small, grassy compound off Lawai Road, not far from where surfers navigate "PK's," a break also named for the prince. The park holds the foundations of the family home, a fishpond that's still connected by a culvert to the sea, the remains of a *heiau* (shrine), and a monument that still receives floral tributes. **Note:** It's considered disrespectful to sit on the rock walls, as tempting as it might be to picnic or don snorkel gear there.

managed by paleoarchaeologists and conservationists David and Lida Pigott Burney, who have opened it for fascinating docent-led tours. After you make the slow, bumpy drive through former cane fields near the Grand Hyatt Kauai, a short walk takes you to the small entrance to the cave—stay hunched until you see sky overhead. Non-native tortoises, abandoned as house pets, help keep the vegetation down; visit their sanctuary outside the cave, where the Burneys are restoring native plants. Admission is free, but please donate toward upkeep and research. *Tip:* Rough roads may make it easier to park near the arena at CJM Country Stables (see p. 552) and follow signposts north.

Near Mahaulepu (Gillin's) Beach, Mahaulepu. www.cavereserve.org. © **808/634-0605** or 808/212-1710. Tours 10am–2pm Wed–Sun. Free admission; donations welcomed. From Poipu, take Poipu Rd. east past the Grand Hyatt Kauai onto dirt road. Follow 2 miles to crossroads, turn right, and turn right again just past green gate and shack. Follow farm road along edge of field and park on left just past signpost 18. Then hike trail over footbridge, turn right, and head to signpost 15; cave entrance is small hole. Tortoise rescue is to left of parking area.

National Tropical Botanical Garden ★★★ HISTORIC SITE/ GARDEN   Formerly owned by the McBryde Sugar Company, which bought the land from Queen Emma in 1886, this lush swath of Lawai

Allerton Garden

Valley contains two major gardens worth visiting, as well as the headquarters and research facilities of the National Tropical Botanical Garden. The 186-acre **McBryde Garden,** open for self-guided tours on mostly unpaved trails, boasts the largest collection of rare and endangered Hawaiian plants in the world, plus numerous varieties of palms, fruit trees, heliconias, orchids, and other colorful flowers. Its Spice of Life trail, which includes cacao and allspice trees, meanders past picturesque Maidenhair Falls. The accessible Diversity Trail follows a 450-million-year timeline as it passes through a misty tunnel and ends at a pavilion with restrooms. Allow at least 90 minutes to explore.

Open only to guided tours, the captivating formal gardens of adjacent **Allerton Garden** are the legacy of wealthy Chicagoan Robert Allerton and his companion John Gregg, whom Allerton later adopted. Allerton bought the land from McBryde in 1938 and with Gregg designed a series of elegant outdoor "rooms," where fountains and European statuary bracket plants collected from Southeast Asia and the Pacific. Garden tours last about 2½ hours; 3-hour sunset tours begin in the afternoon and end with a peek inside the oceanfront Allerton estate (normally off-limits), plus appetizers and drinks on the lanai. A new, 2½-hour guided Discovery Combination Tour offers highlights of both gardens, plus a peek inside the research-oriented horticultural center.

All valley garden tours require a tram ride and reservations by credit card. It's free, however, to tour the **Southshore Visitors Center Garden,** where the trams depart. Although somewhat neglected, its several acres include separate areas for ornamental flowers and trees, a plantation-era home garden, Hawaiian native plants, and the profusion of color and textures known as the Gates Garden at the entrance.

4425 Lawai Rd. (across the street from Spouting Horn), Poipu. www.ntbg.org. © **808/742-2623. Visitors Center Garden:** Self-guided tours daily 8:30am–5pm; free admission. **McBryde Garden:** Self-guided tours daily 9:30am–5pm; $30 adults, $15 children 6–12, free for children 5 and under. Trams leave hourly on the half-hour, last tram 3:30pm. **Allerton Garden:** Guided tours on the hour daily 9am–3pm; $50 adults, $25 children 6–12, free for children 5 and under. Sunset tours daily (hours vary), $95 adults, $45 children 6–12, free for children 5 and under. Discovery Combination Tour: Daily 10:30am and 2:30pm; $60 adults, children 6–12 $30, free for children 5 and under. All tours require reservations and check-in 30 min. in advance.

Spouting Horn ★★ NATURAL ATTRACTION The Hawaiian equivalent to Old Faithful—at least in regularity, if not temperature—is an impressive plume of seawater that jettisons anywhere from 10 to 50 or so feet into the air above the rocky shoreline (fenced for safety reasons). The spout comes from the force of ocean swells funneling waves through a lava tube, with the most spectacular displays in winter and other high-surf days. The *whoosh* of the spraying water is often followed by a load moaning sound, created by air being pushed through another nearby hole. There's an ample parking lot (as well as restrooms) on the site, but if you spot tour buses, don't try to compete with the crowds for a Spouting Horn photo. Instead, browse the vendors of arts, crafts, and jewelry (from $5 bangles to Niihau shell leis costing hundreds of dollars) under the tents along the bluff, or watch the wild chickens put on a show until the buses pull out 15 to 20 minutes later. Keep an eye out for whales in winter.

Lawai Rd., *makai* side, Poipu, 2 miles west of the traffic circle with Poipu Rd. Free admission. Daily during daylight hours.

WEST SIDE

Kokee State Park ★★★ PARK It's only 16 miles from Waimea to Kokee, but the two feel worlds apart: With 4,345 acres of rainforest, Kokee is another climate zone altogether, where the breeze has a bite and trees look quite continental. This is a cloud forest on the edge of the Alakai Swamp, the largest swamp in Hawaii, on the summit plateau of Kauai. Days are cool and wet, with intermittent bright sunshine, not unlike Seattle on a good day. Bring your sweater, and, if you're staying over, be sure you know how to light a fire (overnight lows dip into the 40s/single-digit Celsius).

Although invasive foreign plants such as strawberry guava, kahili ginger, and Australian tree ferns have crowded out native plants, the forest still holds many treasures, including several species that only grow on Kauai: mokihana trees, whose anise-scented green berries adorn the island's signature lei; iliau, a spiky plant similar to Maui's silversword; and the endangered white hibiscus, one of the few with a fragrance.

Kokee State Park

Before exploring the area, though, be sure to stop by the **Kokee Natural History Museum** ★★ (www.kokee.org; ✆ **808/335-9975;** daily 9am–4:30pm). It's right next to the restaurant/gift shop of the Lodge at Kokee, in the meadow off Kokee Road (Hwy. 550), 5 miles past the first official Waimea Canyon lookout. Admission is free, but it deserves at least the $1 donation requested per person. The museum shop has great trail information as well as local books and maps, including the official park trail map. A .1-mile nature walk with labeled plants starts just behind the museum.

Another 2.7 miles up the road from Kokee Lodge is **Kalalau Overlook** ★★★, the spectacular climax of your drive through Waimea Canyon and Kokee—unless the gate is open to the Puu O Kila Lookout 1 mile farther, the true end of the road. The latter lookout is usually closed in inclement weather, which is frequent: Nearby Waialeale is playing catch for clouds that have crossed thousands of miles of ocean. The view from Kalalau Overlook can be Brigadoon-like, too, but when the mists part, it's breathtaking. Shadows dance cross the green cliffs dappled with red and orange, white tropicbirds soar over a valley almost 4,000 feet below, and the turquoise sea sparkles on the horizon. Just below the railing, look for the fluffy red honeycreepers ('*apapane*) darting among the scarlet-tufted ohia lehua trees. Mornings tend to offer the clearest views.

With so many trails to hike up here, including the boardwalk through the Alakai Swamp (p. 552), some choose to stay overnight, either by pitching a tent in one of several campsites (by permit only) or opting for one of the cabins run by West Kauai Lodging or the YWCA's Camp Sloggett (see "Where to Stay," p. 556). You'll need to plan carefully, though, when it comes to food and drink: The Kokee Lodge Restaurant (see "Where to Eat," p. 574) is the only game in town, does not serve dinner, and may close early when business is slow. After 4pm, your best hope may be a snack vendor at a Waimea Canyon overlook; otherwise, it's a slow, 15-mile drive down to Waimea.

Kokee Rd., 7 miles north of its merge with Waimea Canyon Rd. (Hwy. 550). http://dlnr.hawaii.gov/dsp/parks/kauai/kokee-state-park. *C* **808/274-3444.** Free admission. Daily during daylight hours.

Russian Fort Elizabeth State Historical Park ★ HISTORIC SITE   To the list of those who tried to conquer Hawaii, add the Russians. In 1815, a German doctor tried to claim Kauai for Russia. He even supervised the construction of this fort in Waimea, named for the wife of Czar Alexander I (spelled "Elisabeth" on some signage), but he and his handful of Russian companions were expelled by Kamehameha I a couple of years later. Only the walls remain today, built with stacked lava rocks in the shape of a star. If the grounds have been recently mowed, you can easily follow a path around the fort's perimeter to the oceanside entrance to the interior; see the interpretive sign by the parking lot. The site also provides panoramic views of the west bank of the Waimea River, where Captain Cook landed, and the island of Niihau. *Note:* Tidy restrooms and a picnic table make this a convenient pit stop.

Ocean side of Kaumualii Hwy., Waimea, just after mile marker 22, east of Waimea River. http://dlnr.hawaii.gov/dsp/parks/kauai/russian-fort-elizabeth-state-historical-park. *C* **808/274-3444.** Free admission. Daily during daylight hours.

Russian Fort Elizabeth

Waimea Canyon State Park ★★★ PARK/NATURAL ATTRACTION   Often called the Grand Canyon of the Pacific—an analogy attributed to Mark Twain, although there's no record he ever visited—Waimea Canyon is indeed spectacular, albeit on a smaller scale. A mile wide, 3,600 feet deep, and 14 miles long, depending on whom you ask, this counterpart to Arizona's icon deserves accolades for its beauty alone. A jumble of red-orange pyramids, striped with gray bands of volcanic rock and stubbled with green and gold vegetation, Waimea Canyon was formed by a series of prehistoric lava flows, earthquakes, and erosion from wind and water, including the narrow Waimea River, still carving its way to the sea. You can stop by the road and look at the canyon, hike into it, admire it from a downhill bicycle tour, or swoop through it in a helicopter. (For more information, see "Organized Tours" and "Other Outdoor Activities," below.)

By car, there are two ways to visit Waimea Canyon and reach Kokee State Park, 15 miles up from Waimea. From the main road of Kaumualii Highway, it's best to head up Waimea Canyon Drive (Hwy. 550) in Waimea town. You can also pass through Waimea and turn up Kokee Road (Hwy. 55) at Kekaha, but it's steeper—one reason the twice-daily downhill bike tours prefer that route—and its vistas, though lovely, are not as eye-popping as those along Waimea Canyon Drive, the narrower rim road. The two routes merge about 7 miles up from the highway and continue as Kokee Road.

Waimea Canyon

The first good vantage point is **Waimea Canyon Lookout,** between mile markers 10 and 11 on Kokee Road; there's a long, gently graded, paved path for those who can't handle the stairs to the observation area. Far across the canyon, two-tiered **Waipoo** *("why-poh-oh")* **Falls** cascades 800 feet; you might spot a nimble mountain goat clambering on the precipices just below. From here, it's about another 5 miles to Kokee. A few more informal and formal lookout points along the way also offer noteworthy views. **Puu Ka Pele Lookout,** between mile markers 12 and 13, reveals the multiple ribbons of water coursing through Waipoo Falls. **Puu Hinahina Lookout,** between mile markers 13 and 14, actually has two different vista points, one with a sweeping view of the canyon down to the Pacific, and another of Niihau, lying 17 miles west.

Waimea Canyon Drive (Hwy. 550) and Kokee Road (Hwy. 55), Waimea. http://dlnr. hawaii.gov/dsp/parks/kauai/waimea-canyon-state-park. ℂ **808/274-3444.** Free admission. Daily during daylight hours.

West Kauai Visitor Center ★ MUSEUM   Although its hours are limited, this center's two free weekly activities and the small but well-curated cultural exhibitions merit a stop here before or after your Waimea Canyon expedition. The **"Keepers of the Culture"** displays include vintage photos, artifacts, and panels on Waimea's natural and cultural history, from traditional Hawaiian practices such as salt-making and herbal medicine to the arrival of Captain Cook, the sugar plantation era, *paniolo* (cowboy) culture, and the modern Pacific Missile Range Facility. Kids will more likely enjoy the **lei-making class,** which takes place at 10am Friday from March to mid-October (when fresh blossoms are available); admission is by donation, but you need to reserve by phone the week before. On Monday, a free **guided walking tour** of historic Waimea Town explores its ancient Hawaiian roots and modern history with stops at the Captain Cook monument, missionary churches, and picturesque Waimea Pier. It starts at 8:30am and lasts about 3 hours; reservations are required by noon the Friday before.

9565 Kaumualii Hwy. (*mauka* side) at Waimea Canyon Rd., Waimea. Park at rear of building, but lot entrance is only from Kaumualii Hwy. www.westkauaivisitorcenter. org. ℂ **808/338-1332.** Free admission. Mon–Fri 10am–4pm.

Organized Tours

Farms, gardens, historic houses, and other points of interest that may be open only to guided tours are listed under "Attractions & Points of Interest" (see p. 502). For boat, kayak, bicycle, hiking, and similar tours, see listings under "Other Outdoor Activities" (p. 544).

HELICOPTER TOURS ★★★

If you forgo touring Kauai by helicopter, you'll miss seeing the vast majority of its untouched ridgelines, emerald valleys, and exhilarating waterfalls. Yes, the rides are expensive (most are $250–$350 per person),

HOLLYWOOD loves KAUAI

More than 50 major Hollywood productions have been shot on Kauai since the studios discovered the island's spectacular natural beauty. Two of the most recent star turns were in 2015's *Jurassic World* (an update of 1993's *Jurassic Park*) and 2011's *The Descendants*. You can visit a number of Kauai film and TV locations—including scenes from *Fantasy Island* and *Gilligan's Island*—on the **Hawaii Movie Tour** from Roberts Hawaii (www.roberts hawaii.com/island/kauai; ℂ **800/831-5541**). Offered daily except Sunday, the narrated minibus tour features singalongs and video clips that play between sightseeing stops. You'll likely see more of Kauai on this 6-hour tour than you could on your own. Tickets are $119 for adults and $61 for children 4 to 11 (free for younger, if seated on an adult's lap); prices include lunch at Wahooo Seafood Grill and pickup/drop-off ($10 extra for Princeville lodgings). *Tip:* Book online for discounted fares—$108 adults, $55 children—and reserve early.

but you'll take home memories—not to mention photos, videos, and/or a professional DVD—of the thrilling ride over Waimea Canyon, into Kalalau Valley on Kauai's wild Napali Coast, and across the green crater of Waialeale, laced with ribbons of water.

Most flights depart from Lihue, last about 55 to 75 minutes, and, regardless of advertising, offer essentially the same experience: narrated flights, noise-canceling headphones with two-way communication, and multicamera videos of your ride or a pre-taped version (often a better souvenir). The risks are roughly the same—the last fatal crash involving a sightseeing helicopter over Kauai was in 2007, with many thousands of flights safely flown since. (If your pilot chooses to bypass Waialeale due to bad weather, appreciate his or her caution.) So how to distinguish among the half-dozen major operators?

Given the noise inflicted on residents, wildlife, and tranquility-seeking hikers by flights that hover as low as 500 feet, I recommend touring with the most eco-friendly of the bunch, and most luxurious: **Blue Hawaiian** ★★★ (www.bluehawaiian.com; ℂ **800/745-2583** or 808/245-5800). Its American Eurocopter Eco-Star choppers have a unique tail design that reduces noise and fuel use, while the roomy interior has six business-class-style leather seats with premium views. The best seats are the two next to the pilot, but the raised row of rear seats won't disappoint (keep in mind seating is usually determined by weight distribution). The 55-minute "Eco Adventure" ride from Lihue costs $247 ($226 when booked online at least 5 days in advance), which also makes Blue Hawaiian the best value. *Note:* In early 2016, passengers on a Blue Hawaiian helicopter suffered serious injuries due to an emergency hard landing; a final report on the cause had not been issued as of press time.

For those staying on the North Shore, it may be more convenient to do a tour with **Sunshine Helicopters** ★★ (www.sunshinehelicopters.com; © **866/501-7738** or 808/270-3999). Its 40- to 50-minute flights from Princeville Airport are in quiet, roomy Whisper Star models, similar in design to Blue Hawaiian's Eco-Stars (it flies different craft out of Lihue). Tours cost $289 for open seating, $364 if you want to reserve an even roomier "first class" seat in the front row; it's $249 and $324, respectively, if you book online, with an extra $10 off on flights before 8:30am or after 2pm.

Although their aircraft are not as quiet as those of Blue Hawaiian and Sunshine, three other companies have unique itineraries deserving of consideration. **Island Helicopters** (www.islandhelicopters.com; © **800/829-5999** or 808/245-8588) has exclusive rights to land at remote 350-foot Manawaiopuna Falls, nicknamed "Jurassic Falls" for its movie cameo. During your 25 minutes on the ground, you'll hear about the geological history and rare native plants in this area of Hanapepe Valley, which like Niihau is owned by the Robinson family. In part due to landing fees and fuel costs, the 75- to 85-minute **Jurassic Falls Tour** ★★ costs $335; you'll see the falls but not land there on the 50-minute Grand Circle Tour ($175). Both leave from Lihue Airport; add 4% to prices for credit card use. The 90-minute **Kauai Refuge Eco-Tour** ★★ of **Safari Helicopters** (www.safarihelicopters.com; © **800/326-3356** or 808/246-0136) includes

Napali coast viewed from helicopter

a 30- to 40-minute stopover at an otherwise inaccessible Robinson-owned site overlooking vast Olokele Canyon; Keith Robinson is occasionally on hand to explain his efforts to preserve rare, endemic plants here (which your landing fees subsidize). The tour costs $314 ($299 booked online) and departs from Lihue.

Mauna Loa Helicopter Tours (www.maunaloahelicoptertours.com; © **808/245-7500**), meanwhile, only offers private tours, with a thrilling doors-off option ($307 for 1 hour, $408 for 75 minutes; 2-passenger minimum), and customizable trips ($693 per hour).

Note: Minimum ages and maximum weights may apply; read fine print before booking. For Niihau helicopter tours, see p. 499.

BEACHES

Note: You'll find relevant sites on the "Kauai" map, p. 488.

Beaches

Kauai's nearly 70 beaches include some of the most beautiful in the world, and all are open to the public, as required by state law. They are also in the middle of the vast, powerful Pacific, where currents and surf patterns are often quite different than those of Mainland beaches. The North Shore sees the highest surf in winter (Oct–Apr), thanks to swells originating in the Arctic that can also wrap around the West Side and turn the East Side's waters rough. In summer, Antarctic storms can send large swells to the South Shore that wrap around the West Side and churn up the East Side.

The good news is there's almost always a swimmable beach somewhere: You just need to know where to look. Start by asking your hotel concierge or checking the daily ocean report at **Kauaiexplorer.com** to find out current conditions. Nine beaches—all of them county or state parks—have lifeguards, who are keen to clue you in on safety.

Below are highlights of the Garden Isle's more accessible beaches. For detailed listings, including maps and videos, of virtually all strands and coves, see **www.kauaibeachscoop.com**.

EAST SIDE

Anahola Beach ★

Anahola is part of the Hawaiian Home Lands federal program, meaning that much of the land here is reserved for lease by Native Hawaiians; you'll pass their modest homes on the road to this secluded, mostly reef-protected golden strand. The 1½-acre **Anahola Beach Park** on the south end feels like the neighborhood's back yard, particularly on weekends, with kids learning to surf or bodyboarding, a hula class on the grass, and picnickers. It's better to explore here during the week, when you might share it with just a few local fishermen (give their poles and nets a wide berth) and campers. There are sandy-bottomed pockets for swimming and

"When in doubt, don't go out" is the mantra of local authorities, who repeat this and other important safety tips in public service announcements. That refers to going into unsafe waters, walking on slippery rocks and ledges that may be hit by high surf, or other heedless acts, such as disregarding beach closed signs in winter. Many of the unguarded beaches have waters that should only be enjoyed from the sand or during calm conditions, which can change rapidly; large waves may come in sets as much as 20 minutes apart. Although you might see locals seemingly ignoring the warning signs that note hazards such as strong currents, steep drop-offs, dangerous shorebreak, and the like, keep in mind they've had years to acclimatize. Don't be afraid to ask for their advice, though, since they'll tailor it for newcomers—no one wants injuries or worse in their home waters. *Do* go out to Kauai's beaches; just use prudence before going in or near the ocean.

reefy areas for snorkeling, safe except in high surf. The Anahola River, usually shallow enough to walk across, bisects the beach. Facilities include picnic tables, restrooms, campsites, and lifeguards.

From Kuhio Hwy. heading north, turn right on Anahola Rd. (between mile markers 13 and 14) and head ¾-mile to the beach park. You can also park north of the Anahola River by taking a right on Aliomanu Rd. ½-mile past Anahola Rd., just after Duane's Ono Char-Burger (p. 583).

Kumukumu (Donkey) Beach ★★

When the only way to reach this beach was by a downhill hike through sugarcane fields near a donkey pasture, nude sunbathers took full advantage of its seclusion. Now it's bordered by large luxury estates and the **Ke Ala Hele Makalae** coastal path, connecting it to Kealia Beach, 1½ miles south; the 10-minute walk down to the ocean is mostly paved, and even starts at a parking lot with restrooms. So keep your clothes on while enjoying the soft golden sand at this tree-lined beach, also known as Paliku ("vertical cliff") and Kuna Bay. The water is too rough for swimming or snorkeling, but you may see advanced surfers and bodyboarders here. The north side has a shallow cove that's safe for wading in calm conditions.

From Kapaa, take Kuhio Hwy. north past mile marker 11; parking is on right, marked by sign with two hiking figures on it. Footpath to beach starts near parking lot entrance.

Kalapaki Beach ★★

This quarter-mile-long swath of golden sand may seem like a private beach, given all the lounge chairs on its border with the Kauai Marriott Resort, which towers behind. But there's generally plenty of room to find your own space to sunbathe, while the jetty stretching across much of Kalapaki Bay offers a protected place to swim or paddle; body-surfing and surfing are also possible at a small break. The view of the mossy-green Haupu Ridge rising out of Nawiliwili Bay is entrancing, as is watching massive cruise ships and Matson barges angle their way in and out of the nearby harbor. The water is a little murkier here, due to stream runoff. Facilities include restrooms and showers, with numerous shops and restaurants within a short walk.

From Lihue Airport, turn left onto Hwy. 51, then turn left on Rice St., and look for the Kauai Marriott Resort entrance on the left. Free beach access parking is in the upper lot, past the hotel's porte-cochère.

Kealia Beach ★

Only very experienced surfers and bodyboarders should try their skill on the usually powerful waves here, but everyone else can enjoy the show from the broad golden sand, a picnic table, or the nearby coastal multiuse path. The lifeguards can advise you if it's calm enough to go for a swim and where to do it. When the wind is up, which is often, you might see kite flyers. The 66-acre **Kealia Beach Park** is just off the main highway, often with food trucks and coconut vendors in the parking lot, making it a convenient place for an impromptu break. Facilities include restrooms and picnic shelters.

Off Kuhio Hwy. in Kapaa, just north of Kapaa River and Mailihuna Rd.

Lydgate Beach ★

Part of the family oasis of 58-acre **Lydgate Park ★** (p. 526) on the south side of the Wailua River mouth, Lydgate Beach has two rock-walled ponds that create the safest swimming and best snorkeling on the East Side—unless storms have pushed branches and other debris into the pond, which can take several days to clear. Families also gravitate here for the immense wooden play structure known as the **Kamalani Playground** and access to a 2.5-mile stretch of the **Ke Ala Hele Makalae coastal path,** suitable for strollers and bikes. Facilities include a pavilion, restrooms, outdoor showers, picnic tables, barbecue grills, lifeguards, campsites, and parking.

Leho Dr. at Nalu Rd., Wailua. From the intersection of Kuhio Hwy. and Hwy. 51 outside of Lihue, head 2½ miles north to Leho Dr. and turn right, just before the Hilton Garden Inn Kauai Wailua Bay. Turn right again on Nalu Rd. and follow to parking areas.

NORTH SHORE

Anini Beach ★★★

Anini is the safest beach on Kauai for swimming and windsurfing, thanks to one of the longest, widest fringing reefs on the island, among the very largest in all of Hawaii. With shallow water 4 to 5 feet deep, it's also a good snorkel spot for beginners (although the coral and varieties of fish are sparse closer to shore). In summer months, divers are attracted to the 60-foot dropoff near the channel in the northwest corner of the nearly 3-mile-long reef. In winter, this channel creates a very dangerous rip current, although the near-shore waters generally stay calm; it can be fun to watch breakers pounding the distant reef from the bathlike lagoon. The

Anini Beach

well-shaded, sinuous beach is very narrow in places, so just keep walking if you'd like more privacy. The 13-acre **Anini Beach Park** on the south-western end has restrooms, picnic facilities, a boat-launch ramp, camp-sites, and often a food truck or two.

From Lihue, follow Kuhio Hwy. past Kilauea to the 2nd Kalihiwai Rd. exit on right (the 1st Kalihiwai Rd. dead-ends at Kalihiwai Beach). Head downhill ½-mile to a left on Anini Rd.

Hanalei Beach ★★★

Easily one of the most majestic settings in Hawaii, and unbelievably just a few blocks from the main road, Hanalei Beach is a gorgeous half-moon of golden-white sand, 2 miles long and 125 feet wide. Hanalei means "lei-shaped," and like a lei, the curving, ironwood-fringed sands adorn Hanalei Bay, the largest inlet on Kauai. While the cliffside St. Regis Princeville dominates the eastern vista, the view west is lush and green; behind you, emerald peaks streaked with waterfalls rise to 4,000 feet. Renowned for experts-only big surf in winter (Sept–May), Hanalei attracts both begin-ners and old hands with steady, gentler waves the rest of the year. In sum-mer, much of the bay turns into a virtual lake. The county manages three different beach parks here, two with lifeguards.

Black Pot Beach Park, near the historic, 300-foot-long pier, is par-ticularly good for swimming, snorkeling, surfing, and fishing—hence its indefinite closure in April 2018 to repair flood damage hit the local com-munity very hard. It's expected to reopen by 2019; note parking can be hard to find on weekends and during holiday periods. Facilities include restrooms, showers, picnic tables, and campsites. **Hanalei Pavilion Beach Park,** in the center of the bay, has wide-open swimming (in calm weather), surfing, and boogie boarding under the watchful eye of life-guards; facilities include restrooms, showers, and pavilions. "Pine Trees" is the widely used moniker for **Waioli Beach Park,** shaded by ironwood trees towards the western edge of the bay. It's another popular surf spot—champions Andy and Bruce Irons grew up riding the waves here and started the children's Pine Trees Classic held here every April. Check with lifeguards in winter about possible strong currents; facilities include showers and restrooms.

From Princeville heading north on Kuhio Hwy., enter Hanalei and turn right at Aku Rd. just after Tahiti Nui; then right on Weke Rd. Hanalei Pavilion Beach Park will be on your left; the road dead-ends at parking lot for Black Pot Beach Park. For Waioli Beach Park (Pine Trees), take Aku Rd. to a left on Weke Rd.; then right on Hee Rd.

Kauapea (Secret) Beach ★★

Not exactly secret, but still wonderfully secluded, this long, broad stretch of light sand below forested bluffs lies snugly between rocky points, with only a few cliff-top homes and Kilauea Point Lighthouse to the east providing signs of civilization. Although strong currents and high surf, especially in winter, make the water unsafe, tide pools at the west end invite exploration when the surf is low, creating beguiling mini-lagoons; a small artesian waterfall to the east is perfect for washing off salt water. *Note:* Despite its reputation as a safe haven for nudists (who hang out at the more remote eastern end), Kauai County does occasionally enforce the "no public nudity" law here. And as with all destinations where your car will be out of sight for extended periods, be sure to take your valuables with you. It's a 15-minute walk downhill to the beach.

Heading north on Kuhio Hwy., pass Kilauea and take 1st Kalihiwai Rd. turnoff on right. Drive about 50 yards, then turn right on unmarked dirt road, and follow to parking area. Trail at end of lot leads downhill to beach, about a 15-min. walk.

Kee Beach ★★★

The road ends here at this iconic tropical beach, hugged by swaying palms and sheltering ironwoods, its pale dunes sloping into a cozy lagoon brimming with a kaleidoscope of reef fish. You could feel like a sardine during summer when the ocean is at its most tranquil; year-round, the parking lot is typically full by 9am. To be fair, many cars are for hikers tackling all or part of the 11-mile **Kalalau Trail** (p. 511), whose trailhead is just before the beach, and some belong to campers. Kee (pronounced *"kay-eh"*) is also subject to high surf in winter when rogue waves can grab unwitting spectators from the shoreline and dangerous currents form in a channel on the reef's western edge. Always check with the lifeguards about the safest areas for swimming or snorkeling. Part of **Haena State Park** (p. 508), Kee has restrooms and showers in the woodsy area east of the parking lot. *Note:* The beach, trail and park closed for flood repairs in April 2018 but are expected to reopen by 2019. This is also a spectacular place to observe sunset, but you won't be alone in that endeavor either.

From Hanalei, take Kuhio Hwy. northwest about 7½ miles to the road's end.

Lumahai Beach ★

Between lush tropical jungle of pandanus and ironwood trees and the brilliant blue ocean lie two crescents of inviting golden-sand beach, separated by a rocky outcropping. Here is Kauai at its most captivating—and where you must exercise the most caution. Locals have nicknamed it "Luma-die," reflecting the sad tally of those drowned or seriously injured here. With no reef protection and a steeply sloping shore, the undertow and shorebreak are exceptionally strong, while the rocky ledges that seemingly invite exploration are often slapped by huge waves that knock sightseers into the tumbling surf and sharp rocks. Flash floods can also make the Lumahai River, which enters the ocean from the western beach, turn from a wading pool into a raging torrent. Plus, it has neither lifeguards nor facilities; parking is in a bumpy, unpaved area or along the narrow highway. So why would one even go here? When summer brings more tranquil surf, it's a gorgeous setting to stretch out on the sand—not too close to the shorebreak—and soak in the untamed beauty. *Note:* The eastern beach, reached by a short, steep trail from the highway, is where Mitzi Gaynor sang "I'm Gonna Wash That Man Right Outta My Hair" in *South Pacific.* Both beaches are accessible only via Kuhio Highway, expected to reopen to by 2019 after repairs to significant flood damage.

From Hanalei, follow Kuhio Hwy. about 2½ miles west. Look for pull-off on *makai* side, near mile marker 4, for trail to eastern beach. For western beach, continue west (downhill) to larger, unpaved parking area on *makai* side by mile marker 5.

Makua (Tunnels) Beach ★★★ & Haena Beach ★★★

Makua Beach earned the nickname of "Tunnels" from the labyrinth of lava tubes that wind through its inner and outer reef, making this Kauai's premiere snorkeling and diving site year-round. But as fascinating as the rainbow of tropical fish and the underwater tunnels, arches, and channels may be, they're more than matched by the beauty above water. The last pinnacle in a row of velvety green mountains, Makana (Bali Hai) rises over the western end of a golden curved beach next to ironwood trees. One issue: The few parking spots on dirt roads fill quickly and "no parking" zones are enforced.

Fortunately, a quarter-mile up the sand is **Haena Beach Park,** a county facility with much more parking—plus restrooms, showers, picnic tables, campsites, and lifeguards. During calm conditions, most frequent in summer, Haena Beach offers good swimming and some snorkeling, though not as enticing as at Makua. Winter brings enormous waves, rip currents, and a strong shorebreak; leave the water then to local surfers. Walk across the road for a gander at **Maniniholo Dry Cave ★★,** another former sea cave (see "Haena State Park," p. 508). *Note:* These beaches are accessible only via Kuhio Highway, damaged by floods but expected to reopen to by 2019.

From Hanalei, Makua (Tunnels) is just after mile marker 8 on Kuhio Hwy., but not visible from the road. Continue ½-mile to Haena Beach Park; parking lot on right.

SOUTH SHORE

Mahaulepu Beaches ★★

Not far from the well-groomed resorts of Poipu is a magical place to leave the crowds—and maybe the last few centuries—behind. To reach the three different beaches of Mahaulepu, framed by lithified sand dunes, former sugarcane fields, and the bold Haupu ridge, you'll have to drive at least 3 miles on an uneven dirt road through private land (gates close at 6pm) or hike the fascinating Mahaulepu Heritage Trail (p. 551). The first tawny strand is **Mahaulepu Beach,** nicknamed Gillin's Beach after the former Grove Farm manager whose house is the only modern structure you'll see for miles; the house is available for rent starting at $3,450 a week (www.gillinbeachhouse.com). Windsurfing is popular here, yet the strong currents prevent swimming or snorkeling. Around the point is **Kawailoa Bay,** also a windsurfing destination, with a rockier shoreline great for beachcombing and fishing. Wedged between dramatically carved ledges, **Haula Beach** is a picturesque pocket of sand with a rocky cove, best for solitude; access may be restricted. *Note:* The coastline here can be very windy and subject to high surf in summer.

By car: From Poipu Rd. in front of Grand Hyatt Kauai, continue on unpaved road 3 miles east, past the golf course and stables. Turn right at the T intersection, go 1 mile to the big sand dune, turn left, and drive ½-mile to a small lot under the trees to reach **Mahaulepu Beach.** Continue on the dirt road (high-clearance 4WD recommended) another ¼-mile to **Kawailoa Bay,** and then, if it's open, drive another

Mahaulepu Beach

½-mile to a short trail to **Haula Beach. By foot:** Follow Mahaulepu Heritage Trail (www.hikemahaulepu.org) 2 miles from east end of Keoneloa (Shipwrecks) Beach; limited public parking is just east of Grand Hyatt Kauai on Ainako Street.

Poipu Beach ★★★

A perennial "best beach" winner, the long swath of Poipu is actually two beaches in one, divided by a tombolo, or sandbar point. On the left, a lava-rock jetty protects a sandy-bottom pool that's perfect for children most of the year; on the right, the open bay attracts swimmers, snorkelers, and surfers. (If the waves are up, check with the lifeguards for the safest place to swim.) The sandy area is not especially large, but the 5½-acre **Poipu Beach Park** offers a spacious lawn for kids to run around in, plus picnic shelters, play structures, restrooms, and showers. There are plenty of palm trees, but not much shade; bring a beach umbrella. Given the lodgings nearby, Poipu understandably stays busy year-round, and on New Year's Eve, it becomes Kauai's version of Times Square with fireworks. *Note:* A third strand, to the west in front of Kiahuna Plantation Resort, is known as **Kiahuna Beach.** A short walk east is **Brennecke's Beach,** a sandy cove beloved by bodysurfers and boogie-boarders; be forewarned that waves can be large, especially in summer, and the rocky sides are always hazard-ous. Injuries do occur at Brennecke's, which has no lifeguard.

From Koloa, follow Poipu Rd. south to traffic circle and then east to a right turn on Hoowili Rd. Parking is on the left at intersection with Hoone Rd.

Keoneloa (Shipwrecks) Beach ★

Makawehi Point, a lithified sand dune, juts out from the eastern end of this beach, whose Hawaiian name means "the long sand." Harrison Ford and Anne Heche jumped off Makawehi in *Six Days, Seven Nights* (don't try it yourself), while bodysurfers and boogie-boarders find the roiling waters equally exhilarating. Novices should enjoy their antics from the shore or follow the ironwood trees to the path to the top of Makawehi Point, which is also the start of the **Mahaulepu Heritage Trail** (p. 551). A paved beach path in front of the Grand Hyatt Kauai leads west past tide pools to the blustery point at Makahuena, perfect for photographing Makawehi Point. Restrooms and showers are by the small parking lot on Ainako Street.

Public access from Ainako St., off Poipu Rd., just east of Grand Hyatt Kauai.

WEST SIDE

Salt Pond Beach ★★

You'll see Hawaii's only salt ponds still in production across from Salt Pond Beach, just outside Hanapepe. Generations of Hawaiians have care-fully tended the beds in which the sun turns seawater into salt crystals. Tinged with red clay, *'alae,* the salt is used as a health remedy as well as for seasoning food and drying fish. Although the salt ponds are off-limits to visitors, 6-acre **Salt Pond Beach Park** is a great place to explore, offer-ing a curved reddish-gold beach between two rocky points, a protective reef that creates lagoonlike conditions for swimming and snorkeling (talk to the lifeguard first if waves are up), tide pools, and a natural wading pool for kids. Locals flock here on weekends for individual recreation and large family gatherings. Facilities include showers, restrooms, a campground, and picnic areas.

From Lihue, take Kaumualii Hwy. to Hanapepe, cross Hanapepe Bridge, and look for Lele Rd. on left (½-mile ahead). Turn left and follow Lele Rd. to a right turn on Lokokai Rd. Salt Pond Beach parking lot is 1 mile ahead.

Polihale Beach ★★

This mini-Sahara on the western end of the island is Hawaii's biggest beach: 17 miles long and as wide as three football fields in places. This is a wonderful place to get away from it all, but don't forget your flip-flops—the midday sand is hotter than a lava flow. The pale golden sands wrap around Kauai's northwestern shore from Kekaha plantation town, just beyond Waimea, to where the ridges of Napali begin. For military reasons, access is highly restricted for a 7-mile stretch along the southeastern end near the Pacific Missile Range Facility, including the famed **Barking Sands Beach,** known to Hawaiians as Nohili. You'll still have miles of sand to explore in 140-acre **Polihale State Park,** provided you (or your car) can handle the 5-mile, often very rutted dirt road leading there; four-wheel drive is recommended. (Avoid driving on the car-trapping sand, too.) The sheer expanse, plus views of Niihau and the first stark cliffs of

Polihale State Park

Napali, make the arduous trek worth it for many. Although strong rip currents and a heavy shorebreak make the water dangerous, especially in winter, **Queen's Pond,** a small, shallow, sandy-bottom inlet, is generally protected from the surf in summer. The park has restrooms, showers, picnic tables, campsites, and drinking water (usually), but no lifeguards or any other facilities nearby, so plan accordingly. As in all remote areas, don't leave any valuables in your car.

From Kekaha, follow Kaumualii Hwy. 7 miles northwest past Pacific Missile Range Facility to fork at Kao Rd., bear right, and look for sign on left to Polihale. Follow dirt road 5 miles to unpaved parking area, bearing right at forks.

WATERSPORTS

Several outfitters on Kauai not only offer equipment rentals and tours, but also dispense expert information on weather forecasts, sea and trail conditions, and other important matters for adventurers. Brothers Micco and Chino Godinez at **Kayak Kauai** (www.kayakkauai.com; ✆ **888/596-3853** or 808/826-9844) are experts on paddling Kauai's rivers and coastline (as well as hiking and camping), offering guided tours and equipment rentals at their store in the Wailua River Marina. You can also learn about ocean and reef conditions and recommended boat operators at **Snorkel Bob's** (www.snorkelbob.com), with two locations in Kapaa and Poipu (see "Snorkeling," later). *Note:* Expect to tip $10 to $20 for the crew or guides on any tours; prices exclude tax.

Boat & Raft (Zodiac) Tours

One of Hawaii's most spectacular natural attractions is Kauai's **Napali Coast.** Unless you're willing to make an arduous 22-mile round-trip hike (see "Hiking" on p. 548), there are only two ways to see it: by helicopter (see "Helicopter Tours" on p. 521) or by water. Cruising to Napali may involve a well-equipped yacht under full sail, a speedy powerboat, or for the very adventurous, a Zodiac inflatable raft, in which you may explore Napali's sea caves or even land at one of Napali's pristine valleys—be prepared to hang on for dear life (it can reach speeds of 60 miles an hour) and get very wet.

You're almost guaranteed daily sightings of pods of spinner dolphins on morning cruises, as well as Pacific humpback whales during their annual visit from December to early April. In season, both sailing and powerboats combine **whale-watching** with their regular adventures. **Sunset cruises,** with cocktails and/or dinner, are another way to get out on the water and appreciate Kauai's coastline from a different angle.

Note: In addition to Captain Andy's (details below), only two other companies have permits to land at Nualolo Kai, home to the ruins of an 800-year-old Hawaiian village below an elevated Napali valley: **Na Pali Explorer** ★★ (www.napaliexplorer.com; ✆ **808/338-9999**), which departs from Kekaha ($169 adults, $149 ages 8–12), and **Kauai Sea**

Tours ★★ (www.kauaiseatours.com; © **800/733-7997** or 808/826-7254), leaving from Port Allen ($159 adults, $149 ages 13–17, $119 ages 7–12); book online for $10 off. All trips are on rigid-hull inflatables, which, unlike larger boats, can pass through the reef opening; landings take place April through October, conditions permitting.

Captain Andy's Sailing Adventures ★★   Captain Andy has been sailing to Napali since 1980, with a fleet that now includes two sleek 55-foot custom catamarans, the *Spirit of Kauai* and *Akialoa;* two luxurious 65-foot catamarans, the *Southern Star* and the *Northern Star;* and the zippy 24-foot Zodiac, which holds about a dozen thrillseekers. The 5½-hour **Napali catamaran cruise** costs $149 for adults and $109 for children 2 to 12, and it includes a continental breakfast, a deli-style lunch, snorkeling, and drinks; aboard the *Southern Star* ($169 adults, $119 children), a barbecue lunch replaces the deli fare. A 4-hour Napali Coast dinner cruise—which sails around the South Shore when Napali's waters are too rough, most often in winter—costs $119 for adults and $89 for children ($149/$109 on the *Southern Star*), with no snorkeling; all Napali catamaran cruises leave from Port Allen. The 2-hour **Poipu cocktail sunset sail** aboard the *Spirit of Kauai* or *Akialoa,* including drinks and pupu (appetizers), is $79 for adults and $59 for children; it sails Saturday only, from Kukuiula Small Boat Harbor near Poipu. **Napali Zodiac cruises** depart from Kikiaola Small Boat Harbor in Kekaha; the 4-hour version ($139 adults, $119 children 5–12) includes snorkeling and snacks, while the 6-hour version ($159/$119) adds a landing at Nualolo Kai (depending on conditions) and expands snacks to a picnic lunch. *Tip:* Book online for a $10-per-person discount.
www.napali.com. © **800/535-0830** or 808/335-6833.

Holo Holo Charters ★★★   Port Allen is the point of departure for Holo Holo's two gleaming catamarans. The 50-foot *Leila,* licensed for 45 passengers but limited to just 37, serves Holo Holo's 5-hour, year-round **Napali snorkel sails:** They're $159 adults and $119 children 6 to 12, including a continental breakfast and deli lunch, and post-snorkel beer and wine. The 65-foot *Holo Holo* power catamaran, the island's largest, was built specifically to handle the channel crossing between Kauai and Niihau, where passengers snorkel in stunningly clear water after Napali sightseeing on 7-hour trips, also with two meals and post-snorkel libations ($215 adults, $149 children 6–12). The 3½-hour **Napali Sunset Tour** ($129 adults, $109 children 5–12), also aboard the *Holo Holo,* offers heavy appetizers, cocktails, and, at sunset, a champagne toast. The **2-hour Aloha Sunset Sail** ($85) aboard the *Leila* serves the same fare but heads south to Poipu. Holo Holo also runs Napali snorkel tours from ultra-convenient Hanalei on comfortable inflatable "rafts," really speedboats with fiberglass hulls, twin motors, stadium seats, and a freshwater shower. The 4-hour trip, including drinks and lunch, costs $199 for ages 6 and older (younger not allowed). *Tip:* Book online at least 1 day in advance for $15 to $20 off per person.

www.holoholokauaiboattours.com. © **800/848-6130** or 808/335-0815.

Liko Kauai & Makana Charters ★ Born and raised on Kauai, in a Native Hawaiian family with roots on Niihau, Captain Liko Hookano offers more than just typical cruises; instead, they're a 5-hour combination Napali Coast tour/snorkel/cultural history class/seasonal whale-watching extravaganza with lunch. Choose from the 49-foot *Na Pali Kai III* power catamaran, limited to 32 passengers and narrow enough to go in the sea caves normally only visited by inflatable craft, or the similarly capable 32-foot *Makana*, limited to 12 passengers. The tours cost $139 for adults (pregnant women not allowed) and $95 for children 4 to 12. (A charter version on a 14-passenger inflatable raft is available for the same price.) Boats depart at 8:30am and 2pm daily from Kikiaola Small Boat Harbor in Kekaha; check in at 4516 Alawai Rd., Waimea (from Kaumualii Hwy., turn right at Alawai Road just west of the Waimea River). Book online for a 10% discount.

www.tournapali.com. © **808/338-9980.**

Bodysurfing & Boogie Boarding

The best places for beginners' bodysurfing and boogie boarding are **Kalapaki Beach** and **Poipu Beach;** only the more advanced should test the more powerful shorebreaks at **Kealia, Shipwrecks (Keoneloa),** and **Brennecke's** beaches (see "Beaches," p. 524). Boogie-board rentals are widely available at surf shops (see "Surfing," p. 542) and beachfront activity desks. On the South Shore, **Nukumoi Surf Shop** (www.nukumoi.com; © **808/742-8019**), right across from Brennecke's Beach at 2100 Hoone Rd., Poipu, has the best rates and selections ($8 a day; $24 a week). On the North Shore, **Hanalei Surf Co.** (www.hanaleisurf.com; © **808/826-9000**), rents boogie boards for $5 a day, $20 a week, or $7 with fins, $22 weekly (3- and 5-day discounts also available); it's in Hanalei Center (the old Hanalei School Building), 5-5161 Kuhio Hwy., *mauka* side, Hanalei.

Kayaking

With the only navigable river (some would say rivers) in Hawaii, numerous bays, and the stunning Napali Coast, Kauai is made for kayaking. The most popular kayaking route is up the Wailua River to Uluwehi (Secret) Falls (limited to permitted kayaks Mon–Sat), but you can also explore the Huleia and Hanalei rivers as they wind through wildlife reserves, go whale-watching in winter along the South Shore, or test your mettle in summer with an ultrastrenuous, 17-mile paddle from Hanalei to Polihale.

   Kayak Kauai (www.kayakkauai.com; © **888/596-3853** or 808/826-9844), the premiere outfitter for all kinds of paddling, offers a range of rentals and tours from its store in Wailua River Marina, 3-5971 Kuhio Hwy., Kapaa (just south of the Wailua River Bridge, *mauka* side). You can even start with a 90-minute class ($75). River kayak rental starts at $29 for a one-person kayak and $54 for a two-person kayak per day. Wailua River–permitted double kayaks cost $95, with just six available per day (launched only 8:30–11:30am Mon–Sat due to local regulations). Rates include paddles, life preservers, back rests, and car racks. The 5-hour guided Wailua River tours with a Secret Falls hike/swim and picnic lunch, offered three times a day, cost $85 for adults and $65 for children 5 to 12. The 5-hour Blue Lagoon tour from the Hanalei River mouth includes a shuttle to/from the Wailua River Marina, snorkeling, bird-watching, and beach time; it's $105 for adults and $95 for children.

Kayak Kauai's Napali tours ($240, including lunch), offered April through September, are only for the very fit who also aren't prone to seasickness; the 12-hour tour requires 5 to 6 hours of paddling, often through large ocean swells, in two-person kayaks. Co-owner Micco Godinez calls it "the Everest of sea kayaking." Trips depart Haena Beach and end at Polihale, with lunch and a rest stop at Milolii Beach, and shuttle to/from Wailua. Guided tours to Kalalau and Milolii for those with camping permits (see "Camping & Cabins," p. 572) are also available, starting at $154 a day (two-person, two-day minimum), as is shuttle service to Haena and Polihale ($60).

Just Live! (www.ziplinetourskauai.com/just-live-kayak-rentals; ℭ **(808) 482-1295**) rents kayaks by reservation and dispenses advice on best beaches and rivers to explore. Single kayaks run $30 a half-day, $50 full; double kayaks, $50 half-day, $70 full. Transport racks are included, but pickup and dropoff can also be arranged. The store is in Harbor Mall, 3501 Rice St., Lihue, between Kalapaki Beach and Nawiliwili Harbor.

Headquartered in Poipu, **Outfitters Kauai** (www.outfitterskauai.com; ℭ **888/742-9887** or 808/742-9667) offers a similar variety of well-organized tours, from a Wailua kayak/waterfall hike ($109 adults, $89 children 5–14, including lunch) to a Napali adventure (mid-May to mid-Sept, $249 ages 15 and older only) and a winter whale-watching paddle from Poipu to Port Allen ($159 adults, $129 children 12–14). The kid-friendly Hidden Valley Falls tour heads 2 miles downwind on the Huleia River and includes a short hike to a swimming hole and a picnic by a small waterfall, with the bonus of a motorized canoe ride back; it's $119 for adults and $99 for children 3 to 14.

Family-owned **Kayak Hanalei** (www.kayakhanalei.com; ℭ **808/826-1881**) offers relaxed, informative guided tours of Hanalei River, with snorkeling in Hanalei Bay, at 8:30am weekdays for $106 adults, $96 children 5 to 12. Daily rentals start at $25 half-day for a single kayak to $75 full-day for a triple, all gear included. No hauling is required; you launch under the colorful "Dock Dynasty" sign behind the store, 5-5070A Kuhio Hwy., *makai* side (behind Hanalei Taro & Juice Co.), Hanalei.

Outrigger Canoe Paddling

The state's official team sport, outrigger canoe paddling epitomizes Hawaiian culture's emphasis on collaboration, understanding of the ocean, and ability to have fun when the opportunity presents itself—that is, to catch a wave. **Kauai Beach Boys** (www.kauaibeachboys.com; ℂ **808/246-6333**) hosts 45-minute outrigger canoe paddling/surfing from Kalapaki Beach at 9am, 11am, and 1pm Sun–Fri, for $50 per person; paddlers must be at least 6 years of age. **Hoku Water Sports** (www.hoku watersports.com; ℂ **808/639-9333**) offers 1-hour paddles ($50) from Kalapaki and Poipu beaches; a steersman helps you spot sea life and, if conditions permit, ride a few exhilarating waves. The rides, which must be booked in advance, depart at 7am and 4pm weekdays; riders must be 10 years or older and weigh no more than 225 lbs.

Scuba Diving

Diving, like all watersports on Kauai, is dictated by the weather. In winter, when heavy swells and high winds hit the island, it's generally limited to the more protected South Shore. Probably the best-known site along the South Shore is **Sheraton Caverns,** located off the Poipu Beach resort area. This site consists of a series of lava tubes interconnected by a chain of archways. A constant parade of fish streams by (even shy lionfish are spotted lurking in crevices), brightly hued Hawaiian lobsters hide in the lava's tiny holes, and turtles often swim past.

In summer, the magnificent North Shore opens up, and you can take a boat dive locally known as the **Oceanarium,** northwest of Hanalei Bay, where you'll find a kaleidoscopic marine world in a horseshoe-shaped cove. From the rare (long-handed spiny lobsters) to the more common (taape, conger eels, and nudibranchs), the resident population is one of the more diverse on the island. The topography, which features pinnacles, ridges, and archways, is covered with cup corals, black-coral trees, and nooks and crannies enough for a dozen dives. Summer is also the best time to go deep in the crystal-clear waters off Niihau, although the afternoon ride back across the channel can still be bumpy.

Seasport Divers ★★★ (www.seasportdivers.com) leads two South Shore boat trips per day; mornings are geared toward experienced divers ($140), early afternoons toward novice or rusty divers ($140 certified, $185 non-certified). From late spring to early autumn, experienced divers shouldn't miss the all-day, 3-tank dive off Niihau and Lehua Rock, home to lobsters, octopus, manta rays, monk seals, and several kinds of generally harmless sharks ($350, Tues and Fri). Seasport operates two well-stocked stores, in Poipu, from where South Shore trips depart (2827 Poipu Rd., across from the fire station; ℂ **808/742-9303**) and Kapaa (4-976 Kuhio Hwy., at Keaka Rd.; ℂ **808/823-9222**).

Also highly rated, and based on the South Shore, **Fathom Five Ocean Quest Divers** (www.fathomfive.com; © **800/972-3078** or 808/742-6991) offers customized boat dives for up to six passengers, starting at $156 for a two-tank dive up to $381 for a three-tank Niihau dive ($43 more for gear rental). The latter uses a custom-built 35-foot boat limited to just six passengers.

Bubbles Below Scuba Charters (www.bubblesbelowkauai.com; © **808/332-7333**) specializes in highly personalized, small-group dives with an emphasis on marine biology. Based in Port Allen, the 36-foot *Kaimanu* is a custom-built Radon dive boat that comes complete with a hot shower, accommodating up to eight passengers; the 31-foot, catamaran-hulled *Dive Rocket,* also custom-built, takes just six. Standard two-tank boat dives cost $140 (if booked directly); it's $255 for the two-tank dive along the Mana Crack, an 11-mile submerged barrier reef, as well as a Napali cruise. Bubbles Below also offers a three-tank trip, for experienced divers only, to more challenging locations such as the "forbidden" island of Niihau, 90 minutes by boat from Kauai, and its nearby islets of Lehua and Kaula; locations vary by time of year and conditions (from $350, including weights, dive computer, lunch, drinks, and marine guide). You should also be willing to share water space with the resident sharks. Ride-alongs for nondivers and crustacean-focused twilight/night dives, as well as bottles of Nitrox, are also available.

GREAT SHORE DIVES Spectacular shoreline dive sites on the North Shore include beautiful **Kee Beach,** where the road ends and the dropoff near the reef begs for underwater exploration (check with lifeguards first). **Cannons,** east of Haena Beach Park, has lots of vibrant marine life in its sloping offshore reef. Another good bet is the intricate underwater topography off **Makua Beach,** widely known as Tunnels. The wide reef here makes for some fabulous snorkeling and diving, especially during the calm summer months. (See "Beaches" on p. 524 for location details.)

On the South Shore, head to the right of the tombolo (sand bar) splitting **Poipu Beach** if you want to catch a glimpse of sea turtles; it's officially known as Nukumoi Point but nicknamed Tortugas (Spanish for "turtle"). The former boat launch at **Koloa Landing,** also known as Whalers Cove, is considered one of the top sites in the Pacific for shore dives for its horseshoe-shaped reef teeming with tropical fish. It's off Hoonani Road, about a quarter-mile south of Lawai Road near the Poipu traffic circle.

If you want a guided shore dive, **Fathom Five Ocean Quest Divers** (see above) will take you out daily for $95 for one tank and $110 for two tanks at Koloa Landing. Spring through fall, it also offers weekday, two-dive shore dives at Tunnels/Makua for $140, with the same rate for a one-tank night dive. **Seasport Divers** (see above) leads twice-daily shore dives from Koloa Landing for both certified divers (1-tank $100, 2-tank $120) and non-certified (1-tank $140, 2-tank $155).

Snorkeling

You can buy snorkel gear at any number of stores on the island, but with luggage fees going up, I find it easier just to rent. **Kauai Bound** (www. kauaiboundstore.com; ✆ **808/320-3779**) provides top-quality snorkel sets, including carrying bags, fish ID card, and no-fog drops, for $8 a day or $28 a week (child's version $5 daily, $20 weekly; full face masks, $10 daily, $45 weekly). You can also rent pro-level underwater cameras ($20–$30 a day), camera accessories, golf clubs, and other gear at its store, in Anchor Cove Shopping Center, 3486 Rice St., Lihue.

Robert Wintner, the quirky founder of the statewide chain **Snorkel Bob's** (www.snorkelbob.com; ✆ **800/262-7725**), is a tireless advocate for reef protection through his Snorkel Bob Foundation. His two stores here rent top snorkel gear for $10 a day ($38 a week) per adult set, $6 a day ($24 a week) per child set; a budget option costs $2.50 a day, $9 a week; masks with corrective lens are also available. The stores also allow 24-hour and interisland drop-offs, and offer discounts on reputable snorkeling cruises. The East Side location (✆ **808/823-9433**) is at 4-734 Kuhio Hwy., Kapaa, just north of Coconut Marketplace, while the South Shore outlet (✆ **808/742-2206**) is at 3236 Poipu Rd., just south of Old Koloa Town.

On the North Shore, **Pedal 'n Paddle** (www.pedalnpaddle.com; ✆ **808/826-9069**) rents adult snorkel sets for $5 a day ($20 weekly) and children's sets for $4 ($15 weekly); it's in Ching Young Village Shopping Center, 5-5190 Kuhio Hwy., *makai* side, in Hanalei.

In general, North Shore snorkeling sites are safest in summer and South Shore sites in winter, but all are subject to changing conditions; check daily ocean reports such as those on **Kauaiexplorer.com** before venturing out. See "Boat & Raft (Zodiac) Tours" for snorkel cruises to the reefs off Napali and Niihau. The following shoreline recommendations apply in times of low surf (see "Beaches" on p. 524 for more detailed descriptions):

EAST SIDE   The two rock-walled ponds at **Lydgate Park** south of the Wailua River are great for novices and children, if it hasn't rained heavily, which makes it too cloudy to see much.

NORTH SHORE   **Kee Beach,** located at the end of Kuhio Hwy., and **Makua (Tunnels) Beach,** about a mile before in Haena, offer the greatest variety of fish; surf is often dangerously high in winter. *Note:* Both are expected to reopen by 2019 after road access was cut off by April 2018 flooding. **Anini Beach,** located off the northern Kalihiwai Road, between Kuhio Hwy. mile markers 25 and 26, south of Princeville, has the most protected waters; avoid the channel in the reef.

SOUTH SHORE   The right side of the tombolo, the narrow strip of sand dividing **Poipu Beach** into two coves, has good snorkeling but can be crowded. You can also follow the beach path west past the Waiohai Marriott to the pocket cove in front of Koa Kea Hotel. A boat ramp leads into the rocky cove of **Koloa Landing** (see "Scuba Diving," above), where on clear days you'll spot large corals, turtles, and plenty of reef fish. (*Note:* Rain brings in stream runoff, which turns the water murky.) Tour groups often visit rock-studded **Lawai Beach** off Lawai Road, next to the Beach House Restaurant; watch out for sea urchins as you swim among parrotfish, Moorish idols, and other reef fish.

WEST SIDE **Salt Pond Beach,** off Kaumualii Hwy. near Hanapepe, has good snorkeling amid hundreds of tropical fish around two rocky points. Check with the lifeguard if you're unsure about the conditions.

Sport Fishing

DEEP-SEA FISHING Kauai's fishing fleet is smaller than others in the islands, but the fish are still out there, and relatively close to shore. All you need to bring is your lunch (no bananas, per local superstition) and your luck. **Sportfish Hawaii** (www.sportfishhawaii.com; ℂ 877/388-1376 or 808/396-2607), which inspects and books boats on all the islands, has prices starting at $675 for a 4-hour exclusive charter (six passengers maximum), up to $1,440 for 8 hours. Rates may be better, though, booking directly through local operators such as Captain Lance Keener at **Ohana Fishing Charters** (www.fishingcharterskauai.com; ℂ 800/713-4682); excursions on the wide and stable 30-foot *Hoo Maikai* out of Kapaa start at $150 per person for a 4-hour shared trip up, to $1,250 for a private 8-hour trip (up to six passengers).

Captain Harry Shigekane of **Happy Hunter Sport Fishing** (www. happyhuntersportfishing.com; ℂ 808/639-4351) offers 4-hour shared charters for $200 per person aboard his 41-foot Pacifica, the *Happy Hunter II,* out of Nawiliwili Small Boat Harbor. Private tours run $700 to $1,300.

FRESHWATER FISHING Freshwater fishing is big on Kauai, thanks to dozens of reservoirs full of largemouth, smallmouth, and peacock bass (also known as *tucunare*). The **Puu Lua Reservoir,** in Kokee State Park, also has rainbow trout and is stocked by the state every year, but has a limited season, in recent years mid-June to late September.

Sportfish Hawaii (www.sportfishhawaii.com; ℂ 877/388-1376 or 808/396-2607) offers guided bass-fishing trips starting at $265 for one or two people for a half-day ($400 for three people) and $375 for one person for a full day ($450 for two, $575 for three), starting at 6:30am in Kapaa. Gear, bait, and beverages are included; gratuity and 4% state tax are not.

Whatever your catch, you're required to first have a **Hawaii Freshwater Fishing License,** available online through the **State Department of Land and Natural Resources** (http://freshwater.ehawaii.gov) or through fishing-supply stores such as **Wal-Mart,** 3-3300 Kuhio Hwy., Lihue (ℂ 808/246-1599), or **Umi's Store,** 4485 Pokole Rd., Waimea (ℂ 808/338-0808). A 7-day tourist license is $11 (plus a $1 convenience fee if purchased online).

Stand-Up Paddleboarding (SUP)

Like everywhere else in Hawaii, stand-up paddleboarding (SUP) has taken off on Kauai. It's easily learned when the ocean is calm, and still easier than traditional surfing if waves are involved. Lessons and equipment are generally available at all beachfront activity desks and the island's surf shops (see "Surfing," below), while Kauai's numerous rivers provide even more opportunities to practice. Kauai native and pro surfer Chava Greenlee runs **Aloha Stand Up Paddle Lessons** (www.aloha suplessonskauai.com; © **808/639-8614**) at Kalapaki Beach, where he first learned to stand-up paddle; the bay offers a large, lagoonlike section ideal for beginners, plus a small surf break for more advanced paddlers. He and his fellow instructors (all licensed lifeguards) also teach SUP in Poipu, just south of the Sheraton Kauai. Two-hour group lessons (eight-person maximum) cost $75 and include 30 minutes on land and 90 minutes on water, both with instructor; sessions are offered four times a day, with private lessons $150 per person. Walk-ups are welcome, but reservations are recommended.

Kauai Beach Boys (www.kauaibeachboys.com) gives 90-minute lessons three times a day at Kalapaki Beach (© **808/246-6333**) and Poipu (© **808/742-4442**); the $79 fee includes a rash guard, which also helps prevent sunburn. Rental gear costs $25 an hour, $70 a day. Also in Poipu, **Hoku Water Sports** (www.hokuwatersports.com; © **808/639-9333**) gives twice-daily 90-minute group lessons ($80); semi-private and private classes are an option ($125–$225). Once you've got the hang of it, rent a board from **Nukumoi Surf Shop,** across from Brennecke's Beach (www. nukumoi.com; © **808/742-8019**), for $20 an hour, $60 for a full day, or $250 a week, including wheels for easy transport.

In Hanalei, launch directly into the river and head to the bay from **Kayak Hanalei** (www.kayakhanalei.com; © **808/826-1881**), 5-5070A Kuhio Hwy., *makai* side, behind Hanalei Taro & Juice. Rental boards are $40 daily, $30 half-day, offered daily; 90-minute lessons are available Monday through Saturday, with group classes $85 for ages 10 and up (semi-private, $110 for ages 8 and up; private, $130 for ages 5 and up). Based in Hanalei Beach Boys Surf Shop, 5-5134 Kuhio Hwy., **Hawaiian Surfing Adventures** (www.hawaiiansurfingadventures.com; © **808/482-0749**) offers 90-minute group classes for $65 to $75; private lessons, for ages 13 and up, costs $100; yoga fans should try the 90-minute SUP yoga class, from $75 per person for a group of four to $150 for a private class.

Outfitters Kauai (www.outfitterskauai.com; © **808/742-9667**) combines a SUP lesson with a 2-mile, downwind paddle on the Huleia River and hike to a swimming hole; a motorized outrigger brings you back up the river. The half-day trip starts at 7:45am and costs $129 for adults and $99 for kids 12 to 14.

Surf's up

Surfing

With the global expansion in surfing's popularity, the most accessible breaks around the island have plenty of contenders. Practice patience and courtesy when lining up to catch a wave, and ask for advice from local surf shops before heading out on your own. **Hanalei Bay**'s winter surf is the most popular on the island, but it's for experts only. **Kalapaki** and **Poipu beaches** are excellent spots to learn to surf; the waves are generally smaller, and—best of all—nobody laughs when you wipe out. To find out where the surf's up, go to **Kauai Explorer Ocean Report** (www.kauaiexplorer.com/ocean_report) or call the **Weather Service** (✆ **808/245-3564**).

Pro surfer and Garden Island native Chava Greenlee runs **Aloha Surf Lessons** (www.alohasurflessonskauai.com; ✆ **808/639-8614**) at both Kalapaki and Poipu, just south of the Sheraton Kauai. Group lessons, offered four times a day, cost $75 and include a short briefing on land, an hour in the water with an instructor, and 30 minutes to surf on your own; private lessons cost $300, but you can include up to four people if you choose. Rates include a rash guard and reef walkers. Reservations are recommended. *Note:* "All-girl" lessons with a female instructor may also be arranged in advance.

Keep practicing in Poipu with a rental from **Nukumoi Surf Shop** (www.nukumoi.com; ✆ **808/742-8019**), right across from Brennecke's Beach at 2100 Hoone Rd., where soft boards cost $8 an hour, $25 a day, or $75 a week; hard (epoxy) boards, for experienced surfers, cost $10 an hour, $30 a day, or $90 a week. Keep surfing at either Kalapaki or Poipu with a rental from **Kauai Beach Boys** (www.kauaibeachboys.com; C **808/246-6333**) for $15 an hour, $25 a day.

If you're staying on the North Shore, consider a lesson from **Hawaiian Surfing Adventures** (www.hawaiiansurfingadventures.com; C **808/ 482-0749**), which offers smaller group lessons (4 students max) that include 90 minutes of instruction, up to an hour of practice, and soft boards for $65; it's $150 for a private class ($100 ages 12 and younger). The exact surf spot in Hanalei will vary by conditions; check-in for lessons is at the **Hawaiian Beach Boys Surf Shop,** 5-5134 Kuhio Hwy., *makai* side (just before Aku Rd. when heading north). Daily rentals start at $20 for soft boards and $25 for the expert epoxy boards, with discounts for longer periods; rent for the same rates at **Hanalei Surf Co.** (www. hanaleisurf.com/rentals; C **808/826-9000**), 5-5161 Kuhio Hwy. (*mauka* side, in Hanalei Center), Hanalei.

Tubing

Back in the days of the sugar plantations, local kids would grab inner tubes and jump in the irrigation ditches crisscrossing the cane fields for an exciting ride. Today you can enjoy this (formerly illegal) activity by "tubing" the flumes and ditches of the old Lihue Plantation with **Kauai Backcountry Adventures** (www.kauaibackcountry.com; C **888/270-0555** or 808/245-2506). Passengers are taken in 4WD vehicles high into the mountains above Lihue to look at vistas generally off-limits to the public. At the flumes, you will be outfitted with a giant tube, gloves, and headlamp (for the long passageways through the tunnels, hand-dug circa 1870). Jump in the water, and the gentle flow will carry you through forests, into tunnels, and finally to a mountain swimming hole, where a picnic lunch is served. The 3-hour tours are $110, open to ages 5 and up (minimum height 43 in., maximum weight 300 pounds). Swimming is not necessary—all you do is relax and drift downstream—but do wear a hat, swimsuit, sunscreen, and shoes that can get wet, and bring a towel, change of clothing, and insect repellent. Tours are offered up to 13 times a day, from 8:30am to 3pm. *Tip:* The water is always cool, so starting midday, when it's warmer, may be more pleasant.

Windsurfing & Kite Surfing

With a long, fringing reef protecting shallow waters, the North Shore's Anini Beach is one of the safest places for beginners to learn windsurfing. Lessons and equipment rental are available at **Windsurf Kauai** (www.windsurf-kauai.com; C **808/828-6838**). Owner Celeste Harzel has been teaching windsurfing on Anini Beach for decades, with special equipment to help beginners learn the sport; she and fellow teacher Lani White offer novice and refresher classes at 10am and 1pm on weekdays and advanced classes by request. A 2-hour lesson is $100 and includes equipment and instruction. Competent windsurfers may rent the equipment for $25 an hour.

Serious windsurfers and kitesurfers (that is, those who travel with their own gear) will want to check out **Haena Beach Park** and **Makua (Tunnels) Beach** on the North Shore (when road access resumes, as expected, before 2019), and the **Mahaulepu** coastline on the South Shore. See "Beaches," p. 524, for details.

OTHER OUTDOOR ACTIVITIES

Biking

Although the main highway has few stretches truly safe for cycling, there are several great places on Kauai for two-wheeling. The **Poipu** area has wide, flat paved roads and several dirt cane roads (especially around Mahaulepu), while the **East Side** has two completed legs of the **Ke Ala Hele Makalae** multi-use trail (www.kauaipath.org/kauaicoastalpath), eventually intended to extend from Anahola to the airport in Lihue. For now, the 2.5-mile Lydgate Park loop connects it with Wailua Beach, while another 4.1-mile leg in Kapaa links Lihi Park to Ahihi Point, just past Kumukumu (Donkey) Beach, 1.5 miles north of Kealia Beach Park. Mountain bikers can also ride the scenic 5-mile **Wai Koa Loop Trail** at the Anaina Hou Community Park (p. 507) in Kilauea (once it repairs flood damages from 2018), or attempt more challenging trails in actual mountains, if it's not too muddy.

Several places rent mountain bikes, road bikes, and beach cruisers, including helmets and locks, with sizeable discounts for multiday rentals. In Poipu, **Outfitters Kauai** (www.outfitterskauai.com; ✆ **888/742-9887** or 808/742-9667) charges $25 a day for hybrid bikes and $25 to $45 for Kona-brand mountain or road bikes; reservations are recommended. The shop is at 2827 Poipu Rd., Poipu, in the Kukuiula Market strip, across from the fire station. Outfitters Kauai also leads twice-daily, 4½-hour **downhill Waimea Canyon bicycle tours** ($109 adults, $89 kids 12–14) that follow the Kokee Road spur to Kekaha. Some find the experience memorable, but I think there are better places on Kauai to cycle, and certainly better ways to see the canyon.

Kapaa has choices for both adventurers itching to explore the single-track trails in the mountains and vacationers just wanting to pedal the coastal path for a couple of hours. **Kauai Cycle** (www.kauaicycle.com; ✆ **808/821-2115**) offers cruisers for $20 a day but specializes in road and mountain bikes for $30 a day ($45 full-suspension), with helmets, locks, maps and advice on current trail conditions. No reservations are needed; just walk in to its store and repair shop, which also sells clothing and gear, at 4-934 Kuhio Hwy., Kapaa, north of Ala Road, *makai* side (across from Taco Bell). Families in particular will want to take note of the shiny Trek beach cruisers, tandems, and trailers from **Coconut Coasters** (www.coconutcoasters.com; ✆ **808/822-7368**) at 4-1586 Kuhio Hwy., Kapaa, just north of Kou Street on the ocean side. Hourly rentals start at $8.50

(half-day, $18); reservations are recommended. **Hele On Kauai Bike Rentals** (www.kauaibeachbikerentals.com; *℡* **(808) 822-4628**) has the best bargains for beach cruisers and children's trailers, at $5 an hour, $15 all day; its main store is on the south end of Ke Ala Hele Makalae, next to Ono Family Restaurant, 4-1286 Kuhio Hwy., Kapaa, with satellite locations in Princeville and Kapaa.

On the North Shore, **Pedal 'n Paddle** in Hanalei (www.pedalnpaddle.com; *℡* **808/826-9069**) rents beach cruisers for $15 a day ($60 weekly) and hybrids for $20 ($80 weekly); reservations are recommended during holidays and summer months. It's in the Ching Young Village Shopping Center, 5-5190 Kuhio Hwy., *makai* side.

Birding

Kauai provides more than 80 species of birds—not counting the "wild" chickens seen at every roadside attraction. Coastal and lowland areas, including the wildlife refuges at Kilauea Point (p. 509) and along the Hanalei River, are home to introduced species and endangered native waterfowl and migratory shorebirds; the cooler uplands of Kokee State Park shelter native woodland species, who were able to escape mosquito-borne diseases that killed off lowland natives. David Kuhn of **Terran Tours** (*℡* **808/335-0398**) leads custom bird-watching excursions that spot some of Hawaii's rarest birds, using a four-wheel-drive (4WD) vehicle to access remote areas. Rate start at $300 for a half-day, with longer periods available; e-mail info@soundshawaiian.com for details.

Many pairs of endangered nene, the endemic state bird, call Princeville's **Makai Golf Club** home, as do mating and nesting Laysan albatross in winter; for $60 a cart, you can ogle them, their carefully marked nests, and spectacular scenery on a self-guided, six-stop **sunset golf cart tour ★★★** (www.makaigolf.com; *℡* **808/826-1863**).

Golf

It's no wonder that Kauai's exceptional beauty has inspired some exceptionally beautiful links. More surprising is the presence of two lovely, inexpensive public courses: the 9-hole **Kukuiolono** on the South Shore, and the even more impressive 18-hole **Wailua Golf Course** on the East Side; see details below. *Note:* Greens fees listed here include cart rentals unless stated otherwise.

Value-seekers who don't mind occasionally playing next to a Costco and suburban homes—amid panoramas of several soaring green ridges—will appreciate **Puakea** (www.puakeagolf.com; *℡* **808/245-8756**), part of AOL founder Steve Case's portfolio. Greens fees for 18 holes are $85 before 11am, $65 after; it's $45 for 9 holes anytime. The links are centrally located, at 4150 Nuhou St., off Nawiliwili Road, Lihue.

To play the newest course on the Garden Island, you'll need to be a guest in one of the Lodge at Kukuiula cottages, bungalows, or villas, starting at $750 a night (www.lodgeatkukuiula.com; ℭ **800/325-5701**). Along with members of **Kukuiula** (www.kukuiula.com; ℭ **855/742-0234**), Lodge guests have exclusive access to Tom Weiskopf's 18-hole, rolling course through gardens, orchards, and grasslands, and a practice facility; greens fees are $210.

Wherever you play, money can't buy your way out of dealing with trade winds, so start early for the best scores.

EAST SIDE

Hokuala Golf Club ★★   The former Kauai Lagoons Golf Club is now part of the new Timbers Resort development, Hokuala, which plans to add a boutique hotel and retail center to its luxurious private homes. Jack Nicklaus originally designed the 18-hole, oceanfront Kiele Course (since renamed the **Ocean Course**) in the late 1980s, returning in 2011 to create even more spectacularly sited links with views of Ninini Point Lighthouse, Kalapaki Bay, and Haupu Mountain. Timbers renovated and reopened the course in late 2016, and it's as stunning as ever. Facilities include a driving range, snack bar, pro shop, practice greens, clubhouse and rentals; Hualani's, the resort's restaurant, is also open to the public.

3351 Hoolaulea Way, Lihue, next to Marriott's Kauai Lagoons–Kalanipuu and Kauai Marriott Resort. www.hokualakauai.com/golf. ℭ **808/241-6000.** Greens fees $198, $167 11am–2pm, $126 after 2pm; 9 holes $159.

Wailua Golf Course ★★   Highly rated by both *Golf Digest* and the Golf Channel, this coconut palm–dotted, largely seafront course in windy Wailua has hosted three U.S. amateur championships. Along the *makai* (ocean) side of the main highway, the first nine holes were built in the 1930s; the late Kauai golf legend Toyo Shirai designed the second nine in 1961. Nonresident rates start at just $48 (plus $20 for a cart) for 18 holes. Facilities include a locker room with showers, driving range, practice greens, and club rentals.

3-5350 Kuhio Hwy., *makai* side, Wailua, 3 miles north of Lihue airport. www.kauai.gov/golf. ℭ **808/241-6666.** Greens fees $48 weekdays (5-round weekday pass good for 3 months, $215), $60 weekends/holidays, half-price after 2pm. Motorized cart $20 ($11 for 9 holes), pull cart $7 ($5 for 9 holes).

NORTH SHORE

Makai Golf Club ★★★   This gem of a course—the first on the island to be designed by Robert Trent Jones, Jr.—has extra luster now that the nearby Prince Course has gone private. It's already gained favor with non-golfers by offering self-guided **sunset golf cart tours** ★★★ ($60 per cart; ℭ **808/826-1863**), with a map to memorable vistas, flora, and fauna (including nesting Laysan albatross in winter), plus **sunrise yoga** on the 7th hole at 7:30am Monday and Wednesday ($20; cash only). For golfers, it's worth noting that Jones returned in 2009 to remake the 27 holes he created here in 1971. The resulting 18-hole championship Makai Course winds around ocean bluffs and tropical forest with compelling sea and mountain views, including Mount Makana. There's a "time par" of 4 hours, 18 minutes, here, to keep golfers on track (otherwise they might be gawking at the scenery all day). Sadly, the family-friendly 9-hole Woods Course is in rough shape, and likely not worth taking a swing at. Other facilities include a clubhouse, a pro shop, practice facilities, the Makai Grill restaurant, and club rentals. *Note:* "Dynamic" pricing means greens fees vary by time, season, and demand, but all guests of a Kauai hotel are eligible for a $225 rate.

4080 Lei O Papa Rd., Princeville. www.makaigolf.com. ℂ **808/826-1912.** Greens fees vary, but standard rate is $270; 3-day and 6-day "flex passes," $500 and $869, respectively. Check online for discounts. Mahalo Mixer at 4pm Mon includes full swing clinic, several holes on the front 9, sparkling wine toast at sunset, and comme- morative glasses for $99/couple. Nonrenovated Woods Course, $65 for adults; $28 for ages 6–15 unaccompanied by adult; free for ages 6–15 with paying adult. From Lihue, take Kuhio Hwy. to the Princeville entrance, turn right, go 1 mile and course is on the left.

SOUTH SHORE

Kiahuna Golf Club ★ This par-70, 6,353-yard course designed by Robert Trent Jones, Jr., is a veritable wildlife sanctuary, where black-crowned night herons, Hawaiian stilts, and moorhens fish along Waikomo Stream, and outcroppings of lava tubes by the second fairway hold rare blind spiders. Keep your eyes peeled for remains of a stone-walled *heiau* (temple) and a Portuguese home from the early 1800s, whose former inhabitants lie in a nearby crypt—and watch out for the mango tree on the par 4, 440-yard hole 6. Facilities include a driving range, practice greens, club rentals, and **Paco's Tacos Cantina**, offering a lovely view and Mexican fare for breakfast and lunch, with American classics (pancakes, omelettes) also on the breakfast menu.

2545 Kiahuna Plantation Dr. (off Poipu Rd.), Koloa. www.kiahunagolf.com. ℂ **808/742-9595.** Greens fees $96, $60 for 9 holes or after 3pm, $47 for juniors 17 and under with paying adult.

Kukuiolono Golf Course ★★ Although not on a resort, this 9-hole hilltop course has unbeatable views to match an unbeatable price: $9 for all day, plus $9 for an optional cart. The course is part of woodsy **Kukui-olono Park ★** (p. 514), which includes a Japanese garden and Hawaiian rock artifacts; both the garden and the course were developed by pineapple tycoon Walter McBryde, who bequeathed it to the public in 1930. The course is well maintained, given the price, with relatively few fairway hazards (barring a wild pig now and then). Facilities include a driving range (just $2), practice greens, club rental, and a **Paco's Tacos Cantina** restaurant in the clubhouse.

Kukuiolono Park, 854 Puu Rd., Kalaheo. ℂ **808/332-9151.** Greens fees $7 weekday, $9 weekend, optional cart rental $9; cash only. From Lihue, take Kaumualii Hwy. west into Kalaheo, turn left on Papalina Rd., and drive uphill for nearly a mile. Look for sign at right; the entrance has huge iron gates and stone pillars.

Poipu Bay Golf Course ★★ This 7,123-yard, par-72 course with a links-style layout was, for years, the home of the PGA Grand Slam of Golf. Designed by Robert Trent Jones, Jr., the challenging course features undulating greens and water hazards on eight of the holes. The par-4 16th hole has the coastline weaving along the entire left side. The most striking hole is the 201-yard par-3 on the 17th, which has an elevated tee next to an ancient *heiau* (place of worship) and a Hawaiian rock wall along the fairway. A twice-weekly self-guided **sunset golf cart tour** ★★ ends at Hole 15, overlooking Kawailoa Bay. Facilities include a restaurant, lounge, locker room, pro shop, club and shoe rentals, and practice facilities (off grass).

2250 Ainako St. (off Poipu Rd., across from the Grand Hyatt Kauai), Poipu. www. poipubaygolf.com. ✆ **808/742-8711.** Greens fees (includes $5 resort fee): $200 before noon; $184 after noon; back 9, 7am–8am, $115; first 7 holes anytime, $85. **Sunset golf cart tour,** times vary Sun and Wed; $50 per cart; call to reserve.

Hiking

As beautiful as Kauai's drive-up beaches and waterfalls are, some of the island's most arresting sights aren't reachable by the road: You've got to hoof it. Highlights are listed below; for descriptions of the 35 trails in Kauai's state parks and forestry reserves, check out **Na Ala Hele Trail & Access System** (http://hawaiitrails.ehawaii.gov; ✆ **808/274-3433**).

Note: When heavy rains fall on Kauai, normally placid rivers and streams overflow, causing flash floods on some roads and trails. Check the weather forecast, especially November through March, and avoid dry streambeds, which flood quickly. Always bring ample drinking water; stream water is unsafe to drink due to the risk of leptospirosis.

For guided hikes, Micco Godinez of **Kayak Kauai** (www.kayak kauai.com; ✆ **888/596-3853** or 808/826-9844) is just as expert on land as he is at sea. He and his savvy guides lead regular trips (with shuttles from the Wailua River Marina) through Waimea Canyon to Waipoo Falls ($126) and through Kokee to dazzling overlooks of Napali via the Nualolo or Awaawapuhi trails ($126). In Kapaa, they lead clients up Nounou, or Sleeping Giant ($81), and Kuilau Ridge ($85), Departing from Poipu Beach Park, naturalists with **Kauai Nature Tours** (www.kauainature tours.com; ✆ **888/233-8365** or 808/742-8305) lead a similar variety of day hikes, focusing on Kauai's unique geology, environment, and culture; they're $155 to $185 adults and $135 to $155 for children 7 to 12, including lunch.

The Kauai chapter of the **Sierra Club** (www.sierraclubkauai.org) offers four to seven different guided hikes around the island each month, varying from easy 2-milers to 7-mile-plus treks for serious hikers only; they may include service work such as beach cleanups and trail clearing. Listings on the online "outings calendar" include descriptions and local phone contacts; requested donation per hike is $5 adults and $1 for children under 18 and Sierra Club members.

WATERFALL ADVENTURE: rappelling

Gain a unique perspective of two hidden waterfalls—by walking down them. Technically, you're rappelling on the 30- and 60-foot cataracts, with help from guide Charlie Cobb-Adams of **Island Adventures** (www.islandadventureskauai.com; ℱ **808/246-6333**). A Native Hawaiian nicknamed "Hawaiian Dundee," Cobb-Adams leads a practice session on a 25-foot wall before a 15-minute hike near the Huleia National Wildlife Refuge to the otherwise off-limits falls. The 5.5-hour tour ($179 per person) departs from Lihue at 8:30am Monday, Wednesday, and Saturday. A more family-friendly, 4.5-hour tour with kayaking instead of rappelling (but including a swim in a waterfall pool) departs at 8:30am Tuesday and 11am Friday ($112 adults, $89 children ages 6–12.) Both tours include cultural insights and a deli lunch.

EAST SIDE

The dappled green wooded ridges of the Lihue-Koloa and Nounou forest reserves provide the best hiking opportunities here. From Kuamoo Road (Hwy. 580) past Opaekaa Falls, you can park at the trailhead for the easy, 2-mile **Kuamoo Trail,** which connects with the steeper, 1.5-mile **Nounou West Trail;** both have picnic shelters. Stay on Kuamoo Road till just before the Keahua Arboretum to pick up the scenic, 2.1-mile **Kuilau Trail,** often used by horses, which can be linked with the more rugged, 2.5-mile **Moalepe Trail,** ending at the top of Olohena Road in Kapaa. In the arboretum, you'll find the trailhead for the challenging **Powerline Trail,** an unmaintained path that follows electric lines all the way to Princeville's Kapaka Street, on the *mauka* side of Kuhio Highway; avoid if it's been raining (the mud can suck your sneakers off, or worse). A steady climb, but worth the vista at the top, is the 2-mile **Nounou East Trail,** which takes you 960 feet up the mountain known as Sleeping Giant (which does look like a giant lying down); the trail ends at a picnic shelter on his "chest," and connects with the west leg about 1.5 miles in. The east trailhead, which has parking, is on Haleilio Road in Kapaa; turn inland just past mile marker 6 on Kuhio Highway and head 1¼ miles uphill.

NORTH SHORE

Traversing Kauai's amazingly beautiful Napali Coast, the 11-mile (one-way) **Kalalau Trail** is the definition of breathtaking: Not only is the scenery magnificent, but even serious hikers will huff and puff over its extremely strenuous up-and-down route, made even trickier to negotiate by winter rains. It's on every serious hiker's bucket list, and a destination for seemingly every young backpacking bohemian on the island. That's one reason a camping permit ($20 per night; http://camping.ehawaii.gov) is required for those heading beyond Hanakapiai Beach; the permits often sell out up to a year in advance (see "Camping & Cabins," p. 572).

The magnificent Kalalau Trail

People in good physical shape can tackle the 2-mile stretch from the trail head at Kee Beach to Hanakapiai, which starts with a mile-long climb; the reward of Napali vistas starts about a half-mile in. You may see a barefoot surfer on the first 2 miles, but wear sturdy shoes (or hiking boots) and a hat, and carry plenty of water. The trail can be very narrow and slippery; don't bring children who need carrying. Sandy in summer and mostly rocks in winter, Hanakapiai Beach has strong currents that have swept more than 80 visitors to their deaths; best just to admire the view. Those able to rock-hop can clamber another 2 miles inland to the 120-foot Hanakapiai Falls, but only when it has not been raining heavily. Allow 3 to 4 hours for the round-trip trek to the beach, and 7 to 8 hours with the falls added in. *Note:* The trail closed indefinitely for repairs after historic flooding in April 2018, which also cut off road access.

Nearly as beautiful, but much less demanding and much less crowded, is the 2.5-mile **Okolehao Trail** in Hanalei, which climbs 1,232 feet to a ridge overlooking Hanalei Bay and the verdant valley. (Avoid during or after heavy rain; it gets slippery fast.) The trail starts at a parking area off Ohiki Road, inland from Kuhio Hwy.; take an immediate left just past the Hanalei Bridge and look for the parking lot on the left and the trailhead across a small bridge to the right. Be sure to brake for nene (geese).

If you don't mind paying for the privilege, **Princeville Ranch Adventures** (www.princevilleranch.com; © **808/826-7669**) leads guided hikes on private land along the five tiers of **Kalihiwai Falls**. The 4.5-hour tour ($129) involves 3 hours of hiking, a 500-foot ascent to a point with sweeping North Shore views, a scramble down a 10-foot rock wall, and swimming below an 80-foot cascade; it's open to ages 5 and up.

SOUTH SHORE

At the end of Keoneloa (Shipwrecks) Beach, in front of the Grand Hyatt Kauai, the limestone headland of Makawehi Point marks the start of the **Mahaulepu Heritage Trail** (www.hikemahaulepu.org), an easy coastal walk—after the first few minutes uphill—along lithified sand dunes, pinnacles, craggy coves, and ancient Hawaiian rock structures. Inland lie the green swath of Poipu Bay Golf Course, Makauwahi Cave Reserve (p. 514), and the Haupu summit. Keep a safe distance from the fragile edges of cliffs, and give the green sea turtles and endangered Hawaiian monk seals a wide berth, too. It's 1.5 miles to the overlook of Mahaulepu (Gillin's) Beach, and then—if the landowner permits it—another 2 miles to windy Haula Beach.

WEST SIDE

Some of Hawaii's best hikes are found among the 45 miles of maintained trails in **Kokee State Park** (p. 517), 4,345 acres of rainforest with striking views of the Napali Coast from up to 4,000 feet above, and the drier but no less dazzling **Waimea Canyon State Park** (p. 520). Pick up a trail map and tips at the **Kokee Museum** (www.kokee.org; © **808/335-9975**), which also describes a number of trails in the two parks on its website.

The best way to experience the bold colors and stark formations of Waimea Canyon is on the **Canyon Trail,** which starts after a .8-mile forested walk down and up unpaved Halemanu Road, off Kokee Road (Hwy. 550) between mile markers 14 and 15. From there, it's another mile to a small waterfall pool, lined with yellow ginger, that lies above the main cascade of 800-foot **Waipoo Falls;** you won't be able to see the latter, but you can hear it and gaze far across the canyon to try to spot the lookout points you passed on the way up. On the way back, check out the short spur called the **Cliff Trail** for more vistas. (*Note:* Families can hike this trail, but be mindful of the steep dropoffs.)

Two more challenging hikes beckon in dry conditions. The 6.2-mile round-trip **Awaawapuhi Trail** takes at least 3 hours—1 hour down, 2 hours coming back up, depending on your fitness level—but it offers a jaw-dropping overlook for two Napali valleys: Awaawapuhi (named for the wild ginger blossom) and Nualolo. Usually well maintained, it drops about 1,600 feet through native forests to a thin precipice with a guardrail at the overlook. The trailhead is just past mile marker 17 on Kokee Road at a clearing on the left. *Note:* After extensive work to repair erosion, the 2-mile Nualolo Cliff Trail once again connects the Awaawapuhi Trail with the even more strenuous 8-mile Nualolo Trail.

Slippery mud can make the **Pihea Trail** impassable, but when the red clay is firm beneath your feet, it's another must-do for fit hikers. Starting at the end of the Puu O Kila Lookout at the end of Kokee Road (Hwy. 550), the trail provides fantastic views of Kalalau Valley and the distant ocean before turning into a boardwalk through a bog that connects with the **Alakai Swamp Trail,** which you'll want to follow to its end at the Kilohana Overlook; if it's not socked in with fog, you'll have an impressive view of Wainiha Valley and the North Shore. The Pihea-Alakai Swamp round-trip route is 8.6 miles; allow at least 4 hours and be prepared for drizzle or rain.

Horseback Riding

Ride a horse across the wide-open pastures of a working ranch under volcanic peaks and rein up near a waterfall pool, or explore a pristine shoreline hidden by former sugarcane fields: You'll see parts of Kauai many have missed, while helping keep its treasured *paniolo* (cowboy) culture alive. Pack a pair of jeans or long pants and closed-toe shoes.

CJM Country Stables ★★ A trail ride through the rugged Mahaulepu region, passing through former plantation fields and natural landscape to the untrammeled sandy beaches under the shadow of Haupu Ridge, may well be the highlight of your trip. CJM's standard rides both include 2 hours of riding, but the **Secret Beach Picnic Ride** ($140) adds an hour for lunch and beach exploration; reserve early. Private rides, which allow paces faster than a walk, are also available for a minimum of 2 riders, starting at $210 per rider for a 90-min. ride. *Note:* CJM also hosts rodeos throughout the year that are open to the public; click "Events" on the website for details.

Off Poipu Rd., Poipu. From Grand Hyatt Kauai, head 1½ miles east on unpaved Poipu Rd. and turn right at sign for stables. www.cjmstables.com. © **808/742-6096. 2-hr. Mahaulepu Beach Ride:** $110; Mon–Sat 9:30am and 2pm. **3-hr Secret Beach Picnic Ride:** $150; Wed and Fri 1pm.

Princeville Ranch Adventures ★★ There's no nose-to-tail riding at this working North Shore ranch, owned by descendants of the area's first missionaries. Instead, horses amble across wide-open pastures with mountain and ocean views as you learn about Kauai's *paniolo* (cowboy) history and distinctive landscape. The popular **"ride n' glide"** option ($149) takes you to a secluded valley that you then traverse via ziplines (see "Ziplining," below), while the **Waterfall Picnic Ride** ($149) leads to a short (but steep) hike down to a trail leading to a swimming pool at the base of an 80-foot waterfall; after a picnic lunch, you'll climb out via a 10-foot rock wall. Both rides last 3 hours, with 90 minutes in the saddle. Less exertion is required on the 2-hour **Paniolo Ride** ($119) through lush pastures and the occasional herd of cattle. *Note:* Tours go out rain or shine, just like the cowboys.

Check in *makai* side of Kuhio Hwy., just north of mile marker 27, Princeville. www. princevilleranch.com. © **888/955-7669** or 808/826-7669. **Ride N' Glide:** $149; Mon–Sat 1:30pm; ages 10 and older. **Waterfall Picnic Ride:** $149; Mon–Sat 9am, noon, and 1pm (also at 8am June–Aug); ages 8 and older. **Paniolo Ride:** $119; Tues–Sat 10am; ages 8 and older. Rental shoes $5.

Silver Falls Ranch Stables ★★   The wide falls here may not be as impressive as the taller ones on Princeville Ranch, but the swimming hole is equally refreshing and the scenery just as stimulating. The 300-acre ranch in Kalihiwai Valley features an 80-acre tropical garden and close-up views of the 2,800-foot-tall Makaleha Range. The 2-hour **Silver Falls Ride** ($119) includes a barbecue picnic that's a cut above the usual sandwich fare, plus a dip in the waterfall pool, while the 90-minute **Hawaiian Discovery Ride** ($99) follows flower-lined streams through the garden, home to more than 150 species of palms. Combine the two itineraries on the 3-hour **Tropical Trail Adventure** ($139). All rides are open to ages 7 and up; private rides and rides for children ages 5 and 6 are also available, for surcharges ranging from $40 to $115 per ride.

Kamookoa Rd., Kilauea. From Lihue, take Kuhio Hwy. north past mile marker 24 to a left turn on Kahiliholo Rd. at Kalihiwai Ridge sign; follow 2¼ miles to a left on Kamookoa Rd. www.silverfallsranch.com. ✆ **808/828-6718. Discovery Ride:** $99. **Silver Falls Ride:** $119. **Tropical Trails:** $139. All rides offered 3 times daily 9am–3:30pm June–Aug, twice daily Sept–May.

Tennis

Public tennis courts are managed by the **Kauai County Parks and Recreation Department** (www.kauai.gov/parks; ✆ **808/241-4460**). Its website (click on "Park Facilities") lists the 24 public tennis courts around the island, 20 of which are lighted and all of which are free. *Note:* Lights are shut off September 15 to December 15 to protect endangered shearwater fledglings, which may be misdirected by them. Other courts open to the public include the eight resurfaced courts (four hard court, four artificial turf) at the Peter Burwash International Facility of **Hanalei Bay Resort,** Princeville (www.hanaleibayresort.com/tennis; ✆ **808/821-8225**). Court fees are $15 per person per day; the resort also offers private lessons, daily clinics, and a pro shop. Also in Princeville, the **Makai Club** (www.makaigolf.com; ✆ **808/826-1912**) charges $15 per player for 90 minutes on one of its four courts, with biweekly drop-in clinics, weekly men's and women's clinics, and private lessons available.

The South Shore is brimming with resort courts—including **Grand Hyatt Kauai, Poipu Kai Resort, Nihi Kai Villas,** and **Kukuiula**—but they're restricted to overnight guests. Guests in **Kiahuna Plantation** units managed by Castle Resorts (see p. 569) have access to the otherwise members-only four tennis courts, resort pool, and other facilities at the **Poipu Beach Athletic Club;** so do guests in rentals of **Great Vacation Retreats** (www.alohagvr.com; ✆ **866/541-1033**) for a $100 weekly fee per property, covering up to 8 people.

On the East Side, the **Hokuala Golf Club** (p. 546) offers access to its lushly landscaped, four-court Tennis Garden for $20 for 2 hours.

Ziplining

Kauai apparently has Costa Rica to thank for its profusion of ziplines, the metal cable-and-pulley systems that allow harness-wearing riders to "zip" over valleys, forests, and other beautiful but inaccessible areas. After reading about Costa Rica's rainforest canopy tours, Outfitters Kauai co-founder Rick Haviland was inspired to build the Garden Isle's first zipline on Kokee Ranch in 2003. Others soon followed, with ever longer, higher, and faster options. It may seem like a splurge, but keep in mind that ziplines not only offer an exhilarating rush and breathtaking views; they also help keep the verdant landscape gloriously undeveloped.

Be sure to book ahead, especially for families or groups—because of the time spent on harness safety checks, tour sizes are limited—and read the fine print about height, age, and/or weight restrictions. Tours usually go out rain or shine, except in the most severe weather, and include a snack. As with all excursions, plan to tip your guides ($10–$20 per rider).

SOUTH SHORE   A 2,500-foot swoop over the Waita Reservoir is the highlight of the eight-line course ($149) at **Koloa Zipline,** opened in 2012 (www.koloazipline.com; © 877/707-7088 or 808/742-2894). For just $10 more, the harness option called Flyin' Kauaian allows you to soar head-first over most of the lines on the 3½- to 4-hour tour. Check in at the office at 3477-A Weliweli Rd., Koloa, in the Kauai ATV office behind the Old Koloa Town shops. **Skyline Eco Adventures** (www.zipline.com/kauai; © **888/864-6947** or 808/878-8400) opened its eight-line course above Poipu in 2013 and shares a different legend of Kauai for each of the progressively longer, faster lines on the 2½- to 3-hour tour. The cost is $140 for eight zips, $100 for five (with 50% off for one child or teen for each paid adult, and 10% online discount for everyone else); check in at the office at Shops at Kukuiula, 2829 Ala Kalanikaumaka St., Poipu.

EAST SIDE   Lush, 4,000-acre Kipu Ranch hosts the nine lines of **Outfitters Kauai** (www.outfitterskauai.com; © **888/742-9887** or 808/742-9667), including suspension bridges, tandem lines, and a "zippel" (a zipline/rappelling combo) over picturesque streams and waterfalls. The scenery will be familiar from hit movies such as *Jurassic Park*, *Raiders of the Lost Ark*, and *The Descendants*. The latest addition is Hawaii's longest zipline, the 4,000-foot FlyLine, which also boasts the tallest launchpad at 50 feet high; you ride it prone like a superhero on tandem lines. At $50 for a 1-hour tour, the FlyLine is ideal for those on a budget or tight schedule. You can also try the FlyLine on the four-zip, 2½-hour **AdrenaLine Kauai Zipline Tour** ($129 adults, $119 ages 7–14), which starts with an 800-foot zipline and also includes an 1,800-foot tandem line and a zip that ends at a swimming hole. The 4½-hour **New Treehouse Plus Tour** adds the FlyLine to six different zips, with stories of Kauai and Kipu Ranch shared along the way ($149 adults, $139 children). Check in for these zips

ESPECIALLY FOR kids

Climbing the Wooden Jungle Gyms at Kamalani Playground (p. 506) Located in Lydgate Park, Wailua, this unique playground has a maze of jungle gyms for kids of all ages, including an actual labyrinth. Spend an afternoon whipping down slides, exploring caves, hanging from bars, and climbing all over.

Exploring a Magical World (p. 510) **Na Aina Kai Botanical Gardens** sits on some 240 acres, sprinkled with around 70 life-size (or larger-than-life-size) whimsical bronze statues, hidden off the beaten path of the North Shore. The tropical children's garden features a gecko maze, a tropical jungle gym, a treehouse in a rubber tree, and a

16-foot-tall Jack-and-the-Beanstalk giant with a 33-foot wading pool below. Family tours take place Tuesday through Friday; book well in advance.

Riding an Open-Sided Train (p. 506) The **Kauai Plantation Railway** at Kilohana Plantation is a trip back in time (albeit on new tracks and replica cars) to the sugarcane era, with younger kids exhilarated just by the ride. Parents can justify it as an informal botany class, since passengers learn about the orchards, gardens, and forests they pass along the 2½-mile journey. Children of all ages will enjoy the stop to feed goats, chickens, and wild pigs (as long as they watch their fingers).

at the new visitor center, 230 Kipu Rd., Lihue. My favorite, the all-day **Kipu Zipline Safari** ($189 adults, $149 children 3 to 14), includes three ziplines (open to ages 7 and up), an easy 2-mile kayak on the Huleia River, a short hike, wagon ride, swimming, and lunch; for check-in and gear rentals, go to the Outfitters Kauai store, 2827 Poipu Rd., across from the fire station, in Poipu.

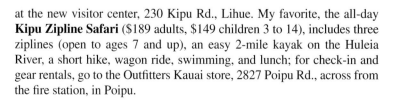

Kauai Backcountry Adventures (www.kauaibackcountry.com; ℂ **888/270-0555** or 800/245-2506) offers excursions through 17,000 acres of former sugarcane fields above Lihue. In addition to its unique tubing ride (see "Tubing," p. 543), the company has a seven-line zip course leading from the lush mountainside to a bamboo grove, where you can take a dip in a swimming hole; the 3-hour tour leaves at 9am and 1pm weekdays ($125). A 5-hour tour ($169) with a side trip to multitiered Halii Falls for a picnic and swim departs at 10am Wed and Fri. Check in at the office at 3-4131 Kuhio Hwy., Hanamaulu, between Hanamaulu Rd. and Laulima St.

Just Live! Zipline Tours (www.ziplinetourskauai.com; ℂ **808/482-1295**) offers three ecology-focused, treetop tours ranging from 2½ to 4½ hours ($79–$125). All glide over a multi-hued forest canopy, and the longest includes a 60-foot rock climbing wall and 100-foot rappelling tower. Check online for daily deals ($10–$15 discounts). Check-in at the Just Live! store in Harbor Mall, 3501 Rice St., Lihue, between Kalapaki Beach and Nawiliwili Harbor.

NORTH SHORE   If you just want to zip nine fast lines over a verdant valley, then take the 3½-hour **Zip Express** ($139) offered by **Princeville Ranch Adventures** (www.princevilleranch.com; ℂ **888/955-7669** or 808/826-7669). But it would be a shame, particularly in summer, to miss the chance to swim in a waterfall pool offered by the 4½-hour **Zip N' Dip** ($159, including picnic lunch). The company also pairs ziplines with its popular horseback rides ($149) and kayak/hike excursions ($159 adults, $99 ages 5–11). *Note:* The latter excursion, called **Jungle Valley Adventure,** is unique in that it allows children as young as 5 and weighing as little as 50 pounds to zip on the two 400-foot-plus lines included on the tour.

WHERE TO STAY ON KAUAI

To avoid long drives, it pays to base your lodgings on the kind of vacation you envision, and consider dividing your time among locations. The island's East Side makes the most sense for those planning to divide their time equally among island sights; however, the best resorts for families and winter weather are on the South Shore. The most gorgeous scenery and best ocean conditions in summer are on the North Shore. If you plan to hike more than a day in Waimea Canyon or Kokee, or want to experience the island's low-key lifestyle, the West Side will suit.

Taxes of 14.42% are added to all hotel bills. Parking is free, and pools are outdoors unless otherwise noted. Parking, Wi-Fi, and resort fees where applicable are charged daily; "cleaning" fees refer to one-time charges for cleaning after your stay, not daily housekeeping—the latter often available for an additional fee for condos and other vacation rentals.

hot-button issue: **VACATION RENTALS & B&BS**

As on other Hawaiian Islands, vacation rentals and bed-and-breakfasts outside of areas zoned for tourism have become a hot-button issue for many on Kauai. Since 2008, owners of all such rentals and B&Bs have needed permits to operate, with special restrictions on agricultural land; the benefit for guests is knowing your lodgings conform to planning and safety codes, the taxes you're paying are actually going to the county, and your stay won't be in jeopardy of a surprise shutdown. B&Bs and vacation rentals must display their permit number (often starting with TVR or TVNC) on any online advertising, and post a sign on the premises listing that number, plus the name and phone number of an on-island emergency contact.

The Kauai Visitors Bureau also urges special caution when booking a vacation rental online from sources other than licensed agencies, such as those listed here. Some visitors, usually those who paid by check or money order, have arrived on island only to discover their unit belongs to somebody else; they had no place to stay and no recourse to recover their payments.

For condos, keep in mind that companies that manage multiple properties in a complex may be able to find you another unit if you're dissatisfied with your view or problems arise during your stay. Happily, more management companies are now advertising their listings on VRBO.com, Airbnb.com, and other DIY sites—but they are eliminating daily maid service and other niceties to remain competitive. Always read the fine print before you arrive to know what to expect.

East Side

Convenient to all parts of the island (except during rush hour), Lihue and the Coconut Coast have the greatest number of budget motels and moderately priced beachfront hotel rooms and condos, along with a couple of posh resorts. Rural Anahola and upcountry Kapaa are outside the official "visitor destination area," so their B&Bs and vacation rentals may not be licensed. *Note:* Much of the East Side's most iconic hotel, the **Coco Palms** (of *Blue Hawaii* fame), was demolished in 2017, 25 years after Hurricane Iniki forced its closure. Plans to rebuild it as a Hyatt Unbound resort have slowed due to permit and ownership disputes.

In addition to the properties below, consider a condo at one of two oceanfront complexes in Kapaa. At the 84-unit **Kapaa Shore ★**, 4-900 Kuhio Hwy., the nine condos managed by Garden Island Properties (www.kauaiproperties.com; © **800/801-0378** or 808/822-4871) start at $145 a day for a one-bedroom, one-bath unit to $185 for a two-bedroom, two-bath unit (plus $115–$130 cleaning and $85 in other fees). At the more upscale **Lae Nani ★★**, 410 Papaloa Rd. (off Kuhio Hwy.), Outrigger (www.outrigger.com; © **866/956-4262** or 808/823-1401) manages about a quarter of the 83 one- and two-bedroom units ($209–$369 nightly; cleaning $175–$225); perks include a lighted tennis court, pool, and beach with child-friendly, rock-walled swimming area.

For more privacy, check out the two elegantly furnished cottages in a leafy setting known as **17 Palms Kauai Vacation Cottages ★★** (www.17palmskauai.com; ✆ **888/725-6799**), a block away from Wailua Bay. Rates for the one-bedroom, one-bathroom Hale Iki (sleeps two adults, plus a small child) start at $189 a night, plus $110 cleaning; the two-bedroom, one-bathroom Meli Meli (sleeps four adults, plus a small child) starts at $239, plus $145 cleaning. Tucked off busy Kuamoo Road in Kapaa, but with easy access to the Wailua River (kayaks provided), the pleasant **Fern Grotto Inn ★** (www.ferngrottoinn.com; ✆ **808/821-9836**) has six quaint cottage units (most sleeping two), for $200 to $275 a night, plus $100 to $150 cleaning, and the upscale, three-bedroom, three-bath **Ohana House ★★** (sleeps up to six), from $325 nightly and $250 cleaning; check online for last-minute 25% discount.

EXPENSIVE

Kauai Marriott Resort ★★★   This 10-story, multiwing hotel—the tallest on Kauai since opening in 1986—may be what prompted the local ordinance that no new structures be higher than a coconut tree, but it would be hard to imagine the island without it. Superlatives include Kauai's largest swimming pool, a sort of Greco-Roman fantasy that would fit in at Hearst Castle; its location on watersports-friendly Kalapaki Beach; and the popular beachfront restaurant, **Duke's Kauai** (p. 575), among other dining choices. The long escalator to the central courtyard lagoon, the immense statuary, and handsome lobby sporting a koa outrigger canoe make you feel like you've arrived somewhere truly unique. Harbor Mall and Anchor Cove shopping centers, with more restaurants, are within a short walk; in the opposite direction lies the 18-hole championship golf course of Hokuala. Rooms tend to be on the smaller side but feel plush and look chic, with hues of taupe and burnt umber. Book at least a partial ocean view—Nawiliwili Harbor, the bay, and the rugged green Haupu ridge provide a mesmerizing backdrop.

Note: The "vacation ownership" **Marriott's Kauai Beach Club** (www.marriott.com/lihka; ✆ **800/845-5279** or 808/245-5050) shares the grounds with access to all its facilities. You can book a guest room, "parlor" room with wall bed and kitchenette, or one-bedroom/two-bathroom and two-bedroom/two-bathroom "villas" with kitchenettes (from $259–$559 nightly). There's no resort fee, or charges for Wi-Fi, but self-parking costs $25. Guests at the newer, nearby **Marriott's Kauai Lagoons—Kalanipuu** (www.marriott.com/lihkn; ✆ **800/845-5279** or 808/632-8200) do *not* have privileges to use the Kauai Marriott's pool or its lounge chairs at Kalapaki Beach (reached by a hillside elevator or free shuttle), but it offers roomier, two-bedroom/two-bathroom and three-bedroom/

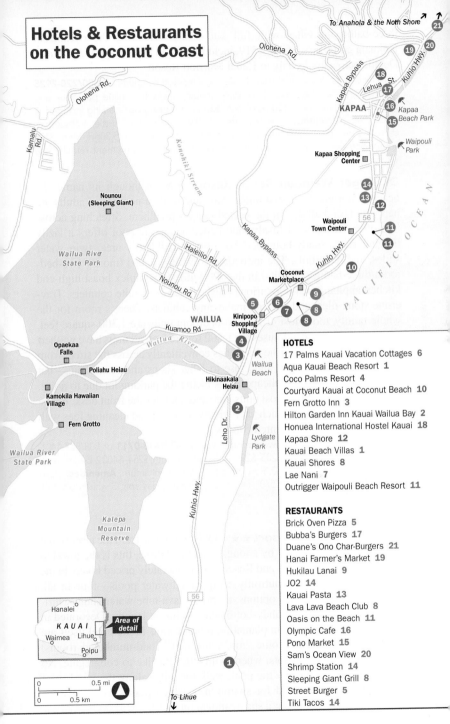

Hotels & Restaurants on the Coconut Coast

To Anahola & the Noth Shore

Olohena Rd.

Kapaa Bypass

Lehua St.

Kuhio Hwy.

KAPAA

Kapaa Beach Park

Waipouli Park

Kamalu Rd.

Olohena Rd.

Konohiki Stream

Nounou (Sleeping Giant)

Kapaa Shopping Center

Kapaa Bypass

Wailua River State Park

Haleilio Rd.

Nounou Rd.

Waipouli Town Center

56

PACIFIC OCEAN

Coconut Marketplace

WAILUA

Kuamoo Rd.

Kinipopo Shopping Village

Kuhio Hwy.

Wailua River

Opaekaa Falls

Poliahu Heiau

Wailua Beach

Hikinaakala Heiau

Kamokila Hawaiian Village

Fern Grotto

Leho Dr.

Lydgate Park

Wailua River State Park

Kalepa Mountain Reserve

56

Kuhio Hwy.

HOTELS

17 Palms Kauai Vacation Cottages **6**
Aqua Kauai Beach Resort **1**
Coco Palms Resort **4**
Courtyard Kauai at Coconut Beach **10**
Fern Grotto Inn **3**
Hilton Garden Inn Kauai Wailua Bay **2**
Honuea International Hostel Kauai **18**
Kapaa Shore **12**
Kauai Beach Villas **1**
Kauai Shores **8**
Lae Nani **7**
Outrigger Waipouli Beach Resort **11**

RESTAURANTS

Brick Oven Pizza **5**
Bubba's Burgers **17**
Duane's Ono Char-Burgers **21**
Hanai Farmer's Market **19**
Hukilau Lanai **9**
JO2 **14**
Kauai Pasta **13**
Lava Lava Beach Club **8**
Oasis on the Beach **11**
Olympic Cafe **16**
Pono Market **15**
Sam's Ocean View **20**
Shrimp Station **14**
Sleeping Giant Grill **8**
Street Burger **5**
Tiki Tacos **14**

KAUAI
Hanalei
Waimea Lihue
Poipu

Area of detail

0   0.5 mi
0   0.5 km

To Lihue

three-bathroom villas with full kitchens, overlooking the oceanfront Hokuala golf course (from $519, including Wi-Fi and self-parking). *Note:* Details below apply only to Kauai Marriott Resort.

3610 Rice St. (at Kalapaki Beach), Lihue. www.marriott.com/lihhi. ℂ **800/220-2925** or 808/245-5050. 356 units. $339–$539 double; check for online packages and discounts. Rollaway $35. $30 resort fee. $30 valet parking (self-parking included in resort fee). **Amenities:** 5 restaurants; 2 bars; free airport shuttle; babysitting; children's program; concierge; fitness center; 5 Jacuzzis; luau (5:30pm Mon; $108 adults, $56 ages 6–12); pool; room service; watersports equipment rentals; free Wi-Fi.

Outrigger Waipouli Beach Resort ★★ Although its namesake beach is not good for swimming, kids and quite a number of adults are happy to spend all day in the heated fantasy pool here. Stretching across two of the resort's 13 lushly landscaped acres, the pool offers a lazily flowing river, sandy-bottomed hot tubs, a children's area, twin water slides, and waterfalls. The individually owned condos (mostly two-bedroom/three-bathroom units) in the $200-million complex boast high-end kitchen appliances and luxurious finishes such as granite counters, Travertine stone tiles, and African mahogany cabinets. There's room for the whole family, too: Most of the two-bedroom units are 1,300 square feet, while a few corner penthouses are 1,800 square feet; all units have washer/dryers and central A/C. The resort lies conveniently across the street from a Safeway grocery store and close to other shops and restaurants—but you'll want to avoid the cheaper units facing the parking lot due to noise. Outrigger manages the most units here and operates the front desk, but be sure to compare rates (which vary widely by view) and cleaning fees with those of independently rented condos.

4-820 Kuhio Hwy., Kapaa. www.outrigger.com. ℂ **877/418-0711** or 808/823-1401. 196 units. From $185 studio; $205–$295 1-bedroom/2-bath; $254–$400 2-bedroom/3-bath. Cleaning fee $140–$250. Resort fee $20. 2-night minimum. **Amenities:** Oasis on the Beach restaurant (p. 578); fitness center; pool; day spa; 3 whirlpools; free Wi-Fi.

MODERATE

Aqua Kauai Beach Resort ★★ Only 5 minutes from the airport, but hidden from the highway by a long, palm-lined drive, this is the jewel in the crown of Aqua Hotels and Resorts' 18 moderately priced hotels in the islands, thanks to its beautifully sculpted saltwater pools—four in all, with adult and children's options, a 75-foot lava-tube water slide, whirlpools, waterfalls, and a sandy-bottomed beachfront lagoon. Decorated in a Balinese wood/Hawaiian plantation motif, rooms in the hotel itself are on the small side, and some "mountain view" (odd-numbered rooms) units overlook parking lots, where wild chickens like to congregate. No matter: You can linger by the pool, walk for miles along the windswept beach (not recommended for swimming), which passes by the Wailua Golf Course, or indulge in a spa treatment onsite.

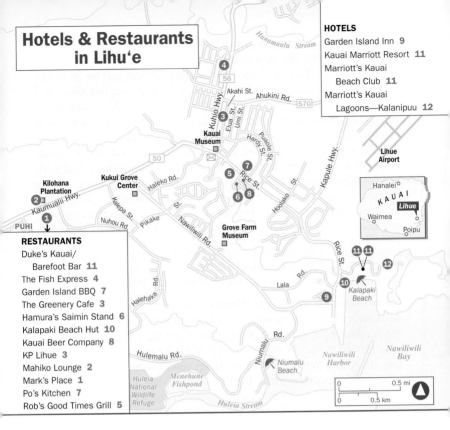

Hotels & Restaurants in Lihuʻe

Hanamaulu Stream

Akahi St. Ahukini Rd. 570

Kuhio Hwy. 56

Elua St. Umi St.

Kauai Museum

Hardy St. Puaole St.

50

Haleko Rd.

Rice St.

Hoolako St.

Kapule Hwy.

Lihue Airport

Inset: **Hanalei** — **KAUAI** — **Lihue** — Waimea — **Poipu**

Kilohana Plantation

Kukui Grove Center

Kaumualii Hwy.

Kalepa St.

Nuhou Rd. Pikake St.

Nawiliwili Rd.

PUHI

Grove Farm Museum

Rice St.

Lala Rd.

Kalapaki Beach

Halehaka Rd.

Hulemalu Rd.

Niumalu Rd.

Niumalu Beach

Nawiliwili Harbor

Nawiliwili Bay

Huleia National Wildlife Refuge

Menehune Fishpond

Huleia Stream

0   0.5 mi
0   0.5 km

Note: A number of hotel rooms are also individually owned "condos"; you'll find lower daily rates when booking through an owner, but you'll pay an extra $80 in resort/cleaning fees, with maid service upon request ($15–$30 daily). The 25-acre resort is also home to the **Kauai Beach Villas,** one- and two-bedroom condos operated as timeshares or privately owned rentals, all with access to the hotel facilities, for a daily resort fee. **Kauai Vacation Rentals** (www.kauaivacationrentals.com; ☏ **800/367-5025** or 808/245-8841) manages the majority of the nontimeshare units, with daily rates starting at $145, plus $125 cleaning and $35 reservation fees. Details below apply only to the Aqua Kauai Beach Resort hotel.

4331 Kauai Beach Dr., Lihue. From the airport, drive 2½ miles northeast on Hwy. 51 (Kapule Hwy.) to Kuhio Hwy. and .6-mile later turn right on Kauai Beach Dr. www.kauaibeachresorthawaii.com. ☏ **866/536-7976** or 808/245-1955. 350 units. $170–$279 double; $370–$580 suite. Check for online specials. Extra person $45. Rollaway $20. Resort fee $25. **Amenities:** 2 restaurants; cafe; lounge; pool bar; free airport/shopping/golf shuttle; babysitting; concierge; fitness center; 2 Jacuzzis; laundry facilities; 4 pools; rental cars; room service; spa and salon; free Wi-Fi.

Courtyard Kauai at Coconut Beach ★★ This centrally located Marriott hotel wins the most raves for its oceanfront courtyard and pool, offering fire pits, fountains, and a large whirlpool spa, and for its twice-weekly, entertaining oceanfront luau (www.luaumakaiwa.com; ☏ **800/763-0120;** $99–$129 adults, $65–$79 ages 4–12). A well-manicured lawn separates the hotel from golden-sand Makaiwa Beach, which is too reefy to do much swimming in, but just the ticket for long walks. Rooms, most of which are just 320 square feet, have lanais with cinnamon-wood shutters (to match the dark-veneered, Hawaiian-style decor), and two-thirds have at least partial ocean views. For more space, book a premium oceanfront room (528 sq. ft.). The comprehensive $20 resort fee includes self-parking, Wi-Fi, two cocktails, yoga class, and beach gear.

650 Aleka Loop, Kapaa. www.courtyardkauai.com. ☏ **877/997-6667** or 808/822-3455. 311 units. $209–$263 standard double, $331 premium room. Check for online packages. Extra person $25. Children 17 and under stay free in parent's room. Resort fee $20. Valet parking $5. **Amenities:** Restaurant; luau; bar; business center; fitness center; Jacuzzi; pool; room service; spa; basketball/tennis court; free Wi-Fi.

Hilton Garden Inn Kauai Wailua Bay ★★ This 10-acre property has a great location for families: next to the protected swimming/snorkeling ponds of Lydgate Beach, the fanciful Kamalani Playground, and historic Hawaiian sites by the Wailua River. Under new management as of late 2017, the "refreshed" rooms, suites, and cottages now have crisp white bedding, contemporary lighting, and splashes of orchid and gold in the room's cushions, artwork, and ottomans to offset the sand-hued carpets and sofa beds. All units come with minifridges, microwaves, and Keurig coffeemakers; some oceanview rooms and all cottages (which are closest to Kamalani Playground) include lanais. *Note:* Wi-Fi and parking are free, but the hotel has added a daily $22 resort fee, which includes bike rentals, a daily cocktail or soft drink, and beach mat and cooler use.

3-5920 Kuhio Hwy., Kapaa. www.hiltongardeninn.com. ☏ **808/823-6000.** 216 units. $159 double, $209 oceanview; $209–$269 oceanview suites with sofa bed; $299 1-bedroom cottage; check online discounts and packages. Extra person $30. Children 18 and under stay free in parent's room. **Amenities:** Restaurant; bar; business center; fitness room; Jacuzzi; coin laundry; 2 pools; free Wi-Fi.

INEXPENSIVE

Young backpackers and adventurous adults on a shoestring budget should consider **Honuea International Hostel Kauai** (www.kauaihostel.com; ☏ **808/823-6142**) in historic Kapaa. Bunks in the three, 10-bed single-sex and mixed dorm rooms (one bathroom per dorm) start at $31 per person, including taxes; for the three female and mixed private rooms, rates range from $53 to $66. The two deluxe private rooms, which share a bathroom, have the nicest setting, in the main house, for $79 a night.

Garden Island Inn ★★ Thrifty travelers will love this cheerily renovated, well-maintained motel within a short walk of Kalapaki Beach, shops, and restaurants, while families will appreciate the large suites (with up to one king-size bed with three twin beds) and extra guest fees of just $10 per person. It's easy to make breakfast on the cheap, too, thanks to the minifridge, microwave, wet bar, and kitchenware, plus standard coffeemaker—the front desk even offers free coffee and snacks. Other freebies include parking, Wi-Fi, and use of beach gear, not to mention happily given advice. Hanalei artist Camile Fontaine's bright, island-inspired murals and paintings make this a welcome antidote to neutral, cookie-cutter resort decor, while owners Lis and Steve Layne work tire-lessly to improve their guests' comfort, even providing DVDs of movies made on Kauai to watch on flatscreen TVs. One caveat: Use earplugs to offset street noise. The inn also manages **Hale Kalapaki,** a pair of two-bedroom condos ($190; sleep six) at nearby, hilltop Banyan Harbor, which boasts an oceanview pool and wooded trail.

3445 Wilcox Rd. (across from Kalapaki Beach, near Nawiliwili Harbor), Lihue. www.gardenislandinn.com. © **800/648-0154** or 808/245-7227. 21 units. $145–$180 double. Extra person $10. **Amenities:** Free watersports and beach gear; free Wi-Fi.

Kauai Shores ★★ This renovated beachfront bargain features small but functional rooms with slightly quirky, IKEA-style furnishings (curvy mirrors, square lamps), bright blue geometric-patterned rugs, and very compact bathrooms. No need to hole up in your room, though: The ocean-view pool is inviting, while the oceanfront **Lava Lava Beach Club** (p. 578) serves three meals daily, with a full bar, indoor/outdoor seating, and nightly live entertainment. Swimming isn't safe here, but children can splash in the rock-walled ocean pool in front of Lae Nani next door, and the Lydgate Beach ponds are just a short drive away. Yoga classes take place on the oceanfront lawn three mornings a week. *Note:* Request a second-floor room for more privacy (if you can carry your own bags), and a room not adjacent to the parking lot.

420 Papaloa Rd. (off Kuhio Hwy.), Kapaa. www.kauaishoreshotel.com. © **855/309-5483** or 808/822-4951. 206 rooms. $139–$169 double; studio suite with kitchenette $185. Check for online discounts. Extra person $25. $21 resort fee (includes Wi-Fi, DVDs, PlayStation, yoga classes, beach chairs and towels, and parking). **Amenities:** 2 pools; barbecue grills; bar; business center; coin laundry; restaurant; free Wi-Fi.

North Shore

Despite this magical region's popularity with visitors, only Princeville is officially one of Kauai County's "visitor destination areas." It's important to be aware that many rural vacation rentals may be unlicensed, and unhappy neighbors have been known to report them to authorities, leading to at least one abrupt shutdown. If you're not staying in a hotel, I recommend booking through one of the following agencies, which manage only licensed properties, or checking closely for the permit number in online listings on VRBO.com or other platforms.

Kauai Vacation Rentals (www.kauaivacationrentals.com; © **800/ 367-5025** or 808/245-8841) has managed well-maintained homes and condos across the island since 1978, with the majority (91 at press time) on the North Shore. Most have a 3- to 5-night minimum that expands to 1 week or 2 weeks from December 15 to January 6, when rates also rise. You can search online listings by location, size, view, air-conditioning (not so common where trade winds blow), and swimming pool; agents can also help you find the perfect match. In **Haena,** for one example, the standard rate for Hale Pua Kai, a one-bedroom, one-bathroom garden-view cottage that's a short walk to Makua (Tunnels) Beach is $235 a night; for Nakea Cottage, an oceanview, two-bedroom, one-and-a-half-bathroom cottage across the road from **Anini Beach,** it's $380 a night, discounted to $1,900 for a weekly stay—a good deal if you're splitting the expenses with another couple. For all rentals, you'll also pay a $35 reservation fee and one-time cleaning fee, anywhere from $90 for a studio condo to as high as $565 for a five-bedroom house.

Parrish Collection Kauai (www.parrishkauai.com; © **800/325-5701** or 808/742-2000), represents 10 homes and cottages from Kilauea to Haena and 40 properties (nearly all condos) in Princeville. Many of the latter are in the **Hanalei Bay Resort ★★**, which has spectacular views rivaling those of the St. Regis, air-conditioning in units, and a recently redone fantasy pool with waterfalls, slides, and so forth; rates start at $209 a night (3-night minimum) for a gardenview one-bedroom with two baths (sleeps four). If you can forgo an ocean view, Parrish's best values are in the **Plantation at Princeville ★**, roomy two- and three-bedroom air-conditioned units in a complex built in 2004 with a pool, spa, barbecues, and fitness center; rates start at $150 for a two-bedroom, two-bathroom unit. Not included in Parrish's rates are the $50 "processing" fee and cleaning fees, starting at $94 for a studio and increasing by size.

Coldwell Banker Bali Hai Realty (www.balihai.com; © **808/826-8000**) manages about 75 luxury vacation rentals, all of them licensed. Expect a 7-night minimum June through August and December 15 to January 5; otherwise, it's 4 to 5 nights. Princeville properties include nine units at the desirable **Pali Ke Kua ★** and **Puu Poa ★★** complexes, less than a half-mile from each other on the bluff above Hideaways Beach. At Pali Ke Kua, nightly rates start as low as $135 for a two-bedroom, two-bathroom mountainview unit, and $200 for a similar unit with ocean view. Its lowest rate at Puu Poa is $330 a night for a two-bedroom, two-bathroom oceanview penthouse unit, ideal for couples to share. Add a reservation fee of $50 and a cleaning fee of $200 to $250 to bookings.

A frequent resource for Hollywood film crews, Mike Lyons of **Kauai Style Vacation Rentals** (www.kauaistyleconcierge.com; © **808/482-1572**) specializes in exquisite, high-end properties on the North Shore; only three (starting at $1,200 a night) are listed online because he prefers to work with clients individually. A passionate surfer, Lyons also enjoys escorting guests on ocean and trail adventures and can arrange private chefs and other services.

EXPENSIVE

In addition to the listings below, consider the posh, residential-style **Cliffs at Princeville** ★★ (www.cliffsatprinceville.com; ✆ **808/826-6129**), on the northern edge of the Princeville bluff. Its 202 one-bedroom, two-bathroom units (sleeping four) offer a full kitchen, living room, and two lanais starting at $375 ($435 for loft units that sleep six), plus a weekly resort fee of $75. The three-story Cliffs has no elevators or A/C, but it does have two tennis courts, fitness center, playground, pool, two hot tubs, and a mini putting green, among other amenities.

Hanalei Colony Resort ★★★ With two bedrooms (separated by louvered wooden doors), 1½ to two bathrooms, full kitchens, and living rooms, these 48 individually owned, updated condos are perfect for families—or anyone who can appreciate being as few as 10 feet from the beach in the shadow of green peaks near the end of the road. It has no TVs, phones, or entertainment systems, although free Wi-Fi means guests don't disconnect quite as much as they used to. The beach is generally not safe for swimming, but you're less than a mile from Makua (Tunnels) Beach, and the barbecue area by the small pool boasts lush landscaping and a koi pond. The resort operates a 13-passenger shuttle to Hanalei, Princeville, and various beaches; the independently run Ayurvedic-themed **Hanalei Day Spa** and Hawaiian fusion **Opakapaka Grill and Bar** (p. 579) restaurant, with excellent cocktails, are on site. Check online for romance and activity packages. *Note:* Undamaged by the April 2018 flood, the resort had to close temporarily while awaiting road access to be restored.

5-7130 Kuhio Hwy., *makai* side, Haena, about 5 miles west of Hanalei. www.hcr.com. ✆ **800/628-3004** or 808/826-6235. 48 units. $309–$476 suite. 2-night minimum; 7th night free. Fourth person $50. Resort fee: $20. **Amenities:** Restaurant; coffee bar/art gallery; free weekly continental breakfast; babysitting; barbecues; concierge; Jacuzzi; coin laundry; luau; pool; spa; free Wi-Fi.

St. Regis Princeville ★★ The state's first and only St. Regis—a brand renowned for its opulence and service—opened in 2009, following a multimillion-dollar transformation of the Princeville Hotel. The dramatic cliffside layout didn't change: You enter on the ninth floor, with a dazzling panorama of Hanalei Bay and Makana (the "Bali Hai" mountain) across the airy lobby and an elevator to take you down to the narrow but pleasant sandy beach and 5,000-square-foot infinity pool. The spacious (540 sq. ft. and up) rooms still feature extra-large bedroom windows as well as "magic" bathroom windows, which toggle between clear and opaque, but no balconies. Families should consider the Ocean View Terrace rooms, which open onto the pool level. A welcome sheen of sophisticated Hawaiiana infuses the resort, typified by the 11,000-square-foot

Halelea Spa, which combines traditional Hawaiian healing practices and local botanicals with Western treatments.

5520 Ka Haku Rd., Princeville. www.stregisprinceville.com. ℂ **877/787-3447** or 808/826-9644. 252 units. $490–$711 double; $830 jr. suite; $1,585–$4,160 St. Regis and larger suites. Extra person $100. Children 17 and under stay free in parent's room; no rollaways. Resort fee $30. Parking (valet only) $34. **Amenities:** 3 restaurants; 3 bars; butler service in suites; children's program; coffee bar; concierge; seasonal Polynesian dinner show ($149 adults, $75 ages 6–12); fitness center; Makai Club golf and tennis access with shuttle by reservation; Jacuzzis; pool; room service; spa; watersports rentals; free Wi-Fi.

Westin Princeville Ocean Villas ★★★   A superb "vacation ownership" property that nonetheless offers nightly rentals, this 18½-acre bluff-side resort is a winner with families and couples seeking condo-style units with resort furnishings and amenities. Besides Westin's justly famed "Heavenly Beds," the roomy studios and one-bedroom suites (which can be combined into two-bedroom units) have immaculate, well-stocked kitchens, washer/dryers, and huge bathrooms with separate glass showers and deep whirlpool tubs. Playful statuary and fountains mark the centrally located children's pool next to the main pool; adults will appreciate the quieter, bluff-side plunge pools. **Nanea Restaurant and Bar,** one of the better hotel restaurants on Kauai, has substantial discounts for children 11 and younger, and creates a bimonthly tasting dinner with wine pairings for a farm tour at the off-site Waipa Foundation. *Note:* Since the nearby unmaintained trail to Anini Beach is steep and often muddy, most guests opt to take the free shuttle to the St. Regis Princeville, where they walk down nearly 200 steps to Puu Poa Beach, or drive themselves to Anini or another beach.

3838 Wyllie Rd., Princeville. www.westinprinceville.com. ℂ **808/827-8700.** 346 units. From $360 studio; $495 1-bedroom; $810 2-bedroom. Parking $13. **Amenities:** 2 restaurants; bar; deli/store; barbecues; children's program; concierge; fitness room w/steam room and sauna, plus use of Makai Club Lap Pool and Fitness Center, 1 mile away; golf at Makai Club; 4 pools; free resort shuttle; free Wi-Fi.

MODERATE

The best values on the North Shore can be found among Princeville's many condo complexes, which vary widely in age and amenities; check the listings of the brokers mentioned above. Larger groups should consider splitting costs in the new oceanfront **Orchid Point** triplex, where the top floor's three-bedroom, 3½-bath unit includes a guest studio with kitchenette (www.vrbo.com/998642); rates average $325 a night, plus $225 cleaning fee and $142 VRBO fee. Also peruse updated units at the dramatically perched, 22-acre **Hanalei Bay Resort ★★** (www.hanaleibayresort.com; ℂ **877/344-0688**), known for its fantasy pool. It participates in timeshare and rental programs but offers direct bookings, too, from $149 for a studio (512 sq. ft.) with kitchen, lanai, and pull-out sofa bed (but no other bed); one-bedroom suites (1,091 sq. ft.) sleep four and start at $269. Rates exclude the $20 daily resort fee.

South Shore

The most popular place to stay year-round, the resort area of Poipu Beach is definitely a "visitor destination area," with hundreds of rental condos, cottages, and houses vying with Kauai's best luxury resorts for families and a romantic boutique hotel. Upcountry Lawai and Kalaheo brim with more modest, not necessarily licensed, B&Bs and vacation homes.

EXPENSIVE

Grand Hyatt Kauai Resort & Spa ★★★   The island's largest hotel aims to have one of the smallest carbon footprints. Its 602 luxurious rooms feature not only pillow-top beds and Toto toilets, but also eco-friendly elements such as recycled-yarn carpets and plush robes made from recycled plastic bottles. Grass-covered roofs and solar panels reduce emissions, a hydroponic garden grows produce for its dining outlets (such as the thatched-roof **Tidepools** restaurant), and used cooking oil becomes biodiesel fuel. But that's just green icing on the cake of this sprawling, family-loving resort where the elaborate, multitiered fantasy pool and saltwater lagoon more than compensate for the rough waters of Keoneloa (Shipwrecks) Beach. The 45,000-square-foot indoor/outdoor **Anara Spa** and adjacent **Poipu Bay Golf Course** offer excellent adult diversions, as do the fire pits overlooking the pool by **Dondero's** Italian restaurant. To feel even more virtuous about splurging on a stay, check out the hotel's volunteer programs with the National Tropical Botanical Garden and Kauai Humane Society, among others.

1571 Poipu Rd., Poipu. www.grandhyattkauai.com. ✆ **800/554-9288** or 808/742-1234. 602 units. $479–$619 double; from $739 Grand Club; from $939 suite. $35 resort fee includes self-parking, Wi-Fi, fitness classes, and more. Children 17 and under stay free in parent's room. Packages available. Valet parking $25. **Amenities:** 6 restaurants; 4 bars; babysitting; bike and car rentals; children's program; club lounge; concierge; fitness center; golf course and clubhouse; 3 Jacuzzis; 1½-acre saltwater swimming lagoon; luau; 2 nonchlorinated pools connected by river pool; room service; spa; 2 tennis courts; watersports rentals; free Wi-Fi.

Koa Kea Hotel & Resort ★★★   This oceanfront jewel box hides between the sprawling Kiahuna Plantation Resort and the densely built Marriott Waiohai Beach Club. A chic boutique inn with arguably the island's best hotel restaurant, **Red Salt ★★★** (p. 586), it takes its name from Hawaiian words for "white coral," which inspires the white and coral accents in the sleek, modern decor. All rooms feature lanais, many with views of the rocky coast (a short walk from sandy beaches). Nespresso coffee makers and L'Occitane bath products suggest Europe, but the staff resounds with pure Hawaiian aloha. *Note:* At these prices, the "garden view" may disappoint—best to spring for an ocean view.

2251 Poipu Rd., Poipu. www.koakea.com. ✆ **888/898-8958** or 808/828-8888. 121 units. $389–$499 gardenview double; $429–$729 oceanview or oceanfront double; from $899 oceanview suite. $39 resort fee includes valet parking, Wi-Fi, fitness

A PERFECT PLACE in poipu

The best way to find a high-quality, licensed vacation rental in Poipu is through **The Parrish Collection Kauai** (www.parrishkauai.com; ✆ **800/325-5701** or 808/742-2000). Parrish manages more than 300 units for 25 different island-wide condo developments, plus dozens of vacation houses ranging from quaint cottages to elite resort homes; about three-quarters are in Poipu. The company maintains resortlike standards, classifying its lodgings into four categories ("premium plus" is the highest, for new or completely renovated units), sending linens for professional laundering, and providing luxe bathroom amenities. **Waikomo Stream Villas** ★, **Nihi Kai Villas** ★★, and **Poipu Kapili** ★★, where the company manages about half the condos (100 in total), each has a concierge desk—with no kickbacks for referrals, according to owner J. P. Parrish. "Our staff knows the island really well and has no agenda; we only recommend what works for each guest," he notes.

Each well-equipped rental offers a full kitchen, washer/dryer, TV/DVD, phone, and free Wi-Fi; you'll pay a one-time cleaning and $50 to $100 in reservation fees. At Nihi Kai Villas, which has a heated pool (a rarity here) and large floor plans, off-peak nightly rates start at $175 for a two-bedroom condo (sleeps six),

plus $166 cleaning; at Waikomo Stream Villas, a garden-view one-bedroom condo (sleeps four) starts at $125 a night, plus a $136 cleaning fee. The more luxurious Poipu Kapili, overlooking the ocean, offers a saltwater pool and two tennis courts; one-bedroom, two-bath units (sleeps four) start at $250 a night, plus $199 cleaning; two-bedroom, three-bath units from $350, plus a $259 cleaning fee. The recently built **Nalo Bungalow,** a cheerily decorated 3-bedroom, 3½ bath, two-story cottage with ocean views, is perfect for multifamily rentals, starting at $400 a night, plus $420 cleaning fee.

Parrish is also the exclusive agent for the luxuriously appointed villas, cottages, and bungalows of the heavenly **Lodge at Kukuiula** ★★★. Guests gain access to the sprawling, residential Kukuiula resort's private, ultra-posh spa, championship golf course, pool, farm, ocean activities and superb clubhouse dining (from $750 a night, plus a $250 cleaning fee; see www.lodgeatkukuiula.com for details).

Condos typically have a 3-night minimum stay and houses, 5 nights. Ask about the **Frommer's Preferred Guest Discount,** good for 5% to 10% off of 5-night or longer stays; Parrish also offers a price-matching guarantee.

center and classes, and more. **Amenities:** Restaurant; 2 bars; bike and watersports rentals; concierge; fitness room; Jacuzzi; pool; room service; spa; free Wi-Fi.

Koloa Landing Resort ★★★ It may not have the best, or any, beachfront, but otherwise this brilliantly transformed 25-acre resort (now part of Marriott's Autograph Collection) deals in several superlatives. Among them are Kauai's largest residential-style hotel villas—studios to three-bedrooms, with Wolf and SubZero appliances. Koloa Landing also has the best pool complex, including a water slide, sprawling main pool with terraces, grottos, and undulating rock walls, plus two outlying pools, all with Jacuzzis. Renowned restaurateur Sam Choy designed the enticing menus for its casual **HoloHolo Grill** (p. 584) and weekly Royal Luau (summer only). It's a short walk to shops and a 5-minute drive to Poipu Beach. *Note:* Rooms with "resort views" may overlook the parking lot.

2641 Poipu Rd., Poipu. www.koloalandingresort.com. ✆ **808/240-6600**. 306 units. From $240 studio; from $309 1-bedroom; from $501 2-bedroom; from $628 3-bedroom. $30 resort fee includes parking, 2 mai tais, Wi-Fi, more. Valet parking $12. **Amenities:** Restaurant; 2 bars; fitness room; 3 pools; 3 Jacuzzis; luau (June–Aug); food market with cafe; spa: free Wi-Fi.

Sheraton Kauai Resort ★★★   This appealingly low-key resort lives up to its ideal beachfront location, where the western horizon sees a riot of color at sunset and rainbows arc over a rocky point after the occasional shower. The oceanfront pool—with rock-lined whirlpool and luxurious bungalows and cabanas (for rent)—provides an inviting place for a dip, conveniently making the traditional pool in the Mauka garden wing a quieter oasis. Nights here are lively, too, thanks to large fire pits in the oceanview courtyard and the tasty libations and wine-tasting social hours at **RumFire Poipu Beach ★★**, an ambitious, island-inspired restaurant/lounge with walls of glass. *Tip:* Ask for a room in the ocean wing, to avoid frequent street crossings; its rooms seem larger, too.

2440 Hoonani Rd., Poipu. www.sheraton-kauai.com. ✆ **866/716-8109** or 808/742-1661. 391 units. $275–$436 double; from $674 suite. $31 resort fee includes self-parking, Wi-Fi, fitness center, bicycles, and more. Extra person $70. Valet parking free first night, $10 nightly after. **Amenities:** 3 restaurants; bar; babysitting; concierge; cultural lessons, fitness room; Jacuzzi; luau; 2 pools; room service; spa services; watersports rentals; torch lighting; free Wi-Fi.

MODERATE

Besides the listings below, the 35-acre, green-lawned **Kiahuna Plantation Resort ★★**, on the sandy beach next to the Sheraton, is also worth considering, although its 333 individually furnished, one- and two-bedroom condos vary widely in taste; they also rely on ceiling fans (and trade winds) for cooling, and there's no elevator in the three-story buildings. **Outrigger** (www.outrigger.com; ✆ **808/742-6411**) manages more than half of the units, but only those rented from **Castle Resorts** (www.castle resorts.com; ✆ **800/367-5004** or 808/545-5310) receive daily housekeeping and access to the tennis courts and resort-style pool of the Poipu Beach Athletic Club across the street. Outrigger's nightly one-bedroom rates start at $169 gardenview and $199 oceanview, plus $175 cleaning, while Castle's equivalent units start at $149 and $209, respectively, plus $50 to $120 cleaning (depending on length of stay). Both Outrigger and Castle include free Wi-Fi and parking in their rates.

Among other options outside of Poipu, **Kauai Banyan Inn ★** (www. kauaibanyan.com; ✆ **808/645-6527**) in rural Lawai offers three airy vacation suites, all with gleaming wood floors, Hawaiian quilts, and kitchenettes or full kitchens. Co-owners Lorna and John Hoff, who live on the

11-acre compound that they helped build years ago, offer detailed advice as well as make-your-own breakfast fixings; rates range from $155 to $230 per night, plus $45 to $55 cleaning.

Kauai Cove ★★ Honeymooners and other romance seekers find a serene oasis on a quiet lane close to the cove at Koloa Landing, and a short walk to a sandier cove known as Baby Beach. The bright cottage provides a four-poster canopy queen-size bed under high vaulted ceilings, private bamboo-walled lanai with barbecue grill, flatscreen TV with DVD player, and full kitchen. Since it can get hot in Poipu, the wall-unit A/C (along with ceiling fan) is a nice touch. Helpful owners E. J. and Diane Olsson live nearby in Poipu Kai, where they also rent out the attractive Palm Room studio and one-bedroom Royal Kauai suite.

Cottage: 2672 Puuholo Rd., Poipu. www.kauaicove.com. ℂ **808/631-9313.** $149–$229 double, cleaning $75. **Studio and suite,** 2367 Hoohu Rd., Poipu. Studio: $129–$159 double, cleaning $60. 1-bedroom: $169–$239 double, cleaning $90. **Amenities:** Barbecue grill, beach gear, use of Poipu Kai pool and hot tub, free Wi-Fi.

Poipu Plantation B&B Inn and Vacation Rentals ★★★ This ultratranquil compound almost defies description. It comprises four adults-only, B&B suites of various sizes in a lovingly restored 1938 plantation house and nine vacation rental units in three modern cottage-style wings behind the B&B. The B&B suites feature handsome hardwood floors, sturdy vintage furnishings, bright tropical art, and (thankfully) modern bathrooms; the 700-square-foot Alii Suite also includes a wet bar, two-person whirlpool tub, and private lanai. The one- and two-bedroom cottage units on the foliage-rich 1-acre lot have less character but offer more space (plus full kitchens); some have ocean views across the rooftops of Sunset Kahili condos across the street. Innkeepers Chris and Javed Moore and their friendly staff delight in offering travel tips. *Note:* When comparing rates, consider that the units here have no cleaning, resort, parking, or Wi-Fi fees; plus, breakfasts for the B&B units include Kauai coffee, hot entrees, and fresh island fruit.

1792 Pee (pronounced "peh-eh") Rd., Poipu. www.poipubeach.com. ℂ **800/643-0263** or 808/742-6757. 12 units. Inn suites: $150–$250, includes breakfast and daily housekeeping; adults only (2 maximum); 3-night minimum (7 for winter holidays). Rental units: $155–$210 1-bedroom; $200–$240 2-bedroom. Condos: $170–$210; extra person $20. **Amenities:** Use of beach gear; laundry facilities; free Wi-Fi.

INEXPENSIVE

In pricey Poipu, staying anywhere under $200 a night—especially if fees and taxes are included—can be a challenge. **Kauai Vacation Rentals** (www.kauaivacationrentals.com; ℂ **800/367-5025** or 808/245-8841), located in the well-kept **Prince Kuhio** ★★ complex across from Lawai Beach, manages 10 garden- and oceanview studios that start at $165 a night (3-night minimum), including taxes, reservation and cleaning fees.

It also has eight one-bedroom/one-bathroom units (some sleeping four) that cost, all told, about $198 a night. During spring and fall, **Suite Paradise** (www.suite-paradise.com; ✆ **800/367-8020**) frequently has garden-view one-bedroom/one-bathroom units in the **Kahala ★** condominium on the 70-acre, verdant Poipu Kai resort for $133 a night, plus $150 cleaning and $9 daily resort fee.

Marjorie's Kauai Inn ★ In keeping with its hilltop setting in Lawai, this unlicensed three-room B&B prides itself on green touches: energy-efficient appliances, eco-friendly cleaning products, and local organic produce (some grown on-site) on the lavish breakfast buffet. You're more likely to notice the sweeping valley views from the private lanais. All rooms have private entrances and kitchenettes, while Sunset View, the largest, boasts its own hot tub in a gazebo and a foldout couch for extra guests. Any guest can use the 50-foot-long saltwater pool and hot tub, down a long flight of stairs (this isn't the best place for young children). Rooms include TV with cable and DVD player, but guests are encouraged to explore the island with a booklet of helpful tips and free use of bikes, a surfboard, a kayak, and beach gear.

Off Hailima Rd., Lawai. www.marjorieskauaiinn.com. ✆ **800/717-8838** or 808/332-8838. 3 units. $210–$260 double, includes breakfast. Extra person $20. **Amenities:** Barbecue; free use of bikes, kayak, and beach gear; Jacuzzi; laundry; pool; free Wi-Fi.

West Side

MODERATE

Waimea Plantation Cottages ★★★ Serenity now: That's what you'll find at this 30-acre oceanfront enclave of 60 restored vintage cottages, spread among large lawns dotted with coconut palms, banyan trees, and tropical flowers. The black-sand beach is not good for swimming (there's a small pool for that), but it offers intriguing driftwood for beach-combers and mesmerizing sunset views; claim a hammock or a lounge chair. The charmingly rustic but airy cottages feature full kitchens, lanais, and modern perks such as Wi-Fi, A/C (window units), and flatscreen TVs. The one- and two-bedroom units have one bathroom, while the three-bedroom versions offer two baths, perfect for families; a few larger houses are also available. Owned by the heirs of Norwegian immigrant Hans Peter Faye, who ran a sugar plantation, it's now managed by Coast Hotels, which has poured money into tasteful upgrades. *Tip:* Gardenview units have the lowest rates.

9400 Kaumualii Hwy., *makai* side, west of Huaki Rd., Waimea. www.coasthotels.com. ✆ **808/338-1625.** 60 units. $188–$286 1-bedroom; $205–$346 2-bedroom; $262–$569 3-bedroom; from $515 4-bedroom; from $633 5-bedroom. $25 resort fee. Children 17 and under stay free in parent's room. Check for online specials. **Amenities:** Barbecues; beach chairs; DVD and game rentals; gift shop; laundry; pool; free Wi-Fi.

The West Inn ★ The closest thing the West Side has to a Holiday Inn Express, the West Inn offers clean, neutral-toned rooms with bright accents and stone counters. One two-story wing of medium-size rooms is just off the highway across from Waimea Theater; some second-story rooms have an ocean view over corrugated metal roofs from the long, shared lanai, and all units have refrigerators, microwaves, A/C, coffee-makers, and cable TV. Another wing of one- and two-bedroom suites, designed for longer stays with full kitchens and living rooms, is tucked off to the side, with a small barbecue area between the wings. *Note:* There's no elevator; call ahead to arrange check-ins after 6pm.

9690 Kaumualii Hwy., *makai* side (at Pokole Rd.), Waimea. www.thewestinn.com. ✆ **808/338-1107.** 20 units. $198 king or double. 3-night minimum for larger rooms: $289 king with kitchen, $325 1-bedroom suite, $359 2-bedroom suite. $30 extra person. **Amenities:** Barbecue grills, coin laundry, free Wi-Fi.

INEXPENSIVE

Inn Waimea/West Kauai Lodging ★★ If you're looking for accommodations with both character and modern conveniences, check out the small lodge and four vacation rentals managed by West Kauai Lodging. A former parsonage that's also known as Halepule ("House of Prayer"), **Inn Waimea** is a Craftsman-style cottage in the center of quaint Waimea, with simple, tropical-tinged, plantation-era decor in its four wood-paneled suites, all but one with a separate living area. The suites offer flatscreen TVs, Wi-Fi, and (in some rooms) air-conditioning, as well as private bathrooms with pedestal sinks, coffeemakers, mini-fridges, and ceiling fans. West Kauai Lodging also manages three moderately priced two-bedroom cottages in Waimea (owned by the Faye family, which has deep roots on the island), plus the newly built five-bedroom, five-bathroom **Hale La** beach house in Kekaha, all with full kitchen and laundry facilities. The plantation-style **Waimea Beach Cottage,** which includes a clawfoot tub, bamboo furniture, and sunset views over the ocean and Waimea Pier, is closest to the inn. The homey, Craftsman-inspired **Ishihara Home** and the tree-shaded **Pali Cottage,** with vintage furnishings and an enclosed lanai, are above town, with sweeping views of ridges and the distant sea. *Note:* Manager Patrick McLean, who owns Hale La, is a former Kauai B&B pro who loves to help visitors plan their days. He also manages the upgraded cabins in Kokee State Park (see "Camping & Cabins," below).

4469 Halepule Rd. (off Kaumualii Hwy.), Waimea. www.westkauailodging.com. ✆ **808/652-6852.** Inn (4 units) $119–$149 ($25 for 3rd person). 3 cottages (sleep 4–6) $179–$229, plus $95–$125 cleaning fee. Hale La beach house (sleeps 11) $495, plus $295 cleaning. **Amenities:** free Wi-Fi.

Camping & Cabins

Kauai offers tent camping in seven county-run beach parks and, for extremely hardy and self-sufficient types, several state-managed, backcountry areas of the **Napali Coast** and **Waimea Canyon.** Tents and simple cabins are also available in the cooler elevations of **Kokee State Park,** and minimal campgrounds at **Polihale State Park;** you have to be hardy and well equipped for the rugged conditions in the latter. With the exception of Kokee cabins, all camping requires permits, which must be purchased in advance; camping in vehicles is not allowed.

County campsites, often busy with local families on weekends, close one day each week for maintenance. The most recommended for visitors, both for scenery and relative safety, are at **Haena, Hanalei Blackpot, Anini,** and **Lydgate** beach parks. Go to **www.kauai.gov/ camping** for schedules, permit applications, hours, and addresses for the neighborhood centers (closed weekends and holidays) where permits are issued in person. Permits for nonresidents cost $3 per adult (free for children 17 and under, with adult), except for Lydgate, which is $25 per site.

For camping in state parks and forest reserves, the **Department of Land & Natural Resources** (http://camping.ehawaii.gov; ℂ **808/274-3444**) prefers to issue online permits; its office in Lihue, 3060 Eiwa St., Suite 306, is also open 8am to 3:30pm weekdays. **Napali Coast State Wilderness Park** allows camping at two sites along the 11-mile Kalalau Trail—Hanakoa Valley, 6 miles in, and Kalalau Valley, at trail's end—for a maximum of 5 nights (no more than 1 consecutive night at Hanakoa). Camping is also permitted at Milolii, for a maximum of 3 nights; it's reached only by kayak or authorized boats mid-May through early September. There's no drinking water, trash must be packed out, and composting toilets are not always in good repair, yet permits ($20 per night) often sell out a year in advance. (*Note:* Rangers conduct periodic permit checks here, so make sure yours is handy.)

Permits for primitive campsites in eight backcountry areas of Waimea Canyon and nearby wilderness preserves cost $18 per night, with a 5-night maximum; see http://camping.ehawaii.gov for detailed descriptions.

In **Kokee State Park,** which gets quite chilly on winter nights, **West Kauai Lodging** (www.westkauailodging.com; ℂ **808/652-6852**) now manages 11 cabins ($79–$129 a night, 2-night minimum) that sleep two to six people and come with fully equipped kitchens and linens. Be sure to book well in advance. Less than a mile away, down a dirt road, the YWCA of Kauai's **Camp Sloggett** (www.campingkauai.com; ℂ **808/245-5959**) allows tent camping in its large forest clearing for $15 per tent per night, with toilets and hot showers available; there's also a four-person cottage ($120–$150). Groups may rent its bunkhouse ($160–$200) or lodge ($200–$225), both of which sleep up to 15.

If you need gear, **Just Live!** (www.ziplinetourskauai.com; ℂ **808/482-1295**) sells and rents top brands of tents, camping stoves, sleep sacks, and more in Harbor Mall, 3501 Rice St., Lihue. **Kayak Kauai** (www.kayakkauai.com; ℂ **888/596-3853** or 808/826-9844) offers camping rentals, supplies, and car and luggage storage at its Wailua River

Marina shop, 3-5971 Kuhio Hwy., Kapaa. **Pedal 'n Paddle** (www.pedal npaddle.com; ✆ **808/826-9069**) sells hiking boots, freeze-dried food, and other necessities and rents tents, backpacks, and sleeping bags; it's in Ching Young Village, 5-5190 Kuhio Hwy., Hanalei.

WHERE TO EAT ON KAUAI

Thanks to a proliferation of hamburger joints, plate-lunch counters, and food trucks, you'll find affordable choices (by local standards) in every town. Even in pricey Princeville, the shopping center food court offers a few tasty bargains. At the gourmet end of the spectrum, Kauai's very expensive restaurants—both on and off the resorts—provide excellent service along with more complex but reliably executed dishes. And nearly every establishment trumpets its Kauai-grown ingredients, which help keep the Garden Island green and the flavors fresh.

The challenge is finding exceptional value in the moderate to expensive range. Costs are indeed higher here, and service is often slower; it's best not to arrive anywhere—even at one of the many food trucks—in a state of starvation. Patience and pleasantness on your part, however, will usually be rewarded. During peak holiday and summer seasons, avoid stress by booking online with **Open Table** (www.opentable.com), currently available for 45 Kauai restaurants and dinner shows. The listings below, not all of which are on Open Table, will note where reservations are recommended.

For those with access to a kitchen (or even just a minifridge), check out "Kauai Farmers Markets" (p. 595). You're guaranteed farm-to-table cuisine at a good price—and at your own pace.

East Side

This populous area yields several unique, moderately priced dining experiences. In Kapaa, former Red Salt executive chef Adam Watten creates a weekly special menu at his locally sourced **Hanai Farmer's Market ★★** (www.hanaikauai.com; ✆ **808/822-2228**) from 3 to 6pm Wednesdays at the Kojima Center, 4-1543 Kuhio Hwy. For happy hour appetizers and cocktails with a dazzling ocean view, head to **Sam's Ocean View ★**, 4-1546 Kuhio Hwy. (www.samsoceanview.com; ✆ **808/822-7887**); Sam's also serves $5 mimosas with Sunday brunch.

In Lihue, microbrew lovers will find hearty, island-grown food pairings on tap at the expanded **Kauai Beer Company ★★**, 4265 Rice St. (www.kauaibeer.com; ✆ **808/245-2337**); don't miss the organic taro fries ($9) or six-beer sampler ($12). The **Greenery Cafe ★★** (www.thegreen-erycafe.com; ✆ **808/246-4567**), in the rear cottage at 3146 Akahi S., will delight health and soul food fans alike with Kauai-grown collard greens, organic rosemary chicken and fresh cornbread.

Note: The restaurants in this section are on either the "Hotels & Restaurants on the Coconut Coast" map (p. 559) or the "Hotels & Restaurants in Lihue" map (p. 561).

EXPENSIVE

Duke's Kauai ★ STEAK/SEAFOOD   The view of Kalapaki Beach, an indoor waterfall, koi pond, and a lively beachfront bar have as much, if not more, to do with the popularity of this outpost of the California–Hawaii TS Restaurants chain as do the fresh seafood, vast salad bar, and belt-straining Hula Pie (an ice cream confection with classic and rotating versions). The downstairs **Barefoot Bar,** which has live music 6 days a week, offers the best values, with burgers, sandwiches, and salads for lunch and dinner, but the dinner-only upstairs dining room shows local flair with Lawai mushroom gnocchi and seared ahi with papaya mustard sauce—among satisfying but less ambitious dishes such as macnut-crusted mahi-mahi. A trip to the island's biggest salad bar costs $4 with any entree upstairs or $18 as a stand-alone meal.

At west end of Kauai Marriott Resort, 3610 Rice St., Lihue (valet parking at restaurant or self-parking in hotel lot). www.dukeskauai.com. © **808/246-9599.** Reservations recommended for dinner. Main courses $14–$20 lunch and dinner in bar; dinner $24–$49 in dining room. $4–$5 taco specials in bar Tues 4–6pm. Bar daily 11am–11pm; dining room daily 5–10pm.

Hukilau Lanai ★★ SEAFOOD/ISLAND FARM   Although his restaurant is hidden inside the nondescript Kauai Coast Resort at the Beachboy, off the main highway in Kapaa, chef/owner Ron Miller has inspired diners to find their way here in droves since 2002. The lure: a hearty menu that's virtually all locally sourced—from Kauai whenever possible, and other islands when not—as well as expertly prepared and presented. Four to five seafood specials, incorporating local produce, are offered nightly; try the coffee-spiced candied ahi, or the hebi (short-billed spearfish) when available. The mushroom meatloaf also packs a savory punch, thanks to grass-fed beef and Big Island mushrooms. Value-conscious diners should try the $32 five-course tasting menu ($50 with wine pairings) offered from 5 to 5:45pm. Reservations are strongly recommended, especially for oceanview seating; the less-scenic lobby bar has nightly music. *Note:* The gluten-free menu includes variants of the five-course tasting menus.

In the Kauai Coast Resort at the Beachboy, 520 Aleka Loop, Kapaa. www.hukilau kauai.com. © **808/822-0600.** Reservations recommended. Main courses $21–$36. Tues–Sun 5–9pm; poolside happy hour daily 3–5pm.

JO2 ★★★ ASIAN/FRENCH   Foodies will want to check out chef Jean-Marie Josselin's triumphant return to Kapaa, in a strip mall not unlike the one where he first gained renown years ago with A Pacific Cafe. A Hawaii Regional Cuisine co-founder and six-time nominee for a James Beard Foundation Award, Josselin's latest victory is JO2, an island-sourced, "natural cuisine" restaurant with Asian-influenced dishes prepared using classic French techniques. The tiny but chic dining room has a neutral palette that makes the artful presentations of brightly hued greens, sauces, and glazes pop. Among the small plates, try the lamb

PLATE LUNCH, BENTO & poke

If you haven't yet tried the Hawaii staples of plate lunch, bento, or poke (seasoned, raw fish), Kauai's inexpensive eateries are a good place to start.

EAST SIDE In Kapaa, the indispensable **Pono Market,** 4-1300 Kuhio Hwy. (*makai* side), Kapaa (© **808/822-4581**), has enticing counters of sashimi, poke, sushi, and a diverse assortment of take-out fare. The roast pork and the potato-macaroni salad are top sellers, but it's also known for plate lunches, including pork and chicken *laulau* (steamed in *ti* leaves), plus flaky *manju* (sweet potato and other fillings in baked crust). It's open Monday to Saturday 6am to 4pm. Kapaa also has **Sleeping Giant Grill,** a renamed branch of Kilauea Fish Market (see "North Shore," below) at 440 Aleka Pl. (© **808/822-3474;** Mon–Sat 11am–8pm); try the mochi ono tacos (battered in rice flour) for a deliciously crisp take on fish tacos.

In Lihue, **Po's Kitchen,** 4100 Rice St. (© **808/246-8617**), packs a lot of goodies in its deluxe bentos ($8.50), including shrimp tempura, chicken katsu, chow fun noodles, spaghetti mac salad, hot dog, ham, and rice balls. It's hidden behind Ace Hardware and open Monday to Saturday from 6am to 2pm (cash only). One block away, **Garden Island BBQ,** 4252 Rice St. (© **808/245-8868**), is the place for Chinese plate lunches, as well as soups and noodle dishes; it's open Monday to Saturday 10am to 9pm, Sunday 11am to 9pm. Across the highway from Wal-Mart, **the Fish Express,** 3343 Kuhio Hwy. (© **808/245-9918**), draws crowds for its wide assortment of poke (the ahi with spicy crab in a light mayo sauce is a favorite), pork laulau, Spam musubi, bentos, and plate lunches, including lighter entree options such as Cajun blackened ahi and smoked fish. The downside: no seating. It's open Monday to Saturday from 10am to 5pm.

Mark's Place, in Puhi Industrial Park at 1610 Haleukana St., Lihue (www.marksplacekauai.com; © **808/245-2722**), fashions daily salad and entree specials with a California-healthy bent: shrimp and grilled-vegetable quinoa salad, say, or cornmeal-crusted mahi with chipotle aioli. But it also serves island standards such as Korean-style chicken, beef stew, and chicken katsu and is famed for its baked goods, including butter mochi and bread pudding. It's open weekdays from 10am to 8pm, with a handful of picnic tables for seating.

dumpling or organic tomato sampler; for larger dishes, seared Hokkaido scallops or the locally caught blackened opah; don't skip the yuzu lemon cheesecake. The early-bird, three-course prix fixe is a bargain at $35. 4-971 Kuhio Hwy., *mauka* side, Kapaa. www.jotwo.com. © **808/212-1627.** Reservations recommended. Main courses $29–$35; small plates $10–$19. Three-course prix fixe 5–6pm $35. Daily 5–9pm.

MODERATE

In addition to the listings below, value seekers will want to visit **Olympic Café ★**, 4-1354 Kuhio Hwy., Kapaa (www.olympiccafekauai.com; © **808/822-5825**), where the portions are almost as large as the sprawling

NORTH SHORE Everything is pricier on the North Shore, and ahi poke and plate lunches are no exception at **Kilauea Fish Market,** 4270 Kilauea Rd. (enter from Keneke St. across the street from Kong Lung Market), Kilauea (*(C)* **808/828-6244**). At $29 a pound, skip the poke and opt for Korean BBQ or grilled teri chicken plates ($11–$12); the burrito-like ahi wrap ($11) is a messy but filling alternative. It's open Monday to Saturday from 11am to 8pm, with outdoor seating only. Locals head to **Village Snack Shop and Bakery,** across from Puka Dog inside Hanalei's Ching Young Village, 5-5190 Kuhio Hwy. (*(C)* **808/826-6841**), for loco moco (eggs, meat, and gravy on rice) at breakfast and chili pepper chicken at lunch; everyone loves the chocolate *haupia* (coconut cream) pies, *malasadas* (doughnut holes), and other pastries. It's open 6:30am to 4pm Monday to Saturday, until 3pm Sunday (kitchen closes an hour earlier). In Wainiha, near the end of the road, **Sushigirl Kauai,** 5-6607 Kuhio Hwy. (*(C)* **808/827-8171**), offers gluten-free takeout, from ahi poke bowls with rice, local organic greens, or quinoa ($12) to seafood and veggie sushi rolls ($12–$15). It's open 11am to 7pm Monday to Saturday, noon to 4pm Sunday.

SOUTH SHORE The **Koloa Fish Market,** 5482 Koloa Rd. (*(C)* **808/742-6199**) in Old Town Koloa, is a tiny corner store with two stools on the veranda. Grab some excellent fresh poke, plate lunches, or seared ahi to go, and don't forgo decadent desserts such as Okinawan sweet potato haupia pie on macadamia nut crust. You can also pick up raw seafood to grill. It's open weekdays from 10am to 6pm and Saturday till 5pm. **Sueoka's Snack Shop** (*(C)* **808/742-1112**), the cash-only window counter of Sueoka grocery store, 5392 Koloa Rd. (www.sueokastore.com; *(C)* **808/742-1611**), offers a wide selection of meat-based lunch plates, such as shoyu chicken or kalua pork for just $6.25. It's open Tuesday to Friday 8:30am to 2pm, weekends 9am to 3pm.

WEST SIDE **Ishihara Market,** 9894 Kaumualii Hwy., Waimea (*(C)* **808/338-1751**), a block past the bridge on the *makai* side, is well worth a stop heading to or from Waimea Canyon. A local favorite founded in 1934, the family-run Ishihara's deli counter stocks an impressive variety of fresh poke and has a grill making plate lunches Tuesday to Saturday. The grocery store is open Monday to Thursday 6am to 7:30pm, Friday and Saturday till 8pm, and Sunday till 7pm.

international menu. Breakfast is your best bet; be prepared to take home leftovers. (There's also a location in Poipu Shopping Village, open for breakfast and lunch only.)

Kauai Pasta/KP Lihue ★ ITALIAN The owners' marital split led to a breakup of the two Kauai Pasta locations, but fortunately you can stick with both. Although the Lihue site changed its name to KP Lihue, both have kept essentially the same menus, emphasizing homemade pasta standards, such as chicken parm and fettuccine Alfredo, and meat specials, such as osso buco or sous vide pork. The larger Kapaa locale also offers $10 lunch specials, a late-night lounge with its own menu (try the truffled prawn "ramen" with angel hair pasta), and, at dinner, pizzetta choices such as rosemary grilled chicken with Gorgonzola. Portions are generous at both sites, but plan to order at least one of the tasty sides to share—I recommend the truffle Parmesan fries with a variety of dipping sauces. The keiki (kids') menus are a good deal too, from $5 pastas to $10 for grilled shrimp with mashed potatoes and vegetable.

Kauai Pasta, 4-939 Kuhio Hwy., *mauka* side, Kapaa (north of Taco Bell). www.kauai pasta.com. © **808/822-7447.** Main courses $13–$27 lunch, $15–$29 dinner. Restaurant daily 11am–9pm; lounge Sun–Thurs 11am–10pm, Fri–Sat 11am–midnight, happy hour daily 3–5pm. Dinner reservations recommended. **KP Lihue:** 3-3142 Kuhio Hwy., Lihue (btw. Poinciana and Hardy sts. in the Garden Island Publishing building). www.kplihue.com. © **808/245-2227.** Daily 11am–9pm. Main courses lunch $13–$24, dinner $13–$30.

Lava Lava Beach Club ★ AMERICAN/ISLAND

On the ocean side of Kauai Shores hotel, Lava Lava Beach Club has the island's only "toes-in-the-sand" dining area, on comfy wicker sofas facing Wailua Bay. It also offers plenty of other oceanview indoor and outdoor seating, a full bar with zippy tropical cocktails and a dozen beers (seven local), and an attentive staff serving American and island-flavored specialties, including a burger made from local beef and Portuguese sausage ($17), from 7am to 10pm. Prices border on the expensive ($22 for a lunch salad with five shrimp) and food quality can vary, but otherwise this is a beachy-keen hideaway, with live music nightly.

At Kauai Shores hotel, 420 Papaloa Rd., Kapaa (off Kuhio Hwy., *makai* side, south of Coconut Marketplace). www.lavalavabeachclub.com. © **808/822-7447.** Main courses $12–$17 breakfast, $15–$19 lunch, $15–$38 dinner. Daily breakfast 7–11am, lunch 11:30am–3pm, happy hour 3–5pm, dinner 5–9pm, bar menu 8–10pm. Lunch and dinner reservations recommended. Free valet parking (required).

Oasis on the Beach ★★ SEAFOOD/ISLAND FARM

Though not actually on the sand, the open-air, oceanfront setting at the Waipouli Beach Resort is still memorable, as are the daily fresh-catch (grilled or pan-seared) and curry specials, the grilled kale salad with whipped Brie, and braised short ribs with bacon-truffle fried rice. Chef de cuisine Sean Smull proudly notes that 90% of ingredients come from Kauai. Luckily, half portions of many dinner entrees make sharing a breeze; save room for the apple banana spring roll with gelato. The handsome canoe bar and sounds of ocean surf make the occasional wait worthwhile. Wednesdays are an ideal time to discover this culinary oasis, with live music and a special "chef's choice" menu from 4 to 6pm. *Note:* Breakfast entrees are tasty but petite by local standards.

In the Waipouli Beach Resort, 4-820 Kuhio Hwy., Kapaa (across from Safeway). www.oasiskauai.com. © **808/822-9332.** Reservations recommended. Main courses $8–$17 breakfast, $9–$24 lunch, $17–$35 dinner. Daily breakfast 8–11am, lunch 11am–3pm, dinner 4–9pm.

INEXPENSIVE

In addition to these listings, and the many in "Plate Lunch, Bento & Poke," below, check out these two Kapaa food counters with limited seating: **Shrimp Station** ★ (p. 590) and **Tiki Tacos** ★★, 4-961 Kuhio Hwy., *mauka* side, in the Waipouli Complex. Billed as "Mexican food with a Hawaiian heart," the latter features sizable tacos ($6–$8) with island fish, kalua pork, and other fillings on handmade tortillas. It's open 11am to 8:30pm daily.

Hamura's Saimin Stand ★★★ JAPANESE NOODLES   Honored by the James Beard Foundation in 2006 as one of "America's Classics," this hole-in-the-wall has been satisfying local palates since 1951. Visitors have also now caught on to the appeal of saimin: large bowls of ramen noodles in salty broth with green onion, cabbage, and slices of fish cake, hard-boiled eggs, and pork, for starters. Here the housemade noodles are served al dente, and sometimes brusquely; figure out what you're going to order before seating yourself at one of the U-shaped counters. The "special regular" includes wontons and diced ham; top off any dish with a barbecued chicken skewer. If your appetite isn't large, order a to-go slice of the ultra-fluffy lilikoi (passion fruit) chiffon pie, just as renowned as the saimin. Shave ice is also delicious, but its separate counter isn't always open. *Note:* There's often a line inside and out; it moves fast, so stay put.
2956 Kress St., Lihue (1 block west of Rice St. in small blue building on left; park farther down the street). ℂ **808/245-3271.** All items under $11. No credit cards. Mon–Thurs 10am–10:30pm; Fri–Sat 10am–midnight; Sun 10am–9:30pm.

North Shore

Change comes slowly to the North Shore, so three new restaurants in one year is big news. In Hanalei, Chef James Moffatt serves three kinds of silky Japanese ramen bowls ($18) plus grilled fish and meat skewers ($10–$11) at **Ama** ★★ (ℂ 808/826-9452), next door to his Bar Acuda (see below) in Hanalei Center; it's dinner only, no reservations. Across the street in the Ching Young Shopping Center, **Northside Grill** ★ (ℂ **808/826-9701**) has replaced long-lived Bouchons; open for lunch and dinner, it's more casual, with affordable seafood and pricey beer.

In Haena, Hanalei Colony Resort, 5–7132 Kuhio Hwy. now hosts **Opakapaka Grill and Bar** ★★, (www.ogbkauai.com; ℂ **808/378-4425**), serving all three meals (and flood relief workers when the road was closed.) Cocktails are pricey ($14), but the Hawaiian fusion happy hour menu (2 to 5pm) and beer list offer good values.

Note: The restaurants in this section are on the "Hotels & Restaurants on Kauai's North Shore" map (p. 581).

EXPENSIVE

For those capable of serious splurges, **Makana Terrace** ★★★ in the Princeville Hotel (p. 565) provides sensational Hanalei Bay and mountain views along with exquisite island-sourced cuisine; try the four-course prix fixe menu ($85; $135 with wine pairing), the Kauai chicken and taro waffle ($37) or the signature Ke Kai seafood medley in a delicate coconut panang emulsion ($51). Also in the posh hotel, Jean-Georges Vongerichten's dark-hued **Kauai Grill ★★** offers similarly delicious island-inspired haute cuisine, at even more *haute* prices.

Bar Acuda ★★★ TAPAS   Named one of *Food & Wine* magazine's "Top 10 New American Chefs" in 1996, when he was still working in San Francisco, chef/owner Jim Moffatt later decided to embrace a low-key lifestyle in Hanalei. But he hasn't relaxed his standards for expertly prepared food, in this case tapas—small plates inspired by several Mediterranean cuisines. Enjoy them on the torch-lit veranda or in the sleek, warm-toned dining room. Given Bar Acuda's deliciously warm, crusty bread, ordering one hearty and one light dish per person, plus a shared starter of spiced olives or crostini, should suffice for a couple. But ask the server for help in ordering the right amount—some dishes, such as the wonderful seared single scallop on mashed potatoes, aren't really suitable for sharing. The menu changes to reflect seasonal tastes and availability but usually includes a seared fresh fish and grilled beef skewers. Note that this is a more smartly dressed crowd than just about anywhere else in Hanalei.

In Hanalei Center, 5-5161 Kuhio Hwy., Hanalei. www.restaurantbaracuda.com. © **808/826-7081.** Reservations recommended. Hearty tapas $8–$23. Daily 5:30–9:30pm (bar open till 10pm).

MODERATE

Bar Acuda's busy chef-owner James Moffatt also runs **Hanalei Bread Company ★★** (© **808/826-6717**), a bakery and coffee house in Hanalei Center, 5-5161 Kuhio Hwy. It's open 7am to 5pm daily, but the delectable breakfast and lunch entrees, including avocado toast and pizza ($10–$12), are only available till 2pm. Locals line up early for chocolate chip scones, lilikoi cinnamon rolls, and other goodies to go with their espresso drinks; don't be in a rush when you arrive. For other moderately priced island and American dining options, see the listings for **Tahiti Nui ★★** in Hanalei and **Tiki Iniki ★** in Princeville under "Kauai Nightlife," p. 596.

The Bistro ★★★ CONTEMPORARY AMERICAN/ISLAND FARM John-Paul Gordon is yet another Kauai chef taking inspiration from the bounty of local fields and fishing grounds, with an admirably inventive palate and a well-practiced eye for presentation. Although his menu is largely seasonal, the "fish rockets" starter of seared ahi in lumpia wrappers with wasabi aioli is a signature dish; Kauai beef sirloin and grilled pork chops are standards. If you crave something lighter, order a salad with local goat cheese and almonds or the grilled fresh catch, perhaps with a baby spinach ragu. Lunch includes simpler but satisfying options such as a Kauai beef burger or fish sandwich. The wine list is reasonably

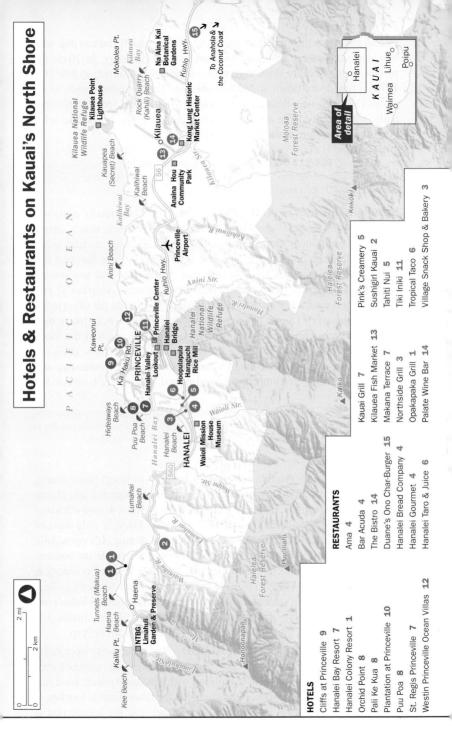

Hotels & Restaurants on Kauai's North Shore

PACIFIC OCEAN

Tunnels (Makua) Beach
Haena Pt.
Kee Beach
Kaliku Pt.
Haena
Haena Beach

NTBG
Limahuli
Garden & Preserve

Lumahai Beach

Hanalei Bay
Hanalei Beach
Waioli Str.
Waioli Mission House Museum

HANALEI

Hideaways Beach
Puu Poa Beach

PRINCEVILLE
Hanalei Valley Lookout
Ka Haku Rd.

Hanalei Bridge
Hoopulapula Haraguchi Rice Mill

Kaweonui Pt.
Princeville Center

Anini Beach
Anini Str.

Kauapea (Secret) Beach
Kalihiwai Beach
Kalihiwai Bay

Kilauea National Wildlife Refuge
Kilauea Point Lighthouse
Mokolea Pt.
Kilauea Bay

Rock Quarry (Kahili) Beach

Na Aina Kai Botanical Gardens

Kong Lung Historic Market Center
Kilauea

Anaina Hou Community Park

Princeville Airport

Kuhio Hwy.

To Anahola & the Coconut Coast

56

Hanalei National Wildlife Refuge

Halelea Forest Reserve
Moloaa Forest Reserve

Kalihiwai R.
Kalihiwai R.
Kilauea R.

Hanalei R.

Kekoki

Kalko

Halelea Forest Reserve

560

Wapa Str.
Mahimahi Str.
Lumahai R.
Waioli R.
Puualiliahi

Pacific
Hononapali
Halelea Forest Reserve

Area of detail

KAUAI
Hanalei
Lihue
Waimea
Poipu

HOTELS

Cliffs at Princeville **9**
Hanalei Bay Resort **7**
Hanalei Colony Resort **1**
Orchid Point **8**
Pali Ke Kua **8**
Plantation at Princeville **10**
Puu Poa **8**
St. Regis Princeville **7**
Westin Princeville Ocean Villas **12**

RESTAURANTS

Ama **4**
Bar Acuda **4**
The Bistro **14**
Duane's Ono Char-Burger **15**
Hanalei Bread Company **4**
Hanalei Gourmet **4**
Hanalei Taro & Juice **6**

Kauai Grill **7**
Kilauea Fish Market **13**
Makana Terrace **7**
Northside Grill **3**
Opakapaka Grill **1**
Palate Wine Bar **14**

Pink's Creamery **5**
Sushigirl Kauai **2**
Tahiti Nui **5**
Tiki Iniki **11**
Tropical Taco **6**
Village Snack Shop & Bakery **3**

priced; ask about the $5 daily happy hour special, which you can pair with live slack-key guitar Thursday and soft jazz on Saturday. In 2015, the owners opened **Palate Wine Bar ★** (www.palatewinebar.net; ℂ **808/212-1974**) a few doors down at 2474 Keneke St. The wine bar serves small plates ($7–$28) and flatbreads and entrees ($20–$36) from 5 to 10pm daily, with quality wine and beer starting at $8 a glass. If you like what you drink, buy more at the Palate Market next door.

In Kong Lung Historic Market Center, 2484 Keneke St., Kilauea. www.thebistro hawaii.com. ℂ **808/828-0480.** Reservations recommended for parties of 6 or more. Lunch $10–$20; dinner main courses $19–$30. Daily noon–2:30pm and 5:30–9pm. Bar noon–9pm. Happy hour 4–6pm.

Hanalei Gourmet ★ AMERICAN   This casual, decidedly nongourmet spot offers the best values (by local standards) at lunch, with a variety of burgers and ample sandwiches on freshly baked bread starting at $8; order the latter to go from the deli. The market-priced beer-battered fish and chips, accompanied by a suitably tart Asian slaw and soy wasabi sauce, is also notable. (If you want a half-papaya, though, skip the $7 version here and walk a few steps to Harvest Market or across the street to the Big Save grocery.) Dinner has rather higher aspirations, not always met, as well as higher prices, but you can still order from much of the lunch menu. The atmosphere tends to be lively if not downright noisy, thanks to wooden floors, the popular bar, TV, and live music on Wednesday and Saturday, drawing an enthusiastic local crowd. Service is laidback but friendly.

In Hanalei Center, 5-5161 Kuhio Hwy., *mauka* side, Hanalei. www.hanaleigourmet. com. ℂ **808/826-2524.** Main courses $8–$13 lunch, $10–$29 dinner. Daily deli 8am–10:30pm; lunch 11am–5:30pm; dinner 5:30–9:30pm; bar 11am–10:30pm.

INEXPENSIVE

Beside plate lunches (see above), the best bargains in North Shore dining usually come from food trucks, often found at Anini, Hanalei, and Haena beach parks, but with fickle hours. **Hanalei Taro & Juice ★** (www.hanalei taro.com; ℂ **808/826-1059**), *makai* side of Kuhio Hwy., a mile west of the Hanalei Bridge, has reliable hours and shaded seating. It's open daily 11am to 3pm, with most items under $10; be sure to sample the banana-bread-like taro butter mochi. Nearby, the tiny storefront **Pink's Creamery ★** (ℂ **808/212-9749**), 4489 Aku Rd., is as justifiably renowned for its grilled-cheese sandwiches on sweet bread with pineapple and optional kalua pork ($8–$9, including chips) as it is for delicious tropical ice creams and housemade frozen yogurt and sorbets; it's open daily 11am to 9pm.

Tropical Taco ★ MEXICAN SEAFOOD   Roger Kennedy operated a North Shore taco wagon for 20-odd years before taking up residence over a decade ago in this cottage-style building with a pleasant porch; food still come on paper plates. Although the menu has local/sustainable touches—the fresh seafood comes from North Shore fishermen, the lettuce mix is

CHEESEBURGERS in paradise

Delicious as Hawaii's fresh seafood is, sometimes what you're really looking for—in the words of Jimmy Buffett—is a cheeseburger in paradise. Luckily, Kauai boasts several joints bound to satisfy.

The first thing to know about **Duane's Ono Char-Burger ★★**, 4-4350 Kuhio Hwy., *makai* side, Anahola (📞 **808/822-9181**), is that its burgers ($5–$8) are not made of the fish called ono (wahoo); they're just *'ono* ("delicious" in Hawaiian). The second thing to know is that waits can be long at this red roadside stand, opened in 1973, where wild chickens, cats, and birds are ready to share your meal with you. Duane's is open Monday to Saturday 10am to 6pm and Sunday 11am to 6pm. Duane's founders also run **Kalapaki Beach Hut ★**, 3474 Rice St., Lihue, near the west end of Kalapaki Beach (www.facebook.com/Kalapaki-BeachHut; 📞 **808/246-6330**). The two-story oceanview "hut" offers grass-fed Kauai beef burgers ($7–$10), a taro burger ($9) made from organic taro grown nearby, and shave ice.

Famed for its sassy slogans ("We Cheat Tourists, Drunks & Attorneys,"

among them) as much as for its burgers ($4–$8) made from grass-fed Kauai beef, **Bubba's ★** (www.bubbaburger.com) claims to have been around since 1936. It's certainly had time to develop a loyal following, even while charging $1 for lettuce and tomato. It also offers a vegan Maui taro burger, hot dogs, and chili rice. The original Bubba's is in **Kapaa,** 4-1421 Kuhio Hwy. (📞 **808/823-0069**), where the deck has a view of the ocean across Kapaa Beach Park; the **Poipu** location is on the *makai* end of the Shops at Kukui-ula, 2829 Ala Kalanikamauka (📞 **808/742-6900**). Both are open daily from 10:30am to 8pm, although the Kukuiula closing time may vary depending on business.

Wailua's more upmarket **Street Burger ★★**, 4-369 Kuhio Hwy. (www.streetburgerkauai.com; 📞 **808/212-1555**), has made a juicy splash with gourmet salads, truffle fries, and toppings such as olive tapenade, jalapeño pineapple marmalade, and brie on its Makaweli beef, Niihau lamb, and veggie burgers ($10–$20). Large parties (6 or more) should call for reservations.

organic, and the fish and chips come with taro fries—the focus here is on satisfying hefty appetites. You might opt for the grilled fish special in soft corn tacos or as a crispy tostada rather than the gut-busting, deep-fried Fat Jack beef or veggie burrito, and be aware that any extras (cheese, sour cream, avocado) drive up prices quickly. *Note:* Hanalei has few places that are open for breakfast, so it's worth the occasional wait for your choice of one of four scrambled-egg burritos (try the taro and cheese, $7).

5-5088 Kuhio Hwy., *makai* side (parking in rear), Hanalei. www.tropicaltaco.com. © **808/827-8226.** Most items $13–$14, breakfast $7–$8. No credit cards. Mon–Fri 8am–8pm; Sat–Sun 11am–4pm.

South Shore

Of all the food trucks you'll encounter on the South Shore, the best are at **Warehouse 3540,** 3540 Koloa Rd. in Lawai (p. 594). **Roots in Culture** ★★ (© **808/631-3622**) prepares healthful versions of local comfort food, typically from 11am to 3pm Tuesday through Saturday, while **Fresh Shave** ★ (www.thefreshshave.com; © **808/631-2222**) serves shave ice made from natural ingredients from 11am to 5pm Tuesday through Saturday. The best poolside restaurant is hidden inside Koloa Landing Resort (p. 568), where Hawaii Regional Cuisine cofounder Sam Choy helped craft the Hawaiian-infused menu at casual **HoloHolo Grill** ★★ (www.holohologrill.com), open for breakfast ($9–$16), lunch ($15–$20), and dinner ($20–$36).

Note: You'll find the restaurants in this section on the "Hotels & Restaurants on Kauai's South Shore" map (p. 585).

EXPENSIVE

In addition to the choices here, see the listing for **Keoki's Paradise** ★★, a perennial favorite for its tropical landscaping, casual vibe, and ambitious, locally sourced island menu (dinner main courses $30–$35), under "Kauai Nightlife," p. 596.

The Beach House ★★ HAWAII REGIONAL CUISINE   Call it dinner and a show: As sunset approaches, diners at this beloved oceanfront restaurant start leaping from their tables to pose for pictures on the grass-covered promontory, while nearby surfers try to catch one last wave. The genial waiters are as used to cameras being thrust upon them as they are reciting specials featuring local ingredients—a staple here long before "farm to table" became a catchphrase. But there are other good reasons to dine here, whether you're splurging on dinner or sampling the more affordable lunch. Among them: the coconut corn chowder, with local kale, tomato, and lemongrass; the house ceviche of fish, prawns, and scallops in a citrus-lilikoi marinade; and the grilled fresh catch with citrus brodo, Parmesan polenta, and candied fennel.

5022 Lawai Rd., Koloa. www.the-beach-house.com. © **808/742-1424.** Reservations recommended. Main courses $13–$23 lunch, $28–$48 dinner. Daily lunch 11am–3pm; dinner 5–10pm; lounge menu 11am–9pm.

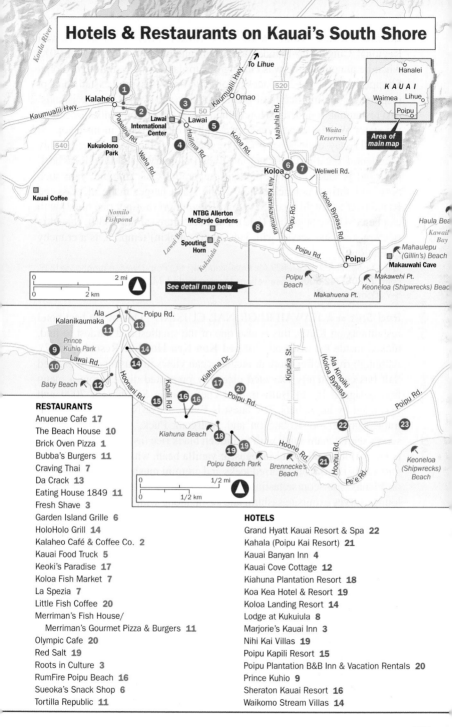

Hotels & Restaurants on Kauai's South Shore

To Lihue

Kaumualii Hwy.

Kalaheo

520
Omao
50

Lawai International Center

Lawai

Kukuiolono Park

540

Kauai Coffee

Papalina Rd.

Waha Rd.

Halima Rd.

Koloa Rd.

Maluhia Rd.

Waita Reservoir

Koloa

Weliweli Rd.

Koloa Bypass Rd.

Ala Kalanikaumaka

Poipu Rd.

NTBG Allerton McBryde Gardens

Spouting Horn

Nomilo Fishpond

Lawai Bay

Kukuiula Bay

Poipu Rd.

Poipu

Poipu Beach

Makahuena Pt.

Makawehi Pt.

Keoneloa (Shipwrecks) Beach

Haula Beach

Kawai Bay

Mahaulepu (Gillin's) Beach

Makauwahi Cave

See detail map below

0   2 mi
0   2 km

KAUAI (inset)

Hanalei

Waimea   Lihue

Poipu

Area of main map

Ala Kalanikaumaka
Poipu Rd.

Prince Kuhio Park

Lawai Rd.

Baby Beach

Hoonani Rd.

Kapili Rd.

Kiahuna Dr.

Kiahuna Beach

Poipu Rd.

Kipuka St.

Ala Kinoiki (Koloa Bypass)

Poipu Rd.

Hoone Rd.

Brennecke's Beach

Poipu Beach Park

Hoohu Rd.

Pe'e Rd.

Keoneloa (Shipwrecks) Beach

0   1/2 mi
0   1/2 km

RESTAURANTS

Anuenue Cafe **17**
The Beach House **10**
Brick Oven Pizza **1**
Bubba's Burgers **11**
Craving Thai **7**
Da Crack **13**
Eating House 1849 **11**
Fresh Shave **3**
Garden Island Grille **6**
HoloHolo Grill **14**
Kalaheo Café & Coffee Co. **2**
Kauai Food Truck **5**
Keoki's Paradise **17**
Koloa Fish Market **7**
La Spezia **7**
Little Fish Coffee **20**
Merriman's Fish House/
    Merriman's Gourmet Pizza & Burgers **11**
Olympic Cafe **20**
Red Salt **19**
Roots in Culture **3**
RumFire Poipu Beach **16**
Sueoka's Snack Shop **6**
Tortilla Republic **11**

HOTELS

Grand Hyatt Kauai Resort & Spa **22**
Kahala (Poipu Kai Resort) **21**
Kauai Banyan Inn **4**
Kauai Cove Cottage **12**
Kiahuna Plantation Resort **18**
Koa Kea Hotel & Resort **19**
Koloa Landing Resort **14**
Lodge at Kukuiula **8**
Marjorie's Kauai Inn **3**
Nihi Kai Villas **19**
Poipu Kapili Resort **15**
Poipu Plantation B&B Inn & Vacation Rentals **20**
Prince Kuhio **9**
Sheraton Kauai Resort **16**
Waikomo Stream Villas **14**

Eating House 1849 ★★★ GOURMET PLANTATION Hawaii Regional Cuisine co-founder Roy Yamaguchi surprised many in 2015 when he announced he was closing his upscale Roy's, a fixture of Poipu Shopping Village for 2 decades, in order to open this more casual concept inspired by the multicultural plantation era (and named for the islands' first restaurant, founded in Honolulu in 1849). The throngs now ascending the stairs to the second-story, open-walled dining room in the Shops at Kukuiula may only be surprised by the noise—the food is predictably excellent. Executive chef Clinton Nuyda's culinary finesse and local beef, fish, and produce ensure excellent preparations of "humble" fare such pork and shrimp potstickers ($15), the Hapa burger made of grass-fed Kauai beef and wild boar ($20), and *kamameshi* (hot-pot rice bowl) with chicken ($18) or butterfish ($42). The bubu arare salmon ($30), coated in rice crackers and served with kabocha (pumpkin) tempura, is a crunchy revelation.

In the Shops at Kukuiula, 2829 Ala Kalanikaumaka St., Poipu. www.eatinghouse1849. com. ✆ **808/742-5000.** Reservations recommended. Main courses $18–$50. Daily 5–9:30pm.

Red Salt ★★ HAWAII REGIONAL CUISINE One of the best hotel restaurants on Kauai, this is also one of the smallest and hardest to find, tucked inside the discreetly located **Koa Kea Hotel & Resort** (p. 567). Although rivals offer more dramatic ocean views in plusher settings, Red Salt has consistently executed elegantly presented dishes from a menu first designed by El Bulli–trained chef Ronnie Sanchez in 2009 and expanded by later chefs. The latest is Kauai native Noelani Planas, who trained under Joel Robuchon and Wolfgang Puck, among others. She serves seared mahi-mahi with forbidden black rice (as the nutritious grain is known) flavored with Madagascar vanilla bean, while her Kona lobster gnocchi benefits from charred leeks and cremini mushrooms. The latter is on Planas' four-course tasting menu ($79). On most nights the adjacent lounge serves exquisite sashimi and sushi, along with small plates such as kalua pork potstickers and crabcakes. Red Salt is also open for breakfast; the house specialty, lemon-souffle pancakes, take 20 minutes, but are worth the wait, and possibly the cost ($22).

In Koa Kea Hotel & Resort, 2251 Poipu Rd., Poipu. www.koakea.com. ✆ **808/828- 8888.** Dinner reservations recommended. Valet parking. Main courses $11–$22 breakfast and $26–$52 dinner (most $35–$39). Daily breakfast 6:30–11am, dinner 6–10pm; sushi lounge Tues–Sat 5:30–9pm.

MODERATE

La Spezia ★★★ ITALIAN The definition of charming, this much-needed stylish but cozy bistro in Old Koloa Town doesn't accept reservations for parties of fewer than six—reason enough to make a few friends at the pool to join you for dinner. Still, walk-ins will find it worth the possible wait for a table, handmade from wine crates by co-owner Dan

Seltzer; don't hesitate to sit at the small but handsome bar either. Stalwarts on the seasonal, home-style menu include spicy veggie arrabiata, rib-sticking lasagna Bolognese, pan-roasted chicken, seared pork tenderloin with capers, and hanger steak with Gorgonzola polenta. At breakfast or the expanded Sunday brunch, French toast made with Hawaiian sweet bread, Brie, bacon, and raspberry jam provides the ultimate guilty plea-sure, balanced by the Caprese-style egg-white frittata. Sunday brunch includes a make-your-own Bloody Mary bar ($7).

5492 Koloa Rd., Koloa (across from the post office). www.laspeziakauai.com. © **808/742-8824.** Reservations accepted for parties of 6 or more. Main courses $10–$14 breakfast, $13–$26 dinner, $12 Sun brunch. Breakfast Tues and Thurs–Sat 8–11:30am, Wed 8:30–11:30am; dinner Tues–Sun 5–10pm; Sun brunch 8am–1pm.

Merriman's Gourmet Pizza & Burgers ★★ AMERICAN/ISLAND FARM   A pioneer in Hawaii Regional Cuisine, Maui-based chef Peter Merriman first expanded onto Kauai with his gourmet restaurant, **Merri-man's Fish House** ★★ (open for dinner Monday–Saturday; main courses $26–$59). Although the elevated dining room still merits a splurge, you're more likely to make repeat trips to the casual restaurant on its ground floor. The thin-crust organic wheat pizzas come with island ingredients such as roasted Hamakua mushrooms or kalua pork with grilled pineap-ple, as well as classics such as pepperoni and sausage. Burgers feature local grass-fed beef and lamb, although the turkey option ($13), with Asian pear, white cheddar, and arugula, is also popular. Fries are extra ($5) but worth ordering. Daily happy hour deals include 25% off all food and wine; entrees on the children's menu cost $9–$10.

In the Shops at Kukuiula, below Merriman's Fish House, 2829 Ala Kalanikaumaka St., Poipu. www.merrimanshawaii.com. © **808/742-2856.** Main courses $13–$20. Daily 11am–10pm, happy hour 3:30–5:30pm. Live music 6:30–8:30pm Tues and Sun.

Tortilla Republic ★★ GOURMET MEXICAN   This vibrant, bi-level restaurant offers two ways to experience its modern, sophisticated take on Mexican cuisine, each with menus based on natural, organic, and local ingredients where possible. Open for dinner only (book for sunset), the **Upstairs** specializes in exotic-for-Kauai seasonings: Sautéed black tiger shrimp are served with a sauce of *pipián rojo* (red squash seeds), while the day's fresh catch comes rubbed in ancho chili with a serrano cilantro cit-rus sauce. Order the table-made guacamole ($16) for sheer entertainment value. At lunch and dinner, the indoor/outdoor **TR Cantina & Margarita Bar** ★★ offers simpler but still delicious dishes, including a trio of gua-jillo-rubbed grilled fish tacos. For weekend brunch at the Cantina, try the avocado toast with poached eggs and pepitas, or the carnitas hash. Happy hour deals include $6 margaritas and $3 beers.

In the Shops at Kukuiula, 2829 Ala Kalanikaumaka St., Poipu. www.tortillarepublic. com. © **808/742-8884.** Reservations recommended. **Upstairs:** Main courses $19–$34; daily 5:30–9pm. **Cantina:** Main courses $13–$22 brunch, lunch, and dinner; daily 11am–10pm. Happy hour daily 3–5pm.

In addition to the listings below, pop into **Little Fish Coffee** ★★ (www. littlefishcoffee.com; ✆ **808/742-2113**) in Poipu for fresh pastries, salads, panini specials, and beautifully swirled coffee and tea drinks, just like its original location in Hanapepe (p. 589). It's at the entrance to the Poipu Beach Athletic Club, 2290 Koloa Rd., and open 6:30am to 3pm daily. **Anuenue Cafe** ★ (www.anuenuecafe.com; ✆ **808/295-0109**) in Poipu Shopping Village opens daily at 6am, serving locally sourced omelets, mac nut pancakes, and kalua pig sandwiches, among other treats, till 12:30pm. In the Kukuiula strip mall, 2827 Poipu Rd., **Da Crack** ★ (✆ **808/742-9505**) is a takeout window where a line often forms for fish tacos with wasabi cream and the massive but relatively healthful burritos (vegan beans, brown rice); it's open 11am to 8pm Monday through Saturday and till 3pm Sunday.

In Old Town Koloa, check out the hearty local fare of **Kauai Food Truck** ★, in Knudsen Park across from Sueoka Market (www.facebook. com/kauaifoodtruck), and **Craving Thai** ★, dishing out noodles and curries at 3477 Weliweli Rd., next to Koloa Zipline (www.cravingthaikauai. com; ✆ **808/634-9959**); their dishes are not as memorable as **Roots in Culture** (p. 584), but are certainly convenient in a pinch. For affordable sit-down, family-friendly fare, including fish tacos, try **Garden Island Grille** ★ (www.gardenislandgrille.com; ✆ **808/639-8444**) at 5404 Koloa Rd; it's open for lunch and dinner 11:30am to 8:30pm daily, with nightly live Hawaiian music.

Brick Oven Pizza ★ PIZZA   This local favorite is relatively easy on the budget—the 12-slice pizzas, featuring hand-tossed crusts, are genuinely large, and there's a bountiful, if not particularly exciting, all-you-can-eat buffet from 5 to 9pm Monday and Thursday ($18 adults, $13 children 4–12). Pastas, subs, and salads are basic but well priced; decadent dessert pizzas come topped with Snickers and the like. For island flavors, order the kimchi tofu or guava-glazed smoked pork appetizers at the bar, which has a broad beer list. *Note:* Gluten-free crusts are available for a $4 surcharge. There's also a branch in Wailua.

Second floor, 2-2555 Kaumualii Hwy., *mauka* side, Kalaheo (across the street from Kalaheo Cafe). www.brickovenpizzahawaii.com. ✆ **808/332-8561. Wailua:** 4-4361 Kuhio Hwy., *mauka* side (across from Kinipopo Shopping Village). ✆ **808/823-8561.** Sandwiches $12–$14; medium (10-slice) pizzas $18–$26. Wed–Mon 11am–9pm; buffet Mon and Thur 5–9pm. Happy hour Wed–Mon 2–6pm.

Kalaheo Café & Coffee Co. ★★ BAKERY CAFE/ISLAND FARM   Whether you just grab a freshly baked cookie and cup of Kauai coffee to go or make a full meal of it, you'll quickly discover why visitors and locals jockey for parking spots at this casual restaurant and bakery. Early hours and hearty breakfasts (including convenient wraps) make it a popular stop on the way to snorkel cruises or Waimea Canyon. About a

15-minute drive from Poipu, the plantation-style cafe also offers a great alternative to high-priced resort dining. Greens grown nearby dominate the extensive salad list, while the rustic housemade buns pair nicely with grass-fed Kauai beef, veggie, or turkey burgers, among other plump sandwiches. Dinner is on the pricier side, but fresh seafood, such as blackened ahi with kale Caesar, and the Hunan-style pork ribs shine.

2-2560 Kaumualii Hwy., *makai* side, Kalaheo (across the street from Brick Oven Pizza). www.kalaheo.com. © **808/332-5858.** Breakfast $5–$13; lunch $7–$15; dinner main courses $17–$32. Breakfast Mon–Sat 6:30–11:30am and Sun 6:30am–2pm; lunch Mon–Sat 11am–2:30pm; dinner Tues–Thurs 5–8:30pm and Fri–Sat 5–9pm.

West Side

With fewer hotels, the West Side offers mostly unassuming food options with limited hours (typically closed Sun). Many visitors just stop in Waimea for shave ice—try **Jo-Jo's Shave Ice ★** at 9691 Kaumualii Hwy., *makai* side, across from the high school (© **808/635-7615**)—or for luscious Roselani ice cream and tropical shakes at **Super Duper ★**, 9889 Waimea Rd. (© **808/338-1590**).

Near Waimea Canyon, visit the **Kokee Lodge ★,** 9400 Kaumualii Hwy. (www.kokeelodge.com; © **808/335-6061**), for inexpensive local-style breakfast and lunch entrees ($4–$12) from 9am to 4pm (although the kitchen may close earlier). Hikers will appreciate the hearty Portuguese bean soup or chili, or a pick-me-up slice of lilikoi chiffon pie with espresso or pour-over coffee from Kauai Roastery. *Note:* The bar takes a dollar off cocktails from 2 to 4pm daily.

In Hanapepe, petite **Little Fish Coffee ★**, 3900 Hanapepe Rd. (www. littlefishcoffee.com; © **808/335-5000**) serves acai bowls, salads, and sandwiches 7am to 3pm daily. The town also holds one of the island's best bakeries, **Midnight Bear Breads ★★★**, 3830 Hanapepe Rd. (www. midnightbearbreads.com; © **808/346-4949**), which makes crusty European loaves, flaky croissants, and other island-sourced, organic baked goods, including pizzas and sandwiches. It's open 6:30am to 5pm Monday and Wednesday, 9am to 5pm Thursday, 9am to 9pm Friday, and 9am to 3pm Saturday. A tiny dining room and excellent Japanese dishes (including sushi) can make it hard to nab a seat at bright **Japanese Grandma's ★★** (www.japanesegrandma.com; © **808/855-5016**), 3871 Hanapepe Rd. It's open for lunch (11am–3pm) and dinner (5:30–9pm) Thursday through Monday.

MODERATE

Kauai Island Brewery & Grill ★★ BREWPUB The founders of the former Waimea Brewing Company opened this snazzy industrial/loft-style microbrewery and restaurant in Port Allen in 2012. The lilikoi ale—one of up to 10 house brews on tap—flavors the batter on fish and chips, but I prefer the silken ahi poke with seaweed salad or the blackened grilled catch of the day. The menu includes fish tacos, burgers (with a falafel veggie option), and other sandwiches. The open-air mezzanine provides an angled view of sunset over the harbor—and it can be mobbed when snorkel boats return midafternoon. *Note:* The kitchen closes at 9pm, but the bar may stay open later.

4350 Waialo Rd., Port Allen. www.kauaiislandbrewing.com. © **808/335-0006.** Main courses $12–$22. Daily 11am–9pm. Happy hour 3:30–5:30pm daily.

Wrangler's Steakhouse ★ STEAK/SEAFOOD   Like a steer in a rodeo, service here can be poky or lightning fast, but as the only full-service restaurant in town, it's often worth it even if you have to sit a spell. At lunch, skip the time-warp salad bar in favor of sandwiches or platters with fresh fish, Niihau free-range lamb, or Makaweli (Kauai) grass-fed beef. Tempura shrimp, teriyaki beef, and rice come in the plantation-style lunchbox known as a kau kau tin ($14); dinner is more steak-focused and pricey. The cozy **Saddle Room ★★** next door serves similar burgers and fish sandwiches, but with a more ambitious, locally sourced cocktail menu, such as the Kokee Mule with passion fruit vodka ($10) Alas, it's only open a few nights for dinner and for Sunday brunch.

9852 Kaumualii Hwy., *makai* side, Waimea (at Halepule Rd.). http://wranglers steakhouse.com. © **808/338-1218. Wrangler's:** Main courses $10–$14 lunch, $18–$34 dinner. Mon–Thurs 11am–8:30pm; Fri 11am–9pm; Sat 5–9pm. **Saddle Room:** Burgers and small plates $7–$17. Thurs 4–9pm; Fri 4–10pm; Sat 11am–10pm; Sun 11am–4pm.

INEXPENSIVE

In Waimea, go to **Gina's Anykine Grinds Cafe ★**, 9734 Kaumualii Hwy., *mauka* side by the theater (© **808/338-1731**), for casual breakfast and lunch ($7–$12), or just killer handheld coconut pies ($5). It's open 7am–2:30pm Tues–Thurs, 7am–1pm Fri, and 8am–1pm Sat. For lunch or early dinner, shrimp platters ($13) are the stars at **The Shrimp Station ★**, 9652 Kaumualii Hwy., Waimea, *makai* side, at Makeke Rd. (www.the shrimpstation.com; © **808/338-1242**). If you don't want to get your hands messy peeling shrimp, order the chopped shrimp tacos, a fried shrimp burger, or the fried coconut shrimp with a zesty papaya ginger tartar sauce. The open-air picnic tables do attract flies, so consider making yours a to-go order. It's open daily 11am to 5pm; the Kapaa location at 4-985 Kuhio Hwy., *mauka* side, at Keaka Rd. (© **808/821-0192**) stays open till 8:30pm. **Ishihara Market ★★** (see "Plate Lunch, Bento & Poke," p. 576) also has good picnic fare.

KAUAI SHOPPING

Kauai has more than a dozen open-air shopping centers and historic districts well suited to browsing, so souvenir and gift hunters are unlikely to leave the island empty-handed. To find something unique to the Garden Isle, look for the purple **Kauai made** logo. The image of a *ho'okupu*, the *ti*-leaf wrapping for special presents, means the county certifies that these handicrafts and food items were made on the island using local materials where possible, and in relatively small batches. Search for them by type of product or region at **www.kauaimade.net**.

Below are some of the island's more distinctive shopping stops.

East Side

LIHUE

The island's largest mall, **Kukui Grove Shopping Center,** 3-2600 Kaumualii Hwy., *makai* side at Nawiliwili Road (www.kukuigrovecenter. com), attracts locals with department stores such as **Macy's** and **Kmart;** visitors on a tight schedule or budget should browse the competitively priced, locally made foodstuffs (coffees, jams, cookies, and the like) at **Longs Drugs** (*©* **808/245-7785**). The mall's family-run **Déjà Vu Surf Hawaii** (www.dejavusurf.com; *©* **808/245-2174**) has a large selection of local and national brands.

Anchor Cove (3416 Rice St.) and **Harbor Mall** (3501 Rice St.), two small shopping centers near Nawiliwili Harbor, mostly offer typical T-shirts, aloha wear, and souvenirs; Harbor Mall has a free trolley for cruise ship passengers. Find tropical-print fabrics and clothes, batiks, and Hawaiian quilts at **Kapaia Stitchery,** 3-3351 Kuhio Hwy., *mauka* side at Laukini Road (www.kapaia-stitchery.com; *©* **808/245-2281**).

9

Hanalei Center shops in Hanalei

The Shops at Kilohana lay within the graceful 1930s mansion of Kilohana Plantation, 3-2087 Kaumualii Hwy., *mauka* side, south of Kauai Commuity College (www.kilohanakauai.com). It's a handsome setting for a half-dozen boutiques selling locally made, Hawaiian-inspired artwork, jewelry, clothing, and vintage Hawaiiana. Don't miss the handmade guava and sea salt caramels at **Kauai Sweet Shoppe** (☎ 808/245-8458) or the stand-alone **Koloa Rum Co.** (www.koloarum.com; ☎ 808/246-8900), which carries six kinds of its locally made rum, rum-based treats, and nonalcoholic goodies.

COCONUT COAST

At press time, **Coconut MarketPlace,** 4-484 Kuhio Hwy., *makai* side (at Aleka Loop), Kapaa (www.coconutmarketplace.com), was nearly done with renovations. It remains a haven for free entertainment (see website for calendar) and low-cost gifts. Check out **Auntie Lynda's Treasures** (www.hawaiianjewelryandgift.com; ☎ 808/821-1780) for an eclectic collection of woodcarvings, jewelry, and tchotchkes. In Wailua, **Pagoda** (4-369 Kuhio Hwy., *makai* side (across from Kintaro restaurant; www.pagodakauai.com; ☎ 808/821-2172), ably fills its niche with Chinese antiques and curios, Hawaiiana, Asian-inspired decor, candles, soaps, and other gifts. *Note:* It's closed Sun and Mon.

The historic (and hippie) district of Kapaa offers an intriguing mix of shops, cafes, and galleries. **Hula Girl,** 4-1340 Kuhio Hwy., *makai* side, at Kauwila St. (☎ 808/822-1950), not only sells women's resort wear (much of it made in Hawaii), but also aloha shirts, boardshorts, and other menswear, plus tiki-style barware, island-made soaps, and accessories. Natural fibers rule the day at **Island Hemp & Cotton,** 4-1373 Kuhio Hwy., *mauka* side (at Huluili St.; www.islandhemp.com; ☎ 808/821-0225), featuring stylish men's and women's clothing lines.

North Shore

KILAUEA

On the way to Kauapea (Secret) Beach and the lighthouse, **Kong Lung Historic Market Center,** 2484 Keneke St. (www.konglungkauai.com), deserves its own slot on the itinerary, with a bakery, bistro, and a half-dozen chic shops in vintage buildings with historical markers. Of the stores, the flagship **Kong Lung Trading** (www.konglung.com; ☎ 808/828-1822) is a showcase for Asian-themed ceramics, jewelry, books, and home accessories, including hand-turned wood bowls. Souvenir seekers can find less pricey options at the factory store of **Island Soap & Candle Works** (www.islandsoap.com; ☎ 808/828-1955), famed for its Surfer's Salve, tropical soaps, and soy candles in coconut shells.

PRINCEVILLE

Although **Princeville Center,** 5-4280 Kuhio Highway, *makai* side, north of the main Princeville entrance (www.princevillecenter.com), is mostly known for its inexpensive dining and resident-focused businesses, the **Hawaiian Music Store** kiosk (no phone) outside Foodland grocery has good deals on a large selection of CDs. **Magic Dragon Toy & Art Supply** (✆ **808/826-9144**) has a compact but cheery array of rainy-day entertainment for kids.

HANALEI

As you enter Hanalei, look for **Ola's Hanalei,** 5-5016 Kuhio Hwy., *makai* side, next to Dolphin restaurant (www.dougbrittart.com/olas-hanale; ✆ **808/826-6937**). Opened in 1982 by award-winning artist Doug Britt and his wife, Sharon, this small gallery features Doug's whimsical paintings, wooden toy boats, and furniture made from *objets trouvés,* plus engaging jewelry, glassware, and other works by Hawaii and Mainland artisans.

The center of town reveals more of Hanalei's bohemian side, with two eclectic shopping and dining complexes in historic buildings facing each other on Kuhio Highway. In the two-story rabbit warren of **Ching Young Village Shopping Center** (www.chingyoungvillage.com), **Divine Planet** (www.divine-planet.com; ✆ **808/826-8970**) brims with beads, star-shaped lanterns, silver jewelry from Thailand and India, and Balinese quilts. **On the Road to Hanalei** (✆ **808/826-7360**) stocks unique gifts from Kauai rooster figurines to Japanese pottery and African masks.

Across the street, the old Hanalei Schoolhouse is now the **Hanalei Center,** with two hidden gems: **Yellowfish Trading Company** (www. yellowfishtradingcompany.com; ✆ **808/826-1227**) and **Havaiki Oceanic and Tribal Art** (www.havaikiart.com; ✆ **808/826-7606**). At Yellowfish, retro hula girl lamps, vintage textiles and pottery, and collectible Hawaiiana mingle with reproduction signs, painted guitars, and other beach-shack musts in ever-changing inventory. The owners of Havaiki have sailed across the Pacific many times to obtain their museum-quality collection of gleaming wood bowls and fishhooks, exotic masks, shell jewelry, and intricately carved weapons and paddles; they also sell CDs, handmade cards, and other less-expensive gifts.

South Shore

KOLOA

Between the tree tunnel road and beaches of Poipu, **Old Koloa Town** (www.oldkoloa.com) has the usual tourist trinkets, but also some well-made local items and the island's best wine shop. The factory store of **Island Soap & Candle Works** (www.islandsoap.com; ✆ **808/742-1945**) is awash in fragrant, brightly hued wares, while the **Koa Store** (www. thekoastore.com; ✆ **808/742-1214**) showcases boxes, picture frames, and other small pieces by local woodworkers. **The Wine Shop** (www.the wineshopkauai.com; ✆ **808/742-7305**) lives up to its name but also sells high-quality, locally made treats such as Monkeypod Jam.

LAWAI

On the road between Koloa and Kalaheo, **Warehouse 3540**, 3540 Koloa Rd. (www.warehouse3540.com), provides a rustic-industrial space for moderately priced, pop-up style boutiques selling gifts, jewelry, home café, and art. Hours vary, with additional vendors and produce at the Friday market from 10am to 2pm. Just up the road, **Lawai Trading Post**, 3427 Koloa Rd., at Kaumualii Highway (✆ 808/332-7404), looks kitschy on the outside (and has a fair amount of kitsch inside), but also sells black pearls, Niihau shells, and other well-made jewelry, gifts, and clothes at decent prices; shop carefully, since returns are not allowed.

POIPU

Poipu Shopping Village, 2360 Kiahuna Plantation Dr. (www.poipushoppingvillage.com), hosts gift shops, independent boutiques, and Hawaii resort and surfwear chains; it also presents a free hula show at 4:30pm Monday and Thursday. The **Shops at Kukuiula,** just off the Poipu Road roundabout (www.kukuiula.com), has even more intriguing—and often expensive—boutiques spread among plantation-style cottages and flowering hibiscus. Amid all the high-end chic, surfers will feel right at home in **Poipu Surf** (www.poipusurf.com; ✆ 808/742-8797) and **Quiksilver** (run by Déjà Vu Surf Hawaii; www.dejavusurf.com; ✆ 808/742-8088). The Shops at Kukuiula is also home to the flagship store of **Malie Organics Lifestyle Boutique** (✆ 808/339-3055; www.malie.com), renowned for its bath and beauty products based on distillations of island plants, including mango, plumeria, and the native, lightly spice-scented *maile* vine.

KALAHEO

The crisp, tropical-flavored butter cookies of the **Kauai Kookie Kompany** are ubiquitous in Hawaii. Even better than a trip to the factory store in Hanapepe (1-3529 Kaumualii Hwy., *makai* side) is a stop at the **Kauai Kookie Bakery & Kitchen** complex in Kalaheo, 2-2436 Kaumualii Hwy., *makai* side (✆ 808/332-0821). One storefront is a small café selling specialty baked goods as well as a variety of "kookies"; the other is a vast gift shop with more fresh treats to consume on the spot.

West Side

HANAPEPE

Known for its Friday-night festival (see "Kauai Nightlife," p. 596), the historic town center of Hanapepe and its dozen-plus art galleries are just as pleasant to peruse by day, especially the cheery paintings at the **Bright Side Gallery,** 3890 Hanapepe Rd. (www.thebrightsidegallery.com; ✆ 808/634-8671), and the playful tiles at **Banana Patch Studio,** 3865 Hanapepe Rd. (www.bananapatchstudio.com; ✆ 808/335-5944). The courtyard passage next to Little Fish Coffee leads to **MoonBow Magic Gift Gallery,** 3900 Hanapepe Rd. (www.moonbowmagic.com;

kauai FARMERS MARKETS

A trip to one of the county-sponsored **Sunshine Markets** is a fun glimpse into island life, with shoppers lined up before the official start—listen for a yell or car honk—to buy fresh produce at rock-bottom prices. Markets end within 2 hours; arrive in time for the start, especially in Koloa and Kapaa. Among the best for visitors:

- **Monday:** noon, **Koloa Ball Park,** off Maluhia Rd., north of Old Town Koloa.

- **Wednesday:** 3pm, **Kapaa New Town Park,** Kahau St. at Olohena Rd.

- **Thursday:** 4:30pm, **Kilauea Neighborhood Center,** Keneke St. off Kilauea (Lighthouse) Rd.

- **Friday:** 3pm, **Vidinha Stadium parking lot,** Hoolako Rd. (off Hwy. 51), Lihue. For an even bigger farmers market, with many prepared foods, head to **Kauai Community College,**

3-1901 Kaumualii Hwy., Lihue, 9:30am to 1pm Saturday.

North Shore farmers markets offer the most organic produce. In **Kilauea,** that includes the privately run **Namahana Farmers Market** (www.anainahou.org; ℭ **808/828-2118**) at Anaina Hou Community Park in Kilauea, *mauka* side of Kuhio Hwy., Saturday 9am to 1pm and Monday 2pm to dusk. In **Hanalei,** the popular **Waipa Farmer's Market** (www.waipafoundation.org; ℭ **808/826-9969**) takes place every Tuesday at 2pm in a field just west of Hanalei, *mauka* side of Kuhio Hwy., between the Waioli and Waipa one-lane bridges. Some vendors also sell baked goods, jewelry, and other crafts, as they also do from 9:30am to noon Saturday at Hanalei's **Hale Halawai** ballpark (www.halehalawai.org; ℭ **808/826-1011**), Kuhio Hwy., *mauka* side at Mahimahi Rd., next to the green church.

9

KAUAI | Kauai Shopping

ℭ **808/335-5890**), which stocks a whimsical potpourri of colorful gifts and baubles, including beaded geckos, Niihau shells, and other jewelry.

If the door is open, the store is open at tiny **Taro Ko Chips Factory,** 3940 Hanapepe Rd. (ℭ **808/335-5586**), where dry-land taro farmer Dale Nagamine slices and fries his harvest—along with potatoes, purple sweet potatoes, and breadfruit—into delectable chips for $5 a bag (cash only). The wares of **Aloha Spice Company,** 3857 Hanapepe Rd. (www.alohaspice.com; ℭ **808/335-5960**), include grill-ready seasonings with a base of Hawaiian sea salt, and Hawaiian cane sugar infused with hibiscus, vanilla, or passion fruit. **Talk Story Bookstore,** 3785 Hanapepe Rd. (www.talkstorybookstore.com; ℭ **808/335-6469**), boasts the island's biggest trove of new, used, and out-of-print books.

PORT ALLEN

Chocolate fiends need to try the luscious handmade truffles, fudge, and "opihi" (chocolate-covered shortbread, caramel, and macadamia nuts in the shape of a shell) at **Kauai Chocolate Company,** 4341 Waialo Rd. (ℭ **808/335-0448**). You can watch them being made on-site, too.

Spice of Life Collectibles and Fine Junque, 9821 Kaumualii Hwy. (*mauka* side, next to the fire station), sell North Shore honey, nursery plants, and solar-powered camping provisions amid vintage Hawaiiana, antiques, and ephemera. Like Kauai Kookies, the passion fruit products of **Aunty Lilikoi**—including jelly, butter, and salad dressing—are often found around the state, but the factory store at 9875 Waimea Rd., across from the Captain Cook statue (www.auntylilikoi.com; ℂ **808/338-1296**), offers shipping and in-store-only delicious baked goods, such as scones, bars, and fudge.

In Kokee State Park (p. 517), the **Kokee Museum** (www.kokee.org; ℂ **808/335-9975**) sells Kauai- and nature-themed books, maps, and DVDs, while **Kokee Lodge** (www.kokeelodge.com; ℂ **808/335-6061**), offers a few souvenirs, island foods, and locally made crafts.

KAUAI NIGHTLIFE

Local nightlife is more suited to moonlight strolls than late-night party-ing, but if you're simply searching for live Hawaiian music, you're in luck. Most nights virtually every hotel lounge presents a slack-key guitar-ist singing Hawaiian *mele,* while many off-resort restaurants offer live Hawaiian music and other genres Thursday to Saturday.

Of the resort nightspots, **Duke's Barefoot Bar** (www.dukeskauai. com; ℂ **808/246-9599**), inside the Kauai Marriott Resort, has long drawn a crowd of visitors and locals, especially at *pau hana* (end of work) on Friday. The downstairs bar has live Hawaiian music Thursday through Monday 4 to 6pm, and Friday and Saturday 8:30 to 10:30pm.

The appetizers are tastier and the music more varied at the lounge of **Hukilau Lanai** (www.hukilaukauai.com; ℂ **808/822-0600**) inside the Kauai Coast Resort at the Beachboy, 520 Aleka Loop, Kapaa; top musi-cians playing Hawaiian, jazz, country, and blues perform Tuesday through Sunday from 6 to 9pm. The Grand Hyatt (www.grandhyattkauai.com; ℂ **808/741-1234**) presents contemporary island music from 8:30 to 11pm nightly at **Stevenson's Library,** a book-lined lounge and sushi bar; the Hyatt's **Seaview Terrace** offers live Hawaiian music from 5 to 8pm nightly, along with sunset views.

You'll meet more locals—and pay a good deal less for your drinks—by leaving the resorts. Here are highlights from around the island:

EAST SIDE   A combination sports bar, family restaurant, and nightclub, **Rob's Good Times Grill,** in the Rice Shopping Center, 4303 Rice St., Lihue (www.kauaisportsbarandgrill.com; ℂ **808/246-0311**), bustles with live music Tuesday through Friday and DJs for club dancing Friday and Saturday 10pm to 2am. **Mahiko Lounge,** the vintage living room of the Kilohana Plantation mansion, *mauka* side of Kaumualii Highway in Lihue (www.kilohanakauai.com; ℂ **808/245-5608**), makes artisan cocktails, served with live jazz 7 to 10pm Friday and $5 happy-hour specials (Mon–Sat 4–5:30pm). In Kapaa, **Trees Lounge**, 440 Aleka Place (www.treesloungekauai.com; © **808/823-0600**) showcases island music from 6pm nightly Monday through Saturday. The first Saturday of the month, Old Kapaa Town's partylike **Art Walk** includes live music from 5 to 9pm.

NORTH SHORE Tiki Iniki (www.tikiiniki.com; © **808/431-4242**), tucked behind Ace Hardware in Princeville Center (p. 592), is a cheeky tiki bar/restaurant owned by Michele Rundgren and her rock-musician husband, Todd. Opened in 1963, **Tahiti Nui**, 5-5134 Kuhio Hwy., Hanalei (www.thenui.com; © **808/826-6277**), morphs from a kid-friendly restaurant into a locals' lounge with nightly live music at 6:30pm. In the Old Hanalei Schoolhouse, **Hanalei Gourmet,** 5-5161 Kuhio Hwy. (www. hanaleigourmet.com; © **808/826-2524**), cranks up live music at 6pm Sunday and 8pm Wednesday. The **Kilauea Night Market**, from 4 to 8pm the last Saturday of the month at Anaina Hou Community Park (p. 507), percolates with live music, food, and art vendors.

SOUTH SHORE Keoki's Paradise, a popular restaurant in Poipu Shopping Village (www.keokisparadise.com; © **808/742-7534**), offers nightly live music in its dining room and on Fridays in its Bamboo Bar. **The Shops at Kukuiula** (www.theshopsatkukuiula.com) hosts a *kani kapila* (jam) from 6:30 to 8:30pm Friday, plus live music and vendors at the **Kukuiula Art Walk,** 6 to 9pm the second Saturday of the month. Don't miss island icon Larry Rivera Sundays at Koloa's **Garden Island Grille** (p. 588), which features music nightly from 6 to 8pm.

WEST SIDE The *tutu* (granddaddy) of local art events, the **Hanapepe Friday Night Festival and Art Walk** (www.hanapepe.org) features food trucks and live music every Friday from 6 to 9pm along Hanapepe Road.

9

KAUAI | Kauai Nightlife

PLANNING YOUR TRIP TO HAWAII

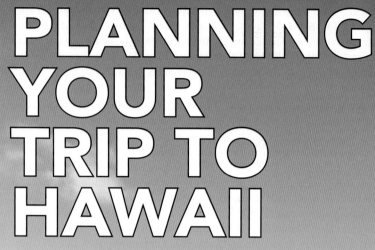

10

H awaii is rich in natural and cultural wonders, and each island has something unique to offer. With so much vying for your attention, planning a trip can be bewildering. Here we've compiled everything you need to know before escaping to the islands.

The first thing to do: **Decide where you want to go.** Read through each chapter to see which islands fit the profile and offer the activities you're looking for. We strongly recommend that you limit your island-hopping to one island per week. If you decide to visit more than one in a week, be warned: You could spend much of your precious vacation time in airports and checking in and out of hotels. Not much fun!

Our second tip is to **fly directly to the island of your choice;** doing so can save you a 2-hour layover in Honolulu and another plane ride. Oahu, the Big Island, Maui, and Kauai all receive direct flights from the Mainland.

So let's get on with the process of planning your trip. For pertinent facts and on-the-ground resources in Hawaii, turn to "Fast Facts: Hawaii," at the end of this chapter on p. 607.

GETTING THERE
By Plane

Most major U.S. and many international carriers fly to the **Daniel K. Inouye International** (HNL)—formerly Honolulu International Airport—on Oahu. Some also offer direct flights to **Kahului Airport** (OGG) on Maui, **Lihue Airport** (LIH) on Kauai, and **Kona International Airport** (KOA) and **Hilo Airport** (ITO) on the Big Island. If you can fly directly to the island of your choice, you'll be spared a 2-hour layover in Honolulu and another plane ride. If you're heading to **Molokai Airport** (MKK) or **Lanai Airport** (LNY), you'll have the easiest connections if you fly into Honolulu or Kahului. See island chapters for detailed information on direct flights to each island.

Hawaiian Airlines offers flights from more mainland U.S. gateways than any other airline. Hawaiian's easy-to-navigate website makes finding the cheapest fares a cinch. Its closest competitor, pricewise, is **Virgin America Airlines,** which flies nonstop from San Francisco and Los Angeles. **Alaska Airlines** offers daily nonstop flights from West Coast cities, including Anchorage, Seattle, Portland, and Oakland. New to the market, **Southwest Airlines** is worth checking out for deals from the West

internet or apps FOR HAWAII HOTEL DISCOUNTS

Hawaii hotels and resorts know they have a captive audience and high prices reflect that. And while it's not impossible to get a good deal by calling a hotel, you're more likely to snag a discount online or with a mobile app. Here are some strategies:

1. **Browse extreme discounts on sites where you reserve or bid for lodgings without knowing which hotel you'll get.** You'll find these on Priceline.com and Hotwire.com, and they can be money-savers, particularly if you're booking within a week of travel (that's when the hotels get nervous and resort to deep discounts). These feature major chains, so it's unlikely you'll book a dump.

2. **Review discounts on the hotel's website.** Hotels tend to give the lowest rates to those who book through their sites rather than through a third party. But you'll only find these truly deep discounts in the loyalty section of these sites—so join the club.

3. **Use the right hotel search engine.** They're not all equal, as we at Frommers.com learned in the spring of 2017 after putting the top 20 sites to the test in 20 destinations around the globe. We discovered that **Booking.com** listed the lowest rates for hotels in the city center, and in the under $200 range, 16 out of 20 times—the best record, by far, of all the sites we tested. And Booking.com includes all taxes and fees in its initial results (not all do, which can make for a frustrating shopping experience). For top-end properties, again in the city center, both Priceline.com and HotelsCombined.com came up with the best rates, tying at 14 wins each.

Coast. From points farther east, **United, American, Continental,** and **Delta** all fly to Hawaii with nonstop service to Honolulu and most neighbor islands. If you're having difficulty finding an affordable fare, try routing your flight through Las Vegas. It's a huge hub for traffic to and from the islands.

For travel from beyond the U.S. mainland, check these airlines: Air Canada, Air New Zealand, Qantas Airways, Japan Air Lines, All Nippon Airways (ANA), the Taiwan-based China Airlines, Korean Air, and Philippine Airlines. Hawaiian Airlines also flies nonstop to Australia, American Samoa, Philippines, Tahiti, South Korea, and Japan.

ARRIVING AT THE AIRPORT

IMMIGRATION & CUSTOMS CLEARANCE International visitors arriving by air should cultivate patience before setting foot on U.S. soil. U.S. airports have considerable security practices in place. Clearing Customs and Immigration can take as long as 2 hours.

AGRICULTURAL SCREENING AT AIRPORTS   At the Honolulu and neighbor-island airports, baggage and passengers bound for the Mainland must be screened by agriculture officials. Officials will confiscate fresh local produce (avocados, bananas, and mangoes) in the name of fruit-fly control. Pineapples, coconuts, and papayas inspected and certified for export; boxed flowers; leis without seeds; and processed foods (macadamia nuts, coffee, jams, dried fruit, and the like) will pass.

GETTING AROUND HAWAII

For additional advice on travel within each island, see "Getting Around" in the individual island chapters.

Interisland Flights

Hawaii has one major interisland carrier, **Hawaiian Airlines** (www.hawaiianair.com; ℂ **800/367-5320**), and a commuter airline **Mokulele Airlines** (www.mokuleleairlines.com; ℂ **866/260-7070**). The commuter flights service the neighbor islands' more remote airports and tend to be on small planes; you'll board from the tarmac and weight restrictions apply. Check-in at least 90 minutes before your flight—especially Oahu or during holidays. You can get by with 60 minutes at the neighbor-island airports.

By Shuttle

Roberts Hawaii Express Shuttle (www.robertshawaii.com; ℂ **800/831-5541** or 808/539-9400), offers curb-to-curb shuttle service to and from the airports on Oahu, Hawaii, Maui, and Kauai. Booking is a breeze (and 15% cheaper) on their website. **SpeediShuttle** (www.speedishuttle.com; ℂ **877/242-5777**) services all of the major airports plus the cruise terminal. For an extra fee, you can request a fresh flower lei greeting.

By Bus

Public transit is spotty—Oahu has adequate bus service, but even so, it's set up for residents, not tourists carrying suitcases or beach toys (all carry-ons must fit on your lap or under the bus seat). **TheBus** (www.thebus.org; ℂ **808/848-5555**) delivers you to destinations around the island for $2.50. If you're traveling on a shoestring and have the patience of a saint, this could be a transportation option for you. Bus nos. 19 and 20 travel regularly between the airport and Waikiki; the trip takes about an hour.

The neighbor-island buses are even less visitor-friendly. One-way rides cost $2. The **Kauai Bus** (www.kauai.gov/bus; ℂ **808/246-8110**) stops at Lihue Airport twice every hour, but connections to towns outside of Lihue are few and far between. On the Valley Isle, the **Maui Bus** (www.mauicounty.gov—hover over the "Services" option and then choose "Bus Service Information"; ℂ **808/871-4838**) picks up at Kahului Airport every 90 minutes and delivers riders to a transfer station at Queen Kaahumanu

Mall. The **Hele-On Bus** (www.heleonbus.org; ℭ **808/961-8744**) on Hawaii Island visits the Hilo Airport every 90 minutes and Kona Airport once a day.

By Car

Bottom line: Rent a car. You will need your own wheels to get around the islands, especially if you plan to explore outside your resort—and you absolutely should. As discussed above, public transit is unreliable, and taxis are obscenely expensive.

That said, Hawaii has some of the priciest car-rental rates in the country. The most expensive is the island of Lanai, where four-wheel-drive (4WD) vehicles cost a small fortune. Rental cars are often at a premium on Kauai, Molokai, and Lanai and may be sold out on any island over holiday weekends, so be sure to book well ahead. In fact, we recommend reserving your car as soon as you book your airfare.

To rent a car in Hawaii, you must be at least 25 years of age and have a valid driver's license and credit card. *Note:* If you're visiting from abroad and plan to rent a car in the United States, keep in mind that foreign driver's licenses are usually recognized in the U.S., but you should get an international one if your home license is not in English.

At the Honolulu and most neighbor-island airports, you'll find many major car-rental agencies, including **Alamo, Avis, Budget, Dollar, Enterprise, Hertz, National,** and **Thrifty.** Most of the islands have independent rental companies that operate outside of the airport, often for cheaper rates; check individual island chapters. If you're traveling with windsurfing or other sports gear on Maui, check out **Aloha Rent a Car** (ℭ **877/5452-5642** or 808/877-4477; www.aloharentacar.com). We highly recommend AutoSlash.com over other online car rental services. It applies every available coupon on the market to the booking, yielding surprisingly low daily rates. And if the cost of a rental drops, it automatically rebooks renters, again lowering the price.

GASOLINE Gas prices in Hawaii, always much higher than on the U.S. mainland, vary from island to island. Expect to pay around $4 a gallon, and as much as $5 a gallon on Lanai and Molokai. Check www.gasbuddy.com to find the cheapest gas in your area.

INSURANCE Hawaii is a no-fault state, which means that if you don't have collision-damage insurance, you are required to pay for all damages before you leave the state, whether or not the accident was your fault. Your personal car insurance may provide rental-car coverage; check before you leave home. Bring your insurance identification card if you decline the optional insurance, which usually costs from $9 to $45 a day. Obtain the name of your company's local claim representative before you go. Some credit card companies also provide collision-damage insurance for their customers; check with yours before you rent.

DRIVING RULES   Hawaii state law mandates that all car passengers must wear a **seat belt** and all infants must be strapped into a car seat. You'll pay a $92 fine if you don't buckle up. **Pedestrians** always have the right of way, even if they're not in the crosswalk. You can turn **right on red** after a full and complete stop, unless otherwise posted. Hand-held electronic devices are prohibited while driving.

> ### Stay Off the Cellphone
>
> Talking on a cellphone while driving in Hawaii is a big no-no. Fines start at $297 and increase in school or construction zones. Save yourself the money; if you *have* to take a photo of that rainbow, pull over.

ROAD MAPS   The best and most detailed maps for activities are published by **Franko Maps** (www.frankosmaps.com); they feature a host of island maps, plus a terrific "Hawaiian Reef Creatures Guide" for snorkelers curious about those fish they spot underwater. Free road maps are published by *This Week* magazine, a visitor publication available on Oahu, the Big Island, Maui, and Kauai.

Another good source is the **University of Hawaii Press maps,** which include a detailed network of island roads, large-scale insets of towns, historical and contemporary points of interest, parks, beaches, and hiking trails. If you can't find them in a bookstore near you, contact **University of Hawaii Press,** 2840 Kolowalu St., Honolulu, HI 96822 (www.uhpress. hawaii.edu; © **888/UH-PRESS** [847-7377]). For topographic maps of the islands, go to the **U.S. Geological Survey** site (https://pubs.er.usgs.gov).

SPECIAL-INTEREST TRIPS & TOURS

This section presents an overview of special-interest trips, tours, and outdoor excursions in Hawaii. See individual island chapters for detailed information on the best local outfitters and tour-guide operators—as well as tips for exploring on your own. Each island chapter discusses the best spots to set out on your own, from the top offshore snorkel and dive spots to great daylong hikes, as well as the federal, state, and county agencies that can help you with hikes on public property. We also list references for spotting birds, plants, and sea life. Always use the resources available to inquire about weather, trail, or surf conditions; water availability; and other conditions before you take off on your adventure.

Air Tours

Nothing beats getting a bird's-eye view of Hawaii. Some of the islands' most stunning scenery can't be seen any other way. You'll have your choice of aircraft here: **helicopter, small fixed-wing plane,** or, on Oahu, **seaplane.** For wide-open spaces such as the lava fields of Hawaii Volcanoes National Park, a fixed-wing plane is the safest and most affordable option. But for exploring tight canyons and valleys, helicopters have an advantage: They can hover. Only a helicopter can bring you face to face with waterfalls in remote places like Mount Waialeale on Kauai and Maui's little-known Wall of Tears, up near the summit of Puu Kukui.

Today's pilots are part historian, part DJ, part amusement-ride operator, and part tour guide, sharing anecdotes about Hawaii's flora, fauna, history, and culture. Top trips include:

o **Napali Coast,** Kauai, where you soar over the painted landscape of Waimea Canyon, known as the "Grand Canyon of the Pacific," and visit the cascading falls of Mount Waialeale, one of the wettest spots on Earth.

o **Haleakala National Park and West Maui,** where you skirt the edges of Haleakala's otherworldly crater before plunging into the deep, pristine valleys of the West Maui Mountains.

o **Hawaii Volcanoes National Park** on the Big Island, where you stare into the molten core of a live volcano and watch lava spill into the sea.

Farm Tours

Overalls and garden spades might fit your image of a Hawaii vacation, but a tour of a lush and bountiful island farm should be on your itinerary. Agritourism has become an important new income stream for Hawaii farmers, who often struggle with the rising costs of doing business in paradise. Farm tours benefit everyone: The farmer gets extra cash, visitors gain an intimate understanding of where and how their food is produced, and fertile farmlands stay in production—preserving Hawaii's rural heritage. There are so many diverse and inspiring farms to choose from: **100-year-old Kona coffee farms,** bean-to-bar **chocolate plantations, orchid nurseries,** an award-winning **goat dairy,** and even a **vodka farm!**

With its massive cattle ranches, tropical flower nurseries, and coffee-covered hillsides, the Big Island is the agricultural heart of Hawaii. But each of the islands has farms worth visiting. Many agritours include sumptuous tasting sessions, fascinating historical accounts, and tips for growing your own food at home. See each island's "Exploring" section for details on visiting local farms.

On the Big Island, **Hawaii Forest & Trail** (www.hawaii-forest.com; ✆ **808/331-8505**) visits tropical fruit and coffee farms as part of their whole-day tours. Individual coffee growers open their orchards up as well (see p. 191).

Maui Country Farm Tours (www.mauicountryfarmtours.com; ✆ **808/283-9131**) offers a gorgeous overview of agriculture on the Valley Isle, traveling through working coffee and pineapple plantations and stopping at a lavender farm, a goat dairy, and a vodka distillery.

National Parks

Hawaii boasts some of the oldest national parks in the system—and the only one with an erupting volcano. The National Park Service manages eight sites on four islands: the **World War II Valor in the Pacific National Monument** on Oahu, **Haleakala National Park** on Maui, **Kalaupapa National Historic Park** on Molokai, and **Hawaii Volcanoes National Park**, **Kaloko-Honokohau National Historic Park**, **Puu o Honaunau Historic Park**, and the **Ala Kahakai National Historic Trail** on the island of Hawaii. Plans to open the **Honouliuli National Monument** commemorating the losses of Japanese citizens interned during WWII are underway.

A Weeklong Cruise Through the Islands

If you're looking for a taste of several islands in 7 days, consider **Norwegian Cruise Line** (www.ncl.com; ✆ **866/234-7350**), the only cruise line that operates year-round in Hawaii. NCL's 2,186-passenger ship *Pride of America* circles Hawaii, stopping on four islands: the Big Island, Maui, Kauai, and Oahu.

Volunteer Vacations & Ecotourism

If you're looking to swap sunbathing for something more memorable on your next trip to Hawaii, consider volunteering while on vacation. Rewards include new friends and access to spectacular wilderness areas that are otherwise off-limits.

If you're looking for eco-friendly tour operators, the **Hawaii Ecotourism Association** website (www.hawaiiecotourism.org; ✆ **808/235-5431**) is a good place to start. The owners of Hale Hookipa Inn on Maui maintain a great list of places to volunteer on the Valley Isle. Check it out at http://volunteer-on-vacation-hawaii.com.

The **Surfrider Foundation** organizes beach and reef cleanups and has several active chapters throughout the islands: Oahu (https://oahu.surfrider.org); Maui (https://maui.surfrider.org); Kauai (https://kauai.surfrider.org); and, on the Big Island, Kona (https://kona.surfrider.org) and Hilo (https://hilo.surfrider.org). And what could be more exciting than keeping watch over nesting sea turtles? Contact the **University of Hawaii Sea Grant College Program** (✆ **808/956-7031**) and the **Hawaii Wildlife Fund** (www.wildhawaii.org; ✆ **808/280-8124**) to see if they need help monitoring marine life.

For a truly novel experience, sign up on the waitlist to volunteer with **Kahoolawe Island Restoration Commission** (www.kahoolawe.hawaii.gov/volunteer.shtml; ✆ **808/243-5020**). You'll travel by boat from Maui to Kahoolawe, an uninhabited island that the U.S. military used as target practice for decades. Plant by plant, volunteers bring life back to the barren island, once a significant site for Hawaiian navigators. A week here is a cultural immersion unlike any other.

A great alternative to hiring a private guide is taking a trip with the **Nature Conservancy** or the **Sierra Club.** Both organizations offer guided hikes in preserves and special areas during the year, as well as day- to week-long volunteer work trips to restore habitats and trails, and root out invasive plants. It's a chance to see the "real" Hawaii—including wilderness areas that are ordinarily off-limits.

The Sierra Club offers half- or all-day hikes to beautiful, remote spots on Oahu, Kauai, the Big Island, and Maui. Knowledgeable volunteers lead the trips and share a wealth of cultural and botanical information. Hikes are classified as easy, moderate, or strenuous; some (but not all) incorporate a few hours of volunteer work. Donations of $3 for Sierra Club members and $5 for nonmembers (bring exact change) are recommended. Contact the **Hawaii Chapter of the Sierra Club** (www.sierra clubhawaii.com; ✆ **808/538-6616** on Oahu).

All Nature Conservancy hikes and work trips are free (donations appreciated). However, you must reserve a spot. Hikes are offered once a month on Maui and Molokai, and occasionally on Oahu. Contact the **Nature Conservancy of Hawaii** (www.nature.org/hawaii; ✆ **808/537-4508** on Oahu; ✆ **808/572-7849** on Maui; ✆ **808/553-5236** on Molokai; and ✆ **808/587-6257** on Kauai).

Watersports Excursions

The same Pacific Ocean surrounds all of the Hawaiian Islands, but the varying topography of each shoreline makes certain spots superior for watersports. If **surfing** is your passion, head to Oahu. You'll find gentle waves at Waikiki and adrenaline-laced action on the famed North Shore. Maui has plenty of surf breaks, too; plus, it's the birthplace of **windsurfing** and a top **kitesurfing** destination. Beginners and pros alike will find perfect conditions for catching air off of Maui's swells.

Kayaking is excellent statewide, particularly on Kauai, where you can take the adventurous Napali Coast challenge, and on Molokai, where you can lazily paddle downwind past ancient fishponds.

Reef-safe Sunscreen

Hawaii recently became the first state to ban the sale of sunscreen containing chemicals that harm coral reefs and other marine life. New studies revealed that oxybenzone and octinoxate—the active ingredients in many sunblocks—contribute to coral bleaching. They may also be detrimental to human health. The good news? You can defend yourself against harmful UV rays without endangering your fishy friends. Invest in a hat and long sleeves. Purchase mineral sunblocks with zinc oxide and titanium dioxide. Look for the "reef safe" label. The new law won't go into effect until 2021, but you can get a head start on protecting yourself and the reef. Check out bereefsafe.com for more information.

Sport fishing fans should head to the Big Island's Kona Coast where billfish tournaments have reeled in monster Pacific blue marlins.

The deep blue Kona waters are also home to giant manta rays, and **scuba diving** among these gentle creatures is a magical experience. Scuba diving is also spectacular off Lanai, where ethereal caverns have formed in the reefs, and on Maui, on the back wall of Molokini Crater.

All of the islands have great **snorkeling** spots, but Maui's two small boat harbors offer the widest range of snorkel and dive tours. Book a half-day cruise out to Molokini or an all-day adventure over to Lanai.

During the winter months, from November to April, **whale-watching** tours launch from every island, but the marine mammals seem to favor Maui's Maalaea Bay. **Dolphin-spotting** is most reliable on Lanai at Manele Bay and on Hawaii at Kealakekua Bay, where the charismatic spinner dolphins come to rest.

Go to each island's "Watersports" sections for detailed information on watersports outfitters and tour providers.

[Fast FACTS] HAWAII

Area Codes Hawaii's area code is 808; it applies to all islands. Use the area code when calling from one island to another; there is a long-distance charge.

Customs For details regarding U.S. Customs and Border Protection, consult your nearest U.S. embassy or consulate, or U.S. Customs (www.cbp.gov). You cannot take home fresh fruit, plants, or seeds (including some leis) unless they are inspected and sealed. You cannot seal and pack them yourself. For information on what you're allowed to bring home, contact one of the following agencies:

U.S. Citizens: U.S. Customs & Border Protection (CBP), 1300 Pennsylvania Ave., NW, Washington, DC 20229 (www.cbp.gov; ☎ 877/CBP-5511).

Canadian Citizens: Canada Border Services Agency (www.cbsa-asfc.gc.ca; ☎ 800/461-9999 in Canada, or 204/983-3500).

U.K. Citizens: HM Customs & Excise (www.hmce.gov.uk; ☎ 0845/010-9000 in the U.K., or 020/8929-0152).

Australian Citizens: Australian Customs Service (www.customs.gov.au; ☎ 1300/363-263).

New Zealand Citizens: New Zealand Customs, The Customhouse, 17–21 Whitmore St., Box 2218, Wellington (www.customs.govt.nz; ☎ 64/9-927-8036 outside of NZ, or 0800/428-786).

Electricity Like Canada, the United States uses 110 to 120 volts AC (60 cycles), compared to 220 to 240 volts AC (50 cycles) in most of Europe, Australia, and New Zealand. Downward converters that change 220–240 volts to 110–120 volts are hard to find in the U.S., so bring one with you if you're traveling to Hawaii from abroad.

Embassies & Consulates All embassies are in the nation's capital, Washington, D.C. Some consulates are in major U.S. cities, and most nations have a mission to the United Nations in New York City. If your country isn't listed below, check **www.embassy.org/embassies**.

The embassy of **Australia** is at 1601 Massachusetts Ave. NW, Washington, DC 20036 (www.usa.embassy.gov.au; ☎ 202/797-3000). Consulates are in New York, Honolulu, Houston, Los Angeles, Denver, Atlanta, Chicago, and San Francisco.

The embassy of **Canada** is at 501 Pennsylvania Ave. NW, Washington, DC 20001 (www.canadianembassy.org; ℂ **202/682-1740**). Consulates are in Chicago, Detroit, San Diego, and other cities. See website for full listing.

The embassy of **Ireland** is at 2234 Massachusetts Ave. NW, Washington, DC 20008 (www.embassyofireland.org; ℂ **202/462-3939**). Irish consulates are in Boston, Chicago, New York, San Francisco, and other cities. See website for full listing.

The embassy of **New Zealand** is at 37 Observatory Circle NW, Washington, DC 20008 (www.nzembassy.com; ℂ **202/328-4800**). Consulates are in Los Angeles and Honolulu.

The embassy of the **United Kingdom** is at 3100 Massachusetts Ave. NW, Washington, DC 20008 (www.gov.uk/government/world/usa; ℂ **202/588-6500**). Other British consulates are in Atlanta, Boston, Chicago, Houston, Los Angeles, New York, San Francisco, and Miami.

Family Travel With

beaches to build castles on, water to splash in, and amazing sights to see, Hawaii is paradise for children. Take a look at "The Best of Hawaii for Kids" in chapter 1.

The larger hotels and resorts offer supervised programs for children and can refer you to qualified babysitters. By state law, hotels can accept only children ages 5 to 12 in supervised activities programs but can often accommodate younger kids by hiring babysitters to watch over them. Contact **People Attentive to Children (PATCH)** for referrals to babysitters who have taken a training course in childcare. On Oahu, call ℂ **808/839-1988;** on the Big Island, call ℂ **808/322-3500** in Kona or ℂ **808/961-3169** in Hilo; on Maui, call ℂ **808/242-9232;** on Kauai, call ℂ **808/246-0622;** on Molokai and Lanai, call ℂ **800/498-4145;** or visit www.patchhawaii.org. The **Nanny Connection** (www.thenannyconnection.com; ℂ **808/875-4777**) on Maui is a reputable business that sends Mary Poppins–esque nannies to resorts and beaches to watch children ($15 per hour and up, with a 3-hour minimum and a $25 booking fee). Tutoring services are also available.

Baby's Away (www.babysaway.com) rents cribs, strollers, highchairs, playpens, infant seats, and the like on Oahu (ℂ **800/496-6386** or 808/729-4214), Maui (ℂ **800/942-9030** or 808/269-4939 and Hawaii Island (ℂ **800/996-9030** or 808/747-9667). The staff will deliver whatever you need to wherever you're staying and pick it up when you're done.

Gay & Lesbian

Travelers The number of gay- or lesbian-specific accommodations on the islands is limited, but Hawaii welcomes all people with aloha. Since 1990, the state's capital has hosted the **Honolulu Pride Parade and Celebration.** Register to participate at www.honolulupride.org.

Pride Guide Hawaii (www.gogayhawaii.com) features gay and lesbian news, blogs, business recommendations, and other information for the entire state. Also check out the website for **Out in Hawaii** (www.outinhawaii.com), which calls itself "Queer Resources and Information for the State of Hawaii," with vacation ideas, a calendar of events, information on Hawaii, and even a chat room.

Health Mosquitoes

Mosquito-borne diseases are rare in Hawaii, though an outbreak of dengue fever did affect Hawaii Island in 2016. The Hawaii State Health Department recommends travelers a) choose lodging with screens or sleep under a mosquito net; b) cover up in long sleeves and pants; and c) use EPA-registered insect repellent. For more info, visit the **Centers for Disease Control and Prevention** website at www.cdc.gov/features/StopMosquitoes.

Centipedes, Scorpions & Other Critters Although insects can get a little close for comfort in Hawaii (expect to see ants, cockroaches, and other critters indoors, even in posh hotels), few cause serious trouble. Giant centipedes—as long as 8 inches—are occasionally seen; scorpions are rare. Around Hilo on the Big Island, little red fire ants can rain down from trees and sting unsuspecting passersby. If you're stung or bitten by an insect and experience extreme pain, swelling, nausea, or any other severe reaction, seek medical help immediately. Geckos—the little lizards circling your porch light—are harmless and considered good luck in Hawaiian homes. Yes, even *inside* homes.

Hiking Safety Before you set out on a hike, let someone know where you're heading and when you plan to return; too many hikers spend cold nights in the wilderness because they don't take this simple precaution. It's always a good idea to hike with a pal. Select your route based on your own fitness level. Check weather conditions with the **National Weather Service** (www.prh.noaa.gov/hnl; ✆ **808/973-5286** on Oahu), even if it looks sunny: The weather here ranges from blistering hot to freezing cold and can change in a matter of hours or miles. Do *not* hike if rain or a storm is predicted; flash floods are common in Hawaii and have resulted in many preventable deaths. Plan to finish your hike at least an hour before sunset; because Hawaii is so close to the equator, it does not have a twilight period, and thus it gets dark quickly after the sun sets. Wear sturdy shoes, a hat, clothes

to protect you from the sun and from getting scratches, and high-SPF sunscreen on all exposed areas. Take plenty of water, a basic first-aid kit, a snack, and a bag to pack out what you pack in. Watch your step. Loose lava rocks are famous for twisting ankles. Don't rely on cellphones; service isn't available in many remote places.

Vog When molten lava from Kilauea pours into the ocean, gases are released, resulting in a brownish, volcanic haze that hovers at the horizon. Some people claim that exposure to the smoglike air causes headaches and bronchial ailments. To date, there's no evidence that vog causes lingering damage to healthy individuals. Vog primarily affects the Big Island—Kona, in particular—but is often felt as far away as Maui and Oahu. You can minimize the effects of vog by closing your windows and using an air conditioner indoors. The University of Hawaii recommends draping a floor fan with a wet cloth saturated in a thin paste of baking soda and water, which captures and neutralizes the sulfur compounds. Cleansing your sinuses with a neti pot and saltwater also helps. ***Word of caution:*** If you're pregnant or have heart or breathing problems, avoid exposure to the sulfuric fumes in and around Hawaii Volcanoes National Park.

Ocean Safety The range of watersports available here is astounding—this is a prime water playground with conditions for every age and ability. But the ocean is also an untamed wilderness; don't expect a calm swimming pool. Many people who visit Hawaii underestimate the power of the ocean. With just a few precautions, your Pacific experience can be a safe and happy one. Before jumping in, familiarize yourself with your equipment. If you're snorkeling, make sure you feel at ease breathing and clearing water from the snorkel. Take a moment to watch where others are swimming. Observe weather conditions, swells, and possible riptides. If you get caught in big surf, dive underneath each wave until the swell subsides. Never turn your back to the ocean; rogue waves catch even experienced water folk unaware. Be realistic about your fitness—more than one visitor has ended his or her vacation with a heart attack in the water. Don't go out alone, or during a storm.

Note that sharks are not a big problem in Hawaii; in fact, local divers look forward to seeing them. Only 2 of the 40 shark species present in Hawaiian waters are known to bite humans, and then usually it's by accident. But here are the general rules for avoiding sharks: Don't swim at dusk or in murky water—sharks may mistake you for one of their usual meals. It should be obvious not to swim where there are bloody fish in the water, as sharks become aggressive around blood.

Seasickness The waters in Hawaii range from calm as glass (off the Kona Coast on the Big Island) to downright turbulent (in storm conditions) and usually fall somewhere in between. In general, expect rougher conditions in winter than in summer and on windward coastlines versus calm, leeward coastlines. If you've never been out on a boat, or if you've been seasick in the past, you might want to heed the following suggestions:

- The day before you go out on the boat, avoid alcohol, caffeine, citrus and other acidic juices, and greasy, spicy, or hard-to-digest foods.

- Get a good night's sleep the night before.

- Take or use whatever seasickness prevention works best for you—medication, an acupressure wristband, ginger tea or capsules, or any combination. But do it **before you board;** once you set sail, it's generally too late.

- While you're on the boat, stay as low and as near the center of the boat as possible. Avoid the fumes (especially if it's a diesel boat); stay out in the fresh air and watch the horizon. Do not read.

- If you start to feel queasy, drink clear fluids like water, and eat something bland, such as a soda cracker.

Stings The most common stings in Hawaii come from **jellyfish,** particularly Portuguese man-of-war and box jellyfish. Since the poisons they inject are very different, you'll need to treat each type of sting differently.

A bluish-purple floating bubble with a long tail, the **Portuguese man-of-war** is responsible for some 6,500 stings a year on Oahu alone. Although painful and a nuisance, these stings are rarely harmful; fewer than 1 in 1,000 requires medical treatment. The best prevention is to watch for these floating bubbles as you snorkel (look for the hanging tentacles below the surface). Get out of the water if anyone near you spots these jellyfish. Reactions to stings range from mild burning and reddening to severe welts and blisters. Most jellyfish stings disappear by themselves within 15 to 20 minutes if you do nothing at all to treat them. *All Stings Considered: First Aid and Medical Treatment of Hawaii's Marine Injuries,* by Craig Thomas, M.D., and Susan Scott (University of Hawaii Press, 1997), recommends the following treatment: First, pick off any visible tentacles with a gloved hand or a stick; then, rinse the sting with salt- or fresh water, and apply ice to prevent swelling. Avoid applying vinegar, baking soda, or urine to the wound, which may actually cause further damage. See a doctor if pain persists or a rash or other symptoms develop.

Transparent, square-shaped **box jellyfish** are nearly impossible to see in the water. Fortunately, they seem to follow a monthly cycle: 8 to 10 days after the full moon, they appear in the waters on the leeward side of each island and hang around for about 3 days. Also, they seem to sting more in the morning, when they're on or near the surface. The stings from a box jellyfish can cause hive-like welts, blisters, and pain lasting from 10 minutes to 8 hours. *All Stings Considered* recommends the following treatment: First, pour regular household vinegar on the sting; this will stop additional burning. Do not rub the area. Pick off any vinegar-soaked tentacles with a stick and apply an ice pack. Seek medical treatment if you experience shortness of breath, weakness, palpitations, or any other severe symptoms.

Punctures Most sea-related punctures come from stepping on or brushing against the needle-like spines of sea urchins (known locally as *wana*). Be careful when you're in the water; don't put your foot down (even if you are wearing booties or fins) if you can't clearly see the bottom.

WHAT THINGS COST IN HAWAII	US$
Hamburger	6.00–22.00
Movie ticket (adult/child)	12.00/9.00
Taxi from Honolulu airport to Waikiki	40.00–45.00
Entry to Bishop Museum (adult/child)	23.00/15.00
Entry to Wet 'n' Wild (adult/child)	50.00/38.00
Entry to Honolulu Zoo (adult/child)	14.00/6.00
Entry to Maui Ocean Center (adult/child)	30.00/20.00
Old Lahaina Luau (adult/child)	115.00/78.00
Entry to Hawaii Volcanoes National Park (car)	25.00
Moderately priced three-course dinner without alcohol	70.00 per person
20-ounce soft drink at convenience store	2.50
16-ounce apple juice	3.50
Cup of coffee	3.00
Moderately priced Waikiki hotel room (double)	165.00–225.00

10

Waves can push you into *wana* in a surge zone in shallow water. The spines can even puncture a wet suit. A sea urchin puncture can result in burning, aching, swelling, and discoloration (black or purple) around the area where the spines entered your skin. The best thing to do is to pull out any protruding spines. The body will absorb the spines within 24 hours to 3 weeks, or the remainder of the spines will work themselves out. Again, contrary to popular thought, urinating or pouring vinegar on the embedded spines will not help.

Cuts Stay out of the ocean if you have an open cut, wound, or new tattoo. The high level of bacteria present in the water means that even small wounds can become infected. Staphylococcus, or "staph," infections start out as swollen, pinkish skin tissue around the wound that spreads and grows rather than dries and heals. Scrub any cuts well with fresh water and avoid the ocean until they heal. Consult a doctor if your wound shows signs of infection.

Also see "Fast Facts" in the individual island chapters for listings of local **doctors, dentists, hospitals,** and **emergency numbers.**

Internet & Wi-Fi   On every island, branches of the **Hawaii State Public Library System** have free computers with Internet access. To find your closest library, check **www.librarieshawaii.org/sitemap.htm**. There is no charge for use of the computers, but you must have a Hawaii library card, which is free to Hawaii residents and members of the military. Visitors can visit any branch to purchase a $10 visitor card that is good for 3 months.

If you have your own laptop, every **Starbucks** in Hawaii has Wi-Fi. For a list of locations, go to www.starbucks.com/retail/find/default.aspx**.** Many, if not most, **hotel lobbies** also have free Wi-Fi. **Whole Foods** is another reliable option. Copy shops like **FedEx Office** offer computer stations with software (as well as Wi-Fi).

Most interisland airports provide basic **Wi-Fi access** for a per-minute fee. The **Daniel K. Inouye International Airport** (http://airports.hawaii.gov/hnl)

US$	Can$	UK£	Euro (€)	Aus$	NZ$
$1	C$1.30	£.69	€.92	A$1.31	NZ$1.36

provides Internet service for a fee through Shaka Net.

Mail   At press time, domestic postage rates were 34¢ for a postcard and 49¢ for a letter. For international mail, a first-class postcard or letter up to 1 ounce costs $1.15. For more information go to **www.usps. com**.

If you aren't sure what your address will be in the United States, mail can be sent to you, in your name, c/o General Delivery at the main post office of the city or region where you expect to be. (Call ℂ **800/275-8777** for information on the nearest post office.) The addressee must pick up mail in person and must produce proof of identity (driver's license, passport, and the like). Most post offices will hold mail for up to 1 month and are open Monday to Friday from 9am to 4pm, and Saturday from 9am to noon.

Always include zip codes when mailing items in the U.S. If you don't know your zip code, visit www.usps.com/zip4.

Medical Requirements   Unless you're arriving from an area known to be suffering from an epidemic (particularly cholera or yellow fever), inoculations or vaccinations are not

required for entry into the United States.

Mobile Phones   Cellphone coverage is decent throughout Hawaii but can be inconsistent in the more remote and mountainous regions of the Islands. AT&T and Verizon tend to get the best reception.

If you are traveling from outside of the U.S., you may want to purchase an international SIM card for your cellphone or buy a prepaid cellphone with local service.

Do *not* use your cellphone while you are driving. Strict laws and heavy fines ($297 and up) are diligently enforced.

Money & Costs   Frommer's lists exact prices in the local currency. The currency conversions quoted below were correct at press time. However, rates fluctuate, so before departing, consult a currency exchange website such as www.oanda.com or www.xe.com/currencyconverter to check up-to-the-minute rates.

ATMs (cashpoints) are everywhere in Hawaii—at banks, supermarkets, Long's Drugs, and Honolulu International Airport, as well as in some resorts and shopping centers.

Note: Many banks impose a fee every time you use a card at another bank's

ATM, and that fee is often higher for international transactions (up to $5 or more) than for domestic ones (rarely more than $2.50). In addition, the bank from which you withdraw cash is likely to charge its own fee. Visitors from outside the U.S. should also find out whether their bank assesses a 1 to 3% fee on charges incurred abroad.

Credit cards are accepted everywhere except on the public buses, most taxicabs (all islands), and some small restaurants and B&B accommodations.

Packing Tips   Hawaii is very informal. Shorts, T-shirts, and sandals will get you by at most restaurants and attractions; a casual dress or a polo shirt and long pants are fine even in the most expensive places. (Restaurants in the Halekulani on Oahu and the Big Island's Mauna Kea Beach Hotel require men to wear long-sleeved collared shirts.) Aloha wear is acceptable everywhere, so you may want to plan on buying an aloha shirt or a Hawaiian-style dress while you're in the islands. If you plan on hiking, horseback riding, or ziplining, bring close-toed shoes; they're required.

The tropical sun poses the greatest threat to

anyone who ventures into the great outdoors, so pack **sun protection:** a good pair of sunglasses, strong sunscreen, a light hat, and a water bottle. Dehydration is common in the tropics.

One last thing: **It can get really cold in Hawaii.** If you plan to see the sunrise from the top of Maui's Haleakala Crater, venture into the Big Island's Hawaii Volcanoes National Park, or spend time in Kokee State Park on Kauai, bring a warm jacket. Temperatures "upcountry" (higher up the mountain) can sink to 40°F (4°C), even in summer when it's 80°F (27°C) at the beach. Bring a windbreaker, sweater, or light jacket. And if you'll be in Hawaii between November and March, toss some **rain gear** into your suitcase, too.

Passports   Virtually every air traveler entering the U.S. is required to show a passport. Children 15 and under may continue entering with only a U.S. birth certificate, or other proof of U.S. citizenship. Bring a photocopy of your passport with you and store it separately. If your passport is lost or stolen, the copy will facilitate the reissuing process at your consulate.

Australia   Australian Passport Information Service (www.passports.gov.au; ℂ **131-232** in Australia).

Canada   Passport Office, Department of Foreign Affairs and International Trade, Ottawa, ON K1A 0G3 (www.canada.ca; ℂ **800/567-6868**).

Ireland   Passport Office, Setanta Centre, Molesworth Street, Dublin 2 (www.foreignaffairs.gov.ie; ℂ **01/671-1633**).

New Zealand   Passports Office, Department of Internal Affairs, 47 Boulcott St., Wellington, 6011 (www.passports.govt.nz; ℂ **0800/225-050** in New Zealand or 04/474-8100).

United Kingdom   Visit your nearest passport office, major post office, or travel agency, or contact the **Identity and Passport Service (IPS),** 89 Eccleston Sq., London, SW1V 1PN (www.ips.gov.uk; ℂ **0300/222-0000**).

United States   To find your regional passport office, check the U.S. State Department website (http://travel.state.gov) or call the **National Passport Information Center** (ℂ **877/487-2778**) for automated information.

Safety   Although tourist areas are generally safe, visitors should always stay alert, even in laidback Hawaii (and especially in Waikiki). If you're in doubt about which neighborhoods are safe, the island tourist office can advise you. Avoid deserted areas, especially at night. Don't go into any city park at night unless there's an event that attracts crowds—for example, the Waikiki Shell concerts in Kapiolani Park. Generally speaking, you can feel safe in areas where there are many people and lots of open establishments.

Avoid carrying valuables with you on the street, and don't display expensive cameras or electronic equipment. Hold on to your purse, and place your billfold in an inside pocket. In theaters, restaurants, and other public places, keep your possessions in sight. Remember also that hotels are open to the public and that security may not be able to screen everyone entering, particularly in large properties. Always lock your room door—don't assume that once inside your hotel you're automatically safe.

Burglaries of tourists' rental cars in hotel parking structures and at beach or hiking parking lots have become more common. Park in well-lit and well-traveled areas, if possible. Never leave any packages or valuables visible in the car. If someone attempts to rob you or steal your car, do not try to resist the thief or carjacker—report the incident to the police department immediately. Ask your rental car agent about specific spots to avoid on each island, and get written directions or a map with the route to your destination clearly marked.

Senior Travel   Getting older pays off! Discounts for seniors are available at almost all of Hawaii's major attractions and occasionally at hotels and restaurants. The Outrigger hotel chain, for instance, offers travelers ages 50 and older a 20% discount on regular published rates—and an additional 5% off for members of AARP. Always ask when making hotel reservations or buying tickets and carry proof of your age with you—it can really pay off. Most major domestic airlines offer senior discounts. Members of **AARP** (www.aarp.org; ✆ **800/424-3410** or 202/434-2277) are usually eligible for extra discounts. AARP also puts together organized tour packages at moderate rates. Some great, low-cost trips to Hawaii are offered to people 55 and older through **Road Scholar (**formerly Elderhostel; 11 Avenue de Lafayette, Boston, MA 02111; www.road-scholar.org; ✆ **800/454-5768**), a nonprofit group that arranges travel and study programs around the world. Write to the address above for a catalog of offerings.

If you're planning to visit Hawaii Volcanoes or Haleakala National Park, you can save sightseeing dollars if you're 62 or older by picking up a **Senior Pass** from any national park, recreation area, or monument. This lifetime pass has a one-time fee of $80 and provides free admission to all of the parks in the system, plus a 50% savings on camping and recreation fees.

Smoking

Smokers will be hard-pressed to find places to light up. It's against the law to smoke in public buildings (including airports, malls, stores, buses, movie theaters,

banks, convention facilities, and all government buildings and facilities). There is no smoking in restaurants, bars, and nightclubs. Neither can you smoke at public beaches or parks. Essentially, you'll be relegated to the tiny smoking section on the edge of your hotel property. More hotels and resorts are becoming nonsmoking, even in public areas, and most B&Bs prohibit smoking indoors. Smoking is prohibited within 20 feet of a doorway, window, or ventilation intake (so no hanging around outside a bar to smoke—you must go 20 ft. away). Smoking **marijuana** is illegal; if you attempt to buy it or light up, you can be arrested.

Taxes

The United States has no value-added tax (VAT) or other indirect tax at the national level. Every state, county, and city may levy its own local tax on all purchases, including hotel and restaurant checks and airline tickets. These taxes will not appear on price tags.

Hawaii state general excise tax is 4.166%, which applies to all items purchased (including hotel rooms). The county of Oahu levies an additional 0.546% tax. On top of that, the state's transient Accommodation Tax (TAT) is 10.25%. These taxes, combined with various resort fees, can add up to 17% to 18% of your room rate. Budget accordingly.

Telephones

All calls on-island are local calls; calls from one island to another via a landline are long distance and you must dial 1, then the Hawaii area code (808), and then the phone number. Convenience stores sell **prepaid calling cards** in denominations up to $50. You are unlikely to see a public pay phone, however. Those at airports now accept American Express, MasterCard, and Visa. **Local calls** made from most pay phones cost 50¢. Most long-distance and international calls can be dialed directly from any phone. **To make calls within the United States and to Canada,** dial 1, followed by the area code and the seven-digit number. **For other international calls,** dial 011, followed by the country code, city code, and the number you are calling.

Calls to area codes **800, 888, 877,** and **866** are toll-free. However, calls to area codes **700** and **900** (chat lines, bulletin boards, "dating" services, and so on) can be expensive—charges of 95¢ to $3 or more per minute. Some numbers have minimum charges that can run $15 or more.

For **reversed-charge or collect calls,** and for person-to-person calls, dial the number 0, then the area code and number; an operator will come on the line, and you should specify whether you are calling collect, person-to-person, or both. If your operator-assisted call is international, ask for the overseas operator.

For **directory assistance** ("Information"), dial 411 for local numbers and national numbers in the U.S. and Canada. For dedicated long-distance information, dial 1, then the appropriate area code plus 555-1212.

Time   The continental United States is divided into **four time zones:** Eastern Standard Time (EST), Central Standard Time (CST), Mountain Standard Time (MST), and Pacific Standard Time (PST). Alaska and Hawaii have their own zones. For example, when it's 7am in Honolulu (HST), it's 9am in Los Angeles (PST), 10am in Denver (MST), 11am in Chicago (CST), noon in New York City (EST), 5pm in London (GMT), and 2am the next day in Sydney.

Daylight saving time, in effect in most of the United States from 2am on the second Sunday in March to 2am on the first Sunday in November, is not observed in Hawaii, Arizona, the U.S. Virgin Islands, and Puerto Rico. Daylight saving time moves the clock 1 hour ahead of standard time.

Tipping   Tips are a major part of certain workers' income, and gratuities are the standard way of showing appreciation for services provided. (Tipping is certainly not compulsory if the service is poor!) In hotels, tip **bellhops** at least $2 per bag ($3–$5 if you have a lot of luggage) and tip the **housekeepers** $2 per person per day (more if you've left a disaster area for them to clean up). Tip the **doorman** or **concierge** only if he or she has provided you with some specific service (for example, calling a cab for you or obtaining difficult-to-get theater tickets). Tip the **valet-parking attendant** $2 to $5 every time you get your car.

In general, tip service staff such **waiters, bartenders, and hairdressers** 18% to 20% of the bill. Tip **cab drivers** 15% of the fare.

Toilets   You won't find public toilets on the streets in Hawaii, but you can find them in hotel lobbies, restaurants, museums, department stores, service stations, and at most beaches (where you'll find showers, too). Large hotels and fast-food restaurants are often the best bet for clean facilities. Restaurants and bars in heavily visited areas may reserve their restrooms for patrons.

Travelers with Disabilities   Travelers with disabilities are made to feel very welcome in Hawaii. There are more than 2,000 ramped curbs in Oahu alone, many hotels are equipped with wheelchair-accessible rooms and pools, and tour companies provide many special services. Beach wheelchairs are available at one beach on Maui (Kamaole I; ask lifeguard) and six beaches on Oahu. Contact the **City and County of Honolulu** **Department of Parks and Recreation** (https://www. honolulu.gov/parks/beach-parks/beach-wheelchair-access.html; ℂ **808/768-3027**) for locations.

For tips on accessible travel in Hawaii, go to the **Hawaii Tourism Authority** website (www.travelsmart-hawaii.com/en/practical-travel-info/before-traveling/travelers-with-special-needs/). The **Statewide Independent Living Council of Hawaii,** 841 Bishop St., Honolulu, HI 96813 (www.hisilc.org; ℂ **808/585-7452**), can provide additional resources about accessibility throughout the Islands.

Access Aloha Travel (www.accessalohatravel. com; ℂ **800/480-1143**) specializes in accommodating travelers with disabilities. Agents book cruises, tours, rental vans (available on Maui and Oahu only), accommodations, and airfare (as part of a package only). On Maui and Kauai, **Gammie Homecare** (www. gammie.com; Maui: ℂ **808/877-4032;** Kauai: ℂ **808/632-2333**) rents everything from motorized scooters to shower chairs.

Travelers with disabilities who wish to do their own driving can rent hand-controlled cars from **Avis** (www.avis.com; ℂ **800/331-1212**) and **Hertz** (www.hertz.com; ℂ **800/654-3131**). The number of hand-controlled cars in Hawaii is limited, so be sure to book well in advance. Hawaii recognizes other states' windshield placards indicating that the driver of the car is disabled, so be sure to bring yours with you. Vision-impaired travelers who use a Seeing Eye dog need to present documentation that the dog is a trained Seeing Eye dog and has had rabies shots. For more information, contact the **Animal Quarantine Facility** (http://hdoa.hawaii.gov/ai/aqs/animal-quarantine-information-page; (℄ **808/483-7151**).

Visas The U.S. State Department has a **Visa Waiver Program (VWP)** allowing citizens of numerous nations to enter the United States without a visa for stays of up to 90 days., Consult **http://usvisas.state.gov** for the most up-to-date list of countries in the VWP. Even though a visa isn't necessary, in an effort to help U.S. officials check travelers against terror watch lists before they arrive at U.S. borders, visitors from VWP countries must register online through the Electronic System for Travel Authorization (ESTA) before boarding a plane or a boat to the U.S. Travelers must complete an electronic application providing basic personal and travel eligibility information. The Department of Homeland Security recommends filling out the form at least 3 days before traveling. Authorizations will be valid for up to 2 years or until the traveler's passport expires, whichever comes first. Currently, there is a US$16 fee for the online application. *Note:* To enter the U.S. without a visa VWP travelers must present an **e-Passport.** E-Passports contain computer chips capable of storing biometric information, such as the required digital photograph of the holder. Citizens of these nations also need to present a round-trip air or cruise ticket upon arrival. For more information, go to **http://usvisas.state.gov**. Under most circumstances, citizens of Canada and Bermuda may enter the United States without a visa but will need to show a passport and proof of residence. See restrictions at: **https://travel.state.gov/content/travel/en/us-visas/tourism-visit/citizens-of-canada-and-bermuda.html**.

Citizens of all other countries must have (1) a valid passport that expires at least 6 months later than the scheduled end of their visit to the U.S., and (2) a tourist visa. For information about U.S. visas, go to **http://usvisas.state.gov**. Or go to one of the following:

U.S. Embassy Canberra (Moonah Place, Yarralumla, ACT 2600; https://au.usembassy.gov; (℄ **02/6214-5600**).

U.S. London Embassy (24 Grosvenor Square, London W1A 2LQ; https://uk.usembassy.gov; (℄)**20/7499-9000**).

U.S. Embassy Dublin (42 Elgin Rd., Ballsbridge, Dublin 4; https://ie.usembassy.gov; (℄ **353 1 668-8777**).

U.S. Embassy New Zealand (29 Fitzherbert Terrace, Thorndon, Wellington; http://nz.usembassy.gov; (℄ **644/462-6000**).

Water Generally the water in your hotel or at public drinking fountains is safe to drink (depending on the island, it may have more chlorine than you like).

Index

See also Accommodations and Restaurant indexes, below.

General Index

A
accessibility, 615
accommodations. see also Accommodations index
  best of, 7–10
  on Big Island, 255–272
  discounts, 600
  on Kauai, 556–574
  on Lanai, 479–481
  on Maui, 354–389
  on Molokai, 450–455
  on Oahu, 127–141
Ackerman Gallery, 288
Ahalanui Park (Hot Pond), 213
Ahihi-Kinau Natural Preserve, 340
Ahuna, Darlene, 292
air tours, 126, 603–604
air travel, 599–601
  to Big Island, 176
  to Kauai, 488–490
  to Lanai, 461
  to Maui, 295–296
  to Molokai, 431–432
  to Oahu, 61–62
Akaka Falls, 6
Akaka Falls State Park, 200
Akaula Cat Garden, 437
Ala Moana, 65, 148–151
Ala Moana Beach Park, 104
Ala Moana Center, 163, 167
Ala Moana Fourth of July Spectacular, 56
Ala Wai Municipal Golf Course, 122
Alii Gardens Marketplace, 286–287
Alii Kula Lavender, 326
Aliiolani Hale, 92–93
Aloha Beach Club, 168
Aloha Festivals, 57
aloha shirts, 163–164
Aloha Spice Company, 595
Altitude, 423
Anaehoomalu Bay, 225–226
Anahola, 494
Anahola Beach, 524–525
Anaina Hou Community Park, 507–508
Anchor Cove, 591
Ancient Fishponds, 440
Anini Beach, 526–527
area codes, 607
Art Night, 420
art shopping, 483–484
Art Walk, 597
ARTafterDARK, 171
As Hawi Returns, 288
As Hawi Turns, 288

Atlantis Submarines, 230–231, 325, 352
ATMs, 612
  on Big Island, 186
  on Molokai, 436
Attic Boutique, 458
ATV tours, 476
Aulani, a Disney Resort & Spa, 13
Auntie Lynda's Treasures, 592
Aunty Lilikoi, 596
authentic experiences, best of, 3–5
Azeka Place II, 423
Azeka Place Shopping Center, 423

B
babysitting, 608
Bailey House Museum, 306
Bailey House Museum Shop, 419–420
Bailey's Antiques and Aloha Shirts, 163
Baldwin Home Museum, 307–308
Ballet Hawaii, 174
Banana Patch Studio, 594
banks, 612
  on Big Island, 186
  on Molokai, 436
Banyan Tree, 308
Bar 35, 172
Barrio Vintage, 166
bars, 171–172
Basically Books, 289
Beach 69, 227
Beach Bar, 171
Beach Break, 458
beaches
  best of, 2–3
  on Big Island, 221–230
  on Kauai, 524–533
  on Lanai, 471–473
  on Maui, 328–334
  on Molokai, 445–447
  on Oahu, 104–112
Bentley's Home & Garden Collection, 289
bento, 576–577
Bergeron, Vic, 45
Big Beach (Maui), 332
Big Island, 175–293
  accommodations, 255–272
  arrival information, 176–177
  attractions, 187–220
  beaches, 221–230
  biking, 243–245
  camping, 271–272
  dining, 273–286
  fast facts, 186–187
  golf, 245–249
  Hamakua Coast neighborhoods, 181
  hiking, 249–252
  Hilo neighborhoods, 181
  horseback riding, 252–253

Kau District neighborhoods, 183
Kohala Coast neighborhoods, 179–181
Kona Coast neighborhoods, 178–179
nightlife, 291–293
Puna District neighborhoods, 181–183
shopping, 286–291
suggested itinerary, 20–23
tennis, 253
tours, 218–220
traveling within, 183–186
visitor information, 177
volcanic activity, 12
watersports, 230–243
ziplining, 254–255
Big Island Bike Tours, 244
Big Island Candies, 167, 289
Big Island Chocolate Festival, 54
Big Island Country Club, 245
Big Island Grown, 289
Big Wind Kite Factory & Plantation Gallery, 458
biking
  on Big Island, 185, 243–245
  on Kauai, 501, 544–545
  on Lanai, 476
  on Maui, 344–345
  on Molokai, 449
  on Oahu, 121–122
bikinis, 423
Bird of Paradise Unique Antiques, 420
birding tours
  on Kauai, 545
  on Molokai, 442
Bishop Museum, 4, 73–74
Blue Ginger, 421
Blue Hawaii Lifestyle, 167
Blue Hawaiian Helicopters, 325
Blue Note Hawaii, 173
boat tours
  on Big Island, 230–235
  on Kauai, 36, 533–535
  on Lanai, 473
boat travel to Lanai, 461
boating
  on Maui, 334–336
  on Oahu, 112–113
Body Glove Cruises, 231
bodyboarding/bodysurfing
  on Big Island, 235
  on Kauai, 535
  on Molokai, 449
  on Oahu, 113
Botanical World Adventures, 201
Bright Side Gallery, 594
Buddha Day, 54
Buffalo's Big Board Surfing Classic, 53
burger joints, 583
bus tours on Big Island, 219–220

PHOTO CREDITS